PAUL WALLACH'S GUIDE TO THE RESTAURANTS OF SAN FRANCISCO AND NORTHERN CALIFORNIA

PAUL WALLACH'S GUIDE TO THE RESTAURANTS OF SAN FRANCISCO AND NORTHERN CALIFORNIA

A Peregrine Smith Book
Gibbs M. Smith, Inc.
Salt Lake City
1985

Published by Gibbs M. Smith, Inc.
Peregrine Smith Books
P.O. Box 667
Layton, Utah 84041

First Peregrine Smith Edition

Book design by J. Scott Knudson,
Layton, Utah

Cover Photo by David James, *Westways Magazine*

Manufactured in the United States of America

Editor-in-Chief
    Cynthia Mushet

Assistant Editor
    Susan Araujo

ISSN 0882-4819

To James A. Nassikas and Alice Waters
For taking us along different paths to new heights.

TRIBUTE

We pay tribute to the advisory board of our first edition. Their participation and moral support have made this guide possible.
Our distinguished panel of experts included:

Cyril Magnin
Chief of Protocol
City of San Francisco

Scott Beach
Epicure/Actor/Broadcaster

Dr. George Delagnes
Wine and Food Societies

Don A. Dianda
Proprietor
Doros

J. Edward Fleishell
Le Club

William P. Gawzner
General Manager
Miramar Hotel

Dr. Benjamin Ichinose
Wine and Food Societies

Robert M. Ivie
President
Guild Wineries and Distilleries

H. Peter Jurgens
Former President
Almaden Vineyards, Beringer Vineyards

Henri Lewin
Sr. Vice President
Hilton Corporation

James A. Nassikas
President
Stanford Court

Harry G. Serlis
President Emeritus
Wine Institute

Professor Robert Wells
Journalist/Enologist

New Members:

Joe Cerrell
President
Cerrell and Associates

Robert Mondavi
Mondavi Vineyards

William J. Beaton, Jr.
KNRY Radio Station

Fifi Chao
Newsletter Publisher

CONTENTS

OFFICE OF THE MAYOR
SAN FRANCISCO

DIANNE FEINSTEIN

MR. PAUL WALLACH, PRESIDENT
PAUL WALLACH, INC.
P.O. Box 1000
Glendale, California 91209

Dear Paul:

All San Franciscans join me in extending our very Best Wishes for every possible success with this exciting new edition, and we are pleased to convey our heartfelt appreciation for what promises to be an invaluable guide to our region's superb cuisines.

Please accept our warmest congratulations on your new restaurant guide and thank you, again, for this superb service to San Francisco.

Warm personal regards,

Sincerely,

Dianne Feinstein
Mayor
DF:BS:lr

ROBERT MONDAVI ON WINE

I found Paul's first edition quite helpful, and I'm pleased to see that many of our new, fine restaurants in Northern California are included here, as well as our older favorites. Fine dining, while still eminently available in Northern California cities, is now also available in many smaller towns.

Throughout the 6,000 year history of wine, its basic purpose has been to be a food beverage, to be enjoyed with other foods. The classic grape varieties, growing in appropriate soils and in the right climate, are the ones which have survived to challenge the skills and art of the world's winemakers.

I had always believed that here in Northern California we had the right grapes, the climate, the soil and thus the prospect of making wines. Now, in a Renaissance of wine in California, we are taking our rightful place as producers of some of the world's finest wines.

For those restaurant patrons who still have some insecurity about wines, please discuss wines with the sommelier or your waiter or waitress—somebody! While some restaurants do not have training programs, by this time most establishments will have an employee who is interested in wine and interested in sharing that knowledge.

Without wine, fine food cannot achieve the rich taste harmonies that are available to the diner. With fine food, wines achieve their highest potential pleasure for the restaurant patron.

PREFACE

My love affair with restaurants began when I was about six years old and my father became the house physician for some of the great hotels of the West. It was a lonely existence for a boy—the luxurious hotels tolerated no other children—and I found my only friends and happiness in the clattering, chattering, behind-the-scenes world of the busy kitchens, where I was immediately adopted by cooks and dishwashers and pantrymen and meat-cutters. After a while, I was allowed to set the tables in the banquet rooms, stir the stockpots and taste the béarnaise and Bordelaise sauces. The huge baker, his florid face dusted with flour, baked special cookies for me. The majestic chef would carry me on his shoulders during his inspection tour of the cooking area, rumbling things to me like, "What do you think, little pigeon, is that soufflé (or ice carving or salad dressing or duckling) *ready* for our people?"

My best friend was a Filipino apprentice, scarcely bigger than I and a superb mimic. We used to sneak into the private rooms favored by wine and food societies, and as the distinguished looking guests would raise their glasses, my friend would ape each expression—the quivering nostrils, the closed, rapt eyes, the pursing of lips, the sage nods of approval—so perfectly that I was reduced to uncontrollable giggling and had to be dragged away to escape detection.

On those occasions when I joined my family for dinner in the main salon, my friends would pretend—except in little undetectable ways—not to know me. The maître d' pinched me—hard—on the rear when I came in, and both of us maintained a straight face. Nor did I crack up when the filling in my baked potato turned out to be neither butter nor sour cream but *bavarois au marasquin* (my favorite cream dessert) nor when my soufflé Grand Marnier had a grotesque cross-eyed face embroidered with *dragées* (sugarcoated bits of fruit). These eccentric, wonderful people were my friends, and I loved them.

I still do, and as a restaurant critic, I am unashamedly prejudiced in favor of the profession. As Oscar Wilde said: "A critic cannot be fair in the ordinary sense of the word. It is only about things that do not interest one that one can give a really unbiased opinion, which is, no doubt, the reason why an unbiased opinion is absolutely valueless."

My bias does not extend to the indifferent restaurateur. Like you, I deplore dirty menus, warm salads, poor service, watery cocktails and overcharging, to mention merely a few of the potential hazards of restaurant roulette that can exasperate the mind as well as the digestive process. The truly professional restaurateur is always striving, never satisfied, never complacent—and, above all, unflappable. He may have a tong war in his kitchen, a drunk passed out in the men's room and a parking attendant who ricochets the Rolls Royces, but the patrons should remain blissfully unaware of these catastrophes.

The profession of restaurant writer or critic is a relatively new one. By "critics," incidentally, I do *not* mean the freeloading "restaurant writers" of many newspapers and magazines who are, first and foremost, advertising salesmen. Their columns directly reflect, in space and enthusiasm, the amount of advertising dollars spent by the individual restaurants, or worse, the bribes (both under and on the table) they receive for the phony accolades—the "tasties" and "yummies" and "fantastics"—they hand out to their sponsors.

For the most part, restaurants have successfully dodged objective evaluation and criticisms. When you buy a set of tires or a pair of skis or a hearing aid, you can consult any one of several impartial rating guides from popular magazines to consumer digests. When you want to go to a movie or a play, you can read reviews beforehand in the daily press—before you invest in a $5 ticket. But if you're looking for a neighborhood pizzeria—or a $100-a-couple *haute cuisine*—you have virtually no reliable guide to differentiate excellence from mediocrity, or worse. This, in spite of the fact that a recent study shows that $2 out of every $5 spent for food in California is spent in restaurants.

The restaurant ratings in this guide are based upon a complex system that takes into account every detail of the dining experience related to the premise of the particular restaurant—specifically, what it is trying to achieve. It would be unfair to measure seven different kinds of restaurants against one set of inflexible criteria, just as it is unfair to criticize the size of the wine list at a small restaurant when that restaurant quite properly offers the limited selection it can afford. My ratings, initially in the form of staff reports, were submitted to the distinguished Advisory Committee, who serve as a blue ribbon jury, before I made the final decisions. It is the fairest method we can use.

Unlike most rating systems, mine accords considerable recognition to the smaller, less pretentious (but no less admirable) restaurateur along with the more familiar superstars.

Bill's Place's hamburgers are the best in the West, maybe in the nation, and they work as hard to achieve high standards as does, say, Don Dianda who operates Doros. At Hang Ah, the *dim sum* has achieved an art form, and the manager leaves nothing to chance. He works as hard as Jeremiah Tower, who has helped steer Stars into the stratosphere of the three-star rating. Bill's Place and Hang Ah are every bit as deserving of a three-star rating as Doros and Stars though I obviously don't mean to suggest that a hamburger, however superbly prepared and presented, is as complex or requires as much culinary expertise to prepare as *lièvre aux pruneaux et marrons*.

This book includes a wide range of restaurants. Like most restaurant writers, I've traveled the *haute cuisine* route and earned my ribbons. One of the early Paris critics commented, "Maxim's is perfection. Perfection can become a bore." Well, I don't totally agree. We have not been exposed to all that much perfection. The grand restaurants can still provide the grand experience. However, it's the unexpected, undiscovered cafe—often concealed by a shabby storefront—that can create that rare, rich dining adventure of which memories and cocktail conversations are made.

I would like to thank Howard Young for his invaluable contribution to this book. Mr. Young knows more about restaurants than anyone I've had the pleasure of working with, and I'd like to make it clear that he does not believe in negative criticisms of restaurants. For that reason, any such critical comments have originated from my smoking typewriter and do not, in any way, represent his point of view. I would also like to thank Howard Young, Jr. for his assistance with the research, and his data with regard to restaurants outside of San Francisco. He possesses a precise palate and a telling pen.

In the years since I became a restaurant critic, I've learned a great deal about what you want—and need—to know. Tangible evidence of the need for this kind of writing is the tremendous amount of mail I get, letters that share comments and criticisms, suggestions, agreements and disagreements. I value that confidence above everything. I hope this revised *Guide to the Restaurants of San Francisco and Northern California* will serve you well. Use it in good appetite.

PAUL WALLACH

RESTAURANT ETIQUETTE

It's time to soften the rigid structures of etiquette to make dining out a more enjoyable experience, one more suited to contemporary life-styles.

Times and attitudes have altered. No longer is the restaurant an aristocratic adversary (with the pouter-pigeon maître d' a sentinel between you and a lovely dinner). Restaurants today are less manipulator and more the servant of their patrons, although I would prefer to think of a good restaurant as "friend."

"Etiquette" has been defined as the rules or procedures required by society that enable people to understand and to get along with one another. Unfortunately, in the early American hunger for status, etiquette became a means of maintaining caste systems. The right people knew how to pour tea, the wrong people didn't. Obviously we've advanced since those feudal, silly times.

The guiding philosophy of the new etiquette can be stated quite simply: "You may do whatever is comfortable for you, as long as it is not offensive to anyone else."

For example, diners should not let Amy Vanderbilt prevent them from dunking good bread into the last exquisite dregs of escargot butter or lamb gravy. If you or your palate are frustrated by not being able to get at the meat closest to the bone, then you should be able to pick up the bone—or drumstick or ear of corn or whatever—without destroying an aura of decorum and neatness.

When you're in a hurry: At a restaurant, you should mention (a) To the host: "We hope to be out by 7:30 because we have tickets to the theatre," and (b) To the waiter: "Please don't let us order anything that takes along time. We have to be finished by 7:30. Do you have any suggestions?"

When you want a leisurely dinner: When the waiter or captain approaches your table, you should tell him: "We would like a relaxed dinner this evening. Perhaps a cocktail or two before you bring the menu." It is always a good idea to ask for suggestions as well, because a dessert soufflé, which may be specialty of the chef, requires a forty-five minute advance notice.

The man should walk ahead: When entering a restaurant without a host, the man should walk ahead of his girlfriend or spouse. Upon reaching the table, it is still considerate to pull the lady's chair out (no tricks, please) and make sure she's comfortable.

The woman should walk ahead: When a host or hostess is leading the way, the woman should walk ahead of the man. Often the host will seat the lady and a waiter will pull the chair out for the man.

Splitting checks: If there are four in the party, the best idea is not to ask the poor waiter for separate checks — it's a devilish nuisance — and generally, paying for your share of the bill will always equalize somehow (perhaps you or your guest drank a little more of the wine ordered, a slightly more expensive dish, what matter?). If you must split the check, be certain to tell the waiter well in advance so he doesn't have to tax his memory or begin a series of interrogations — "Let's see, who had the side dish of creamed spinach?" If there are more than two separate checks the mathematics should be performed by the patrons.

At the table: Some of the most fundamental acts in dining are silly. Like cutting meat. Somehow, one day, someone decided that we should begin with the fork in the left hand, the knife in the right hand (step one); then after cutting the meat, lay the knife across the plate (step two); transfer the fork to the right hand (step three); then after taking the bite of food, transfer the fork and knife back again (step four and five). How absurd to perform these manual calisthenics while your steak gets cold.

The European manner is much simpler and far less effort. You cut the meat (knife and fork as before), but instead of fighting a duel with your cutlery, you merely bring the meat on the fork in your left hand to your mouth and that's the end of that. One step as opposed to five. So why not learn the basic — and more elegant — manner.

Speaking of cutlery, begin with the outside-in — use the fork farthest to the outside first. Signals are changed, however, when a fork is placed across the top of your plate just prior to the serving of a dish (usually seafood or salad). Another switch occurs when restaurants adopt the barbarous practice of handing you an icy salad fork in the mistaken belief that this somehow will assure a chilled salad. Actually, all it assures is a chilled and rather wet hand, and is more often used — I have noted — in restaurants that might have done better to ice the lettuce rather than the forks. At best, it's a silly pretension.

At the risk of sounding like a clod; when I have enjoyed my soup and the last few spoonfuls elude my every effort — due mainly to artfully shaped crockery — I will pick up my cup or small bowl and finish it off. If I can, you can. After all, better we than the garbage disposal.

We tell our children not to use bread as a "pusher" to entrap the last bit or morsel of some delicacy. How silly. The bread stick or roll can indeed be useful in cornering such bites and we should be allowed to use them in that manner without incurring a national guilt complex.

When the check arrives: Don't be reluctant to take your time and see to it that you were charged correctly on the check. It is not an indication that you cannot afford the dinner or that you are paranoid, merely that you are not to be taken advantage of as a pigeon. Mistakes are made. Misunderstandings ofter occur.

No less an epicure than Roy Andries de Groot was a victim of a restaurant's greedy manipulation. He wandered into a ristorante in Venice with his dog (Europeans often bring their pets) and was pleased at the fuss made over his canine friend. They placed a napkin on the ground, brought a dish of spaghetti, morsels of chicken, water and then even wiped the animal's mouth at the conclusion. Mr. de Groot was pleased — that is, until he got his check that included full service for two. He paid.

American restaurants rarely are knowingly dishonest, but in the clamor and shouting of the back, the kitchen cashier may perhaps make an honest error.

Wine etiquette: The wine etiquette procedure or series of rituals have meaning. It is valuable for you to know and understand the rules. (Also see the section on wine in the appendix.)

When it is time to serve the first wine, the sommelier or waiter or waitress must bring you an unopened bottle so that the label (and the vintage year) may be confirmed and the bottle checked for leakage (indicating it has been improperly sealed.) The bottle is opened and you are handed the cork to smell (look for vinegary, stale scents) and feel (roll between your fingers to make sure the cork is moist and firm). Moistness indicates the bottle has been properly stored on its side. Then, take your time and swirl the wine around in the glass, inhale the "nose," taste, and approve the temperature. Don't feel rushed — the wine server waits for your approval before pouring. If you want to keep the label as either a souvenir or for your gastronomic notes, don't be at all reluctant to ask your waiter to soak off the label and present it to you.

You should drink what you like, and not be bullied into ordering a wine because it would be "proper." House wines, *vin ordinaire,* are always the least expensive and often among the most pleasant — if unpretentious — wines in an honorable restaurant. Always ask what the house wine is. If it's the cheapest wine available, it will tell you a great deal about the restaurant. It should be a wine that the proprietor or manager has personally selected for his patrons, be priced reasonably and be served by the half or full liter.

A FEW INSIDE TIPS

When you are going to visit a restaurant for the first time, and it is an important occasion, it's always a good idea to pay an advance call on the maître d' to study the menu.

An advance look at the menu provides several advantages. First, I would eliminate everything that you can prepare well, or easily, or out of a can—at home. I would not be interested in an hors d' oeuvre of sardines or a glamorous sounding *"le demi pamplemousse,"* which turns out to be half a grapefruit. Rather, both you and I should explore the artistry or specialty of the chef—he may have trained twenty years to make a few dishes perfectly.

If yours is a party of four or more, you might consider ordering the dinner in advance. Your guests may be immensely flattered by your thoughtfulness, and the restaurant will be better able to prepare and serve each dish to the best of their ability.

Never but never, order your dinner in increments. By that, I mean do not say, "We'll order the appetizer now and then decide on the soup later." This throws the kitchen into a confused depression; it does not enable them to coordinate the timing of each course properly, and may result in unnecessary delays for you. (You may, of course, wish to withhold your desert order until you finish your dinner.)

Don't over-order. Everything looks good when you're hungry, and there's always a tendency to order an eleven course marathon when a salad and an entrée would have sufficed.

Some of the more knowledgeable diners call beforehand to discuss their wine preferences—and budgets—with the maître d'. (Few restaurants have sommeliers these days.) If such a learned discussion is not feasible and you are not a wine connoisseur, you should ask the waiter or captain for advice. Some key words to remember: When you ask for a "nice little wine," you're telling him "inexpensive." If you mention a "good wine," you probably mean something in the mid-range of the wine list's price range. If you say, "I'd like a really great wine," you'd better be on a heavy expense account. Rule of thumb: For unspecial occasions, the price of the wine should not exceed half the price of your dinner.

If you are served a dish that is obviously wrong—spoiled or curdled sauce, stringy or fat meat, cold soup, the wrong dish—do not hesitate to send it back. It is neither rude nor inconsiderate. You should, however, be prepared to explain precisely your objection. Any restaurant of integrity will whisk away the offending dish and either suggest an alternative order or start over with your original one.

Restaurateurs, when hearing a complaint related through a third party, often groan with exasperation. They'd much prefer to keep you as a customer by correcting the real (or imagined) error. The prospect of customers walking out muttering malevolently ("I ain't never coming back to this joint") is an operator's nightmare. If you've had unusually good—or bad—service, you should write a letter to the restaurant. Most restaurants are starved for recognition, and a complimentary letter will place you permanently in their hall of fame. A letter of complaint, if it's intelligent and precise, not just splitting hairs or raging, will often be appreciated more than the compliment. The professional restaurateurs I know tell me such letters are more valuable than accolades – praise is nice, but they can't improve with it.

If you make reservations and find yourself running late, by all means call the restaurant to let them know. Most maître d's can juggle the tables to accommodate you. If you simply show up a half-hour late, your table may be gone, you'll be furious, and the restaurant will be upset.

Should you make a reservation and, for some reason find yourself unable to keep it, for heaven's sake call and cancel. Many still cling to the fear that the restaurant will roar in anger or, at the very least, acidly acquiese. Nothing (well, hardly anything) could be farther from the truth. They will be pleased that you were considerate enough to call. There may be patrons waiting restlessly, staring dramatically at your empty table.

You should be aware, though, of some of the problems the restaurant faces in handling reservations. Often people will overstay, tying up a table for hours and making your eight o'clock reservation impossible to handle. (Although he'd probably like to, the maître d' can't very well push the dawdlers out the door.) Another common error is made when a hungry visitor without a reservation is turned away by the maître d' "even though," as letters to me often rage, "there were several empty tables staring me in the face." Actually, those tables were probably reserved by other parties and the fact that the restaurant holds them is a mark of integrity.

Don't get smashed before dinner. In spite of the myths about restaurants shunting you off to the bar to make a buck from booze, the good restaurants would prefer that you not anesthetize your palate with more than two cocktails.

And do have some feeling for the restaurant people. Most try very hard to please you. Most restaurateurs are unflappable: the parking lot attendant may be ricocheting the Rolls, the kitchen ceiling may be leaking, the chef may be rendered *hors de combat* by a lean broilerman who has finally erupted, and the freshly laundered napkins may have been lost, but he (or she) will not flutter an eyelash. It is an impossible, absurd, insane business hounded by bureaucracy and a million variables that can be the difference between success and failure. Most who work in restaurants are not primarily motivated by money and many have spent their youth apprenticed to the kitchen. The pride and the sense of satisfaction after a busy night is a great reward to the staff and it's helpful if you are on the same wavelength.

I have a friend who prides himself on using his wits to obtain the ultimate in service. He has his wife, using a somewhat affected English accent, call ahead for reservations. She sternly admonishes the maître d', "Mr. Black is *not* to be bothered by newspaper reporters or photographers during his dinner." The restaurant staff may fumble the flambé trying to identify Mr. Black, but he'll be sure to get the best possible treatment.

ON DINING ALONE

Some of my richest experiences have occurred on the infrequent occasions when I have dined alone. I do not, of course, refer to efficient, hurried meals, the sole purpose of which is to fulfill our obligation to the stomach. What I have in mind is a leisurely appointment with one's self to savor special foods — perhaps an extravagant delicacy — with simple dignity.

It has been written that Lucullus, the Roman consul famous for his lavish feasts, decided one night to dine alone. He noticed the sauces were a touch indifferent and the fowl less succulent than usual. When summoned, his major-domo explained he thought there was no need to prepare a banquet "for just my lord alone."

"It is precisely when I am alone," the great epicurean replied, "that you will take special care. At such times you must remember that Lucullus dines with Lucullus."

You are dining alone. If it is your intention to have a fine leisurely dinner, it is important that you let the restaurant know your plans in advance.

When placing the reservation, indicate, "I will be dining alone this evening, but I'm looking forward to a fine dinner. Please seat me at a comfortable table." Failure to do this may allow the maître d' to reach the understandable — if mistaken — conclusion that you are traveling alone and simply want to be refueled.

If you are shown to a table that is unsatisfactory (too close to the kitchen or to a service center), you should politely decline the table. Inform the host that you are willing to wait a bit longer, if necessary, to obtain a better table.

When you are seated, indicate to your captain that you are indeed looking forward to dinner at the restaurant and ask him for his recommendation. This also tells him that you expect good service and appeals to his sense of pride. Always find a way to ask his name. "I may be returning here again, and I want to be sure I know who to ask for," is a polite way of getting the information. It also, gently, puts him on notice that you consider him the responsible party.

Take your time over both the menu and the wine list. Consult with your waiter and/or captain. Ask questions. Your concern with your dinner will be communicated to the staff and will generally bring you the best service the establishment has to offer.

It is quite common for a single diner to feel conspicuous and self-conscious. Thus some diners' process of placing the order is perfunctory, as though it were a ritual to be hastily concluded. The restaurant personnel feel that if you don't care, why should they?

When dining in unfamiliar cities at a new restaurant, I enjoy settling back and observing the patrons and the service. We all of us have the habit of fantasy. Dining alone can be marvelously entertaining.

When a women dines alone, it brings up a few unique but conquerable problems. She should definitely reach an understanding with the maître d' at the time she places the reservations. "I will be dining alone this evening, and I know that some restaurants do not like to serve a woman who dines alone. Your restaurant has been recommended to me." This introduction to the establishment will almost guarantee the pampering you deserve and the extra special attention it requires. After all, you might be a restaurant writer or the public relations director of a large company. Again, you should involve the restaurant in your total experience. When arriving at the desk, you should tell the maître d' that you would like a lovely table to observe his restaurant. Consult with the captain about each individual dish you are considering, and take particular pains to talk with the wine steward. When the wine arrives, make sure that you follow the ritual and take a few seconds to inhale the aroma, take a little sip, and then—if acceptable—nod to the server, indicating permission to fill your glass. It is often more comfortable to request wine at the outset so you aren't sitting like a statue awaiting your first course.

I would like to emphasize the importance of working with the restaurant and letting them know your plans. Failure to do so makes you fair game.

TIPPING MADE EASY

As a restaurant authority I've often been asked to appear before groups. Invariably during the question and answer period the subject most frequently mentioned is tipping. The word "tip," so historians tell us, is the acronym for the phrase, "to insure promptness." (They also told us the one about George Washington and the cherry tree, remember?)

I have begun to suspect that tipping might rate just below adultery or moral rearmament as a national concern. Reasonable men and women seem to dissemble in a restaurant.

Audiences tell me that a good portion of their deals are made in restaurants and yet they have trouble concentrating. They're constantly wondering who to tip, when to tip, how much to tip, how to tip, who's waiting on them, who the captain is, and more. When I suggest that 90% of all their tipping problems can be solved by uttering a single sentence, their eyebrows raise like a field of brown butterflies taking off.

Tipping in America has always been shrouded in mystery. Even the act of giving the tip has become somewhat like a Masonic handshake . You "slip" the tip to the head waiter. You hide the tip under the plate. And for some silly reason you think it rude to ask how much to tip. But sillier yet are the restaurant people who rely on gratuities for their livelihood and still shy away from that question, mumbling something about, "Whatever you feel is fair, sir." Balderdash! We need to know the cost of things if we're going to pay for them. But I digress.

The single sentence I alluded to that will not only solve your tipping problems but save you money as well is:

"KINDLY ADD 15% TO THE NET AMOUNT OF MY BILL AND SEE THAT IT IS DISTRIBUTED TO THE PEOPLE WHO WAITED ON ME."

The reason for specifying the "net" amount is to avoid paying gratuity on top of taxes, something we all do.

In a splendid restaurant, you may want to tip 20%. If the experience warrants.

While acknowledging that the tip or "gratuity" is a vital part of their income, service personnel seemingly engage in a conspiracy of silence about specific amounts, as though tipping were some sort of secret rite like a Masonic handshake or, at the least, a source of embarrassment. For that matter, tipping itself has somehow become a covert operation, with the money being slipped to maître d's or left on dressers or tucked into pockets.

If tipping is *not* a bribe – and it isn't – and *is* a significant budgetable portion of living and traveling expenses, then it becomes necessary to put price tags on the services. We would be appalled at a department store that made us guess how much each item cost; yet, that's the dilemma most face when trying to arrive at the specific amounts to give the waitress or bell captain, the tour guide or red cap, the beautician, barber, bartender, masseuse, washroom attendant, doorman or beach boy: How much is just enough without being ostentatiously overgenerous or unintentionally stingy? To find the answers, I talked to San Francisco service personnel representing virtually every tippable occupation. Here is what I found out.

Planes and trains: Sky-caps or red caps, $.50 minimum, with $.50 for each bag over two. On train sleeping cars, $1.00 a day per person to porter.

At the hotel: Bellmen, $1 for up to three bags, $.50 a bag thereafter. The doorman gets a dollar if he hails you a taxi and handles your bags. Maids: In a transient hotel or motel, nothing; in a resort hotel (for reasons that are difficult to understand), $.50 a day is the accepted rate. Room service: 25% of the tab. Beach boys are accustomed to $.50 per person for locating chairs and providing towels, $1 if it's a plush resort. The caddy at the golf course expects 50% of the green fee or $3 if golf is free.

Restaurants: It is not necessary to tip the maître d' unless he has performed a special service for you. Where there is captain service, and you are pleased, indicate 15% as a tip plus an additional 5% specified for the captain. (If you do not specify the captain's share, he may not receive anything, depending on the policy of the house.) There are few sommeliers or wine stewards left; but if you have one, he should be tipped $1 to $2 per bottle depending on how helpful he has been. Checking your coat: $1 for all services. Restroom attendants: Your small change—$.50 is sufficient.

In smaller restaurants with counters and booths, the percentages sometimes should be disregarded—for example, if you spend two hours over coffee in a romantic tête-a-tête, and if your total bill is under $2, your tip is really "rent" and should be at least a dollar (more if it's a busy restaurant and you've deprived the waitress of other parties). In the case of a small bill, $.50 should be the minimum tip.

Bartenders get 10% of your drink tab, cocktail waitresses 15%.

Food to go? Zero. **Food delivered to the home or hotel?** Fifty cents to $1, depending upon the bulk of the order. **Food service at national parks and camp sites?** 15% or more. These facilities are often staffed primarily by college students who depend on their tips to pay for their educations.

Touring and sight-seeing: Airport coach drivers: Not usually tipped. Tour drivers are also rarely tipped, but if you do wish to express your gratuity, $1 is ample for a full day. Full-day or extended tours (week or more) with both driver and guide: The guide expects about $1 per person per day, the driver $.50. Guides at Disneyland, Disney World, and such, are not allowed to accept tips. Offer the hostess or guide at a historical monument $.50. Fishing charters or boat tours: $2 per half-day per person, or 20% of any jackpot that is won.

Taxis, limousines, car rentals: A New York cabby told me they give undertippers an evil glare that's described as the "curse of the uncrossed palm." To avoid this curse, tip between 15 and 20%. If he juggles your bags any distance, an additional $.50 per bag is in order. In private limousines, 15% is the norm for a day. Car rental agencies rarely expect or accept tipping.

Personal services: Have a massage? (A real one, I mean.) Standard tip is 10 to 15%. Good barber shops: $1 minimum for a haircut, depending on the price; $1 for a shave; $1 to $1.50 for a shoe shine or brush-down; and $1 minimum to the manicurist. At better beauty salons, tip about 15% per operation.

It is a good idea when planning an extensive trip to include the necessary expense of tipping in the overall budget. As a rule, you can expect the same standards in small towns and big cities alike, because the amount of the tip is most often calculated on a percentage of the bill.

While this may provide guidelines, tipping itself will always be a matter of some controversy. There are organizations dedicated to the abolishment of gratuities whose members refuse to leave a tip, often penalizing a waitress who is merely a part of the system. There have been movements to include the tip as a service charge, in the European manner, by adding 10 to 15% on the bill; unfortunately, these attempts have met with universal failure. Payment for service has become an American characteristic, unlikely to change in the foreseeable future.

What is needed is better communication between the tipper and the "tippee" so that both can survive with their dignity intact, at least 15 or 20% of the time.

HOW TO USE THIS GUIDE

The restaurants selected for this guide are all listed alphabetically, with the various categories indexed in the back of the book. Obviously, the guide will never list *all* the restaurants that should be here, and I apologize in advance for blatant oversights. But the more than ten thousand restaurants in Northern California have been screened (and rescreened) to the ones that we felt would be of most importance to the reader.

Just as many of the rules of etiquette are obsolete, so are the ways in which guide books are alphabetized. Technically, "Le Restaurant" should be filed under "R," but *you* don't think of it that way, so we start out with the first letter of the restaurant's full title. The only exception to this rule would be restaurants that start with the English word "The."

Each listing contains the restaurant name, street address and area number plus all the data as to days and hours, credit cards, price, etc. Restaurants are rated from zero to three stars.

RATING SYSTEM

Stars are awarded and restaurants are judged primarily on what the restaurants purport to be. If a restaurant says it is a veritable temple of *haute cuisine* it will be judged on that basis and its success or failure indicated.

Restaurants are evaluated carefully. Staff recommendations are submitted to the Advisory Committee who, in effect, serves as a blue ribbon jury.

(No stars) Not necessarily recommended but important enough to include as a listing, to give you basic information. Perhaps too new.

★ Definitely above average, worth visiting.

★ ★ Excellent.

★ ★ ★ Among the best in the nation.

D A Signifies a "dining adventure," that rare and colorful instance in which the total experience transcends any of the component parts—food, service and decor.

PRICES

It is virtually impossible to come up with a simple price formula. A $5 breakfast may be inexpensive at a hotel dining room and expensive in Jack in the Box. For those who insist on figures, here are our rules of thumb:

Inexpensive: $12 or less for dinner.
Moderate: $25 or less for dinner
Expensive: Don't expect to get away for less than $30 per person.

The menus of a large proportion of the restaurants offer both à la carte and complete dinners. Our classification of the cost refers to an "average" dinner.

DRESS DESCRIPTIONS

Casual—Even those restaurants in which "causal" dress is appropriate draw the line at tank tops and bathing suits. "Casual" means that men in sportshirts and women in slacks will feel comfortable. Usually, even jeans would be fine.

Semi-dressy—Men in sportcoats (but not necessarily with a tie); women in what are called, for want of a better term, "after-five" dresses or pant suits.

Dressy—Where this term is used, the restaurant insists upon men in coat and tie and women in semi-formal to formal dress. San Francisco is more formal than most other cities, but the restaurants are worth dressing up for.

HOURS

The hours given show, to our best knowledge at the time of publication, the normal hours during which food is served. When dinner is described as being from 6:00 to 10:00 P.M., the restaurant may stay open later to serve cocktails or to allow diners time to finish their dinners.

CREDIT CARD SYMBOLS

> AX American Express
> CB Carte Blanche
> DC Diners Club
> MC MasterCard
> Visa

Restaurants pay a fee ranging up to 10% for the use of some credit cards, thus it is understandable if they opt to honor no cards at all (as indicated in the listings). The bank cards, MasterCard and Visa, cost the restaurant substantially less than the status cards.

MAP SYMBOLS

The map on the following page indicates areas of Northern California that have been numbered for convenience. The area numbers appear on most listings to enable you to look up the restaurants in a particular locale without necessarily knowing the name of the county or city.

MAP OF NORTHERN CALIFORNIA

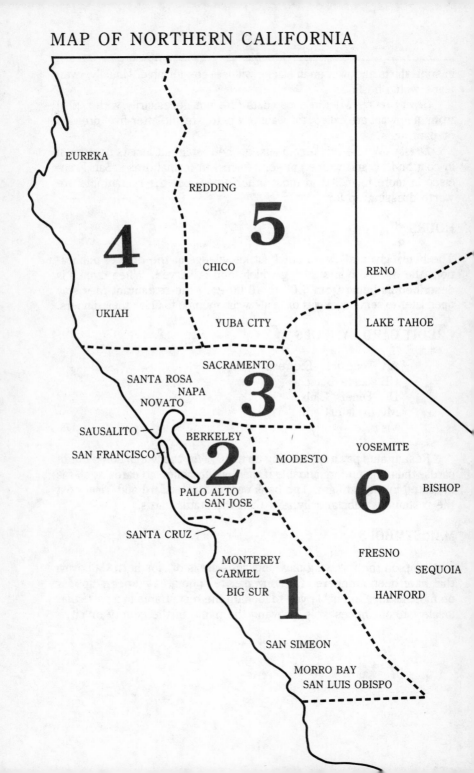

★
ABBEY/California/Continental
3020 St. Helena Highway North/St. Helena/Area 3/(707) 963-2706

Silent stone walls stand at attention as you enter through the carved doors of this monastery-type building. The friendly atmosphere, which Mr. and Mrs. John Pappas (formerly of Ondine's in Sausalito) offer, is best expressed in their comment, "Every customer is a celebrity." The food is prepared with the same feeling . . . celebrity status. There's no attempt at excess here . . . either with rich sauces or enormous servings. A variety of classics are available for luncheon; especially pleasing was the *cannelloni* supreme, crêpes stuffed with pork, veal, chicken and mushrooms. A whisper of vodka is apparent in the sauce served over breast of chicken Vladimir. There are daily specials. Ask to sit on the patio where you can see the changing colors of the mountains as the sun sets. There is a dignity in this Napa establishment that's hard to find in the big cities.

Moderate. Open for lunch seven days from noon to 3:30 P.M. Dinner served Wednesday through Sunday from 5 to 8:30 P.M. Reservations preferred, especially dinner and weekends. Visa, MC, AX. Full bar. Patio. Mountain and garden view. Child's menu. Ample lot parking. Casual to semi-dressy.

In order to obtain the best results from this Guide, be sure to read the French, German, Italian and Oriental menu translators on pages 399 to 404 of this Guide.

★
ACAPULCO/Mexican
2104 Lincoln Avenue/Alameda/Area 2/(415) 523-4935

In 1953, Modesto and Rose Quintero came to Alameda and started Acapulco. At that time there was only one table for dining. Now after more than three decades, this independent is thriving. And with good reason. In a time when we've been cautioned from every rooftop, pulpit and government office to curb our national appetite—that less is better in all things from speed limits to sugar consumption—those of us who can't quite accept the message will find solace at the Quintero family's Acapulco. The portions are Bunyan-sized, hefty enough for even the most . . . well, hefty. Moderate prices for above-average food—a winning combination. Specialties include chile verde and chile Colorado. **Moderate.** Open Tuesday through Sunday. Dinner served Tuesday through Thursday from 11:30 A.M. to 9 P.M., Friday and Saturday from 11:30 A.M. to 10 P.M. Sunday 4 to 9 P.M. No reservations. Visa, MC, AX. Wine and beer only. Free parking. Casual.

★
ADOLPH'S/Italian
641 Vallejo Street/San Francisco/Area 2/(415) 392-6333

Since 1956, Adolph's has served northern Italian dishes to a group of devoted regulars. There are many who claim that Adolph's is the best Italian restaurant in San Francisco. They're wrong. But it can be quite good. Adolph left his place in good hands when he sold to then-chef Alberto Mourino and Paolo Carboni, and their pride in this narrow, atmospheric (crystal chandeliers, wall mural and wine bottles galore) charmer is obvious. There are a number of *table d'hôte* dinners that run the predictable gamut of Italian fare, but the real finds are à la carte. Specialties include a capon, boned breast of chicken stuffed with prosciutto, mozzarella, artichoke and veal, rolled in bread crumbs and baked. It appears with "fresh mushrooms" which turn out to be a thick mushroom sauce. Try their rigatoni vodka—another specialty. Spumoni or *zabaglione* may be just the right dessert—it's stomach-stretching good. **Moderate.** Open for lunch weekdays from 11:30 A.M. to 2:30 P.M. Dinner Tuesday through Sunday from 5:30 to 11:30 P.M. Reservations accepted. All major credit cards. Full bar. Valet parking. Casual.

In order to obtain the best results from this Guide, please consult "A Few Inside Tips" on page 18.

AFFAGOTTSO'S/Italian
1995 North Main Street/Walnut Creek/Area 3/(415) 938-4040
290 Highway 4/Oakley/Area 2/(415) 625-1700

Forget ambiance (there isn't any—it consists of oil cloth table coverings, plastic grapes, masonite wainscoting). But remember the menu! It's crammed full of Italian goodies, some not often seen on California menus. Deep dish pizza (baked in squares), *melenzania parmigiana* (breaded eggplant, topped with mozzarella cheese, tomato sauce, mushrooms and baked), and *baccala parmigiana en forno*, (basically the same as the *melenzania*, but with cod replacing the eggplant) are some of the house specialties. The portions are generally large with entrées reminiscent of southern Italian fare. Fair to good original oil paintings are a nod toward sprucing up the place . . . but three hundred of them? **Inexpensive to moderate.** Open seven days from 11:30 A.M. to 10:30 P.M. Reservations accepted. Visa, MC. Wine and beer only. Casual to semi-dressy.

DA ★
THE AHWAHNEE/Continental/American
The Ahwahnee Hotel Inn/Yosemite National Park/Area 6/(209) 372-1489

If you're willing to make reservations by putting your name in a lottery one year in advance, you can enjoy a traditional old English Christmas dinner in what has been described as the most beautiful dining room in the world, at $75 a person and worth every penny of it. It's a fantastic adventure with choirs, beefeaters, parades of chefs and festive fare that must be seen to be believed. On less special days, The Ahwahnee serves just good food . . . somewhat of a miracle considering its remote location. As for the scenery, even poets have trouble describing Yosemite. The hotel has a breakfast terrace and a huge old hall which is a dining adventure of the first magnitude. Fresh mountain trout are popped from stream to pan to you in record time, with steaks, veal and a good duckling rounding out the limited menu. Also included are a fresh relish dish, soup or salad, entrée, vegetable, baked potato, and beverage. All in the moderate price range. Several entrées are available in smaller portions for children and the "conservative diner."

For best results, consult "How to Use This Guide" on page 25.

Moderate. Open seven days. Breakfast from 7 to 10 A.M. Lunch from noon to 1:20 P.M. Dinner from 5:45 to 8:30 P.M. Sunday brunch from 7:30 to 10 A.M. Reservations advised for dinner only. All major credit cards. Piano music. Full bar. View of Yosemite Valley. Smaller portions for children and the "conservative diner." Free self-parking on Hotel grounds. Casual for breakfast and lunch. Dressy (jackets required, ties preferred) for dinner.

★
AKASAKA/Japanese
1723 Buchanan Road/Japanese Cultural Center/San Francisco/Area 2
(415) 921-5360

Food virtuosity is an everyday occurrence. Some of the most attractively presented food is available here . . . the appetizer plate is arranged in columns — from galantine of roast pork and thin-sliced radish, to clam shells stuffed with assorted sea food. This appetizer is priced on the high end of the scale. It's gorgeous and wonderful. But not for those who like their Oriental food Americanized. The connoisseur of Japanese dining will find Akasaka a total experience of sight and sound and taste in the tradition of the Nippon family restaurant.
Moderate. Open Monday through Saturday. Lunch served Monday through Friday 11:30 A.M. to 2:30 P.M. Dinner Monday through Saturday 5:30 to 11:30 P.M. No reservations. Visa, MC. Full bar. Validated lot parking. Semi-dressy.

★ ★
ALDO'S/Continental
Town and Country Village/Sacramento/Area 3/(916) 483-5031

This ultra-smart haven of continental cuisine could take its place in any world capital. Urbanely cosmopolitan in every respect, patronized by social leaders, the elite of the business world, sports celebrities, TV and motion picture personalities and virtually every western politician at one time or another, this beautiful dining place is one of the capital's best.

Commodious booths encircle the room's undulating brick walls. Shaded, hanging lamps over each table have three, variable light settings, controlled by diners. Tuxedoed waiters are kept alert under owner Aldo Bovero's eyes. As he surveys his busy, sophisticated dining room, he pauses to pour wine, comment on the day's specials and chat with guests in any of the five languages in which he is fluent.

The all-encompassing menu details a myriad of culinary temptations, from *vichyssoise,* scampi, escargots and Beluga caviar to *cannelloni* and fettuccine, abalone, seafood creations, flamed-at-your-table steaks, rack of lamb and the chef's specialties. Try the breast of chicken *Valdostana.* Aldo's is really three restaurants in one—a fish house, steak house and a French *haute cuisine maison.* Aldo is responsible for the wines, priced somewhat higher than in many Sacramento establishments but justified by what Aldo's has to offer.

In addition to several private party rooms, there is a chic opera-bar lounge where concert pianist Mario Ferrari plays. Volunteer opera, light opera and would-be club singers at serendipitous times.
Expensive. Open Monday through Saturday. Lunch from 11:30 A.M. to 2:30 P.M. Dinner from 6 to 10:30 P.M. Reservations advised. All major credit cards. Fashion show daily during lunch. Classic pianist during dinner. Full bar. Parking in shopping center lot. Semi-dressy to dressy.

★
ALEJANDRO'S SOCIEDAD GASTRONOMICA/South American
1840 Clement Street/San Francisco/Area 2/(415) 668-1184

There are a number of things about Alejandro's which might throw you off. It boasts of Mexican, Spanish, AND Peruvian cuisine . . . and that usually translates as another taco joint. A mysterious group of self-proclaimed epicures calling themselves the "Sociedad Gastronomica" evaluated the restaurant's food and deigned to lend their initials as endorsement of dishes they considered noteworthy. Finally, the place is on Clement in the Richmond area . . . where you find a good restaurant only half the time, and parking spots never!

Happily, the paranoia from which all restaurant critics seem to suffer was unjustified. The cuisine is Latin—but varied, authentic, and superb. Outside, it looks like another remodeled (though handsomely), neighborhood store-front establishment. There are shuttered second-story windows and a few elegant flourishes including an impressively gleaming solid brass insignia by the door. It hardly prepares you for what you'll find inside that door.

A stylized Spanish decor sets the tone. There are groupings of ancient Peruvian gilded mirrors and illuminated glass-covered shelves display old, recognizably genuine pre-Columbian artifacts. The leather chairs are comfortable; the china expensive; the linens starched and spotless.

You order from an extensive menu—so long that experienced diners quickly request a plate (or two) of *Alejandrinos* before they even look at the day's offerings. These morsels are tiny fried pastries filled with cheese and peppers, eggs, onions, and any number of secret things.

More than two dozen entrées are described; many of them not often encountered in this area, and most of these bear the initialed approval of the Sociedad Gastronomica. Rabbit, trout, seafood, chile rellenos – all with tantalizing sauces – never an easy decision.

I took the easy way out the first time I went there, and ordered their highly-recommended *paella a la Valenciana*. It contained chicken, pork, sausage, mussels, green beans, tomatoes, peas and moist saffron rice. When presented, it could have been the cover illustration of a classic volume on Spanish gastronomy. And it tasted even better than it looked. It was the best *paella* I've had in recent memory. Good selection of Spanish and California wines.

Moderate. Open seven days. Monday through Thursday from 5 to 11 P.M. Friday and Saturday from 5 P.M. to midnight. Sunday from 4 to 11 P.M. Reservations essential. All major credit cards. Entertainment. Full bar. Street parking. Casual.

★ ★

ALEXIS/Continental/French
1001 California Street (at Mason)/San Francisco/Area 2/(415) 885-6400

There are enough flaming swords and icons and Russian artifacts to provide the setting for a Rudolph Valentino movie – and the best lamb in the city. On a hungry evening, I scarcely noticed the doorman in my eagerness to get to the rack of lamb Karski, always perfectly prepared and artfully served. The herbs, I'm sure, are a chef's secret, but the tapestry of flavors has never varied. The *yalanji dolma*, an appetizer of grape leaves filled with spices, pine nuts and sour cream, is a good choice beginning. The many appetizers, soups and entrées, representative of the French talent in Alexis' kitchen, will reward you. My starter favorites are crêpes Bengal, enlivened with curry, as the name indicates, and the *quenelles*, delicate and ambrosial. The sole Waleska, accompanied by a lobster and cream sauce, is a specialty, but the all-time favorite of most of the regulars is the *koulebiaka à la russe* of salmon that must be ordered a day in advance. It consists of layer upon layer of salmon, mushrooms and sliced egg in a pastry shell shaped similar to a brioche. Desserts are a triumph – strawberries Romanoff and meringue glacé, crêpes Suzette, mangoes and more – all presented with appropriate drama. If you can afford Alexis, you can't afford not to have dessert with a dessert wine selected from the long wine list. Your accomplished host, André Jouanjus, will see to every detail. André opened Alexis in 1960 and is the managing partner. I join with him in recommending that you visit Alexis' Gypsy Cellar, not just for a libation, but to listen to the lovely melodies of a gifted pianist and a talented violinist.

Expensive. Open Monday through Saturday. Dinner served from 5:30 to 11 P.M. Reservations advised. All major credit cards. Entertainment. Full bar. Valet parking. Dressy (coat and tie).

ALFRED'S/Italian/Steak
886 Broadway/San Francisco/Area 2/(415) 781-7058

In a city full of Italian restaurants, it is always difficult for me to understand the success of the pseudo-Italian trattorìa. Surely at Alfred's the specialties of Italian dishes and eastern corn-fed steaks are a strong indication they are after the best of all worlds — but offer the best of none. The "world famous" *cannelloni* and fettuccine would bring tears to the eyes of Michelangelo's David. The best part of this operation is the wine list, with good values at fair prices; and the steaks *are* OK.

Moderate. Dinner daily from 5:30 to 10:30 P.M. Reservations accepted. All major credit cards. Full bar. Valet parking. Casual to semi-dressy.

DA ★
ALTA MIRA HOTEL/Continental
125 Bulkley/Sausalito/Area 3/(415) 332-1350

If anyone tells you to be sure and have "eggs Benedict at the Alta Mira," be sure you know what day it is. On weekends, this old favorite is so jammed with tourists packed elbow to elbow in the waiting room until their names are called, that you'll be lucky to glimpse the magnificent bay view between the tourists' Hawaiian sport shirts and the Jeanette MacDonald hats. On less-crowded weekdays, it can be the closest thing to paradise to sit on the long veranda, sip a Bloody Mary and enjoy a really good eggs Benedict and the breathtaking view. Since prices have kept considerably ahead of inflation, you'll not find this an inexpensive thrill, but money can seem a trifling thing at times (only when you have it, of course).

Moderate. Open seven days. Lunch served from noon to 4 P.M. Dinner from 5 to 10 P.M. Sunday brunch from 7:30 A.M. to 3:30 P.M. Reservations advised. Visa, MC, AX, CB. Full bar. Patio. View of Bay. Valet parking. Semi-dressy.

Please be sure to consult "Tipping Made Easy" on page 22 of this Guide.

★
ALTA PLAZA/California/Continental
2201 Fillmore Street/San Francisco/Area 2/(415) 921-4646

Fillmore Street on the edge of Pacific Heights has changed a great deal in the past decade. Alta Plaza has helped to anchor the upscale conversion, serving excellent food in their understated gray shingled building, now a landmark in the area.

Chef Gary Harrell is yet another graduate of Chez Panisse and was, for a time, the private cook for John Wayne. A dinner here may be as light as a bowl of carrot-ginger soup and a fresh salad of beautifully ripe sliced tomatoes, thin slices of sweet onion, and Sonoma goat cheese. Specials change daily and might include Southern fried chicken with homemade biscuits or salmon cooked in parchment with a confit of red onions and zinfandel butter. Grilled fish is served, at times, with a delectable fresh salsa. Pork loin is stuffed with figs and walnuts, then served with a red butter sauce. Fettuccine with sausage, cream and red chard is another favorite.

Moderate to expensive. Open for lunch weekdays from 11:30 A.M. to 2:30 P.M. Dinner nightly from 5:30 to 11 p.m. Reservations advised. Visa, MC, AX. Full bar. Street parking. Semi-dressy.

★★
AMELIO'S/Continental/Classic/Nouvelle
1630 Powell Street/San Francisco/Area 2/(415) 397-4339

Chris Shearman, owner-host, continually receives praise from his numerous, long-time guests for the innovative dishes of his celebrated kitchen staff. Travel-Holiday Magazine states, in bestowing its Award for Fine Dining, as it has for decades, "The superb food matches the refined atmosphere — filet of veal with fresh forest mushrooms, loin of lamb with coriander sauce, boned duck sautéed with raspberry vinegar sauce." Even the gravlox is made here. Chris maintains and polishes Amelio's traditions, dating back to its 1926 opening. The ambiance is intimate, romantic, pleasantly subdued — a welcome relief from a sometimes turbulent world. Visit the gem of a bar. Service is impeccable as is the wine book.

Expensive. Open seven days. Dinner from 5:30 to 10:30 P.M. Reservations advised. AX, MC, V and DC. Full bar. Street parking; valet parking weekends. Dressy.

For best results, consult "How to Use This Guide" on page 25.

★
ANDALOU/California/Continental
824 "E" Street/San Rafael/Area 2/(415) 454-4900

Enjoying the challenge of preparing food well and interestingly, and serving it to a loyal clientele — these are the pleasures of Andalou, which is housed in a Northern California Victorian house-cum-restaurant, but offers cuisine with a soupçon of southern Spain. Specialties are the hors d'oeuvres which range from barbecued oysters to ceviche, swordfish, and snapper marinated in lime juice, to an attractive, almost Oriental arrangement of crunchy snowpeas and tomatoes dressed in a sesame paste — all tempting and tantalizing. Entrées are basic, but then liberally adapted: snapper with soy and ginger sauce; chicken salad with cilantro; orange and rosemary sauce over boned chicken breasts. See what I mean? Also featured in varying preparations are pasta, veal, lamb and beef dishes. Desserts run to those brought in from outside vendors such as homemade chocolate cake with apricot and brandy glacé.
Moderate. Open Monday through Saturday. Lunch from 11:30 A.M. to 2 P.M. Dinner from 6 to 9 P.M. Reservations advised. Visa, MC, AX. Wine and beer only. Patio dining. Parking lot. Semi-dressy.

★
ANTHONY'S PIER 9/Seafood/Continental
10745 North De Anza Boulevard/Cupertino/Area 2/(408) 255-4711

Anthony is owner Michael Del Monaco's son, and the very nautical dining rooms and exterior, even to the appearance of being waterside, justify the "Pier" theme. The menu emphasizes Italian specialties.

After we placed our order with the smartly-attired, mess-jacketed waiter, we agreed that the marine influence, even to an unusual complex of large aquariums with fantastic fish that centers the spacious main room, conveyed the impression that we were dining in the salon of an ocean liner. Stop and observe the unbelievable Lion-head goldfish which is as graceful as a prima ballerina.

We were impressed with the quality of our entire meal; the fresh al dente vegetables, the tender white veal, the choice meats and all the accompaniments. Since that first visit, some of my scouts and I have returned, covering the extensive scope of the kitchen's talents, from Blue Points and scampi to the six regular pastas and a few specials plus deep fried calamari, abalone sauté, *saltimbocca alla Romana,* sweetbreads in Madeira, and much more, including oysters Rockefeller. The dessert menu describes almost twenty sweets. Consider the Cassata ice cream cake and the Italian ice cream *bombe.* Wines are well-balanced in selections. Ask to see the special Blue Book, also.

A few words about Michael Del Monaco, born near Naples, a keen gentleman whose grandfather and father were restaurateurs. He enjoyed our praise for his pastas. "I own my own pasta factory," he remarked. We also learned that he owns two other dining places, both named The Florentine, in Cupertino and Mountain View. He is proud to give anyone a tour of his spotless, large kitchen and the comfortable bar lounge "the Captain's Cabin," where we later disposed of some espressos.

Moderate. Open seven days. Lunch served weekdays from 11 A.M. to 3 P.M. Dinner from 5 to 11 P.M. Saturday brunch from 11 A.M. to 3 P.M. Sunday champagne brunch from 10 A.M. to 3 P.M., and dinner from 4 to 10 P.M. Visa, MC, AX. Piano bar. Full bar. Child's menu. Parking lot. Semi-dressy to dressy.

★ ★

ANTON & MICHEL/Continental
Mission between Ocean and 7th/Carmel/Area 1/(408) 624-2406

This charming Old World restaurant presents patrons with a view, through tall windows, of a splashing fountain, bricked courtyard and the ivy-covered walls of the inner court—pastoral sight for city eyes. The ambiance is somewhat formal, with designer wallpaper, handsome carpeting and attentive service by tuxedo-clad waiters. The fireplaces that enhance almost every room soften the subdued lighting, melting years from each diner's countenance, making for a romantic, memorable evening.

Anton and Michel are graduates of the famous Hotel School of Lausanne and they do credit to their antecedents. The elaborate menu describes such offerings as Armenian lamb chops, chicken Jerusalem, veal Oscar, tournedos Rossini, duckling Montmorency, roast rack of lamb (for two), fresh seafood, and exceptional appetizers and salads.

To complement the cuisine, the cellar holds both California and imported wines. The spacious bar lounge is as well-appointed as a private club.

Moderate to expensive. Open daily from 5 to 9 P.M. Sunday brunch 10 A.M. to 2 P.M. Reservations accepted. All major credit cards. Full bar. Patio. Street parking. Semi-dressy.

To obtain the best results from this Guide, be sure to consult the map on the various Northern California areas on page 28.

★
ARCHIL'S/Russian
3011 Steiner Street/San Francisco/Area 2/(415) 921-2141

A **Russian** restaurant sans kitsch . . . no samovars or Balalaikas. It's just plain elegant, with good food at reasonable prices and splendid service. This is a restaurant whose roots are in the family of Archil Merab: his mother supervises the kitchen. With love and interest, Archil has arranged a presentation of full dinners—with borscht, romaine salad, desserts—and entrées ranging from rabbit *chakhokhbili* (a Georgian stew in white wine sauce with onions and garlic), fish *kotlety* (ground "cutlets" with mustard sauce) and *kufta* (lamb meatballs in tomato sauce). Exotic tongue is a meat that Americans have never taken to heart, but Archil prepares it with tangy sauce and so much gusto that I find it as fine an entrée as any on the menu. The headcheese appetizer served in spicy jelly is another item not often encountered, but one worth experiencing.

Moderate. Open Tuesday through Saturday. Dinner served from 5:30 to 10 P.M. Reservations advised. Visa, MC. Wine and beer only. Street parking; garage nearby. Casual.

★
ASIA GARDEN/Chinese
772 Pacific Street/San Francisco/Area 2/(415) 398-5112

I **am not,** for the most part, a fan of the oversized Hong Kong-style *dim sum* houses. Though I can appreciate these vast, barnlike structures as a sort of Oriental art form, I often emerge from them with something of a headache from the endless din and cacophony that echoes off the walls and the formica tables. Still, if you can bear the noise and the ruckus, Asia Garden is one of the best of the big dim summeries.

Since you'll have to wait for a table (there may be a time when Asia Garden is less than mobbed, though I have yet to discover it), the first thing to do is to admire the speed and zip with which the women at the to-go counter fill orders of *dim sum* for people who prefer their *char siu bao* at home. All *dim sum* to-go orders, in all *dim sum* restaurants, seem to be packed in pink boxes. I suspect there is some sort of symbolism involved, though what it is eludes me.

In order to obtain the best results from this Guide, be sure to read the French, German, Italian and Oriental menu translators on pages 399 to 404 of this Guide.

When you're finally seated, you'll have to get into the eye contact game with the waitresses who push around the various *dim sums* on rolling carts (usually no more than two types per cart). Without eye contact, they can easily go zipping by. Tea is an important part of the ritual, since it alone has the power to cut through the unfortunate greasiness that's sometimes part and parcel of *dim sum*. Expect a fairly good selection of the tea cakes, like rice flour noodle rolls, green peppers stuffed with a shrimp ball, and terrific *har gow* (minced shrimp inside a half-moon shaped dumpling). The desserts, as ever, are an acquired taste. **Moderate.** Open seven days. Lunch from 9 A.M. to 2:30 P.M. Dinner from 5 to 9:30 P.M. Reservations essential (none Saturday or Sunday). Visa, MC, AX at dinner only. Full bar at dinner. Street parking is difficult. Casual.

★
ATLANTIS SEAFOOD/Seafood
361 West Portal Avenue/San Francisco/Area 2/(415) 665-7920

Owner Cherdpoom "Pinky" Markpol has combined sea fare and good service at this pleasant restaurant. Food is fresh and seasonal so there are variances throughout the year. A Boston clam chowder or shrimp bisque or salad are indicators of the well-prepared food at this neighborhood restaurant. Available entrées on the dinner include calamari sautéed in garlic, tomatoes and herbs; curried prawns; a *cannelloni* stuffed with crab, shrimp, scallops and Jack cheese; *cannelloni* topped with a Mornay sauce; and an almost every-fish-in-the-sea stew that's very pleasing and filling. A family-style seafood house.
Moderate. Open weekdays from 11 A.M. to 10 P.M. Saturday from 4 to 11 P.M. Reservations accepted. Visa, MC, AX. Wine and beer only. Lot parking. Casual.

★ ★
AUBERGE DU SOLEIL/French/Nouvelle
180 Rutherford Hill Road/Rutherford/Area 3/(707) 963-1211

A wine country fantasy, this magnificent French restaurant with unsurpassed views of olive groves, vineyards and the Mayacamas mountains, would be popular even if the food was merely average, which, happily, it's not. The irregular stuccoed walls and the fireplace are surrounded with simplicity to emphasize the view. This has always been a restaurant dedicated to fine cooking, and the late Masa Kobayashi embellished his nearly legendary reputation before leaving to open his own restaurant. Now Michel Cornu, who formerly worked at the Adolphus Hotel in Dallas, has a firm hold on the kitchen, and the French nouvelle dishes are a delight. The menu was in the process of changing when we last contacted Auberge du Soleil, but they were to have $40 multi-course dinners with two seatings: 6 and 9 P.M., and at lunch 11:30 A.M. and 1:30 P.M. ($25). The wine list contains some treasures that are fairly priced.

Expensive. Open Thursday through Tuesday. Dinner seatings at 6 and 9 P.M., lunch seatings at 11:30 A.M. and 1:30 P.M. Reservations advised. All major credit cards. Entertainment. Full bar. Patio. View. Lot parking. Semi-dressy to dressy.

★
AUBURN HOTEL/Basque
853 Lincoln Way/Auburn/Area 5/(916) 885-8132

When the Auburn Hotel opened in the historic Mother Lode in 1917, it was a marvel: two-stories with a canopied porch running the length of the structure, gables, and other late-Victorian architectural accoutrements. The six-course family-style dinner starts with a relish tray, followed by minestrone, salad, pasta, spinach soufflé, the entrée — steak, or a choice of two chef's specialties like stuffed pork chops or chicken cacciatore — dessert and coffee. Few frills; substantial sustenance.
Moderate. Open seven days. Lunch weekdays from 11:30 A.M. to 4 P.M. Dinner Tuesday through Saturday from 6 to 10 P.M. Sunday from 2 to 10 P.M. Reservations accepted. Visa, MC. Entertainment. Full bar. Parking lot. Casual.

★
AUGUSTA'S/Seafood/Pasta
2955 Telegraph Avenue/Berkeley/Area 2/(415) 548-3140

The simplicity of the foods at Augusta's is a rare treat for palates that are overwhelmed with over-done menu offerings. Simplicity is reflected even in the blue and white checkered cloths, fresh flowers, wooden chairs (I don't think any one has a matching mate) and a cheerful fireplace. One dining room overlooks an open kitchen on one side and a patio on the other. Patio service is available on balmy days. Fresh seafood, from grilled halibut to sautéed calamari is the house specialty, along with the homemade fettuccine served in a variety of styles. The fish: grilled, sautéed, fried, or baked; retains its own flavor . . . simply. Even vegetables are given a treat instead of a treatment: potatoes, quartered, in skins brushed with butter and grilled with garlic cloves, and a special favorite, the sautéed zucchini julienne, with sweet basil, retains the appropriate crunch. Augusta's special fudge pie is a kingly dessert.
Moderate. Open Tuesday through Sunday. Lunch served Tuesday

through Friday 11:30 A.M. to 2:30 P.M. Dinner served Tuesday through Sunday 5:30 to 10 P.M. Sunday brunch 10 A.M. to 2:30 P.M. Reservations advised for dinner. Visa, MC. Wine and beer only. Patio. Street parking. Casual.

★ ★
AU RELAIS RESTAURANT/French
691 Broadway/Sonoma/Area 3/(707) 996-1031

Take an old farmhouse, sprinkle liberally with redwood and art deco furnishings, enclose a lovely garden for looking at or in, *et voila*. In this way, co-owner/chef Harold Marsden has blended the elegance of Paris with Sonoma's charm to create a very tasteful restaurant.

Under revision at this writing, the menu can, nonetheless, be relied upon to offer seasonally fresh seafood specials, and lamb, pork, veal, and pasta dishes. Desserts, concocted on the premises, are a specialty; the *tart tatin* (apple tart) is particularly popular. The extensive wine list features California vintages, but does include French and Italian labels. Operating hours vary with the season.

Mr. Marsden and his wife/partner, Dorothy, are also proud of the bed and breakfast inn they have opened in a refurbished Victorian house next door to Au Relais.
Moderate. Open seven days. Lunch Monday, and Thursday through Saturday from 11 A.M. to 5 P.M., Tuesday and Wednesday from 11 A.M. to 2:30 P.M. Dinner Monday, and Thursday through Saturday from 5 to 9 P.M., Sunday from 4 to 9 P.M. Sunday brunch from 10 A.M. to 4 P.M. Reservations advised. All major cards. Full bar. Patio. Parking in rear lot. Casual to semi-dressy.

★
AUX DELICES/Vietnamese
23 Orinda Way/Orinda/Area 2/(415) 254-3410

Despite a very French name, this restaurant serves Vietnamese food—which, when you place Viet Nam in historical perspective, is not so far off—since the French were influential in the area for decades. The owner of Aux Delices is one of the many high-ranking officials who fled to the U.S. and opened a restaurant—as so many of his compatriots have done. The decor here is strictly early 1950's diner; it provides a very non-descript background for some mostly descriptive fare. The chicken ginger, chicken flambé and chicken steamed with green mustard were all accoutred with an interesting taste texture. House specialties include spicy crab, the fire pot, and prawns on sugar cane. A selection that blends Oriental and French touches is a rice flour batter and eggs, fried omelette style, bursting with onions, sprouts, beef and bay shrimp. It sounds and looks better than it tastes. An interesting note about Vietnamese cooking procedures — food is sautéed in water, not oil — resulting in lower cholesterol and a lighter, more flavorful taste. **Moderate.** Open Tuesday through Saturday 11 A.M. to 9 P.M. Reservations advised. Visa, MC. Wine and beer only. Street and lot parking.

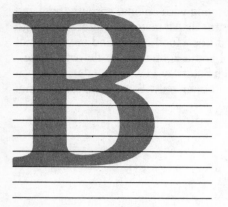

★
BACCHI'S INN/Italian
2905 Lake Forest Road/Lake Forest/Area 6/(916) 583-3324

Diners from as far away as the South Shore drive up for the bounteous dinners and the pleasantly ageless dining experience in this legendary favorite. Recipes of the late chef, Sara Bacchi Hunter, are still faithfully followed in the tradition of fine Italian family-style food. Modestly priced evening meals are cheerfully served in attractive, mountain-lodge surroundings, complete with red-checked tablecloths, walnut paneling, windows overlooking scenic vistas, roaring (at times) fireplace in the happy, uncrowded bar lounge and a mellow ambiance of *bonhomie.*

When "Bonanza" was filming nearby, it was like one of their sets.

Sara's parents built the beginnings of this great, old place back in 1932 as a combination restaurant, grocery store, gas pump. It was built of logs, by their own hand work. Bill Hunter, Sr. and Bill, Jr., both hosts, will be glad to point out the original logs. They cellar a nice collection of wines.

Moderate. Open seven days from 5:30 to 10 P.M. Closed the first two weeks of May and November. Reservations necessary. All major credit cards. Full bar. Child's menu. Casual.

Please be sure to consult "Tipping Made Easy" on page 22 of this Guide.

★
BAGATELLE/Continental
215 West Portal Avenue/San Francisco/Area 2/(415) 566-5700

Set back from the street, approached by a brick walk, between lawn and shrubs, Bagatelle is a charming French country-style restaurant. In two spacious rooms, old-fashioned brass chandeliers with frosted globes oversee white napery, papered walls hung with large mirrors, tapestry, paintings, deep-grey carpeting, terra cotta trim and gleaming kitchen copper pans. It has a relaxed, laid-back ambiance.

Owner-host Guy Francoz's professional staff pleasantly attends, shifting some of the profusion of blooms. The menu runs the gamut of the efforts of a splendid chef and culinary assistants.

Seven appetizers include filets of herring in wine, and smoked salmon. Entrées offer seven chef's specialties, all with either soup or salad (a *large* salad), eleven seafood dishes, five veal creations, six beef dishes, including *boeuf Bourguignon* (hearty and inexpensive) plus four miscellaneous attractions, like chicken sauté *toscana* and calf's liver. Also, each day of the week there is a Specialty of the Day: Wednesday—roast turkey; Friday, Saturday, Sunday—a roasted leg of lamb, etc. The usual mousse cheese cake but the heavenly, rich pastries are diet-breakers, for sure. M. Francoz's wines are all the selections of a connoisseur, yet modestly tabbed. The lively, cheerful bar lounge merits your looksee. **Moderate.** Open seven days. Dinner Monday through Thursday from 5 to 10 P.M., Friday from 5 to 10:30 P.M., Saturday from 4:30 to 10:30 P.M., Sunday from 4:30 to 10 P.M. Reservations advised. Visa, MC, AX, CB. Full bar. Child's menu. Street parking. Semi-dressy to dressy.

★
BALBOA CAFE RESTAURANT/Sandwiches
3199 Fillmore/San Francisco/Area 2/(415) 922-4595

When the U.S. entered World War I, the Balboa Cafe had already been serving its clientele for four years. Six decades later when it was spruced up, the owners opted to retain the patina. Using old photographs as a guide, they restored the cafe to its former glory. There are tables—all antique—that, if they could but speak would tell such stories. . . . Take a peek through the portals for a glimpse into yesterday. Under the influence of Jeremiah Tower, a more sophisticated California-cafe type of food goes hand in hand with the old pub favorites. Start with beef carpaccio or onion soup gratinee. Then try the famous foot-long sandwich—served on a baguette. Half of mine went home in a people bag—no pooch was going to get these goodies! Muffins, French rolls as well as the baguettes underscore such combination as the Balboa burger (with one-half pound of ground beef) and Jack's BLT. The lasagna is a must, and the daily fish dishes are always popular. Balboa is a hangout and always packed.

Inexpensive. Open seven days 11 A.M. to 11 P.M. No reservations. Visa, MC, AX, DC. Full bar. Casual.

★
BANCHEROS/Italian
20102 Mission Boulevard/Hayward/Area 2/(415) 276-7355

For some reason, this place is one of my favorites in the area, although the service – inclined to be a bit daffy at times – and the food are not exceptional. It's one of those cheap, cheap, eat, eat emporiums with eight-course dinners, fat patrons and thin wine. It's a good family spot and great to take the children to if they're ravenous, because you couldn't begin to feed them at home for the small price you'll pay here.

Inexpensive. Open Tuesday through Sunday. Dinner Tuesday through Thursday from 4 to 9 P.M., Friday from 4 P.M. and Saturday from 3:30 to 9:30 P.M. Sunday from 1 to 9 P.M. Reservations required for five or more. No credit cards. Full bar. Child's menu. Parking lot. Casual.

★
THE BANK EXCHANGE/Continental
600 Montgomery/San Francisco/Area 2/(415) 983-4800

Joe Betz is the energetic owner of this dual-personality restaurant/disco, and he runs the place with flair and efficiency. The Bank Exchange is snugly esconced within the impressive supports of the towering Transamerica Pyramid. Naturally, the liveliest of the financial district's workers of all ages are regular patrons.

Only luncheon is served and Joe tells me that it is the busiest lunch restaurant in all Northern California. There are a number of solid reasons for this: the handsome location, the rooms entirely encased with high windows that afford spreading views of the lovely park beyond, young redwood trees, lush lawns, shrubs, plantings and scattered benches. Within are custom-designed, modern tables and chairs. All is airy and light, largely owing to the glass roof. The contrast with the building's columns and beams is intriguing.

The menu changes daily but there are always salads, sandwiches and hot dishes, including omelettes. The wines are priced well and the bar is a busy one.

Tuesday through Saturday the disco certainly moves. After 2 A.M. Joe's cabaret license allows non-alcoholic beverages and his special club dancing permit holds back the dawn for the "I'd rather be dancing" set.

Moderate. Open weekdays from 11:30 A.M. to 2:30 P.M. Disco and bar only at night. Reservations advised. All major credit cards. Full bar. Garage parking, valet after 9 P.M. Casual to semi-dressy.

★
BARDELLI'S/Continental
243 O'Farrell Street/San Francisco/Area 2/(415) 982-0243

Around 1906, when San Francisco was shaking out her ashes, two characters, Darby and Immel, built an oyster house at 243 O'Farrell Street, where it prospered until 1911. Then it became the Charles Fashion Grill, catering to the little ladies from Nob Hill, with portions so small that one of the sandwiches could have been called "roastbrief." In 1949, with a new proprietor from Milan, by way of New York, Charles' became Bardelli's. This is not a place where booths can become your vinyl resting place, nor is there chrome or plastic. A row of classic columns supports the lofty ceiling, the lighting is soft and the rich red carpets and the stained glass entry vestibule — a colorful portrayal of a peacock — provide the tone. Chicken Jerusalem or scampi *à la Deovola,* or filet beef tips sauté are choice among the wide assortment of entrées. Desserts are well-presented and an after-dinner cognac or Amaretto can make you feel what Lucius Beebe used to describe as "amiable."
Expensive. Open weekdays for lunch from 11:30 A.M. to 3:30 P.M. Dinner from 3:30 to 10 P.M. Reservations accepted. Visa, MC, AX. Full bar. Parking lot. Casual to semi-dressy.

DA ★
BASQUE HOTEL RESTAURANT/Basque/French
15 Romolo Place/San Francisco/Area 2/(415) 788-9404

This is the real thing; a hard-to-find boarding-house-type restaurant clinging to a steep hill off Broadway. Enormous dinners of home-made soup, entrées served with potatoes, salad, and dessert, with coffee in the same glass that's used for wine attest to the authenticity of this large, husband (he's Spanish) and wife (she's French) dining hall with long tables that provide a kind of picnic atmosphere. Francisco and Antoinette Oroz's menu is unpredictable; nothing's great but everything's good. Specialties may include sweetbreads, oxtail stew or lamb. You will go away stuffed to the gills. To pick a single night of the week, the menu would be thick pea soup, clams served on rice, scalloped veal, vegetables, salad, cheese, fruit and coffee. This is a dining adventure that everyone in the family can share and will probably long remember.

Moderate. Open Tuesday through Sunday from 5 to 10 P.M. Reservations accepted. No credit cards. Full bar. Child's menu. Street parking. Casual.

DA ★
BASTA PASTA/Italian/Seafood
1268 Grant/San Francisco/Area 2/(415) 434-2248

The name – Italian for "enough pasta"– is accurate, but it doesn't go far enough. There are a dozen fettuccines and spaghettinis and *gnocchis*, including most of the classic styles – but there are at least twice as many seafood specialties.

The pasta is prepared each morning in the downstairs portion of this two-story restaurant, and it's something to watch. My personal favorite is fettuccine Basta Pasta; it's an eating experience which should be shared for two reasons: loving friendship and the generous helpings. The house specialty consists of mushrooms, veal, prosciutto (made here), and fresh tomatoes . . . it's easily worth the calories!

The wine list is mainly Italian, selected by someone who has actually tasted the wines before putting them on the list. Most of the important areas of the vast vineyard called Italy are included, but the best buy may very well be the Italian house wine – a chianti reputed to be made in a small winery by friends of Basta Pasta's owner, Lorenzo Petroni.

We didn't expect so many fish dishes on the menu, but an even greater surprise was the kind of fish which possesses two priceless attributes of seafood gastronomy: it is impeccably fresh and the preparation is simple. Most interesting could very well be the "catch of the day." The restaurant, together with its sister establishment, the nearby North Beach Restaurant, whose chef, Bruno Orsi, is Lorenzo's partner, owns and operates a sixty-foot fishing boat to supply fish for both kitchens.

Our "catch of the day" was rex sole; the menu promised "a whole broiled fish with lemon"– we got *two*. A squeeze of lemon provided just enough accent to bring out the sweet, natural flavor of the fish. The same restraint is used with other dishes – a trick the French discovered, with much ballyhoo, a few years ago.

Other than a painted claw-foot bathtub on the second floor left over from a previous tenant, the place lacks atmosphere. Vinyl walls, plastic tables and crowded seating contribute to a casual, relaxed ambiance, if not to a feeling of luxury.

Inexpensive to moderate. Open seven days. Lunch from 11:30 A.M. to 4 P.M. Dinner from 4 P.M. to 1 A.M. No reservations. All major credit cards. Full bar. Valet parking. Casual.

★ ★
BAY WOLF CAFE AND RESTAURANT/Mediterranean
3853 Piedmont Avenue/Oakland/Area 2/(415) 655-6004

The cuisine is Mediterranean with the California influence of local, seasonal, fresh-fresh-fresh ingredients on the constantly changing menu. On a Wednesday night, you might choose sautéed lamb chops with roasted eggplant, red pepper, potatoes and whiskey shallot sauce; or grilled swordfish with tomato *buerre blanc* and pink grapefruit. Appetizers and petite entrées can be as simple as a green salad, or more complex, like duck and calf's liver flan with pecans, figs and brandy. The three young owners grow their own herbs and must have weekly cuisine-storming sessions to arrive at the interesting combinations that chef/owner Michael Wild turns out.

In addition to pre-scheduled dishes, there are nightly specials by the veteran kitchen staff, and, according to owner/partner Larry Goldman, "the longer we work together, the better the food is." The restaurant is housed, literally, in a restored Victorian home for a comfortable unpretentious feeling. Sunday brunch continues the dynamic tradition of food preparation, and there are special menus and celebration dinners throughout the year, including "Double Duck" dinners, where you'll be sure to go quackers over the various preparations.

Moderate. Open seven days. Lunch served weekdays from 11:30 A.M. to 2 P.M. Dinner from 6 to 9:30 P.M. Sunday brunch from 10 A.M. to 3 P.M. Reservations accepted for dinner only. Visa, MC. Beer and wine only. Patio. Street parking. Casual.

★
BEETHOVEN/German/Continental
1701 Powell Street/San Francisco/Area 2/(415) 391-4488

No where else locally can you dine sumptuously and listen to the soothing, uplifting compositions of Ludwig von Beethoven and his classic contemporaries as soft background to the hum of light conversation and muted laughter. Alfred Baumann, owner/host, has created a sophisticated, ideal retreat reminiscent of a dining room-parlor in turn-of-the-century Europe. While Alfred serves roast pork and veal specialties such as wienerschnitzel and sauerbraten with fresh-made potato pancakes, I am an admirer of that rarely encountered roast goose, cooked slowly and virtually fat free. The stuffed leg of veal, another rarity, is also a favorite.

For best results, consult "How to Use This Guide" on page 25.

The seafood is fresh, properly prepared and likely to please. I favor the scallops, sautéed, and the absolutely fresh trout will remind the angler of the joys of rod and reel. Mr. Baumann is justly proud of his apple strudel with vanilla sauce. Naturally, there are fine German wines, some twenty of them, and, perhaps thirty California selections. Good German beers, of course.

Moderate. Open Tuesday through Saturday from 5:30 to 10:30 P.M. Reservations advised. Visa, MC, AX. Wine and beer only. Valet parking. Casual to semi-dressy.

★
BENBOW INN/Continental
445 Lake Benbow Drive/Garberville/Area 4/(707) 923-2124

Far ahead of its time when completed in 1926, the Benbow Inn is happily now far behind its time, dedicated as it is to the old and best traditions of hostelry. This complete resort lies nestled in a bucolic valley of Humboldt redwood country. Its Tudor-style windows look out over the Eel River. Patsy and Chuck Watts rescued this dignified edifice four years ago and are restoring it to its expected grace and elegance. The Inn continues to offer quality foods from its kitchen. Dinners are served complete with the day's soup and house salad and are topped off by a selection of desserts. If you prefer dining *au natural* (the surroundings, not you), then by all means opt for *al fresco* dining on the terrace.

Moderate. Open seven days. Buffet lunch served noon to 1:30 P.M. Brunch 8 A.M. to 2 P.M. Dinner from 6 to 9 P.M. Closed January-March. Reservations requested. Visa, MC. Full bar. Patio. Casual.

★
BENIHANA OF TOKYO/Japanese
1737 Post Street/Japan Center/San Francisco/Area 2/(415) 563-4844
1496 Old Bayshore Highway/Burlingame/Area 2/(415) 342-5202
2074 Vallco Fashion Park/Cupertino/Area 2/(408) 253-1221

The success Rocky Aoki has enjoyed with his Benihana chain is a myth come to life. And little wonder, for he offers a dining experience that is at once exotic and familiar, combining showmanship with the very best of ingredients and cooking right before your eyes. Even chopstick novices are sure to enjoy the house specialty—tender, well-aged filets of beef grilled *teppan* style and accompanied by mushrooms, onions, zucchini and bean sprouts flavored with soy and sake and sugar and spice. To enjoy this dish in true Japanese style, ask for a raw egg which you beat with your chopsticks and use as a dip to coat each bite-size morsel. Or you can eat Western style with a fork, and satisfy even the most obdurate meat and potatoes die-hard. Two first courses suggest themselves: for the less adventurous, order the tempura of shrimp and vegetables coated in the frothiest of batters and fried crisp and light; the initiated or adventuresome will want to try the *sashimi* of delicately flavorful raw tuna served with a paste of hot green *wasabi* radish.

Moderate. Open for lunch 11:30 A.M. to 2 P.M. Monday through Saturday. Dinner weekdays 5 to 10 P.M., Saturday 5:30 to 11 P.M., Sunday 4:30 to 10 P.M. Reservations advised. All major credit cards. Full bar. Casual to semi-dressy.

★
BENTLEY'S/Seafood/Oyster Bar
185 Sutter Street/Galleria Park Hotel/San Francisco/Area 2/(415) 989-6895

Conveniently placed in the heart of the Financial District, on the first and second (mezzanine) floors, this unpretentiously-accoutered restaurant has already won its spurs, if only for the scrupulous concern with the intriguing varieties of oysters and fish from the east, New Orleans and Pacific waters. A quite unusual, cleverly-conceived menu clearly describes the day's offerings and the waiters' advice is up to the minute. You will find that the chowders are correctly made, without flour, that the New Orleans blackened redfish is both crisp-skinned and still thoroughly cooked, unspoiled by a raw center. On the ground floor, fronting on Sutter Street, awaits the oyster bar, tables, an open kitchen and counter. It can be a bit noisy, but the mezzanine dining area is quieter and carpeted, with views of the ground floor, the street and a portion of the hotel lobby. There is a small, adequate list of California wines. Have the great sweet potato pecan pie. Go ahead. Enjoy.

Moderate to expensive. Open Monday through Friday for lunch, 11:30 A.M. to 3 P.M. Dinner Monday through Thursday 5 to 9 P.M., Friday and Saturday till 11 P.M. Oyster bar open 3 to 5 P.M. Reservations necessary for lunch, recommended for dinner. All major cards. Entertainment. Full bar. Street parking. Casual.

★
BEPPINO'S RISTORANTE/Continental/Italian
San Franciscan Hotel/1231 Market Street/San Francisco/Area 2/(415) 626-8000

San Francisco's serious lack of a good restaurant near the Opera House for pre-performance dining was remedied when Beppino's opened in the refurbished San Franciscan Hotel. No need to worry that you'll be faced with standard hotel fare, for although the hotel houses the kitchen, that's where the connection ends. The veal dishes are up to the city's standards; veal *agro* in a lemon sauce with a hint of garlic, veal with eggplant Napoletana and a really good stuffed breast of veal. Either of the two best pasta courses here—linguine with white clam sauce or seafood *cannelloni*—makes an excellent choice for a light repast before a heavy opera. If you have no fear of falling asleep before the intermission, go ahead and order the grenadine of beef, which is accompanied by *cannelloni*. If there's still room—and time before the curtain—you can top off with *zabaglione*; rich custard with sweet Marsala wine.

Moderate. Open seven days. Breakfast from 6:30 to 11 A.M. Lunch from 11:30 A.M. to 5 P.M. Dinner from 5 to 10 P.M. Reservations advised. All major credit cards. Entertainment. Full bar. Street parking. Semi-dressy.

★ ★
BERTOLUCCI'S/Northern Italian
421 Cypress Avenue/San Francisco/Area 2/(415) 588-1625

This restaurant had its roots in 1928 when the Bertolucci family opened a humble boarding house, the Liberty Hotel, serving hearty northern Italian dinners to laborers in nearby steel and packing plants. Tisbe "Mama" Bertolucci toiled long hours in the kitchen preparing wondrously fragrant pastas, veal and chicken in her cucina Toscana. As Prohibition ended, husband Joe opened an adjacent bar, Joe's Blue Room. So popular did their table become, that they opened to the public as a restaurant. Now Bertolucci's is not only patronized by fourth generation descendants of former lodgers, but by celebrities from the world-over like John Forsythe of "Dynasty," actor Clint Eastwood, columnist Ann Landers and figures from the world of politics, sports, industry, society and media. Mama's children, Larry and Lola, take an active part in the kitchen and management of the restaurant which, in spite of a sophisticated Florentine mirror-and-dark-wood-elegance, is as friendly and relaxing as a trattoria. Northern Italian cuisine is marked by lighter, subtly flavored sauces, a marriage of Italian and French cuisine. Specialties are chicken *Toscana*, veal *picatta* and *linguine carbonara*, but the crowning achievement is their *cannelloni rossini*, made fresh daily by Mama and Lola. These are airy crêpes encasing a frothy pink mixture of meats, prosciutto and spices—as light and haunting as a South San Francisco fog. They get orders for these from Hollywood, and as far away as Denver.

Among the last of the great Depression-born family restaurants, Bertolucci's recently celebrated its 50th anniversary. The walls are currently covered with congratulatory messages from such diverse fans as President Reagan, Frank Sinatra, Governor Deukmejian and countless others. Mama, at eighty-seven, still keeps a watchful, matriarchal eye on the kitchen to be sure her recipes are followed to the letter, and that all ingredients are the freshest and of highest quality. In her apron, she sits at a table dubbed "Mission Control" to greet her friends, all treated as her "family." Located near Candlestick Park, San Francisco Airport, the Cow Palace and hotels, Bertolucci's enjoys a convenient location for travelers and sports devotees.

Moderate. Open seven days. Lunch from 11:30 A.M. to 3 P.M. on weekdays. Dinner from 5 to 10 P.M. Reservations advised. Visa, MC, AX. Full bar. Child's menu. Parking lot. Casual.

★ ★

BETTE'S OCEANVIEW DINER/American Diner
1807 A Fourth Street/Berkeley/Area 2/(415) 644-3230

If you fondly recall the '40s, '50s, and '60s, you will not delay in visiting this wonderful, small modernized version of the diner, with truly far superior food. The best Bay Area jukebox, a Seeburg from 1957 with a collection of eight hundred records of the past, brightens the air, and guests relax at the counter or in booths. The atmosphere is simple, comfortable, and the food ranges from great breakfasts to huge sandwiches on interesting breads (from Acme, in Berkeley) to loin of pork, with potato pancakes and, perhaps sliced turkey, or any of several salads. Daily hot specialties are highlighted on a board. Currently, they're not putting out burgers or French fries, but as you can get these old-hat items anywhere, settle down and revel in the '50s feeling. Yes, you can go home again. And, when you do, have a thick, tall shake and a generous cut of pie, perhaps apple, like Mom used to try to bake. Real casual.

Inexpensive. Open seven days. Breakfast and lunch Monday 6:30 A.M. to 2:30 P.M.; Tuesday through Saturday 6:30 A.M. to 4 P.M. Sunday 8 A.M. to 4 P.M. No reservations. No credit cards. Wine and beer only. Street parking. Casual.

★ ★ ★

THE BIG FOUR/Continental
1075 California Street/San Francisco/Area 2/(415) 771-1140

Oscar de la Renta called this magnificently appointed dining place "the most beautiful restaurant in America" when it opened in 1976. Local describers of the dining out scene, and several widely syndicated columnists have written glowingly of the impressive design's concept and execution. Yet regular patrons say, somewhat smugly but really most accurately, that the Big Four is "one of the better-kept secrets in San Francisco."

Operated in and by the Huntington Hotel, this compelling monument to the finer, more solid components of the late 1880s honors four magnates whose combined efforts made possible the junction at Promontory Point, Utah in 1869, of the Union Pacific and Central Pacific railroads, completing the transcontinental rail link. Already famous on Nob Hill (in fact, they were the most prominent "Nobs"), Collis P. Huntington, Mark Hopkins, Charles Crocker and Leland Stanford would certainly have approved and patronized this handsome establishment. The Big Four just may be, for most of us, the closest we'll ever get to an elegant, private, millionaire's club.

The design is smashing—all green leather club chairs and banquettes, stained glass, cut glass, green-shade wall sconces created from rams' horns and set in brass, oak-paneled walls, a bar of properly polished copper, too many details to record here. You enter the outer lobby to an array of 1880 memorabilia so well displayed and intriguing that you'll tarry on your departure to study the collection, all of which is museum-worthy. Check the restrooms, even.

The gentlemen responsible for all this, Newton Cope, Sr. and Newton, Jr., who also have the impressive St. George in St. Helena, have striven mightily over the last six years to improve their cuisine to match the opulent decor. Their success is borne out by the fact that many residents of the Nob Hill area, who can well afford to eat anywhere they wish, including at least five world-famous places within a block of the Big Four, are wont to dine with the Copes as often as twice weekly. Newton, Jr. says that some come thrice (nice word; how often can you use "thrice").

The menu is constantly revised to maintain an innovative, creative cuisine, with nightly specials which are frequently seafood dishes. Rather than a classic dinner dining place, this is a specialty house. I won't describe the entrées other than to cite that here you may order filet of buffalo (Wyoming ranch-raised) with *chanterelles,* evoking *déjà-vu* recollections of western plains. Oh, yes, choice among last course offerings—grasshopper pie, the best in town. The constantly expanding wine book (we now have 450 wineries in California, alone) lists many treasures. The Copes' frequent visits to their Napa Valley restaurant keep them *au courant* to the nth.

Moderate to expensive. Open seven days. Breakfast 7:30 to 9:30 A.M. Lunch from 11:30 A.M. to 3 P.M. Dinner from 5:30 to 11 P.M. Sunday brunch 9 A.M. to 3 P.M. Reservations essential. Visa, MC, AX. Full bar. Parking garages and valet parking. Dressy.

For best results, consult "How to Use This Guide" on page 25.

★
BILLBOARD CAFE/California/Continental
299 9th Street/San Francisco/Area 2/(415) 558-9500

Mark Rennie, Hastings law graduate and computer artist, is the unofficial mayor of this Soho-like area south of Market Street. His Billboard Cafe is noisy, funky and new wave, appealing to the yuppies of the Bay Area. Billboard waiters border on punk with barely controlled hairstyles and a funny kind of informality. It is not uncommon for your waiter to draw up a chair as he waits for you to decide betwixt such good and well prepared dishes as marinated roast chicken, or grilled swordfish. Quiche is a cloud-light concoction in a great crust, and is served with wafer thin slices of red onion and a watercress, spinach and red leaf lettuce salad. The hamburgers will add fuel to the ongoing hamburger debate—here they are served near perfect—charcoal grilled with sesame seed rolls. Tables are jammed together, but that's part of the fun and people don't mind waiting. Lunch is a little quieter. One of the best food bargains in town.
Moderate. Lunch Monday through Saturday from 11 A.M. to 5:30 P.M. Dinner Monday through Thursday from 5:30 to 10 P.M., Friday and Saturday till 11:30 P.M. No reservations. No credit cards. Wine and beer only. Street parking. Casual.

★ ★ ★
BILL'S PLACE/American
2315 Clement Street/San Francisco/Area 2/(415) 221-5262
★ ★
56 Lake Shore Plaza/San Francisco/Area 2/(415) 566-1146

Bill's serves the best hamburgers in town. Most everyone has spent some good times in this inspired, flower-bedecked, American-style restaurant. There are some who feel these are the best hamburgers *anywhere*—I don't—but the homemade carrot cake may be. I love the admonition on the menu: "Children are most welcome . . . however, because we must consider all our customers, children are not allowed to make undue noise . . . must remain seated at all times." Shoulder chuck is ground fresh daily, the French fries are hand cut, and soups are homemade. Though desserts are not made in-house, they are some of the best; Double Rainbow ice cream and cakes by Just Desserts. I like everything but the hotdogs, and strongly recommend just plain Bill's for a quick and easy lunch.

Inexpensive. Open seven days from 11:30 A.M. to 9:30 P.M. Reservations accepted. No credit cards. Beer and wine only. Patio dining at Clement St. location. Child's menu. Parking lot at Lake Shore, valet at Clement. Casual.

★
BINI'S BAR & GRILLE/Homestyle American
337 East Taylor Street/San Jose/Area 2/(408) 279-9996

Harsh fluorescent lights cast shadows on the greasy walls and dust-laden fixtures at Bini's. But the cannery employees and attorneys don't seem to mind. They enjoy this unusual establishment with its view of the railroad tracks. Probably one of the oldest bars and restaurants in the heart of the produce market and industrial area, Bini's offers inexpensive homestyle food. Here, the American workingman can sit at the bar where the barkeep doesn't measure the sauce, and where the breakfasts and lunches keep the locals' bread baskets filled unto dinner. No *cuisine minceur* here, just hearty dishes. Liver and onions, beef stew, stuffed bell peppers, sandwiches served with French fries, cole slaw or vegetable, depending on selection. No delicacies. No nonsense. No frills. No high prices, either.
Inexpensive. Open Monday through Saturday for breakfast and lunch only from 6 A.M. to 2:30 P.M. No reservations. No credit cards. Cocktails. Casual.

★ ★
BLANCHE'S/Continental/Art Gallery
998 Fourth Street/San Francisco/Area 2/(415) 397-4191

Blanche Pastorino has owned and run this diminutive "in" delight since 1959, in the course of years winning a distinctive clientele from all walks of life. Often called the Galerie de Blanche, a small gesture to her Gallic antecedents, this charmer is, as she says, "five minutes from the heart of The City but a million miles away in peace and quietude." Situated on a waterside pier on the Mission Channel, the city skyline views from this intimate dining place are rarely seen even by the locals, unless they come here. The interior views of the works of carefully screened artists are alone worth your visit. Some of the simple menu's suggestions: shrimp Louie salad, Blanche's home-cooked meat and cheese rolls, hot specialties, hearty sandwiches on proper rolls and good bread, fresh crab when available and "simply wonderful" (quoting discerning patrons, such as Mayor Feinstein) desserts. This is a unique find.

Inexpensive. Open Monday through Friday for lunch from 11 A.M. to 2:30 P.M. Reservations for large parties. MC. Wine and beer only. Street parking. Casual.

★ ★
BLUE BOAR INN/French/California/British
1713 Lombard Street/San Francisco/Area 2/(415) 567-8424

When I asked owners Brian Weatherhill and Bernard Jansen just how they regarded themselves in the complex restaurant profession, both smiled and Brian replied, "We are practitioners in the art of innovative cuisine." Well, they really are. When my guests, including associate Steve Knight of KIEV radio, and I dined recently in this replica of an English inn, charmingly authentic in detail, we feasted upon roast rack of lamb, beef Wellington, prime rib and Yorkshire pudding and London mixed grill (boar is no longer served here, and I won't miss it). While these are classics, there were subtle touches in their creation, as there were with accompanying courses. We received tasty tidbits, courtesy of diners at the next table, who happened to recognize me, of a fantastic country goose and quail. Their award-winning cellar is now housed in an adjoining building which the Boar has acquired, with tasting and banquet rooms, and the bottlings presently exceed thirty thousand. Unusual in the San Francisco Bay Area—you can come in here as late as 1 A.M. and be served. Patrons of theater, ballet, opera and symphony seem to be aware of this unusual boon.
Moderate to expensive. Open Monday through Saturday from 6 P.M. to 1 A.M. Sunday from 5 to 11 P.M. Reservations advised. All major credit cards. Full bar. Valet parking. Semi-dressy.

★ ★
BLUE FOX/Continental/Northern Italian
659 Merchant Street/San Francisco/Area 2/(415) 981-1177

The prestigious elegance of the Blue Fox has prospered—except for a brief period of uncertainty—despite its improbable site on dingy Merchant Street, where a few winos and ragged individualists prowl for handouts. Impervious to the surroundings and under the demanding direction of Mario Mondin, the Blue Fox has nearly returned to its former glory as one of the hedonist temples of a sophisticated city. There are high-backed velvet chairs from Italy, French impressionist paintings and a main salon with Roman columns is paneled in Florentine gold. The menu presents the classic dishes of many regions—with emphasis on the *alta cucina* of northern Italy—and it's not a place for bargains (money, after all, doesn't grow on sprees).

There is usually a delay in seating, despite reservations – diners like to linger and thus are apt to tie up your table – but the wait is not unpleasant in the dramatic cocktail lounge. Appetizers? You might try the *tortellini* that have been simmering in chicken broth and are served with a herb-cream sauce, or the *pâté maison* with truffles, or the most exotic: the *bitello tonnato,* a lovely dish of cold veal in a sauce rich with capers, anchovy and tuna. The cream of spinach soup is one of the best cream soups I've tasted. The Roquefort salad is made, oddly these days, with Roquefort that is crushed at your table, oil and vinegar and tossed onto heart of romaine lettuce garnished with tiny tomatoes. The Caesar salad is the best in the city.

The list of entrées is seemingly without end, and includes the expected – Long Island duckling, rack of lamb, tournedos – along with lesser known dishes from Venice and small French provinces. You might ask about the *entrecôte* of beef – it's not on the menu – sliced, tender beef in truffle sauce served from a grandiloquent silver cart. The Blue Fox is one of the few restaurants in America that serves an outstanding selection of cheeses at the proper temperature (most restaurants serve their cheese from the refrigerator, because of the waste or left-over factor). The Camembert, Bel Paese, Brie and Port du Salut are presented beautifully. The blueberry crêpes flambé (for two) are served with a curacao base sauce, filled with soft pudding and festooned with blueberries. The wine cellar is an incomparable setting for banquets, though I find the wines overpriced.

Historic note: A few yards away is old Portsmouth Square where the vigilantes rendered their peculiar "justice" and Robert Louis Stevenson sunned himself in the afternoons.

Financial note: At this writing, there is an "early bird special," available 6 to 7 P.M., that features a four-course dinner for about $22.50. **Expensive.** Open Monday through Saturday. Dinner served from 6 to 11 P.M. Reservations advised. All major credit cards. Full bar. Valet parking. Dressy.

★
BLUE LIGHT CAFE/American/Southern
1979 Union/San Francisco/Area 2/(415) 922-5510

San Francisco's own Boz Scaggs, pop singer extraordinaire, opened this lively, innovative restaurant as "a labor of love." The type of food at the Blue Light is the kind of food that Boz grew up on in Oklahoma and Texas. The eclectic menu includes stuffed and grilled Maine lobster from an aquarium. Chicken-fried steak and bacon fat white gravy always sounds horrible, but tastes good, even to the more finicky gourmets.

Boz's famous fried chicken is his own recipe that he has prepared for charitable events, sometimes on and sometimes off the menu. A near-pound T-bone is done to a fair-thee-well. The full bar serves generously. There are often some interesting dishes on the Sunday brunch. **Moderate.** Open daily from 4 P.M. to 2 A.M. Sunday brunch 10 A.M. to 3 P.M. Reservations accepted. All major credit cards. Full bar. Street parking. Casual.

★
BLUE NILE/Ethiopian
2525 Telegraph/Berkeley/Area 2/(415) 540-6777

The first ethnic restaurants in California seem to all have started in the Berkeley area, usually with a modest storefront and a few travel posters. In this small, unpretentious upstairs location, eating "family style" is similar to the Morrocan custom of eating with bread rather than knife and fork, and, though it sounds messy, there is a grand communal spirit about such gastronomic adventuring. Chef Alem Mamo previously worked at a restaurant in Ethiopia and the authenticity of the food is undeniable. *Doro wat* is chicken marinated in hot sauce, *ye-beg alecha* is curried lamb stew and *ye-siga wat* is a form of spicy beef stew. *Kitfo* is Ethiopian-style tartar (sic) steak. Owner/host Seyoum Kebede is there to interpret and consult. **Inexpensive.** Open seven days from 11:30 A.M. to 10 P.M., Sunday 5 to 10 P.M. Reservations accepted. Visa, MC. Wine and beer only. Validated parking. Casual to semi-dressy.

BODEGA GALLERY/California/Continental
17110 Bodega Lane/Bodega/Area 3/(707) 876-3257

Good food and fine art have always gone cheek by jowl from the earliest times. The Potter School was built in Bodega in 1873 for the then-staggering sum of $5,000,000 and has since become a landmark in the area. Alfred Hitchcock, the artist of the macabre, used the edifice for the 1962 scare, *The Birds*. It is now also an art gallery, housing paintings and drawings of local artists, a boutique and gift shop. It also features one of Sonoma County's better restaurants. Fresh local fish are highlighted on the menu: poached salmon with *beurre blanc,* snapper Créole, scallops *Provençale*, roast duck with ginger plum sauce, and home-made pasta . . . and the view of the surrounding rural area and gardens makes it especially palatable.

Inexpensive to moderate. Open Wednesday through Sunday. Lunch Thursday through Saturday noon to 2:30 P.M. Dinner from 5 to 9:30 P.M. Sunday brunch 10 A.M. to 2:30 P.M. Reservations advised. Visa, MC. Classical guitar in evening. Wine and beer only. View. Lot parking. Semi-dressy.

★★

BON APPÉTIT/French/Continental
Almond Orchard Center/11773 Fair Oaks Boulevard at Madison Avenue
Fair Oaks/Area 3/(916) 966-9666

Neatly situated in a corner of this smart shopping center (meaning that you'll have no parking problems), this gem of a dining place is lovingly tended by owners David O'Dell and his wife Lin, whose precepts reach far higher than many restaurants. The comfort of a gracious home distinguishes Bon Appétit, and you settle back in your upholstered arm-chair as you survey ceiling-high bookcases against a brick wall. The crystal placed meticulously on the heavy linen tablecloth reflects the light as you peruse a menu that underlines the O'Dells' comprehension of a fine dining experience. Take special note of the *poisson du jour,* the fresh fish of the evening, and the *caneton aux sauce de miel et amande.* The roasted Petaluma duckling, first glazed with a blend of duck stock, honey and Amaretto, is topped with crystalized almonds. The classic tournedos "Helder" is two broiled filet steaks, wrapped in bacon and served on toasted croutons. Chopped tomatoes and béarnaise fill artichoke hearts, which are then placed atop the meat. Here is elegance without formality. The bar lounge is a quiet retreat. Wine devotees will admire the cellar. **Expensive.** Open Tuesday through Sunday. Lunch from 11:30 A.M. to 2 P.M. Dinner 6 to 10 P.M.; 7 to 10 P.M. Tuesday. Sunday brunch from 10 A.M. to 2 P.M. Reservations recommended. MC, Visa. Entertainment Friday and Saturday night. Full bar. Lot parking. Semi-dressy.

★

THE BRAMBLES DINNER HOUSE/American
4005 Burton Drive/Cambria/Area 1/(805) 927-4716

1985 was the 20th anniversary of this Cambria mainstay. The house itself has begun its second century. The gradual additions have ex-tended the seating capacity from 35 to 200, but the increases in size have not altered the friendly family feeling. New owners Nick and Deb-bie Kaperonis are continuing the tradition of a sturdily American menu — steaks cooked over an oak wood pit, sautéed seafood, and chicken. Boston chowder, oyster or split pea soup, salad (green or Caesar), potato and

vegetable accompany all entrées. A homey restaurant with an "ours," not "mine" feeling.
Moderate. Open seven days. Dinner Monday through Saturday from 5 to 10 P.M.; Sunday 4 to 9 P.M. Reservations required. Visa, MC, AX. Wine and beer only. Casual.

★

BRENTWOOD LODGE/Continental
101 Brentwood Drive/South San Francisco/Area 2/(415) 583-6263

It's perhaps a sign of the times that the least expensive dinner offered here is upstaging the rest of the menu. This solid value is the special "supper steak"—a healthy cut of sirloin that comes with soup, salad, spaghetti and dessert. The other end of the menu boasts prime rib and châteaubriand, with a sprinkling of standard veal and chicken dishes in between. Lunch choices are topped by an adequate London broil. Not the most imaginative menu, but the service is amiable, the food is good and the Lodge is convenient to three freeways.
Moderate. Open seven days. Lunch served Monday through Saturday 11 A.M. to 2:30 P.M. Dinner Tuesday through Sunday 5 to 10 P.M. Reservations accepted. Visa, MC. Full bar. Lot parking. Casual.

★

THE BRITISH BANKERS CLUB/Continental
1090 El Camino Real/Menlo Park/Area 2/(415) 327-8769

The pinstriped crowd from the "Old Lady of Threadneedle Street" would find themselves at home here at the BBC (as the logo on the window indicates). This was, indeed, a bank building (brick) that Anglophile Dennis Grimsman converted into an "establishment" British club and restaurant. The decor, as might be expected, is from Victoria's era: dark woods, cut glass screens, burgundy velvet drapes, a tartan rug downstairs – and, oddly – a magnificent back bar from Roseburg, Oregon. There are no adventurous food surprises here. What is done is done well – including really splendid service. Prime rib is thick and juicy; calf's liver, veal scalloppine, and prawns are all done properly and all reasonably priced. Fish and chips, on Fridays only, is popular fare. A British dish flagged "Union Jack" (turkey, bacon, avocado, on egg bread open face) is a popular lunch offering. There has been considerable thought expended on shaping the wine list: twenty California whites, twenty-one reds; Souverain, the house wine, is served in carafes.
Moderate. Open Monday through Friday for lunch from 11 A.M. to 3 P.M. Dinner Monday through Thursday from 6 to 10 P.M.; Friday and Saturday to 11 P.M. Reservations accepted for parties of eight or more. Visa, MC, AX, DC. Full bar. Parking lot. Casual.

★ ★ ★
BROADWAY TERRACE CAFE/California
5891 Broadway Terrace/Oakland/Area 2/(415) 652-4442

This wonderful dining adventure is situated improbably in Oakland, and has had to compete with such stalwarts as Chez Panisse and Greens on the east bay for attention. While the ubiquitous mesquite grill is in evidence, it is used with sensitivity, and the four fresh fish featured each day are flawlessly executed. Located in what used to be a garage or filling station, the small thirty-four seat restaurant is rather undistinguished as to decor—fresh flowers provide the only real color in the room. Menus change every six weeks, but the current one lists, under "starters," wild rice crêpe with goat cheese and country ham and pasta of the day. "Salads" offers a bouquet of mixed greens along with a more complex salad made of romaine, gorgonzola, pears and walnuts with a gorgonzola vinaigrette. Entrées include a grilled and dry marinated rib-eye steak with a black pepper anchovy chili butter; sautéed loin of veal with paprika, red peppers, almonds and cream; and grilled loin of pork with an apple-currant chutney. Desserts offer a silky smooth "sour cream chocolate cake," bourbon orange poundcake, fruit tarte and homemade ice cream or sorbet. Owner/chef/maître d' Albert Katz shops each day for the freshest and best raw materials. In a reversal of form he will not accept credit cards but will take personal checks, and, while he isn't open for luncheon, there is a Sunday sit-down brunch.

Moderate. Open Tuesday through Saturday from 5:30 to 10 P.M., Sunday 5 to 9 P.M. Sunday brunch from 10:30 A.M. to 2 P.M. Reservations necessary. Personal checks. Wine and beer only. View. Lot parking. Casual.

DA ★
BUENA VISTA CAFE/American
2765 Hyde Street/San Francisco/Area 2/(415) 474-5044

That Buena Vista is most famous for their Irish coffee is kind of unfair. While their bar menu is the best in town, with a good wine list featuring some California greats and near-greats, the food is not insignificant. On those mornings when the sky is so blue you can see three months in any direction, I'll wander on down to the corner of Beach and Hyde (Hyde is one of those hills you can lean against when you get tired of walking) and begin with a sumptuous breakfast: perhaps a chilled aquavit or king-sized Bloody Mary, and the JLK special, an omelette with fresh, crisp bacon bits, onion, green pepper and mushrooms. There's a menu that's both varied and limited, if that's not a contradiction, with changing daily specials like pot roast, ravioli, and Hungarian goulash. This is where the intellectuals have gathered to play trivia or argue politics since 1895. Some of them look it.

Incidentally, the recipe for Irish coffee Buena Vista: (1) Preheat glass with very hot water; empty. (2) Fill glass three quarters full of hot black coffee. Drop in three cubes of sugar. (3) Stir until sugar is dissolved completely. (4) Add a full ounce of Irish whiskey. (5) Pour in lightly whipped cream over a spoon to make a "head." (6) Enjoy.

Tour note: There are four historic ships moored across the way as part of the San Francisco Maritime State Monument.

Inexpensive. Open seven days. Lunch and dinner served from 11 A.M. to 9:30 P.M. Breakfast 9 A.M. (Saturday and Sunday 8 A.M.) to 9:30 P.M. No reservations. No credit cards. Full bar. View of bay, Alcatraz, Golden Gate Bridge, cable car turnaround. Street parking. Casual (no tank shirts).

★
BULL VALLEY INN/Continental
14 Canyon Lake Drive/Port Costa/Area 2/(415) 787-2244

Setting foot in Port Costa today is like stepping back into early California, and the port that once dared to rival San Francisco has, happily, been saved from decay by enterprise and tourism. The fine old stone-faced building across from the hotel was one of seventeen town saloons when it was built in 1897; now it's one of two. The well-preserved bar dates from 1885 — it still basks in the warm glow of Tiffany lamps, and Saturday nights are filled with the sound of a local ragtime group. The little dining room which adjoins the bar presents dinners reminiscent of Diamond Jim Brady. Early California's penchant for massive meals is well served by roast duck smothered in a fresh fruit glaze, three double lamb chops in a mild curry sauce, and oysters with a fresh vegetable dressing baked in the shell and flamed at your table. Even Big Jim's appetite would falter at the filet mignon à la Louis XIV, a full pound-and-a-half planked filet dressed fit to kill.

Moderate. Open Wednesday through Sunday. Lunch served 11:30 A.M. to 2:30 P.M. Dinner served Wednesday through Friday 5:30 to 9:30 P.M.; Saturday 5:30 to 10 P.M.; Sunday 4:30 to 9 P.M. Sunday brunch served from 11 A.M. to 2:30 P.M. Reservations advised. All major credit cards. Entertainment. Full bar. Patio. Ample parking. Casual.

In order to obtain the best results from this Guide, be sure to read the French, German, Italian and Oriental menu translators on pages 399 to 404 of this Guide.

★
BUY-TH-BUCKET/Take-out
4565 Stevens Creek Boulevard/Santa Clara/Area 2/(408) 248-6244

Buy-Th-Bucket doesn't fool around with pretensions – it knows what it is. The Bucket is a non-service dinner house, strictly cash and carry, that has immortalized its stripped-down operation by offering family-size buckets of plain good food – quarts, half gallons, or gallons of spaghetti, ravioli, clams or any other number of items – to the hungering masses.

A gourmand's paradise, the menu that never quits lists Italian specials like fresh catfish, lasagna, linguine and clams (just to mention a few), and the Bucket's deservedly famous steamed clams Bordelaise with its garlic and lemon broth and large, sweet, chewy clams – the likes of which turned us into fans – proved conclusively that the chef at Buy-Th-Bucket knows what food is all about.

The ambiance can best be described as Early Tennis Shoe, but who needs decor? People-watching is the thing, next to eating and drinking, that is. Order an ice-cold pitcher of beer or some Sebastiani, wait for your order, and join the crowds who have made the Bucket almost an institution.

Inexpensive to moderate. Open Monday through Saturday 11 A.M. to 2 A.M.; Sunday from 11 A.M. to midnight. No reservations. No credit cards. Full bar. Parking lot. Casual.

★
BY THE SQUARE/Breakfast/Continental/Italian
433 Powell Street/San Francisco/Area 2/(415) 362-2004

By The Square Restaurant, located in the Chancellor Hotel on the Powell cable car line half a block up from San Francisco's famous Union Square, is owned and operated by Nancy and Jimmy Ng. The warm atmosphere is reflected from the skylight ceiling to the brightly papered walls, oriental art and beautiful green foliage. Efficient hostess/manager Nancy greets patrons with a smile. Jimmy presides over breakfasts and chef Carmelo DiGrande creates the Florentine Italian-continental lunches and dinners. Besides the daily specials, some of the regular features are shrimp scampi style, chicken secco, stuffed prawns and petrale, calamari, tender veal dishes, marvelous pastas, homemade soups, crisp, generous salads and an array of desserts. There's a full bar in the intimate lounge and a good list of California and imported wines.

Moderate. Open for breakfast and lunch seven days a week and dinner Monday through Saturday. Breakfast 7 to 11:30 A.M. Lunch from 11:30 A.M. to 3 P.M. Dinner 5 to 9:30 P.M. Sunday brunch. Reservations accepted. MC, Visa. Full bar. Street parking. Casual.

★
CADEMARTORI'S CASA MARIA/Italian/American
First and San Jose Streets/San Juan Bautista/Area 1/(408) 623-4511

This rambling mansion was the original "parish house" on the grounds of California's largest mission, San Juan Bautista, that faces out on an interesting old plaza, originally the site of bullfights and fandangoes. The historic square remains virtually unchanged in appearance since the days of the Dons. The tiled-roof restaurant serves visitors and locals alike with low priced Italian pasta, and the patio is a peaceful retreat from the crowded highways. The *cannelloni* is the best of the huge menu offerings, but it's only fair.

Moderate. Lunch Tuesday through Saturday 11:30 A.M. to 2 P.M. Dinner weeknights from 5 to 9 P.M., Saturday until 10 P.M., Sunday from 1 to 9 P.M. Reservations accepted. Visa, MC, DC, AX. Full bar. Patio. Parking lot. Casual.

★ ★
CAESAR'S/Northern Italian
2299 Powell Street/San Francisco/Area 2/(415) 989-6000

Here's an Italian family restaurant near the Embarcadero that manages to rise above the plastic grapevines and candled wine bottles of so many in the area. One can imagine the upper-class families of Milan enjoying the daily specials and the traditional mid-Italian entrées with a scattering of American dishes. The dinners are enormous (seven courses) and full-filling, all the way from antipasto to dessert. If this restaurant were not in San Francisco, the home of so many fine Italian ristorantes, it would be a sensation. Here it's merely good and completely honest.

The wine list is better than at most such restaurants and the prices are reasonable.

Inexpensive to moderate. Open Tuesday through Sunday. Lunch served from 11:30 A.M. to 2 P.M. Dinner served from 4:30 to 9:30 P.M. Reservations advised. Visa, MC, AX. Full bar. Child's menu. Valet parking. Casual.

★
CAFE AMERICAIN/Continental/Eclectic
317 Columbus/San Francisco/Area 2/(415) 981-8266

A **light,** bright restaurant in every way – in a neighborhood filled with the grand old-fashioned Italian "family" restaurants that look like an Alka Seltzer commercial. There are skylights, whitewashed walls, greenery and an open exhibition kitchen to support a menu that seems to feature fresh fish and oak-fired pizzas. Smoked chicken salad; spinach linguine with sun-dried tomatoes, garlic and mushrooms; fetuccine with pork, cilantro, hot green chile sauce and red peppers; and twilight zone desserts like floating island (when was the last time you saw that on a menu?) and white chocolate mousse will give you an idea of the menu. Dishes are prepared competently, but there is an overabundance of these kinds of restaurants and you have the feeling that all the food could be prepared by one commissary.

Moderate. Lunch weekdays from 11:30 A.M. to 3 P.M. Dinner Monday through Thursday from 6 to 10 P.M., Friday and Saturday till 11 P.M. Reservations advised. Visa, MC. Wine and beer only. Valet parking. Casual.

★ ★
CAFE AT CHEZ PANISSE/Continental
1517 Shattuck/Berkeley/Area 2/(415) 548-5525

W**hat** more can be written of the legendary Alice Waters and her gastronome? Cafe at Chez Panisse is upstairs (the dining room downstairs serves the famous *prix fixe* menu) and provides lighter and more accessible food – open from 11:30 in the morning until 11:30 at night. The open kitchen, skylight and general feeling is a perfect setting for the food, which if not drop-dead stunning, is at least original. There are three salads including a fresh garden salad that is literally hand-picked from the garden. There are pizzas, of course, folded over (calzone), flat, and with interesting combinations. Other menu categories include appetizers, salads, light entrées, plats du jour and desserts (prepared by the same pastry chef for Chez Panisse). Chef Paul Bertolli has previously cooked for the Fourth St. Grill.

Moderate to expensive. Open daily from 11:30 A.M. to 11:30 P.M. No reservations. No credit cards. Wine and beer only. Street parking. Casual to semi-dressy.

★
CAFE BEAUJOLAIS/American/Continental
961 Ukiah Street/Mendocino/Area 3/(707) 937-5614

Cafe Beaujolais is a converted house on a side street, three blocks away from the noise of downtown, with a beautiful deck overlooking their one-half acre garden and the Pacific, which makes for an enchanted setting.

Many claim the breakfasts here as the finest in Northern California. A fresh mushroom and Swiss cheese omelette is one of a long list of egg specialities. And if you long for a *real* waffle, this is where you find it – dark brown, hearty, and crunchy with Vermont maple syrup – no imitations here. Owner Margaret Fox bakes the muffins and coffee cake. The French-roast coffee *is* French roasted.
Moderate. Open seven days. Breakfast from 7:30 A.M. to 2 P.M. Lunch from 11:30 A.M. to 2 P.M. Dinner served Friday through Monday 6 to 9:30 A.M. in the summer. Serving times change seasonally. Reservations advised. Wine and beer only. Casual.

★
CAFE DELICIAS/Mexican
1591 Lincoln Way/Auburn/Area 5/(916) 885-2050
211 Harding/Roseville/Area 5/(916) 782-4004

Mexican food at almost Mexican prices is the big draw here. Nothing fancy in these small, Old West cafes, but then fancy Mexican food would be out of place in this setting. All of the usual combination plates are served with rice, beans and tortillas. The chef takes justifiable pride in his *chile rellenos* and steak *chicana*, slices of sirloin in a spicy tomato and green pepper sauce, as well as his steak *rancheros*, sirloin or pork steak topped with special sauce. The Mexican wedding cake is enough to make you dash to the altar.
Inexpensive. Open Wednesday through Monday 11 A.M. to 9 P.M. No reservations. Visa, MC, AX (Roseville only). Beer and wine only. Ample free parking. Casual to semi-dressy.

Please be sure to consult "Tipping Made Easy" on page 22 of this Guide.

★
CAFE DU NORD/Basque/French
2170 Market Street/San Francisco/Area 2/(415) 626-0977

Basque fare is hearty, often served family style, and is essentially *cocina campesina*, peasant food originally intended for sheepherders and farmers. Like so many foods of humble origin (soul food, *cassoulet* of French cuisine), it is now considered more "haute" than not and is served here as well as anywhere in San Francisco. Located in the basement of a somewhat shabby building, with individual tables in a wood-paneled room, there is a spacious feeling, as compared with the Basque tradition of communal dining. Pre-set dinners change nightly. Entrées like sweetbreads, lamb stew and beef tongue are favorites. There's always a good soup and a dish of fresh beets vinaigrette or kidney beans and onions in egg sauce. A simple salad follows the main course and dessert is mostly flan. The only à la carte dinner is filet mignon. Jean Louis Arteta and William Davenport, co-owners and operators, have a winner on their hands.
Moderate. Open Wednesday through Sunday from 5:30 to 9:45 P.M. Reservations accepted for eight or more. Visa, MC. Full bar. Child's menu. Street parking. Casual.

★
CAFE FANNY/California
1603 San Pablo Avenue/Berkeley/Area 2/(415) 524-5447

This newest of Alice Waters' creations has no kitchen or tables, and is not in the best part of town, but, nonetheless, it is a winner. A skylight glows above the handsome interior with tile floors, an espresso machine tucked behind a hand-carved counter, a toaster and an egg cooker—all the equipment needed to keep the place buzzing with friendly conversation. The wine bar seems always to be crowded, and though patrons eat while standing, as in some of the Roman trattorìas, it is fun and some how relaxing. Good individual pizzas under $5 are brought in from a nearby bakery.
Inexpensive. Open Tuesday through Saturday from 7 A.M. to 6 P.M. No reservations. No credit cards. Wine and beer only. Lot parking. Casual.

In order to obtain the best results from this Guide, be sure to read the French, German, Italian and Oriental menu translators on pages 399 to 404 of this Guide.

★
CAFE GIGI/French
MGM Grand Hotel/Reno, Nevada/Area 5/(702) 789-2266

This is a place for high rollers. Dinners are available on an à la carte basis only and can run in excess of $50 per person, without wine. It's a bit cutesy to call this a "cafe" since this establishment indicates that its atmosphere is as "regal as the Palace of Versailles." The entrées include the specialty, roast saddle of veal (for two), roast Long Island duckling with a choice of bigarde or Montmorency sauce and imported Dover sole. The menu tends toward the beefy side: beef à la Stroganoff, sirloin steak, filet mignon, pepper steak, and châteaubriand—all prime. It's romantic (private dining alcoves are available) and very French.
Expensive. Open Thursday through Monday. Dinner from 6 to 11 P.M. Reservations advised. All major credit cards. Full bar. Free valet and self-parking. Semi-dressy.

★
CAFE GITANES/Tunisian
3214 16th Street/San Francisco/Area 2/(415) 431-5838

This tiny thirty-seater is one of the few places we can go for *couscous* without having to order an elaborate, heavy dinner in and around it. There are six kinds of *couscous* served here, all authentic, all good. Lamb *m'hammer* is served on the bone with prunes and almonds in a honey sauce. *Brik* are deep-fried pastries stuffed with egg or tuna, and you can order them on the combination plate that includes *merguez,* a delectably spicy Tunisian sausage. Mint tea and conversation usually follow. Open for breakfast with omelettes, lunch with unusual sandwiches and dinner is served until roughly 10 P.M.
Moderate. Open Monday through Saturday from 9:30 A.M. to 10:30 P.M. (Closed from 3 to 5 P.M. daily.) Reservations accepted. No credit cards. Wine and beer only. Street parking. Casual.

★★
CAFE JACQUELINE/French
1454 Grant Avenue/San Francisco/Area 2/(415) 981-5565

Chef/owner Jacqueline Margulis serves up the best soufflés in town in this modest storefront conversion. The various ambrosial concoctions start with a gruyère soufflé and then are built by adding broccoli, ham, mushrooms, prosciutto, spinach and much more. But soufflés do not exhaust the talents of this gracious French lady. She also offers onion soup topped with melted gruyère, good salads and, occasionally, marvelous stewed rabbit served with pâté made of rabbit liver. Best of all dessert soufflés are the bitter chocolate or Grand Marnier. **Moderate to expensive.** Open Wednesday through Saturday. Lunch from 11 A.M. to 2 P.M., dinner 5:30 to 9 P.M. Reservations accepted. Visa, MC. Wine only. Street parking. Casual.

★
CAFE LA SALLE/Continental
1028 Second Street/Sacramento/Area 3/(916) 442-9000

When so many of our capital's restaurants are little more than over-decorated steak houses, Cafe La Salle is unique. Surroundings are traditional European — the dining room's muted pink walls are dotted with statuary, and deep greens warm the room where brick wine cabinets arch gracefully. Seated comfortably in your armchair, you are not bound to a rigid course meal. Rather, you can devise your meal as you wish — possibly just two hearty appetizers followed by a dessert flambé. Or, a salad, an appetizer and liqueur coffee. Again, simply an entrée and light dessert. The tuxedo-clad staff is adroitly professional in the smooth presentation of your dinner.

The numbers are tantalizing. Ten appetizers, from escargots to fettuccine La Salle. A list of dressings for your salad specifies each dressing's ingredients. Entrées could begin with boneless trout Aurora or the specialty, beef Wellington with Perigourdline sauce. If it's flames you desire, there's medallions of beef Diane. There are special selections that change each day.

I can't end without revealing that no other place locally serves a wider selection of desserts. Cafe La Salle's range from fresh kiwi to strawberries or apple flambé, with cognac enticing the flames, served over vanilla ice cream. There are twenty-seven in all. The *real* Old Sacramento was never like this.

Moderate to expensive. Open seven days. Lunch Monday through Friday from 11:30 A.M. to 2 P.M. Dinner nightly from 5:30 to 10 P.M., Sunday 5 to 8:30 P.M. Reservations advised. All major credit cards. Entertainment. Full bar. Patio. Parking in public lots. Semi-dressy.

★ ★
CAFE PASTORAL/Asian/Nouvelle
1981 Shattuck Avenue/Berkeley/Area 2/(415) 540-7514

One might expect that Berkeley would be the first good restaurant region to boast "nouvelle Asian" cuisine, and this restaurant appeals to all the senses in a dramatic and quite wonderful manner. It may be crowded, small and noisy, but once into appetizers like chef San-ju Dong's version of steak tartare — paper thin slices of beef in sesame oil, sesame seeds, topped with a raw egg yolk; or (at luncheon) the *fettuccine de la casa* with tomato, bacon, goat cheese, pine nuts, parmesan and black pepper; or (at dinner) a baby chicken with red wine sauce and apricots; or boned chicken breast in a tarragon sauce; or, well, you get the idea. Casual at lunch, more formal at dinner with table linens and flowers, this is one of the dining adventures of the Berkeley area. **Moderate.** Lunch weekdays from 11:30 A.M. to 2:30 P.M. Dinner Monday through Saturday from 5:30 to 10 P.M. Reservations advised. No credit cards. Wine and beer only. Street parking. Semi-dressy.

★
CAFE RIGGIO/Italian
4112 Geary Boulevard/San Francisco/Area 2/(415) 221-2114

Cafe Riggio's distinctive adaptations of traditional regional dishes of Italy—*nuovo cucina*—under the direction of two talented chef/owners, are quickly building a large following; the place is jammed every night.

The restaurant is small, only twenty-six tables, with a certain New York-special-find charm about it: whitewashed walls, contrasting with polished dark wood, and large framed menus decorate the room. The crisp white tablecloths seem to announce a no-nonsense approach to what is clearly a restaurant that takes itself seriously. The service is attentive and sensitive.

The steamed clams, which are best shared, are served in a delicious broth, rich in basil, fresh whole tomatoes, butter and onions. Try the exquisitely prepared *cannelloni* or any of the white *provimi* veal dishes. The scalloppine, sautéed in lemon, wine and capers, was flawless. Al dente garden vegetables and crusty, fresh-baked baguettes complete a finely prepared dinner.

Plan to arrive early, as they don't take reservations. The bar can get very crowded, but just remember it's all worth it. The response to this young restaurant is well deserved. **Moderate.** Open seven days. Dinner only from 5 to 11 P.M.; Sunday from 4:30 to 10:30 P.M. No reservations. Visa, MC. Full bar. Casual to semi-dressy.

★ ★
CAFE ROYALE/California/Continental
2080 Van Ness Avenue/San Francisco/Area 2/(415) 441-1300

Sam Duvall is an entrepreneur extraordinaire—his restaurants, always good, are even better these days, in spite of the fact that he has stretched himself clear to Southern California. Cafe Royale is painted an eye-boggling rosy-mauve inside and outside. It's a theme restaurant, glamourous in the mirrored ways of the thirties, with art deco of that period along with touches like live piano music playing tunes of the twenties to the fourties. Like all Duvall's establishments, the food is good, particularly the seafood. The ubiquitous mesquite grill doesn't dominate the menu as much as in Californians; there are poached and sautéed dishes as well. Poached Norwegian salmon is served with a creamy cucumber sauce and watercress purée. Smoked chicken is served with apples in a contemporary Waldorf-style salad, and the loin of lamb is marinated in cranberry juice and wine before placed on the coals. Chef Farnham Hogue has been at Royale since the 1983 opening yet he keeps renewing the menu and is clearly happy with what he's doing.

The oyster bar serves up golden caviar with cucumber and pumpernickel, marinated calamari with capers and black olives, and prawns that have been steamed in beer and served with rémoulade sauce, as well as the Appalachicola oysters. Perhaps my favorite dish from the kitchen is curried lobster fish with papaya ginger chutney. Good desserts include warm mince meat compote with brandy ice cream, *crème brûlée* with oranges and walnuts, fresh fruit sorbets and a pear and ginger tart with chantilly cream.

Moderate to expensive. Open for dinner seven nights from 6 P.M. to midnight. Reservations necesssary. Visa, MC, AX. Entertainment. Full bar. Semi-dressy to dressy.

★
CAFE SN. MARCOS/Continental
2367 Market Street/San Francisco/Area 2/(415) 861-3846

Named for the beautiful gardens in the fabled city of Aguascalientes, in central Mexico, this strikingly different restaurant occupies three levels. The bar lounge is on the uppermost, thus only the ablest are the most likely patrons of this lofty oasis. The city's name means "hot waters," appropriate for the mineral baths responsible for the prominent health resorts there. As you enter Cafe Sn. Marcos, the entire right wall is a depiction of the portals to the famous gardens. Carved by hand, in Mexico, the antique fountain in the dining room's rear does enhance the water theme. You'll be pleased with the tall street lights, the dining balcony, the feel of a European coffeehouse, and with all that owner-creator Hector Romo has accomplished in this very "in" place not far from the entrance to the Twin Peaks Tunnel.

Hector devised most of the dishes and recipes on the long menu. In addition to the many breakfast specials, there are some exciting, spicy Mexican *desayunos,* as well. I can vouch for the hearty, delectable half-pound broiled sirloin hamburgers—in eight versions. Continental seafood and meats at dinner. The twenty-five liqueured coffee drinks alone merit a visit.

Moderate to expensive. Open seven days from 10 A.M. to midnight. Saturday and Sunday brunch from 10 A.M. to 4 P.M. Reservations for seven or more. Visa, MC, AX, DC. Full bar. Patio for cocktails. Street parking. Casual.

★
CAFFE GIOVANNI/Italian
2420 Shattuck/Berkeley/Area 2/(415) 843-6678

This little cafe (which is only cafe-like when, weather permitting, the bar opens up for al fresco dining and drinking) has some of the best homemade minestrone soup this side of Italy. But everything here from pizza to pasta is well prepared. Service is good and the surroundings are relaxing . . . *"Il Bar"* can make it a little more relaxing. **Moderate to expensive.** Open seven days. Lunch weekdays 11:30 A.M. to 2:30 P.M. Sunday through Thursday from 11:30 A.M. to 11:30 P.M. Friday and Saturday to 12:30 A.M. Reservations accepted. Visa, MC, AX, DC. Full bar. Lot and street parking. Casual.

★ ★
CAFFE SPORT/Italian
574 Green Street/San Francisco/Area 2/(415) 981-1251

Walk into Caffe Sport and you walk into a world that literally assaults the senses. The walls, the ceiling and even the tables are completely covered with knick knacks from the old world. The noise level never descends below that of a rock concert hall. And yet, Caffe Sport is always crowded. Why? Because the chef/owner/artist Antonio Latona has combined the casual North Beach atmosphere with some of the finest Italian cuisine found in the Bay Area. Garlic-laden pasta and seafood are the best bets. For lunch, try one of the many Italian sandwiches. In any event, Caffe Sport is one of the hottest spots in San Francisco.
Moderate. Open Tuesday through Saturday. Lunch from noon to 2 P.M. Dinner seatings 6:30, 8:30 and 10:30 P.M. Reservations accepted for four or more only. No credit cards. Wine and beer only. Parking at Vallejo and Powell. Casual.

To obtain the best results from this Guide, be sure to consult the map on the various Northern California areas on page 28.

DA ★
CAFFE TRIESTE/Italian Coffeehouse
601 Vallejo Street/San Francisco/Area 2/(415) 392-6739
★
1000 Bridgeway/Sausalito/Area 3/(415) 332-7770

There are two Triestes, one in San Francisco and the newer addition in Sausalito. The original SF Trieste was an innovation, a coffeehouse long before it was fashionable, for the perfect good reason that *paisanos* wanted to read the Italian sport papers' soccer scores and leisurely sip *caffe latte* or cappuccino. There's a folk concert on Saturday afternoons from noon to 2 P.M. Giotta has seen to it that the atmosphere remains unchanged, and he serves just enough nourishing sandwiches (Italian-style ice cream in Sausalito) to keep his sociable clientele happy. Coffee drinking is raised to a fine art here.
Inexpensive. Open seven days from 7 A.M. to 11 P.M. Friday and Saturday to midnight. No reservations. No credit cards. Entertainment. Wine and beer only. Street parking. Casual.

★ ★
CALIFORNIA CAFE/American
60 Belvedere Drive/Mill Valley/Area 3/(415) 381-0800
3111 North St. Helena Highway/St. Helena/Area 3/(707) 963-5300
1540 North California Boulevard/Walnut Creek/Area 2/(415) 938-9977
3211 J. Crow Canyon Place/San Ramon/Area 2/(415) 837-4488

Another "California" style cuisine series, not particularly original, but quite good. The founder has been around long enough to profit from other restaurant excesses (Victoria Station) and the interesting menu contains up-to-the-minute favorites. At brunch you can select from dishes like a fresh-from-the-garden vegetable omelette with Calico bay scallops, Boucheron goat cheese, apple segments and roasted walnuts; Cajun omelette of hot sausage, spicy chicken, sweet peppers and Créole sauce; and eight or nine other entrées.

Cold mussels *aioli* is a stunning dish of mussels with a zippy garlic sauce; and there are salads galore (sounds like a James Bond character). Naturally there is grilled Sonoma duck breast, fettuccine with veal, and especially good and tender lamb.

California Cafe brings some creativity to banquet menus with such specialties as grilled chicken paillard with curry chutney butter, Chinese chicken salad with sesame soy vinaigrette and much more. Service is deft, there is decaf, wine by the glass, and lots of good touches.
Moderate. Lunch Monday through Friday 11 A.M. to 2:30 P.M. Dinner Monday through Thursday 5:30 to 10 P.M., Friday and Saturday 5 to

11 P.M., Sunday 5 to 9:30 P.M. Sunday brunch 11 A.M. to 3 P.M. (Hours vary at each location.) Reservations accepted (except St. Helena location). All major credit cards. Full bar. Lot parking (valet parking at Walnut Creek location). Casual.

DA ★
CALIFORNIA CULINARY ACADEMY/Continental
215 Fremont Street/San Francisco/Area 2/(415) 546-1316

It's a card game but the cards are stacked in your favor when you reserve at the California Culinary Academy. Your meal is in the hands of one hundred amateurs—but *such* amateurs! Dedicated young people who are willing to spend $7,000 each and put in sixteen months of their respective male and female lives to learn to cook; your dining experience is their assignment.

Menus are truly inspired and, almost always the execution does live up to the promise. Meals include an appetizer, main dish, dessert and beverage (non-alcoholic). Choices are extremely limited but the prices are certainly reasonable for this quality food. Because there is an excess of willing hands, pasta, bread, sherbets and pastries are all produced right here. The sparkling kitchen is clearly visible through the gleaming glass window which separates the culinary preparation from the guests who are seated in a bright, large, functional dining room.

I seriously doubt that you'll find any other restaurant in the West with the ambitious selection of appetizers, entrées and desserts from which each day's menu is chosen. Roast partridge, lamb cutlets with cherries, mussels baked with shallots and prosciutto, squab, duck mousse, salmon stew with Oriental pepper, salmon tartare, *pistou*—the list is as long and boundless as a master chef's imagination. There's no way of knowing which of these enticements will be served on any particular evening but you can call ahead to ask.

Of course, there are times when the impeccably fresh fish will be dry as a bone—from overcooking. Sometimes, the duck skin is not crisp and the cake is heavy as a weight. Perhaps the pudding will be pasty. These, however, are not common faults. The talented students corps is working its collective aspics off for grades and their efforts for you are judged critically before you're served.

Dining here is always an adventure. You are taking a chance with cooks who possess more enthusiasm than experience. But—when you can't have both—*this* is the more exciting way to go.

Expensive. Open Monday through Friday. Two lunch seatings, 12:20 and 12:30 P.M.. Three dinner seatings, 6, 6:30, 7 P.M. Thursday and Friday nights are buffet with seatings at 6:30, 7 and 7:30 P.M. Reservations essential. Visa, MC, AX. Wine only. Street parking for lunch, lot parking for dinner. Semi-dressy.

★
CALISTOGA INN/Seafood/Continental
1250 Lincoln Avenue/Calistoga/Area 3/(707) 942-4101

This Inn is exactly that, actually containing seventeen rooms on the second floor that rarely lack for occupants and which can be booked solid for weeks ahead. This is a landmark, dating back to the century's advent, a nostalgically pleasing vestige of Calistoga's social period.

The personable owner, Phil Rogers, acquired this fine location in early 1979, giving it a handsome restoration all around. He had been a line chef at Scott's Seafood in San Francisco, eventually becoming general manager. His first move was to establish the Calistoga Inn with local residents as a worthwhile place to dine. So successful was he that word-of-mouth spread his fame and many diners come from fifty to one hundred miles away, some remaining as overnight guests.

There are two spacious, high-ceilinged dining rooms, with tables set decently apart. The bar lounge has a pub-like quality, and Napa Valley wines can be purchased by the glass, a nice touch if you have arrived early for your reservation, as you should do. There's also a lush patio for outdoor dining.

Phil's two daughters have their duties here and he delegates his host and maître d' duties one evening a week, so that he can cook, his first love. His concepts are to serve very good, simple, non-pretentious food of top quality, utilizing the freshest of vegetables, seafood, fowl and meats, in generous portions, at very modest prices. He wants his chefs to be imaginative and creative, not bound by tradition. When you dine here, you realize at once how well he has been able to follow his concepts, and how well his chef, Keith Filipello, makes it all a reality.

You'll note, first off, a heartening item – the menu bears the particular day's date.

Usually there are about ten entrées and soup or salad is included. Appetizers could be fried calamari, duck liver mousse and cracked crab (seasonal), à la carte. Main courses – perhaps sautéed scallops with garlic butter sauce, braised veal with tarragon-mushroom sauce or, even *fettuccini con pollo*. Desserts might include fresh Napa Valley walnut pie, Italian cream with raspberry sauce, and *crème caramel* – one to set the standard.

Even if you don't have wine with your meal (what an ignoble thought) ask to see the wine book. At last count there were almost 150 north coast selections, all fairly priced. Phil Rogers' cellar attests to his superb taste. Any wine buff will be a happier person after a bottle of Chateau St. Jean's Fume Blanc. The bar also features a comprehensive list of beers (lager, ale, steam, and draft) from all over the world.
Moderate to expensive. Open Tuesday through Sunday. Dinner Tuesday through Friday from 5:30 to 10 P.M., Saturday from 5 to 10 P.M., Sunday from 5 to 9 P.M. Reservations essential. Visa, MC. Full bar. Street parking. Casual.

★
CAMBRIA PINES/American/Continental
2905 Burton Drive/Cambria/Area 1/(805) 927-4200

The Cambria Pines Lodge was opened in 1927 when it served as a bedding place, watering hole and eatery for the land speculators of the times. The lodge has been improved—so some would describe it—into a Las Vegas style motel; but the restaurant is still good. Fresh fish, veal, and good salads fancy up what would otherwise be a mundane menu of steak fare. The cioppino is to be avoided at any price but the calamari is prepared scampi style and served with rice pilaf and vegetables. The breakfast menu serves as a hearty base for those who are off to explore Hearst country.
Moderate. Open seven days. Breakfast served Monday through Saturday from 7 to 11:30 A.M. Lunch from 11:30 A.M. to 2 P.M. Dinner from 5 to 9 P.M. Sunday breakfast from 7 A.M. to 1 P.M. Reservations advised. Visa, MC. Entertainment. Full bar. Garden patio. Child's menu. Easy street parking. Casual to semi-dressy.

★ ★ ★
CAMPTON PLACE/California/Continental
340 Stockton/San Francisco/Area 2/(415) 781-5155

Campton Place has emerged as one of the most important restaurants in America today. It is consistently listed as one of the best, and chef Bradly Ogden is likewise touted as one of the nation's finest chefs. Ogden, only in his early 30s, was raised in Michigan, and graduated with honors from the Culinary Institute of America. He is uninfluenced by what most chefs consider the imperative culinary tour of France. Ogden, in fact, has never traveled in Europe and interprets regional American dishes only as he knows them in this country. It is his execution of the cuisine that sets him apart from most of his peers.

Located in the Union Square hotel of the same name, Campton Place is an intimate, charming restaurant—the perfect setting for stylish food to be enjoyed morning, noon, and night. Seating only sixty the comfortable decor consists of banquettes and wall upholstery, mostly in tones of peach and ivory with a splash of chocolate brown. Tables are laid with white linen, and exquisite small amenities complete the visual pleasure.

Creatively conceived dishes such as lamb on a bed of wild greens, spiny lobster on fluffy blue corn cakes, apple-ham pâté, grilled quail served atop fried sweet potato sticks, Dungeness crab chowder, and panfried trout strewn with black walnuts inspire both the eye and the palate. Superb desserts include a blackberry poundcake, Concord grape sorbet, orange pecan pie and flourless chocolate pecan cake.

A more interesting day will dawn when you start with a fruit compote of figs, plums and raspberries, or poached eggs topped with orange hollandaise sitting on paper-thin slices of Smithfield ham. The baskets of mixed hot breads, fresh from the oven, accompanying all meals are a rare treat in themselves. Succinctly stated, Campton Place and chef Bradly Ogden provide a rare dining experience. It is cuisine à la mode, executed with great care.

Expensive. Open daily from 7 A.M. to 11 P.M., breakfast, lunch and dinner. Reservations necessary. All major credit cards. Full bar. Valet parking. Dressy.

★
CANTINA LOS TRES HOMBRES/Mexican
8791 North Lake Boulevard/Kings Beach/Area 6/(916) 546-4052

This lively Cantina—a collage of awning stripes, hanging plants, stained glass windows, and Technicolor margueritas—makes no claim to exotic Mexican dishes. Their focus is the burrito. In fact, their pride and joy is the *"hombre"* burrito—an ample beauty—a meal in itself, stuffed with rice, beans and beef colorado, topped with red chili sauce and abundant melted cheese. All this for a (Mexican) song.

Other dishes are good (*carnitas,* enchilada *Suissa*) California-gone-Mexican fare—but it's the single "Hombre" of Los Tres Hombres that seems to be the favorite of the locals and *turistas* here.

Inexpensive. Open seven days from 5 to 10:30 P.M. No reservations. Visa, MC. Full bar. Casual.

In order to obtain the best results from this Guide, please consult "A Few Inside Tips" on page 18.

★ ★
CAPE COD HOUSE/Seafood/American
3666 Mount Diablo Boulevard/Lafayette/Area 2/(415) 283-8288

Sometimes the nostalgic past overshadows the present, but here the pleasant past melds with the better elements of today so smoothly that devotees of yesteryear may happily relax over some mighty fine seafood and good drinks.

In the 1920s this building housed a series of restaurants, culminating in the once-famous "Curve" (old Highway 24 curved right past the front door). Now, by-passed by the handsome freeway from Berkeley and Oakland, Cape Cod House rests securely in the heart of Lafayette. The exterior has that nautical New England solidarity, a feeling developed within the cheerful, casually refined interior. Shuttered windows, a natural stone fireplace, ship models, captain's chairs, hooked rugs, ships' wheels, a hand-carved Cape Cod street scene behind the long bar, and miniature carved fishermen — authentic down to the knobby pipes. Rimming the marine-scened walls are tankards, mugs and plates of copper and brass.

Each and any fresh fish will be on the day's menu and Maine lobster, of course. Waiters are friendly but crisply efficient. It's busy, busy. Consider the three-decade's famous "House" salad, tossed with crab, prawns, anchovies and house dressing.

Moderate to expensive. Open seven days. Lunch weekdays from 11:30 A.M. to 4 P.M.; Saturday and Sunday from noon to 4 P.M. Dinner from 4 to 10 P.M. Reservations strongly advised. All major credit cards. Piano bar. Full bar. Parking lot. Casual.

★ ★
THE CAPRICE/French/Continental
2000 Paradise Drive/Tiburon/Area 3/(415) 435-3400

There are those who solemnly declare that The Caprice, a restaurant of astonishing charm, in Tiburon (across the Bay from San Francisco), provides the greatest dining experience in the West. I can understand their enthusiasm.

The lengthy menu presents *piroshki* in a masterful fashion. Any of the four salads (*coeurs de palmier,* Caesar, *salade verte* and Stephan) are beautifully dressed and served. The seventeen entrées, tending to the classic, include a notable *scampi Provençale,* but the triumph, *canard rôti flambé* (roast duckling with cherries), is reminiscent of a fine Parisian specialty restaurant. Steak Diane and the rack of lamb (both for two) would be astute choices. Wine may be ordered either by glass or bottle. Owner Kirby Atterbury is highly respected for his wine knowledge, reflected in the Caprice's vast cellar and select California bottlings. The view of the skyline, the Bay and the bridge presents a majestic mural of living, twinkling color that contributes to the enjoyment of an unhurried dinner. Certainly The Caprice should rate at the top of the list of those who find that their old favorites in San Francisco have become less than great. You will receive special attention at this gracious establishment. **Moderate to expensive.** Open seven days. Lunch served from 11:30 A.M. to 2:30 P.M. Dinner served from 5:30 to 10 P.M. Sunday brunch 11:30 A.M. to 2:30 P.M. Reservations advised. All major credit cards. View of Bay, Golden Gate Bridge. Full bar. Very limited parking lot. Semi-dressy.

★ ★
CARAVANSARY/Armenian/Mediterranean
2263 Chestnut Street/San Francisco/Area 2/(415) 921-3466
310 Sutter Street/San Francisco/Area 2/(415) 362-4640
Stanford Park Hotel/100 El Camino Real/Menlo Park/Area 2/(415) 322-1234

What you see is what you can buy in these half shop/half restaurants that manage to score well on both counts. Established by some of the old waiters at Bali's, the food (in my opinion, at least) has surpassed that venerable restaurant which deteriorated since its relocation. Three of the best entrées on the menu are shish kebab, spinach quiche and chicken *tabaka*. In addition, there is a daily special which might include sensational rack of lamb. The house coffee is sensational, the best I've had in this country, probably because it's freshly roasted to order. You'll like the desserts, although it takes some getting used to the use of honey as a sweetener. (Try the cheesecake if it's available.) **Moderate.** Lunch Monday through Saturday from 11 A.M. to 3 P.M. Dinner from 5 to 10 P.M. Sunday brunch from 11 A.M. to 3 P.M. (Chestnut location only). Reservations advised. All major credit cards. Full bar (Sutter location), wine and beer only (Chestnut location). Street and lot parking. Casual.

★
THE CARMEL BUTCHER SHOP/American/Continental
Ocean Avenue near Dolores/Carmel/Area 1/(408) 624-2569

Easily one of the mellowest and most exciting of this city's restaurants — even the locals call it "very Carmel." Indeed. The Tudor-influenced outer façade, window-walled, is attractive. So is the inviting, softly lit interior, with generous use of woods and a fireplace. Even an occasional celebrity is accepted graciously. In this cheerful ambiance, excellent food and wines taste that much better, and you can be sure that the seafood, much of it from Monterey and Carmel bays, is but hours out of its briny home. Meats are choice, and fowl is delicious. Very civilized bar. Kim Novak was one of the first regulars here, minus her llamas and wildlife, of course. In the heart of downtown.

Moderate to expensive. Open seven days from 4:30 to 11 P.M. Reservations advised. All major credit cards. Full bar. Child's menu. Street parking only. Casual.

CARMEN'S/Mexican
1700 McHenry Avenue/Modesto/Area 6/(209) 529-0208

Modesto is known as the geographic center of the state, as an access point to the Sonora Pass and for its hot summers. It is not known for good food, and nothing that appears in this book will disrupt that longtime image.

Carmen's would be tolerable anywhere else, but is notable here. The combination plates are "MexiTexican": heavy, predictable and not very good. If trapped, try "Al's Special," a big chicken enchilada with green chili sauce. The margueritas are good, however.

Inexpensive. Open seven days. Lunch and dinner served Sunday through Thursday from 11 A.M. to 10 P.M., Friday and Saturday until 11 P.M. Reservations accepted. Visa, MC, AX, DC. Full bar. Excellent parking. Casual.

DA ★★
CARNELIAN ROOM/French
52nd Floor—Bank of America Center/555 California Street/San Francisco
Area 2/(415) 433-7500

There's little to say about the Carnelian Room—good or bad—that hasn't been said fervently and frequently since the elegant skyroom opened in 1970. My strong opinion is that too much was expected too soon of this magnificently appointed restaurant.

From the moment the elevator whisks you in thirty-five seconds to the penthouse opulence of The Carnelian, with its rust and gold carpeting, elegant Louis XV and XVI antiques, Aubusson tapestries, dark-paneled hallways and crystal chandeliers, you step into another world— the classic French restaurant where, under the influence of affluence, gustatory greatness is sought, if not always achieved. The *table d'hôte* dinner and Sunday brunch are inexpensive for both the lavish menu and the setting. There is also a sunset dinner with appetizer, entrée and dessert for $21.

One can spend a great deal more here by selecting from the à la carte section of the menu. Specialties include roast breast of pheasant, medallions of venison with baked pear and glazed chestnuts, and veal scallopini with pippin apples and Calvados sauce. The award-winning wine cellar holds more than twenty-five thousand bottles of domestic and imported wines.

For the ultimate in romantic tête-a-tête, there is the Tamalpais Room, which is one of ten private suites where you privately dine by candlelight and summon your waiter by a special call button.

At lunch, this is a private club for the bankers of the city, but you can ask to be shown some of the exquisite banquet rooms like the Sierra Room, the Golden Gate Room or the more intimate Yosemite Room. **Expensive.** Dinner nightly from 6 to 10:30 P.M. Sunday brunch from 10 A.M. to 2:30 P.M. Reservations advised. All major credit cards. Full bar. View. Parking in building. Dressy.

DA ★
THE CARRIAGE HOUSE/Continental/American
1775 Clay Street/Napa/Area 3/(707) 255-4744

A **historical** monument (it really was a carriage house for the Noyes mansion around the turn of the century) rarely converts into a good restaurant, but this is a happy exception. Here in wine country, where palates are attuned to the slightest nuance of flavor, this combination reconstruction and restaurant talent proves more than equal to the challenge. Many of the third and fourth-generation wine makers sit on the lovely terrace and discuss the plantings with a refreshing candor and intensity common in the area. The ancient brick building is a department store of ideas — art galleries, a stage for homespun entertainment, an antique bar carved out of a single massive piece of wood — and innovative cookery. A long wine list is part of the attraction with many limited bottlings from surrounding vineyards.
Moderate. Open Monday through Saturday. Lunch served from 11:30 A.M. to 2:30 P.M. Dinner served from 5:30 to 9:30 P.M. Reservations advised. Visa, MC, AX. Full bar. Patio. Parking lot. Casual.

★
CARS/California/Continental
478 Green Street/San Francisco/Area 2/(415) 433-7733

C **ars** has been described as a clone of the fabulously successful Hard Rock Cafe in London and Hollywood, but the comparison is unfair. Actually Cars is a better and more ambitious undertaking than the Hard Rock, although there are similarities: a police car is frozen as it crashes through a "brick" wall and there are racing car murals, but most of all there is good, light bistro fare coming out of the kitchen. This used to be the old Spaghetti Factory, until it was acquired by Pascal Chevillot, scion of a fashionable European family. It is a large restaurant that seats two hundred, with an additional one hundred in fine weather. An oyster bar, a mesquite grill and unusual eclectic fare is available here for under $10. Richard Limstrom formerly cooked at Windshapes in Sausalito and he has come into his own at Cars. There's entertainment on the weekend with "salsa" music livening up the action.

Moderate. Open for lunch daily from 11:30 A.M. to 3 P.M. Dinner Monday through Saturday from 6 P.M. to 12:30 A.M. Reservations accepted. Visa, MC, AX. Full bar. Patio. Valet parking. Casual.

★
CASABLANCA/French/Continental
2323 Polk Street/San Francisco/Area 2/(415) 441-2244

Robert **DiFranco** has an interesting theme here: part Warner Brothers, part nursery and part incongruity. The framed photographs of the old Humphrey Bogart movie give the idea that Robert considers himself the "Rick" of the movie's "Rick's American Cafe." The lush greenery and dark polished woods attest to Robert's green thumb. French onion soup and — surprise — good roast duck with cassis and lime sauce or veal with pippin apples and Calvados brandy sauce are some of the selections. Robert's got something going here, currently the "in" place with the superannuated rich ex-hippies who have graduated from the law or medical school they were rebelling against and wear prewashed $250 denim outfits as a memento. Desserts are fair, with white chocolate cheesecake with raspberry at the top of the list. The wine list is rather poorly thought out and overpriced.

Moderate. Open Tuesday through Sunday. Dinner served Tuesday through Thursday from 6 P.M. to midnight, Friday and Saturday until 1 A.M., Sunday 6 to 10 P.M. Reservations advised. All major credit cards. Valet parking. Casual.

★
CASA DE EVA/Mexican
2826 Telegraph Avenue/Berkeley/Area 2/(415) 540-9092

Probably the best Mexican food in Berkeley is served at Casa de Eva, in the most attractive atmosphere, both because there is an "Eva" (Lopez) and because it is a family operation in the style of a Mexico City restaurant. The front of the building is an authentic replica of a fine Mexican restaurant, although the prices are extremely reasonable. Specialties include *flautas, chalupas, chihuahuenas* and enchiladas, but the menu provides a wide selection. From the time they opened in 1964, this has been a very special place for upper-class academia, and they can be seen waiting in line on weekends, wearing their tweeds and jeans.

Inexpensive. Open Monday through Saturday. Lunch and dinner served weekdays from 11 A.M. to 10 P.M. Saturday from 3:30 to 10 P.M. Reservations advised. No credit cards. Wine and beer only. Street parking. Casual.

★
CASA MADRONA/French/California
801 Bridgeway/Sausalito/Area 3/(415) 331-5888

Casa Madrona is one of the newer old restaurants, located in a hotel by the same name. Actually, the dining room here has had its ups and downs, but it has never been better than its present incarnation, a professional, dedicated approach to the lighter French cuisine. Chef Rob Larman worked at Cafe Riggio, across the bay, where he learned the techniques of preparing dishes like soft shell crab, poached salmon, rabbit grilled with zinfandel sauce, quail with cabbage and some extraordinary fish dishes. This has long been regarded as a romantic hideaway – the restaurant in a charming old house full of flowers – with a spectacular view of Oakland and Berkeley.

Expensive. Lunch weekdays from 11:30 A.M. to 2:30 P.M. Dinner Monday through Thursday from 6 to 10 P.M., Friday and Saturday until 11 P.M. Reservations accepted. Visa, MC, AX, DC. Wine and beer only. Patio. View. Validated parking. Casual.

★
CASTLE GRAND BRASSERIE/French
1600 Folsom Street (at 12th)/San Francisco/Area 2/(415) 626-2723

We didn't expect to find it – I mean you could drive right by. It's plunk in the heart of an industrial area, and there's not much to delineate it from the neighboring buildings. But it is worth the hunt. It's a warming place – from the leaded glass room divider to the ram's head above the bar, and the nightly live piano music and lots of greenery – with some pleasant surprises on the menu. A luncheon specialty (the sandwiches change daily) on our visit was a dish with the fowl name "turkey gobble-up"; layers of turkey breast, avocado, and tomatoes on a half French roll, slathered with melted cheese. It's much better than the name suggests. Salad of greens, beets, garbanzo beans (they're the ones you have trouble chasing about the bowl) and onion dressed in an oil and vinegar dressing with the unusual ingredients of grated cheese and orange juice . . . a bit cloying. Other grand selections were a fine salad Nicoise and a béarnaise burger. *Tournedos au poivre vert* (filets sautéed with imported green peppercorns) is a dinner menu delight. Especially tangy, announced my companion, was the *canard aux pêches* (duckling in a Grand Marnier peach sauce). White linen and fresh carnations and gracious service create a grand place . . . convenient before or after the theater.

Moderate. Open seven days. Lunch Monday through Friday from 11:30 A.M. to 2:30 P.M. Dinner served Sunday through Thursday 6 to 11 P.M., Friday and Saturday to midnight. Reservations advised. Visa, MC, AX, DC. Live music. Full bar. Street parking. Semi-dressy to dressy.

★
CAVALIER INN RESTAURANT/Seafood
Highway 1/San Simeon/Area 1/(805) 927-3276

Just three miles south of the Hearst Castle gates is this better-than-average seafood restaurant located in a fine old motel-hotel with fireplaces, ocean view and terraces. Prices are not tourist-inflated, and the Cavalier attracts a local following (a reassuring fact).
Inexpensive to moderate. Open seven days. Breakfast served from 7 to 11:30 A.M. Lunch served from 11:30 A.M. to 5 P.M. Dinner served from 5 to 9:30 P.M. Reservations advised. All major credit cards. Wine and beer only. Ocean view. Child's menu. Lot parking. Casual.

★ ★
CELADON/Chinese
881 Clay Street/San Francisco/Area 2/(415) 982-1168

You might almost anticipate the sound of ancient gongs being struck as you enter the premises of this temple of Chinese cuisine, for your very presence anticipates the feast to come from a kitchen staff who offer you 150 selections. These are derived from the entire range of all the Chinese provinces.

The Epicurean Review society bestowed their Four Star Award of Excellence on Celadon. When you have enjoyed a dining experience here, you will understand why. The professional staff suggests such delicacies as: coconut seafood bisque, sautéed Imperial lobster, minced squab wrapped in lettuce, prawns sautéed in black bean sauce and a myriad of other fantasies come to life.

Celadon is a beautiful composition, with dining on several levels, lovely, fresh appointments and a feeling of intimacy which is not offset by the airy spaciousness of the rooms. I always feel—after saying goodbye—that if I suddenly re-entered the restaurant, the staff would still be smiling without manifesting any surprise.
Moderate to expensive. Open seven days. Lunch from 11:30 A.M. to 3 P.M. Dinner from 5 to 11 P.M. Reservations advised. All major credit cards. Full bar. Street parking, and lot two blocks down. Casual to semi-dressy.

In order to obtain the best results from this Guide, be sure to read the French, German, Italian and Oriental menu translators on pages 399 to 404 of this Guide.

★ ★
CHANTILLY/French
530 Ramona Street/Palo Alto/Area 2/(415) 321-4080

This thoroughly professional, subtly sophisticated oasis of fine dining might well be your personal find of the year. Owned and operated by Michel Fischtein and Gus Talasaz with the talented, French-born André Guerguy, once a mainstay of Ernie's as chef de cuisine, Chantilly has won worldwide fame as one of California's most-respected restaurants. Never advertised, it counts among its patrons most of nearby Stanford University's prominent professors, the elite of the Peninsula and high-income electronic executives from Silicon Valley a few miles south.

The "Restaurant Français" sub-title is nicely supported by the unencumbered, somewhat romantic design, a mellow ambiance and the attentive, distinguished staff. Michel and Guz are active in the dining room, alert to every nuance.

The extensive menu offers the epitome of Gallic cuisine. Notables are *selle d'agneau à la Dijonnaise,* roast duckling Chantilly, *l'escalopine de veau melanzana* and *supreme de poulet à la Cynthia*. A sterling wine book is available and the house wine is Foppiano, an astute choice. **Expensive.** Open Monday through Saturday. Lunch served weekdays from 11:30 A.M. to 3 P.M. Dinner from 5:30 P.M. to midnight. Reservations required. Visa, MC, AX, DC. Full bar. Patio. Semi-dressy to dressy.

★
CHARLIE BOLTON'S ROAD HOUSE/International/Eclectic
6090 Redwood Boulevard/Novato/Area 3/(415) 892-0779

Large, rambling dining rooms—the terraced first room and the Black Bart Room—suggest San Francisco in the gilded era of the 1890s. Waiters and waitresses dress neatly and sport small, dark bow-ties. Their enthusiasm and professionalism meld to your advantage. There are so many tempting course possibilities and extras that it would be a diner of sturdier character than I who could resist some of the offerings. For example, consider Charlie's nachos—mounded chips with homemade salsa, guacamole, sour cream and melted cheeses. You may have just a half order. Do that and you can have the deep fried zucchini and sautéed mushrooms. Or, guacamole and chips. Or, soup. Entrées: sherried scallops, calamari sauté, or grilled pork chops. There is always some fresh fish. All entrées are served with soup or salad. More dinner courses: veal Oscar, veal Marsala, garlic chicken, and sautéed prawns.

There is dancing nightly and during Sunday brunch. Some evenings it's to disc jockey selections, some nights (Tuesday, Thursday) it's Country and Western with free dancing lessons. Some evenings there are live

bands, and on Monday it's Comedy Night, with three comedians and later, dancing until closing. No cover charge if you come for dinner. Otherwise the charge varies a bit depending upon the night's format.
Moderate. Open seven days. Lunch Monday through Friday from 11:30 A.M. to 2:30 P.M. Dinner Monday through Thursday from 5:30 to 9:30 P.M., Friday through Sunday from 5 to 9:30 P.M. Reservations advised. Visa, MC. Entertainment. Full bar. Lot parking. Casual to semi-dressy.

★
CHEERS/California/Continental
127 Clement Street/San Francisco/Area 2/(415) 387-6966

Best on the pizza list of this somewhat charming cafe is their "four seasons pizza" with prosciutto, artichoke hearts, capers and fresh mushrooms, each topping on a quarter of the round. Pasta is their thing, as well, and they have some interesting salads and a dynamite lasagna. There's also a sit-down Sunday brunch.
Inexpensive to moderate. Open daily from 7 A.M. to midnight. Reservations accepted. Visa, MC. Wine and beer only. Street parking. Casual.

★ ★
THE CHERRY FLOWER/Vietnamese
124 Columbus Avenue/San Francisco/Area 2/(415) 398-9101

The floor above the tumult of Columbus and Jackson is an oasis of tranquility and beauty, the most graceful Vietnamese restaurant in the city. This is a highly professional, authentic operation that is to other Vietnamese restaurants what the Empress of China is to a local chopsuery. Decor and cuisine are the best of North and South Vietnam – the South: Saigon fish soup; the North: beef broth with noodles and slices of beef, called *pho*. In addition to the à la carte offerings, there are four inexpensive complete dinners and two moderately priced: a "deluxe" sea food or "deluxe" beef that include *pho, cha bo* (a beef ball), steak and salad, beef and mushroom, fried rice, lychee in syrup, and tea. The *"hoa mai"* is roast crab, especially delicious whether as an appetizer or in a dinner. Bangkok beer, made with rice, heads the exotic beer/wine card. You would do well to let your enthusiastic host explain and assist.
Inexpensive. Open seven days. Lunch served 11:30 A.M. to 2 P.M. Dinner from 6 to 10 P.M. Reservations accepted. Visa, MC, AX. Beer and wine only. Casual.

For best results, consult "How to Use This Guide" on page 25.

★ ★
CHEZ LOUIS/French Provincial
4170 El Camino Real/Palo Alto/Area 2/(415) 493-1660

This French country inn is set back nicely so that there is parking space right in front for many cars plus a stadium-size lot in the rear. A fenced garden area parallels the cottage windows on one side, buffering the diner from the parked autos and freshening the view. Mellow, best describes the quite spacious main dining room, the staff at their posts or attending to patrons. Very civilized. Patrice moves about smoothly, seating guests, pausing for a suggestion, perhaps about the latest California boutique wines stocked in the far-underground cellar. Occasionally chef Veron leaves his kitchen in the care of one of his chefs and sallies forth to greet a regular guest or discuss a special dish with a party. You have the feeling that everyone here cares – and does something worthwhile about it.

Owner Louis Borel has been involved with restaurants and hotels since he went to hotel school in Paris at age seventeen. He even worked under the famous chef, Roger Verge, in Southern Rhodesia, from whom Louis learned many of the fine points and with whom he is still friendly. Asked to recommend for our readers, the following dishes were suggested: *crêpe de fruits de mer, Nantua; pâté de maison; soupe a l'oignon; paupiette de sole, deauville; canard à la Normande; côte de veau aux parfums des sous bois*, and *tournedos au poivre vert;* then a *salade* of butter lettuce, followed by Louis' special *café* and, perhaps, fresh strawberries Romanoff.

You might like to stop in the lively bar lounge, where there is a working fireplace, and view Chez Louis' collection of historic *chapeaux* – even one of Maurice Chevalier's straws. And, you can't miss the piano bar where there is singing and dancing. No, you can't hear them in the dining room.

Moderate to expensive. Open Monday through Saturday. Lunch weekdays from 11:30 A.M. to 2 P.M. Dinner from 5:30 to 10 P.M. Reservations advised. All major credit cards. Entertainment except Monday. Full bar. Ample lot parking. Casual to semi-dressy.

★
CHEZ MARGUERITE/French/Belgian
2330 Taylor Street/San Francisco/Area 2/(415) 775-9785

Although a succession of chefs and owners usually augers badly for the quality of a French restaurant, Chez Marguerite has remained constant through the changes and is still that tucked-away hide-and-chic spot for many of the locals. Occupying the bottom of one of those old

Victorian mansions on Taylor Street, the vibes and the food are alluring. A tiny wait-till-your-name-is-called bar, candlelit tables (some in intimate alcoves), and correct, vested waiters provide just the right setting for the above-average Belgian fare, and dishes like sweetbreads "Parisienne." The ducking *à l'orange* is better than most.

Moderate. Open Tuesday through Sunday. Dinner from 6 to 10 P.M. Tuesday through Saturday; Sunday 5:30 to 9:30 P.M. No reservations. All major credit cards. Full bar. Street parking. Casual to semi-dressy.

★★
CHEZ MICHEL/French
804 North Point/San Francisco/Area 2/(415) 771-6077

Now one of the area's most beautiful restaurants, it wasn't always so. Michel Elkaim acquired the grocery store adjoining his bistro, closed for three months of massive interior architectural surgery, and reopened as an important restaurant. It's among the smartest places in town—for dinner and after-the-whatever. Chez Michel has become one of "the" places. The elegant French menu lists dishes that are well prepared, and the service is a fine combination of attention and unobtrusiveness that most restaurants seek but never attain. A chicken breast, exquisitely browned and served with an almond sauce (*le poulet sauté amandine*) is my favorite here. The white baby veal (*l'escalope ce veau*) is a close second. Another notable culinary achievement is the lamb chops covered with spinach and baked in puff pastry (*les côtes d'agneau pied nus*). The complete dinners are most reasonable, but the à la carte selections are exotic and often exciting. Be sure to make at least a one-drink stop at the bar . . . it's a remarkable sculpture.

Moderate to expensive. Open Tuesday through Sunday. Dinner served from 6 P.M. to 12:30 A.M. Reservations necessary. Visa, MC. Full bar. Parking available in area. Casual to semi-dressy.

★★★
CHEZ PANISSE/French
1517 Shattuck Avenue/Berkeley/Area 2/(415) 548-5525

Chez Panisse is one of my favorite restaurants in America. I know that sounds a bit extreme, but someplace has got to be my favorite, and Chez Panisse is close. Chez Panisse is a lovely little wooden house, nestled inconspicuously across the street from the Shattuck Avenue Co-op. All that marks Chez Panisse is a modest sign, and a small glass case in which the menu for the week is posted.

Chez Panisse serves a different meal every day. There are no options (except for dessert and, of course, wine) on the dinner menu, and dishes rarely repeat. During a recent week, for instance, the Wednesday night meal consisted of a fresh Sonoma goat cheese soufflé flavored with thyme; a warm spinach salad with fresh scallops; roast duck served with a red wine sauce and fresh figs; and a choice of cheese and fruit for dessert. Saturday night included *croûtons Provençale;* a fresh fish charcoal-grilled, served with a saffron butter and caramelized pearl onion; and a pressed double breast of chicken, sautéed and served with a vinegar and Italian parsley sauce.

Five nights a week, Chez Panisse serves some of the best food in and of the land; food highly dependent on fresh *local* ingredients (spring lamb from a farm in Amador County, for instance; and salad vegetables grown in Berkeley). Sometimes the dishes are not quite right at Chez Panisse; but this isn't because of lack of skill. It's more because duck cooked in rock salt is sometimes hard to bring off.

Chez Panisse has long served lunch, but since the last time I was there, lunch has gone through a change and has become an all-day affair. The restaurant's second floor has been turned into a cafe open from lunchtime until midnight. (See Cafe at Chez Panisse.)

But above everything else, there are the people at Chez Panisse. From guiding spirit and founder Alice Waters on down, everyone cares. Pretension is not the point. The point at Chez Panisse is a conspiracy whereby all concerned are involved in creating a meal that goes beyond being memorable, into the realm of the truly unforgettable.

Expensive. Open Tuesday through Saturday by reservation only. No credit cards. Beer and wine only. Difficult street parking. Casual.

★ ★
CHEZ VILLARET/French
Highway 89 and 15th Street/South Lake Tahoe/Area 6/(916) 541-7868

It would be easy to miss this little restaurant, almost hidden in a row of nondescript motels on the highway, but playing the sleuth is worth it when you open its door and discover a French country inn beyond — down to the provincial flowered wallpaper and the finely set tables with fresh flowers.

À *la française,* the Chez Villaret menu is à la carte; *à l'Américain,* bring at least $30 per person. However, chef Villaret's appetizers will make you forget things like money. His duck and salmon pâté are both delicious. For hot hors d'oeuvres, the eastern mussels with mustard sauce are reminiscent of Marseilles. Select the scampi — good and garlicky — and you'll envision France with a clear view of the Italian coast.

The boned sole Veronique and the pheasant with mushroom-cognac sauce are fine choices from an extensive list of entrées, but the rack of lamb for two was *the* event at our table. Menus here are changed quarterly and the wine list has over two hundred selections.

Cap the evening with a Grand Marnier soufflé. You may want to hum a bar of "La Marseillaise"–or at least think about it.

Expensive. Open seven days. Dinner from 6 to 11 P.M. Reservations advised. All major credit cards. Beer and wine only. Lot parking. Semi-dressy.

CHILI'S/Chili Parlor/Saloon
20060 Stevens Creek Boulevard/Cupertino/Area 2/(408) 257-4664

This chili parlor is more saloon than salon. It does serve chili and burgers and such in an ersatz Texas setting: cactus (complete with sharp needles), brick floor, low, wood ceiling and chili cook-off posters (I didn't realize there was a market for such memorabilia). It gets so crowded here on the weekends that if they did take reservations, you'd need a shoe horn just to belly up to the bar. The most popular drink is a ten-ounce frozen marguerita dispensed from a Slurpy machine. The burgers are big and juicy and the chili will warm your innards.

Inexpensive. Open seven days. Monday through Thursday 11 A.M. to 11 P.M.; Friday and Saturday to midnight. Sunday from noon to 10:30 P.M. No reservations. Visa, MC, AX, DC. Full bar. Adjacent parking. Casual.

★ ★
CHINA FIRST/Szechwan/Hunan
675 El Camino Real/Palo Alto/Area 2/(415) 326-3900

Start planning right now for your initial meal in this truly sensational restaurant that is the Hunan/Szechwan favorite for those who recognize superlative northern Chinese food.

Set beneath large trees beside the humming freeway, China First has drawn rave reviews from every critic for the freshness and high quality as well as for the generous servings of its uniquely seasoned, tantalizing, spicy Mandarin dishes. The large, square dining room is low-key in design with hand-carved teak screens, white tablecloths and orange-net lamps. Here one comes to savor and to exclaim over the potstickers, *mu shu* beef (that delicious blending of egg, vegetables and beef), sliced leg of lamb, shredded pork with garlic sauce and delectable *lake tung ting* shrimp or ingredient fried rice.

Moderate. Open seven days. Lunch 11:30 A.M. to 2 P.M. Dinner served Sunday through Thursday from 5 to 9:30 P.M., Friday and Saturday to 10 P.M. Reservations advised. Visa, MC. Full bar. Lot parking. Casual.

★
CHINA STATION/Chinese
700 University Avenue/Berkeley/Area 2/(415) 548-7880

Alon Yu, managing co-owner of this impressive Cantonese dining place, says that it is really far more than just a handsome restaurant—it is "a gift of love, for all to share." Alon points out that it is sincerely dedicated to the thousands of Chinese who built the very railroad where this former Southern Pacific Depot is sited.

My Berkeley friends tell me that when they were children, it was the thing to preface Sunday dinner with a trip down to this station, by streetcar, to watch the Overland Limited pull out for mysterious cities to the East. Now, they drive here from all over the Bay Area for the Chinatown food at Chinatown prices, often dining on some of the favorite dishes of those same Chinese pioneers.

The conversion, from architect Harry Lim's plans, under the vigilant eyes of partner Leon Paulos, is beguiling. Credit, also, to executive chef Pak Lam Ho, whose efforts have resulted in the strong support of U.C. Berkeley's students and professorial staff. Cantonese and Mandarin dishes are masterfully prepared; fresh oysters in ginger sauce, crab in black bean sauce, and, the old favorite, lemon chicken. Sup, quaff and enjoy the passing trains.

Inexpensive to moderate. Open daily from 11:30 A.M. to 12:45 A.M. Visa, MC, AX. Full bar. Parking lot. Casual.

★★
CHIN SZCHAWN/Chinese
1166 Solano Avenue/Albany/Area 2/(415) 525-0909

In ancient China, the chef was literally treated like a king. Homeowners who wanted to entertain guests would respectfully engage one of the few chefs available who would send his minions ahead to prepare the foods just the way he wanted them. There was always a seat at the head table reserved for the chef. When the soup was served, he would take a sip . . . then bow to the host as though to say: "I am able to eat it. I think you will be, too." Then he would return to the kitchen. After the dinner, the Chinese chef would share a cup of tea with the host and hostess in their home as a gesture of courtesy. He would take usually just one sip, then leave to be transported to his own home in a sedan chair.

It is at this kind of restaurant, little changed from its counterpart of centuries past, that the great Chinese chefs learned their trade. The Ngs came from Singapore in 1970 and brought with them a knowledge not only of many styles of Chinese cooking, but of Burmese and Malaysian food, too. *Mu shu* pork is a stateside favorite, even in its frequently unauthentic forms. The Ngs' *mu shu* pork is a perfectly blended concoction of cabbage, "cloud ears," eggs, peppers, bamboo shoots and other ingredients I couldn't quite pick out, wrapped in a plum sauce-covered pancake.

Moderate. Open Monday through Saturday from 5 to 10 P.M. Reservations essential on weekends. Visa, MC. Wine and beer only. Street parking. Casual.

★ ★
CHO CHO/Japanese
1020 Kearny Street/San Francisco/Area 2/(415) 397-3066

James Sakata wanted a departure from the sukiyaki emporiums that have become virtually commonplace in San Francisco, so he remodeled in the style of a rural Japanese farmhouse and opened one of the few tempura bars around. Choice beef is prepared to taste at the *irori* hearth. Specialties include farmer's chicken, grilled at your table with bean sprouts, onions, mushrooms and a fascinating barbecue sauce; *shabu shabu* and *yakitori*. Convenient to the financial district and North Beach, they're busy. It's a good idea to make reservations, particularly for lunch. Cocktails are so-so, and it's a little noisy.

Inexpensive to moderate. Open Monday through Saturday. Lunch from 11:45 A.M. to 2 P.M. Dinner from 5:30 to 10 P.M. Friday and Saturday to 11 P.M. Reservations advised. All major credit cards. Street and lot parking. Casual to semi-dressy.

★ ★ ★
CHRIS' SUPER DUPER HOT DOGS & HAMBURGERS/American
4366 Broadway/Oakland/Area 2/(415) 652-9538

We never close!" boasts Constance Foster, owner of Chris' for the last forty-five years. And a good thing, too, because patrons ranging from students, professional baseball and football players to movie stars and pop singers vie for a table at this no-frills stand where old-fashioned, hand-packed hot dogs are served. The same vendor who supplied the epicurean dog to Chris' more than two generations ago is still providing this eight-inch long treat. Garnished with specially blended mustard, relish, and fresh tomato, these hot dogs are more than a hot dog; they put on the dog. Yes, Virginia, you *can* order hamburgers, fries, cheeseburgers and chili dogs, too.

Inexpensive. Open seven days, 9 A.M. to 1 A.M. No reservations. No credit cards. Parking lot. Casual.

94

DA ★
CHRISTIANIA INN/Continental
3819 Saddle Road/South Lake Tahoe/Area 6/(916) 544-7337

A wonderful place for lovers, this European inn sits high above Lake Tahoe, overlooking the lower slopes of the Heavenly Valley ski area, and features elegant fireside dining. It's the next best thing to an Alpine hideaway.

There is a large continental menu here, with a tip of the hat to some American fare, but beef Wellington is the house specialty, and properly so. Its crust is flaky and the beef is prime and pale-pink tender. The Christiania also bakes its own delicious bread, and their pastry chef turns out artful pâtisserie that would shake a stoic's resolve.

Moderate to expensive. Open seven days. Dinner from 6 to 10 P.M., summer months; 6:30 to 10 P.M., winter. Reservations advised. Visa, MC, AX. Full bar. Casual.

DA ★
CHUTNEY KITCHEN/American/Continental
Vintage 1870 (shops)/Yountville/Area 3/(707) 944-2788

Just off the St. Helena Highway (Route 29), is my favorite place to shop for lunch in the wine country. My first visit was in the company of Maynard Monahan of BV wines, one of those thoroughly dedicated, thoroughly charming, thoroughly honest people who seem to flourish in the wine industry. As we sat in the patio of this ancient winery, now converted to an utterly enchanting restaurant complex, Maynard was enthusing about a zinfandel BV had turned out a year or so before. "It was so good," he recalled, "that I took the bottle to bed with me and uncorked it several times during the night just to made sure I hadn't imagined the whole thing." The restaurant that Maynard selected had a good selection of Napa Valley wines and—at adjoining tables—the cordial people that made them. The food had to be good to pass the test of the winemakers' palates, and it passed mine as well. There are fresh salads, sandwiches that are different—cheese combinations and smoked salmon or tongue—and soups as fine and savory as you'll encounter anywhere. Real homemade chutney in a dozen varieties is available by the mason jar in the gift shop, along with other colorful artifacts, many produced in the area.

Inexpensive. Open seven days. Lunch served 11:30 A.M. to 4 P.M. weekdays. Weekends from 11:30 A.M. to 3:30 P.M. Reservations advised. Visa, MC. Entertainment. Full bar. Patio, vineyard. Child's menu. Parking lot. Casual.

★ ★
CIAO/Northern Italian
230 Jackson Street/San Francisco/Area 2/(415) 982-9500

Ciao is more than just something agents say to each other as they leave the Polo Lounge. It's the Italian way of saying both "Hello" and "Goodbye," though ironically it translates literally as "I am your slave." Ciao is situated down by the Golden Gateway Center, just around the corner from MacArthur Park, and both restaurants share the same ownership. In some ways, Ciao reminds me of the stage set for the play of *Dracula,* the one designed by Edward Gorey. Most of the restaurant is done in stark white, except for the occasional touch of bright red – a red carnation on each table, the lipstick red Ciao logo on the napkins, menus and T-shirts worn by the busboys.

There's a minibike up on one wall of Ciao, and pasta hangs from the open kitchen area like strands of Spanish moss. The *antipasto misto* is one of the finest mixed salads I've encountered outside of Italy. Heaps of squid, sardines, beans and tiny salad islands are piled on top of a landmass of cheeses and meats, and served with a cruet of greenish olive oil on the side. The buffalo milk mozzarella also comes with a cruet of olive oil, and is served to you comfortably seated on a slice of tomato with a basil leaf nuzzled on top.

The main pasta at Ciao is homemade egg noodles, which are served decidedly al dente. The *pesto Genovese* is nothing short of ambrosial, with an honest garlic kick and a green freshness which reminds me of walks along the ocean, as the fog begins to seep in. There's a very fine *vitello tonnato,* which is cold veal topped with a tuna sauce, and tastes a lot better than it sounds. You can also get brochettes of quail and scallops, but I advise leaving room for the dessert ices – the melon is served in half a frozen melon, the banana inside half a frozen banana, and so forth, although the strawberry ice is *not* served inside half a frozen strawberry. It comes inside half a frozen orange, in the name of fairness. **Moderate.** Open seven days. Monday through Saturday from 11 A.M. to midnight. Sunday from 4 P.M. to midnight. Reservations advised. Visa, MC, AX, CB. Full bar. Valet parking at night. Casual to semi-dressy.

★
CITY HOTEL/French
Main Street/Columbia/Area 6/(209) 532-1479

By entering this 125-year-old hostelry, you will be taking a step back into a gentler era. City Hotel is operated by the City Hotel Corporation, a non-profit organization offering on-the-job training to the students from the Hospitality Management Program of Columbia Junior College.

The hotel rents out its nine upstairs rooms and serves à la carte meals in a typical-of-the-era dining room with handsome accoutrements that include properly, almost lavishly, set tables, fresh flowers, crystal, and small brass table lamps.

Waiters sport vests with black ties and waitresses are most feminine in floor-length dresses. You almost expect someone to inquire "Did you hear about the last Lincoln-Douglas debate?" Should this occur, better not take more wine.

Tom Bender, a genial host, says that they even have the custom of offering glasses of sherry in the parlor to overnight guests before dinner. Filet Helder heads the impressive menu. Other specialties include oysters and a delightful chocolate soufflé. Barry Marcillac, a former, illustrious chef from Ernie's, works his excellent wiles in the spacious kitchen, responsible for chicken champagne Cynthia as well as *ris de veau* and châteaubriand.

Expensive. Open Tuesday through Sunday. Lunch served 11:30 A.M. to 2 P.M. Dinner from 5:30 to 9 P.M. Sunday brunch from 11 A.M. to 2 P.M. Reservations essential. Visa, MC. Full bar. Parking lot. Casual to semi-dressy.

CLAM BOX RESTAURANT/Seafood
Mission Street/Carmel/Area 1/(408) 624-8597

It's not the principle—fresh seafood is served all along the coast—it's the money, the low prices, that attract throngs to this popular-with-locals little place that does its thing fairly well. Chicken, pot roast and ham are offered for the non-purists. A good place to take the kids, but you'll probably have to stand in line for this finny gold mine.

Inexpensive. Open Tuesday through Sunday. Dinner served from 4:30 to 9 P.M. No reservations. No credit cards. Full bar. Limited patio service for bar only. Child's menu. Street parking. Casual.

★
THE CLOCK GARDEN RESTAURANT/Continental
565 Abrego Street/Monterey/Area 1/(408) 375-6100

To discover this hidden rendezvous in old Monterey, look for the tall, antique, jeweler's street clock behind the high, blue gates of the garden patio. You can dine casually, yet sumptuously, at both lunch and dinner (weather permitting) in the sunny, flowery, outdoor area or in a colorful lounge and dining room created from a one-time adobe carriage house which is highlighted by more flowers, an artistic fountain and gaslight. The kitchen's versatility is indicated by such subtleties as Greek lemon soup, fresh sole *meunière*, London broil, filet teriyaki and veal *Vallarta*. Better make reservations too, especially for the Sunday brunch which is served both in the garden patio and dining room. The "intime" bar is admirably stocked and staffed.

Moderate. Open seven days. Breakfast weekdays 10 to 11:30 A.M. Lunch served 11 A.M. to 3 P.M. Dinner from 5 to 10 P.M. Reservations accepted only for dinner. Visa, MC, AX. Full bar. Patio. Street parking. Casual.

★★
CLUB XIX/French
The Lodge at Pebble Beach/Pebble Beach/Area 1/(408) 625-1880

A beautiful view overlooking the Pebble Beach golf course makes this lovely—and expensive—restaurant one of the beautiful luncheon places in the area. Eggs Benedict (our old friend with the gangster movie name) and salade Nicoise are my favorites here, but the roast chicken with mushrooms is delicate, succulent and savory. In the evening, the room caters mostly to guests of the Lodge in which it is situated; nights are a little chilly for the patio. Manager Pierre Bain is an experienced professional whose very presence is reassuring. Sunday brunch can be a nearly spectacular experience, but in Carmel, spectacular is par for the course. Lunching at Club XIX also grants you free admission to the seventeen-mile drive.

Moderate to expensive. Open seven days. Lunch from 11:30 A.M. to 4:45 P.M. Dinner from 6:30 to 10 P.M. Sunday brunch from 11:30 A.M. to 4:45 P.M. Reservations required. All major credit cards. Full bar. Patio. View. Lot and valet parking. Dressy.

DA ★★
COATEPEQUE RESTAURANT/Salvadorean
2240 Mission Street (at Eighteenth)/San Francisco/Area 2/(415) 863-5237

This immaculate little place, with a long counter and formica tables, offers one of the more exciting dining adventures in the Bay Area. The foods of El Salvadore are distinctively different from most of the foods of Mexico and South and Central America, and they have their own style. The unfamiliar dishes—unfamiliar to North American palates anyway—are astonishingly good. The *guineos, frijoles, y crema* are fried bananas, beans, and thick, chilled cream. *Relleno de pescado* is stuffed rock cod with a bouquet of flavors achieved by the use of many herbs and native spices. Tamales, Salvadorean style, are filled with morsels of rare beef and whole beans. The desserts are super. *Torrejas* are pastries with a light sauce of honey. There's even a dessert tamale (*de azucar*) made with sweet corn and sour cream. A specialty beverage – called *refrescos Salvadorenos* – is exotic. You could come back to this inexpensive gem a dozen times and always find new and exciting dishes. **Inexpensive.** Open Friday through Tuesday. Lunch served from noon. Dinner Monday and Tuesday to 8:30 P.M.; Friday through Sunday to 9:30 P.M. No reservations. No credit cards. Beer only. Casual.

COFFEE CANTATA/Continental/You-name-it
2030 Union Street/San Francisco/Area 2/(415) 931-0770

Despite the name, this is not a coffeehouse. I'm not sure what it is, because the entrées range from Greek (grape leaves stuffed with ground lamb) to Indian (chicken curry) and back again, by way of Copenhagen (*smorrebrod*). The restaurant is also an art gallery where the exhibits change every six or eight weeks. The bar has a palate-boggling array of spirited suggestions from a banana banshee to a green lizard. There are coffees, of course – Irish with real whipped cream, Jamaican with Tia Maria, and many more. There is also a large selection of homemade desserts. In addition to this pastiche, there is a classical guitar player, an outdoor dining area (great for days when the fog doesn't erase the city) and weekend brunches (from 10:30 A.M. to 3:30 P.M.) with blintzes, lox and cream cheese, baked eggs with chopped ham, tomatoes, cheese and scallions. Sidewalk bar on sunny days. **Inexpensive.** Open seven days. Lunch served from 11:30 A.M. to 5 P.M. Dinner served Sunday through Thursday 11:30 A.M. to 11:30 P.M. Friday and Saturday 11:30 to 12:30 A.M. Saturday and Sunday brunch served from 10:30 A.M. to 3:30 P.M. No reservations. All major credit cards. Classical guitar. Full bar. Patio (limited). Street parking and in lot across the street. Casual.

★
COFFEE TREE/American
Nut Tree/Area 3/(707) 448-8435

The eye appeal of the cleanly designed exterior and the spacious interior of this sparkling-fresh oasis for Tahoe/Reno or Sacramento-bound freewayers extends agreeably to the food. Hospitably portioned burgers are offered, along with the unusual sandwich board, delicious entrées, hearty steaks, and desserts to conquer even the sternest calorie counter. The Coffee Tree complements The Nut Tree's good taste by also offering its own distinctively made pastries, breads and bakery goods. Substantial breakfasts and a clever problem-solver – a children's

menu for those under ten; yes, there's a peanut butter and jelly sandwich. Pleasant waitresses, prompt service.
Inexpensive. Open daily 5:30 A.M. to midnight. No reservations. AX, Visa, MC. Beer and wine only. Child's menu. Lot parking. Casual.

★
COLUMBUS/Italian
611 Broadway/San Francisco/Area 2/(415) 781-2939

In 1927 this was one of the first ristorantes at which "northern" Italian food was served. Fish, veal and pasta are cooked to order at prices that should embarrass some of the more pompous purveyors of *alta cucina*. Calamari is prepared with respect and the "calamari club," an organization of professional men that meet often to sample variations of their favorite dish, have pronounced Columbus a winner. The most expensive dinner on the long list is under $10, and that is real veal *saltimbocca* served—as are all the entrées—with a choice of spaghetti, vegetables, rice or macaroni. For some reason pot roast shows up as a dinner entrée (this is Italian?). Beef tongue, roast lamb, Italian sausage and veal *piccata* are some other selections. Among the daily specials—different each day of the week—*osso bucco* (veal shanks) are a favorite.

The Ditano family wants you to call for directions—it isn't the easiest place to find for out-of-towners, but is well worth whatever trouble you may take. Lively Italian music in this house of aromas finishes off the mood of *bon homie*.
Moderate. Open Monday through Saturday. Lunch from 11 A.M. to 4 P.M. Dinner 5:30 to 9 P.M. Reservations accepted. No credit cards. Wine and beer only. Lot parking. Casual to semi-dressy.

★★
COLUMBUS STREET RESTAURANT & BAR/Italian
4898 El Camino Real/Los Altos/Area 2/(415) 968-7251

I envy those who dine here regularly. My occupation does not permit frequent repeat meals; we all have our crosses. Anyway, it's a delectable experience in this outpost of North Beach. In fact, only a few dining places in that historic Italian sector of San Francisco approach this restaurant in either its *alta cucina* standards of fresh ingredients, or in the talents of the chef. Michael Ghilarducci, executive chef, and co-owner Bobby Sadri have that perfect relationship that produces a fine, balanced restaurant.

Michael is from a restaurant family. He grew up eating very well and learning his complex profession the best way—by doing. He has a way with anything edible and is remarkably proficient with his veal specialties and the pasta dishes. All his pastas are made fresh here: fettuccine, *gnocchi, taglierini*. My favorite, and everything else is excellent as well, is the *cannelloni* – delicate, incredibly tasteful. Of course, the extensive menu describes a generous plenitude of appetizers, soups and entrées, all that you'd expect from such an inspired kitchen. I can never pass up Michael's veal scaloppine, often having it *marsala* style. Gia Ghilarducci, the chef's lovely wife, frequently creates such tempting desserts as chocolate tortes, chocolate mousse cake and others of this caloric fraternity. The wine list emphasizes Californias with some refreshing Italian imports. The regular clientele includes many from nearby Silicon Valley, and Stanford University has contributed its scholarly quota since the restaurant's 1983 advent. The interior design is mellow and low-key, with soft lighting, yet ample enough for perusing the menu and wine list. **Moderate.** Lunch weekdays from 11:30 A.M., served all day. Dinner seven days from 5:30 to 10:30 P.M. Reservations recommended. Visa, MC, AX and DC. Full bar. Lot parking. Casual.

CONSUELO'S MEXICAN RESTAURANT/Mexican
361 Lighthouse Avenue/Monterey/Area 1/(408) 372-8111

I once had a date with a well-known young movie actress. I remember how I groomed for hours, arrived early, had to wait in my car, and finally – heart pounding – I took the lady out. The evening was a disaster. She was too beautiful, too contrived, too much the *poseur* and too boring. That's the feeling I get about Consuelo's. It's beautiful – located in a restored Victorian gingerbread mansion with a stairwell rising to the second floor, complimentary quesadillas, everything served hot and everyone cheerful as hell – but I didn't like it. You may, however, if your palate is not spoiled by the real restaurants of Mexico City. Besides, it's a showy place for entertaining and great for families as well.
Inexpensive. Open seven days. Lunch and dinner served from 11:30 A.M. to 9:30 P.M., Friday and Saturday to 10 P.M. Sunday brunch noon to 2 P.M. Reservations advised. All major credit cards. Wine and beer only. Patio. Street parking and lot off Drake Street. Casual.

In order to obtain the best results from this Guide, please consult "A Few Inside Tips" on page 18.

★
THE COOK BOOK/American
787 Emerald Bay Road/South Lake Tahoe/Area 6/(916) 541-8400

South Lake Tahoe is fortunate to have this all-American place that faithfully serves every day of the year, at modest prices, with an endearing consistency of quality and service.

There are several other Cook Books around California – the original in San Jose's Pruneyard Shopping Center, another in Palo Alto, one more in Tustin and two others, one each in Laguna Hills and Chino. White leghorns have to strain to increase production, for these restaurants are already famous for the tremendous number of eggs they use in making over three hundred varieties of huge omelettes.

Of course, there is also a standard menu at all meals and steaks, chicken and seafood have their loyal supporters here. The restaurant is family-oriented, and its location, near the junction of Highway 89 and Highway 50, makes The Cook Book convenient to locals and visitors alike. Summertime finds many patrons dining outdoors here. The design is mountain-rustic with wood panels and overhead beams. There's freshly squeezed orange juice, beer and wine.

Inexpensive to moderate. Open daily from 7 A.M. to 3 P.M. No reservations. No credit cards. Wine and beer only. Patio. Parking lot. Casual.

★
COQUELICOT/French/Nouvelle
23 Ross Common/Ross/Area 3/(415) 461-4782

Ross is to the Bay Area what Pasadena is to Hollywood – an exclusive domain of old-money families who maintain a low profile and a high balance. Coquelicot was started in 1981 by Maxime and Susan Schacher, Maxime in the kitchen at Chez Michel for three years before opening this charming, clubby, *prix fixe* ($30) whimsical restaurant. Actually, $30 is quite modest for the multi-course menu dégustatif that covers a wide range from Chinois to Japanese to French to "California." The tasting menu changes every night, but luncheon is another matter, and on a lovely day the patio provides a touch of serendipity with lunches priced generally under $10.

Expensive. Open for lunch Tuesday through Friday from 11:30 A.M. to 2 P.M. Dinner Tuesday through Saturday from 6 to 10 P.M. Reservations advised. Visa, MC. Wine and beer only. Patio. Child's menu. Street parking. Casual.

★
CORDON BLEU RESTAURANT/Vietnamese
1574 California Street/San Francisco/Area 2/(415) 673-5637
771 O'Farrell Street/San Francisco/Area 2/(415) 441-4581

The decor is sparse, the prices reasonable and the aroma from the kitchen is distinctly Vietnamese, as Trung Nguyen oversees the preparation of the dinners. If you've not tried the soup of this relatively unfamiliar cuisine, I'd recommend the asparagus (served in firm chunks in chicken broth) or the *hu tieu*, a noodle soup with tangy pork and bean sprouts, or the crab and corn soup. The five-spice chicken is barbecued with ginger, anise, cloves and cardamon. There's imperial roll and a form of shish kebab and some good desserts. A few wines, but beer goes especially well with this food. The O'Farrell location is larger and serves a greater variety of dishes and, although no longer owned by Trung, it seems to be holding up just fine.
Inexpensive. Open Tuesday through Sunday. Lunch served from 11:30 A.M. to 2:30 P.M. Dinner served from 5 to 10 P.M. Reservations advised. Visa, MC. (No reservations or credit cards at California location.) Wine and beer only at O'Farrell Street. Street parking. Casual.

★★
THE COURTYARD/California/Continental
2436 Clement/San Francisco/Area 2/(415) 387-7616

This is a relaxing place to enjoy some fine California continental cuisine in beautiful, spacious surroundings. Architect-designer Bruce Heiser's son, Kirk, completed the creative work half-way along, after his father's untimely demise. Partners Jonathan Holbrook and Jim Lyons assisted on a day and night basis — long hours to meet the constant demands of running a food and service business. There are two-story glass ceilings, natural woods, tile and gleaming brass, with an elevated dining section. A bold wall with woodsy murals projects an airy garden setting. The casual bar lounge restates the theme, its wide windows fronting on the street. Even the foyer is lush with greenery which provides a pleasant preview.

Pachi Calvo-Perez, the chef de cuisine, possesses culinary talents evident in every dish; from soups, special salads, huge sandwiches, burgers, omelettes, quiche, seafood and pasta at lunch, to fifteen dinner entrées, served with soup or salad, homemade French bread piping-hot from his ovens and fresh vegetables with cottage fries. Chicken American and double lamb chops are worthies typifying the choice-full menu. Many regulars order Pachi's nightly specials; possibly rack of spring lamb, perhaps corned beef and cabbage — let the staff rhapsodize for you. Oh, yes, they know their wines.

Sunday brunch is ample; I counted twenty-five items listed, a menu drawn from the luncheon with intriguing additions: eggs with Dungeness crab and poached eggs on English muffin with either Mornay or hollandaise.

Moderate. Open seven days for lunch from 11:30 A.M. to 2:30 P.M. Dinner from 5 to 9:30 P.M., Friday and Saturday until 10 P.M. Reservations accepted. All major credit cards. Full bar. Validated parking. Casual to semi-dressy.

★ ★ ★
THE COVEY AT QUAIL LODGE/Continental
8205 Valley Greens Drive/Carmel/Area 1/(408) 624-1581

You come here expecting to be impressed—and you are. The sole dining room in the Lodge is The Covey, a quiet, wood-enhanced retreat with a warm, dark blending of earth tones and tables lighted with brass oil lamps. It overlooks a pleasant man-made lake through broad windows and the luxuriously rustic effect pervades from the moment you enter the lobby with its huge fireplace that rises toward overhead beams and towering ceiling. Guests, attired casually but richly (jackets for gentlemen), dine on three levels, attended by properly trained waiters and staff. Owner Edgar Haber is a perfectionist and most capable overseer.

Now that the scene is set, on to the dining. All is what you would expect, from the hors d'oeuvres, soups and salads to the perfect entrées and sinful desserts. The *quenelles* of fresh sole would be an astute choice, then, perhaps, soup of the day rather than the classic onion soup. Fresh spinach salad *maison* is ideal. Seafood entrées emphasize locally caught fish. *Crab en chemise* is a rich, satisfying delight in pastry and *médaillons de veau aux champignons,* a delicate loin of veal sautéed and served in a light cream sauce. There are usually six or so sturdier meats, such as *steak au poivre, flambé.* At the risk of sounding like a press agent, I must go on to chronicle another triumph of The Covey—the desserts, although dessert is really too modest a word for such as the *vacherin au chocolat.* Chocolate mousse tarte defies adequate description.

Expensive. (Dinner is about $25 per person). Open seven days from 6:30 to 10 P.M. Reservations required. Visa, MC, AX, DC. Full bar. View. Ample lot parking. Semi-dressy to dressy.

In order to obtain the best results from this Guide, be sure to read the French, German, Italian and Oriental menu translators on pages 399 to 404 of this Guide.

★ ★
CRICKLEWOOD/Steak
4618 Old Redwood Highway/Santa Rosa/Area 3/(707) 527-7768

Beef" is owner/host Mike O'Brien's succinct description of what Cricklewood, "an eating & drinking place," is mainly about. There's no question that the affable Mr. O'Brien takes his meat seriously, for he buys choice-aged Colorado beef and carves the cuts himself. Diners can choose from prime rib large and small, top sirloin, New York steak, and porterhouse or T-bone steak "for the hearty appetite." For smaller appetites, smaller cuts are offered.

The menu is given balance with a grilled daily fresh fish— salmon, swordfish, and sea bass, among others—as well as lobster and prawn combinations. In addition to his fresh produce, Mr. O'Brien takes pride in his homemade soup.

Cricklewood's wine list, devoted exclusively to Sonoma County bottlings, is revised each year to accommodate winners of the annual county Harvest Fair competition.

The decor—wood and soft lighting, including Tiffany-style hanging lamps—provides a cozy atmosphere, especially in the room consisting entirely of booths.

Moderate. Open seven days. Lunch Monday through Friday from 11:30 A.M. to 2:30 P.M. Dinner Monday through Thursday from 5:30 to 10 P.M., Friday and Saturday from 5 to 11 P.M., and Sunday from 5 to 10 P.M. Reservations for six or more only. Visa, MC, AX. Full bar. Parking in adjacent lot. Casual.

★
THE CROW'S NEST/Steak/Seafood
2218 E. Cliff/Santa Cruz Yacht Harbor/Santa Cruz/Area 1/(408) 476-4560

Oh, hell, we're great!" modestly claims owner Robert Munsey. If a view of sea and sky and boats and harbor, predictable menu, attractive decor, and overly loud live bar entertainment makes a great restaurant . . . then, yes, this establishment is great. The name of the restaurant is derived from the lookout sitting high atop the restaurant, which the Coast Guard uses to direct sea rescue operations. The wonderful view from the greenhouse-like interior (glass walls and ceilings) brings the outdoors to your table. The menu offerings are in themselves not noteworthy, but the quality of all fare is high, from fish and seafood (especially the lobster tails) to beef selections (top sirloin, New York) to the chicken. Few food frills here, just basics well prepared and served by a better than average crew. Recently expanded, the restaurant can now accommodate even more of its fans.

Moderate. Open seven days. Lunch from 11:30 A.M. to 2:30 P.M. Dinner Monday through Thursday from 5:30 to 10 P.M., Friday 5:30 to 10:30 P.M., Saturday and Sunday 4 to 10 P.M. Visa, MC. Entertainment. Full bar. Patio. View. Child's menu. Validated parking. Casual to semi-dressy.

★
CUBA RESTAURANT/Cuban/Spanish
2886 Sixteenth Street/San Francisco/Area 2/(415) 864-9871

Cuban cooking can be exquisite, but it's usually served in tacky storefront restaurants with waitresses who all have the attitude that anything that could be done today is just as well done tomorrow. Cuba is no exception, but if you can ignore the atmosphere (or lack of it) and plan to spend an evening sipping beer and soaking up the *"mañana"* attitude, you can enjoy an exciting dining experience. The seafood is exceptional; be brave and try the squid in black sauce, a favorite at the pre-Castro Havana Hilton. The shrimp Cuban style is also exceptional, and many of the entrées here are served with yucca, and a bowl of black beans in a thick dark sauce. Neither are familiar to the typical American palate, but after trying them you may find yourself craving Cuban food at all hours of the night. The *paella* is somewhat of a disappointment as is the veal.

Moderate. Open Friday through Wednesday from noon to midnight. Reservations accepted. Visa, MC, DC, AX. Wine and beer only. Child's menu. Street parking. Casual.

★
THE CUSTOMS HOUSE/Continental
979 Edgewater Boulevard/Foster City/Area 2/(415) 574-7904

In this restaurant, set by the Foster City lagoon, you may be dining within an enormous packing crate, quite private, with a dimmer light switch. All views on the eastern exposure are of the lagoon and the elbow-to-elbow homes across the usually calm water. Although the Customs House seats quite a few, you are never aware of other diners nearby. The youthful, casually attired staff serves with dispatch and courtesy. You will be handed a cargo inventory clipboard—the extensive menu and list of the unusual, often exotic libations. Patrons marvel at the floor-to-ceiling piles of crates, bales, casks, barrels and containers of imaginary cargo. Note the maritime objects, the theme carried out to the nth. A sound-track subliminally underlines your experience—sounds of tropical birds, water slapping the pier and a faint steamer whistle.

"Just the Beginning" starts out the menu offerings with "Pago Pago potato skins," fried crispy, to dip into sour cream and chives. Twelve other starters, from pork ribs and egg rolls to Mexican pizza. Uncle Louie's shrimp Louie opens "From the Cold Hold," rich with salads, tacos and even tostadas. Omelettes, quiche and egg dishes from "Around the World in Eighty Eggs." Next page—"Robinson Potato," five tempting versions of richly stuffed potatoes. "Overland Cargo" vividly describes ten hamburgers and five startling sandwiches, including a "Drunken Chicken." Moving right along—a number of entrées, all served with extra goodies, actually a dinner special—"Adventurer's Manifest," from mahi mahi to a choice top sirloin teriyaki steak. Dessert is well-named "Precious Cargo," and is a fitting end. Wines are sold by the glass, half litre and litre, all from Taylor. They serve Anchor Steam Beer and the fantastic Foster's, in twenty-five ounce cans, from Australia. Sensational tropical drinks.

Check out the spacious bar lounge for entertainment Wednesday through Saturday.

Inexpensive to moderate. Open seven days. Lunch served Monday through Saturday from 11:30 A.M. to 2 P.M. Appetizers and sandwiches served from 2:30 to 5 P.M. Full menu for dinner from 5 to 10 P.M. Open Sunday from 5 to 9 P.M. for dinner; Sunday brunch from 11 A.M. to 2 P.M. Visa, MC, AX, DC. Entertainment. Full bar. Patio. Parking lot. Casual.

★
DAL BAFFO/Continental
878 Santa Cruz Avenue/Menlo Park/Area 2/(415) 325-1588

This is the restaurant that understands ladies. The rose-hued neon lights are most flattering to the female face. Chef/proprietor Vincenzo Lo Grasso is a gracious host and every attempt is made to make the customer feel like a guest and not a dollar sign. The general feeling is European elegance. Vincenzo's pastas, including his famous pasta dumpling, are well prepared and attractively served: fettuccine Alfredo (al dente noodles with a velvet cheese and cream sauce) and *angelotti manicotti*, (pasta shells bursting with a cheese filling, dressed in cream and butter) make memorable beginnings. There is a wide range of seafood, but the specialty is the veal. From parmigiana and Oscar to Marsala and Cordon Bleu, we found it flavorful and fork-tender.
Moderate to expensive. Open Tuesday through Saturday. Lunch served weekdays from 11:30 A.M. to 2:30 P.M. Dinner Tuesday through Thursday from 6 to 10 P.M., Friday and Saturday until 10:30 P.M. Reservations advised. All major credit cards. Ample parking. Dressy.

★ ★
DANTE'S/Italian
430 Columbus Avenue/San Francisco/Area 2/(415) 956-0676

Located in the heart of San Francisco's famous North Beach, Dante's is a favorite with tourists and locals alike for both its charming atmosphere and its Italian Tuscany cuisine. The entire sliding glass-windowed front (including the cozy, full bar) opens onto colorful Columbus Avenue. Dante Serafini is host/manager, but it's Mama Louise who's head chef, cooking family recipes in huge ovens. Some of her specialties are chicken *coteghino* (stuffed with sausage in wine sauce), *saltimbocca,* roast and sautéed veal, and fresh fish of the day such as prawns *della casa,* trout *alla Toscana* and sautéed calamari. Also pleasing are appetizers, pastas, salads, homemade soups, delicious desserts, Italian coffees and a good list of California wines and champagnes.

Moderate. Open seven days. Lunch Monday through Friday 11:30 A.M. to 3 P.M. Dinner Sunday through Thursday, 5:30 to 11 P.M. Friday and Saturday till midnight. Reservations recommended. AX, Visa, MC, DC. Full bar. Street parking. Casual.

★★
DAVID'S/Jewish Deli
474 Geary Street/ San Francisco/Area 2/(415) 771-1600

This is the "Stage Door" or "Lindy's" of San Francisco, a really good Kosher deli located in the theatrical district. David's is far more than The City's most celebrated restaurant-delicatessen-bakery. Here, all is prepared with what David calls *love.* The ambiance is comfortable and unharried, in the fine European cafe tradition. Everything is the best of its kind: bagels, blintzes, borscht. All breads and pastries are baked here. David's is situated on the ground floor of Hotel David, another jewel, whose guests breakfast here on whatever they wish, price included with their room. David Apfelbaum, wearing a sportshirt behind the deli counter, often greets his guests by name. If you order corned beef lean, it really comes out that way. The stuffed cabbage, goulash and Kosher knockwurst are also excellent—and the sauerbraten is the best in town. Don't miss the "hors d'oeuvrye," a hybrid of French and rye with whipped cream cheese. It's a no-nonsense place that caters to serious eaters (as opposed to diners).

Moderate to expensive. Open seven days, 8 A.M. to 1 A.M. No reservations. All major credit cards. Wine and beer only. Child's menu. Parking lot. Casual.

★
DEER PARK VILLA/Italian
367 Bolinas Road/Fairfax/Area 3/(415) 456-8084

This appealing restaurant is on what was once a Mexican land grant, and later a cattle ranch. A hunting lodge was extensively remodeled into the current spacious building, originally opened as a dining place in late 1922, and expanded by Joseph and Antoinette Ghiringhelli who purchased it in 1937. Their family carries on, graciously receiving patrons in the several dining rooms and wide deck (open seasonally). Two outer areas, amidst towering redwoods planted by Joseph, are popular for wedding receptions and parties. "Like dining in a lovely park," is often heard. Cuisine includes really good Italian and American specialties, even a roast turkey (Sunday) and prime rib on weekends plus roast leg of lamb. The seafood is always the freshest and includes petrale sole whenever it has been caught that day. Blackboards show the specials. **Moderate.** Open Wednesday through Sunday. Dinner Wednesday through Saturday from 5:30 to 10 P.M. Sunday from 4 to 10 P.M. Reservations advised. Visa, MC, AX. Full bar. Patio. View overlooking redwood and oak trees and gardens. Child's menu. Parking lot. Semi-dressy.

DA ★
DEETJEN'S/American/Continental
South Highway 1/Big Sur/Area 1/(408) 667-2377

When on occasion I lecture before journalism classes, the classic ethical dilemma is always proposed: What if a restaurateur—whether he wishes to avoid a bad review or for reasons of privacy—does not *want* to appear in this book? What then?

The answer is simple. The premise of this kind of guide is to seek out those places that are special and to criticize restaurants we feel deserve to be criticized.

I must say that this delightful letter from the owner of Deetjen's gave me pause: "In reference to your letter and request for information . . . I'm writing to ask that you not publicize the inn in your forthcoming guide. It has always been a tradition . . . that 'discovery' was the best way to be introduced to the inn. Surely there's no reason to change what has always been the policy. . . ."

My reply: "While I respect your request to not be included in our book, particularly *because* the inn is an exciting and valuable restaurant, I must point out that our job is to tell readers about places like yours.

"The lovely dinners we've had there, simple, but with homemade freshness in every bite, and the sensational pies, should be shared with our readers. Yours is a dining adventure. Your attitude of serving dinner at 6:30 and 8 P.M. only is intelligent for the area. Your warm and cozy interior should not be missed. Thanks for all the lovely times we've spent in your inn."

Be sure to make reservations and show up on time . . . or else. **Moderate.** Open seven days. Breakfast from 8 to 11:30 A.M. Dinner seatings at 6, 7 and 8 P.M. Tuesday and Wednesday they serve only a continental breakfast and supper at night. Reservations accepted. No credit cards. Wine and beer only. Parking lot. Casual.

★
THE DELI/Deli/Continental
1980 Union Street/San Francisco/Area 2/(415) 563-7274

A **Jewish deli** with a patio? Stained glass? Fresh flowers??? Improbable, you say. True, but Mr. Benjamin has provided a gracious setting that is far more appropriate to this good food than the grease-and-holler shops that bellow out great draughts of essence of dill pickle. The sandwiches are all one might expect. And the dinners—baked chicken, sweet and sour meatballs, blintzes—are lovely, with marinated herring (ah!), chopped liver (sigh!) and savory rye bread. If Jewish deli foods are unfamiliar to you (and I'm sorry if they are), then this is the place to "Eat! Eat!" **Inexpensive to moderate.** Open seven days from 11 A.M. to 12:30 A.M. Reservations accepted. All major credit cards. Full bar. Patio. Parking garages nearby. Casual.

DA ★
DE PAULA'S/Brazilian
2114 Fillmore/San Francisco/Area 2/(415) 346-9888

B **razilian** restaurants seem to come and go in San Francisco, but De Paula's was established in 1978 and is still going strong. *Feijoada combleda* is Brazilian soul food, black beans simmered with pork stew, sometimes with a touch of orange peel. *Camarao a bahiama* is a favorite here, sautéed prawns with herbs and spices. Chef Luis Antonio is direct from Brazil and people who know and appreciate the food are quick to praise him. This is a lively, sometimes rocking, place with occasional live bands and Brazilian music on the system. For some reason, De Paula's delivers anything on their menu, including a pretty good version of pizza. **Moderate.** Lunch weekdays from 11:30 A.M. to 2:30 P.M. Dinner Sunday through Thursday from 5 to 11:30 P.M., Friday and Saturday to 1 A.M. Reservations accepted. All major credit cards. Entertainment. Wine and beer only. Street parking. Casual.

★
DES ALPES/Basque
732 Broadway/San Francisco/Area 2/(415) 391-4249

C **limb** the highest mountain and you might just be able to prepare yourself for the enormous fare placed before you here. The incredible amount of food presented begins with a warming tureen of soup and sourdough bread . . . followed by a salad which some restaurants would serve as a main course—string beans, hard-boiled eggs, onions. Then comes—no, not the entrée—but a meat or seafood course, lamb stew or maybe steamed clams. That's enough, you say. Nay! The main course is yet to arrive: maybe roast beef with fries and . . . another salad . . . this one a tossed green. These family-style dinners are served under the auspices of the Iturris, who are amazingly able to keep the prices in the moderate range. You probably can't eat at home as well for the price.

Moderate. Open Tuesday through Sunday. Dinner served from 5:30 to 10 P.M.; Sunday from 5 to 9:30 P.M. Reservations accepted. Visa, MC. Full bar. Street parking. Casual.

★
DIAMOND STREET RESTAURANT/Indian/Vegetarian
737 Diamond Street/San Francisco/Area 2/(415) 285-6988

You and your karma will flourish in this congenial restaurant that specializes in unusual vegetarian dishes. The homemade soups are perked up with tantalizing hints of Indian spices. And the fresh-daily molasses bread tastes like it. But why, oh why, do they serve a mini-butter pat for two? A variety of vegetarian dinners are offered nightly: spinach and walnut lasagna or maybe a French artichoke and mushroom and cheese pie. There's chicken in lemon sauce that is better than expected, fresh fish and pastas. Art from some of the top New York artists brightens up the cleanly modern interior.

Inexpensive to moderate. Open seven days. Dinner Sunday through Thursday 5:30 to 10 P.M., Friday and Saturday until 10:30 P.M. Reservations accepted. Visa, MC. Wine and beer only. Street parking. Casual to semi-dressy.

DIGGER DANS/American
7793 Wren Avenue/Gilroy/Area 2/(408) 842-0609

There's a touch of the old mining days in this serve-yourself soup and salad bar operation. Beamed ceilings, picks and shovels, lanterns and a large map of the nearby mines provide the atmosphere, and there are about a dozen dinners on the menu centering around beef and the ubiquitous steak and lobster combo's. "Miners Stew" is fun, served in a small loaf of hollowed out sourdough bread.

Moderate to expensive. Open seven days. Lunch served weekdays from 11:30 A.M. to 2:30 P.M. Dinner Monday through Saturday from 5:30 to 10 P.M. Sunday 4:30 to 9 P.M. Brunch on each first Sunday of the month from 10 A.M. to 2 P.M. Reservations advised. All major credit cards. Entertainment. Full bar. Child's menu for dinner. Lot parking. Casual to semi-dressy.

★
DI GRANDE RESTAURANT/Seafood/Italian
1439 Taraval/San Francisco/Area 2/(415) 665-0325

Owner Vincent Di Grande serves good *cannelloni* as an appetizer and specializes in *saltimbocca* (rolled veal) served in an herb sauce. This is one of the better North Beach restaurants, a step up from its compadres, with some fine entrées, (as opposed to the "who cares, there's *so* much food" kind) like veal *dore,* and petrale sole. The *zabaglione* was not good (*zabaglione,* that gold froth made with eggs and Marsala is either fantastic or not good) and the other desserts were lackluster. **Moderate.** Open Sunday and Tuesday through Thursday from 4:30 to 10:30 P.M., weekends to 11 P.M. Reservations advised. Visa, MC, AX. Full bar. Street parking. Casual to semi-dressy.

★
DINAH'S SHACK/Smorgasbord
4269 El Camino Real/Palo Alto/Area 2/(415) 493-9510

Founded as a Southern fried chicken house in 1927, this delightful, rambling old favorite is renowned primarily for its excellent smorgasbord (and for the soothing harpist's melodies), with forty selections that include many seafood dishes. Yes, the original Dinah's chicken recipe is still followed faithfully. American and continental offerings: prime rib, steaks and daily fresh fish head the large menu. The late Herman Rickey, respected citizen of the restaurant profession, owned and operated Dinah's since 1950. Ambiance reflects New Orleans of the past, mellow, softly lighted, comfortable. There is also a beguiling lounge with long bar and pianist (Tuesday-Saturday). **Moderate.** Open seven days. Lunch served from 11 A.M. to 2:30 P.M. weekdays. Dinner served Monday through Saturday from 5 to 10 P.M. Sunday from 4 to 9:30 P.M. Reservations advised. All major credit cards. Entertainment. Child's menu. Ample parking. Casual.

★★
THE DOCK/American/Continental
25 Main Street/Tiburon/Area 3/(415) 435-4550

You may tie up your yacht for al fresco dining on this dramatic deck, high above Tiburon's quiet harbor. San Francisco's skyline appears here as backdrop on a huge stage. Attention to the menu has not been forgotten, however. It features seafood and beef, with a wide choice of brunch combinations served early in the day. If there's ever a competition for the best sautéed abalone on the coast, I'd be tempted to back the version prepared here, for it presents the mollusk's delicate flavor at its purest with no outside enhancers. Only problem is it's not always available. Daily specials take advantage of whatever's freshest. Over two decades of popularity attest to the care with which everything is handled. The wine list is a rarity, not in choices but in prices, which are about the same as you'd pay in a retail store. Souverain wines are featured with Fetzer chardonnay and Mondavi chardonnay also available. It's little wonder the place is always filled.

Moderate. Open seven days. Breakfast and lunch served Monday through Friday from 11 A.M. to 4:30 P.M. Dinner served from 5 to 10 P.M. Saturday and Sunday brunch served from 10 A.M. to 4:30 P.M. Reservations advised. All major credit cards. Entertainment, dancing. Full bar. Patio. View of San Francisco and Bay. Validated parking. Casual.

★
DOIDGE'S KITCHEN/Continental
2217 Union Street/San Francisco/Area 2/(415) 921-2149

Everything on Union Street is a delight, from the old Victorian mansions—be sure to visit the Octagon House, built in 1857 and carefully restored by the Colonial Dames—to the boutiques, antique shops and restaurants. Doidge's is a favorite, a charmingly unpretentious luncheonette where home-baked cakes and unusual grilled sandwich combinations are served at low prices.

Although everything here is good, brunch is the real event. French toast is made from six different varieties of bread and covered with your choice of toppings. Omelettes range from the familiar (Spanish, mushroom and herb) to the exotic (peach and walnut chutney). The only problem here is in limiting your order to one item and passing by all the creations you see being brought to adjoining tables.

Inexpensive to moderate. Open seven days. Monday through Wednesday from 8 A.M. to 2:15 P.M. Thursday through Sunday 8 A.M. to 9 P.M. Reservations advised. Visa, MC. No alcohol. Street and lot parking. Casual.

★ ★
DOMAINE CHANDON/French
California Drive/Yountville/Area 3/(707) 944-2892

One of the finest champagne type wines is produced at the winery and served in this exquisite restaurant. (The winery is an American invasion by Moet and Chandon.) A fresh, green springtime look to the interior is a pleasant setting for really splendid food. The *prix fixe* luncheon includes an appetizer or salad, entrée and dessert. Specialties like lamb noisettes with rosemary and balsamic vinegar, grilled yellow fin tuna, and cream of tomato in a puff pastry keep people, other than tourists, coming back to this wine country gem. **Expensive.** (Dinner approximately $40). Open seven days for lunch from May to November and Wednesday through Sunday from November to May and for dinner all year. Lunch from 11:30 A.M. to 2:30 P.M. Dinner from 6 to 9 P.M. Reservations suggested two weeks in advance. Visa, MC, AX. Wine only. Patio. Parking lot. Semi-dressy.

★★
DOMENICO'S ON THE WHARF/Seafood/Italian
50 Fisherman's Wharf/Monterey/Area 1/(408) 372-3655

Dominic Mercurio, himself, will probably greet you in this perfectly placed, blue and white sparkler. Dominic, partner here with uncle John Pisto, whose own fine Whaling Station Inn is reviewed in this book, is one of those youthful, competent professionals who can handle any position on his staff, from bus boy to bartender to pasta maker. Yes, he does have an imported pasta machine and produces interesting dishes like crab ravioli. You will be seated in a window-walled room that looks out on moored yachts, cruisers in the harbor, barking seals, seagulls, pelicans, and possibly even a sea otter – swimming on its back, shellfish held firmly on its chest, pounding away with a paw-held rock: a lively floor show for your meal. Waiters are invariably young, handsome, and able to describe the unusual seafood salads, pastas and Italian-inspired creations on the innovative menu. Dominic's kitchen is gourmet-worthy with choice meats, fresh-that-morning seafood, crisp greens, and house-made pastries. In the marble-floored foyer, a long bar flanks displays of many nautical offerings. Enjoy generous libations, snacks or lunch at the bar. California wines are offered by the glass or the bottle. **Moderate.** Open seven days. Lunch weekdays from 11:30 A.M. to 2:30 P.M.; Saturday 11:30 A.M. to 3:30 P.M. Dinner nightly 5 to 10 P.M. Sunday brunch from 10 A.M. to 3:30 P.M. Reservations necessary. All major cards. Full bar. Parking on the wharf. Casual.

★
DOMINIC'S HARBOR/Seafood/Italian
507 Francisco Boulevard/San Rafael/Area 3/(415) 456-1383

Dominic's has been an integral part of the San Rafael social goings-on for nearly two decades. His tiny-to-large and beautifully appointed banquet rooms have been the scene of many marriages, anniversaries and other happy occasions. The public dining room combines a marine view with a sort of French-Swiss ambiance in which continental dinners are served virtually around the clock. Dominic's two brothers have their own fishing boats and supply Dominic with fresh fish. Other specialties include pasta and veal dishes. There's a sky-high fishing boat as a landmark-sign, a spacious over-the-water outdoor terrace, good waiter and captain service, and a fair wine list. Fisherman's Wharf should have such a place.

Moderate. Open seven days. Lunch served from 11:30 A.M. to 4:30 P.M. Dinner served from 4:30 to 10:30 P.M. Sunday brunch served from 10 A.M. to 3 P.M. Reservations advised. Visa, MC, AX, DC. Organ. Full bar. Patio. San Rafael Canal view. Child's menu. Two-acre free parking. Casual.

★ ★
DONATELLO RISTORANTE/Northern Italian
501 Post Street/San Francisco/Area 2/(415) 441-7182

Cal Rossi inherited a love and understanding of fine food that he manifests in his Donatello (named for the Italian sculptor), who was one of the leaders in and founders of Renaissance art. Cal, let us presume a bit, is responsible not only for his hotel's concept and execution but for the highly refined cuisine wherein he has imprinted his own refined tastes (he is a remarkable cook) as well as some imported dishes that are rarely attempted in this country. The culinary achievements routinely presented here are regarded as some of the finest in this city of Italian dining places. The menu changes daily and allows chef Michael Hart the freedom to prepare specials with the freshest of ingredients. I shall not detail the kitchen's accomplishments but will reveal that the two dining rooms—The Fortuny Room and The Stucco Room, each distinct—glow with Venetian glass, Fortuny fabric walls, Carpaccio lamps, marble floors, and too much to mention. The wine list is extensive and reasonably priced. It is a pleasure to see the return of fine dining in first class hotels.

Expensive. Open seven days. Breakfast from 7:30 to 10:30 A.M. Lunch from 11:30 A.M. to 2:30 P.M. Dinner from 6 to 10:30 P.M. Reservations essential. All major credit cards. Full bar. Parking in hotel, validated partly. Dressy.

★ ★
DON THE BEACHCOMBER/Polynesian
5580 Stevens Creek Boulevard/San Jose/Area 2/(408) 996-3547

Depending on your point of view, Don Beach should be given the credit or the blame for starting the first Polynesian restaurant anywhere. (He also invented *rumaki*.) These tastefully designed locations have been quietly turning out high-quality food and good rum drinks for so long that there is a tendency to take them for granted. The usual

"Polynesian" dishes are prepared unusually well here, and the rum drinks are a sensation. There is more to the menu than South Seas fare – good seafood dishes and some less exotic staples.
Moderate to expensive. Open seven days. Lunch served weekdays from 11:30 A.M. to 2:30 P.M. Dinner Monday through Thursday from 5 to 10 P.M. Friday and Saturday until 11 P.M. Sunday brunch from 10 A.M. to 3 P.M. All major credit cards. Full bar. Parking lot. Casual.

★ ★ ★
DOROS/Continental
714 Montgomery Street/San Francisco/Area 2/(415) 397-6822

Don Dianda has achieved new heights for preparation and service of the elaborate dishes of northern Italy. In this ambiance of understated elegance (red banquettes against white brick walls and dark paneled woods), a carefully assembled staff of professional waiters serve some spectacular dishes by chef Paul Bermani, who has been with Doros for a quarter of a century. The *saltimbocca a la romana* with *risotto* is the most extraordinary version of this classic dish I've tasted anywhere, including a memorable dinner at La Fenice in Venice. The veal cutlet parmigiana may sound mundane, but it might be one of the rare opportunities to taste a real veal classic ("I didn't know veal looked like that," said the man at the next table. Sad. For years he's been eating pork soaked in milk as a counterfeit of one of the most delicate meats of any cuisine.) While you can order spaghetti at lunch, I would hope you'd try their specialty-of-the-house *cannelloni* or the fettuccine *al' Alfredo*. The selections range to French, not surprising when you realize that no less an authority than Brillat-Savarin (historic French epicure) agreed with the great chef Escoffier that many *haute cuisine* dishes were inspired by the chefs of northern Italy. A couple of noteworthy specials: tournedos of beef Rossini and veal courvoiseur. Whatever you order here will be superb; we've never been disappointed nor have our hard-to-convince friends from New York who still cling to the ancient theory that the Big Apple is America's capital of cuisine. Doros confuses, depresses and delights them. At a price. Outstanding wine selection.
Expensive. Open Monday through Saturday. Lunch served from 11:30 A.M. to 2:30 P.M. Dinner served from 6 to 10:30 P.M. Reservations required. All major credit cards. Full bar. Valet parking at dinner. Dressy.

For best results, consult "How to Use This Guide" on page 25.

★
DOUBLE RAINBOW/Ice Cream
(Many locations in San Francisco and one in Oakland.
See your phone book for listings.)

The avid ice creamaholic can spend hours debating the merits and shortcomings of Baskin-Robbins vs. Haagen Dazs vs. Dreyer's. And the Double Rainbow is moving up as a contender. The waiters here are really the customers — there's always a line — but the wait is worth it. What distinguishes their ice cream is that no artificial colorings or flavors are used. Just fresh quality ingredients like rich dark chocolate, fresh peaches, blueberries and strawberries and crunchy fresh walnuts. As a purist in matters of ice cream, I like mine straight, but my companion seemed to get lost in ice cream heaven over one of their sundaes. Espresso and cappuccino are also available to go with the richness of the ice cream. **Inexpensive.** Open seven days. Sunday through Thursday from 11 A.M. to midnight, Friday and Saturday from 11 A.M. to 1 A.M. Hours vary with the location. Street parking. Casual.

★
DRAKE'S TAVERN/English
Sir Francis Drake Hotel/450 Powell (at Sutter)/San Francisco/Area 2
(415) 392-7755

Step in from the chill, dank fog outside to the warmth of this tudor dining room, and if you squint your eyes just right, you might mistake it for a fashionable West End hotel. The illusion is sustained by the service, smartly conducted by your captain and a covey of waiters, attentive to your every whim. The menu consists of such standbys as fresh fish of the day, prime rib, lamb chops and double breast of chicken almondine. The wine list is one of the more extensive in the city. This is a good place to go looking for an old, neglected bottle of cabernet or a really vintage glass of port alongside a piece of Cheshire cheese, should it suit your whimsey. **Moderate to expensive.** Open seven days. Lunch Monday through Saturday from 11 A.M. to 6 P.M. Dinner from 6 to 10 P.M. Reservations advised. All major credit cards. Full bar. Street parking. Semi-dressy.

★ ★
DUARTE'S TAVERN/American
202 Stage Road/Pescadero/Area 2/(415) 879-0464

Duarte's began life in 1894 when Frank Duarte started his tavern with hard spirits for neighboring farmers and travelers en route from San Francisco to Santa Cruz along what is now Highway One. Fifty miles south of The City, thirty-five miles up from "Holy Cross," about an hour's scenic drive west from San Mateo and set inland two miles from the Pacific awaits this unusual down-to-earth find. It's worth the trip to this glorious segment of the ever-dwindling, nostalgic past.

Frank's grandson, Ronald, and wife, Lynn, work harder than you and I ever have, or will, to feed the sea-air-provoked appetites of their patrons. Everything is good, just plain American country food—but fresh, fresh as you almost never find it.

Duarte's serves all day, everyday, modestly tabbed complete meals at dinner, country breakfasts, the works. Everything is made fresh— soups to gladden the soul; the artichoke (from hearts of the Duarte-grown delights) are alone worth your excursion. Seasonal vegetables Ronald nurses from seed through infancy to you; apples emerge from his own orchard for the pies (and the memorable applesauce that accompanies huge pork chops). If you've never had olallie berries, which Ron picks himself from bushes on Pescadero's bordering hills, just taste the heavenly olallie pie.

Seafood often reaches the kitchen less than an hour from the ocean, from Ronald's private sources. He drives up and along the coast searching for marine bounty. He buys quality meats for his steaks and chops. If he could, he would even coax extra eggs from neighbors' chickens, I suspect.

Moderate to expensive. Open seven days from 7:30 A.M. to 9 P.M. Reservations advised. Visa, MC, AX. Full bar. Parking lot. Casual.

★
DUTCH EAST INDIES/Indonesian
368 Second Street/Oakland/Area 2/(415) 444-9358

It is becoming increasing difficult to find Indonesian restaurants that serve up *rijsttafel,* that banquet of exquisite small tastes on small plates. I don't particularly like the shrimp puffs served here, it's kind of a chemical concoction that puffs up under heat from a poker chip-sized kernel, but I covet everything else on the menu. *Rijsttafel* for two includes *frikadel,* a spiced sausage; *gado gado,* a mixed salad of raw and cooked vegetables with hardboiled eggs in a coconut peanut sauce; *ajam pangang,* marinated charcoal broiled chicken; and *satay,* a skewer of marinated beef topped with spicy peanut sauce, along with a special curry of the day. Chef Andy Suyatno previously worked in the Orient, where this kind of food is appreciated. Indonesian beer is a fair enough accompaniment to the spicy fare.

Inexpensive to moderate. Open Tuesday through Sunday. Lunch from 11:30 A.M. to 2 P.M., dinner 5:30 to 9:30 P.M. Sunday brunch from 10:30 A.M. to 2:30 P.M. Reservations accepted. All major credit cards. Wine and beer only. Patio for lunch. Street parking. Semi-dressy.

★ ★
E'ANGELO/Northern Italian
2234 Chestnut/San Francisco/Area 2/(415) 567-6164

When I inquired of owner-chef Ezio A. Rastelli about that "E" in the name of his popular local favorite, I learned that his former partner was the "Angelo" and, when Ezio bought him out in 1979, he wanted a little credit himself, and so . . .

This is a simple place with small paintings depicting many Italian legends and an open kitchen where you can see Ezio working his miracles, facing his oft-rapt audience. It's a rather crowded room with busy waiters, and quite European for the heart of the Marina's commercial district, amidst elbow-to-elbow shops, many purveying foodstuffs.

Ezio is from northern Italy, near Genoa, and so his cuisine is lighter, easy on the garlic without ignoring it. In addition to pastas, there are small, appetizer-type pizzas of merit, also *antipasti* and minestrone. Entrées are typical and flavorful; scalloppine, veal dishes, sole, a remarkable roast lamb, roast chicken—but, you come here for pasta.

There are twenty, count 'em, specialty pastas, starting with lasagna Bolognese, green lasagna, *cannelloni* Eduardo's, eggplant parmigiana, fettuccine *carbonara* and on to *tortellini*—four versions. Linguine *alla vongole, gnocchi al sugo* and some spaghettis, what else? *Buono appetito!* **Inexpensive to moderate.** Open Tuesday through Sunday for dinner from 5 to 11 P.M. No reservations. No credit cards. Wine and beer only. Public parking. Casual.

Please be sure to consult "Tipping Made Easy" on page 22 of this Guide.

★ ★
ECCO/Italian/American
Hyatt Palo Alto/4290 El Camino Real/Palo Alto/Area 2/(415) 493-0800

Where do you find good Italian food in this area, when almost all is dried, frozen or canned? Surprisingly, in this handsome Hyatt operation. This famous hotel chain is known for its dedication to good food and they have not spared the budget in Ecco's spacious, airy premises, with comfortable, commodious booths and well-spaced tables. At lunch, there is a help-yourself salad bar of impressive variety. All the right things are fresh and I filled my plate twice. (Or was it three times?) The Sunday brunch uses the same technique, and the buffet table actually groans. A pitiful sound, rather like mine when the bus boy removes my plate while there is still one last bite. Evenings a pianist works his wiles. The hot dishes are generously portioned and I discovered some choice wines here.

Moderate to expensive. Open daily. Monday through Saturday from 6:30 A.M. to 10:30 P.M. Sunday from 7 A.M. to 10 P.M. Sunday brunch 10:30 A.M. to 2:30 P.M. Reservations advised. All major credit cards. Entertainment. Full bar. Child's menu. Ample parking. Casual.

EL CALDERON/Salvadorean/Mexican
699 Calderon/Mountain View/Area 2/(415) 940-9533

The foods of El Salvadore: rich *sopas,* fried bananas in a cream sauce, and sliced tongue in Salvadorean sauce are worth getting into, if you're in the area. It's just a little storefront in Mountain View, but I know some pretty knowledgeable palates that have returned several times in the last year. *Paposas* – mini tortillas stuffed with pork, cheese or beans – are the specialty. But the *pollo Encebolla* (chicken in a marvelous sauce) is my favorite.

Inexpensive. Open Monday through Saturday. Lunch from 11 A.M. to 1:45 P.M. Dinner from 5 to 8:45 P.M. Reservations accepted. No credit cards. Entertainment. Beer only. Ample parking. Casual.

In order to obtain the best results from this Guide, please consult "A Few Inside Tips" on page 18.

★
THE ELEGANT BIB/American/Continental
3201 Danville Boulevard/Alamo/Area 2/(415) 837-5123

You're never going to find any friendlier place than this old (1969) favorite of the Alamo/Danville/Walnut Creek/Dublin/San Ramon folks. After you sit down in the somewhat Victorian-influenced restaurant, if you're wearing anything red, owner Brian Kahng bids you a fond welcome and reels off the features of the house and menu specials. Next arrives courtesy hors d'oeuvres and the salad is accompanied by a small glass of wine. At the end of the meal, the house treats you to brandy in a snifter. Many diners like to wear the bibs—I don't—which are immediately offered. Some nights the visual effect can be that of a very junior crowd. Food here is good, not truly epicurean, but portions are large. Both the seafood and the veal are wise picks. **Moderate to expensive.** Open seven days. Dinner served Monday through Thursday from 5:30 to 9:30 P.M. Friday to 10 P.M. Saturdays 5 to 10 P.M., Sunday from 4:30 to 9 P.M. Reservations accepted. Visa, MC, AX. Entertainment. Full bar. Child's menu. Parking lot. Casual.

★
THE ELITE CAFE/Créole/Seafood
2049 Fillmore Street/San Francisco/Area 2/(415) 346-8668

Sam Duvall keeps repeating himself, only doing it even better every time. First, he gave us the Front Room, then The Back Room, next to Casablanca (the San Francisco version), followed by Duvall's Good Eats and then the delightful Albatross. Then, Southern-born Sam created his hard-to-get-into Elite Cafe, bringing us genuine New Orleans style cooking—not the fancy French dishes, but of the people, especially the Cajuns and Créoles. He has since sold the establishment to Tom Clandening and Rahim Talia, who are doing their best to follow in Sam's tradition.

The small front oyster bar appeases some of the always-waiting patrons. In the brightly lighted, fairly long room, diners are packed into the old, wood booths with others at the counter and still more filling the tables beneath ancient ceiling fans and Art Deco light fixtures. Everyone is eating, almost ravenously, surprised that The Elite is so remarkably satisfying. Although it is not feasible to fly in all the gulf prawns, oysters and fish, the local products are nearly as good after the superb handling of Elite's chef (from a top restaurant of New Orleans) and his adroit employment of the true native spices makes the dishes authentic.

Names and dishes to conjure with—shrimp rémoulade, Créole gumbo, redfish with pecan sauce(!!!), redfish Carolyn, Créole eggplant with shrimp and crab, to list a few. Don't ignore roast pork loin with the sweet potato and cornbread dressing. Desserts are exceptional—pecan pie, the real thing, with flaky creamy cheese crust and bread pudding for those pudding lovers, sometimes with bourbon sauce or lemon rum. Sunday brunch is busy, offering fruit, cornbread and six entrées.

Moderate. Open seven days from 5 to 11 P.M., Sunday 5 to 10 P.M. Sunday brunch from 10 A.M. to 3 P.M. No reservations. No credit cards. Full bar. Street parking. Semi-dressy.

★

EL PASEO/French/Continental
17 Throckmorton Avenue/Mill Valley/Area 3/(415) 388-0741

El **Paseo** is tucked into a Carmel-like, verdantly attired small alley off of Throckmorton where you can enjoy a quiet, rather romantic adventure. Brick walls, high-beamed ceiling, thoughtfully selected antiques and soft but adequate lighting, set the scene. Service is gently formal but cordial. The staff in large part consists of owners Mark Bottermeyer and Gunter Kollner. Schooled in Europe, with local service in Ernie's, these gentlemen do *everything* correctly. Seated, perhaps, at the small wine-apéritif bar, ask to see the comprehensive wine book—impressive indeed with some delightful, rare selections.

I recommend the complete dinner, rich with special soups, fine appetizers and over a dozen tantalizing entrées. *Les médaillons de veau Dijonnaise* and *le lapin à la Bohemienne* are typical. Sweet-toothers will revel in the tempting desserts.

Moderate. Open seven days from 5:30 to 10 P.M. Reservations strongly advised. No credit cards. Wine and beer only. Street parking. Casual to semi-dressy.

★ ★

EL SOMBRERO/Mexican
5800 Geary Boulevard/San Francisco/Area 2/(415) 221-2382

After an enjoyable Taxco-style meal in Los Angeles, I asked what there was for dessert. The waitress checked the kitchen and zinged, "We have Alka-Seltzer." Masochism should not be the underlying motive of Mexican dining. Only Texans and border Mexicans serve blistering hot chilis, but that has been enough to shape the popular conception. There are certain minimum standards for any Mexican restaurant worth its salsa. Mild salsa and fiery chile colorado should be on the table so that each diner can add appropriate bite to the kitchen's preparations.

Shredded beef should be used instead of hamburger; tortillas should be freshly made *in* the dining room, not by machine but patted out by a tortillera (and she should be tipped separately). El Sombrero is hands-down the highest class *comida* in the city; its cool colonial architecture is loaded with blue tiles and wrought iron, dark wooden beams and tasteful color accents. To my mind, their best dish is one of the least expensive: enchiladas *suizas* filled with melted jack cheese and slathered in sour cream and green chile salsa. The top of the line dishes are quite good too: *arroz con pollo* (chicken with yellow rice) and *gallina en mole* (spicy, dark chocolate, sauced hen).

Moderate. Open Tuesday through Saturday from 11:45 A.M. to 10:30 P.M. No reservations. No credit cards. Full bar. Street parking. Casual.

★
EL TAZUMAL/Salvadorean/Mexican
3522 20th Street/San Francisco/Area 2/(415) 550-0935

Tazumal is the name of a Mayan ruin and El Tazumal is run by a Salvadorean couple. They have made this a cheerful neighborhood hangout with ample portions and more than reasonable prices. *Chile rellenos* employs fresh green chiles and Jack cheese and is covered in rich, dark tomato sauce. *Lengua en salsa* is a Salvadorean favorite of beef tongue cooked with peppers and tomatoes and seasoned with fresh coriander, cumin and garlic. At these prices you can afford to be adventuresome. Exotic as some dishes may sound, I've never been disappointed.

Inexpensive. Open seven days. Lunch from 10 A.M. to 3 P.M. Dinner from 5 to 10:45 P.M. Reservations accepted for large parties only. Visa, MC. Wine and beer only. Child's menu. Street parking. Casual.

★ ★
EL ZARAPE ROOM/Mexican
3349 23rd Street/San Francisco/Area 2/(415) 282-1168

If you accept the local examples of Mexican cuisine as a fair cross-section, then you have to believe that Mexicans eat nothing but variations of tortillas served with limp salads, mushy beans and exploded rice. You also can't help but believe that our friendly neighbors to the south drink a lot of beer. The funny thing is that, to a large degree, this is all true. I spent some months in Mexico a while back and mostly I ate either beans and rice or rice and beans. And I drank a lot of beer.

If that was all there was to Mexican food I would probably have hot-footed it back to Mexicali-Calexico and headed for a good hamburger in Kansas City. But there were moments—in the fondas at the marketplace and under *japalas* along the beachfronts—where, by nothing more than serendipity, I'd find spectacular local dishes which were as unique to Mexico as the cheeseburger is indigenous to America. So few of these dishes have found their way to America that it came as a real thrill to browse over the menu in El Zarape and find beloved words like *camarones, albondigas* and *molé* which brought back happy memories of drunken debauches in cantinas and heroic battles with the fabled Revenge of Montezuma.

El Zarape is certainly better designed than most of the Bay Area's Mexican restaurants. Blue decorative tiles surrounded by wood borders make for soothing tabletops, in heavy-duty contrast to the incredible blacklight scenes of the Mexican countryside that surround a blacklight Aztec calendar on the back wall. Not a poster, mind you, but a full-size carved calendar with menacing dayglo serpents. Which is about as far as proprietors Panchito and Celia Venegas have allowed funk to creep into El Zarape. Everything else, including the liveried waiter, is in the best of taste, which brings me, circuitously, to the food.

Overwhelmed by El Zarape's choice of twenty-six dinners, I'll start with the excellent guacamole, a bit stiff for the smallish portion, but very fresh and good with chunks of avocado floating about with the tomato and onion—it's hard to resist licking out the bowl. If you order a dinner, the next course will be a *botana,* a snack which runs to tasty little meatballs or fried chunks of fish in batter, then a soup with rough-cut chunks of potato, carrot and what-not swimming in a beefish broth.

At the top of the dinner choices are the six *camarone* (prawn) dishes, served on enormous plates with the ubiquitous sides of rice, beans and salad. Ignore this filler for the moment and sate yourself upon *camarones rellenos estilo Cozumel,* giant prawns split, then stuffed with crab, wrapped in bacon, then broiled—a dish worth betraying your family for. Or indulge in the *camarones alcaparrados estolo Campeche,* a healthy portion of butterflied prawns covered with a palate-dazzling sauce of tomatoes, capers, onions and olives.

Though it's hard to tear away from the spectacular *camarone* dishes, I will admit the *molé poblana* to be the best I've ever tasted outside of Oaxaca. *Molé* is an acquired taste (like calamata olives and cottage cheese)—at heart it's a thick sauce of bitter chocolate and puréed chiles: from there it's a field day for any chef to add *tomatilloes,* raisins, garlic, almonds, whatever. In *molé poblano* the sauce covers a juicy breast of chicken, at once overwhelming the tastebuds and enhancing the bland taste of chicken.

Though the *camarones* and *molé* are the superstars of El Zarape, all the dishes are fascinatingly good. If you go to El Zarape to eat enchiladas, you should have your taste buds examined.

Moderate. Open Tuesday through Sunday from 11 A.M. to 11 P.M. Reservations accepted. Visa, MC, AX, DC. Entertainment. Full bar. Street parking. Casual.

★ ★
EMILE'S/Continental/Swiss
545 S. Second Street/San Jose/Area 2/(408) 289-1960

A n evening here is a fine dining experience, reminiscent of Europe's choicest inns. Emile travels regularly through the Continent, often with his chef de cuisine and junior partner, James Connolly, trying the world's reputedly greatest restaurants. Emile Mooser, of French-Swiss heritage, *chef-propriétaire* of Emile's and a dedicated perfectionist, changes his menus bi-weekly, using nothing but the freshest ingredients. As air travel has become simpler, so has Emile's become a destination for discerning Europeans, often involved with high technology in nearby Silicon Valley. Magnificent wines are cellared, to match the superlative dinners. Increasing numbers of patrons order, with a week's advance notice, *"la table du chef,"* a unique, elegant dinner with many creative courses, for four or more. One thought for you—have the *emincé de veau Zurichoise,* thinly sliced veal and pork, with shallot butter, mushrooms and heavy cream, *en casserole.*
Moderate to expensive. Lunch Tuesday through Friday from 11:30 A.M. to 2:30 P.M. Dinner Tuesday through Saturday 5:30 to 10 P.M. Reservations advised. AX, Visa, MC, DC. Full bar. Valet parking. Semi-dressy.

DA ★ ★
EMPRESS OF CHINA/Chinese
838 Grant Avenue/San Francisco/Area 2/(415) 434-1345

F or years Cantonese food in America has been the unfair victim of the little storefront restaurants' inability to cope with the highly sophisticated dishes of Canton. Here, in a magnificent rooftop pavilion, it is served in a setting appropriate to the cuisine that grew in art form during the age of the five Emperors, that begin in 2674 B.C. The restaurant has been composed, as one would a poem, with priceless artifacts, stunning architecture, magnificent table settings, continental service and a seventy-one-foot cooking range (we paced it off) having the largest Chinese oven and wok units in the United States. The cocktail lounge reflects the Han period motif, with teak canopy and fifteen-foot-high panels. The mirrors here are artfully arranged to provide kaleidoscopic reflections of the Western skyline of Nob Hill and the busy street below (the vistas of Telegraph Hill, Coit Tower, Russian Hill and the Bay may be enjoyed from the huge picture windows in the dining rooms). Dishes from all provinces of China are served, but I tend to think of the Empress as a lady from Canton, and even the set dinners—unlike most Chinese establishments—provide a fair sampling of the kitchen artistry. The least expensive includes fried won ton in an exquisite Mandarin orange sauce, a soup of the chef, and "Empress beef" (tender sirloin, cut fine, with snow peas, bamboo shoots and vegetables, topped with a vermicelli-type crisp noodle). You can spend a lot of money here—wine and food societies have been known to go as high as $100 per person—but you can also enjoy the priceless surroundings for very little, particularly at lunch. The Empress is a tourist attraction in her own right, and it is a bonus to find such beautiful food and service at comparatively reasonable prices.

Moderate to expensive. Open seven days. Lunch served from 11:30 A.M. to 3 P.M. Dinner served from 5 to 11 P.M. Sundays from 12:30 to 11 P.M. Reservations advised. All major credit cards. Full bar. View of San Francisco. Public parking one-half block away. Semi-dressy.

★ ★
THE ENGLISH GRILL/Continental
Powell at Geary/San Francisco/Area 2/(415) 397-7000

Once, pre-Prohibition, this was the Men's Bar, a masculine stronghold. It still has that solid, no-nonsense feeling, with its fine oak paneling and ample silver and linen, embodying its definitive name. Formerly famous for meat and continental specialties, the English Grill's theme is now "fresh catch." At lunch recently, I noted that there were twelve fresh fish on the menu and almost that many on public view in the display offered daily. The Hotel St. Francis, where this "must see" dining room is set, is guided by corporate executives who shrewdly and sensibly determine not only the basics but even the finest details of their food and service operations. The Cobb salad, either as an appetizer or as an entrée, is a remarkable mélange of deviled egg, bacon, avocado, tomato, and diced chicken with romaine lettuce. Prime rib, medallions of beef, and the entrecôte are still served, of course. But come here for the seafood, proper service and solid comfort in a distinguished ambiance. One further inducement—California's most prestigious wines can be ordered by the glass. Currently, a number of these are served in a generous goblet at a most modest price. Also, the luncheon check here is reasonable indeed.

Moderate to expensive. Open for lunch Monday through Saturday from 11:30 A.M. to 2:30 P.M. Dinner from 6 to 10 P.M. weekdays, weekends until 10:30 P.M. Reservations advised. All major credit cards. Full bar. Child's menu. Hotel garage parking. Casual to semi-dressy.

DA
ENRICO'S/Coffee Shop/Continental
504 Broadway/San Francisco/Area 2/(415) 392-6220

Even the proprietor's name, Enrico Banducci, has an operatic ring to it, and his establishment is the premier sidewalk cafe in the city. One thing: it's not on the sidewalk (health laws, you know). But it is set back and open and serves a full range of cocktails, coffees (twenty-five varieties), light lunches, snacks and good apple pancakes. The expansive menu has something for everybody at almost any time, day or night. The intellectuals and show people gather here for a pre- or post-theatre round of drinks and voluble discussion. There's a great deal of camaraderie between parties—shouting and walking over to visit and compare impressions of the opera, play or concert. **Inexpensive to moderate.** Open seven days from 11 A.M. to 3 A.M. Reservations advised. Visa, MC, AX. Full bar. Outside eating terrace. Street parking. Casual.

★
EQUINOX/Continental
2062 Mountain Boulevard/Oakland/Area 2/(415) 339-8472

Comfortably nestled in the Carmel-like environs of Montclair, in the forested slopes of the Oakland hills, this perennial local favorite continues its cheery way, combating inflation—and winning.

The principal dining room is all in redwood, as is the adjacent Garden Room with its wicker chairs and potted plants. An honest fireplace, in which only oak wood is burned, honors the main room and can be enjoyed visually from the second room. As you enter through thick glass doors, there is a bar lounge on the right with sliding glass doors beyond, opening to The Cave, a hideaway with a piano where a pianist-singer holds forth with light jazz. Lighting by table candles is romantic.

Soup or salad come with entrées such as petit filet, teriyaki sirloin, medallions of beef, sole, scallops, large gulf shrimp with a scampi-type sauce, and individual rack of lamb. Nightly specials may include beef Wellington. Appetizers range from shrimp quiche and *coquilles St. Jacques* to fried zucchini. The croutons for salads are house-made. At the end—coffee-and-Kahlua cheesecake and homemade pastries from The Gourmet Express. Choice wines are available; Equinox is known for its many unusual Chardonnays. Ask them why they selected Equinox as their name. **Moderate.** Open for lunch Tuesday through Friday from 11:30 A.M. to 2 P.M. Dinner Sunday through Thursday from 5 to 10 P.M., Friday and Saturday to 11 P.M. Reservations accepted. Visa, MC, AX, DC. Piano entertainment. Full bar. Street parking. Casual.

ERNIE'S NEPTUNE FISH GROTTO/Seafood
1816 Irving Street/San Francisco/Area 2/(415) 566-3344

I'm sure the seafood *is* fresh and the prices are fairly low for the fish plates preceded by a passable white or red chowder and a slightly overcooked shrimp cocktail followed by a fair dessert. The waitresses are busy, with no time for small talk. On my last visit, a tourist with a nameplate attached to his lapel (I presume, to help him remember his name) bespoke to his waitress: "Hi, I'm from New Jersey, where're you from." "The kitchen," was the reply delivered on the run. There's beer and wine and not enough selection of the latter; but seafood places are a disappearing national resource, and if you're in the Sunset district you could do a lot worse.

Moderate. Open Tuesday through Saturday. Lunch weekdays from 11 A.M. to 3 P.M. Dinner from 3 to 8:45 P.M. Reservations accepted. No credit cards. Wine and beer only. Street parking. Casual.

DA ★ ★ ★
ERNIE'S RESTAURANT/French
847 Montgomery Street/San Francisco/Area 2/(415) 397-5969

This is both a nitpicker's and an epicurean's paradise. There are those who feel a legend — particularly a high-priced one — should attain perfection, and thus they quibble about purely subjective matters. To the epicures, experts like Paul Bocuse, the great French chef, and Graham Kerr, the great Australian galloper, Ernie's rates among the top restaurants in the nation. Opulently gracious, with maroon walls and crystal accents of Victorian times, Ernie's could rest on their impressive laurels and still attract crowds of the curious. But Victor and Roland Gotti are perfectionists. Every dish on the extensive menu is meticulously prepared. Every move by the waiters and captains has been rehearsed and choreographed. The wine list is a collector's delight, and some of the more enlightened wine discussions of our time have occurred in the Baccus Cellar or at the tables with the amiable proprietors. The menu is straight from the pages of *L'Escoffier*, with a few creative touches here and there; the veal dishes are the specialty of this grand house. In addition to the classic dishes, chef Jacky Robert has been acclaimed for his interpretation of nouvelle dishes. It's expensive but not outrageously so, although

To obtain the best results from this Guide, be sure to consult the map on the various Northern California areas on page 28.

the patrons always appear to be the shell-out or expense-account crowd. I would recommend that you discuss your dinner carefully with the captain, order it complete with the lavish desserts, and relax. Ernie's can give you an evening like no other restaurant, if you're fortunate. At the very least, it will give you a memorable one.

Expensive. Open seven days. Dinner served from 6:30 to 10:30 P.M. Closed January 1-15. Reservations required. All major credit cards. Full bar. Valet parking. Dressy.

★
FAR EAST CAFE/Chinese/Cantonese
631 Grant Avenue/San Francisco/Area 2/(415) 982-3245

As the gateway to the Orient, it's not surprising that San Francisco has the largest Chinese population outside either China, Mainland or Nationalist. When the Far East first opened its doors over a half century ago, it was to accommodate the immigrants from Canton who used to call the city "Gum San Dai Fow"–"Great City of the Golden Hill." That was back in the days when the hills were golden, when "Smoke Gets In Your Eyes" was a song instead of a weather report — before the grotesque high-rise buildings, like giant granite spears thrown from another planet, interrupted the soft curves of the skyline.

San Francisco's Chinatown lifts the bamboo curtain on the mysterious continent and exposes the Chinese taste and lifestyle in authentic style. The bustling shops, herb stores and markets, with unfamiliar vegetables and roots, still outnumber the souvenir stands. Restaurants like the Far East were palaces to the poorer Chinese; the Far East is still impressive, like a great Oriental banquet hall emblazoned with panels, golden portals, murals and antiques.

Since the quota was lifted in 1965, the Chinese population in San Francisco has doubled to one hundred thousand mostly from Canton; and the Chinese are a substantial portion of the business at Far East, where the chicken salad (as unlike the Western version as Woody Allen is unlike Bruce Jenner), Chinese roast pork and fried won ton bring back the good memories of home.

For best results, consult "How to Use This Guide" on page 25.

Authentic Chinese restaurants do not seem to handle cocktails well, and the Far East is no exception; if you're one of the two-before-dinner crowd, there are a lot of plusher lounges up the hill, and besides, beer goes great with this kind of fare. (If you must have wine, try a gewurtztraminer.)

Moderate. Open seven days. Lunch served from 11:30 A.M. to 3 P.M. Dinner from 3 to 10 P.M. Saturday and Sunday from noon to 10 P.M. No reservations. All major credit cards. Full bar. Street parking. Casual.

★
THE FARRELL HOUSE/Continental/California
222 Weller/Petaluma/Area 3/(707) 778-6600

Located beside the turning basin on the Petaluma River, the Farrell House provides guests with a pleasant view of waterway activities. The peaceful atmosphere surrounding the handsome two hundred-year-old Victorian house makes meals there all the more enjoyable.

Particularly strong in seafood, the menu includes live Maine lobster, scallop sautée, swordfish steak, and the fresh catch of the day, as well as rack of lamb Dijonnaise and pepper steak. Several scrumptious-sounding desserts complicate decision-making. The wine list, though not large, is balanced.

In warm weather, guests can watch pleasure boats dock nearby while lunching on the riverside terrace.

Moderate. Open seven days. Lunch Monday through Saturday from 11:30 A.M. to 2:30 P.M. Dinner Monday and Tuesday from 5:30 to 9 P.M., Wednesday through Saturday from 5:30 to 10 P.M., Sunday from 5 to 9 P.M. Sunday brunch from 10 A.M. to 2 P.M. Reservations advised. Major credit cards. Live music Friday and Saturday evenings. Full bar. Parking in adjacent lot. Casual.

★
FIOR D'ITALIA/Italian
601 Union Street/San Francisco/Area 2/(415) 986-1886

An honest establishment that claims, among other things, to be the oldest Italian restaurant in San Francisco. It was opened in May 1886, in the bawdy times when the Barbary Coast was swarming with miners, gamblers, and the ladies of the evening (as a friend once said, "If you really want to know why they're called that, just see them in the daytime sometime").

A young Italian immigrant, Armido Marianetti, helped found the Fior. It was demolished by the towering inferno of 1906, but reopened a week later in a shack and continued through all the wars, pestilence and political conventions that followed. You'll still get the fine, homemade *cannelloni*, *tortellini* and *malfatti* — abundant, albeit Americanized. For a special treat, try the Italian sausage sauté with peppers or the *radichetta*, dandelion leaves with anchovies, tomatoes and chopped egg topped with vinaigrette dressing. The Fior is a favorite for opera buffs because the late Gaetana Merola, founder of the San Francisco Opera, used to hold court there. **Moderate.** Open seven days. Lunch weekdays from 11:30 A.M. to 3:30 P.M. Dinner from 3:30 to 10:30 P.M. Reservations accepted. All major credit cards. Full bar. Valet parking. Semi-dressy.

DA ★ ★
THE FIREHOUSE/Continental
1112 Second Street/Sacramento/Area 3/(916) 442-4772

From the august year 1853 to 1921, nothing other than hay and a possible carry-in sandwich was consumed in this compelling dining place. Sacramento No. 3, a volunteer fire company located in the elongated structure, responded only to the dire needs of a most exclusive list of subscribers. The fire-horses were stabled in the deep basement, now the site of handsome banquet rooms, and came pounding up a ramp to be harnessed to the primitive engine.

The Firehouse owes its rebirth to brothers Newton, Larry and Carl Cope, the last now deceased, who opened the Firehouse as a saloon in 1960, pending a selection of a proper kitchen staff. They planned to create a restaurant that would reflect Sacramento's historical prominence. For three years they had browsed, collecting bric-a-brac, antique lamps and *objets d'art* to add to their veritable museum of the Gold Rush era and following decades. They were the ones who did the most to redevelop Old Sacramento, rescuing it from its skid row obscurity.

The Cope brothers left the interior relatively undisturbed architecturally, retaining the circular iron stairway and tradition brass fireman's pole. They sandblasted old brick walls, papered here and painted there. Nineteenth century engravings, prints, Florentine cherubim, Victorian mirrors and furniture, plus Firehouse Windsor chairs polished off their creation. In the main dining room—The Central Pacific Room—you return again to that oft-missed nostalgic past. Ivory and gold-fluted columns rise to a twenty-foot ceiling. Ornate chandeliers, framed mirrors, flocked paper, white brick, and oils of The Big Four, painted by Mrs. Newton A. Cope, grace the room.

Every dining room nicety is observed and you will dine well on fine continental dishes. I rather fancied a steak Diane here that the maître d' prepared with the usual and expected theatrics. With suitable advance notice, the chef will cook any special dish of your choosing.

The Firehouse Courtyard, serving in summertime for lunches only is a verdant, tree-blessed and parasoled-table haven that is extremely popular when the weather is agreeable. The Golden Eagle Room, recently added, serves dinner only in winter.
Moderate to expensive. Open Monday through Friday for lunch from 11:30 A.M. to 2:15 P.M. Dinner Monday through Saturday from 6 to 10 P.M. Reservations accepted. Visa, MC, AX. Full bar. Patio April through October. Parking lot in rear. Casual for lunch, dressy for dinner.

★
FIREHOUSE BAR-B-QUE/Barbecue
501 Clement/San Francisco/Area 2/(415) 386-5882
2401 Larkspur Landing Circle/Larkspur/Area 2/(415) 461-4994

I've got the best barbecue in the whole damn town," says owner Carl T. English, Jr. (a vet of the San Francisco Fire Department). Despite the hokey appearance, the Firehouse does make some of the better barbecue in town. The spicy, extremely smokey Firehouse links are dandy. The Firehouse sampler gives you enough ribs, chicken and links to get you and a friend happily through an afternoon with the '49ers. There's a fine Firehouse sandwich made up of a quarter pound of diced pork and doused in a fiery sauce. All dishes can be ordered in three forms: one alarm, two alarm, and three alarm (about which the menu coyly says "Watch out"). The latest addition to the family, in Larkspur, dispenses the same fare in a larger setting with great views of Alcatraz and Angel Island.
Inexpensive. Open seven days. Monday through Thursday from 11:30 A.M. to 10 P.M., Friday from 11:30 A.M. to 11 P.M. Saturday and Sunday from noon to 10 P.M. No reservations. Visa, MC, AX. Wine and beer only. Street parking. Casual.

★
FIRE SIGN CAFE/American
1785 Westlake Boulevard/Tahoe City/Area 6/(916) 583-0871

Our old friend the espresso house is dressed up these days, and while you'll still find the coffees, fresh juices, herbal teas and imported beer, the look is more franchise than fifties. The Fire Sign is notable because there are few places to recommend around Tahoe City and this one would be a winner anywhere. Ethnic dinners blossom irregularly on the menu with *dolmades,* curries and quiches as well as vegetarian fare, omelettes and (these are good!) fruit pancakes.
Inexpensive. Open seven days from 7 A.M. to 3 P.M. No reservations. Visa, MC. Wine and beer only. Patio. Lot parking. Casual.

FISHERMEN'S GROTTO/Seafood
9 Fisherman's Wharf/San Francisco/Area 2/(415) 673-7025

The upstairs room at Fishermen's Grotto is one of my favorite places on Fisherman's Wharf, more a tourist attraction than a legitimate commercial fishing area. The Grotto opened in 1935 to accommodate the lusty appetites of Italian fishermen, and the cioppino's still about as close to real peasant fish stew as you can get this side of Europe. Service is apt to be a touch surly and impatient, and tourists are sometimes intimidated by a waiter who wants more turnover of his tables. However, in an imperfect wharf, the Grotto is one of the better places — family owned-and-operated by the Geraldis, you'll get honest, if not fancy, fare. **Moderate.** Open seven days from 10:30 A.M. to midnight. Reservations accepted. Visa, MC, AX. Two full bars. Child's menu. Validated parking adjacent to restaurant. Casual to semi-dressy.

★ ★
FLEUR DE LYS/French
777 Sutter Street/San Francisco/Area 2/(415) 673-7779

Owners here are also owners of the more formal L'Etoile, but we found substantial differences. Where L'Etoile can be haughty-haute, Fleur de Lys is a stunning setting, with hundreds of yards of hand-painted fabric which billow and drape around the diner in the facsimile of a tent-like enclosure. The pattern, executed by local artists Judith Azur and Cedric Smith (with twenty-six assistants), is a European adaptation of the sixteenth-century Indian design.

The classic *L'Escoffier* menu is well handled here. The *nantua* sauce for the *quenelles* was perfectly made, with crayfish, butter and béchamel. The whole artichoke (*l'artichaute maison*) was a bit overcooked, something that can be remedied when placing your order. The fresh, cold asparagus in mustard sauce is smashing. Self-professed specialties are *composé de homard et de laup de mer au vinaigre dexeres, tournedos de boeuf venaison aux baies de genievre,* and *panaché gourmand mousse chocolat blanc et noir fruits frais du jour.* Menu is à la carte. **Expensive.** Open Tuesday through Sunday from 6 to 11 P.M. Reservations required. All major credit cards. Full bar. Valet parking. Dressy.

To obtain the best results from this Guide, be sure to consult the map on the various Northern California areas on page 28.

★ ★
FLINT'S/Barbecue
6672 East 14th Street/Oakland/Area 2/(415) 569-1312
3114 San Pablo Avenue/Oakland/Area 2/Take-out only/(415) 658-9912
6609 Shattuck Avenue/Oakland/Area 2/Take-out only/(415) 653-0593

There is much controversy about the definition of the word "barbecue," some preferring that searing hot sauce slathered over huge stacks of ribs, other opting for more exotic preparations. So many people spoke up for this spot—there are two other Flint's—that I felt I *had* to try it, and I can do no more than agree with some reviewer who proclaimed their pork ribs to be the best *anywhere*. The dining room has a view—although barbecue fanatics scarcely look up from scarfing—and the aroma of the barbecue pulls people in off the street with a glazed look in their eyes. Marilyn Flint does the cooking here, and the beef ribs, hot links, brisket of beef and chicken are served with a wide variety of side dishes, all of them homemade. This is a questionable neighborhood and you would do well to come in the daylight hours.
Inexpensive. Open seven days 11 A.M. to midnight (San Pablo and Shattuck locations stay open much later). No reservations. No credit cards. No alcohol. Street parking. Casual.

★
THE FONDUE POT/American/Fondue
213 Beach Street/Morro Bay/Area 1/(805) 772-8900

Fondue Bourguignonne, according to legend, had its beginning in the famous vineyards of the Burgundy region of France. During the harvest, the grapes had to be picked at the precise time of ripeness without even giving the workers time to eat. Someone had the idea of keeping a pot of fat boiling so each worker could quickly cook his own pieces of meat in spare moments and voila . . . La Fondue. In Morro Bay, this idea has been slightly refined and you will find beef, shrimp, chicken and squid available for cooking and dunking in the "dipping sauces."

In addition to the oil fondues are the cheese fondues which originated in Switzerland out of a fervent desire to utilize hardened cheese and bread. I'm afraid I could not quite bring myself to try some of the modernized versions of this tradition: "Pizza Fondue" and "Mexican Fondue."

Breakfast is really the best thing, offering massive three-egg omelettes that are served with country fries, muffins and steamy, hot coffee. The baked goods are all homebaked and the honeybran muffins alone are enough to head me toward the Fondue Pot.

Inexpensive to moderate. Open daily from 7 A.M. to 9 P.M., Friday and Saturday until 10 P.M. Reservations accepted. All major credit cards. Wine and beer only. Child's menu. Parking lot. Casual.

DA ★★★
FOURNOU'S OVENS/Continental
905 California Street/San Francisco/Area 2/(415) 989-1910

The story of this dining place of wide repute and epicurean stature is essentially the story of one man, James Nassikas, president and managing director of The Stanford Court, within which reposes Fournou's Ovens. Nassikas, who has dedicated his life to fine hotels and restaurants, is a *Chavalier de la Confrerie des Chevaliers de Tastevin,* has held high office in *Les Anciens Elèves de L'Ecole Hotelier de la Societé Suisse* and is a member of many other distinguished organizations.

In a cosmopolis such as San Francisco, a restaurant wishing to acquire the respect of epicures must excite more than their palates to win a devoted clientele. The Stanford Court recently celebrated a decade of dedicated and well-rewarded service. Formerly a famous building of elaborate apartments, the hotel brings to this relatively young city the grandeur of the old world, a certain European magnificence it sustains so handsomely that it has created its own traditions.

James Nassikas, from the first, was determined to place a restaurant in his hotel that would never be marred by the stigma that most hotels suffer because of their failure to provide a dining experience for their room guests. Fournou's Ovens was given a separate entrance, at California and Powell Streets and its own telephone number. It is not an extension of the Stanford Court but an entirely separate entity. Mobil Guide, in awarding its rare Five Stars, states, in part, ". . . incomparable culinary masterpieces." George Christy: ". . . among the most exciting dining hideaways in the country." Harper and Queen, London: "a unique place of great charm . . . creative dining at its best."

Fournou's Ovens is two distinct restaurants. The original is a complex of nine dining areas on three levels, utilizing a sturdy beamed ceiling, wrought-iron, floors of handsome tile, impressive pillars, and the famous ovens, faced with blue and white Portuguese tile. On the lowest level, stepping down Powell Street, it is all Victorian conservatories with glass and metal airy domes, and views of close-by cable cars and highrise vistas. Only luncheon and cocktails are served in the glassed-in conservatory setting and only dinner in the original restaurant. Andrew Delfino, world-famous decorator, holds the credits for the hotel and both the Fournou's Ovens distinct dining rooms.

Jim Nassikas modestly describes his luxurious creation as "a typical, Provincial roast restaurant . . . with a touch of fantasy." Specialties include roast rack of lamb and a superb roast duckling. For dessert, try either the *dacquoise* or praline ice cream pie. Ah, yes, forty thousand bottlings from over three hundred labels.

Expensive. Open seven days. Lunch served weekdays from 11:30 A.M. to 2:30 P.M. Dinner every day from 5:30 to 11 P.M. Reservations essential. All major credit cards. Entertainment. Full bar. View. Valet parking. Dressy.

★
FOUR SEAS/Chinese/Grand
731 Grant Avenue/San Francisco/Area 2/(415) 397-5577

This seven hundred-seat restaurant is less expensive and intimidating than it first appears. Of all the Chinese restaurants that aspire to grandeur, the Four Seas is the most reasonable, though how manager Hing Tse can keep such tight reins on the cavernous restaurant is more than I can understand. The menu offers surprisingly creative fare — baby sweetcorn, boneless chicken, prawns lightly dusted with graham crackers, and the dinner specialty "Chicken Gold Coin" (served for a minimum of eight, and consisting of layers of pork, ham and chicken served with freshly baked rolls). Cocktails are not particularly good here, but as I've indicated before, a beer or light wine is the best accompaniment to Chinese food.

Moderate. Open seven days. Lunch from 10:30 A.M. to 3 P.M. Dinner from 3 to 10 P.M. Reservations advised. All major credit cards. Entertainment. Full bar. Garage parking nearby. Casual.

★
FOURTH STREET GRILL/Seafood/Continental
1820 Fourth Street/Berkeley/Area 2/(415) 849-0526

Fresh fish can only be so fresh, right? I'm still convinced that the chef has an underground (or is that underwater) seafood connection that manages to get the catch of the day to him so fast that they can't even take time to see what they have caught. The fresh fish is cooked over a mesquite charcoal grill, giving it a delicate, smokey flavor. Other grilled specialties range from hamburgers to New York steak. The smokey flavor enhances the meat as well as the fish and keeps the house packed.

Please be sure to consult "Tipping Made Easy" on page 22 of this Guide.

Although The Grill is not primarily Italian, they can dish up a mean pasta (seafood, of course). The Yucatan white sausage (chicken, pork and jalapeño peppers) and the Ceasar salad are favorites of the house. There are no reservations so come extra early or late, or expect to wait (one hour is not unusual).

Moderate. Open seven days. Lunch served Monday through Friday from 11:30 A.M. to 2:30 P.M. Dinner from 5:30 to 10 P.M., Saturday till 10:30 P.M., Sunday till 9:30 P.M. No reservations. MC, Visa. Wine and beer only. Easy street parking. Casual.

DA ★
FRANCOIS' COFFEE HOUSE/Continental
The Village Fair—2nd Floor/777 Bridgeway/Sausalito/Area 3/(415) 332-3350

Guests here may dine at outside redwood picnic tables and enjoy a view of the yacht harbor directly below, plus the Bay traffic with Belvedere and Angel Island beyond. Of course, you may want to eat indoors, anything from a late breakfast (don't count on bacon and eggs here, though) to lunch, snacks and what might satisfy you for an early dinner.

The dining room is cheerful, not busily decorated but it does have an ancient coffee grinder. The window wall side offers the same views as the outer tables and you get to size up the interesting attire that visitors and locals wear when wandering about Sausalito.

A youthful staff, under the ever-watchful eye of operating owner-manager Cathy Patterson, attends your needs. It is self-service at its best for the huge, quality sandwiches, excellent soups, flaky cheesecake, magnificent Napoleons (from the same bakery that supplies Ernie's Restaurant), superb coffee and espresso, iced or hot whipped chocolate—an eater's Nirvana.

Expensive. Open seven days. Monday through Friday from 9:30 A.M. to 5 P.M. Saturday and Sunday from 9:30 A.M. to 6 P.M. No reservations. No credit cards. Parking lot across the street. Casual.

★ ★ ★
THE FRENCH LAUNDRY/California/Continental
Washington and Creek Streets/Yountville/Area 3/(707) 944-2380

Not identified by any kind of sign, this two-story stone structure was built over eighty years ago and is enhanced by a lovely side garden. It originally housed a bar, then a laundry during Prohibition, emerging as a rooming house and eventually, in 1978, reached its pinnacle as The French Laundry—one of the reasons for visiting Napa Valley.

Husband/wife team, Sally and Don Schmitt are perfectionists. Sally is the inspired chef and Don handles the "front of the house" and is responsible for the near-two hundred selected wines, principally from the wine country of California. They are so successful in what they do that reservations for weekend dining are booked solid four months ahead at any time.

The interior design is low-key—white walls, a few extremely fine paintings, fresh flowers on every table, crisp linen covering floor-length printed tablecloths, a fireplace in the downstairs room and French doors in the room above that present an outdoor descent to the garden. Incidentally, you may stroll in the garden between courses, taking along a glass of wine, if you wish. Don will advise you that the dining room table is yours for the entire evening; how gratifying. There is one seating only with reservations somewhat offset to ease the kitchen, and dining is at your selected pace. Dinner consists of five courses; appetizers, soup, entrée of the evening with delicate pasta, salad and house-made dessert. There is a choice of appetizer—usually one vegetable, one seafood and one of meat. Three excellent cheeses accompany the salad and there is a choice of three desserts, almost always one with chocolate (for all those chocoholics out there, like yours truly), another of fresh fruit, such as rhubarb shortcake or sliced marinated oranges and perhaps, a pastry treat such as chocolate Amaretto torte.

Entrées can be Sally's duckling with green peppercorn sauce, braised oxtails or lamb shanks (those flavor-blessed morsels of the tenderest and most delectable of close-to-the-bone meats), or possibly, chicken with lemon and mint cream. You will have, on occasion, the chef's miraculous sweetbreads, done in any of several ways, all of which are magnificent. (By the way, Don and Sally prefer no smoking.)
Expensive. Open Wednesday through Sunday with one seating 7 to 8:30 P.M. Reservations essential. No credit cards. Wine and beer only. Street and lot parking. Semi-dressy.

★ ★
FRENCH POODLE/French
Junipero and Fifth Avenue/Carmel/Area 1/(408) 624-8643

An elongated building with only awnings and shrubbery to set it off, this honorable French restaurant and chef/owner Marc Vedrines have been serving consistently good food since 1961. The fact has not gone unappreciated by the locals in the area who keep the thirty-six seats heavily booked year round. The *poulet chaumière* (chicken in wine sauce with truffles) and the sole *Marinette* are wonderful. *Noisettes d'agneau* and *le magnet de canard au dieux porto* are quite possibly the favorite dishes of the house. The floating island dessert is fantastic, as is *la marquise au chocolat,* the specialty of the house.

Moderate. Open for dinner Thursday through Saturday and Monday and Tuesday from 5:30 to 9:30 P.M. Reservations required. AX, DC only. Wine only. Street parking. Dressy.

★★
THE FRENCH ROOM RESTAURANT/Continental
Four Seasons Clift Hotel/San Francisco/Area 2/(415) 775-4700

One of only eight hotels to be recognized with the coveted Mobil Travel Guide Five Star Award, the Four Seasons Clift Hotel has become a favorite at both luncheon and dinner. The magnificent French Room Restaurant, with its eighteenth century French-cut crystal chandeliers, solid armchairs upholstered in needlepoint, and graceful palms, exemplifies the concept that, to be a great hotel in a city such as San Francisco, one must cater to the requirements and desires of that segment of the area residents whose life-style dictates their dining out decisions.

The hotel was acquired in 1976 by Four Seasons, the Canadian-based hotel group which now includes some of the world's elegant hostelries such as the Pierre in New York and the Ritz-Carlton in Chicago. The sixty-five-year-old Four Seasons Clift was already a California landmark when its renovation was completed in 1978. In addition to careful restoration in The French Room and other hotel projects, the historic Redwood Room Bar and Cafe, a gathering place for locals and travelers, gleams as never before, from the twenty-foot redwood burl panels to the Art Deco lighting and bar, typifying the original opulence and grandeur of the 1933 era.

All three meals are served in this ivory-enameled, velvet-draped room. There are seasonal food festivals and a series of special dinners throughout the year. If this aura and concept lies within your means, check periodically with the hotel's able food and beverage manager. The exemplary fare is prepared in a continental style with somewhat lighter variations of the classics. At special holidays, traditional four to five course menus, featuring roast turkey, roast goose and prime rib (from the silver Simpson-style carts), carved at your table, are worth reserving for far in advance.

Expensive. Open seven days. Breakfast from 7 to 11 A.M. Lunch from noon to 2 P.M. Dinner from 6 to 11 P.M. Sunday brunch from 11 A.M. to 2 P.M. Reservations essential. All major credit cards. Entertainment. Full bar. Valet parking. Dressy.

★ ★
FRESH CREAM/Continental
Corner of Scott and Pacific/Heritage Harbor/Monterey/Area 1/(408) 375-9798

This captivating, intimate dining place, a study in complementing pastels – creamy white walls, pink trim, grey carpet – offers a dining adventure. Guests seated in black chairs at snowy-top tables can enjoy such worthies as roast boned duckling with currant sauce, loin of veal with wine butter, prawns "Opo" stuffed with lobster mousse, tournedos in various styles and, always, fresh seafood. Desserts may include wickedly rich chocolate cake, fresh berries (in season) and, soufflé Grand Marnier, which you, of course, order at the start of the meal. Chef/owner Robert Kinkaid is a chef of broad expertise. A bit difficult to locate, but well worth the effort.

Moderate to expensive. Open for dinner Tuesday through Sunday from 6 to 10 P.M. Reservations recommended. MC, Visa. Beer and wine. Garage parking across the street. Casual.

★
FUJI SUKIYAKI RESTAURANT/Japanese
2422 Thirteenth Street/Sacramento/Area 3/(916) 446-4135

In a bleak neighborhood with a bleak converted-storefront entrance, Fuji is a house of surprises. The classic dishes of Japan are done well here, and served in an immaculate, scrubbed interior. For my palate, this is one of the best places to dine in Sacramento, although expense account buffs may prefer the showy steakhouses where lobbyists used to practice the arts of persuasion on imminently persuadable legislators. Now that our state assemblymen have to pay for their own lunches, they are more likely to come to a place like Fuji where all the dinners are reasonable. Kirin, my favorite beer, is available here, and I recommend my own version of a Japanese boilermaker: hot saki served with ice cold Kirin. Ah, the tranquil feeling that combination creates, without numbing the palate, is in a class beyond liquid valium.

Inexpensive to moderate. Open seven days. Lunch weekdays 11:30 A.M. to 2:30 P.M. Dinner from 5 to 10 P.M., Saturday and Sunday from 4:30 to 10 P.M. Reservations advised on weekends. All major credit cards. Full bar. Street parking. Casual.

In order to obtain the best results from this Guide, be sure to read the French, German, Italian and Oriental menu translators on pages 399 to 404 of this Guide.

★
FUKI-YA/Japanese
22 Peace Plaza/San Francisco/Area 2/(415) 929-0127

The first *robata-yaki* in the United States was served at this casual restaurant, located at the indoor mall of the Japanese Center. "Ro" means fire, "robata" means fireplace. It is the Japanese version of backyard barbecue, served on paper plates (as here) as a background to socializing (as here). Appetizers include *shishamo,* a smelt-like fish from the Bering Strait stuffed with its own roe. There are skewers of grilled salmon, and skewers of chicken, salmon or shrimp. Sashimi is splendid here, and there is an active sushi bar. Rick Duran is a Caucasian smitten with all things Japanese—he speaks the language fluently—and his kitchen turns out delicate dishes at low prices.

Moderate. Open Monday through Saturday from 5 to 11:30 P.M. (closed second Monday of each month). Reservations advised. Visa, MC. Wine and beer only. Japan Center lot. Casual.

★★
FUNG LUM/Chinese/Cantonese
1815 South Bascom Avenue/Campbell/Area 2/(408) 377-6955

An offspring of the Hong Kong Fung Lum that has been in business for three decades, the Pang Brothers decided to open stateside in 1975 with their mammoth operation that somehow—with all the screaming confusion in the kitchen—manages to turn out lemon chicken and special spareribs that are light years and eggrolls above the usual chop-suery. Fung Lum is a celebration of Chinese art and cuisine. All the chefs are from Hong Kong and Taiwan and the entire staff exudes a feeling of warmth as though each customer was a member of the family returning from a long journey. The atmosphere is that of a royal courtyard, with jade sculptures, hand-carved wood murals, enormous brass chandeliers and many other bits of Oriental art creating an overall effect of harmony and tasteful magnificence. Cocktails are not the forte, however.

Moderate. Open seven days. Lunch Sunday through Friday 11:30 A.M. to 2 P.M. Dinner Monday through Thursday 5 to 10 P.M. Friday and Saturday 5 to 10:30 P.M. Sunday brunch 11 A.M. to 3 P.M. Sunday dinner 3 to 9 P.M. Reservations for larger parties only. Visa, MC, AX, DC. Full bar. Parking lot. Casual.

For best results, consult "How to Use This Guide" on page 25.

★ ★
GALLEY RESTAURANT/Seafood
899 Embarcadero/Morro Bay/Area 1/(805) 772-3434

This is one of my favorite small seafood restaurants. The proximity to the ocean is important not only in the scenic sense, but most particularly because this gem buys its fish directly from the boats at their own dock—salmon, halibut, sea bass, swordfish, sole, rock cod and shrimp—and wastes as little time as possible between the catch and the cooking. Bud Anderson and his sons and daughter are the owners/operators and they're justifiably proud of the success they've enjoyed since the 1966 opening.
Moderate. Open seven days. Lunch and dinner served from 11 A.M. to 9 P.M. Reservations advised. No credit cards. Wine and beer only. View. Child's menu. Lot parking. Casual.

DA ★ ★ ★
GAYLORD (INDIA) RESTAURANT/Northern Indian
Ghirardelli Square/San Francisco/Area 2/(415) 771-8822
★ ★
1 Embarcadero Center/San Francisco/Area 2/(415) 397-7775
Stanford Shopping Center/Palo Alto/Area 2/(415) 326-8761

So thoroughly Indian is this proud standard bearer of the farflung Gaylord chain of distinguished restaurants that you will always note Indians dining sumptuously in the lovely, elegant, spacious room. First opened in New Delhi in 1941, there are now Gaylords in other world capitals— Bombay, London, Hong Kong, Kobe and New York. Each is individually owned but the chefs are trained in New Delhi. There are four chefs in the lofty Ghirardelli Square location—each a specialist, like the curry chef and the *tandoori* chef. Proper, formal waiters describe the intriguing dinners, breads and spices. Let them guide you.

The design is breathtaking—draped from ceiling to floor around eight-foot windows with panoramic views of the Square, the Bay and all it contains. A sophisticated, harmonious warmth envelops you as you find yourself surrounded by potted palms, Chippendale pieces, Indian hangings, crisp tablecloths and a waiting area with sofas where you can be served cocktails.

Ghirardelli Square location: Expensive. Open seven days. Lunch from 11:45 A.M. to 1:45 P.M. Dinner from 5 to 10:45 P.M. Sunday brunch from noon to 2:45 P.M. Reservations advised. All major credit cards. Entertainment at brunch. Live music and dancing. Full bar. View of bay. Validated parking for one hour in Ghirardelli Square. Casual.

1 Embarcadero Center and Stanford Court: Expensive. Open seven days. Lunch Monday through Saturday from 11:30 A.M. to 3 P.M. dinner from 5 to 10 P.M. Reservations advised. All major credit cards. Full bar. Free parking after 5 p.m. and weekends in Embarcadero Center garage. Parking lot in Stanford Court. Dressy.

★★
GELCO'S/Continental/Yugoslavian
1450 Lombard Street/San Francisco/Area 2/(415) 928-1054

What is Yugoslavian cuisine? It's really a mélange of flavors and recipes absorbed from the surrounding nations of Turkey, Austria and Greece. The biggest impact of Yugoslavian influence in San Francisco is the great seafood restaurants (Sam's, Tadich's), but it is presented here with a broader range of dishes that bring an exciting adventure into lesser known gastronomic territory. Vlaho Buich served his time in many fine restaurants where he developed the talent for subtly manipulating his patrons into dishes he thinks they will enjoy. For openers, he'll likely steer you into the *antipasto* or the cheese-filled pastry and then suggest brother/chef Luko's lamb paprika, served with creamed spinach (our night), topped off with a stunning chocolate cake. There's more: moussaka, *raznijici* (brochette) and seafood. The pita can be ordered with the spectacular hors d'oeuvres platter as a late supper. There are some unusual wines offered and you would do well to let the proprietor guide you here as well.

Moderate to expensive. Open Monday through Saturday. Dinner served from 5:30 to 11 P.M. Reservations advised. All major credit cards. Full bar. Lot parking. Casual.

★ ★ ★

GEORGE'S SPECIALTIES/Russian
3420 Balboa Street/San Francisco/Area 2/(415) 752-4009

A **deceptive** name for this Russian treasure with food that has been created around George Semenoff's memories of Mother Russia. Every dish is prepared to order with the ceremony that would be appropriate to a special guest. Every scrap of meat is the finest money can purchase and most of the food is purchased retail in good markets. Angelina Semenoff is the proprietor and the chef as well, and her *blini* (buckwheat pancakes, crisp and buttery on the outside and satiny smooth on the inside with the taste of butter, sour cream, red roe smoked salmon and scallions) is extraordinary. *Sashliks* — chicken or lamb — and the chicken Stroganoff are the best Russian entrées in the city.

The atmosphere is part formica and part Cost Plus, but soon everything evaporates into memories of long Russian feasts in palatial surroundings. With twenty-four hours notice Angelina will prepare a gustatory orgy for you.

Moderate to expensive. Open Tuesday through Saturday. Dinner from 6 to 9 P.M. Reservations essential. Visa, MC. Wine and beer only. Semi-dressy.

★ ★

GERMAN COOK/German
612 O'Farrell/San Francisco/Area 2/(415) 776-9022

Until proved otherwise, or water-tortured into submission, I am going to insist that the best food is cooked by small, family-run restaurants. Especially those with counter-service where you can see the cook at work (studiously noting that he is not throwing sawdust into the meatloaf), kibbitz with the owner, and generally appreciate the maxim that good food comes from happy, laughing people, and bad food from dour, underpaid workhorses who bear a grudge against the boss. The German Cook has three small booths and seven counter stools, a small phonograph playing scratchy waltzes and the best bargain German cookery in town. The food is pretty basic, leaning toward hearty wurst, well prepared wienerschnitzel, and topnotch daily specials like once-a-week sauerbraten. All dinners are served with fried potatoes and tasty cabbage, accompanied by wine or German beer. And the German chocolate cake is a dark, sweet dream from *Schlaraffenland*.

Inexpensive to moderate. Open Tuesday through Saturday from 4:30 to 9:30 P.M. No reservations. No credit cards. Wine and beer only. Street parking. Casual.

★ ★
GERVAIS RESTAURANT FRANCAIS/French
1798 Park Avenue/San Jose/Area 2/(408) 275-8631

This quiet, bistro-like place serves classic French cuisine, expertly presented by tuxedoed waiters. Master chef Gervais Henric, for my taste, could be creating his culinary gems in any of the world's premiere establishments. The most discerning and demanding of gourmets will be delighted. Only the freshest and best of every product — seafood, meats and vegetables.

The ambiance has considerable charm, blending a high, white ceiling, blue carpeting, gold chandeliers and white on white napery in two spacious rooms. Even the background music demonstrates taste, evidencing the sensitivity of Marylou Henric. She and husband Gervais share the concern of the "mama-papa" bistro proprietors, but have constructed a dining place that would be at home on Nob Hill.

Gervais offers only an à la carte menu and the soufflés are legendary (you should definitely include one in your selection). Gervais is proud of his full liquor license but uses his bar purely for service by waiters to the tables. His cellar holds an admirable array of California and foreign wines.

Expensive. Open Tuesday through Saturday. Lunch served Tuesday through Friday from 11 A.M. to 2 P.M. Dinner from 5:30 to 10 P.M. Reservations necessary. Visa, MC, AX. Wine and beer only. Parking lot. Semi-dressy.

★
GINGERBREAD HOUSE/American/Cajun/Créole
741 Fifth Street/Oakland/Area 2/(415) 444-7373

I closed my eyes and tried to imagine that I was at K-Paul's in New Orleans, but my taste buds told me I was really in Oakland, a gustatory light year away. The jambalaya and gingercakes are quite respectable and the restaurant is a great deal fancier than I'm accustomed to for Cajun Créole cooking. There are some tremendous dishes here though, that show a great deal of love in the kitchen. Whiskey-stuffed lobster is served with shrimp and mushrooms, topped with melted cheese; rabbit "piquante" is marinated in a combination of herbs and sauces; and the appetizers called "TJ's own barbecued plankettes of ribs" are glazed with a spicy sauce — and very good. The jambalaya is a revelation. It's kind of touristy with a gift shop and strolling musicians and a singer on weekends, and not a bad place to take the kids.

Moderate to expensive. Lunch seatings Tuesday through Friday at noon and 1:30 P.M. Dinner seatings Tuesday through Thursday at 6 and 8 P.M., Friday at 6, 8, and 10 P.M., Saturday at 4, 6, 8, and 10 P.M. Reservations necessary. All major credit cards. Entertainment on weekends. Wine and beer only. Patio. Semi-dressy to dressy.

★
GINO'S RESTAURANT/Italian
7 Spring Street/San Francisco/Area 2/(415) 989-8006

Gino's was founded in 1947 by James Battaglieri (whose two sons Joseph and Tony now own and operate the restaurant with Nick Andros), Gino Tagliaferro, and a member of San Francisco's finest (still the finest, strikes or no), Inspector Engler of the homicide squad who used to collect recipes and memories from the *trattorìas* of the city as he made his rounds. The veal dishes are particularly enticing and the chicken is allowed to simmer long enough to absorb the flavors of the herbs and other ingredients. Specialties include fettuccine Alfredo, steak, seafood and the classic Ceasar salad.
Moderate. Open Monday through Saturday. Lunch weekdays from 11:30 A.M. to 3:30 P.M. Dinner from 5 to 10:30 P.M. Reservations advised. Visa, MC, AX, DC. Full bar. Garage parking next door. Casual to semi-dressy.

★★
GIORGIO'S/Italian/Pizzeria
25 Grant Avenue/Healdsburg/Area 3/(707) 433-1106

In the unrelenting search for the best pizza in the Bay Area—if not the world—the name Giorgio's will crop up with satisfying frequency. Now moved to Healdsburg (formerly known as the "Healdsburg House"), the pizza tastes as good in Sonoma County as it did in San Francisco. There are daily specials of veal, poultry, pasta and beef but pizza is the thing here and you shouldn't go home without it.
Inexpensive to moderate. Open seven days. Lunch served weekdays 11:30 A.M. to 2:30 P.M. Dinner Monday through Friday 2:30 to 10 P.M. Saturday and Sunday from 2 to 10 P.M. Reservations advised, essential on weekends. Visa, MC. Full bar. Child's menu. Parking lot. Casual.

For best results, consult "How to Use This Guide" on page 25.

★★
THE GOLDEN ACORN/Continental
1120 Crane Street/Menlo Park/Area 2/(415) 322-6201

Owner Sam Petrakis, multi-talented chef of many cuisines, and his vibrant wife, Maria, have such love for this once-pastoral and still peaceful city that they named their intimate, three dining-room restaurant The Golden Acorn to identify with the city's oak tree emblem. Murals, paintings, prints and photographs of Menlo Park's early days adorn the walls. The interior design reflects the pleasant past and your welcome is a bit more sincere, perhaps, than in a larger, colder area. Paralleling the warm atmosphere and personalized attention are the reasonable prices for complete dinners, with entrées from Italy, France, Greece and America. Luncheon menus describe soups, sandwiches, salads and hot specialties.

Moderate. Lunch Monday through Friday 11:30 A.M. to 2:30 P.M. Dinner Monday through Saturday from 5 to 10 P.M. MC, Visa, AX, DC. Full bar. Street and lot parking. Casual to semi-dressy.

★★
GOLDEN TURTLE/Vietnamese
308 5th Avenue/San Francisco/Area 2/(415) 221-5285

Arguably one of the best Vietnamese restaurants in the area, the Golden Turtle presents a setting appropriate to the complexity of these fine dishes. A touch of color, the roses and the napery at each table let you know immediately that this is no off-campus production.

The "Imperial roll" is sliced into rounds and served with cold rice noodles along with a spicy dipping sauce. Vietnamese pork kebabs are grilled over charcoal and artistically presented, as is the beef served with lemon grass, vinegar and hot peppers. The "seven jewel beef"–seven different preparations of beef–may be the most memorable in a long list of impressive selections.

There are set dinners for parties of six or more that are well worth the time and trouble to arrange.

Moderate. Open Tuesday through Sunday. Lunch served weekends 11 A.M. to 5 P.M. Dinner weekdays 5 to 10:30 P.M. Reservations accepted for large parties only–and before 7 P.M. Visa, MC, AX. Wine and beer only. Street parking. Semi-dressy.

In order to obtain the best results from this Guide, please consult "A Few Inside Tips" on page 18.

★★
GOLD MIRROR/Italian
800 Taraval Street/San Francisco/Area 2/(415) 564-0401

It's **easy** to believe the seventeen-year-old Gold Mirror was recently voted on a radio opinion poll "most popular Italian restaurant in the San Francisco Bay Area." Operated by partners, chef Guiseppe DiGrande and host/manager Mike Bushati, the place has a colorful, lively candlelit atmosphere, reflected in a large antique gold-framed mirror (a gift from a patron) from which it acquired its name. The full old-fashioned bar and wine cellar offer California and imported wines to please the palates of any connoisseurs. Florentine-continental cuisine is featured. Some of the many specialties include Icelandic scampi in meunière-lemon sauce, prawns stuffed with crabmeat, tender veal dishes, eggplant parmigiana, fresh pastas, homemade soups, beautiful steaks and prime rib, as well as a marvelous *antipasto* for hearty appetites. Try Joe's terrific *zabbioni*, Italian cream cake, fresh fruit tarts or cheesecake.

Moderate. Open seven days. Lunch weekends from 11:30 A.M. to 3 P.M. Dinner from 5 to 10 P.M. Reservations advised. All major credit cards. Full bar. Child's menu. Casual to semi-dressy.

★★
GOLD SPIKE/Italian/Home Style
527 Columbus Avenue/San Francisco/Area 2/(415) 986-9747

The **name** conjures visions of sleek plastic menus and a steakhouse ambiance, but it's far (seven thousand miles) from the truth. This is the mamacita of Italian family establishments, one of the best dining bargains in town. While waiting to be seated for your six-course dinner you can browse among the pistols, rifles, mounted elk and stuffed marlin on display.

You don't get a menu here, you get a meal. An enormous meal. The dishes vary and might likely consist of a tureen of aromatic minestrone soup (all you want); a basket of fresh sourdough bread; a dish of home-cured olives; a salad of beet-root, tomatoes, lettuce, carrots and onions; a plate of ravioli with Parmesan cheese; and a main dish like crab cioppino or veal sauté with spinach, peas and celery. Then, finally, a heaped plate of cookies with spumoni and a *cuppa*. If you're counting calories, bring a pocket computer, or better yet, have a few good drinks in the bar and to hell with it! This third-generation restaurant (now owned by Paul Mechetti and managed by Paul Mechetti, Jr.) was famous the year Joltin' Joe was born (1920), and even though there are no reservations, the competence of the staff will keep your wait—but not your weight—down to less than an hour.

Moderate. Open Thursday through Tuesday. Dinner from 5 to 10 P.M., weekends to 10:30 P.M. Reservations accepted for six or more. Visa, MC, DC. Full bar. Child's menu. Street parking. Casual.

THE GOOD EARTH/Organic
(Locations in Berkeley, Concord, Larkspur, Los Gatos, Palo Alto, Pleasanton, Sacramento, San Francisco, San Jose, Santa Clara, Santa Rosa. See your phone book for listings.)

More than likely the mention of nutritious food conjures up the thought of a parsnip parfait consumed at a bleak counter in a health food store. Well, not anymore. While care has been taken to avoid refined sugar and over-processed foods, one bite of their homebaked whole grain rolls asks the question: Can anything that tastes so good really be good for you?

Breakfasts include omelettes, sourdough cakes and hot or cold granola cereal. At lunch the sandwiches are made with freshly-baked ten-grain bread or there are interesting salads and the Good Earth's burrito or tostada.

Dinner is reasonably priced. My favorite was the country French lasagna—spinach pasta, three cheeses and a white-and-red sauce with almond slivers—not your usual lasagna, healthy or no. Other choices include Zhivago's beef stroganoff, curried chicken or shrimp, Malaysian cashew beef and more. Fresh juices and shakes are provided along with beer and not-so-good homemade wine sold by the carafe.

Moderate. Open seven days. Breakfast from 9 to 11 A.M. Full lunch and dinner menu 11 A.M. to 11 P.M. Sunday through Thursday; to midnight Friday, Saturday. Sunday brunch 9 A.M. to 3 P.M. Hours may differ at each location. No reservations. Visa, MC, DC. Wine and beer. Lot parking. Casual.

★
GOOD KARMA CAFE/Organic/Natural
501 Dolores Street/San Francisco/Area 2/(415) 621-4112

This is an innocent vegetarian place that has been around for quite a while. As a prelude to writing this guide, we sent out rather detailed questionnaires asking a number of questions. To the question: "Do you ban certain attire?" came the reply, "Nudity—sometimes." The Karma is proof in itself of the theory of reincarnation, for it has been dead and resuscitated—mouth to mouth—several times. In its current incarnation, it has more of an international flair, offering specialties from many different cultures. There is the obligatory variety of salads and eggplant parmesan, and just to add a little confusion to the menu, enchiladas and tofu tempura. Both the home-baked bread and the desserts are made without dairy products, oil, sugar or synthetics. **Inexpensive.** Open seven days. Lunch weekdays 11:30 A.M. to 2:30 P.M. Dinner from 5 to 11 P.M. Reservations accepted. No credit cards. Entertainment. No alcohol. Street parking. Casual.

★
GRAPE VINE INN/American/Italian
7331 St. Helena Highway/Napa/Area 3/(707) 944-2488

Every day of the week for more than forty years, this venerable eatery has greeted the winemakers and winetasters who flock in from the surrounding vineyards. Fresh from tasting a dozen or so red wines, what could be more welcome than a plateful of steaming hot pasta? The Grape Vine obliges with fresh homemade pasta in a variety of sauces and that almost relic of the past: real homemade ravioli. For second courses there's veal parmigiana and chicken cacciatore. The main problem facing a restaurant with such a large clientele of wine-wise patrons is the wine list. Suffice to say that only Napa Valley wines appear on the list. I mean, after all. **Moderate.** Open seven days. Lunch from 11:30 A.M. to 4 P.M. Dinner from 4 to 10 P.M. Reservations accepted. Visa, MC, AX. Entertainment Friday and Saturday. Full bar. Child's menu. Parking lot. Casual.

★
GRAZIANO'S/Italian/Continental
453 Pine Street/San Francisco/Area 2/(415) 981-4800

Anyone can finish this sentence in twenty-five words or less: "San Francisco needs *another* Italian restaurant . . . ." Apparently Tom Duffy thought it did, anyway. He opened here in 1970 on the site of some illustrious forebears, bought some banquettes and chandeliers, steered the menu north and is doing a good business. The *cannelloni*, veal a la Buster and veal *zingara* are all faultless. Graziano's must attract a particular following—they're closed weekends and only open for lunch—because only loyalty could make someone pass up the better Italian restaurants with which San Francisco is gratefully endowed. The Dow Jones and Dow Janes hang out here, when they're tickered out. **Moderate to expensive.** Open weekdays for lunch only from 11:30 A.M. to 4 P.M. Reservations required. All major credit cards. Full bar. Garage parking. Semi-dressy.

★
GREAT EASTERN/Chinese/Cantonese
649 Jackson Street/San Francisco/Area 2/(415) 397-0554

The distinct advantage this restaurant has over many others in Chinatown is its gracious and helpful manager, Pearl Wong. How she can be always at hand, cheerfully advising diners from 11 one morning until 3 the next morning is a mystery to me. Her personal favorites from the extensive menu are Mongolian lamb, cubed steak with tender greens, stuffed prawns and, when it's in season, crab in either ginger or black bean sauce. Prices are so moderate that you're sorely tempted to keep ordering just one more dish. An unusually broad selection of California wines is also a pleasant surprise here.

Moderate. Open seven days. Lunch and dinner served from 11 A.M. to 3 A.M. Reservations advised. Visa, MC. Entertainment. Full bar. No parking. Casual.

DA ★ ★ ★
GREENS/Vegetarian
Building A, Fort Mason/San Francisco/Area 2/(415) 771-6222

Even an agressively non-vegetarian like me does not miss the meat at Greens where the dishes are prepared with the exquisite care more common to the hautiest of *haute cuisine* establishments.

For more than a decade the Tassajara Zen Mountain Center has been attracting guests to their natural hot springs and open air cabinets – but it is the food that always draws the raves. The breads are so popular that they have opened their own bakery – the Tassajara Bread bakery – that sells thousands of loaves each week. Vegetables are grown at the center-owned Green Gulch Farm and are same-morning fresh.

The restaurant is situated in a high-ceilinged open space with exposed steel beams and a great view of the Golden Gate Bridge. The room is painted flat white, enlivened by good original oils. Dishes include: ragoût of peppers, home-grown tomatoes, sweet corn and summer squash; sorrel and new potato soup; open faced sandwiches (on that bread!); tostadas with black beans and much, much more. This is as exciting a dining adventure as Northern California has to offer.

Moderate. Open Tuesday through Saturday. Lunch from 11:30 A.M. to 2:30 P.M. Dinner Tuesday through Thursday 6 to 9 P.M., Friday and Saturday 6 to 8:15 P.M. Sunday brunch 10:30 A.M. to 2 P.M. Reservations advised. Visa, MC, AX. Wine and beer only. Parking at Fort Mason lot. Semi-dressy.

★ ★
GREY FOX INN/Continental
4095 Burton Drive/Cambria/Area 1/(805) 927-3305

This beguiling gem peacefully awaits the appetite-conscious sightseers from Hearst Castle, just six miles north, and travelers who by-passed Morro Bay's restaurant row, about a half-hour south. Once the home of Frank Souza, head building foreman of the noted Castle, this wayfarer's dining retreat recently changed hands with new owner Ken Colby assuming all responsibilities but wisely retaining the entire staff—including a fine chef. Their only change has been to begin serving breakfast while still serving lunch, and Saturday and Sunday brunch. In cooler weather, the dining room's wood-burning fireplace cheerily blazes. It is faced by tiles from the Hearst's monument, courtesy of Frank. Warm days find guests dining al fresco on the heated terrace deck, with broad vistas of pines and mountains. The dining room has a romantic country ambiance created by lighted candles, touches of greenery and even stained glass in the front.

Complete dinners include an appetizer, homemade soups and salads, freshly baked sourdough rolls, rice or potato and fresh vegetables. Entrées may be teriyaki chicken, chicken Kiev, vegetarian dinner, fresh catch of the day, steaks, prime rib, sautéed jumbo prawns, scallops in wine sauce, French lamb chops and Australian lobster tail. Desserts include a brandied walnut pie. There is coffee, six teas, espresso and an extensive wine list.

Saturday and Sunday brunch, besides the standards, include lox and bagels, German potato pancakes, lots of omelettes and their special French toast *Parisienne*. Lunch affords you a chance to sample unusually imaginative sandwiches, and the soup and salad bar.

Moderate to expensive. Open daily. Breakfast weekdays 7:30 to 11:30 A.M. Lunch from 11:30 A.M. to 2 P.M. Dinner from 5:30 to 10 P.M. Saturday and Sunday brunch from 9 A.M. to 2 P.M. Reservations advised. Visa, MC, AX. Wine and beer only. Patio. Parking lot. Casual to semi-dressy.

★ ★
GRISON'S/Continental/Steaks
1536 Newell Avenue/Walnut Creek/Area 2/(415) 930-0888

Perhaps some of you have yet to learn what happened to Grison's Steak House, the 1936-founded San Francisco favorite that seemingly vanished a couple of years back, when Harris' Restaurant opened in the old location. So pay attention and do yourself a favor, for Grison's is well-established in an attractive building in downtown Walnut Creek. Better yet, owner and executive chef Eddie Armendizo is still working his kitchen wizardry with his prime meats and continental dishes of fine veal. Prime rib is on the nightly menu and those great steaks are as thick and juicy as ever. Don't worry about the famous onion rings. Yes, they are still on Eddie's menu, to which he has added such attractions as swordfish steaks, all broiled on his mesquite grill. Perfection is assured in view of the chef's skill, honed during his thirty years as part owner and chef of the original Grison's. Wines here are a connoisseur's joy. Piano bar and piano during dinner.

Moderate to expensive. Lunch Monday through Friday 11 A.M. to 3 P.M. Dinner Monday through Saturday 4 to 11 P.M. Reservations advised. All major cards. Entertainment. Full bar. Child's menu. Street parking. Casual.

★
THE GROTTO/Seafood/Steak
70 Jack London Square/Oakland/Area 2/(415) 893-2244

All steaks are not cremated equal in this fine, scenic seafood and steak restaurant-with-a-view. The proof is when you order it "charred rare" as I do, and it's crusty and black on the outside, pink and juicy as you slice it. The Grotto has been serving the East Bay for forty years now (eighteen at the present location) and you can still get a good bottle of wine, a beautiful view (particularly at night) and a satisfying dinner.

Moderate. Open seven days. Lunch Monday through Saturday from 11:30 A.M. to 3 P.M. Dinner Monday through Thursday from 3 to 10 P.M., Friday and Saturday from 11:30 A.M. to 11 P.M., Sunday from 11:30 A.M. to 10 P.M. Reservations accepted. All major credit cards. Full bar. View. Child's menu. Valet and lot parking. Casual to semi-dressy.

★
THE GROUND COW/American
3129 Penryn Road/Penryn/Area 6/(916) 652-7261

Don't let the name deter you. The Ground Cow got its start in Berkeley about 1945, after the split of partners who owned the very successful and still operating, Zim's—a hamburger haven in San Francisco. Owners Zimmerman and Strauss split, and the latter agreed to stay out of The City but could use the Zim's menu. Zim's was to remain within San Francisco's forty-nine square miles and the Ground Cow in the outlying area. The Ground Cow did well in Oakland and, later, in Reno for a time, but now has settled down in solitary splendor overlooking Highway I-80, only twenty minutes north of Sacramento—a tribute to the astute stewardship of owner Elmo Rua.

Mr. Rua has kept all the right parts of the basic concept of hamburgers, chili and thick milkshakes "in the can" from which you can pour two overflowing glasses of one of the best shakes in the state. He has further converted his handsome, almost ski chateau-design to a wayside dining place. For here, with a pastoral view of the foothills, you can also eat in the covered porch-like dining room such classic choices as sirloin tips, spare ribs and shrimp Créole plus an expanded menu of choice entrées and delicious salads and sandwiches. Rua believes in making all his sauces and dressings on the premises. He has a penchant for high quality, as my scouts aver, and this 1963 landmark is an oasis on those trips to and from Reno or Tahoe when you prefer not to delay the start of your drive. The Ground Cow is an air-conditioned, cheerful bargain. Wines, beers and even a gift shop.

Inexpensive to moderate. Open seven days. Monday through Friday from 11 A.M. to 9:30 P.M., Saturday and Sunday from 7:30 A.M. to 9:30 P.M. No reservations. Visa, MC. Wine and beer only. Patio. View of the foothills. Child's menu. Lot parking. Casual.

★ ★
GUERNICA/French/Basque
2009 Bridgeway/Sausalito/Area 3/(415) 332-1512

This captivating, romantic home of exquisite food was founded in 1974 by executive chef/owner Roger Minhondo, a Basque gentleman who, years past, created the fine food that contributed strongly to the fame of several of San Francisco's leading restaurants. Now, his Guernica is a veritable *must* in any respectable dining out guide. His low building, with its spacious window booths, intimate lighting, dark woods, verdant plants, and paintings fairly radiates a rare appeal. Roger and his well-trained staff serve dinners (only); rack of lamb *Guernica, quenelles nantua, entrecôte* for two, duckling with olive sauce and other entrées, plus nightly specials such as the incomparable bouillabaisse.

Moderate to expensive. Open seven days for dinner only. Sunday through Thursday 5 to 10:30 P.M., Friday and Saturday till 11 P.M. Reservations recommended. All major cards. Entertainment. Beer and wine only. Lot parking. Casual.

In order to obtain the best results from this Guide, be sure to read the French, German, Italian and Oriental menu translators on pages 399 to 404 of this Guide.

★ ★
GUIDO'S/Italian/Old-style
1555 Fourth Street/San Rafael/Area 3/(415) 453-7877

This mellow, intimate dining-place is the personal statement of owner-chef Andy Scopazzi, son of a master Italian chef and related to other chefs of note, all of whom cooked years ago at the beloved Scopazzi's in Boulder Creek, California. Andy's father, John, still leaves his retirement (quite early) to visit and cook *gnocchi* with his son here weekly. This low-key citadel of fine food doesn't even have an illuminated sign outside. Andy designed, built, even mixed paints and painted Guido's. The walls and ceiling are burgundy and off-white. Andy conveys the feeling of the old-style Italian family restaurant, even to adorning the walls with blown-up photos from his family album. Two-thirds of the patrons are regulars, many enjoying their ravioli or veal on one of the seven rear counter stools from Original Joe's. Here all is done properly and quality prevails. Each dish is cooked to your order in the open display kitchen and the coffee is from Graffeo in North Beach. Here are some of the favorite dishes: *tortellini, cannelloni,* veal parmigiana, chicken *dore,* calamari sauté, linguine with baby clams, sweetbreads, and veal scaloppine. Fine California and Italian bottlings.
Moderate. Open for lunch Tuesday through Friday 11:30 A.M. to 2 P.M. Dinner Tuesday through Saturday 5:30 to 10 P.M. Reservations recommended. MC, Visa. Wine and beer only. Street parking. Casual.

★
GYPSY CELLAR/Czechoslovakian/Hungarian
932 Middlefield/Redwood City/Area 2/(415) 367-1166

Don't let the dingy exterior discourage you—opening the door leads you into an enchanting world that will have you longing to run away with the gypsies. Dark print fabric is hung like a canopy above the tables. Prints, drawings and other knick knacks are tastefully disarranged and the owner, John Novak, plays haunting old European melodies as well as some of the more popular tunes.

John's wife, Antoinette, is the creative force in the kitchen who turns out some wonderful selections. *Caravan dore,* tender breaded veal served with Bohemian potato salad, is a good choice as is *fuliska paprikas,* chicken with a sour cream paprika sauce. All of her central European dishes taste homemade and the *"bohemia,"* mildly seasoned pork chops with caraway

---

For best results, consult "How to Use This Guide" on page 25.

seeds and served with enormous dumplings is a delightful feast. The more Americanized dishes are not handled quite as well.

Moderate. Open Tuesday through Saturday from 6 to 10 P.M. Reservations recommended. All major credit cards. Entertainment. Full bar. Child's menu. Parking lot. Casual.

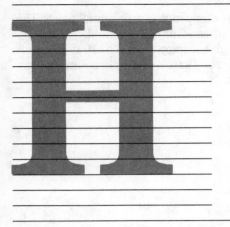

★

HAHN'S HIBACHI/Korean
2121 Clement/San Francisco/Area 2/(415) 221-4246

Hahn's is a relaxed Korean restaurant that has developed a strong local following for the *buhl-goghi* (Korean barbecue) and the pot-boiled dishes. It looks as Japanese to me as it does Korean and there is a Japanese influence in the clear broths that are so artfully served. The gas-fueled hot plates are table centerpieces here, and while they don't do much for the ambiance, they assure hot, freshly prepared dishes. **Inexpensive.** Open Wednesday through Monday from 11 A.M. to 9:30 P.M. Reservations advised. Visa, MC, AX. Wine and beer only. Street parking. Casual.

★

HAMBURGER MARY'S/Hamburgers
1582 Folsom Street/San Francisco/Area 2/(415) 626-6653

This happy place embodies the best of San Francisco's funky side, and you should be prepared for an unusual experience that may leave members of the moral majority a bit shaken. On my last visit, I found myself seated amidst a surprising mélange of people who could have nothing in common but the fact that they enjoyed hamburgers. Two girls to my left had their hair dyed in blue and green streaks. A man joined another girl sitting to my right and was apparently upset with the girl for not remembering a promise she had made to him in a past life. Rather than being miffed by the intrusion, she tried earnestly to remember the promise. A group of what had to be Hell's Angels recruits were just leaving as I arrived. Somehow, amidst all this madness, I felt perfectly comfortable eating a Mary burger with avocado and a side of home fries. A number of vegetarian sandwiches are available like: cheese and mushrooms; cream cheese with spiced olives; or avocado, lettuce and tomato. This is a crazy place that can be a lot of fun if you don't mind an occasional Corporal Klinger-type waiter.

Inexpensive. Open daily from 10 A.M. to 1:30 A.M. No reservations. Visa, MC, AX. Dancing. Full bar. Street parking. Casual.

★★
HANA/Japanese
408 Irving Street/San Francisco/Area 2/(415) 665-3952

The hostess greeted us affably, if not coherently, and guided us to our table. Unfortunately, there was a bit more of the language problem from that point on and even my pantomime gestures that had worked so well in Paris only got me escorted to the men's room—twice. In spite of the language difficulty, Hana is a popular place. It's tiny, and there is often a line of waiting patrons outside on the sidewalk. The food is consistently of high quality, yet below rock-bottom prices. The vegetables are done well, which is to say that they're not well done. The teriyaki dishes are lightly seasoned—not drowning in a sea of teriyaki. The tempura is thinly battered so that you can really taste shrimp, vegetables, or whatever, instead of just the batter. Impeccably fresh seafood—I think Japanese restaurants have the corner on the fresh seafood market—is the highlight. But every dish is full of flavor and the portions are substantial.

Inexpensive to moderate. Open Monday through Friday for lunch 11:30 A.M. to 2 P.M. Dinner Monday through Saturday from 5 to 9:30 P.M. No reservations. No credit cards. Street parking. Casual.

DA ★★
HANG AH TEA ROOM/Chinese/Cantonese/Dim Sum
1 Pagoda Place/San Francisco/Area 2/(415) 982-5686

It's hard to believe that Hang Ah has been serving that Oriental treasure, *dim sum,* for sixty years without more people knowing it. *Dim sum* is a Chinese tea pastry that is simply exquisite—and often exquisitely simple. Browse among the different colors and textures of pastries, filled with steamed shrimp or pork in bell-shaped pastry, crunchy shrimp toast, parchment wrapped chicken . . . the list goes on. There are also sweet *dim sum* with rice cake that are somewhat like a sturdy rice jello or custard tart of coconut juice or deep-fried sesame ball. Tucked up an alley across from the Chinatown YMCA, the one hundred-seat restaurant has a steady following for their Cantonese food; but I like them best as a place to load up for an unusual picnic in any of the lovely parks around San Francisco, or for eating while taking the forty-nine-mile scenic drive. You can order by phone, too, and they'll have everything boxed and ready when you come.

Inexpensive. Open Tuesday through Saturday from 10 A.M. to 9 P.M. Reservations accepted. No credit cards. Wine and beer only. Street parking. Casual to semi-dressy.

★ ★
HANS SPECKMANN'S/German
1550 Church Street/San Francisco/Area 2/(415) 282-6850

Simply speaking, Hans Speckmann's serves virtually the best German cuisine in San Francisco, and some of the best food this side of the Meinekestrasse in Berlin.

There is some competition here in the City, but Speckmann's, with almost no ambiance, has one concern in mind — serving the best of German cuisine to the incredibly discerning palates of the many *Deutschlanders* who come from all over the Bay Area to shop and eat here. At first glance, Speckmann's does not look at all like a restaurant. There's a delicatessen/*Konditorei* in front selling *rollmops, lachs schinken,* and imported sauerkraut. You walk through a narrow passageway into a small restaurant in the back with a blessedly non-redundant menu. For dinner, you have a choice of hot and cold dishes. The cold dishes are wonderful for a flagging appetite, especially the steak tartare, served German style with a raw egg broken in the center surrounded by small plates of delicacies like capers, anchovies, chopped onion, and parsley, along with salt and pepper to mix with the top-quality chopped meat and spread on dark bread. There are also cold plates of *Westfalischer schinken, gerauchter lachs mit creme kaese* (smoked salmon with cream cheese), and salad plates of *fleisch* (meat) of herring. The hot dishes range from *warmer leberkaese mit kartoffelpuree and erbsen* (hot liver cheese with mashed potatoes and peas), through *kassler rippchen* and excellent sauerbraten, to a superb *rahm schnitzel* (veal in cream sauce). Dishes are accompanied variously by excellent *gurkensalot* (cucumber salad), *gemischtersalat* (potato salad), sauerkraut, and *rotkohl* (red cabbage). And for dessert, there's a rolling pastry tray including a *schwartzwalder kirschtorte* worthy of the *Nibelungen.*

Moderate. Open seven days. Lunch weekdays from 11 A.M. to 2 P.M. Dinner Monday through Thursday from 5 to 9 P.M., Friday and Saturday to 10 P.M., Sunday from noon to 9 P.M. Reservations recommended. Visa, MC, AX. Wine and beer only. Street parking. Casual.

★ ★
HARBIN/Chinese/Mandarin
327 Balboa Street/San Francisco/Area 2/(415) 387-0274

Dick Williams and Eva Chang have guided this essentially Mandarin style restaurant to its present size and success. Set dinners in Chinese restaurants are usually not very representative, but the Shanghai Dinner here will offer a good first-time exposure. The dinner includes a good soup of the day, steamed rice, *kud tieh* (pot stickers) and a choice of a wide range of entrées from Manchurian-style fish to curried chicken. There's a Mongolian "fire pot" that's fun—you cook it yourself on the table in a chicken-base broth with assorted thin sliced beef, pork, chicken, shrimp, fish, scallops, meat balls, bean cake and vegetables. Nothing here is pre-cooked and the service may take a bit longer than you are accustomed to, but the fresh flavors are worth the wait and the cocktails are better than at most Chinese restaurants. The extensive menu, one of the largest Mandarin lists in the area, offers some innovations and all northern specialties except basic Hunan. The waitresses are especially trained to assist you with your order, and though this is not near the grandeur of Madame Chiang's Mandarin, it is a strikingly lovely atmosphere in which to enjoy the centuries-old dishes served better in San Francisco than anywhere in the Western Hemisphere.

Moderate. Open seven days. Lunch and dinner from 11 A.M. to 11 P.M. Reservations accepted. Visa, MC, AX, DC. Full bar. Patio by a pond. Street parking. Casual.

★
HARBOR VIEW GROTTO/Seafood
Citizens Dock Road/Crescent City/Area 4/(707) 464-3815

There's an old lighthouse in Crescent City with one of the more fascinating collections of seafaring memorabilia—historic photographs of shipwrecks, old log books, the original light and antique clocks—that is accessible only at low tide. It's not surprising that a good seafood restaurant that emblazons the word "grotto" across its front would flourish in this fast-growing port on the northern coast. The multilevel building on stilts over the water has a deceptively fragile appearance. It managed to survive the great tidal wave of 1964 that wiped out a major part of the surrounding area. Dinners are inexpensive and offer everything that's fresh from halibut to snapper to clams. There's much more (including choice steaks) on the vast menu, and it's all "the best in town," according to our friend, the oboist, who docks her boat nearby.

Moderate. Open seven days. Lunch from noon to 3 P.M. Dinner from 3 to 10 P.M. No reservations. No credit cards. Full bar. View of ocean. Child's menu. Lot parking. Casual to semi-dressy.

★ ★
HARRAH'S TAHOE/Continental
Stateline, Nevada/South Lake Tahoe/Area 6/(702) 588-6611

I enjoy returning to Harrah's Tahoe, and it's not necessarily for the gaming, although I'm sure the management would not object. Some of the reasons involve the dining that is available in this beautiful hotel. For descriptive purposes, let us start at the top, literally—The Summit Restaurant, with views of the lake, is sumptuous, elegant, and handsomely accoutered from the impressive booths to the luxurious ambiance. Much of the cooking is done tableside and a professional staff prepares such dishes as: *piccata de veau,* steak Diane, *coeur de filet,* sauce béarnaise, *tournedos de boeuf aux fleurs des bois* and so on. You've probably noted that all are flamed, and may be interested in flaming desserts: bananas Foster, crêpes Suzette, and even a soufflé Grand Marnier. The wine list has won awards. You may be intrigued by the menu of The Forest Buffet, on the same floor as the Summit, featuring specialties of the season. All three meals are served here, and featured are fourteen chilled salads, soups such as seafood bisque, and hot dishes like veal stew Madeira, broiled chicken and pork tenderloin. The dessert bar supplies enough sweets to make an entire meal (and, probably another ten pounds) with the likes of Harrah's cheesecake and sweet tarts. Oh, yes, on Fridays, fresh seafood is brought in via air from Boston and, on Saturday, the prime rib is hearty and plentiful. Don't overlook Friday Station, with the more elegant features of Old West design: lots of brass, oak, cut glass, a fancy bar, and the same wine cellar that supports The Summit. Hi, Ho, Silver. Away.

Expensive. The Summit Restaurant is open seven nights for dinner, 6 P.M. to midnight. Reservations necessary. All major cards. Entertainment. Full bar. Valet parking. Semi-dressy.

To obtain the best results from this Guide, be sure to consult the map on the various Northern California areas on page 28.

★ ★ ★
HARRIS'/American/Steaks
2100 Van Ness Avenue/San Francisco/Area 2/(415) 673-1888

Entering Harris', the new steakhouse on the site of the old Grison's in San Francisco, is like stepping into the twilight zone. If Smithsonian had preserved a top-of-the-line establishment of the '50s, with comfortable booths, gleaming dark woods, white napery and full sized palms, it would look much like this. There is a massive mural by Barnaby Conrad, and the greatest luxury of all in this era of high rents — spaciousness. Wide aisles, high ceilings and an uncomplicated decor provide a serene setting for magnificent quality beef, and the service manages to be attentive without hovering.

Ann Harris, who operated the Harris' Ranch in Coalinga with her late husband, has a firm fix on her priorities. The display window that looks out upon the avenue is actually a working meat case filled with exquisite beef, seemingly by the ton. Just inside, visitors encounter another illuminated glass case with retail prices on various cuts. To the right of the main room, there is a majestic mahogany bar, and to the right of that, a skylit garden room with floral print upholstery and another long mural. The rear of the spacious restaurant is divided into private rooms that accommodate small groups from about a dozen to several dozen.

The round of drinks we ordered provided the first of many touches of class that distinguish this solid restaurant. Martinis were brought in individual redwood buckets, a flask imbedded in ice to be poured into the simple old-fashioned V-glass. Appetizers included a beef pâté, herbed and spiced and made from sweetbreads, served with crisp home-baked melba-style toast from the Harris' bakery. A fresh crabmeat cocktail was served with good cocktail sauce on the side, and the fried zucchini was crisp on the outside, yet moist and succulent within.

Beef is all-important here, and chef Goetz Boje turned out the more difficult order, "rare and charred," perfectly. There is a choice of filet mignon, petit filet, ribeye, T-bone and sliced filet Bordelaise, along with tender cuts of roast prime rib served with a freshly grated horseradish dressing. Rarer dishes, evocative of steakhouses like Gallaghers in New York, include brains and brown butter, broiled sweetbreads, mixed grill, steak tartare, and the more common, but no less delectable, duck à la Boje. All main courses are accompanied by fresh vegetables, but the à la carte section lists a dynamite creamed spinach, and full-sized baked potatoes. If I were to nit pick, I'd prefer the baked potato served on a separate plate, and I missed seeing shrimp cocktail on the menu, harking back to the days when the shrimp, steak and baked potato were accompanied – in our innocence – by a bottle of Lancers, now regarded as strawberry pop.

Desserts are all prepared in the bakery, an eye boggling assortment of pastries,including a good apple pie. The wine list is a marvel, with very moderate pricing.

Moderate to expensive. Open seven days. Lunch weekdays from 11:30 A.M. to 2 P.M. Dinner Monday through Saturday from 5 to 11 P.M., Sunday from 4 to 10 P.M. Reservations advised. Visa, MC, AX, DC. Full bar. Valet parking. Semi-dressy to dressy.

★
HARRY'S HOFBRAU/American
390 Saratoga Avenue/San Jose/Area 2/(408) 243-0434

Harry's is steam table all the way, with turkey and ham that are sliced by lightning fast cooks in sort of an American Benihana style. The commodious interior is frequently silent as the concentration of hundreds of hungry hordes methodically refuel themselves. There are times when a restaurant like this can restore the soul and the stomach.

Sandwiches are generous with the meat piled high on several choices of rolls. Desserts are tacky, a glass shelf filled with puddings and pies that you should assiduously avoid. The Bavarian interior adds little to the experience which is essentially one for the gourmands of the world.

Inexpensive. Open seven days. Sunday and Monday 11 A.M. to 11 P.M., Tuesday through Thursday 11 A.M. to midnight, Friday and Saturday to 1 A.M. No reservations. Full bar. Parking lot. Casual.

★ ★
HARVEY'S RESORT HOTEL AND CASINO/Continental/Variety
Stateline, Nevada/South Lake Tahoe/Area 6/(702) 588-2411

This four decades-plus destination resort for countless travelers offers more dining possibilities than many small towns, Jack Palance states. You can ride the glass elevator to the Top of the Wheel restaurant, where Polynesian design decrees that appropriate food is served, including Cantonese dishes, as well as American and continental specialties. Views of the lake are memorable and, if your John Travolta shoes agree, dance a while in the nearby Tiki lounge to a real orchestra. Or, have dinner awaiting in the Sage Room, on the casino floor, but removed from extraneous noise of all kinds. This gourmet-worthy, quietly stated room attracts a wide range of patrons. The wines are impressive and the list is long. Of course, service is of the highest standards here. I always enjoy El Vaquero, in the hotel's lowest level, where all guests are seated in large, comfortable booths, served by costumed waitresses. What is the cuisine, you neophytes inquire? Why, it's Mexican and some of the finest versions of this often lively and piquant cuisine around. The Carriage House serves, for twenty-four hours daily, a cut above the usual coffee house. Next on my list of "where to dine (or eat) at Harvey's" is the Garden Restaurant, open twenty-four hours during the summer and from 7 A.M. to 10 P.M. in winter. I like this for a fast breakfast, promptly and cheerfully served. The general menu has some light suggestions, as well. Many of you will be in tune with El Dorado, where a daily buffet, all that you can eat, begins on weekends at 4 and at 5 P.M. on other days. There are always at least seven hot dishes, with veggies, in addition to the array of tempters. There are thirty varieties of pastries, alone. Or perhaps you'll be drawn to the twenty salads with choice of dressing. Mmmmmm. **Top of the Wheel: Moderate to expensive.** Open seven days. Dinner only from 5 to 1 P.M., till midnight Saturday. Reservations necessary. All major cards. Entertainment. Full bar. Valet parking. Casual to semi-dressy.

★
HAYES STREET GRILL/California/Seafood
324 Hayes Street/San Francisco/Area 2/(415) 863-5545

If you like fresh fish, and I'm an addict, you'll find it at its freshest in this restaurant. It's very crowded — and you didn't think really fresh seafood cooked over mesquite charcoal could be kept a secret long, did you — but fortunately, they take reservations so your wait will be kept to a minimum. The fish really is fresh, fresh, fresh and sauces are served in tiny condiment dishes on the side so that you can really taste seafood instead of just the béarnaise, tartar or herb-shallot butter (my favorite).

In addition to the fish, there are the standard offerings of chicken, steaks or hamburgers. All entrées are served with *pommes frites*, an excellent kind of French fries done in the French style so that there is no grease, just crisp strips of potato. Outside of the entrées, the Hayes Street Grill doesn't lose any ground. Their salads are reasonably priced and could be a meal by themselves. Fresh fish Nicoise, spinach salad or "composed salads" (varied kinds of antipasto) are worth trying. The desserts, supplied by a Berkeley pastry chef, are also uniformly good, particularly the rum-soaked brioche.

Moderate to expensive. Open weekdays for lunch from 11:30 A.M. to 3 P.M. Dinner served Monday through Thursday from 5 to 10 P.M., Friday and Saturday from 6 to 11 P.M. Reservations accepted. Visa, MC. Wine and beer only. Street and public parking. Casual.

★
HERITAGE HOUSE/American/Home Cooking
5200 North Highway 1/Little River/Area 4/(707) 937-5885

Sheltered in the trees on a hillside above the Mendocino coast sits a one hundred-year-old farmhouse surrounded by tidy cottages. Since 1949, the Dennens have maintained the property as a country inn with accommodations on the modified American plan, which here means that no lunch is served. The dining room is, however, open to the public, but only by reservation. They describe the style of cooking as "somewhere between home and gourmet," a territory as rewarding as the seascapes visible from the tables. The key to maintaining a happy resident population is a variety in the daily offerings, so a two-week's menu scarcely repeats a single dish. Soups range from vegetable, chunky tomato and potato with leek to Greek lemon, cheddar, lettuce and cream of cauliflower. Salads are a forte, presenting combinations such as asparagus with mushrooms, cherry tomatoes and heart of palm, artichokes with herbed mayonnaise, avocado, pear and cheddar, and butter lettuce with a cucumber sauce *verte*. There is no choice of entrée except on weekends, when a fish course is offered, but who could be less than pleased by rack of lamb, baked ham with fresh pineapple, roast loin of pork with fresh plum sauce, ginger-glazed corned beef, or prime rib served with any of a number of sauces? The variety even extends to the breads, where hot rolls, biscuits or corn muffins may turn up on any given night. And for the truly stout stomached, there's still dessert. It is not the sort of place to show up in jeans and sandals; the guests most often dress for dinner.

Expensive. Open seven days. Breakfast from 8 to 11 A.M. Dinner from 6 to 8 P.M. Sunday brunch from 8 to 11 A.M. Closed December and January. Reservations essential. No credit cards. Full bar. Patio. View of ocean. Lot parking. Semi-dressy to dressy.

DA ★ ★
THE HILLTOP CAFE/Continental
850 Lamont Avenue/Novato/Area 3/(415) 892-0796

Host-general manager John Wiedwald will probably greet and seat your party as you enter this spacious and airy restaurant atop a hill, only minutes from the heart of this pleasant bedroom community. Aside from the over three hundred-degree views from what was decades ago a sumptuous private mansion, the cleverly planned, extensive menu and its perfectly prepared and cooked offerings will reward you handsomely. The seafood, such as the lobster on Tuesday nights (only) is ocean fresh, as are all of John's products. His certified Black Angus beef guarantees, quite possibly, one of the finest and juiciest steaks you'll ever have. Charcoal broiled, of course. Pastas are fresh, also. In fact, everything is really good. **Moderate.** Lunch Monday through Friday 11:30 A.M. to 3 P.M. Dinner Monday through Thursday 5 to 10 P.M., till 11 P.M. Friday and Saturday. Sunday brunch 11 A.M. Reservations necessary. All major credit cards. Lot parking. Casual.

★ ★

THE HIPPO/American/Hamburger
2025 Van Ness (at Pacific)/San Francisco/Area 2/(415) 771-3939

More famous than Heinz for their fifty-seven varieties — of hamburgers, that is. They range from the improbable (hamburger with pineapple) to the incredible (the Cantonese burger) to the inedible (hamburger topped with ice cream, chopped nuts and Kosher dill pickle) to what could be called the "haut-burger" (béarnaise, tarragon, fresh eggs and shallots). Of course, there are just plain hamburgers in this Hippo fantasia with huge murals that delight the children and stagger the sensibilities. There is not one in the Bay Area with a soul so dead that he hasn't visited the Hippopotamus, as much an institution here as Alcatraz — which it outlasted. Around 2 A.M., a lot of the tired girls from the massage parlors wend their way here for a comforting pound or two of burger and some good coffee.

Inexpensive. Open seven days. Sunday through Wednesday 11:30 A.M. to 1 A.M., Thursday through Saturday until 3 A.M. No reservations. Visa, MC. Wine and beer only. Child's menu. Lot parking. Casual.

★

HOG HEAVEN/Ribs
770 Stanyan Street/San Francisco/Area 2/(415) 668-2038
244 Front Street/San Francisco/Area 2/(415) 989-1866

It's places like this that have people regressing to more primal instincts as they contentedly gnaw on slabs of pork ribs. The meats are smoked in an almost room-sized brick structure over hickory wood and mesquite charcoal, and they emerge hours later with a real smoked flavor and a light barbecue sauce. The barbecued pork shoulder and pork ribs are one of the happiest ways I know of getting some of that good ol' vitamin 'que, and the baked beans are homemade and cooked in the barbecue oven. The atmosphere is sleekly modern with some of owner Andrea R. Martin's pig art humorously decorating the walls (Napoleon Bonapork, Pignic in the Grass). And no one minds if you "pork out" on the good eatin's.

Moderate. Open seven days from 11 A.M. to 10 P.M. No reservations. Visa, MC. Full bar. Street parking or pay lot parking across the street. Casual.

★
HONG KONG CAFE/Chinese
501 Broadway/Sacramento/Area 3/(916) 442-7963

This is not the kind of place you would ordinarily look at twice," cautioned my friend who was dragging me along to his latest "find." He was right—but if you're looking for hefty portions of good Chinese food then it's worth taking that second look.

As the waiter brought my order, I warily surveyed the mountain of noodles piled before me and wondered how they would taste reheated at home later. After the first bite, I gave up wondering and happily devoured them on the spot.

The menu is simple, but extensive and includes endless variations of chicken or beef concoctions, chow mein, chop suey, steamed fish, egg foo yung and much more that I would certainly take the time to explore. **Inexpensive.** Open Thursday through Tuesday from 11:30 A.M. to 9 P.M. No reservations. No credit cards. Wine and beer only. Parking lot. Casual.

★ ★
HORKY'S/Mexican/Creative
1316 El Camino Real/Belmont/Area 2/(415) 591-7177

Horky Schy and her husband (manufacturer of Maxi's Snax, apart from Horky's) opened this small, charming bit of Mexico in 1955. Her cuisine is based upon old family recipes, but Horky has forged ahead creatively. In the comfortable, casual interior, Mexican woods are in contrast with knotty pine, metal artifacts, and lush plants. The extensive menu offerings include: *molé en gallina* (rarely found elsewhere), *nopales y chile con carne* (tender cactus morsels with chunky beef in chili sauce), Pancho's pastel (my favorite), and handmade husk tamales. The guacamole is sensational. So are the *chile rellenos* and the house tostadas. **Inexpensive to moderate.** Open seven days. Monday and Tuesday 11:30 A.M. to 2 P.M. for lunch, 5 to 10 P.M. for dinner. Wednesday through Friday 11:30 A.M. to 10 P.M. Saturday noon to 10 P.M. Sunday 4 to 10 P.M. Reservations accepted weeknights only. All major cards. Wine and beer only. Child's menu. Street parking. Casual.

Please be sure to consult "Tipping Made Easy" on page 22 of this Guide.

★ ★
HOTEL MAC/Continental
50 Washington Avenue/Point Richmond/Area 3/(415) 233-0576

In 1911, this was the Colonial Hotel for boarders and it was upgraded in 1915 . . . with stained-glass windows yet. The 1930s saw the emergence of Hotel Mac as a gourmet's word-of-mouth mecca, praised even by that old praiser Duncan Hines. In 1970, a fire devastated the premises, but in 1978 Bill Burnett completely rebuilt the hotel with resplendence it had never known before.

Diners still come from all over Northern California to stop at the long bar and lounge, then mount the staircase to the main dining room, rich with reproductions of those famous windows. Brass chandeliers, green walls adorned with hunting prints, a pressed-tin ceiling and polished dark woods are reminders of the hotel's history. Even cushioned bentwood chairs.

The menu has some imaginative touches along with such time-tested dishes as rack of lamb, roast duckling, Australian lobster tail and fresh seafood. The clientele is eager to relax and relive the pre-plastic past. Waiters have tasted every wine and can discuss the selections from the impressive cellar intelligently. Be sure to arrive early in this quaint, tiny village and drive along the shady hilly streets, suddenly coming upon unexpected, spectacular views of the Bay.

Moderate to expensive. Open seven days. Lunch served weekdays from 11:30 A.M. to 2:30 P.M. Dinner served Tuesday through Sunday from 5:30 to 10 P.M. Sunday brunch 10:30 A.M. to 2:30 P.M. Reservations essential. All major credit cards. Full bar. Parking lot, and valet parking for lunch and weekend dinners. Semi-dressy.

★
HOUSE OF PRIME RIB/American
1906 Van Ness Avenue/San Francisco/Area 2/(415) 885-4605

The limited menu reduced to the ultimate — one entrée. This kind of Queen Mary camp restaurant serves just prime rib at dinner, following a huge salad of beets and chopped egg and special dressing with celery salt. The baked potato is for real (I eat the jacket), but the creamed spinach has a gooey consistency and a bland neutral flavor. Good desserts à la carte.

Expensive. Open seven days. Dinner served weekdays from 5:15 to 10 P.M., Sundays from 4 to 10 P.M., major holidays from 3:30 to 10 P.M. No reservations. All major credit cards. Full bar. Child's menu. Lot parking. Casual to semi-dressy.

★
HUGO'S ROTISSERIE/Continental/Seafood
Hyatt Lake Tahoe/Incline Village, Nevada/Area 6/(702) 831-1111

The Hyatt hotels are leaders in restoring the good name and reputation of hotel restaurants. Hugo's Rotisserie at the Hyatt Lake Tahoe is located right on the shore of the lake. The decor is charming and hospitable, but it is the food that is the big surprise here. A bountiful salad bar is followed by your choice of continental style entrées, including spit-roasted duckling that would do credit to any establishment. Sauce for the duckling includes a choice of green pepper, honey almond, orange or Chinese spice. The herb encrusted rack of spring lamb Dijon and chicken Sicilia are several notches above what we have been led to expect from hotel food operations.

Expensive. Open seven days. Dinner from 6 to 10 P.M., Saturday until 11 P.M. Alll major credit cards. Live guitarist. Full bar. View of Lake Tahoe. Parking lot. Semi-dressy.

DA ★ ★
HUNAN/Chinese
853 Kearny Street/San Francisco/Area 2/(415) 788-2234
★ ★
924 Sansome Street/San Francisco/Area 2/(415) 956-7727

A tiny, exciting restaurant if you like the rarer and more exotic cuisine of Hunan – and I do. For openers, your "attendant" will size you up and serve you the size portion he believes you would want to eat – and pay for. The selection of eight noodles is sensational; I've had them all. Under "rice and food in plate," you'll find all manner of beef and seafood and sauced dishes, but the most interesting is rice with sliced, boiled, deep-fried and steamed bacon and pickled vegetables.

The soups are good and hot, but it is in the "country-style dishes" that you will exult – masterpieces like Hunan smoked ham sautéed with bamboo shoots, green pepper and black bean garlic-mash sauce; smoked chicken or duck; or the most unusual spareribs you've probably ever tasted, coated with rice crumbs and steamed in a bamboo steamer.

In the back of the menu, written in not very good English (no criticism implied; you should see my Chinese) there is a section entitled "My Country and My People" that provides some diverting claims. For example, "A Taoist priest can fetch whatever you need from a thousand miles away in half an hour through his intensive meditation." Or, how about, "A Kung Fu expert can paralyze . . . by tapping one's blood vessels with his fingertips and he is the only one . . . who can revive the victim." The colorful commentary goes on for quite a few pages, and makes delightful reading.

Perhaps you detect my zeal of approval in this review. That's what I intended, because this is just the kind of dining adventure that's really the most fun and one you'll be talking about for weeks. I love the Chungs, their ideas and their improbable restaurant, and I hope you find your way there soon.

Moderate. Open Monday to Friday. Lunch from 11:30 A.M. to 3 P.M. Dinner from 3 to 9:30 P.M. No reservations. All major credit cards at Sansome Street. No credit cards at Kearny Street. Full bar at Sansome Street. Wine and beer only at Kearny Street. Street parking. Casual.

★
HUNAN VILLAGE/Chinese/Hunan
839 Kearny/San Francisco/Area 2/(415) 956-7868
272 Sutter Street/San Francisco/Area 2/(415) 433-7878

Notable if only for the fact that the spicy northern Chinese dishes are not toned down for the American palate. Specialties include Hunan smoked pork, *kung pao* chicken and *tungan* chicken. Not many Chinese restaurants have specials, but this one does, and manager May Chin will be glad to explain the menu if the waiter doesn't. "Sliced rolls" is a Hunan dinner roll that will rest your palate between spicy courses.

Inexpensive to moderate. Open seven days from 11 A.M. to 9:30 P.M., Friday and Saturday till 10 P.M. Reservations accepted. Visa, MC, AX. Wine and beer only. Street and public lots. Casual.

HUNGRY TIGER/Seafood/Steaks
2801 Leavenworth/San Francisco/Area 2/(415) 776-3839
1375 Exposition Boulevard/Sacramento/Area 3/(916)920-1331

I approach my review of this restaurant as warily as if I were literally approaching a hungry tiger; whatever the Latin word for "inconsistency" is, it should be emblazoned across the Hungry Tiger's coat of arms. This chain—for the most part in the purgatory of mediocrity—can, on occasion, rise to great heights. Fresh oysters, cherrystone clams, Maine lobster and a seafood bar sound great, right? But somehow, some of the locations muck it up. One day the food may be good enough to shout about, another day it may be barely good enough to eat. Frustratingly, the two extremes can be—and often are—experienced at the same location. So with the forewarning above, I suggest you explore a location or two and look into their great cocktail hour bargains—oysters and fresh clams at giveaway prices. You might be one of the lucky ones.

Moderate to expensive. Open sevens days. Lunch 11:30 A.M. to 3:30 P.M. Dinner daily from 4 to 10 P.M., 4 to 11:30 P.M. on Friday and Saturday. Hours may vary. Sacramento location open for lunch Monday through Friday only. Reservations advised. All major credit cards. Full bar. Child's menu. Casual to semi-dressy.

★
IL GIGLIO/Northern Italian
545 Franscisco Street/San Francisco/Area 2/(415) 441-1040

An intimate aristocratic little room with dark pink tablecloths, red, red roses and crystal chandeliers. The dishes here are especially well prepared and served, and the plates are "dressed" to be appealing to the eye as well as the palate. The best hors d'oeuvre is crab Etruscan, glistening in garlic butter. *Cannelloni Romano* is a good beginning, and the veal dishes, particularly veal a la Henry VIII with mushrooms, are exquisite. Lorenzo Picchi knows how to operate a fine restaurant, it's a family tradition.

Moderate. Open Monday through Saturday. Lunch Monday through Friday from 11:30 A.M. to 2 P.M. Dinner Monday through Saturday from 5 to 10 P.M. Reservations advised. Visa, MC. Wine and beer only. Ample street parking. Semi-dressy.

DA ★ ★ ★
IMPERIAL DYNASTY/Chinois/Continental
2 China Alley/Hanford/Area 6/(209) 582-0087

The pleasantly buccolic community of Hanford, about thirty-five miles southeast of Fresno, is an improbable location for an epicurean restaurant. Yet it was in Hanford, where there are more livestock than people, that I had one of my most memorable dining adventures.

The Imperial Dynasty stands on China Alley, an ancient back street of shaded buildings where herbs, opium and all night gambling were once dispensed to Chinese laborers who worked on the railroads and in the mines around the turn of the century. The restaurant has been part of the Wing family since Henry Gong Wing, an acclaimed chef, established it in 1883.

The Imperial Dynasty is merely one of the jammed-together buildings with Chinese markings that give no clue to the pleasures inside. Behind the massive, somewhat forbidding door, there is a surprising jumble of vivid Oriental color, wall hangings, huge lanterns with red tassels, exquisitely carved jade, and the murmur of people happily dining.

Richard Wing presides here. A creative artist, he blends the classic French cuisine with touches of Mandarin. His *escargot à la bourguignon*, stuffed into shells with chopsticks and prepared with the unorthodox ingredient of cashew butter, has won two major awards as "Best Dish of the Year" from national wine and food societies. Most dinners include a soup du jour (my night: consomme of oxtail with whole mushrooms), half a head of lettuce with special house dressing, crab fu yung, an entrée (there are forty), dessert and coffee – or tea.

I tasted petite lobster tails in sauce diablo under crisp leaves of fried spinach, *coquilles St. Jacque* (scallops in a delicate white wine sauce) topped with shrimps and Mandarin orange, and tournedos of beef Bordelaise covered with a gigantic mushroom cap, followed by a dessert of honey pastry (similar to the Greek baklava) laid across a circle of crenshaw melon, then drenched with Grand Marnier.

There was a teenaged couple at the next table – straight out of Norman Rockwell's "First Date"– who were matter-of-factly enjoying a similar culinary triumph.

Service is informal, mostly by members of the family. Richard himself makes frequent trips from the kitchen to see how his guests are faring, and chuckles appreciatively over the compliments. He may disappear for a moment into the wine cellar that once served as an escape tunnel for opium smugglers, to emerge with a bottle he feels would be particularly suitable. The private party facility – more museum than banquet hall – contains four hundred pieces of art, some priceless, in recessed wall cabinets.

The most magnificent room of all, the highlight of the interior, is . . . the ladies' room. It is about the size of a hotel lobby, with a foyer surrounded by richly upholstered chairs. Two ornate, hand-carved wooden pagodas contain the essentials, and they are surrounded by wall tapestries, paintings, screens and Oriental carpets. Mr. Wing's ladies' room was used for a cocktail party by the San Joaquin press corps on one occasion, an honor which has not before been bestowed on any lavatory of my acquaintance.

Hanford is located on State 99 about 120 miles north of Los Angeles (look for China Alley).

Expensive. Open Tuesday through Sunday from 4:30 to 10 P.M. Reservations advised. V, MC, AX. Full bar. Ample parking behind restaurant. Casual.

DA ★ ★ ★
IMPERIAL PALACE/Chinese/Elegant
919 Grant Avenue/San Francisco/Area 2/(415) 982-4440

Minced squab mixed with herbs and almond-like hearts of olive pits, spooned onto a chilled iceberg lettuce leaf and dressed with plum sauce to be cupped in your hand and eaten like a taco; it's a sumptuous appetizer at one of the more sumptuous Chinese restaurants in San Francisco . . . or anywhere. Tommy Toy operates this Oriental treasure where huge vases of fresh roses, gold napery, silver candlesticks and metallic wallpaper provide a setting for luxurious dishes. They cannot be classified by region (Cantonese or Mandarin) but by the artistry with which they are prepared and served. At lunch once, we left the choice of menu entirely to the proprietor. We had sweet and sour pork with sesame, magnificent imported mushrooms, chicken with bamboo shoots, water chestnuts and brown sauce with scallions. We tasted snow peas with beef and oysters; four-season rice with diced chicken, pork, ham and shrimp; and a soup of bean curd, mushrooms, melon and shrimp that was practically a purée.

Prices are a bit more than at most fine restaurants serving the foods of Mainland China, but the setting is exquisite and the experience can be priceless.

Expensive. Open seven days. Sunday through Thursday 11:30 A.M. to 1 A.M. Friday and Saturday to 2 A.M. Reservations advised. All major credit cards. Full bar and extensive wine list. Street parking. Semi-dressy to dressy.

★
INDIA HOUSE/Indian
350 Jackson Street/San Francisco/Area 2/(415) 392-0744

Curry powders do not a curry make, but this is a superfluous warning if you are going to India House where the chefs have managed to develop a flawless curry (if there can be such a thing in the many varieties possible to be had). In addition to the curries there is creamed chicken Bermuda with Dry Sack, *tandoori* dishes, and many other interesting items which I have not yet been able to sample. But the curries are the thing: chicken, beef, prawn, crab, egg, lamb, and vegetable. A tray of *sambals*, or condiments, is served to enhance the curry and your rice, and these could be a meal to themselves: raisins, chutney, vegetables, coconut, onions and spices. In addition to the main entrées, don't ignore the lentil soup or the breads which may be ordered à la carte.

If the food weren't authentic enough by itself, there is a carefully planned decor to get you in the spirit of exotic dining. Tapestries of Bengal tigers, skins, ornate gold mirrors, and framed menus from legendary hotels like the Raffles in Singapore, cover the walls. Costumed waiters and soft native music complete the illusion of dining in India. **Moderate.** Open Monday through Saturday. Lunch Monday through Friday from 11:30 A.M. to 2 P.M. Dinner from 5:30 to 10 P.M. Reservations advised. All major credit cards. Full bar. Valet parking on weekends. Semi-dressy.

★
INDIA KASHMIR/Indian
1888 Solano Avenue/Berkeley/Area 2/(415) 525-1122
350 Jackson Street/San Francisco/Area 2/(415) 525-1122
707 Redwood Highway/Mill Valley/Area 3/(415) 388-3350

If the United Nations has failed in some respects, and most would agree that it has, it did make a significant contribution to the epicurean legend of San Francisco. When the United Nations was located here, virtually all of the member nations inspired restaurants with the cuisine of their homelands. The spicy foods of northern India were unknown here until the late forties, and now the tastes have grown so discerning and sophisticated that restaurants like India Kashmir find an interested and eager reception. The *tandoori* and lamb curry are specialties of this restaurant, a close relative to the India House in San Francisco.
Moderate. Open seven days. Lunch weekdays from 11:30 A.M. to 2 P.M. Dinner from 5:30 to 9:30 P.M. Reservations accepted. All major credit cards. Wine and beer only. Street parking. Semi-dressy.

INO SUSHI/Sushi
1620 Webster Street/San Francisco/Area 2/(415) 922-3121

Why put a fourteen-seat sushi bar in the book? Because it is as good as any sushi in San Francisco. In this simple restaurant, where the costumes of the sushi chef and hostess provide most of the color, the eight stools at the counter seem almost always to be full. Sushi take-out is at its best here with fancy foil boxes, tucked-in chopsticks and soy sauce that are much healthier and a lot more fun than giving boxes of candy.
Moderate. Open Tuesday through Saturday from 5:30 to 10:30 P.M. No reservations. V, MC. Wine and beer only. Street parking. Casual.

★ ★
IRON GATE/Italian/Continental
1360 El Camino Real/Belmont/Area 2/(415) 592-7893

Owned and operated by Al Malatesta and chef Ed Zago, this is an elegant spot to dine. Conveniently located next to the Circle Star Theatre for dining before or after the show, there is mood music for your dancing pleasure Wednesday through Sunday. Each day there are different specialities such as lamb tips Bombay, *osso buco à la liverness*, poached salmon and breast of veal with Italian dressing. Dinners are cart service and candlelight. Al Malatesta takes great pride in his work. Just watch him prepare one of his gourmet salads at your table, or perhaps one of his flaming crêpes for dessert. All dinners include a relish tray, tossed green salad, soup or homemade ravioli, dessert and beverage. This is one of those rare restaurants that serve *gnocchi al pesto* or Neapolitan, homemade, right from scratch by chef Zago. **Moderate.** Open Monday through Friday for lunch, 11:30 A.M. to 2:30 P.M. Dinner Monday through Saturday 5 to 9:45 P.M. Reservations necessary. All major credit cards. Entertainment. Full bar. Child's menu. Lot parking. Casual.

★ ★
THE IRON HORSE/Italian/Continental
19 Maiden Lane/San Francisco/Area 2/(415) 362-8133

San Francisco is filled with charming surprises, none more delightful than an alley called Maiden Lane, named after London's street of fine jewelers. While millions throng Union Square every year, most walk unknowingly right past the little alley that extends for two blocks toward the Bay, a brick-paved mall of intimate boutiques, galleries, jewelers and, of course, restaurants. The Iron Horse provides just the kind of understated elegance you would expect of Maiden Lane, with a continental menu that's heavy—both figuratively and literally—with the dishes of northern Italy. Specialties are the veal *ruggero*, chicken Toscana and veal *piccata*. I had to eye-wrestle for a few minutes with the maître d' who couldn't find my reservation, but they finally found a table for me, and I had a long, leisurely lunch. Cocktails are fine here and this has been a hideaway (until now) for older executives since 1955. **Moderate to expensive.** Open Monday through Saturday. Lunch from 11:30 A.M. to 4 P.M. Dinner from 5:30 to 10:45 P.M. Reservations accepted. All major credit cards. Full bar. Street parking and garage nearby. Semi-dressy to dressy.

★
ITALIAN COTTAGE/Italian
2234 Esplanade/Chico/Area 5/(916) 343-7000
1630 Hilltop Drive/Redding/Area 5/(916) 221-6433

The sandwiches here are all hero—you deserve a medal if you can finish one—in this sawdust-on-the-floor popular pizzeria where you can gorge at bargain prices. Neither Redding nor Chico are renowned as a gustatory haven, but this bright, spright, checked-tableclothed little restaurant/deli would be successful anywhere. There's a neat artsy-craftsy shop immediately adjoining that's great for browsing.

Inexpensive. Open seven days. Breakfast from 6 to 11 A.M. Lunch and dinner Friday and Saturday from 11 A.M. to midnight, Sunday through Thursday to 11 P.M. Sunday brunch 6 A.M. to 1 P.M. No reservations. Visa, MC. Wine and beer only. Child's menu. Lot parking. Casual.

★
JACK'S/French
615 Sacramento Street (near Montgomery)/San Francisco/Area 2
(415) 986-9854

OK, so Jack's *is* San Francisco, a century-old restaurant with paneled walls and third-generation waiters – a favorite of the financial crowd that can still afford to eat there (or anywhere, for that matter). But that doesn't mean I have to love it. I don't. The food is among the best and the most authentic French cuisine in San Francisco – high praise indeed – but the acoustics, or lack thereof, is intolerable to me. Even the great lamb kidneys and the cold poached salmon with *remoulade* sauce and the perfect béarnaise turn to ashes on my palate as I try, unsuccessfully, to deal with the high-volume clatter and chatter, the din of dishes, the shouted conversations or the blasé waiters and the indifferent reception. Upstairs is a different matter, however. There are small banquet rooms and a few seduction chambers where the roar below is reduced to a mere rumble. According to legend, there have been more transactions arranged here – business and otherwise – than anywhere else in the Bay Area. If you're in an epicurean mood, you might order Lucius Beebe's favorite, the mutton chop, a massive cut of lamb that is exquisitely prepared in a manner that is, to my knowledge, unique unto Jack's. Vegetables are done well here, which is to say that they are not well-done.

Moderate to expensive. Open seven days. Lunch Monday through Saturday 11:30 A.M. to 5 P.M. Dinner served seven days 5 to 9:30 P.M. Reservations advised. No credit cards. Full bar. Lot parking. Dressy.

★
JACK'S GRILL/American/Steak
1743 California Street/Redding/Area 5/(916) 241-9705

What could be more masculine or steak-sounding than Jack's Grill managed by Don Conly. Actually, this fifty-seat restaurant is a steak-eaters paradise with a one-pound filet mignon as the house specialty—prepared precisely the way you like it. Everything—steak, seafood, chicken—is cooked with care, and they've built a strong local following since they opened in 1938. It's a favorite place to thaw out for the snow-mobile set, who fill up with their own version of antifreeze after a long day's jouncing.
Moderate. Open Monday through Saturday from 5 to 11 P.M. No reservations. Visa, MC, AX. Full bar. Street and lot parking. Casual.

★ ★
JADE VILLA/Dim Sum/Chinese
800 Broadway Street/Oakland/Area 2/(415) 839-1688

It **was** a surprise to find superb *dim sum* here, really as good as any across the bay. Francis H. Tse, M.D.—an anesthesiologist and one of the majority partners—must have known that there was no *dim sum* of any consequence in the Oakland area, and was determined to provide it here in both familiar and exotic forms. If I can digress from the *dim sum* briefly—there are also excellent live seafood dishes in fresh and saltwater tanks.

But luncheon is the thing, when *dim sum* is the king, and you need reservations for weekend lunches. The interior is like a Hong Kong banquet hall, a large busy room with high ceilings and a continual buzz of conversation. Jade Villa seats nearly five hundred and is just beginning to attract the attention of the Caucasian foodies.
Moderate. Open seven days from 9 A.M. to 9:30 P.M. Reservations advised. V, MC. Wine and beer only. Street and nearby lot parking. Casual.

In order to obtain the best results from this Guide, please consult "A Few Inside Tips" on page 18.

★
JAKE'S ON THE LAKE/American/Continental
780 North Lake Boulevard/Tahoe City/Area 6/(916) 583-0188

This beautiful restaurant is located right on the lake at the Boatworks in Tahoe City. Natural wood, lots of windows, a waterfall behind the bar and a deck overlooking the lake for al fresco dining make this an enjoyable place to relax. The kitchen generally provides some well-done selections. There is chicken tarragon, individual rack of lamb, New York steak, scallops *maison* (in herb butter and Parmesan cheese), filet mignon and lobster (very reasonable), and baked stuffed trout. The cafe menu offers lighter fare such as Jake's burgers with cheddar or gruyère, *cannelloni,* fish 'n fries and the steak board of bite-sized teriyaki steak pieces.

The owners are from Hawaii, where they own Kimo's restaurant, which may explain the "hula pie" dessert. I'm afraid I didn't have the stomach to ask what this one was, so I settled for the homemade cheesecake instead. The bar pours only prime labels as their regular well drinks. **Moderate.** Open seven days for lunch in July and August only from 11:30 A.M. to 2:30 P.M. Dinner from 5:30 to 11 P.M. Reservations accepted. Visa, MC, AX. Full bar. Ample parking. Casual to dressy.

★ ★
J. M. ROSEN'S/New American
135 Fourth Street/Santa Rosa/Area 3/(707) 544-9550

Guests don't simply have a meal at J. M. Rosen's; they have an experience. All elements, from the glittering silverware and crystal to the ornate mahagany bar, contribute to an aura of elegance found in very few establishments in Sonoma County. Co-owners Jan (chef) and Michele (hostess) Rosen (hence the "J. M.") even keep a Rolls Royce, an eye-catching symbol, parked across the street.

At this writing, the menu was about to be revised, but two very popular items, stuffed pork chops and duck cassis, will undoubtedly remain as offerings, as well, naturally, as Jan's famous cheesecake, now also served in such prominent Southern California restaurants as Chasen's. It seems likely, too, that at least one fresh seafood will continue to be served each night. A vegetable dish (always fresh) can be specially ordered.

In addition to one of the most extensive wine lists (including major French labels) in the area, J. M. Rosen's carries a very substantial collection of ports and cognacs.

All this does not come cheap. Dinners and lunches at Rosen's are generally considered the most expensive in Sonoma County.

Moderate to expensive. Open Monday through Saturday. Lunch Monday through Friday from 11:30 A.M. to 2:30 P.M. Dinner Monday through Saturday from 6 to 10 P.M. Reservations advised. Visa, MC. Piano with dinner. Full bar. Parking on street and in nearby lot. Semi-dressy.

★
JOANN'S/American
1131 El Camino Real/South San Francisco/Area 2/(415) 872-2810

JoAnn's is the coffee shop of the '80s, with an eclectic range that seems made up—in equal parts—of American, Italian and Spanish dishes. The atmosphere is formica-linoleum-flourescent, but they serve one of the best breakfasts in town with a selection of twenty-four omelettes and such exotica as pumpkin pancakes, home-baked muffins and French toast made from orange nut bread. One of my favorite breakfast combinations is sometimes known as a "Diamond Jim," and it is served here with scrambled eggs, freshly ground beef and spinach. JoAnn and husband Tony have roots in good kitchens, both French and Italian, but they seem to have taken the best dishes for this unpretentious diner. José Rivera does the cooking when the owners are out of town, and the quality doesn't descend an iota.

Inexpensive. Open Tuesday through Friday from 7 A.M. to 2:30 P.M., Saturday and Sunday from 8 A.M. to 2:30 P.M. No reservations. No credit cards. Wine and beer only. Street parking. Casual.

★
JOHN ASH & CO./Californian/French
2324 Montgomery Drive/Santa Rosa/Area 3/(707) 527-7687

Properly describing itself in full as a restaurant and wine shop, John Ash & Co. has attracted national attention for both activities. Guiding spirit John Ash has been profiled in a book entitled *New American Chefs*, and the restaurant has been honored by the *Wine Spectator* for having one of the "100 best wine lists" in America. Once or twice each month special limited-seating wine (and beer) dinners are held, featuring tasting and discussion with winemakers or brewers.

Taking advantage of nearby farms and ranches (and airplanes, for some seafood), John Ash uses only fresh products in his creations. A typical dinner menu (selections change fairly often) includes a plate of varied local mushrooms, a vegetable dish (seasonal and fresh), chicken, quail, a fish du jour, pork, veal, and lamb. In addition to wine list offerings, new releases are available by the glass.

Located in a rather rustic-looking shopping center, the restaurant itself features white walls and a high ceiling hung with banners. Definitely worth your time.

Moderate. Open seven days. Lunch Monday through Friday from 11:30 A.M. to 2:30 P.M. Dinner Tuesday through Sunday from 6 to 9:30 P.M. Sunday brunch from 10:30 A.M. to 2 P.M. Reservations advised. Visa, MC, AX. Live music occasionally. Wine and beer only. Parking in adjacent lot. Casual.

DA ★
JOHN'S GRILL/Seafood/Continental
63 Ellis (between Powell and Stockton)/San Francisco/Area 2/(415) 986-3274

From "The Eye," Pinkerton's Security house organ: "The memory of Dashiell Hammett, a one-time Pinkerton Investigator, lives on at John's Grill in San Francisco where a room was dedicated in his honor."

As you trivia freaks know, Sam Spade in Dashiell Hammett's *The Maltese Falcon* lunched often at John's Grill on Ellis. Then why is it an item that the new owner of the Grill, having purchased it from Mike Cawley, is Gus Konstin? Right! Because in the book, the Fat Man talks about a Greek dealer, Konstantinides, who found the bird—the falcon—in an obscure shop in Paris.

Dashiell Hammett, who worked as a Pinkerton "eye" in 1920 (coincidentally, at the same address that houses the restaurant) used to fill his Sam Spade stories with real places and people, with names sometimes slightly, whimsically changed. No place is more real than John's Grill where Spade ate chops, a baked potato and sliced tomatoes ($.75 in 1920, $17.95 today).

The room is still dark paneled and—surprisingly—serves good food. The semi-continental, mostly American menu provides a wide selection of fish. House wine is Robert Mondavi, very reasonably priced. For those who think John's Grill is opportunistic, taking advantage of a brief literary spin, I disagree. Dashiell Hammett captured the essence of San Francisco as did Ross McDonald with his Lew Archer adventures in Los Angeles as did Sir Arthur Conan Doyle with the magnificent Sherlock in London. I get the vibes of the place—my first visit having been after seeing *The Maltese Falcon* at a nearby theatre—and you will, too. The fact that the food is good is simply a plus, here.

Moderate. Open Monday through Saturday. Lunch from 11 A.M. to 4 P.M. Dinner from 4 to 10 P.M. Reservations taken. Visa, MC, AX. Full bar. Street and lot parking. Semi-dressy.

★ ★
JONESY'S FAMOUS STEAK HOUSE/American
2044 Airport Road/Napa County Airport/Napa/Area 3/(707) 255-2003

In **1955,** Hugh Jones (an ex-pilot) opened a country-eatery at the Napa County Airport, providing basic food for private plane owners and guests. Hugh (Jonesy) did so well, giving thoughtful attention to the needs of his growing clientele that his little place reached its present generous proportions many years ago. Now, this fine steak house is always cheerfully busy and on weekend nights, it is usual to expect a wait for your table anytime after 6 P.M.

After Mr. Jones' death in 1976, Everett (Pinky) Dering (for many years the executive chef here and recently retired) joined with genial host Bill Tuthill (produce business veteran in the nearby Napa Valley) in acquiring this highly acclaimed place. Now, Connie Cavallero, Bill's daughter, runs this restaurant with her father.

Basically family-oriented, Jonesy's windows face the airfield and guests can observe the small-airport traffic while devouring the kitchen's bounty. The "Famous Steak Dinners" include tossed green salad (almost a meal) with "Jonesy's Bleu Cheese Dressing," special potatoes (hashed browns topped with melted cheese and an onion slice), your choice of steak—sirloin club, filet mignon, New York or the top sirloin (for two), French roll and coffee. Steaks are thick, juicy and tender, with some fat. There is no oil used on the grill but instead, each steak is weighted down with a large, smooth, Sacramento River rock, sealing in all the juices! Some guests, like Arnold Palmer, fly in from five hundred miles away.

To appease non-steak-eaters, there is excellent Southern fried chicken, and usually four seafood entrées. The breaded mushrooms and fried onion rings are both sensational. The wines are indicative of the owners' love affair with Napa Valley. Coming soon is an informal lounge/waiting area that will serve drinks.

Moderate. Open Tuesday through Sunday from 11:30 A.M. to 9 P.M. Hours may vary, according to the season. Reservations essential for large parties. Visa, MC, AX. Full bar. View. Lot parking. Casual.

Please be sure to consult "Tipping Made Easy" on page 22 of this Guide.

★★
J. R. CHOPS/Creative Continental
Mervyn's Shopping Plaza/El Camino Real at Scott/Santa Clara/Area 2
(408) 244-3700

Don't allow the shopping center association to give you pause. It only indicates ample, free parking in the evenings. This is one of my most gratifying finds, recommended to me by a number of Silicon Valley's high tech executives. The man who makes this all work, executive chef Gerard Sinotte, also manages every phase of his handsome restaurant and spacious bar lounge. Gerard is a big, vital man, but his subtle touches and instinctive comprehension of superb food lifts him above many other chefs. He uses the freshest of ingredients, and everything possible is made right here. Try his *tortellini al pesto.* As the "J. R. Chops" would indicate, all types of domestic chops can be ordered. I admire the triple-cut chops of lamb, with Gerard's piquant green peppercorn sauce. The impressive, easy-to-read menu describes several Provimi veal specialities, smoked baby back ribs, thick steaks, prime rib, fresh pastas, seafood concoctions, chicken and scallops. My salad of Chinese cabbage and diced prosciutto with hazelnut dressing was so tantalizing that, after clearing my plate, I sopped up the dressing with French bread. Chef Gerard likes his sweets, too, and his Grand Marnier soufflé is frothy-light. The coffee is a European blend—heady with its French roast beans. Gerard will prepare special dinners for eight and more, to your order.

Moderate to expensive. Open Monday through Friday for lunch 11:30 A.M. to 3 P.M., dinner 5 to 10 P.M.; Saturday til 10:30 P.M. Reservations necessary for lunch, advised for dinner. MC, V, AX. Full bar. Lot parking. Semi-dressy.

DA ★★
JULIUS CASTLE/Continental
302 Greenwich Street/San Francisco/Area 2/(415) 362-3042

First it was "in," then it was out. Now this ancient, romantic restaurant perched precariously atop Telegraph Hill has come back to the real San Francisco, and the real San Franciscans—replacing the tourist-on-a-package—have come back to it in an unprecedented reconciliation. (Usually when a restaurant has had it, it's *had* it.)

The miracle worker was Jeffrey Pollack, who fell in love with the turreted house that provides one of the more spectacular views of this spectacular city (ask for a table by the window, or better yet, ask for "the" table by the bar that provides a 180 degree bay panorama). Under the direction of the maestro, the kitchen has reawakened, turning out the *alta cucina* of northern Italy along with some classic French dishes.

Even getting there is a trip, in both senses of the word. At night, patrons cluster in a bleak commercial garage at 1541 Powell to await the mini-bus that winds its way up to the Castle door. Our group consisted of some tourists ("Hi, we're the Robertsons from Grand Rapids"), some locals ("that's nice") and us (silence). Once inside the paneled rooms, we were seized with the sense of adventure that anticipates a fine evening. The black-tied waiters are competent and very professional. If you ask their advice, they'll take as long as necessary to discuss what's good and fresh and to recommend wines from the large selection, remarkably inexpensive for an otherwise not inexpensive restaurant.

The menu is extensive, with some of the less familiar appetizers and entrées offered along with the *luigi nono* (large firm prawns in a good garlic sauce), fettuccine Alfredo and an exquisite veal *piccata* — all veal dishes are handled well. Desserts are something special, enhanced, I believe, by the view and the leisurely pace.

I particularly relished the banana fritters, but the *zabaglione au Cointreau* was a step down (I prefer mine made with Marsala, adding a less obtrusive flavor to the lovely golden-brown, warm cloud of Italian heaven).

Although the food is not perfect and the ambiance is a shade worn and the prices are a bit high, the combination of everything adds up to an evening that could be an important memory. Here is not the place to talk business or chatter about inconsequential things. Here one absorbs, discusses, lingers and — if one is lucky — loves.

Lunch is not nearly the same adventure. Like a still beautiful but aging lady, the makeup is a little too obvious in the daytime, the atmosphere a bit brittle and hurried.

Expensive. Open seven days. Lunch Monday through Friday 11:30 A.M. to 3:30 P.M. Dinner served seven days from 5:30 to 9:30 P.M. Reservations advised. All major credit cards. Full bar. View of the Bay. Valet parking. Dressy.

In order to obtain the best results from this Guide, please consult "A Few Inside Tips" on page 18.

★ ★
KABUTO/Sushi
5116 Geary/San Francisco/Area 2/(415) 752-5652

Imagine a chef with flashing knives at twice the speed of the chef in the Benihana commercials, and imagine him as a new-wave character shouting judo-type explicatives as he works and cuts and kibitzes in a small, sensational sushi bar open until 2 A.M. Sachio is his name and sushi is his game and he owns this small enterprise, and the small traditional restaurant adjacent. Fresh water eel, fresh halibut, and raw shrimp (the only sushi I didn't like), and, my favorite, *ikura* — with sparkling red salmon roe atop vinegared rice — are some of the many, many choices offered here. Sachio formerly worked at Kinokawa and has his own following, an interesting mix of San Francisco sushi and Sachio lovers. **Moderate.** Open Thursday through Tuesday from 5 P.M. to 2 A.M., Sunday from 5 to 11 P.M. Reservations accepted. V, MC, AX. Sake and beer. Street parking. Casual.

★
KAN'S/Chinese/Cantonese
708 Grant Avenue/San Francisco/Area 2/(415) 982-2388

Fine Chinese restaurants have existed for such a long time in Chinatown that they are taken for granted; most people believe that fine Chinese food was intermingled with the history of the city. Wrong. The Chinese restaurant of quality — a gastronomic light-year away from the soggy eggroll and watery egg flower soup — began to emerge in the late forties and early fifties, about the time the late Johnny Kan opened his famous restaurant on Grant Street. Mr. Kan was honorary Mayor of Chinatown, but he was more than that — he was a great ambassador of fine Cantonese cuisine to the world. There are still scores of pictures of Mr. Kan through the decades posing unselfconsciously with the stars, but I remember him best as a friend who patiently introduced me to the then-exotic dishes: melon cup soup and Peking duck.

Sadly, the cuisine is not what it once was—although manager Guy Wong does a commendable job of keeping things together—and now there are other important temples of Chinese gastronomy: the Empress of China, Imperial Palace and the Mandarin. But here is where it all began for me, the delightful adventure into the centuries-old art of Chinese food that was magnificent during the time of Confucius and can still be so, if somebody cares enough. Johnny Kan did care, and San Francisco is indebted to him and, I'm certain, will never forget him.

Moderate. Open seven days. Monday through Friday from noon to 10 P.M. Saturday 4:30 to 11 P.M., Sunday 4:30 to 10 P.M. Reservations accepted. All major credit cards. Full bar. Lot parking. Semi-dressy.

★ ★ ★

KEE JOON'S CUISINE OF CHINA/Chinese/Grand
433 Airport Boulevard/Burlingame/Area 2/(415) 348-1122

Next to the late Johnny Kan, I would have to feel that Kee Joon had the greatest influence on the development of the "fine" Chinese restaurant. Thus it was with great interest that the epicurean set in the Bay Area watched him build and open the lavish penthouse restaurant in Burlingame, so near the airport you can watch the planes come winking in during the evening.

The restaurant is, as one would expect, elaborately and carefully ornate. There are trees, an aviary with multicolored live birds in the foyer and a goldfish pond. There are marble fountains, priceless antiques, magnificent table settings and comfortable, upholstered chairs to accomodate the potential of four hundred visitors (including banquet facilities).

The menu is where Kee Joon has made his greatest imprint, however, with *haute cuisine* from all the regions of China, and service by captains and waiters who have trained for years to earn their position. Special condiment dishes, some shaped like a curved fish that frames the plate with sauces in porcelain compartments—artist's palette-like—were especially designed by Kee Joon for his new restaurant.

I began one memorable evening with an appetizer of baby quail flamed in brandy—fantastic. To dissect them, you first cut off each tiny drumstick, then slice down each side of the breast, dust with a pinch of five-season salt or a touch of plum sauce. The tip of the wing, bones and all, are a special, crunchy delicacy.

Next we ordered *moo shu* pork with Chinese truffle in crêpe, then hot and spicy Szechwan soup with pine fungus (like morsels of crunchy mushrooms). The main course was Mongolian lamb with a flat onion bread which was moist and aromatic, accompanied by stir-fried vegetables (snow peas, broccoli, asparagus).

The sweet and sour chicken is as close to a dessert as chicken can be, with a honey coating that is difficult to describe. The actual dessert was "mixed fruit powder," a custard made of the essence of banana, pineapple, orange, papaya, and guava which is reduced to powders and imported from China.

The only jarring note is not of Kee Joon's making. But I do object to the suburbanites who insist on wearing sportshirts or mumus to a restaurant of this character. Call me snob, or whatever—I feel it detracts from the pleasure of other diners in the room.

The wine list is one of the best ever for an Oriental restaurant, and I found that a modest California chablis went well with the entire dinner. Of course, a gewurtztraminer complements Chinese food, as it usually suggests something of lichee. Kee Joon's continues to win awards, such as the Mobil Travel Guide's four star and, as always, the Travel Holiday Magazine's award.

Moderate to expensive. Open seven days. Lunch weekdays from 11:30 A.M. to 2 P.M. Dinner daily from 5 to 10:30 P.M. Reservations advised. Visa, MC, AX. Full bar. View of the bay. Parking lot. Semi-dressy.

★ ★ ★
KHAN TOKE THAI HOUSE/Thai
5937 Geary Boulevard/San Francisco/Area 2/(415) 668-6654

Thai food can be as spicy as a bullfighter's language—after he's just tripped over his cape. Khan Toke can rival any Thai restaurant for spiciness, if that is your desire, but in general the spices have been carefully calculated to emerge through the heat as an exotic bouquet with a distinctive flavor that seeks to enliven rather than kill your taste buds.

At first glance, the extensive fold-out menu looks too exotic to many Westerners, but this authentic Thai cuisine may have even the most diehard "meat and potatoes people" leaning slightly to the East.

We started with an appetizer of pork balls with Oriental fine herbs—a platter of meatballs with ginger, garlic, peppers and peanuts to be put in a wrapping with tamarind sauce . . . a pleasant contradiction of flavors. Another dish which I can only describe as eclectic is *satea*, marinated beef cooked with peanut sauce and cucumber and dipped first in a hot sauce then a cold one.

The *mus-a-mun* is beef with red curry, peanuts, onions and coconut milk. One of my companions claimed to love spicy food and told the waiter to "make it spicy." Impervious to our warnings that the chef's idea of spicy was not going to be what she was used to, she defiantly took a large bite . . . and promptly disappeared behind her large glass of water which she followed with the pitcher of water snatched from our understanding, if somewhat amused, waiter. Everything is good here—just watch how spicy you designate.

Inexpensive to moderate. Open daily for dinner from 5 to 11 P.M. Reservations essential. Visa, MC, AX. Wine and Thai beer only. Entertainment on Sunday. Street or lot parking behind bank at 24th Avenue. Casual.

★ ★ ★
KICHIHEI/Japanese
2084 Chestnut Street/San Francisco/Area 2/(415) 929-1670

This may be the best Japanese restaurant in San Francisco—another way of saying it may be one of the best Japanese restaurants in America. The skill of Mr. Kichihei, an experienced Japanese chef, is the main attraction, although the tiny, thirty-six-seat restaurant (half table service and half *tatami* mats) is attractive in the classical sense and overlooks a beautiful garden. The *nabemono* (one pot cookery) are served in iron pots and range from the *shabu shabu* (beef and vegetables) to a vegetarian *yasainabe*. The Kichihei dinner selection offers a classical assortment of dishes like salmon *shioyaki*, fresh salmon broiled with salt; *shabu shabu*, paper-thin slices of beef with fresh spinach and mushrooms; and a sensational *nasu shigiyaki*, eggplant broiled in its skin, blended with cream, sesame seeds and bean sauce. All the familiar dishes are available—tempura, sukiyaki—but if you really want a lesson in Japanese cuisine, ask your kimono'd waitress to serve you "Japanese style." Incidentally, the sashimi is the best in town, served perfectly to appeal to both the palate and the eye. We've been here often and found it without a flaw.

Moderate. Open seven days. Dinner from 5 to 10 P.M., Sunday 4:30 to 9:30 P.M. Reservations advised. Visa, MC, AX, DC. Wine and beer only. View of Japanese garden. Street and lot parking. Casual.

For best results, consult "How to Use This Guide" on page 25.

★ ★

KINOKAWA/Japanese
347 Grant Avenue/San Francisco/Area 2/(415) 956-6085

If sushi turns you on, this place is made to order. With the popularity of sushi now, sushi places have been proliferating like a precious fungus. Unfortunately, the number of sushi bars outnumbers the sushi chefs (who train for years) — a sad state of affairs that leaves too many places in willing, but untrained hands. The sushi chef here is a trained professional who moves with lightning precision. The barman pulls a ball of sticky rice out of a steamer, slaps it around his palm until it becomes an oval shape, and smears *wasabi*, the hot, green horseradish paste on it, followed by the fish. The sushi bar also makes up cardboard-box lunches for take-out.

The hibachi dinners are a varied selection which proves a good alternative to a sushi dinner. Beef, chicken and pork are put together with sashimi and the dinners include soup, salad, rice, dessert and tea. The seafood combo is a good choice from this section.

Moderate. Open Monday through Saturday. Lunch served weekdays from 11:30 A.M. to 2:30 P.M. Dinner from 5 to 11 P.M., Sushi bar to 1:30 A.M. All major credit cards. Full bar. Entertainment. Street and garage parking. Casual.

★ ★

KIRIN/Chinese
6135 Geary Boulevard/San Francisco/Area 2/(415) 752-2412

Go to Kirin," said my friend, the Chinese food maven. "For what?" asked I. "A bottle of Japanese beer?" Muttering that I was a fool to be reckoned with, the maven hustled me out one foggy night to the Kirin Restaurant, just a wonton's throw away from the Cliff House and the briny Pacific. Kirin is not named for the beer, but rather is the Oriental name for the unicorn, a whimsical beast that fits this exceptional Chinese restaurant like a glove.

Kirin is special, first of all, because it's a Chinese restaurant with a Korean filigree (rather than the usually encountered other way around). *Kim chee* arrives right after your tea, a holdover from the migration of chef/owner Chen-Hsien Chu's family from China to Korea many years ago. But Kirin is even more exceptional because of its way with noodles. Chef Chu is a master of the hand-pulled noodle, and if you're lucky, you'll see him working his magic back in the kitchen. Exactly how he turns the dough into noodles is more than a mystery to me. I've watched as chef Chu stretches and twirls a lump of dough over and over again until, in the twinkling of an eye, the dough becomes transformed into exquisitely thin noodles – hundreds of them. They're called "no knife" noodles, and come pan-fried in hot plum sauce (extraordinary!) with squid, chicken, beef, pork or shrimp and an assortment of perfectly cooked vegetables.

There are other wonders at Kirin, some of which are not listed on the menu. Try the special hot dried fish, which blends plum sauce with brown bean sauce, and still manages to maintain its integrity. Enjoy the incredible cherry pork, a deceptively subtle sweet and sour dish, which isn't actually created with cherry, but rather with sweetened tomato sauce (à la catsup, if you must know). And by all means, do order a Kirin beer with your dinner. It's only right.

Moderate. Open Tuesday through Sunday from 11:30 A.M. to 9:30 P.M. Reservations required. Visa, MC. Wine and beer only. Lot and street parking. Casual.

★
KIRK'S/American/Hamburger
361 California/Palo Alto/Area 2/(415) 326-6159

Kirk's serves up the best hamburger in Palo Alto, and while he has not been the recipient of a Travel Holiday Award, his recognition comes from the generations served here since 1950. It's a put-it-together-yourself burger buffet where you are handed the perfectly ground beef on a good bun and can decorate to your heart's delight. On a nice day it's healing to sit at one of the awning-covered tables munching away on good hot dogs and – don't order the pineapple cheeseburger, please – basic, honest, satisfying burgers with fresh produce.

Inexpensive. Open seven days. Monday through Saturday from 11 A.M. to 10 P.M., Sunday from 11:30 A.M. No reservations. No credit cards. No alcohol. Patio. Lot parking. Casual.

★ ★
KOREA HOUSE/Korean
1640 Post Street/San Francisco/Area 2/(415) 563-1388

There's little good to be said for war, right? However, one of its side benefits is the palate broadening that occurs when doughboys from Dubuque are exposed to crêpes in Cannes or – as in the case here – to Korean foods they enjoyed (grew accustomed to) during that hideous conflagration. This is *it*, the Korean restaurant of Inchon or wherever, without frills or thrills but with the spicy-good food that is similar – yet apart from – the foods of the Orient. *Kim chee* (hot pickles) always start the dinner. You'll find *nang myon*, a cold but zingy soup; *saeng sun hae* (raw fish like sashimi); and chicken with sesame oil and red peppers. The Korea House is located in a walk-up, but ambiance is long lost in the sole concentration on cuisine. It's authentic, and good. **Moderate.** Open seven days from 11 A.M. to 3 A.M. Reservations accepted. Visa, MC. Full bar. Street parking. Casual.

★ ★
KOYA'S/Continental
6693 Folsom-Auburn Road/Folsom/Area 3/(916) 989-4926

Ismail and Stefanie Koya indulge appreciative guests with true privacy in high-back booths. Fabric-dressed walls in soothing earth tones are lit by the soft glow of gleaming brass lamps creating a warm, soothing atmosphere.

Perhaps no other menu area better defines a restaurant's character than the appetizers selected to introduce guests to its style. Here they include – *escargots Bourguignonne, crôute Forestière*, creamed mushrooms in pastry; Oregon Bay shrimp and Dungeness crab cocktail.

Innovation is the rule at Koya's: No exception is the *supreme de volaille* with raspberry vinegar. The boneless chicken has a texture contrast of roasted almond slivers. One of the specialties is shrimp and crab in white wine sauce, served with mushrooms in flaky pastry then glazed with hollandaise. Prepared for two is châteaubriand, with green peppercorns and mustard *glacé.* Also for two – *noisette d'agneau en croute*, roasted loin of lamb sliced, *duxelle* in puff pastry.

Another example of Koya's distinction is the desserts: raspberry and strawberry mousse, apple hazelnut custard tart and kiwi flan in pastry. The chef produces a dessert du jour, providing everchanging variety.

If you can, stop for a relaxant either before your meal or post-prandial, in the delightful bar lounge. This is one dining place where I believe that I could just sit with a glass and absorb the all-encompassing details of the interior design. **Moderate to expensive.** Open Tuesday through Sunday. Lunch Tuesday through Friday from 11 A.M. to 2 P.M. Dinner from 5:30 to 10 P.M. Sunday brunch from 10 A.M. to 1:30 P.M. Reservations necessary. Visa, MC, AX. Full bar. Piano lounge. Lot parking. Semi-dressy.

★
KUM MOON/Chinese
2109 Clement Street/San Francisco/Area 2/(415) 221-5656

Fifteen years ago, Cantonese food was just about the only way to go if you had a yen for Chinese food. Now, with the proliferation of Szechwan, Hunan and Thai restaurants, it seems to be the trend for people to snub what they consider to be the blandness of Cantonese food. At Kum Moon, a lack of chili peppers and garlic does not mean bland. The bare bones atmosphere may be the only bland thing about the place. The clams in their shells are pure essence of shellfish covered in a pungent black bean sauce. The lettuce blossom is one of my favorite dishes. Minced pork and vegetables are stir-fried and then put in a shell of Chinese winter lettuce covered in plum sauce. The menu is a staggering ten pages long, mostly of Cantonese dishes, but with a bow to the Szechwan region. Rather than try to detail all the possibilities, suffice to say there is enough variation and innovation to wake up even the most lackluster palate—or those permanently numbed from Szechwan chili oil. **Inexpensive to moderate.** Open seven days from 11 A.M. to 9:30 P.M. Reservations accepted for large parties only. Visa, MC, AX. Wine and beer only. Lot parking. Casual to semi-dressy.

★ ★
KUNDAN/Indian
601 Van Ness Avenue/San Francisco/Area 2/(415) 673-5600

C hef **Aziz Khan** turns out good, colorful dishes, subtly spiced, in what is far and away the best Indian restaurant in Northern California. This is not the *pukka sahib* food regularly served in the States, but admirable concoctions served in generous portions at somewhat high prices. Most Indian restaurants have at least one eccentricity which sets them apart, here it is the lack of combination or sampler dinners that might provide the first timer with an overview of the cuisine. Indian breads are exquisite, the chicken *tandoori* is moist (usually it is served dry at Indian establishments), chicken Makhani served from the *tandoori* is outstanding, and the homemade sausages (*seekh kabab zafrani*) are wonderful.

Kundan is a spinoff of the London Kundan, at which the chef trained, and both are comfortable, graceful, opulent restaurants . . . an appropriate setting for the high art of the kitchen. Maître d' Mohammed Akram choreographs the service and Akram, along with manager Jalal Ahmed, will consult with hesitant patrons.

Moderate to expensive. Open seven days. Lunch Monday through Saturday from 11 A.M. to 2:30 P.M. Dinner 5 to 11 P.M. Sunday brunch from 11 A.M. to 2:30 P.M. Reservations advised. All major credit cards. Full bar. Lot parking. Semi-dressy.

In order to obtain the best results from this Guide, be sure to read the French, German, Italian and Oriental menu translators on pages 399 to 404 of this Guide.

★ ★
LA BELLE HELENE/French
1345 Railroad Avenue/St. Helena/Area 3/(707) 963-1234

Highway 29 extends just twenty-nine miles from Napa to Calistoga, right through the very heart of Napa Valley wine country. I assume that by the time you are anticipating a fine dinner, you have already visited at least two wineries with famous names and are eager to match some of your tastings with more substantial fare.

The setting of La Belle Helene is a century-old, one-time hatchery; a quarried stone building with white walls and bright paintings where guests dine beneath broad beams in French Provincial style.

Chef Marc Dullin is innovative, mixing classic dishes with nouvelle inspirations. The menu is changed daily to take advantage of the best available ingredients. Appetizers may include grilled quail with pear sauce, cold pheasant "parfait" with huckleberry sauce, or mousseline of scallops with butter sauce. The inevitable green salad with walnut oil dressing appears regularly. Entrées offered range from medallions of venison with apple and lightly creamed walnut sauce and rack of lamb to breast of duck with pear sauce and veal stew. There are fruit tarts, in season and chocolate mousse, of course, but the chocolate cheesecake has been accused of being "satanically delicious." Proper coffee that calls for a second cup and a cellar that gives credit to the choicest bottlings of the surrounding area.

Moderate to expensive. Open Wednesday through Monday. (Closed on Tuesdays during summer.) Lunch served weekdays from noon to 2:30 P.M. Dinner from 6 to 9:30 P.M. Sunday brunch from 11:30 A.M. to 3 P.M. Reservations necessary. MC, Visa, AX. Beer and wine only. Adequate parking. Casual.

★

LA BODEGA/Spanish
1337 Grant Avenue/San Francisco/Area 2/(415) 433-0439

As rare as caterpillar's spectacles is a truly authentic Spanish restaurant in America. But the spirit of Spain resides and may be visited on Grant Avenue. Bernardo and Carla provide the entertainment; Carla dances to Bernardo's flamenco guitar and spirits soar from 6:30 P.M. till . . . Only one dinner is offered: a steaming *paella* crammed full of chicken, shrimps, clams and *chorizo* on a bed of saffron rice. A typical *ensalada mista* and pastries round out the meal. Sauterne and zinfandel are available. The room is small, with seats for only forty, so reservations are a must.

Moderate. Open Thursday through Sunday from 6:30 to 10:30 P.M. Reservations advised. No credit cards. Wine and beer only. Flamenco dancing. Street parking. Casual.

★

LA BONNE AUBERGE/French
2075 South El Camino Real/San Mateo/Area 2/(415) 341-2525

There is a rumor that around the turn of the century, a chef by the name of Augustín Saboureau wouldn't let his customers salt and pepper their own food. If a diner was foolish enough to ask for extra seasoning, a grumbling Saboureau would leave the kitchen and personally season the dish . . . using a set of jewel-encrusted shakers he carried on a chain around his neck. Chef Philippe Perugia is not quite so eccentric but he is equally a perfectionist. The béarnaise sauce — more tangy than most — brings the filet mignon to life. The rabbit in white wine sauce and the scallops sautéed in sherry are far and away the best dishes of their complexity in this suburban community. The pleasant dining room is an authentic transplant of a Breton country cafe. There are red and white checkered cloths, candlelight, leaded glass windows, high-backed wooden chairs and paneled walls. If you have too many glasses of the French wines, you might forget you were in California and expect to leave and go strolling down the Champs d'Elysees.

Moderate. Open Wednesday through Sunday. Dinner Wednesday through Saturday from 5:30 to 10 P.M. Sunday 5 to 9 P.M. Reservations essential. Visa, MC, AX. Wine and beer only. Street parking. Semi-dressy.

To obtain the best results from this Guide, be sure to consult the map on the various Northern California areas on page 28.

★ ★
LA BOUCANE/French
1778 Second Street/Napa/Area 3/(707) 253-1177

Celebrities vie with famous local wine-makers, such as Robert Mondavi, for a table in this highly acclaimed dining favorite. Devotees of "Falcon Crest" just might be seated near Jane Wyman. This intriguing information is not given to provide you with a reason for visiting La Boucane but merely to let you know that even television actors appreciate classic French cuisine. The gentleman who is responsible for this veritable gem is also one of the most knowledgeable – Jacques Mokrani, owner and master chef. M. Jacques opened his doors here in 1972 after becoming famous in San Francisco for his earlier La Boucane, which has now been transplanted to Napa in this one hundred-year old country inn. You will dine in a room of true dignity, a red rose in a silver vase and a candle reflecting light from the crystal on your table, while listening to the mellow strains of classic music.

On my last visit to the Napa Valley vineyards, we were rewarded with a dinner beginning with poached salmon in champagne sauce, soup, and the Macedoine salad, consisting of avocado, fresh mushrooms, vine-ripened tomatoes, onions, and walnuts, with an olive oil dressing. Our entrées included crisp, roast duckling with orange sauce; a remarkable rack of lamb, teasingly herbed; a simple, perfect filet of petrale sole; and prawns *Provençale* with just a hint of garlic. Our desserts were outstanding – a mousse that has won awards, a praline soufflé, not to die over but to live for, and strawberries in red wine (local, of course). Wines are entirely from Napa and Sonoma vintners, except for a couple of California selections that Jacques respects. Jacques Mokrani is also partner in the delightful Le Chardonnay, not too many miles north, in Yountville, described in this book.

Expensive. Open for dinner Monday through Saturday 5:30 to 10:30 P.M. Reservations recommended. MC, Visa, AX. Wine and beer only. Lot parking. Casual.

In order to obtain the best results from this Guide, be sure to read the French, German, Italian and Oriental menu translators on pages 399 to 404 of this Guide.

★ ★ ★
LA BOURGOGNE/French
330 Mason Street/San Francisco/Area 2/(415) 362-7352

Almost everyone who dines well can describe the "front" of a great restaurant. The subdued opulence of La Bourgogne is familiar to thousands: the gold booths and silver platters and rich draperies and fresh flowers and deep carpeting that provide a setting for one of America's great restaurants. Few patrons, however, are aware of the world that exists behind the swinging doors where dedicated, hardworking professionals perform as a unit in intricate and eleaborate rites under the direction of the chef/maestro. They transform a daily river of raw materials into the *poulard demi deuil*, the *faisan rôti a la flamande*, the *courte de bomard Brillat-Savarin* and all the noble dishes that must begin with someone peeling a potato, washing spinach, cutting meat. Here are the cooks that the late Ludwig Bemelmans wrote about: "fat fingers sliding around the insides of pots, buttering them; fat fingers on a carrot, feeding it slowly to the chopping knife. Here, have a look: yes, I know my fingers are thin. But the thumb is thickened with the scar tissues of a million tiny cuts – the tiny knife that, with which vegetables are trimmed. Called a turning knife. And the thick callous at the root of the first finger, there – there is where the base of a chopping knife fits into a cook's hand. The permanently misshapen nail is in memory of a lobster; and that thick scarred knuckle that can no longer bend properly: it was poisoned, that cut, and for a fortnight I thought I would lose the finger."

The constant hubbub, clattering, rattling, disagreements and waiters arguing for their orders – cooks and *sous* chefs work under intense pressure but carefully, ever so carefully, so that the radish should be carved into a rose for garnish or the rack should be perfectly trimmed or the sauce exquisitely balanced.

Inside such a kitchen there is often a rigid caste system. The sauce cooks and larder cooks are the aristocracy of the kitchen. Pastry cooks are loners because, in fact, they work independent of the team. Grill and soup cooks are still working their way up and the rotation chef (he works on the chef's day off) is generally a man who once had his own room. There is little humor here except for the small kitchen jokes; everyone knows his job and he knows if he doesn't perform he'll be sacked. In the eye of this raging cyclone, generally imperturbable, generally a great man whose slightest approval can send the spirits of the lowly *commis* soaring and whose icy disdain is a major catastrophe – is the chef. At La Bourgogne, the chef is Louis Marticorena.

For best results, consult "How to Use This Guide" on page 25.

The main difference between European and American kitchens? European kitchens – even those of many great restaurants – are often unbelievably dirty, with grime-covered uniforms, slippery floors and garbage accumulating as the day moves on, to be cleaned only after the final pot has been washed. With the American preoccupation with hygiene (sometimes too much so), the kitchens are immaculate and stay relatively clean with the help of all kinds of modern equipment.

La Bourgogne is a masterpiece. It would score high marks in Paris, let alone New York, which must watch in frustration as its once-great restaurants slowly but assuredly disappear.

There are those who feel it is chic to criticize a great restaurant. I'm sure *monsieur le propriétore* Jean Lapuyade would agree that La Bourgogne is not perfect (I never knew a perfect restaurant) but it has set and maintained the gastronomic standards by which all other restaurants are now compared. It has pleased the discerning and affluent patrons of the most demanding restaurant city in the Western Hemisphere. La Bourgogne is the last of its kind – there's neither the money nor the talent to create new restaurants in the Grand Manner – and I pray that it will endure forever.

Expensive. (About $40 minimum per person). Open Monday through Saturday from 5:30 to 11:45 P.M. Reservations advised. All major credit cards. Full bar. Valet parking. Dressy.

★
LA CASA/Mexican
121 East Spain Street/Sonoma/Area 3/(707) 996-3406

It's entirely fitting that the plaza in Sonoma, with the northernmost of Alta California's Spanish missions, should boast a Mexican restaurant *muy típico*. Just across the street from the Mission San Francisco de Solano is La Casa, where the authentic wrought iron, dark wood beams and whitewashed adobe walls promise equally authentic Mexican food. La Casa fulfills that promise, offering a menu of regional specialties that reflect the diversity of Mexican cooking.

Seafood, unfortunately seldom seen on Mexican menus north of the border, is a feature here. You can order broiled snapper Vera Cruzana (broiled with tomatoes, olives, and onions) as well as *ceviche*, a happy marriage of snapper and lime juice. The cheese soup is a favorite with patrons, as are the margueritas and such desserts as flan and ice box cake. A lively establishment, popular with families.

Inexpensive to moderate. Open seven days from 11:30 A.M. to 10 P.M. Sunday brunch from 11 A.M. to 2 P.M. Reservations advised. All major cards. Full bar. View of Mission. Parking in lot and on street. Casual.

★
LA CASA ROSA/American
107 3rd Street/San Juan Bautista/Area 1/(408) 623-4563

Gracing one end of the main street in this quiet, little Old California town of one thousand is "The Pink House." Just as the name implies, the quaint 1885 building wears its pink mantle as it has since it first became a restaurant in 1935.

Since 1964, the Shockey family has personally run this charming luncheon retreat, which has the feel of a tasteful home. Charles and Linda Shockey acquired the restaurant in 1973 and have continued to run it in the grand tradition of their forebearers. Weather allowing, there is also patio dining in the midst of an herb garden, from which come most of the seasonings employed in such dishes as their "Old California casserole," "New California casserole" and "chicken soufflé." Both casseroles have a corn polenta base; sharp cheddar cheese and beef sauce are in the "Old" version while the "New" is made with Monterey jack cheese and chopped green chiles. The chicken soufflé has a batter-bread top with the chicken bathed in a wine and cream sauce. A generous salad of local lettuce and herb dressing (buy some to take home) with wonderful rolls from the nearby Paradise Bakery accompanies your entrée. Be sure to order a carafe of the unique Ash Blond, a chilled, apéritif fortified wine.

Atop an impressive grand piano is a display of enticing chutneys, jams, jellies and marmalades that are made here by the Shockeys. Guests are cordially invited, nay, expected to taste one and all. You'll want to take some along or have them shipped home and to friends.

Luncheon, or even just a walk in the herb garden and a sampling of those delicious homemade goodies will enhance memories you will gain from the minutes-short side-trip to this marvelous mission town, a state monument, where part of Hitchcock's *Vertigo* was filmed. **Inexpensive to moderate.** Open Wednesday through Monday from 11:30 A.M. to 3:30 P.M. June through October also open Friday and Saturday nights from 5:30 to 9 P.M. Reservations advised. Visa, MC. Wine and beer only. Street parking. Casual.

In order to obtain the best results from this Guide, please consult "A Few Inside Tips" on page 18.

★ ★
LA CIGOGNE/Alsatian
201 Baldwin Avenue/San Mateo/Area 2/(415) 348-7444

This handsome, exquisitely detailed restaurant dates back to 1781, when Cardinal Rohan, Bishop of Strasbourg, issued a proclamation granting the Wagner family authority to operate an inn. Continuing a two hundred-year tradition, chef/co-owner Fernand Wagner presents the excellent authentic food and atmosphere of his homeland, Alsace. The eclectic menu features French classics and Alsatian dishes including *filet d'agneau rohan, le trois rosettes de filet balzac, Dover sole au chambertin and choucroute du cardinal au champagne*. Co-owner, René Chagniot, presides over an intimate full bar and extensive wine list. Recently moved, everyone is now at home at this new address in a red brick building with a stately Alsatian castle-like setting, and European-trained staff.
Moderate to expensive. Open for lunch Tuesday through Friday 11:30 A.M. to 2 P.M. Dinner Tuesday through Saturday from 6 to 10 P.M. Reservations necessary on weekends. AX, Visa, MC. Full bar. Lot parking. Semi-dressy.

★
LA FORET/Continental
21747 Bertram Road/San Jose/Area 2/(408) 997-3458

You'll know why they call them "picture windows" when you gaze out upon the living forest at this serendipity of a restaurant, owned by John Davoudi. Built-in wine racks, good paintings and the choreography of tuxedoed waiters serving *haute cuisine* completes the interior view. The fact that soup and salad come with the dinner may deprive you of some intriguing appetizers like snails poached in garlic butter or prawns Bordelaise in a lemony butter sauce.

The veal sweetbreads Brettone are succulent in a sauce rich with mushrooms. Tournedos of veal *au morilles* is two fist-sized filets of milk-fed veal glazed in a sauce made from wild morel mushrooms. Performing at your table are a good steak Diane and a nearly perfect pepper steak flambé covered with peppercorns and flamed in brandy sauce. Desserts include the fried cream which is beginning to become a gastronomic legend in the area. La Foret is virtually a landmark that used to be a boarding house in years past. It is an index by which the growing sophistication of San Jose might be measured.
Moderate to expensive. Open Tuesday through Sunday from 5:30 to 10 P.M. Sunday brunch from 10 A.M. to 2 P.M. Reservations necessary. Visa, MC, AX. Full bar. Piano bar Friday and Saturday. Child's menu. Ample parking. Semi-dressy.

★
LA FUENTE/Mexican/Spanish
#2 Embarcadero Center – Podium Level/San Francisco/Area 2/(415) 982-3363

While there seems to be an unwritten law to the effect that Mexican food diminishes in quality the farther it is removed from the border, this is – nonetheless – a sturdy operation. The full range of that complex cuisine is explored here in a setting that much resembles a fine Mexico City establishment. Seafood is prepared with Mexican panache and is indubitably fresh. The *paella* here is a specialty. The beef is sauced with *salsa de pipian*, a gorgeous medley of pumpkin seeds. There is meaty turtle soup, *ceviche* (raw fish that has "cooked" in lime, served with cilantro) and a hot salad. Vicente, Raymond and Manuel Aguilar have been carefully building a loyal clientele since 1976.
Inexpensive to moderate. Open Monday through Saturday. Lunch from 11 A.M. to 5 P.M. Dinner from 5 to 10 P.M. Reservations advised. All major credit cards. Entertainment. Dancing. Full bar. Patio. Underground parking at center. Casual to semi-dressy.

★★
LA GARE/Swiss French
208 Wilson Street/Santa Rosa/Area 3/(707) 528-4355

Although only a few years old, La Gare seems already on its way to becoming a Santa Rosa institution. Owners/hosts Marc and Gladys Praplan have combined an attractive, balanced menu, an extensive wine list, efficient service and a friendly, intimate setting to produce a restaurant that is very popular with serious diners as well as those simply looking for a good time. An animated atmosphere prevails.

Essential to the operation of a restaurant of this quality are daily trips to the market for produce from nearby farms; nothing served at La Gare has been frozen. The menu, which has something for everyone, includes veal with mustard sauce, beef with tarragon sauce, sautéed prawns, duck with orange sauce, and even a vegetarian special. Though devoted largely to California vintages, the impressive wine list does carry some prominent imports.
Moderate. Open Tuesday through Sunday. Dinner Tuesday through Thursday from 5:30 to 10 P.M., Friday and Saturday from 5 to 10 P.M., and Sunday from 5 to 9 P.M. Reservations strongly advised. All major cards. Wine and beer only. Street parking. Casual.

Please be sure to consult "Tipping Made Easy" on page 22 of this Guide.

★ ★
LA GUINGUETTE/Seafood/French
593 Woodside Road/Redwood City/Area 2/(415) 369-7364

La Guinguette means "a roadside inn" which is quite appropriate; this fine little restaurant is set neatly with shops and two other dining places by the side of Woodside Road. There are two cozy dining rooms, simply designed, pleasant and comfortable – a proper setting for excellent French Provincial cuisine.

Chef/owner Raoul Michel prepares such specialties as fresh filet of sea bass *en croute,* and calamari steak. Or, consider his quail sautéed with brandy, cream and green peppercorns. Michel, himself, favors the *canard à l'orange* – young duckling roasted and flamed in an orange brandy sauce. One of my guests, last visit, was taken with the traditional dish, so dear to Frenchmen, *lapin Provençale* – rabbit rich with tomato, mushrooms, garlic and red wine. Delicious. Everything of Chef Raoul's has a touch of style. His *carre d'agneau* is one of the juiciest, most favorable racks of lamb, ever. He always presents three fresh vegetables with the entrées.

A word about the desserts: I like the *profiteroles,* small pastry-encased balls of ice cream, covered with chocolate syrup, but I am also moved by the strawberries Romanoff (in season), and the *coupe aux marrons,* (the cream of chestnuts with rum, ice cream and whipped cream). We all have our temptations.

Moderate. Open Tuesday through Sunday from 5:30 to 9:30 P.M. Reservations advised. Visa, MC. Wine and beer only. Lot and street parking. Casual.

DA ★ ★
LA HACIENDA INN/Italian/Continental
18840 Saratoga-Los Gatos Road/Monte Sereno/Area 1/(408) 354-6669

The gracious warmth of early California continues to pervade this popular, rambling restaurant, where reservations are essential for dinner. In 1776, the governor of the state had his hunting lodge on this section of his Rinconada Grant. A century ago this was an overnight stage stop on the long run from the Midwest to Monterey. Today, the knowledgeable come here from fifty miles around to enjoy choice Italian and continental specialties. The large menu includes many veal dishes, rack of lamb, steak Diane, tournedos, even châteaubriand *boquietière. Saltimbocca alla Romana* is one of many choices, and I almost always ask for the delicate *cannelloni.* You just might favor the *fettuccine al pesto,* if you enjoy *basilico* as much as do I. The staff is attentive and personable. Superior wines complement the menu selections.

Moderate. Open seven days. Monday to Saturday from 11 A.M. to 11 P.M. Sunday from 10 A.M. to 10 P.M. Reservations accepted. MC, Visa, AX. Full bar. Lot parking. Semi-dressy.

★
LA MEXICANA/Mexican
3930 E. 14th Street/Oakland/Area 2/(415) 436-8388

While Mexican food is never quite so good as it is in Mexico, this may be the best basic enchilada-taco-burrito-tamale in the area. Owner Olympia Gudina has been turning out homemade start-from-scratch food for the better part of three decades, and the plain decor — flourescent lights and linoleum — is almost always full of people. Steak Mexicana is my favorite dish, but you can't go wrong with anything you order.
Moderate. Open Wednesday through Sunday from 12:30 to 8 P.M. No reservations. Visa, MC. Beer only. Street parking. Casual.

★ ★
LA MIRABELLE/French/Continental
1326 Powell/San Francisco/Area 2/(415) 421-3374

There is a tendency among locals to compare their blessings. La Mirabelle is often judged alongside La Bourgogne, which is not quite fair to either establishment. La Mirabelle is less expensive, appeals less to celebrants — more to serious diners. La Mirabelle is not so haute or atmospheric, but fulfills a need every bit as important as the better-known Bourgogne. Duck with black currants or pears (*le canard aux cassis*) is one of the house specialties along with filet of veal served with crab legs and béarnaise sauce (*médaillons de veau*) and rack of lamb. Perhaps a fairer comparison — if you've the unrelenting urge to compare — might be with the fine boulevard restaurants of Paris (not the cafes). In that case, La Mirabelle rates favorably, with both service and cuisine, and pricewise, it's about a third of the going menu rates in France.
Expensive. Open Tuesday through Saturday 5:30 to 10 P.M. Lunch weekdays from 11:30 A.M. to 2 P.M. Reservations essential. Visa, MC, AX. Full bar. Valet parking. Semi-dressy.

For best results, consult "How to Use This Guide" on page 25.

★
LANAI/Polynesian/Cantonese
4060 South El Camino Real/San Mateo/Area 2/(415) 345-1242

The bar is like a nautical museum with a rattan rain forest and impressive aquarium. Rum drinks—the comparison to Trader Vic is inevitable—are the thing on the long and colorful drink list, topped with a Navy grog that's made with rum-soaked ice, packed to look like a banana.

The menu is large and tries to be all things to all diners—and succeeds surprisingly well, especially with the Cantonese dishes. The hors d'oeuvres could serve as a meal: gulf prawns with diced bamboo shoots, "crêpes" of eggroll, *pulao* (spiced chicken livers and water chestnuts wrapped in bacon and deep fried in peanut oil) and much more.

The specialties include a "plantain plate" consisting of Mandarin duck, almond chicken, pork chow mein, ham foo yung and fried rice and the "Lanai plate" of egg roll, *mo goo gai pin*, pineapple pork, barbecued spare ribs, prawns Cantonese and fried rice. There are curries galore and more epicurean fare like barbecued suckling pig and "gold braid imperial duck" which is a whole duck, boned and stuffed with diced mushrooms, ham, water chestnuts, bamboo shoots and lotus seeds (order three days in advance).

Altogether a Polynesian Technicolor production that provides quality in a theme that usually adds up to indifferent fare. Prepare for a wait, the Lanai is very popular.

Moderate. Open seven days from 5 to 11:30 P.M. Reservations accepted. All major credit cards. Full bar. Parking lot. Casual.

★
LA PANTERA/Italian
1234 Grant Avenue/San Francisco/Area 2/(415) 392-0170

The favorite "boardinghouse" family restaurant in the North Beach area is this quaint *rotticceria* where you can get a stomach-bursting feast for about $9. There's an innocent, personal touch here—with a picture of Joe Alioto where the picture of FDR must have hung—but the service is a bit brusque: "Look pass this platter down, willya, I can't stand here all day." The hungry hordes at the long tables look like an Alka-Seltzer commercial or a scene from *Godfather II,* with huge crocks of soup and platter upon platter upon platter of good homemade food. Wine, included in the low price, is not very good.

Moderate. Open Tuesday through Sunday. Lunch Tuesday through Friday from noon to 2:30 P.M. Dinner Tuesday through Thursday from 6 to 10 P.M., Friday through Sunday from 6 to 11 P.M. Reservations for eight or more. No credit cards. Full bar. Street parking. Casual.

★ ★
LA PERGOLA/Northern Italian
2060 Chestnut Street/San Francisco/Area 2/(415) 563-4500

Owner/chef Angelo Piccinini is the guiding force behind this cozy, authentic favorite of both neighboring Marina-ites and Bay Area diners who value top northern Italian cuisine. La Pergola means "arbor" in Italian, and this is what physically characterizes the small, busy dining room— trellises suspended somewhat below the ceiling, giving the effect of lattice-work employed in vineyards. Racks of wine bottles cover the walls on two sides, so it would be a pity if no one in your party ordered a sniff of the grape.

Chef Angelo has long been locally famous for his kitchen artistry in several of our most illustrious Italian restaurants. Some of his most popular specialties are: *vitèllo all'agro di limóne*—lemon veal prepared, with no little effort, so that the sauce is sublime; chicken *vecchia usanza*— artichokes, zucchini, mushrooms and white wine embellishing the fowl; petrale sole; abalone from the highly-regarded Cal-Mex firm; spaghetti *carbonara*, fettuccine Alfredo, with fresh noodles and cream; and veal *piccata* finished with a topping of artichoke hearts and a pinch of capers. **Moderate to expensive.** Open Monday through Saturday from 5 to 10:30 P.M. Reservations essential. Visa, MC. Wine and beer only. Parking lot. Casual to semi-dressy.

★ ★
LA PETITE AUBERGE/French/Continental
704 Fourth Street/San Rafael/Area 3/(415) 456-5808

The highlight is the skylight, a massive ceiling of glass supported by sturdy rafters. A fresh flower arrangement, usually something spectacular—like birds of paradise—sprouts from the old, stone fountain in the center of the room. Murals, red-checkered tablecloths and a giant tree branch that forms a lattice for the skylight complete a dramatic setting for what could be a memorable dining experience. All the correct dishes are here, the rack of lamb, *canard à l'orange* even the soufflé Grand Marnier (order in advance, please). The menu is the slickest, simplest and most original I've seen, and it does credit to the establishment. One can dine well here, but only after a careful consultation with the maître d' to see what is recommended particularly. The accordionist is a pleasant and unobtrusive background to the colorful ambiance. **Moderate to expensive.** Open Tuesday through Sunday. Dinner served Tuesday through Saturday from 5:30 to 11 P.M., Sunday 4 to 9:30 P.M. Reservations advised. All major credit cards. Accordionist. Full bar. Street parking. Semi-dressy.

★
LA PIÑATA/Mexican
1205 Burlingame Avenue/Burlingame/Area 2/(415) 375-1070

This is a quaint Mexican restaurant, the decor of which greatly enhances this unpretentious spot and reminds one of a trip to mañana land. Delicious food is served in festive dining rooms, with ceilings festooned with colorful piñatas. There are fifteen combination plates, plus another fifteen super specials to keep your sombrero spinning. A great variety of exotic drinks are offered, including their famous double marguerita. Children are welcome, and they always take home a complimentary gift from La Piñata. Everything is completely fresh, prepared daily on the premises. Personable owner Chris Vlassis is on hand to greet his patrons. Ideal for families who enjoy true Mexican cuisine at candlelit tables.
Inexpensive. Open seven days. Lunch served weekdays. Saturday and Sunday 3 to 10 P.M. Dinner nightly til 10 P.M. No reservations. All major credit cards. Entertainment. Full bar. Child's menu. Parking in rear. Casual.

LA PIÑATA/Mexican
510 Larkin Street/San Francisco/Area 2/(415) 771-1850

The dishes are good, the corn tortillas are made on the premises, the atmosphere is attractive — beamed ceiling, overlooking a patio — but it's about as Mexican as Frank Sinatra. The only big score is the tostada spread with guacamole (the avocado was fresh) and combination plate number five, two green enchiladas (one beef and one cheese) in a sensational sauce of sour cream and fresh garden onions. Nice touch: La Piñata closes Mother's Day — generally the biggest restaurant day of the year — because, as owner Armando Rodriguez puts it, "Mother does the cooking here."
Inexpensive. Open Monday through Saturday. Lunch from 11:30 A.M. to 2 P.M. Dinner from 5 to 10 P.M. No reservations. Visa, MC. Full bar. Street parking. Casual.

In order to obtain the best results from this Guide, be sure to read the French, German, Italian and Oriental menu translators on pages 399 to 404 of this Guide.

★ ★
LA PROVINCE/Continental
521-525 College Avenue/Santa Rosa/Area 3/(707) 526-6233

To study the menu at La Province is to risk the agony of deciding among a number of irresistible choices. Will it be the *truite farçie au pernod* (trout stuffed with mushrooms and herbs in Pernod butter sauce)? Or the *émincé de veau Zurichoise* (diced veal in a mushroom cream sauce)? Or the shrimp, the duckling, the lamb? Having selected your entrée, you're still not off the hook, for there are dozens of appropriate French and California wines to consider. And finally dessert. The best solution is to have one of each.

Owner/host Helmut Pauer, who insists on fresh seafood, Sonoma County lamb, and Provimi milk-fed veal, has brought the same high standards to the attentive staff and quietly elegant decor of the restaurant, which occupies two joined 1920s-era homes. A favorite among serious diners.

Moderate. Open Monday through Saturday. Lunch Tuesday through Friday from 10 A.M. to 2 P.M. Dinner Monday through Saturday from 5:30 to 9:30 P.M. Reservations recommended. Visa, MC. Wine and beer only. Parking in rear lot. Semi-dressy.

★
LA QUICHE/French/Crêpes
550 Taylor Street/San Francisco/Area 2/(415) 441-2711

A friendly little downtown bistro, where two can dine quite well and quite cheaply. Delectable crêpes served for lunch include ratatouille, Parisian ham, creamed chicken and mushroom, and more. And more crêpes still for desserts, that ooze with apples or ice cream or strawberry jam. In addition to crêpes, there are beef, chicken and seafood dishes and each day two specials of the chef are featured. There's an unusual blue cheese quiche, and splendid chicken *Provençale*—food, plus prices, to warm the Gallic heart.

Inexpensive to moderate. Open Monday through Saturday. Lunch from 11:30 A.M. to 2:30 P.M. Dinner from 5:30 to 10 P.M. Reservations accepted. All major credit cards. Wine and beer only. Street parking. Casual.

★ ★
LARK CREEK INN/Continental
234 Magnolia Avenue/Larkspur/Area 2/(415) 924-7766

Originally a private home, in 1888, this lovely Victorian was known as "the Murphy place" until Victor and Roland Gotti, the owners of Ernie's, acquired it about ten years ago and set about completing the restoration begun by the previous occupant. A wing had been added to the existing two-story premises and now serves as the main dining room. Outdoors, beneath a huge bay tree and stand of redwoods, weather permitting, patrons lunch or brunch at festive tables. Still more redwoods guard the front of the home which, despite its name, is not a true bedroom inn.

The Gotti's term this pleasant oasis their "cookery and saloon"—sort of a country Ernie's. The menu is not in competition with the famous San Francisco restaurant but the food is very good and they provide an excellent drink in a cozy bar-lounge where photographs of early-days Marin set the nostalgic mood.

The staff is youthful and devoted to fine service. Luncheon leans heavily to salads and sandwiches, with a quiche or omelette, of course. Dinner has entrées in all departments: seafood, fowl, beef and other meats — even linguine and clams. You can begin with snails in mushroom caps or *piroshki* and more. Oysters on the half shell are a good choice here. In season, the fresh asparagus vinaigrette is ideal. Roast rack of lamb and beef Wellington are two of the more ambitious entrées. My scouts in the area dine often in this old-timer, gazing up at the glass ceiling, admiring the inside and outside greenery, sipping their California wine and feeling very Marin-ish.

Moderate. Open Tuesday through Sunday. Lunch served Tuesday through Saturday from 11:30 A.M. to 2:30 P.M. Dinner from 5:30 to 10 P.M., Friday and Saturday to 10:30 P.M. Sunday brunch from 11 A.M. to 2:30 P.M. Reservations strongly advised. All major credit cards. Full bar. Patio. Parking lot. Casual to semi-dressy.

To obtain the best results from this Guide, be sure to consult the map on the various Northern California areas on page 28.

★
LA ROCCA'S/Seafood
3519 California/San Francisco/Area 2/(415) 387-4100

It's places like this that prove some of the best fresh fish can be found away from the more touristy areas by the ocean. Pasquale La Rocca is the son of a Sicilian fisherman who has managed to get the local fishermen with small boats to deliver to him the freshest clams, shrimp, salmon, swordfish, sea bass, sand dabs and any other sea life available. The oyster bar is a delight and the Boston clam chowder is a big steaming bowl of thick white ambrosia.

You could practically write the menu yourself, it's that familiar, but with fish as fresh as this, a lack of originality is beside the point. Your fish can be served grilled or broiled and, for Pasquale's Sicilian touch, upon request the chef will baste your selection in a garlicky olive oil mixture.

Inexpensive to moderate. Open Monday through Saturday from 11 A.M. to 8 P.M. No reservations. No credit cards. Wine and beer only. Parking lot. Casual.

DA ★
LA RONDALLA/Mexican
901 Valencia Street/San Francisco/Area 2/(415) 647-7474

Day and night. . .it's Fiesta! The tinsel and lights are left over from Christmas. The sexy Aztec maidens painted on velvet do honor to a juggler in the plaza. Mariachis materialize magically to take over from the juke box. Bells and gongs of the old-fashioned pinball machines join in.

But—the sweetest music here comes from the clatter of pots and pans, the scrape of knife and spatula, the bang of plates and spoons. Sit at the counter—there are four rooms of booths and tables—for here the concert is best and you can watch the grill-side musicians, hear the musical clatter and ogle the chorus line of lively waitresses. And, suddenly, quicker than you imagined possible, the climax of all this cacophony appears before you, steamy and fragrant.

Many pub-crawlers are convinced that La Rondalla is the best true cantina north of the Rio Grande. All the tested and true Mexican standbys are there: burritos, enchiladas, chile rellenos and flautas. However, these energetic chefs performing just a scant half-yard from you are capable of much more, of the unusual. The *adobada*, for example, is a tender pork steak, stewed in a cunning blend of hot spices and cool veggies. Goat meat, far more popular south of the border than here, is cleverly converted to *birria de chivo*, a kid stew for adults. And, *menudo*—that fiery tripe soup—tames any hangover. As this place jumps until sun-up, if huevos rancheros is your dish, La Rondalla is your destination. **Inexpensive.** Open Tuesday through Sunday from 11:30 A.M. to 3:30 A.M. Reservations advised. No credit cards. Mariachis nightly. Full bar. Street parking. Casual.

★ ★
LA RUE/French/Continental
3740 Mount Diablo Boulevard/Lafayette/Area 2/(415) 284-5700

A **favorite** dining place of the discerning locals since its founding by Erich Astl and his successor Karl Niederer. La Rue has been steadily upgraded by owner/executive chef Ghassan Jarrouj since his acquisition in 1981. In the French country-style interior, guests dine in three distinct areas with pleasant views through beveled glass windows. The extensive menu offers as many as four veal specialties, fresh fish and other classic dishes, of which I found the breast of duck especially appealing. Dinner is six courses, *prix fixe.* Each guest is served a palate-clearing fruit sherbet. Regular entrées are enlivened with nightly specials. The full bar is a recent, happy addition.
Moderate to expensive. Open seven days. Lunch Monday through Friday 11:30 A.M. to 2:30 P.M. Dinner 5:30 to 10 P.M., Sunday from 4 to 8:30 P.M. Reservations essential. Visa, MC, AX. Full bar. Easy parking. Casual to semi-dressy.

★
LA SCALA/Seafood/Italian
1980 Union Street/San Francisco/Area 2/(415) 885-2222

H **osts** can be intimidating, especially maître d's of French or Italian restaurants. With the American trait of seeking approval from the man in charge—ship's captains, railway conductors, airline pilots—we have a conditioned reflex to dissemble in the presence of a man carrying a clipboard or standing behind a podium. It is in restaurants where this quirk in our otherwise aggressive personalities becomes troublesome. We order and accept dishes in a language we do not understand and, because they may think us stupid, we're reluctant to ask questions. This is a long preamble to La Scala (where the maître d' even has a pompadour), and my firm suggestion that you ask about the dishes unfamiliar to you.

Owner Fred Delmarva has created a ristorante of very high-quality, with red tablecloths over white ones, tuxedoed waiters, dim lighting, and a chef who doesn't skimp or take short-cuts. The *tortoni* is a heavenly creation of whipped cream, egg whites, toasted almonds and Marsala. This is the true *tortoni* which is *not* a form of ice cream.

The chicken dishes all begin with a fresh hen, not one that has been blanched to reduce the cooking time. The veal dishes are all from top round of veal sirloin. But seafood is the real specialty: scampi, fresh mussels and clams, calamari, scallops *meunière* and three versions of petrale are all done with a flair.

Moderate. Open Monday through Saturday. Dinner from 5:30 P.M. to midnight. Reservations accepted. Visa, MC, AX. Piano bar. Full bar. Patio. Street parking. Casual.

★ ★
LAS MAÑANITAS/Mexican
850 Montgomery Street/San Francisco/Area 2/(415) 434-2088

In the last edition of this guide, I belabored the point about the virtual absence of good Mexican food in San Francisco. While I do not flatter myself with the fantasy that Las Mañanitas opened, subsequent to that edition, because of my remarks, I'm delighted they are here. Most Mexican restaurant menus hold no surprises. The dishes listed are fast food items, prepared to order. Many of the "Mexican" restaurants in this area buy their tamales and tacos and enchiladas from a central commissary. And you might as well get used to the fact that lard is the cooking medium of Mexico—fresh lard—not vegetable oil.

Osiel Malagon, chef since the opening in 1981, prepares splendid dishes like *ostiones Mañanitas* (half a dozen baked oysters with cheese and bacon); *huachinango Veracruzana*; (fresh snapper in a sauce of tomatoes, onions, olives and green peppers); *chiles en nogada* stuffed with pork, beef, raisins and pine nuts; and *pollo en mole poblano,* chicken cooked with an improbable, but delicious, sauce made of chocolate and chilies. The tortilla soup is made with melted cheese, avocado and tortilla shreds with a whole black chile. I was disappointed to find the bar did not know how to make a sangrita (not sangria), a wonderful concoction that is a straight shot of tequila (preferably gold) with a "back" of tomato juice, orange juice, hot spices and more.

You'll pay more than you've paid at Mexican restaurants in the past, but it's well worth it.

Moderate. Lunch weekdays from 11 A.M. to 4 P.M. Dinner seven nights from 5 to midnight. Reservations accepted. All major credit cards. Entertainment. Full bar. Patio. Lot parking. Semi-dressy.

In order to obtain the best results from this Guide, please consult "A Few Inside Tips" on page 18.

★
LATE FOR THE TRAIN/American/Natural
561 Oak Grove Street/Menlo Park/Area 2/(415) 321-6124

This is one of those places you just *want* to like — cutesy name and
all. The decor lends an ambiance of comfortable domesticity: fresh
flowers, doilies, bits and pieces of china and little odds and ends make
this a happy little retreat back to simpler times.

The menu is on the simple side also, but simple is a far cry from
boring. Fresh fruit, homemade scones and real home-fried potatoes are
all good choices to go with an entrée. The omelettes are three egg masterpieces of: avocado, scallions, tomatoes, cheese and sour cream; turkey,
mushrooms, green peppers and onions with Mornay sauce; chicken liver;
mushrooms, and more. The tabbouli salad is a wonderfully natural selection
that doesn't make "natural" a synonym for "yuck" . . . marinated bulgar
(cracked wheat), raisins, chopped vegetables and tomato. The service
is unhurried in spite of the waiting throngs that congregate in the parking lot — enjoy a leisurely breakfast and drink a champagne Mimosa toast
to the people still waiting.
Inexpensive. Open Tuesday through Friday from 7 A.M. to 3 P.M.,
8:30 A.M. to 2:30 P.M. on weekends. No reservations. No credit cards.
Wine and beer only. Ample parking. Casual.

★★
LA TOUR/French
3610 Clayton Road/Concord/Area 2/(415) 825-9955

Fine French chefs like owner Frank Dickinson are wise to bring their
talents to outlying communities (Concord is northeast of Berkeley)
where they are needed and appreciated. (Besides, another French
restaurant or two and San Francisco would explode in a cloud of béarnaise,
Bordelaise and chocolate mousse). Here, Frank has a tiny window
overlooking the golden-toned dining room from his chef's office to see
how his finely executed dishes, like filet of beef cordon bleu, are received.
Escargot is the only à la carte appetizer on the otherwise complete dinner that includes a choice of crabmeat cocktail or *pâté maison*, potage,
and green salad that is better dressed than many of the patrons, with
choice of Roquefort, Caesar or Thousand Island. Main courses range
from veal sweetbreads to *le coq au vin*, (boned chicken sautéed in burgundy
wine with mushrooms, artichoke hearts and pearl onions), to even salmon
in a pastry shell with *nantua* sauce. A few entrées that determine the
cost of the complete dinner range up to $15, but the three I've men-
tioned are quite lovely. *Gnocchi*, a form of potato dumpling, is served
with the main courses as a distinctive touch. The limited wine list is

an all-star team of California and imported well-knowns. One exceptional bargain: a very drinkable champagne, Château Madeleine.

Note: The annual Concord Summer Festival, featuring pop, jazz, and classical music, is held in August.

Moderate. Open Tuesday through Saturday 5:30 to 10:30 P.M. Reservations advised. Visa, AX, MC. Wine and beer only. Lot parking. Semi-dressy.

★ ★
L'AUBERGE/French
2826 El Camino Real/Redwood City/Area 2/(415) 365-3735

It **is true** that dining critics proclaim this bastion of French gastronomy as among the finest, but the important fact is that the well-traveled and affluent of the peninsula have favored L'Auberge for over twenty years. One of the basic reasons for this patronage is the owner, Louis Frutschi, whose charm and sincere concern with the well-being of his guests is paramount. Another reason lies in the talents of chef de cuisine Rudolph Camozzi. Backing up Louis' distinct personality is maître d' Eddie Woodford, one of the very few restaurateurs of my acquaintance who dines out frequently.

This trio continues to attend to this French provincial, or country inn, with its comfortable atmosphere, so well that the Mobil Travel Guide awards it three stars, excellent. The professional service, a sterling cellar, the exquisite tableside salad-making and dramatic cooking, plus the fireside bar lounge help retain the guests' loyalty.

Some of my personal favorites here are: Rex sole, petrale sole, poached fish, London broil, the hard-to-find culotte steak and dishes like steak Diane. The crêpes Suzette and soufflés make one feel so very French. You'll like the *bon homie* and Louis' special Gallic touch.

Expensive. Open for lunch weekdays from 11:30 A.M. to 2:30 P.M. Dinner Monday through Saturday from 6 to 10:30 P.M. Reservations advised. All major credit cards. Full bar. Parking lot. Semi-dressy.

★
LA VAL'S GARDENS/Italian
1834 Euclid Avenue/Berkeley/Area 2/(415) 843-5617

Italian eating places are divided into four kinds: a *ristorante* is deluxe; a *trattoria* is simpler and more reasonably priced; a *rosticceria* specializes in a few simple preparations that are snack-shop priced; and an *osteria* is a hole-in-the-wall, the Roman equivalent to a small hot dog stand.

La Val's is a *rosticceria*, but with really pleasant outdoor dining facilities. The pizza, ravioli and lasagna are respectable, hearty and more

often adequate rather than good. Since the house opened in 1956, it's been serving these filling meals at student prices.
Inexpensive. Open seven days. Sunday through Tuesday from 11 A.M. to 11:30 P.M., Wednesday and Thursday from 11 A.M. to midnight. Friday and Saturday from 11 A.M. to 1 A.M. No reservations. Visa, MC. Wine and beer only. Patio. Street parking. Casual.

★ ★
LAZIO'S SEA FOODS/Seafood
Foot of C Street/Eureka/Area 4/(707) 442-2337

What we have here is a no-nonsense seafood place that's been holding forth at dockside since 1944. Owner Tom Lazio puts a glistening array of fresh seafood, that is caught by the restaurant's own boats, right out front for all to see. If you're interested in preparing seafood at home, Lazio's offers a fully stocked retail counter. The glass-walled refrigerator is so large that it takes up one whole wall of this mid-sized dining room. With a name like Lazio, you'd expect some Italian seafood dishes and you'll not be disappointed. Crêpe *cannelloni* is wrapped around Dungeness crab swathed in Mornay sauce and broiled until it begins to bubble. Calamari and cioppino are cooked with a sure Sicilian touch. And if you're lucky enough to be here on a Friday, the bouillabaisse is not to be believed! **Moderate to expensive.** Open seven days. Breakfast from 7 to 11 A.M., Saturday and Sunday till noon. Lunch from 11 A.M. to 3 P.M. Dinner 3 to 9 P.M. No reservations. All major credit cards. Full bar. View of Humboldt Bay. Child's menu. Lot parking. Casual.

★
LE CAMEMBERT/French
200 Shoreline Highway/Mill Valley/Area 3/(415) 383-8000

North from San Francisco on 101, turn off at the Stinson Beach exit and continue — on the road to Mill Valley — until you reach an inspired restaurant which evokes the comfort and charm of a French country château, and which has been overlooked by tourist guides and the print media. Yet here Gilbert Duquesne entertains some of the best palates in the Bay Area, those who seem more than willing to undertake the drive. You find in the dining room, precisely as one might expect in a well-to-do Normandie restaurant, ladderback chairs, fresh flowers, lovely tableware and antiques on little shelves. Tripe may be a bit too ethnic for the average American taste, but they are considered a good test of the kitchen and here they get an "A." The *escalope de veau a crème* is a rich and generous cut of veal with mushroom sauce. The wine list is essentially imports, but the too-short list of Californias includes some fine labels. Prices for wine are reasonable and the Mouton Cadet (by Baron Philippe de Rothschild) is an especially good French bordeaux (have it opened immediately upon being seated, it requires a half hour of breathing time at least). For the gourmet on the go, there's a delicatessen/charcuterie adjacent to the restaurant.

Moderate to expensive. Open seven days. Lunch from 11:30 A.M. to 4 P.M. Dinner from 5 to 10 P.M. Sunday brunch from 10 A.M. to 3 P.M. Reservations advised. Visa, MC, AX. Full bar. Patio. Lot parking. Semi-dressy.

★ ★
LE CANDIDE/French
301 Kearny/San Francisco/Area 2/(415) 981-2213

Neatly ensconced in the heart of the Financial District, this veritable Parisian *brasserie* vividly recalls memories of similar places in the Boulevard St. Michel. Rather than expand their intimate favorite, Le Central, brothers Pierre and Claude Cappelle opened this delightful place in 1979. At both lunch and dinner the smart set of the business community, politicians and some fortunate visitors keep the cash register ringing a merry tune. And rightly so.

Le Candide is quietly elegant – an entire bar top of flawless brass, etched glass windows, cafe curtains, tiled floor, lush green plants, dark wood partitions, marble-topped tables, a mirrored bar and high ceiling. French artists' paintings brighten the walls. Altogether perfect for the authentic Gallic cuisine – lentil salad, cold beef, tongue *ravigotte*, onion tarte, fresh red snapper *meunière, boudin aux pommes*, Manhattan mixed grill, and on. Daily specials are chalked on a board by the bar – such as *boeuf Bourguignon*, salmon steak, perhaps *sauté de veau Marengo*. Many enjoy pâté or escargots in this French charmer.

Expensive. (Lunch in the $25 range – for two, dinner in the $45 range). Open weekdays from 11:30 A.M. to 10 P.M. Reservations advised. Visa, MC, AX, DC. Full bar. City parking lot. Semi-dressy.

In order to obtain the best results from this Guide, be sure to read the French, German, Italian and Oriental menu translators on pages 399 to 404 of this Guide.

★ ★ ★

LE CASTEL/Alsatian
3235 Sacramento Street/San Francisco/Area 2/(415) 921-7115

Le Castel is a relatively new dinner restaurant but the word "new" does not apply in its normal usage, for owner/host Fritz Frankel is a long-time San Franciscan. He is a sincere, professional restaurateur who has long attended the needs of those of impeccable taste and the means with which to satisfy them. Further, Fritz's chef worked with him in another local dining place for some years where mutual respect developed, to the benefit of their guests.

The cuisine of Le Castel is actually Alsatian, one to which few restaurants aspire, and even fewer succeed. Here, you will not find *"nouvelle"* dishes. You will find the classic Alsatian dishes but with a lighter treatment and not an iota of the time-honored ingredients left out. My recent dinners have included perfect Islandic *scampi, terrine,* cream of asparagus soup, *ris de veau Madeira,* with the sweetbreads perfectly trimmed, a wonderful creation involving goose liver upon a bed of cabbage, and desserts that would put pounds on you if I merely mentioned them.

The building is a handsome Victorian with three dining room areas, all yielding the effect of the private home it was for many years. Astute blends of off-white with peach-tone walls, several ceiling-to-wall arches, one above a nostalgic bay window, unusual lighting, fringed lamps, green palms, and bud vases on each table. *Bon appétit.*

Expensive. Open Monday through Saturday. Dinner served from 6 to 10:30 P.M. Reservations essential. All major credit cards. Beer and wine only. Valet parking. Dressy.

★

LE CENTRAL/French/Provincial
453 Bush Street/San Francisco/Area 2/(415) 391-2233

There are brass rails, a copper top bar, fresh flowers and white tiled floors in the high ceilinged room, and the food is what it should be in a brasserie. Hot sausage and potatoes, *pâté de campagne,* steak *boudin noir* and roast chicken are all good. The *cassoulet Central,* for which the restaurant is famous, is a concoction of white beans, sausage and much more which has supposedly cooked in the same pot since the night the restaurant opened (of course that's not *entirely* true, but each new batch does start with a bit of the one before). The place is packed at lunch when people come as much for the sights as for the food. It's noisy. It's crowded. And it's unabashedly fun.

Moderate to expensive. Open Monday through Saturday. Lunch Monday through Friday from 11:45 A.M. to 3:30 P.M. Dinner from 5:30 to 10:30 P.M. Reservations advised. Visa, MC, AX, DC. Full bar. Street parking. Casual.

★
LE CHALET BASQUE/French/Basque
405 North San Pedro Road/San Rafael/Area 3/(415) 479-1070

Basque, a combination of French and Spanish cuisines, should not be downgraded because it is inexpensive and of incredibly gargantuan portions. The Basque art of cooking was developed at a time when peasants were near starvation and cooks had to make the most out of the least at the cheapest prices. As in the history of all cuisines, the humble food was cooked with the resourcefulness and skill to reach epicurean levels of its own, here showing the whim of the chef, the hospitality of the house and the creativity of the entire operation. This is not peasant-Basque, nor is it French, but it manages to hold and sustain a balance (somewhere between bass and treble) that is uniformly good. The complete dinners include the homemade soup of the day, garlic bread, hors d'oeuvres, salad, vegetables, entrée, dessert and coffee. The extensive menu includes a succulent *"Azouria Basque"*: marinated leg of lamb diced with shallots, pimentoes, mushrooms, tomatoes and Madeira wine gravy.

The wine list is exceptional—a fine mix of good imports and some of the better California wines at reasonable prices.

Moderate. Open Tuesday through Sunday. Lunch from 11:30 A.M. to 2 P.M., Sunday brunch from 10:30 A.M. Dinner from 5 to 10 P.M. Reservations advised. Visa, MC. Full bar. Patio. View of forest. Child's menu. Street and lot parking. Casual.

★★
LE CHARDONNAY/Classic French
6534 Washington Street/Yountville/Area 3/(707) 944-2521

Soft lighting and tall French windows enhance the antiques, as well as the silver and cut crystal on the linen tablecloths of this Napa wine country dining place. Classic French cuisine is deftly prepared by chef/partner Bernard Moutal. Some of the menu selections: fresh de-veined prawns sautéed in cognac and butter; poached salmon in red wine butter; filet of beef in crust; duckling in two fashions (one with champagne and grapes); *coquille St. Jacques* with ginger cream; and grenadine of veal with tarragon. Hungry, yet? Besides à la carte ordering, there are three-course dinners. Sweets include a great mousse, sorbets

with fresh fruit (seasonal) and pastries. Bernard's partner, Jacques Mokrani, is also chef/owner of the La Boucane in Napa.
Expensive. Open Tuesday through Sunday. Lunch 11:30 A.M. to 2:30 P.M. Dinner 6 P.M. to 10:30 P.M. Reservations recommended. Visa, MC, AX. Wine and beer only. Lot parking. Casual to semi-dressy.

★ ★ ★
LE CLUB/French
Clay-Jones Apartments/1250 Jones Street/San Francisco/Area 2/(415) 771-5400

Every major city has a soul — a quintessence — of mode and elegance. From that source emanate the vibrations that guide the life-style of other restaurants and the influential, affluential crowd. Le Club now has the distinction of occupying that exalted position — formerly it was Ernie's, once it was The Blue Fox, as in New York it was the "21" and in London, Parkes. That Le Club was the caprice of a wealthy attorney makes it all the more unlikely; that it has been accepted as the new standard of relaxed elegance in its short life is remarkable.

J. Edward Fleishell wanted a restaurant that embodied all the components he felt essential to its objective. It musn't be too large (for that would remove the aura of exclusivity) and it should serve exquisite food with the air of competence that borders on — but never quite becomes — the new snobbism. The result is this tasteful, luxurious establishment where such dishes as saddle of lamb with chestnuts and artichoke hearts and classic *Escoffier* are served to a clientele as interested in the peering as the palate. The wine list is a superb collection that covers the entire range of imports and locals with meticulous care.

Perhaps Mr. Fleishell acquired his professionalism of knowledge as sort of an unpaid legman for his good friend Stan Delaplane, or maybe he's one of those extraordinary perfectionists who is able to accomplish with deceptive ease the success that is so frantically sought by his colleagues. But whatever, however, Le Club has become the swinging social center of a sophisticated city and it looks like it will continue indefinitely.

Expensive. Open Monday through Saturday from 5:30 to 11:30 P.M. Reservations advised. All major credit cards. Full bar. Valet parking. Dressy.

For best results, consult "How to Use This Guide" on page 25.

★
LE CYRANO/French
4134 Geary Boulevard/San Francisco/Area 2/(415) 387-1090

One doesn't usually expect *table d'hôte* dinners in surroundings of such tranquil luxury. Yet Cyrano is statusfying—pristine white napery, gold touches—as well as unreasonably reasonable. The *boeuf en daube Beaune Village* is a rich stew in wine sauce with distinctive herbs and spices. The *coquilles St. Jacques* are ringed, not with that out-of-a-toothpaste-tube potato, but real mashed and creamed potatoes. Hostess Janine Bovigny (her husband is co-owner along with Jacques Gaiddon) closely supervises the small dining room. This is perhaps the best example of an authentic small cafe, direct from Paris—except the prices here are much lower.

Moderate. Open Monday through Saturday from 5 to 10:30 P.M. Reservations advised. No credit cards. Full bar. Street parking. Casual to semi-dressy.

DA ★ ★
THE LEDFORD HOUSE/American/Continental
7051 N. Highway 1/Little River/Area 4/(707) 937-0282

Built in 1862, Ledford House is steeped in that sense of the historic past that is so much the essence of the Mendocino Coast. Harold and Loretta Mathers believe that all food is good if it is prepared with love and care, and their five entrées are veritable gustatory gems, including such seasonal specialties as freshly caught salmon served in thick cuts, accompanied by a béarnaise-type sauce made with fresh sorrel, green peppercorns, herbs and fresh, rich cream. Lamb is presented in a variety of fashions, depending upon the chef's whim—rack of lamb with pastry crust in Madeira sauce, or braised or whatever—and all dinners include homemade brioche, homemade soup, fresh garden salad and a special blend of coffee or tea. Desserts are (what else?) homemade and splendid. There's an ocean view and fireside dining for chilly evenings and a simple wine list that is as carefully prepared as virtually everything else. Little River is near the town of Mendocino and very much worth the detour.

Moderate. Open seven nights 6 to 9 P.M. Saturday and Sunday brunch is served during the summer months from 9 A.M. to 2 P.M. Reservations advised. No credit cards. Wine only. View of ocean. Lot parking. Casual.

Please be sure to consult "Tipping Made Easy" on page 22 of this Guide.

★
LEE'S CANTON/Chinese/American
511 Reeves Avenue/Yuba City/Area 5/(916)673-2970

Just west of Yuba City on Highway 20 is Jerry Lee's restaurant, a place that shouldn't be as good as it is. The menu is too vast (there are over one hundred items), the cuisine is mixed (steak and ham!), and it's in an area not noted for its appreciation of Chinese food. Somehow, though, everything seems to come out OK in this bilious yellow and crimson emporium. I've had brandy fried chicken that was terrific, and except for the blah chow mein, there's little else the matter with this busy place.
Inexpensive. Open Tuesday through Sunday 11 A.M. to 10 P.M. Reservations accepted. No credit cards. Wine and beer only. Lot parking. Casual.

DA ★ ★
LEHR'S GREENHOUSE RESTAURANT & FLORIST/American
740 Sutter Street/San Francisco/Area 2/(415) 474-6464

Why not dine surrounded by a garden in full bloom? This veritable San Francisco institution offers a relaxing and restoring dining experience. You'll be seated in a true arboretum, possibly within a gazebo of white wicker. All is white and green, with many flowers, plants, blooms, even a banana palm or two, towering overhead. Chef Randy Lehr has composed "The Great American Soup and Salad Bar," with seventy offerings. There is also the "Fish and Game" menu to tempt the most diet-conscious. Restaurant manager Jon Lehr commented upon the patrons who have been regulars in past years and continue to enjoy themselves with the entirely new format. When in the San Diego area, consider visiting the impressively spacious sister place, in Mission Valley, run by Dean Lehr, brother of Randy and Jon.
Moderate to expensive. Open seven days. Lunch from noon to 4 P.M. Dinner 5 to 11 P.M. Sunday brunch from 9:30 A.M. to 2:30 P.M. Reservations advised. Visa, MC, AX. Full bar. Street parking. Casual.

★ ★ ★
LE MOUTON NOIR/French
14560 Big Basin Way/Saratoga/Area 2/(408) 867-7017

Perhaps you should not be reading this. Le Mouton Noir, the "Black Sheep," is definitely not for everyone. It's really too good for many diners-out, those who care little for the perfect dining experience and tolerate the canned soups, frozen entrées and a chocolate ice cream sundae.

Don Durante buys only the freshest of seafood, vegetables, prime eastern beef from Wichita, Kansas and milk-fed Provimi veal. He plans his menu selections each season, utilizing California's bounty. The fowl dishes he presents could be duckling, pheasant, pigeon, or quail. Possibly an entrée of two delicate, flavorful quail, each stuffed with a mousse of a spicy veal blend, roasted, then blessed with a noble sauce based upon stock from duck (he prepares his own stocks each morning); ask about this one when you reserve.

Seafood is only hours away and what Don creates with scallops is celestial. One of his favorite fish is salmon, with its several possibilities as to sauces. Another is fresh halibut, with its firm, white flaky-texture meat of unusually delicious flavor. I digress to comment that halibut, around the fourteenth to fifteenth centuries was the favorite fish for holy day meals. Called "halybutte," as in Olde Englishe, "hally" was holy and "butte" meant flat fish.

Chef Don changes about thirty percent of the hors d'oeuvres and salads monthly. He varies his specialties of the day and avoids being bound to a set menu. His concept of appropriate vegetables to accompany certain entrées is to be lauded. How many times have you encountered a frozen peas-and-carrots mixture? I relish indeed the way that he has with one of the most overlooked greens—Swiss chard.

To most of us, desserts are a highpoint, but first, please know that hot, individual baguette-like rolls are brought to your table about every fifteen minutes, politely tendered from a lidded basket by some member of the staff, possibly even Don himself. He likes to view his patrons close up now and then.

Probably the most requested sweet is the French silk pie. You will never, *ever*, taste anything its equal in the way of chocolate desserts. Indescribably luscious. Besides other pastry concoctions, the fresh fruit suggestions are amazing—raspberries and blackberries from New Zealand, stemmed strawberries from Mexico, to be consumed with brown sugar, and *crème fraiche*.

The wine list contains about eighty-five percent California bottlings, many from the most prestigious boutique vineyards. A problem with the smaller, distinctive wineries is that, due to their relatively limited production, they often restrict the number of cases allocated to any one restaurant. If certain issues receive too much favorable publicity, they sell out more rapidly than anticipated and must be deleted from the wine book.

To obtain the best results from this Guide, be sure to consult the map on the various Northern California areas on page 28.

Now, where do all these good things take place? In a veritable country cottage, dating from over a century ago. A simple, clapboard pastel structure that is graced by two most delightful dining rooms – one with a free-standing fireplace. Ambiance is literally flowerful, quiet, and low-key. You dine leisurely and romantically with a perfectly trained staff in attendance.

Expensive. Open Tuesday through Friday for lunch from 11:30 A.M. to 2 P.M. Dinner Tuesday through Saturday from 6 to 10 P.M. Reservations essential. All major credit cards. Wine and beer only. Lot and street parking. Semi-dressy.

★
L'ENTRECÔTE DE PARIS/French
2032 Union Street/San Francisco/Area 2/(415) 931-5006

There are few steakhouses in Paris, the best of which is Les Trois Limousins off the Champs d' Elysee. But even that establishment is not as plush, nor perhaps as self-conscious as L'Entrecôte de Paris. By European standards, Americans consume incredible slabs of beef and portions are large here, as they should be. There are two main courses, steak and a fresh fish of the day. The French serve both with herb butter, and so it is in this restaurant. Salads are fresh – lettuce and walnuts – and the Caesar salad is one of the best in the city. The dessert list would do credit to a more pretentious French restaurant, and though the menu focuses in on specials, I do hope they have the chocolate Grand Marnier mousse on the evening you visit them.

Moderate. Open seven days. Lunch from 11:30 A.M. to 4 P.M., dinner 5:30 to 11 P.M. Saturday and Sunday brunch. Reservations recommended. All major credit cards. Full bar. Patio. Valet parking. Casual to semi-dressy.

★ ★
LE PETIT PIER/French
7252 North Lake Boulevard/Tahoe Vista/Area 6/(916) 546-4464

Owner Jean DuFau, a chef's chef, opened here in 1976, expanding from a nearby location that had proven so successful that he was encouraged, nay, almost forced, to move to satisfy the desires of his social, wealthy clientele. I recommend that, on any trip to Lake Tahoe's North Shore, you set aside one evening to share the dining experience that will be your reward in this so-French lakeside favorite. Ambiance is completely Gallic-romantic with sparkling appointments, unsurpassed views of the lake, fresh flowers and concerned service.

Culinary feats, rarely encountered away from urban areas, can be mussels *marinière*, or smoked fresh king salmon, as appetizers, followed by any of an array of salads, such as Belgian endive with shrimps and spinach *salade*. Chef Jean's entrées range from *pheasant braise Forestière*, duckling with oysters, to baby rack of lamb, and lobster *à l'américaine*. Oh, yes – lamb within a fine pastry shell, prepared for you and your companion is a DuFau specialty.

Expensive. (About $30 per person). Open seven days 6 P.M. to 9 P.M. Reservations essential. Visa, MC, AX, DC. Full bar. Patio. View. Parking lot and valet. Casual-chic.

★
LE POMMIER/French
1015 Gravenstein Highway South/Sebastopol/Area 3/(707) 823-9865

Have you a reservation?" inquired our hostess as the waiting throng threatened to surge us into the dining room. "Yes," I replied, digging my heels into the carpet, but I had forgotten the assumed name I had given (I keep making up improbable names like Homer Illiad as a cover for restaurant reviews). After convincing the lady to give me a peek at the reservations card (not easily done), the error was rectified, we were mollified and seated inside. The vegetables, as you might hope in a town just five miles away from Luther Burbank's birthplace and memorial, were served fresh. Specialities here are veal dishes (sweetbreads, cordon bleu), duck (breast of duck accompanied by cherry sauce), and seafood (salmon with *buerre blanc*). The French cooking was not especially noteworthy, but the dishes were correct and service was swift – if anything, too much so. The artichoke is a g-e-m, not to be missed. Wines are good, but not with the extra spicy salad dressings.

Moderate. Open seven days. Lunch Tuesday through Thursday from 11:30 A.M. to 3 P.M. Dinner Monday through Saturday from 5 to 9 P.M. Reservations accepted. Visa, MC. Wine and beer only. Lot parking. Semi-dressy.

★
LE POT AU FEU/French
1149 El Camino Real/Menlo Park/Area 2/(415) 322-4343

Pot-au-feu is the standby for Parisian housewives, who can turn boiled brisket of beef and vegetables into an incredible meal, served with hot Dijon mustard and gherkins. Naturally, it is one of the specialties at this charming cafe. The specialty the day we were there, *mardi*, was *foie de veau persillade* – calf liver sautéed in butter and garlic and sprinkled with parsley. My companion didn't think she even liked calf liver until she tried a bite of mine. Another specialty is the *saumon en croute au beurre blanc* – salmon in a light, fish-shaped pastry with a light herbed cream sauce.

The atmosphere is reminiscent of the south of France with large umbrellas over some of the tables, kerosene lamps and copperware hanging on the walls. Very provincial, if you catch my drift. The service is prompt and efficient. As this book goes to press, a patio is on the drawing board and should be open for dining soon.

Moderate. Lunch served Tuesday through Friday from 11:30 A.M. to 2 P.M. Dinner Tuesday through Saturday from 6 to 10 P.M. Reservations accepted. Visa, MC. Wine and beer only. Parking lot. Semi-dressy.

★ ★
L'ESCARGOT/French
Mission at 4th/Carmel/Area 1/(408) 624-4914

This authentic, chic and "in" country French restaurant won fame, and the Holiday Magazine Award for fine dining, under the aegis of founder Yvan Nopert back in the late '50s. M. Nopert retired and sold the restaurant to his affable, accomplished *maître d'hotel*, André Francot, in late 1979. André has been with this intimate dining place for over fifteen years, as both a chef and maître d'.

While we're dealing with names, you'll like Paul Poffenberger, manager-host, who is seemingly everywhere at once, suggesting one of the distinctive wines or assisting a waiter. He will detail the limited but more than adequate menu, describing how executive chef Tom Goode creates such temptations as the ambrosial *poulet à la creme avec foie gras et truffes* (chicken in cream with duck liver and truffles), *rôti de veau au poivre vert* (veal in green peppercorns), *selle d'agneau* (twenty-four hours advance), *moules marinières* (seasonal), a delectable *filet de sole*, fragrant with tomatoes, herbs, cream and champagne, and others of comparable stature. Naturally, the house namesake – *escargots à la Bourguignonne* sets the standard for this choice starter. Other beginnings could be the delicate *quenelles de saumon* and *distinctive saumon fumé* (both seasonal). Desserts are, as is everything here, quite special. *Tartes* of the season top the list; I rather admire the housemade almost foamy *mousse au chocolat*.

Setting the scene for this experience are beamed ceilings, sideboards, plate rails, antique copper pans, bursts of fresh flowers, old prints, hangings, ladder-back chairs, dividers and banquette seating. This is France in the Carmel you've yearned about.

Moderate to expensive. Open Monday through Saturday. Dinner from 6 to 9:30 P.M. Reservations necessary. Visa, MC, AX. Wine and beer only. Lot parking. Semi-dressy.

★ ★
L'ETOILE/French
1075 California Street/San Francisco/Area 2/(415) 771-1529

As the French might observe, "The Star *(l'étoile)* is in its correct place — on top." And rightly so, for L'Etoile is on the crest of Nob Hill, San Francisco's repository for several first class dining places. Gracing lower levels of the exceptional Huntington Hotel, L'Etoile is owned and operated by two astute, charming Frenchmen — Claude Rouas and Henri Barberis.

One descends a wide staircase to the cocktail lounge where Peter Mintun plays piano in nostalgic style. On this level, you will be received by either of the owners or the *maître d'hotel*, or all — if your name shines brightly enough. Then, you will be graciously conducted to your booth or banquette in the compellingly attractive room — all latticework and rose-hued with an abundance of fresh flowers, crystal, glittering silver and jewels.

So much has been written about the truly fine cuisine and sterling cellar that I'll dispense with details other than to state that every effort of kitchen and dining room staff will be made to persuade you to recall your dining experience here.

Expensive. Open Monday through Saturday from 6 to 10:30 P.M. Reservations essential. All major credit cards. Pianist. Full bar. Valet parking. Dressy.

★ ★
LE VIRAGE/French
2211 North Main Street/Walnut Creek/Area 2/(415) 933-8484

In this completely captivating Gallic bistro, you will instantly feel that your party has been accorded absolutely the very best table in the house and that you are privileged guests. Owner/host Lolek Jasinski is the resident genius responsible for this particularly gratifying reception and for the many polished facets, from the staff's professionalism to the choice cuisine and generous pourings at the intimate bar.

The waiters observe team service, a cooperative effort that too few reataurants encourage. The current chef, Gary Boyer, is a classicist but enjoys his imaginative touch. You could try the crêpes rich with seafood; *ris de veau sauté* (perfectly trimmed), the day's catch (invariably the most fresh) and, perhaps, lead off with escargots. Lolek is a true master of

the flames, flambéeing a number of gourmet dishes tableside. You wouldn't believe what he does with desserts, even tossing glasses and objects over his shoulder, from the rear! Le Virage translates to "The corner," where you'll find it, a block from BART.
Expensive. Open Tuesday through Sunday. Lunch Tuesday through Friday from 11:30 A.M. to 2:30 P.M. Dinner from 5:30 to 10:30 P.M. Reservations advised. All major credit cards. Strolling musicians. Full bar. Lot and valet parking. Semi-dressy to dressy.

★
LIAISON/Italian/French
4101 El Camino Way/Palo Alto/Area 2/(415) 494-8848

The "liaison" here is one of Italian and French cooking and the menu jumps back and forth across the border like a smuggler with one hand on linguine *con Vongole*, fettuccine Alfredo and roast saddle of lamb Florentine, and the other hand on medallions of beef with sauce béarnaise, sole sauté *meunière* and veal sweetbreads sauté "Liaison." The ambitious menu offers some fine appetizers such as the Dungeness crab cocktail and prawns Bordelaise. Try a soufflé for dessert.
Moderate. Open seven days. Lunch served weekdays from 11:30 A.M. to 2:30 P.M. Dinner from 5:30 to 10:30 P.M., Sunday from 4:30 to 10 P.M. Reservations essential. Visa, MC, AX. Full bar. Parking lot. Semi-dressy.

★
LICHEE GARDEN/Chinese/Cantonese
1416 Powell Street/San Francisco/Area 2/(415) 397-2290

This is a large, new-style Cantonese restaurant and chef Chuck Siu probably never heard of chow mein. "Cold chicken" is typical of the Chinese inclination to understate. It is actually shredded crisp chicken mixed with crunchy dried jellyfish in a dressing of sesame oil and rice vinegar. "Boned duck webs stir-fried with snowpeas" sounds dreadful—but isn't. Minced squab in a firm lettuce leaf is eaten like a taco, and their specialty—pork spare ribs—are deep fried, not the sweet and sour-sauced variety. My favorite dish is walnut beef. However, there are some real language problems and you might need manager Myron Lui to help you decipher the menu. There are also long lines at dinner, but they move along pretty well. Chinese beer is excellent.
Moderate. Open daily from 11:30 A.M. to 9:30 P.M. Wine and beer only. Reservations advised. Visa, MC. Street parking and lots nearby. Semi-dressy.

★ ★
LIPIZZANER/Viennese/French
2223 Union Street/San Francisco/Area 2/(415) 921-3424

When Lipizzaner opened in 1983, I was interested to find out if they could capture the elusive and subtle wonders of Viennese cooking. Indeed, this little restaurant, named after the famous horses of Europe, touches all bases, managing the Viennese fare with French cooking—a seemingly perfect blend that captures the essence of both. Thus lobster Parisienne is balanced by loin of veal with fresh goose liver, and there are strudels and *nuss palatschinken* (warm Viennese crêpes with chocolate and hazelnuts) and, perhaps best of all on the changing menu, wienerschnitzel, the mellow brown breading made from fresh bread crumbs. Holidays bring out the best of chef-owner Josef Roettig's cooking with fixed menus usually under $30. Prices generally range from $25 to $40 for dinner, and reservations—there are only thirty-four seats—are essential.

Expensive. Dinner served Tuesday through Saturday from 5:30 to 10 P.M. Reservations necessary. Visa, MC. Wine and beer only. Street parking. Casual to semi-dressy.

★ ★
LITTLE JOE'S—BABY JOE'S/Italian
523 Broadway/San Francisco/Area 2/(415) 433-4343

Since Frank Montarello took over in 1971, the cuisine has become peasant-perfect. The veal parmigiana is made with real veal (much "veal" is pork soaked in milk) in a fantastic *sugo di carne* sauce (which translates to a sort of meat "gravy sauce" that is virtually indescribable). The minestrone is savory on a cold day and the calamari (squid) served on Friday and Saturday only is the best in town. There's wine and beer only, and not much selection, but don't nitpick.

Inexpensive. Open Monday through Saturday from 11 A.M. to 10 P.M. No reservations. No credit cards. Singing cooks. Wine and beer only. Garage and street parking. Casual.

In order to obtain the best results from this Guide, be sure to read the French, German, Italian and Oriental menu translators on pages 399 to 404 of this Guide.

★
LIVERPOOL LIL'S/Continental/Saloon
2942 Lyon Street/San Francisco/Area 2/(415) 921-6664

While the food is fine in this little pub, its location near the Golden Gate Bridge makes it a favorite meeting place for locals to meet for a pint after football games or for commuters to down a couple martinis before continuing on home. "Manchester Wellington" is the specialty—ground round steak that's wrapped in ham and baked in a pastry crust—but I like the third-of-a-pound hamburgers with sautéed onion and cheese on an egg roll. Altogether, this good-natured pub is an ideal place for people who get wound up in the daytime to unwind at night, and it's a damn good food bargain for everyone. An ample Sunday brunch deserves more recognition than it gets.

Inexpensive. Open seven days. Monday through Friday 4 P.M. to 2 A.M. Saturday and Sunday 10 to 4 P.M. Reservations advised. Visa, MC. Full bar. Street parking. Casual.

★
LoCOCO'S/Italian/Sicilian
4270 Piedmont Avenue/Oakland/Area 2/(415) 652-6222
631 Del Granada Road/Terra Linda/Area 3/(415) 472-3323
1400 Shattuck Avenue/Berkeley/Area 2/(415) 843-3745

Another only-in-America story: two brothers, Nicola and Filippo LoCoco, arrived from Sicily in 1970 with $20 between them. They took jobs as busboys and a few years later scraped together enough to rent a storefront. Pizza is delectable here in all its guises, the crust is sheer joy. It's a very casual family-run restaurant these days, somewhat boisterous but a lot of fun. Everything has a Sicilian accent—including the family—and there are low prices for food and wine.

Moderate. Open Sunday and Tuesday through Thursday from 4 to 10 P.M., Friday and Saturday to 11 P.M. Hours may vary. Reservations for six or more only. No credit cards. Wine and beer only. Child's menu. Street parking. Casual.

For best results, consult "How to Use This Guide" on page 25.

★ ★
L'OLIVIER/French
465 Davis Court/San Francisco/Area 2/(415) 981-7824

If you are seeking an authentic French provincial restaurant that presents classic (not *"nouvelle"*) cuisine in an ambiance neither too formal nor too rustic, it will likely be found at L'Olivier.

Owner/host Christian Francoz, the very essence of genteel urbanity, has created a quietly charming, low-key favorite that personifies exactly what travelers hope to discover in France. Of course, the setting—in a bricked courtyard within the very heart of the Golden Gateway apartment complex—differs vastly, but the adroit realization suspends disbelief and, there you are, studying *la carte*, considering *les hors d'oeuvres froid et chaud* as you nibble on a sliced baguette and sip, perhaps, a *domaine "les roures"* from the *Côtes du Rhone*.

Gaze about before ordering—two dining rooms, the outer "Greenhouse" rather like an outdoor sidewalk cafe, but glassed-in, and the main room which is high-ceilinged with chandeliers of softly lit globes, walls of flower-patterned paper, antique sideboards, dark wood wall panels behind banquettes, mirrors and prints, tables double-clothed to the floor, fresh flowered vases, tapestries, brass-based candle lamps, and off-white, curtained twelve-foot windows fronting on the other dining room.

While mere numbers do not always mean a great deal where a restaurant is involved, here they do have meaning, for each of the individual dishes represents skillful handling and care. Eleven cold and hot appetizers head the menu, with four soups, five salads, eighteen entrées and nine desserts. My personal recommendations: *mousse froide de poisson panachee, huitres chaudes aux herbes de Provence, filet de lapin en Chartreuse, ris de veau braises en cocotte* (braised sweetbreads), and *carré d'agneau aux herbs seches* (rack of lamb with herbs). Service is exactly correct, by tuxedoed, very professional waiters who are alert to your every whim. M. Francoz, when not receiving his patrons, surveys all that transpires, occasionally pausing at a table to exchange a pleasantry. **Moderate.** Open Monday through Saturday. Lunch served Monday through Friday from 11:30 A.M. to 4 P.M. Dinner from 6 to 10 P.M. Reservations advised. All major credit cards. Full bar. Valet parking for dinner. Semi-dressy.

★ ★
LOS ROBLES LODGE/Continental
Highway 101 at Steele Lane/Santa Rosa/Area 3/(707) 545-6330

For years one of Sonoma County's most highly regarded restaurants, Los Robles Lodge reflects owner/host Claus Neumann's attention to detail. Mr. Neumann has created a comfortable, elegant setting that features a crimson carpet, deep-red flocked wallpaper, soft lighting, and sinfully cozy chairs. One wall is devoted to large foliage-framed windows. The restaurant's menu, developed by Mr. Neumann and executive chef Russell Heald, describes a tantalizing variety of selections, with seafood (including three different prawn and two salmon dishes) and beef (including filet of beef teriyaki, and châteaubriand for two) dominating. Popular chicken, veal, and lamb preparations are also offered, as well as a vegetarian entrée. There is a light entrée, and a bargain hunter's daily special. Some choice dishes are also available in the coffee shop, which shares the kitchen.

The wine list, carrying forty-eight Sonoma County labels (includng Mr. Neumann's "Claus Vineyards" bottlings), is one of the most extensive in the county. Service is cordial and thoroughly professional. **Moderate.** Open seven days. Lunch Monday through Saturday from 11 A.M. to 2:30 P.M. Dinner Monday through Thursday from 5 to 10 P.M., Friday and Saturday from 5 to 11 P.M., Sunday from 4:30 to 9:30 P.M. Sunday brunch from 10 A.M. to 2 P.M. Reservations advised. All major cards. Dancing in the cocktail lounge Wednesday through Saturday. Full bar. Parking in adjacent lot. Casual to semi-dressy.

★
LUNG FUNG/Chinese/Mandarin
3038 Clement Street/San Francisco/Area 2/(415) 668-3038

Pot stickers," those mincemeat dumplings wrapped in noodles, are authentic here, guaranteed to chase the chill on a cold day. This Richmond district restaurant attracts the dinner crowd with Mongolian lamb and *mussee* pork, a favorite Chinese dish. Lung Fung is not worth making a special trip for, but if you're near, it's worth visiting. **Moderate.** Open seven days. Monday through Saturday from 11:30 A.M. to 10 P.M., Sunday from 4 to 10 P.M. Reservations advised for parties of five or more. All major credit cards. Wine and beer only. Street parking. Casual.

★ ★
LUZERN RESTAURANT/French/Swiss
1431 Noriega Street/San Francisco/Area 2/(415) 664-2353

Many travelers, when in a large city, seek the smaller neighborhood restaurants, often finding finer food than in most of the downtown dining places. In San Francisco, probably the finest place of this type serving French cuisine is Luzern, a local favorite that you will probably talk about to your haute-y friends.

Owner/chef Rolf Tschudi and his wife/hostess, Louise, are the dedicated proprietors of this charmer, named for their favorite city—Lucerne to us outlanders. A commanding photo-mural of the Kappell tower bridge in that lovely city occupies one wall of the neatly appointed, intimate (twelve tables) Luzern. The Tschudis are Swiss-born and the menu's two fondues (à la carte) reflect that gesture to their heritage. Rolf was personal chef, at one time, to Laurence Rockefeller—I happen to know, but he modestly refrains from making a point of that in conversation or on his menu. The superb dinners in this appealing place speak for his talents.

If you prefer to savor an hors d'oeuvre before your multicourse meal, the *pâté maison* and *escargots de Bourgogne* are each an example in perfection. Leek and potato is usually the soup and as good as is served anywhere. The simple *salade* follows. Then your entrée: rack of lamb, *saumon poche nantua* (the sauce is incredible), *l'escalope de veau Murat*, with artichoke and mushrooms (my personal choice), or *escalope de veau aux morilles*, the veal scallops enhanced with the delicate mushroom sauce. *Coquilles St. Jacques*, a traditional seashell-encased dish of crab, scallops and shrimp, finds new meaning here. Consider, also a true German specialty, the only one on the menu—wienerschnitzel; breaded veal cutlets were never like this.

Your dessert can be ice cream or sherbet, if you like, but I must strongly recommend that you take the *crème caramel*, a sweet that sets the standard for this often-avoided temptation. Of course, if you wish, there are also *meringue glacée* and *mousse au chocolat*, plus three cheeses. But for your first time . . . order that *crème caramel*. You'll never order it again anywhere else.

The wine list is not long but there are some Swiss bottlings that may vary, depending on importers. Some admire *Fendant de Valais*, occasionally there is *Vaudois Dézalley* (not always listed) and *Chateau de Mont* is crisp and clean on the palate. When you reserve, ask for driving directions. An easy trip.

Moderate. Open Wednesday through Saturday from 5 to 10 P.M., Sunday from 4 to 9 P.M. Reservations advised. No credit cards. Wine and beer only. Easy street parking. Casual.

DA ★ ★
MacARTHUR PARK/American
607 Front Street/San Francisco/Area 2/(415) 398-5700
27 University Avenue/Palo Alto/Area 2/(415) 321-9990

This beautiful park/restaurant was composed rather than constructed; its poetry, which took a little while to understand, has finally touched the hearts and minds (and palates) of San Franciscans, usually slow to accept a new concept. Wherever you sit in MacArthur Park, you're looking at water, trees, flowers, birds, and—most colorful of all—bouquets of people.

Weekdays at cocktail hour, guests may sit outside in a heated sidewalk café, nibbling on imaginative hors d'oeuvres, sipping cocktails.

The food (yes, there is food here) ranges from picnic style (peasant lunch: soup, loaf of bread, cheese, fresh fruit and wine) to a varied assortment of salads (very fresh fruit with yogurt) to barbecued ribs (the specialty), hot sandwiches, cold sandwiches, casseroles, exciting ratatouille, teriyaki steak, steak tartare, omelettes, fresh juices, pot teas, exotic coffees and sumptuous desserts. In addition, MacArthur Park has the broadest array of brunch dishes in the city. Just so you know that it's not all poetry and date-nut sandwiches, the steaks and duck and fresh lobster and trout favorites are for the less aesthetic set. The wine list is the result of a lot of tastings and discussions and is subject to change, as the wineries themselves are subject to change.

Moderate. Open seven days. Lunch Monday through Friday from 11:30 A.M. to 2:30 P.M. Dinner daily from 5 to 10:30 P.M. Sunday brunch from 9:30 A.M. at Palo Alto. Reservations advised. Visa, MC, AX. Entertainment at Palo Alto. Full bar. Patio. Valet parking in evening. Casual.

★
MAC'S OF LOS ALTOS/American
325 Main Street/Los Altos/Area 2/(415) 941-0234

Mac's is the hopping social center for the over 50s set of Los Altos locals. I'm not quite sure what the attraction is that pulls in the throngs nightly, but the feel is definitely that of a social event. Diners and staff seem to know each other, and if you're an outsider, as I was, a couple rounds at the piano bar can pull you into all the merry-making. The crowded bar lounge is alive with casually dressed patrons. Dark woods, paintings and the piano give this a club-like feeling. The second and larger room is solid with comfortable upholstered booths and more formally attired guests.

Only complete dinners are served, including soup or salad, potatoes, fresh vegetables and desserts. Service can be very personal — you may hear, "Mrs. Miller, we have your fresh scallops tonight." But even if you aren't a regular, the waitresses try to make suggestions and describe dishes to you. The shrimp sauté was tender, well-seasoned prawns in a garlicky lemon sauce. The broiled red snapper Vera Cruz was not quite as well done — I could barely find the taste of snapper in the overpowering sauce. Owners Ron and Dianne Shanholtz are good people who have been well received by the surrounding population. It's an enjoyable place to stop in and feel like part of the gang.
Moderate to expensive. Open Monday through Saturday. Lunch from 11:30 A.M. to 3 P.M. Dinner from 5:30 to 10:30 P.M. Reservations accepted. Visa, MC, AX, DC. Piano bar. Full bar. Lot and street parking. Casual.

★
MADDALENA'S/Continental
544 Emerson Street/Palo Alto/Area 2/(415) 326-6082

Freddie Maddalena is a fine restaurateur who must also be an incurable romantic. You'd have to be to create a restaurant this warm, intimate, and well . . . romantic. Teal blue walls are bordered with dark wood beams. Long stemmed roses grace each white-naped table.

Dover sole *meunière* is sautéed with butter in a wine, lemon, and parsley sauce. The veal *piccata* was an impeccable dish served with a tart lemon and butter sauce. The entrées are well prepared, and tuxedoed waiters know, as they should in any romantic restaurant, the art of subdued, unobtrusive serving.

Moderate to expensive. Open Monday through Saturday. Lunch served from 11:30 A.M. to 2 P.M. Dinner from 6 to 10 P.M. Reservations essential. Visa, MC, AX, CB. Entertainment and dancing. Full bar. Parking lot. Semi-dressy to dressy.

MADONNA INN/Continental/Seafood
100 Madonna Road/San Luis Obispo/Area 1/(805) 543-3000

Probably everyone knows the story of Alex and Phyllis Madonna's rambling Inn, where no two rooms are decorated alike and all have the interior appointments of a Caliph's dream (or nightmare, depending on which room you get). It would be too much to expect the food here to be as imaginative as the lodgings—it isn't—with a mundane menu that is tourist-French and coffeeshop-Danish. An exception is the abalone. Delivered fresh from nearby waters, the delicacy is served tender, light and fresh. Incidentally, this is a fine place to stay when visiting San Simeon. The opulence of the rooms at the Inn creates less of a culture shock than an average hotel-motel as you re-enter the real world after spending a couple of hours in Hearst's.
Moderate to expensive. Coffee shop open seven days from 7 A.M. to 10 P.M., dining room open seven days from 5:30 to 10 P.M. Reservations advised. No credit cards. Entertainment. Dancing. Full bar. Lot parking. Casual to semi-dressy.

★★
MADRONA MANOR/California/Continental
1001 Westside Road/Healdsburg/Area 3/(707) 433-4231

John Paxton, banker and politician in San Francisco, built Madrona Knoll as a summer retreat in 1881, but it wasn't long before the Paxton family made it their permanent home. One hundred years later John and Carol Muir acquired the property and spent several years working hard, but with great love for the old Victorian retreat, to restore its dignity and elegance. Now there are sixteen rooms at the inn, and, surprisingly, one of the fine restaurants of the area.

On 5 January 1985, the year this review was written, the fixed menu consisted of: puff pastry tart with carmelized onions, sundried tomatoes, olives and cheese; barley soup with sausages, spinach and ham; mesquite grilled duck breast on a wild rice waffle with cassis sauce and red currants—served with broccoli and hollandaise; salad of young greens and cheese; chocolate decadence and coffee for $32.50 per person. Todd Muir came home after a string at Chez Panisse (has everyone in the world worked there?) and the menus come as close to a definition of California cuisine as we're likely to see. Todd's sister Denise Fitzgerald is the pastry chef.

Madrona Manor is one of the treasures of the Russian River area and not to be missed if you're wine-touring.
Expensive. Open seven nights from 6 to 9 P.M. Sunday brunch 10:30 A.M. to 2 P.M. Reservations advised. Visa, MC, AX. Wine and beer only. Patio. View. Lot parking. Semi-dressy.

★
MAI'S VIETNAMESE RESTAURANT/Vietnamese
316 Clement Street/San Francisco/Area 2/(415) 221-3046
1360 9th Avenue/San Francisco/Area 2/(415) 753-6863
1838 Union Street/San Francisco/Area 2/(415) 921-2861

The tremendous success of Mai's on Clement Street was followed by progressively more upscale locations, with the last on Union Street quite elegant with dark wood paneling, white linens and red roses. The "imperial rolls" are lighter than eggrolls in a Chinese restaurant, and stuffed with a delicate combination of flavors. Hanoi-style soup is a meal in itself with tender morsels of beef and noodles in a broth with a light touch of cilantro, garlic, lemon and scallions. Sautéed shrimp balls, coconut chicken and spicy prawns are among the favorites. Freshly squeezed lemonade and the aromatic Vietnamese coffee are refreshing touches, although there is a full bar serving standard drinks as well. **Moderate.** Open seven days 11 A.M. to 11 P.M.; closed Sunday for lunch. Reservations advised. Visa, MC, AX. Full bar. Street parking. Casual.

MALEVILLE'S CORAL REEF/Chinese/American
2795 Fulton Avenue/Sacramento/Area 3/(916) 483-5552

Since 1948, the Maleville brothers' founding year, the Coral Reef has burgeoned from the initial one-dining-room operation into a rambling village of inviting rooms that can easily accomodate over four hundred diners. To Sacramentans, the tiki-front mask signifies a happy place, with memories of good food and drink, anniversaries, receptions, business functions and all the good times humans share and employ to highlight the passing years.

The Coral Reef is currently run by Mr. and Mrs. Anello, who have taken over from the Malevilles. Nothing has been changed, and the new owners follow in the decades-old tradition of their predecessors.

The Coral Reef might be the movie-goer's concept of a discriminating beachcomber's abode in Pago Pago or Tahiti. Weathered dock piles loom at the entry to the airy Marlin Room. Among the many nautical charms abundant here are ships' wheels, lanterns, life rings and binnacles. Each room has a South Seas theme, some use giant shells, some nets, some with ship models, others with impressive leafy plants. Even an outrigger. No off-notes in this tropical symphony—all native woods and fibres.

You'll find it easy to order from the Chinese and American menus. Fried prawns, barbecued spareribs, shrimp curry and chicken foo yung are some of the Cantonese suggestions. There is a moderately tabbed Chinese gourmet dinner, although how gourmet-ish it is might be hard to decide. American meals offer succulent chicken, steaks and more. **Moderate to expensive.** Open seven days. Dinner Monday through Thursday from 5 to 11 P.M. Friday and Saturday from 5 to 11:30 P.M., Sunday from 3 to 10:15 P.M. Reservations advised. Visa, MC, AX, DC. Full bar. Lot parking. Casual.

★
MAMA'S OF SAN FRANCISCO/American
(Locations in Palo Alto, San Francisco, San Jose, and San Mateo. See phone book for listings.)

Frances and Michael Sanchez are the mama and papa of these fine American cafes that serve a mixed cuisine (mostly American) to shoppers and busy people. They started ten years ago at Macy's on Union Square, and they have been adding new locations ever since. Breakfasts are especially good, although there is an avid following for dinner as well. Incidentally, chain restaurants do not always mean diluted quality and are not necessarily an American concept. A friend of Alexander Dumas, named Duval, opened a restaurant called Bouillons in the mid-nineteenth century. He served simple fare on marble tables with chairs that were deliberately uncomfortable so that patrons would not tie up the tables for a long time, as in the coffeehouses of that era. The operation was such a success that he opened more of them; Duval was perhaps the first restaurant entrepreneur in gastronomic history. **Moderate.** Open seven days. Breakfast, lunch and dinner served all day. Sunday brunch from 9 A.M. to 5 P.M. (Hours may vary at different locations.) Reservations accepted. No credit cards. Full bar. Child's menu. Garage parking. Casual to semi-dressy.

DA ★ ★
MAMOUNIA/Moroccan
4411 Balboa Street/San Francisco/Area 2/(415) 752-6566
200 Merrydale Drive/San Rafael/Area 3/(415) 472-1372

I **first** heard about Mamounia from an Oriental carpet salesman who had taken his wares to my home. "Marrakech—fooey, strictly for the tourists, you know what I mean?" He leaned his massive body back amongst the pillows of the couch, closed his eyes and smacked his lips in reflection: "But Mamounia . . . ah, there's cooking just like in Beirut."

His geography might have been wrong, but his taste buds were functioning perfectly, as I found out after a visit the very next evening to this ornamented but untheatrical restaurant with banquettes. There are similarities with Marrakech, understandable when you realize the master chef used to work there, but the important difference is in the quality— not the serving—of the food. There are towels and frequent laving of hands in rose water by an attentive staff. The food—spicy lemon soup, exotic salad, pastry stuffed with chicken and nuts and honey and cinnamon and hard-boiled eggs and lamb with honey and almonds is simply ambrosial. Of course, one eats with the fingers here (your own), and the essence of the total experience adds up to two stars . . . pushing for three.

Moderate to expensive. Open seven days from 6 to 10 P.M. Reservations essential. Visa, MC. Wine and beer only. Street parking. Casual to semi-dressy.

DA ★ ★ ★
THE MANDARIN/Chinese/Mandarin
Ghirardelli Square/San Francisco/Area 2/(415) 673-8812

Cecelia Chiang recalls: "There were no red eggs sent out on my first birthday. A child is one year old at birth in China. If a boy, his birth is an occasion for celebration, a feast, with presents of eggs dyed red sent out by the happy parents. Since I was a girl, with twelve brothers and sisters, rejoicing at my birth was naturally subdued."

Mrs. Chiang solved her identity crisis by becoming resourceful, shrewd and an expert in the dishes of northern China. She opened her first restaurant in Tokyo after World War II simply because she could not find there the good food she had become accustomed to as the daughter of a family of great wealth. In 1961, she opened the Mandarin on Polk Street in San Francisco, where it enjoyed such success that she moved it to Ghirardelli Square seven years later.

Designed by the diminutive, yet tough, Chinese proprietress, the interior is a fascinating re-creation of her palatial home and the great homes of pre-revolutionary China when subtlety was the essence of design. Madame Chiang feels that in most Chinese restaurants, decor is "too exaggerated."

The spacious dining areas are partitioned by carved screens from China, not unlike an Oriental temple. The rich interior is accented by quarry floor tiles and a burnt-orange carpet with flashes of red. Sitting beneath the gigantic rafters of this vast space, one can feel he is in the home of an ancient Mandarin; even the luxurious chairs were custom designed. There is a lovely view of the Bay on one side, and the rest of Ghirardelli Square on the other.

The Mandarin achieved early attention as one of the first restaurants in America to serve the dramatic dishes of Szechwan and northern China: smoked tea duck, beggar's chicken (a whole chicken baked in clay), prawns a la Szechwan and Mongolian fire pot, a charcoal-burning chafing pot containing highly flavored chicken broth with thinly sliced meats, seafood and vegetables. The focal point of the restaurant is the Mongolian fire pit, where up to a dozen diners can grill their own food or have the chef do it for them.

Madame Chiang spent much of her youth in Peking and learned to prepare the Peking duck as art form from those restaurants that specialized only in duck, many of them run by Mohammedans who cannot eat pork. As in China, as soon as a seven-pound duck is killed, a bamboo tube is inserted just below the neck and the skin gradually separates from the flesh as air is blown into the tube. The neck and vent are tied to prevent the collapse of the skin and the duck is hung to dry for more than twenty-four hours. It's then coated with honey — no seasoning — and hung in a hot oven for an hour to allow the fat to drip down.

The duck is carved in front of the guests: first the skin, then the meat. The skin, regarded as the choicest part, is a delicate, deep translucent brown, crisp and luscious. The waiter next spreads *hoisin* (duck sauce) on the *pao-ping* (crêpe-like Peking pancakes), adds scallions, puts the duck meat on top and rolls up the pancake to be eaten with the hands. It's ambrosial.

One aside: I learned, to my astonishment, that *jujubes*, those tough-as-taffy (and hard-as-rock) little candies I used to eat at matinees, actually came from China where they are little, red dessert dates.

Madame Chiang conducts cooking classes in the restaurant whenever she can schedule them; you'll have to call for latest information. The Mandarin is an epicurean and visual treasure of San Francisco, a "must visit" for out-of-towners.

Moderate to expensive. Open seven days. Lunch from noon to 4 P.M.
Dinner from 4 to 11 P.M. Reservations advised. All major credit cards.
Full bar. Garage parking. Casual.

★ ★
MANDARIN DELIGHT/Chinese
941 Kearny Street/San Francisco/Area 2/(415) 362-8299

The funny thing about most Chinese restaurants is that there's often
no difference in appearance between a great one and a mediocre
one. They can easily share the same red banquets, the same Texas-
Ware bowls and plates, the same stoical service. Yet one will serve the
greatest *kung pao* shrimp you've ever tasted, while the other will leave
you gasping for Pepto-Bismol. As James Clavell wrote so often in *Noble
House*, it's all just "joss."

Mandarin Delight looks like any of a hundred Chinese restaurants.
The menu is posted in the window. The tables are formica. The overhead lights are too bright. The only difference is, the food is among
the best Oriental cuisine in San Francisco, a town that's no slouch when
it comes to Chinese cooking.

One sure test of a Chinese restaurant is the potsticker hors d'oeuvre.
The potstickers at Mandarin Delight pass with flying colors—the pastry skin is firm without being tough, the pork filling is neither too salty
nor too bland, and the grease level is eminently well controlled. Right
next to the potstickers on the menu are a type of steamed *dim sum*
called *shao lung pao*. They arrived still in their steamer basket, all pink
and plump and delicious. They also arrived early in the course of the
meal (the random arrival of appetizers, I have found, is a problem at
many Chinese restaurants).

The best way to eat at Mandarin Delight is to order too much. That
way you'll be able to take home some of those coy little white containers
which look so good when you wake up hungry at two in the morning.
Imagine opening your refrigerator and finding things as good as fish flavor
eggplant (one of the best eggplant dishes I've ever had the pleasure
of devouring). Or perhaps "ants climbing a tree" (actually chopped pork
on crystalline rice noodles, rolled in lettuce leaves), shrimp with pork
kidneys, pan-fried noodles Shanghai style, or egg white blended with
chicken. With the exception of a disappointing order of green onion
pancakes, I haven't found a failed dish at Mandarin Delight. For a change,
I even like their sweet rice dumpling with black sesame seed paste,
except that it does get stuck in my teeth.

Moderate. Open Friday through Wednesday. Lunch served weekdays (except Thursdays) from 11:30 A.M. to 3 P.M. Dinner served 3 to 10 P.M. Reservations accepted. Visa, MC, AX. Entertainment. Wine and beer only. Street parking. Casual.

DA★
MANKA'S CZECH RESTAURANT/Czech/European
30 Callender Way (at Argyle)/Inverness/Area 3/(415) 669-1034

Inverness is a Finian's Rainbow sort of place, so far removed from ordinary cares it can make you a bit spacey. All this tranquility in an honest-to-God Czech country inn perched on the hillside overlooking Tomales Bay is dreamlike. Since 1956, the Prokupek family has been warmly welcoming guests for dinner. If you desire, comfortable overnight accomodations are often available, but be sure to reserve. Dinners are as exciting as a new stamp on your passport. Rather than a single appetizer, Manka's offers a veritable cornucopia of Scandanavian cheeses, herring, and sausages, plus cold cuts and crisps. A variety of country-style soups threaten to dispose of what's left of your appetite. The veal dishes are especially good; either *smetana* in sour cream and lemon, "paprika," or Viennese schnitzel. Czechoslovakia has a national penchant for duckling, and the caraway-sauced version is far better than the sweet sauce usually ladled on in America. Local oysters are baked on the half shell with anchovy butter, unusual and remarkable for its freshness of flavor. Dessert is selected from a cart of Czech pastries and are a fitting ending.

Moderate. Open Friday through Sunday in winter, Thursday through Monday in summer. Breakfast 8:30 to 11 A.M. Dinner from 6 to 8:30 P.M. Sunday brunch from 8:30 to 11 A.M. Reservations essential. Visa, MC, AX. Wine and beer only. View. Lot and street parking. Semi-dressy.

In order to obtain the best results from this Guide, be sure to read the French, German, Italian and Oriental menu translators on pages 399 to 404 of this Guide.

★ ★
MARCELLO'S/Northern Italian
1 Orinda Way/Orinda/Area 2/(415) 254-5433

Owner/chef Pierangelo Bigotti has brough his own style of northern Italian cuisine to Orinda, where it flourishes in a plain, old storefront in an inelegant part of town. He considers his *vitello* (veal) *all agro di limóne*, the specialty of the house, and it is special, but I prefer the chicken Toscana—perfectly herbed—with zucchini, mushrooms and sliced onions. If Marcello's were down the coast with waiters instead of waitresses and some polished paneling, it could easily become one of San Francisco's little favorites. Here, the artistry is not as appreciated but the tab is lower, and business is good.
Moderate. Lunch Tuesday through Friday from 11:30 A.M. to 2:30 P.M. Dinner nightly from 5 to 10:30 P.M., Sunday to 9 P.M. Reservations advised. Visa, MC, AX, DC. Full bar. Lot parking. Casual to semi-dressy.

★ ★
MARK THOMAS' OUTRIGGER/Polynesian
700 Cannery Row/Monterey/Area 1/(408) 372-8540

Since 1955, guests have enjoyed not only the excellent steaks, fresh seafood, Polynesian specialties and continental dishes, as well as numerous, exotic, tropically inspired beverages, but also the panoramic views of Monterey Bay, its marine and bird life and water traffic. Built out over the bay on sturdy pilings, at Cannery Row's water's edge, The Outrigger has consistently improved with age.

At lunch you may select from the tempting buffet or be served at your window-side table. The array of huge sandwiches and salads includes: a Reuben, roast beef on choice of English muffin or bun, burgers, and the "Back-to-Nature" (my favorite) made with avocado, tomato, cream cheese, bean sprouts, mushrooms and walnuts, on whole grain bread. I go very tourist here, preceding my meal, day or night, with either a piña colada, chi chi or Cuba libre. Oysters & Company, a New York-style oyster bar, separately ensconced within the spacious building, is a happy plus. In this airy dining room, oysters (Eastern, Blue Points and local pearl-makers) are prepared just about any way you prefer.

Dinners are romantic; with the sunset, lights appear all around the bay and on maritime crafts. Ask about the fresh local seafood which is always a discerning selection. The wine list includes a choice of bottlings from area vineyards. Consider the Durneys and Lohrs.

Moderate to expensive. Open seven days. Lunch from 11:30 A.M. to 2:30 P.M. Dinner from 5 to 10:30 P.M. weekdays, 4 to 11 P.M. weekends. Sunday brunch from 10:30 A.M. to 2:30 P.M. Reservations advised. Visa, MC, AX, DC. Entertainment. Dancing. Full bar. View. Child's menu. Parking lot. Casual to semi-dressy.

★ ★
MARQUIS/French
Corner of 4th and San Carlos/Carmel/Area 1/(408) 624-8068

Rated as one of the best French restaurants on the Monterey Peninsula by our advisory board, the Marquis, under the direction of owners Walter and Maxi (his charming wife) Becker, is one of those rare, personal dining places that caters to the same, loyal clientele year round. Their classic French cuisine does not deal with faddy new trends, but all is prepared and presented so perfectly that the scene here looks as though it might be a television commercial for a very expensive champagne. The Beckers seem to be everywhere in the two Louis XV accoutered rooms with gold, green and white accents. Crystal chandeliers grace the intimate dining rooms, one of which is invariably reserved by ex-president Gerald Ford when he dines out in this superlative, small town. Walter stops by each table, unobtrusively orchestrating his patrons' dinners. Maxi, hostess and manager, smilingly oversees the delightful, professional waitresses as they tend their guests.
Moderate to expensive. Open Monday through Saturday for dinner from 6 to 9:30 P.M. Reservations recommended. Visa, MC, AX. Wine only. Street parking. Semi-dressy to dressy.

DA ★ ★
MARRAKECH/Mid-Eastern
417 O'Farrell/San Francisco/Area 2/(415) 776-6717

Just for fun (certainly not just for the food) everyone should visit Marrakech, where you can lounge on huge pillows like Sidney Greenstreet or Merle Oberon while eating *couscous* with your fingers from dishes served on brass tables by waiters in theatrical Turkish costumes. The lamb with almonds and honey is good—and sticky—but warm water from the samovar is poured over your hands and thick (Turkish?) towels are provided. Chicken with lemon sauce and a community platter of salad that you scoop up with a kind of pita bread should be topped off with thick, sweet mint tea, poured from a height of three feet into a tall glass. All the food and most of the decor is Americanized—perhaps "touristized" is the word—and the Marrakech is no longer a favorite among the locals as in the days when founder Pierre Dupart was operating here.

Expensive. Open Monday through Saturday from 6 to 11 P.M. Reservations advised. All major credit cards. Entertainment. Full bar. Valet parking. Semi-dressy.

MASA 'S/French
650 Bush Street/San Francisco/Area 2/(415) 989-7154

This restaurant has had to overcome a great tragedy and seems to be regaining its composure. A note I received from manager John Cumin contained this message: "Masa Kobayashi our founder, owner and creator was found murdered in his San Francisco apartment. We continue with our kitchen under the supervision of William Calloway who was Masa's sous chef for three years. We offer dishes from Masa's repetoire with the same commitment to quality of ingredient and technique. Masa's death was a tragedy. He was arguably one of the finest chefs ever to practice his art in the United States. We are proud to be able to continue to offer his work to the dining public."

It is too soon to say if the restaurant will survive the shock. Specialities like pasta with truffles, *foie gras*, pheasant with morels are still served in the superb tradition of Masa. The restaurant will either become a memorial or it will have to change its name and direction. Time will tell.

Expensive. Open for dinner Tuesday through Saturday from 6 to 9 P.M. Reservations advised. Visa, MC, AX. Full bar. Valet parking. Dressy.

★ ★
MASONS/American/Seafood
Fairmont Hotel/San Francisco/Area 2/(415) 392-0113

Quiet, sophisticated, and oh so elegant, this spacious dining room places much emphasis on natural stone and woods. Large bay windows overlook the activity on California Avenue with its colorful cable cars. The copper-plated charcoal broiler is the focal point of the room; and well it should be as diners eagerly anticipate the next specialty to emerge from this open hearth broiler. Tender milk-fed squab, and French lamb chops are broiled to your individual taste. Pacific *mahi-mahi*, fresh poached salmon, shrimp "Canlis" and crab legs are the best selections of the fresh seafood that is flown in from the East and Pacific Northwest. Lovely, Kimono-clad waitresses serve gracefully, with great attention to detail, and manager Peter Seely is always on hand overseeing his staff, with Chris Canlis dropping in from Seattle to keep an eye on things. There is a friendly piano bar and a very extensive wine cellar featuring many hard to find California vintages.

Expensive. (Average $35 a person). Open seven days. Dinner served from 6 to 11:30 P.M. Reservations advised. All major credit cards. Full bar. View. Fairmont Hotel parking. Dressy.

***

★ ★ ★
MAURICE ET CHARLES BISTROT/French
901 Lincoln Avenue/San Rafael/Area 3/(415) 456-2010

One of the best "little" French restaurants in town (and, some say, in the country) and only thirteen years old. Co-owner Maurice Amazallag is the consummate host with hands as deft as Blackstone's—at the serving cart.

Chef Marcel Cathala is the other co-owner—and the balance between each partner's area of responsibility and expertise results in near perfection. The *quenelles* are so light they dissolve like a snowflake on the tongue, and there are special dishes daily in addition to the half dozen or so on the constantly changing, but never disappointing, menu.

Decor is romantic-bistro, with white walls highlighting striking flower paintings from M. Amazallag's personal collection.

Perhaps the finest dish in the house is the *selle d'agneau au poivre vert*, a majestic presentation of succulent, pink saddle of lamb in a flaky pastry crust with green peppercorns.

Chef Cathala shows his Lyons background in his handling of game— the wild boar in chestnut sauce is marvelous (boar is usually as salty as Alexander Haig and twice as tough)—and the venison, when available, is carefully trimmed and bursting with flavor. Desserts, in keeping with the tradition of the kitchen, are superb. The wine list is extensive. When you call for reservations, it's a good idea to ask about the off-menu items that are available; they will reserve portions if you like. **Moderate to expensive.** Open Monday through Saturday from 6:30 to 10:30 P.M. Reservations necessary. Visa, MC, AX. Wine and beer only. Lot parking. Semi-dressy.

***

DA ★ ★
MAXWELL'S PLUM/Continental
Ghirardelli Square/San Francisco/Area 2/(415) 441-1161

Warner LeRoy, Hollywood producer Mervyn LeRoy's son, created this spectacular restaurant, cafe and gathering place. It is, to say the least, visually exciting. For almost eight million dollars, here is what you get: nine magnificent crystal chandeliers from Baccarat, Ossler and Strauss crystals; fifty Art Nouveau and Art Deco statues; seven painted murals; a forty-foot *lalique* fountain; hand-loomed fabric wall coverings; custom carpeting; brass and copper chandeliers and beautifully colorful Tiffany-designed stained-glass overhead.

The indoor/outdoor cafe overlooks Ghirardelli Square Plaza, the Ruth Asawa fountain and throngs of interestingly attired sightseers and shoppers, most of whom stare right back at you. After all, it's a free country, even with inflation. For a first visit, I recommend the impressive Bay Room, with breathtaking vistas of the Bay and Golden Gate Bridge plus everything between and beyond. Even here though, dress is what you wish. You'll see non-designer jeans and tennis shoes alongside the latest fancy label clothing.

You can order anything from seventeen appetizers, three soups, two pastas, seven seafood dishes, five beef entrées, including châteaubriand *garni* (for two), eleven other entrées, even marianated roasted spareribs, chicken on the spit and wild boar, six salads (hot chicken salad!), nine miscellaneous goodies—cottage fries, French fries, baked potato, onion rings, some vegetables and Maxwell's beef chili, with beans, sour cream, chopped onions and cheddar cheese—wow. Fifteen desserts include five flavors of ice cream with either chocolate or butterscotch sauce and a banana split.

Now that you have memorized the statistics, I must say that everything is good with some items downright wonderful. The large, capable, youthful staff is on the ball and quite cheerful. They are right up front about the food, telling you the facts: only the very freshest ingredients; fresh string beans from France; prime beef from Chicago and New York; hearts of palm—not from Brazil—from the Seminole Indians. The wines cellared are your favorites. The man who keeps everything running so smoothly here is manager Dino La Rosa.

Children go mad over the unique design of Warner LeRoy, with special balloons and razz-ma-tazz at their parties.

Moderate to expensive. Open seven days. Lunch served from 11:30 A.M. to 4 P.M. Dinner served every night from 5:30 P.M. to 1 A.M. All major credit cards. Full bar. Garage parking. Semi-dressy.

★
MAYE'S OYSTER HOUSE/Seafood
1233 Polk Street/San Francisco/Area 2/(415) 474-7674

Inexpensive" and "seafood" would seem to be a contradiction in terms, but not in this unpretentious house that has managed to keep the prices in line, somehow, without reducing the portions or the quality. The rex sole stuffed with creamed crab meat *en casserole* is as sensational a dish as it was back in 1867 when the restaurant opened. There are multi-course feasts here—homemade soup, salad or fresh seafood cocktail, pasta course, entrée, dessert and coffee. Manager/partner Dave Berosh sees to it that everyone is comfortable, and the service efficient.

When steamed clams are in season, they are served Bordelaise here, either on the dinner or à la carte, and people come from afar on those special days. The wine list is a bit sparse, and I wasn't crazy about the Yugoslavian imports. This is a no-nonsense eatery; don't come expecting atmosphere.

Moderate. Open seven days 11 A.M. to 10 P.M. Sunday from 2 to 9:30 P.M. Reservations advised. Visa, MC. Full bar. Lot and street parking. Casual.

★★
McCALLUM'S/Ice Cream
1825 Solano Avenue/Berkeley/Area 2/(415) 525-3510

Rich McCallum may just be the man who is responsible for some of the extra pounds I'm carrying around. His huge, rich sundaes have been responsible for some wonderful ice cream orgies. Vanilla ice cream topped with house-made caramel, hot fudge, marshmallow and a mountain of whipped cream. His butter pecan ice cream has won the gold medal at the California State Fair for the last twenty years. I like the butter pecan, but my weakness is the orange fudge ice cream which, much to my dismay nine months out of twelve, is only served in the fall. In addition to the ice cream there are also homemade Danishes and cakes – but really, if you can pass up that rich ice cream, you have more control than I.

Inexpensive. Open Monday through Thursday from 8 A.M. to 11 P.M., Friday till midnight, Saturday 10 A.M. to midnight, Sunday 11 A.M. to 11 P.M. No credit cards. No alcohol. Street parking. Casual.

★
MEAT MARKET COFFEEHOUSE/Coffeehouse
4123 Twenty-fourth Street/San Francisco/Area 2/(415) 285-5598

A Berkeley-style, community-oriented coffeehouse of the sort that was common when students had a full schedule of clashes . . . when wrongs were rioted. The same ragged individualists – a little older now – gather here to compare poverty and intellects (some pay with their welfare checks), drink good espresso or choose from a wide variety of coffees and teas.

The homemade soups, salads and pastries are often delicious, and the sandwiches are hearty and reasonable. I like their espresso cheesecake and the ice cream and Italian sodas. This is a good place to enjoy relaxed conversation, read or play chess. The cappuccino here won first place at the San Francisco fair in both 1982 and 1983.

Inexpensive. Open seven days from 8 A.M. to 8 P.M., Friday and Saturday to 11 P.M. No reservations. No credit cards. Entertainment Friday and Saturday evening. Street parking. Casual.

★ ★
MEKONG/Vietnamese
288 Castro Street/Mountain View/Area 2/(415) 968-2604

In 1964, shortly before he opened one of the best Vietnamese restaurants in Paris, Mr. Nguyen Ton Hoan was Vice-Premier of South Vietnam. Today, he presides over this unusual cuisine in his restaurant in downtown Mountain View, of all places. Reflecting the cultural and political influences in the lives of its people, Vietnamese cooking blends culinary techniques of China, India and Indonesia with French attention to subtleties and desserts. Chinese influence appears in the use of rice or noodles, stir-frying and a deftly balanced sweet-sour sauce. The idea of curry was borrowed from India, but here the accent is on the aromatic while pungency is played down. From Indonesia comes the barbecuing of meats and brochettes with extremely flavorful sauces. These techniques, when applied to fish or shrimp, beef, pork or chicken, create a diversity of effect more complex than most national cuisines. For starters, try the imperial roll (an overstuffed egg roll) and creamy, thick rice soup, garnished with shellfish or abalone. Under no circumstances should you skip dessert here, for the deep-fried *beignets* of fresh banana, apple or pineapple are not only luscious but also soothing to the spice-assaulted palate. The best strategy is to order à la carte, for the complete dinners afford little, if any, saving.
Inexpensive to moderate. Open Monday through Saturday. Lunch from 11:30 A.M. to 2 P.M. Dinner from 5:30 to 9:30 P.M. Reservations advised. Visa, MC, AX. Wine and beer only. Street and lot parking. Casual.

★ ★
MEKONG/Vietnamese
730 Larkin Street/San Francisco/Area 2/(415) 928-8989

It is ghastly to look for some benefit from the Vietnamese war, but it is, nonetheless, a fact that American servicemen supported and encouraged Yamato after WWII, Korean food, and, finally (we pray) the food of Vietnam. That cuisine is a curious amalgam of many influences, including Indo-Chinese, French, Philippine, Thai, and Indonesian. "Imperial rolls" on Mekong's menu would be "lumpia" on a Philippine list. Much of the six page menu is closely related to other cuisines, yet distinctive on its own.

This slightly bleak restaurant near the Civic Center provides dishes for breakfast, lunch and dinner, mostly prepared by Vietnamese housewives under the supervision of chef Min Chin. "Imperial seven beef," seven kinds of beef you cook at your table, is far and away the house favorite, and owner Betty Chin has enjoyed much success at this small—fifty-seat—establishment that opened in mid 1984.
Inexpensive. Open seven days from 9 A.M. to 9 P.M. Reservations accepted. No credit cards. Wine and beer only. Street parking. Casual.

★
THE MELTING POT/Fondue
1532 North Main Street/Walnut Creek/Area 2/(415) 937-1006
1975 Diamond Boulevard/The Willows/Concord/Area 2/(415) 676-3368

The name is apt description of both the food and the patrons in these thoroughly professional, highly popular little cafes that specialize in fondue. The dinner menu is on a lantern lighted by candle power. Wine list is on a wine bottle. There's entertainment intermittently, usually on Friday and Saturday and usually student/youth oriented. An old tradition, both charming and profitable for the house, is that should a person lose his or her bread in the bubbling cheese, he/she/it provides the next round of wine. In addition to the multitude of fondue variations from beef to chive, there's a good crisp salad, homemade soup, and hamburgers—and then it's back to fondue again for the chocolate with fresh fruit. The wine list is so intelligently conceived, you won't mind the fact it's limited. In all, terrific operations with good food, exceptional service, low prices and fun.
Inexpensive. Open seven days. Lunch served daily from 11:30 A.M. to 4 P.M. Dinner served from 4 to 10 P.M. Reservations advised for six or more. Visa, MC, AX. Entertainment in Walnut Creek. Wine and beer only. Patio at Willows. Street and lot parking. Casual.

★
MENARA/Moroccan
41 East Gish Road/San Jose/Area 2/(408) 998-1583

I never thought the road to Morocco would lead to such improbable places, but Moroccan cuisine is sweeping the country, and was bound to show up in San Jose sooner or later. I've never had bad Moroccan food, only variations of "good." There are two rooms opulently decorated with tile, rugs, Moorish arches and ornate partitions. Lush colored cushions are piled luxuriously high to provide comfortable nesting places while eating this fare with your fingers. Soup—*harira*—is a spicy, warming blend that's drunk from the bowl. You begin with a hand laving ceremony over an impressive silver bowl. Then course after course is brought to you whilst you groan with the attempt to keep up. **Expensive.** Open Monday through Saturday from 6 to 10 P.M. Reservations advised. Visa, MC, AX. Belly dancing. Full bar. Parking lot. Casual.

★ ★
MICHAEL'S/Seafood/Continental
830 East El Camino/Sunnyvale/Area 2/(408) 245-2925

Winning a large, profit-making clientele is the ultimate goal of most restaurateurs, but Ted Faravelli, co-owner of Michael's, set his sights still higher, and consequently has earned the respect of virtually all of his contemporaries in the devastatingly wicked hospitality trade. He acquired this fine seafood-continental favorite in 1969, and since then has completed a third of a million dollar redecoration and renovation. The spacious interior features etched glass dividers, sturdy chairs and tables, and the *esprit de corps* is reflected in the smiles and brisk service of the large staff.

Frankly, I have tried to find specific faults here because of the unusually high compliments that come to me about Michael's. I'm still trying, but not so hard. The tall menu details not only the wealth of New England and eastern seafood, from lobsters to Blue Points, but many other versions of west coast finny and crustacean specialties which are cooked up by award-winning executive chef Alfred Saarne and his most professional kitchen staff. Chef Alfred is an impressive artist in both oils and water colors as well and a number of his paintings brighten the paneled walls above the roomy booths. Oh, yes, here you receive four fresh vegetables with your entrée.

Expensive. Open seven days. Monday through Thursday from 5:30 to 10:30 P.M. Friday and Saturday from 5 to 11 P.M., Sunday from 4 to 9 P.M. Reservations strongly advised. Visa, MC, AX. Piano bar. Full bar. Child's menu. Parking lot. Casual to semi-dressy.

To obtain the best results from this Guide, be sure to consult the map on the various Northern California areas on page 28.

MIFUNE/Japanese
1737 Post Street/San Francisco/Area 2/(415) 922-0337

Noodles are the name of the game here, either *udan* (thick noodles made of white flour) or *soba* (thin noodles made of buckwheat flour). All noodle dishes come with dipping sauces and condiments which you can mix to your own desired flavor, and most come with a bowl of seaweed soup. The tempura is lightly battered and never greasy. The *soba* beef is noodles topped with grilled beef and scallions.

Mifune is a kind of fast food noodle shop chain in Japan—if the idea catches on here we may be seeing more rice instead of French fries in the near future.

Moderate. Open seven days, Monday through Saturday from 11 A.M. to 9 P.M., Sunday 11 A.M. to 9 P.M. No reservations. Visa, MC, AX. Beer and sake only. Validated parking downstairs. Casual.

★ ★
MIKE'S CHINESE CUISINE/Chinese/Cantonese
5145 Geary Boulevard/San Francisco/Area 2/(415) 752-0120

Plain as its name, with no atmosphere whatsoever, yet the food is really good and Lily (Mike's wife) is attentive to even the tiniest detail. Crystal shrimp is my favorite, although you should be sure to have the egg roll if only to see how this often abused dish should taste. The sweet and sour sauce, particularly on pork, is exceptional—more vivid and less gluey than at most Chinese restaurants. Comparatively new—they opened in 1970—Mike Won knew he had to be good to survive in a city with the best Chinese restaurants in the Western Hemisphere, and he's making it.

Moderate. Open Wednesday through Monday from 4:30 to 10 P.M. Reservations accepted. Visa, MC. Full bar. Street parking. Casual.

MING'S/Chinese/Cantonese
1700 Embarcadero Road/Palo Alto/Area 2/(415) 856-7700

Ming's is one of those monstrous Cantonese restaurants with paper umbrellas in the tropical drinks and touches of technicolor Polynesia. The egg roll is a punishment, but the chicken salad (Chinese chicken salad bears about as much resemblance to the American variety as, say, Brooke Shields to Wilt Chamberlain) and the sweet and sour pork are at least a step or two above a chop suery. Specialties are Ming's beef and Mandarin orange beef. Winter melon soup is also a specialty here—halves of white melon filled with hot broth—and the whole fish (in season) is steamed in its natural juices with fresh ginger slivers, soy sauce, black mushrooms and scallion strips added. Served as a course in a feast, the steamed fish usually signifies the end of the meal—dessert generally follows. Desserts here are an afterthought though, and that may be giving them more credit than they deserve. **Moderate.** Open seven days. Lunch from 11:30 A.M. to 2 P.M. Dinner from 5 to 10 P.M. Reservations advised. Visa, MC, AX. Full bar. Lot parking. Semi-dressy.

★
MIRABEAU RESTAURANT/French/Continental
344 Twentieth Street/Oakland/Area 2/(415) 834-6575

If **you** didn't know it was there you would probably pass right by . . . and you would miss a dining experience unequaled in the East Bay. Hidden inside of the massive Kaiser Center complex in the heart of the financial district of Oakland, Mirabeau has played host to society, corporate moguls, and discerning patrons for years. An elevator ride from the parking lot or lobby wisks you into the restaurant.

The cuisine is French, with only a slight nod to the best of *nouvelle* cuisine. Portions are generous, as are the prices, but the experience is worth it.

Chef Michael Rech changes his menu four times a year, to follow the European tradition of preparing only the freshest ingredients at the height of their season. The night we dined we enjoyed tournedos of lamb with trumpet mushrooms and mint, and medallions of salmon in puff pastry with truffle sauce. Duckling, roast pheasant, rack of lamb and many fresh seafood dishes were offered as well on this impressive menu. Desserts on the pastry cart kept passing us all evening and by the time it came time for us to order, we knew what our selection would be. The Mirabeau cake is a cognac cream cake with white and dark chocolate and it was divine. Having had the foresight to order the Grand Mariner soufflé ahead of time, we were not disappointed. All the pastries and ice cream are made fresh daily in the Mirabeau kitchen. The five hundred plus wine list is what you would expect of a restaurant of this caliber and the harp music during dinner added an extra special touch to the evening. Service by waiters and captains is attentive without being intrusive, and the art of tableside cooking and flambé is still alive and well and executed with flair in the European tradition.

Parking is validated in the building and we suggest you ask for directions when you call for reservations, to avoid getting lost.

Moderate to expensive. Open Tuesday through Saturday. Luncheon weekdays 11:30 A.M. to 2 P.M. Dinner Tuesday through Saturday 5:30 P.M. to 10 P.M. *Prix fixe* pre-theatre dinner Tuesday through Saturday 5:30 P.M. to 6:45 P.M. Reservations advised. All major credit cards. Harp music during dinner. Full bar. Validated parking in the building. Semi-dressy to dressy.

★ ★ ★
MIRAMONTE/French
1327 Railroad Avenue/St. Helena/Area 3/(707) 963-3970

Until the mid 1960s, it was rare to hear of a restaurant of any distinction that served a multi-course *prix fixe* dinner for one sitting only. Economics were such that a dinner could not be truly profitable in competition with the usual dining place. Nevertheless, when Maison Bergerac, in Pacific Grove, began to receive high praise for instituting exactly such a format, other restaurateurs (just a few) adopted this formula with agreeable success, and I believe we shall see many more of this genre.

Miramonte was conceived for the discriminating diner, and its gratifying success attests to the truly fine experience you will enjoy here. Chefs/partners Edouard Platel and Udo Nechutnys acquired the old stone Miramonte Hotel and completely renovated the premises with cheerful colors and light woods to give an open feeling that is rather cozy at night when the fireplace is lit. The owners' wives oversee a gracious dining room staff.

Chef Udo, once an apprentice to Paul Bocuse, a former instructor at the prestigious California Culinary Academy, and now very much his own man, sometimes will prepare for your first course a delicate mussel soup, perhaps a fresh turtle soup, then smoked German ham, followed by your entrée. Menus are changed seasonally and you can be pleasantly surprised with your meal's elements. Perhaps steak *canard* or beef tenderloin will be your main course. Depending upon season and other basic factors, you might even be presented with a trout from a nearby pond. The chefs utilize salmon, sole, sturgeon, sea bass, duckling, true veal and lamb.

Desserts are in keeping with the kitchen's creativity. You can be sure that you'll be delighted, whether it be fresh fruit or homemade ice cream. Only California wines are cellared, many from vineyards just minutes away.

Moderate to expensive. Open Wednesday through Sunday from 6 to 9:30 P.M., (group luncheons only). Reservations essential. No credit cards. Wine and apéritifs. Lot and street parking. Semi-dressy.

★ ★

MISSION DELICATESSEN/Deli
155 Anza/Fremont/Area 2/(415) 657-8062

A deli that offers catering and a gourmet cooking school? Mary Chamberlin feels a gourmet revolution is taking place in America. People are moving away from the preservatives and fillers that are part and parcel of most fast food places and delis and moving towards healthier fare. In addition to the standard deli sandwich offerings of lean corned beef, polish sausage, liverwurst, hot pastrami and German bologna, Chamberlin offers such diverse selections as: "brunch in a bag" (eggs Benedict wrapped in a crêpe with béarnaise sauce), the beef bunion (roast beef on an onion roll with swiss cheese, tomato, onion, lettuce and corn relish), the *torta prima Vera* (seventeen layer crêpe sandwich with turkey, ham, two kinds of cheese, sliced eggs and avocado), the "moron's ecstacy" (served on pillow French or dark rye with turkey, roast beef, ham, cheese, cucumber, tomatoes, sour cream and horseradish). Just to add a little more confusion to the menu, there is also a Mission Deli falafel, *piroshki*, and a Bavarian pancake with sautéed vegetables, meat, sour cream, cheese and tomato. New dinner dishes are fresh fish: Portuguese fish stew, Greek style scampi, and snapper. Soups are homemade daily, and salads are individually built masterpieces. **Inexpensive.** Open Monday through Saturday. Monday through Wednesday from 11 A.M. to 8 P.M., Thursday and Friday until 9 P.M., and Saturday until 5 P.M. Reservations accepted. No credit cards. Wine and beer only. Parking lot. Casual.

★

MITOYA/Japanese
1855 Post Street/San Francisco/Area 2/(415) 653-2156

A schizophrenic restaurant with the personality of a sedate and very good Japanese tatami restaurant until nine o'clock, when it turns into a touch of the Ginza with Japanese hostesses like Geisha girls, and "entertainment" that is often less than professional—Japanese songs sung to a taped background. Among the treats here are fried chicken wings with black mushrooms (a Nipponese version of the "Buffalo wings"), *komochi shiitake*, deep fried mushrooms, and many interesting grilled dishes that are less common than the usual fare. Specials are chalked on a blackboard and manager Naoto Matsuda will be glad to make you comfortable.

Moderate. Open seven days. Sunday through Thursday from 6 p.m. to midnight, Friday and Saturday til 3 A.M. Reservations accepted. Visa, MC, AX. Full bar. Entertainment. Parking in Japanese Center lot. Casual.

★ ★
MODESTO LANZONE'S/Italian
900 North Point/San Francisco/Area 2/(415) 771-2880

Remember the gangster movies, circa prohibition era, when there were the lovable heavies that — as played by Robert Stack — wore chalk-striped double-breasted suits, silk shirts and ascots? That's our man, Modesto Lanzone, a Latin charmer who has realized his long-time fantasy in a lush, overdecorated house of *alta cucina*. His *cima Genovese*, veal stuffed with pine nuts, cheese, herbs and vegetables, is a typically pretentious dish, but I like Lanzone's for the veal *piccata*. All the opulent dishes of *la dolce vita* are here — generous portions lavishly served by professionals — although tourists often nervously read their menus from right to left as it is expensive.
Moderate to expensive. Open Tuesday through Friday noon to 11 P.M., Saturday and Sunday from 4 P.M. to midnight. Reservations accepted. All major credit cards. Full bar. Validated garage parking. Casual.

★ ★
MODESTO LANZONE'S OPERA PLAZA/Italian
601 Van Ness Avenue/San Francisco/Area 2/(415) 928-0400

Two years ago, Modesto Lanzone (he also owns the restaurant bearing his name in Ghirardelli Square) opened this spacious establishment to house his impressively large art collection, a gallery that one could spend days viewing and admiring. I am not going to comment in detail upon the superb cuisine — classic Italian — but there are a few off-beat treatments that sparkle in their own imaginative creation. Suffice it to note that you will find an extensive treasure of gourmet-worthy Italian dishes. Modesto's gallery occupies every nook and cranny of this seven-area dining place.
Moderate to expensive. Monday through Friday for lunch 11:30 A.M. to 4:30 P.M. Dinner Monday through Saturday 5 to 11:30 P.M. Reservations advised. All major credit cards. Full bar. Parking under Opera Plaza. Semi-dressy to dressy.

MONDELLO'S/Italian
337 Rheem Boulevard/Moraga/Area 2/(415) 376-2533

A sophisticated Italian couple was visiting me and I debated where to take them when they claimed they were homesick for some food from their home country. Well, let's face it, Moraga is a long way from Basilica, but I decided we'd give it a shot. We were all glad we did. The *vitella con funghi freschi* is billed as Mondello's favorite: veal scaloppine sautéed with fresh mushrooms in a light wine sauce. Another *"specialita della casa"* is the *scampi alla Mondello*: Icelandic baby lobster tails sautéed in a delicate butter, garlic, lemon and wine sauce. For dessert we had *cannoli*, which was a light flaky pastry shell filled with sweetened ricotta cheese and pieces of chocolate and vanilla. It's a bit pricey, but well worth it.

Moderate to expensive. Open Monday through Saturday from 5:30 to 9:30 P.M. Reservations accepted. Visa, MC, AX. Wine and beer only. Ample parking. Casual.

★ ★
MONROE'S/Continental
1968 Lombard Street/San Francisco/Area 2/(415) 567-4550

The rather select clientele appreciates the warm and friendly feeling this delightful place imparts. Peter Lomax, English-born gentleman-owner and host, and Irish-born Brendan O'Donnell, co-host, make you feel like a privileged member of a smart club. Pause at the intimate, copper-top bar before dining or for a liqueur later, a civilized experience. The interior design is understated-masculine, with English hunting prints and original pastoral scenes. Good use is made of brass and pewter, and a tempting dessert display centers the mellow room. Diners order from a menu rich in the superb creations of a talented French kitchen. Cream of hearts of artichoke soup, tournedos Wellington and roast rack of lamb are good choices. I admire the "breast of chicken Monroe's," a celestial dish. The wine list reflects Peter's expertise with vintages, especially California's top wineries.

Moderate to expensive. Open Monday through Saturday from 5:30 to 11 P.M. Reservations accepted. Full bar. Parking in nearby motels. Semi-dressy.

For best results, consult "How to Use This Guide" on page 25.

★
MOONRAKER/Continental/Seafood
105 Rockaway Beach Avenue/Pacifica/Area 2/(415) 359-0303

A moonraker is the topmost sail of the Clipper ships of years ago, sometimes carried in light winds," so the menu tells us. "Often called the moonsail, this small canvas swept through the heavens, in the brilliant, clear air aloft. All about you are authentic reminders of that romantic era." Surprisingly enough for a restaurant with this kind of emphasis, and the ocean view to boot, they do not feel obliged to restrict themselves to an entirely seafood menu. Veal *saltimbocca* is tender slices of sautéed veal, topped with prosciutto and muenster cheese, served with vermicelli. The roast rack of lamb is served with a special sauce flavored with mint—real mint, not the mint jelly flavorings used by some. The roast smoked duckling is a wonderful raspberry-laced choice.

I have been ignoring the seafood though, and there is no lack of skill in the preparation of these dishes. Bouillabaise à la Parisienne is served in a casserole with garlic croutons, and there are daily seafood specials. The Pacific salmon was—hoorah—fresh, and finished with a light herb butter. The side dish of creamed spinach (how is it that kids can hate a vegetable that's this good?) was a large portion of spinach blended with fresh cream and seasoned with tarragon, basil and nutmeg.

This is a good place to go with someone you're really compatible with, as some of the best appetizers (Caesar salad) and desserts (baked Alaska flambé and crêpes Suzette) are served for two people. The portions are very large, so by the time you reach dessert you could be very happy to be sharing instead of facing a chocolate mousse all by yourself.

Moderate to expensive. Open Tuesday through Sunday from 5 to 10 P.M. Reservations necessary. Visa, MC, AX, DC. Full bar. Lot parking. Semi-dressy.

★ ★
MOUNT VIEW HOTEL/French/Continental
1457 Lincoln Avenue/Calistoga/Area 3/(707) 942-6877

In the late 1800s it was fashionable to "take the waters" in Calistoga, a quiet town at the top of the lush Napa Valley, where mineral waters abounded with many a spa, in accordance with European custom.

The European Hotel then occupied the present site of the Mount View Hotel and flourished until the 1910 fire that razed almost all of Calistoga. In 1917 Johnny Ghisolfo, the mayor, built the Mt. View—a handsome, spacious, stylish place for the swells. It did well until

Prohibition, the 1929 Depression, the following Recession and World War II. Then came lean years until its relatively recent restoration and renovation in the art deco style, enhancing the basic, beautiful architecture, enlarging rooms and suites, and utilizing much of the original furniture, lighting and bath fixtures.

This description is partly to advise those readers who will want to remain overnight after an exceptional dining experience. Overnight guests relax with many of the little niceties of the '20s of the Riviera — fresh flowers, fresh-squeezed orange juice with the morning continental breakfast that is a perk for room guests, as well as *cafe au lait* and fresh croissants.

However, the main thing is the food, especially the evening meal. Chef Diane Paiseau does a superb job all around. Everything is cooked to your order from the freshest of products. *Table d'hôte* dinners include five courses — appetizer to sweet.

The wine book is all that one might expect. As you settle back with your coffee or a liqueur, with the Casablanca fans revolving overhead, potted palms and plants completing the image, plan your next day's visits to nearby vineyards or to one of the several spas, possibly "taking the waters."

Expensive. Open seven days. Lunch seven days from 11:30 A.M. to 2 P.M. Dinner seven days from 6 to 9 P.M. Sunday brunch from 9 A.M. to 2 P.M. Poolside lunch and barbecues (5 to 9:30 P.M.) start in June and continue as long as the weather is good. Reservations necessary. All major credit cards. Swing music seven nights. Dancing. Full bar. Lot parking. Semi-dressy.

★ ★

THE MOVABLE FEAST/Creative/California
601 Munroe Street at Fulton/Sacramento/Area 3/(916) 971-1677

Much more than a bistro but with the same feeling, the Movable Feast, under the direction of owners/creators Anik Vickers and Ashley Barden, just may become one of your favorites. French doors open to the highwalled courtyard where dining is an occasion in mild weather. A skylight brightens the long bar lounge, which is enhanced by a fireplace. The restaurant's unusual name will not seem mystifying to fans of Ernest Hemingway and relates to the take-out feature, where you can take-out anything on the menu. Also, Movable Feast combines a much-enlisted catering service. Try the endive salad with smoked *poussin* and, at the least, a small or large pasta. I favor the duck breast and a guest praised the individual rack of lamb. Jumbo prawns are sautéed with sauce of lobster, herbs and a sensitive touch of garlic. The *poulet Paulette* is named in honor of its creator, the luncheon chef, who also makes a wicked *coquilles St. Jacques Paulette*.

Moderate. Open Monday through Friday 11:30 A.M. to 10 P.M., Saturday and Sunday 5 to 10 P.M. Reservations advised. Visa, MC. Full bar. Ample lot parking. Casual.

★
MURILLO'S/Mexican
633 Merchant Street/Vacaville/Area 3/(707) 448-3395
1581 E. Monte Vista Avenue/Vacaville/Area 3/(707) 447-3704

A friend of mine was complaining that highway robbers are not found as frequently in Mexico as they are found running Mexican restaurants north of the border. This place could prove him wrong—or at least is the exception that proves the rule. You'd have to really work hard to spend over $8 here. The menu is comprised of all the items you've seen on a hundred other menus, but at Murillo's you're getting a unique dining bargain. Portions are large, prices are low and the place is packed. The chicken and avocado tostada is an all-time favorite. By now the owners must realize they have a winning formula (they've expanded to a second location on Monte Vista) and they're sticking to it in their success.

Inexpensive. Open Monday through Thursday from 10 A.M. to 9 P.M. Friday and Saturday to 10 P.M., Sunday from 2 to 9:30 P.M. Reservations accepted. No credit cards. Wine and beer only. Child's menu. Parking lot. Casual.

Please be sure to consult "Tipping Made Easy" on page 22 of this Guide.

★
NAM YUEN/Chinese/Cantonese
740 Washington Street/San Francisco/Area 2/(415) 781-5636

Seating is strictly on a first-come, first-served basis; the maître d' hands you a number to await your turn (unless he recognizes you as one of the regulars, who are immediately seated upstairs). It would be very easy to become a regular here, requiring only enough spirit to venture beyond almond chicken and sweet and sour pork. You're not likely to find better interpretations of this classic cuisine at even luxury prices. Three daily *prix fixe* dinners are offered with individual dishes varying according to the chef's whim. The menu is not as extensive as most; it has been pared down to a very reliable selection. Regrettably, shark's fin soup is now so expensive that it would be a major splurge, but their famous bird's nest soup is much less and worth trying. Lobster Cantonese with wonderfully fresh peas and long string beans with beef and black bean sauce are excellent choices. Nothing is precooked, so be prepared to sip tea, a cocktail or a sprightly Riesling wine while you wait. **Moderate.** Open Tuesday through Friday from 11:30 A.M. to 11:00 P.M., Saturday and Sunday from 2:30 to 11:30 P.M. Reservations accepted. Visa, MC. Full bar. Child's menu. Lot parking. Casual.

In order to obtain the best results from this Guide, please consult "A Few Inside Tips" on page 18.

★
NAPOLI/Pasta
2435 Clement/San Francisco/Area 2/(415) 752-3003

Mati Ndrekaj and G. Darbe are unlikely names for the proprie-
tors/chefs of an Italian restaurant. But the carbonara sauce was
just right, the pastas all fresh, the portions ample and the place delightful. Pasta *matriciana* is a seldom offered blend of peppers and tomatoes,
seasoned with basil. The chicken baked in butter and sherry requires
a half hour wait, but it can be worth it. Try going on a Monday when
the place is rarely crowded and whichever owner is in the kitchen will
take requests for items not on the menu.
Moderate. Open Thursday through Tuesday from 5 to 11 P.M. Reservations advised. Visa, MC. Full bar. Parking lot. Casual.

★
NAUTILUS/Seafood
Pier 39/San Francisco/Area 2/(415) 433-3721

Nautilus is many things to many people. To some it's an exercise
system designed to tear tendons and wear down excessive masses
of flesh. To others, it's a curious little creature that lives near the bottom
of the sea, a mollusk that grabs passing shrimp with its tentacles and
zips along the sea bottom thanks to a cleverly evolved jet siphon. To
those visiting Pier 39, Nautilus is one of the facility's many seafood restaurants which differentiates itself mostly through a mild patina of Oriental
cooking, in the Hawaiian Oriental style.

Thus, the menu is dotted with pan fried *mahi mahi aloha* (I hate
dishes that feature the word aloha because it almost always means there's
an irrelevant chunk of pineapple on one side of your plate). The top of
the menu "invites" you to try mai tais, chi chis, piña coladas and Singapore slings. There's a pineapple chicken offered which is entirely too
sweet. The road from Nautilus the restaurant, leads directly to Nautilus
the exercise machine.
Moderate. Open seven days from 11:30 A.M. to 4 P.M. Dinner from 5
to 9 P.M. 10 P.M. on Friday and Saturday. No reservations. Full bar. Parking lot. Casual.

For best results, consult "How to Use This Guide" on page 25.

★
N-B CAFE/American
7875 E. Highway 99/Los Molinos/Area 5/(916) 384-2310

Since **1949,** Tom Nagos, along with his wife Patricia, has been serving what he describes as "just good food." A modest man, whose claim to fame is that everything from his kitchen tastes like mother wishes hers did. Meals here come complete with soup, salad and coffee. The soup is so well built and carefully simmered (tomato rice, chicken noodle, vegetable, navy bean and Boston clam chowder) that each spoonful speaks love. As for Tom Nagos, well, he's partial to the roast leg of pork. His cafe seats only sixty; you can sense why it's most often full. Try a Grecian burger.

Inexpensive. Open Friday through Tuesday. Breakfast served all day. Lunch from 10 A.M. to 3:30 P.M. Dinner from 4:30 to 8 P.M. No reservations. No credit cards. Wine and beer only. Street parking. Casual.

DA ★
NEGRI'S/Italian
3700 Bohemian Highway/Occidental/Area 3/(707) 823-5301

This is not Occidental cuisine — as opposed to Oriental — but Occidental is the name of a community that is a beautiful drive north, along the coast, from San Francisco. The huge restaurant serves the hearty fare of southern Italy with homemade ravioli and chicken cacciatore at small-town prices. Cocktails are unusually good, service is swift and the atmosphere is informal.

Inexpensive to moderate. Open seven days from 11:30 A.M. to 9 P.M. Reservations advised. Visa, MC, AX, DC. Full bar. Child's menu. Street and lot parking. Casual.

DA ★★
NEIL DE VAUGHN'S/Continental
654 Cannery Row/Monterey/Area 1/(408) 372-2141

Don't hesitate to request a small tour by general manager Werner Braun, long-time mainstay of this famous dinner house in one of the most storied areas in our country, let alone the Monterey Peninsula. This waterside favorite, with window walls above the beach affording vistas of Monterey Bay, was completely rebuilt, from the bare columns and beams up, and reopened in mid-1984. According to host Werner, this is the most elegant new dining place in the area, a beautifully conceived design and execution costing over $1,000,000. In the sumptuous, enlarged dining rooms, a fireplace reflects dancing flames in ornate mirrors and on the fabulous paintings of renowned artist Leroy Niemann. You will have to pause to admire the Michael Leed stained-glass window. The menu describes the same, long-favored steaks and seafood specialties, all prefaced by complimentary cheese fondue. The cellar matches the food. Now open atop the restaurant—The Spindrift Inn, featuring lovely, expensive lodgings.

Moderate. Open for dinner Tuesday through Sunday from 5 to 10:30 P.M. Reservations necessary. Visa, MC. Full bar. Child's menu. Street parking. Casual.

★
THE NEON CHICKEN/American/Funky
4063 Eighteenth Street/San Francisco/Area 2/(415) 863-0484

This is an exciting little (forty-five-seat) house of inventiveness, both in cuisine and decor. Owner Michael Chmelik has captured a mood, sort of a forties feeling, in which he serves four homemade specials every night, from *paella* to lamb shanks to steak and kidney pie. Service is unusually competent, prices are reasonable and the limited wine list represents a great deal of thought (the house wine was Mondavi). Sunday brunch is especially sumptuous, with fresh fruit cups and fresh baked biscuits and an array of egg dishes that would do credit to a hautier—and less fun—establishment.

Moderate. Open seven days from 5:30 to 10:30 P.M. No reservations. Visa, MC, AX. Wine and beer only. Lot parking. Casual.

DA ★ ★
NEPENTHE/American
Highway 1/Big Sur/Area 1/(408) 667-2345

The term "romantic," when applied to a restaurant, is frustratingly ambiguous. To some, it conjures visions of strolling musicians and a single red rose placed across madam's plate. To others, it may be a favorite downstairs bistro, all bread sticks and checkered tablecloths (with that rare, discreet waiter who understands the precise moment when not to serve). But whether it's an intimate countryside pub or a cozy cafe with a jukebox, we've all got one—our personal place more valued for the memory than the menu.

To me, the truly romantic restaurant must possess a special aura that affects the mood by everything that is seen, heard, smelled and touched. It should be a private fantasyland—an emotional light-year away from the real world. Of course, these are few. One of the best of the few is Nepenthe. Located amidst the rugged, wild beauty of Big Sur, the restaurant has been handcrafted from natural elements—adobe, rock, oak and redwood—which make it seem part of the cliff it tops. Man strives to establish himself in proportion to this beauty. Some ninety miles south, William Randolph Hearst met the challenge by building a castle on a mountain at San Simeon and filling it with priceless treasures. William Fassett, however, decided that Big Sur itself was the treasure, and designed Nepenthe as an unobtrusive entity from which the spectacle of nature can be absorbed fully. Hearst's achievement seems somehow less significant when compared to a single exquisite sunset at Big Sur.

At Nepenthe, vast windows surround the room to provide a breathtaking living gallery. Raging white surf crashes against the huge rocks some eight hundred feet below, and beyond is a Pacific sometimes so blue that it blends almost imperceptibly with the horizon. Landward, dense pine and redwood forests tower cloud high above sheer cliffs and precipitous gorges. Nepenthe is a gathering place for the intellectuals – the writers and artists of Big Sur drawn from the world over – who sip liqueur and draft beer around the enormous fire pit on the terrace. Occasional al fresco entertainment is as unplanned as it is unpaid: chamber music ensembles creating a fragmentary Bach festival, or folk dancers, or those gentle musicians who play the music of the air – primitive rhythms in which the musician himself seems an instrument of the environment.

Inside, oak logs crackle to life as the dusk chill draws the crowd around the circular fireplace, to the tables, or best of all, to the long stretches of wooden window seats that surround the dining area. A profusion of cushions in every size and color provide comfortable backrests for gazing at the outside view or sharing the inside warmth and rapprochement.

Modern conveniences have been accepted reluctantly at Nepenthe. The room is lighted by candles only, and it was not until recently that Nepenthe acceded to the need for a telephone. The food is simple though perfectly prepared. Lunch consists mostly of good sandwiches, desserts and the "cheese board with port wine," which seems to be preferred by the chess players. For dinner, I enjoyed the "cheddar steak," lean ground steak topped with melted cheddar cheese and chopped green onions, served with fresh green salad and herb dressing. The French fries are of the quality I've found in Europe. The limited menu includes excellent steaks, broiled chicken and a local favorite, roast squab – served on weekends only. Every entrée has a wine recommendation on the menu, and the list is surprisingly diverse.

Cocktails are served, though there seems more concern about liqueurs (C&C – Chartreuse and Cognac – is a favorite), reflecting the sophisticated taste of the patrons. On a level beneath the restaurant is the Phoenix, a gift shop and art and craft gallery where much of the local talent is represented.

Nepenthe is thirty-two miles south of Carmel on Highway 1. Look for a rustic gate, leave your car in the compound and follow the footpath.

Moderate. Open seven days. Lunch from 11:30 A.M. to 4:30 P.M. Dinner from 5 to 10 P.M. No reservations. Visa, MC, AX. Full bar. Patio. View. Lot parking. Casual.

★

NEPTUNE'S PALACE/Seafood
Pier 39/San Francisco/Area 2/(415) 434-2260

The best thing about the new generation of seafood restaurants to appear on Pier 39 (which, were it not for the bay and the surrounding mountains, would not look out of place somewhere in the wilds of Ohio, where it might function as a theme park built to indulge indolent teenagers) is that they have a commitment to fresh seafood. Using fresh food at least puts them several lengths ahead of the old warhorses along Fisherman's Wharf.

Neptune's Palace is a pleasant, somewhat less than palatial restaurant, with a fine view of Angel Island. You'll be told what's fresh and what's not soon after being taken to your table. If it's available, order the smoked trout appetizer, which is treated over applewood. It's quite good. The best choices are usually the simplest—the grilled petrale, Pacific snapper, flounder and shark (thresher steaks, delicious, and served without cello music). To their shame, Neptune's serves a nine-ounce steak with half a Maine lobster, which is one of the worst American inventions. **Moderate to expensive**. Open seven days. Lunch served weekdays from 11 A.M. to 4 P.M. Dinner from 5 to 11 P.M. Reservations advised. All major credit cards. Full bar. Harbor view. Parking lot. Casual to semi-dressy.

DA ★ ★ ★

NEW BOONEVILLE HOTEL/California/American
14050 Highway 128/Booneville/Area 4/(707) 895-3478

This is everything a restaurant ought to be. Caring people, innovative cooking, vegetables fresh from the garden, local game and ingredients, a view of the surrounding hills, mesquite and hardwood fire for cooking home baked bread, homemade preserves, classical, improvisational jazz on a grand piano and even a *compris* policy by which the fifteen percent tip is included in the menu prices.

Please be sure to consult "Tipping Made Easy" on page 22 of this Guide.

Charlene and Vernon Rollins (she in the kitchen and he in the front of the house) took all they learned at Chez Panisse and all they dreamed about in their restaurant fantasy and somehow made it all come true. Their menu covers a wide and unpredictable range from suckling pig, rabbit, duck, lamb, goat kid and veal to their all-Anderson Valley wine list. Smoked ham braised in bourbon and served with red cabbage is a knockout dish.

The building has been divided into dining areas, some filled with the art and memorabilia of the region, particularly the cozy bar. In the winter, much of the illumination of my favorite room is provided by a crackling fireplace. The aroma of fresh bread emerging from the brick pizza oven is a palate aphrodisiac that is worth the drive — two hours and some minutes north of San Francisco.

Moderate to expensive. Open seven days from noon to 9:30 P.M. Closed on Wednesdays during the winter. Reservations advised. No credit cards. Entertainment. Full bar. Patio. View. Ample street parking. Casual to dressy.

★
NEW PISA/Italian
550 Green Street/San Francisco/Area 2/(415) 362-5188

The Pisa was new when Rudolph Valentino was still an extra, but if they served just one dish — just *osso bucco* — that braised shin of veal, full of succulent marrow, cooked with chopped vegetables and garlic and herb sauce — I'd come back to this ancient trattorìa six times a year. But they do have the North Beach specialties — home-cooked Italian dishes — unchanged in recipe or portion for a half-century. There's homemade ravioli and veal sauté ("as pink as a baby's ass" according to the waiter). The name of the owner sounds like a dish: Dante Benedetti, and New Pisa has been in the family since 1930. The walls are festooned with momentos and baseball paraphenalia. It's a homey North Beach institution. **Moderate**. Open Thursday through Tuesday. Lunch from 11:30 A.M. to 2:30 P.M. Dinner from 2:30 to 11 P.M. No reservations. No credit cards. Full bar. Child's menu. Valet parking. Casual.

To obtain the best results from this Guide, be sure to consult the map on the various Northern California areas on page 28.

★
THE NEW SAN REMO RESTAURANT/Italian
2237 Mason Street/San Francisco/Area 2/(415) 673-9090

Frank Romaguera and his charming wife/hostess, Eleanor, have done wonders with this four decades-plus old-timer. While the original place was, for its time, a pleasant eating place, the renovation (completed in 1978) presents the delightful parodox of a completely new turn-of-the-century ambiance. Passing the intimate piano-bar alcove, you are seated by Eleanor, or Frank, in a handsome dining room, divided by shoulder-high wood paneling. The ceiling is of pressed tin, floors of gleaming hardwood and cafe curtains screen the windows' lower half, allowing views of the street-bordering trees. Casablanca ceiling fans turn lazily, reflecting on polished mahogany. Everything is freshly painted in light tones, white-naped tables are well spaced. *Si*, the *New* San Remo.

Anything might taste good in such an attractive, airy room, but the food is of top quality and dishes are created by a skillful chef and staff. Prices are very modestly set, amazingly so.

Appetizers begin with escargot, *antipasto* or calamari vinaigrette. There are always two soups and three salads. Pastas are the thing— from *fettuccine vongole, tortellini alla crema* and, of course, *cannelloni,* to *ravioli Piedmontese* and three spaghettis.

Seafood specialties range from petrale Florentine to the rare *bouillebesina!* The *saltimboca alla Romana* and veal *piccata* are my choices. True spumoni and Amaretto cheesecake are typical desserts. After this— an espresso or cappuccino.

Moderate. Open seven days. Monday through Saturday from 5 to 11 P.M., Sunday from 3 to 10 P.M. Open for lunch only to parties of fifty to hundred people. Reservations advised. All major credit cards. Piano Wednesday through Saturday. Full bar. Child's menu. Valet parking. Casual to semi-dressy.

★
NEW SUNSHINE PIZZA/Italian/Pizza
3891 Piedmont Avenue/Oakland/Area 2/(415) 428-2500

An original eastern type family pizzeria in a converted Victorian home, this is on the way to elegance and pizza heaven. Nothing but the freshest ingredients are used by owners/operators John and Shari Glatzer and the crusts are thin and crunchy. Situated on Oakland's oldest street with an open air patio, this pizzeria will compete favorably with the best in San Francisco. Some will even go so far as to say—as the menu does—"the finest pizza this side of the Mississippi." I won't, but it's close.

268

Moderate. Open Tuesday through Sunday from 5 to 11 P.M. No reservations. No credit cards. Wine and beer only. Patio. Street parking. Casual.

★
NICARAGUA/Nicaraguan
3015 Mission/San Francisco/Area 2/(415) 550-9283

Part of the life of the Nicaragua restaurant is on its walls. Surrounding the counter and diners is an open-air clothes closet of brightly embroidered Nicaragua shirts, broad-brimmed hats, a Nicaraguan flag of blue and white and, inexplicably, a blue, white and gold foil saint's altar in the rear. Some of the items on the wall are for sale (*se venden camisas guayaberas* . . .), though certainly not the flag or saint. The food's top notch: try the *indio viéjo,* a beef mixture with corn flour, much better than its colorful name (which means "old Indian") implies; or the *baho,* long-simmered to bring out and meld the flavors of beef, *yuca* and plantain.

Inexpensive. Open seven days. Sunday through Thursday from 11 A.M. to 10 P.M. Friday and Saturday to midnight. Reservations accepted. No credit cards. Wine and beer only. Street parking. Casual.

★ ★
NOB HILL CAFE/Continental
1152 Taylor Street/San Francisco/Area 2/(415) 776-6915

Literally "Top of the Hill" in more ways than one, and praised extravagantly by every usually caustic critic who has somehow managed to secure one of the seven tables, this veritable gemlet of a miniature restaurant has won a fiercely loyal clientele away from nearby illustrious dining places.

Reservations are absolutely necessary, something you will understand with your very first taste of the delectable food. Owner Gerardo Boccara, who is responsible for the meal cooking, counts among his patrons the social leaders, old money and new money as well as delegates from the intelligentsia. One thing these usually diverse types share — appreciation of the finest in food and drink, with their corollaries of service and ambiance. Gerardo offers all, with exquisite specialties, some choice wines (try the Navarro gewurtztraminer), a dedicated, most knowledgeable waiter and a delightfully simple interior, all off-white and pastel, entered through an always half-open Dutch door.

Gerardo is internationally experienced in his profession, with background in such exotics as Marrakech, Casablanca, Paris (where he opened their first disco), etc. Their loss was our gain for he arrived in San Francisco during the '60s, captaining at Canlis where Michiko, his wife, was head waitress. Together they opened Nob Hill in 1978, nobly replacing what for four decades had been a hamburger-type eatery in a store-front. Half the cafe holds the glass-over-linen topped tables, each bearing a crystal vase with flowers. A silver napkin ring encloses your crisp cloth. Well-modulated modern jazz melodies from KJAZ background the crosscurrents of conversation while he prepares your meal. Large blackboards above the kitchen-half of Nob Hill are chalked daily with the numerous specials and certain standards, perhaps, at luncheon, a seafood quiche with salad, omelettes (always) or the sautéed prawns. Some of his dinner entrées (served with a light, thin soup, such as tomato or cauliflower and delicious salad, Japanese in concept) are sautéed scallops Nicoise, canard orange (one of the most vaunted here) and filet of lamb with cumin, to name a few. Coffee is just right, not too strong but with satisfying flavor; I noted the French roast with pleasure. Desserts are remarkably good, as expected. Both the pecan tart and the chocolate truffle with Grand Marnier are typical. I admit—I put away one of each. **Moderate.** Open seven days. Lunch Tuesday through Friday from 11 A.M. to 2:30 P.M. Dinner Tuesday through Saturday from 5:30 to 11 P.M. Reservations necessary. No credit cards. Wine and beer only. Street parking. Casual.

★ ★
NORMAN'S RESTAURANT/California/Continental
3204 College Avenue/Berkeley/Area 2/(415) 655-5291

The philosophy of Norman's owner, Howard Sylvester, appears on the menu: "The owner may be your bus boy, your bartender, or your waiter. Hopefully, we all fully represent the owner to you." It's no idle boast that the prompt, careful service and attention to detail make dining here a warm and pleasant experience. Fresh flowers, solid fir beams, and framed floral prints lend a modern yet homey look to the clean lines of the restaurant. Tables are surrounded by Breuer chairs and simply appointed with white linen and candlelight. Not to be upstaged, the kitchen presents unusual dishes conceived with imagination and executed with care. When in season, salmon receives a perfect poaching and is served with a golden caviar. Roast duckling *à l'orange* is done to a turn, the skin crisp and the flesh succulent, with no trace of greasiness. An unusual dish is roast beef blintzes, crêpes surrounding a mixture of diced roast, kasha, mushrooms, seasoned with sherry and burgundy and served with sour cream. There are also nightly specials which may include blackened red snapper with Créole spices or swordfish with rosemary-orange butter. Dinners are preceded by either a chilled artichoke, tossed salad

or soup and are accompanied with rice, vegetable and a solid Bulgar wheat bread. The wine list presents a good selection of California cabernets and rieslings, Bordeaux and German whites.
Moderate. Open seven days. Lunch Monday through Friday from 11:30 A.M. to 2 P.M. Dinner served Monday through Thursday from 6 to 10 P.M., Friday and Saturday from 6 to 10:30 P.M., Sunday from 5:30 to 9:30 P.M. Reservations advised. All major credit cards. Full bar. Street parking. Casual to semi-dressy.

★ ★
NORTH BEACH/Italian/Continental
1512 Stockton Street/San Francisco/Area 2/(415) 392-1587

This is the best of the "I can't believe I ate the whole thing" Italian restaurants, because it is an unusual combination of *alta cucina* (particularly on the sauces) and hearty peasant fare brought to new heights. My last visit, I had a gargantuan *antipasto* with generous slices of expensive prosciutto and calamari (squid); a fresh green salad, not just lettuce, served chilled, with zingy homemade Italian dressing; minestrone like mama used to make; a dish of pasta with savory sauce; a selection of entrées from veal Milanese to *calamari livornese* or sole *mugnàia* or trout hollandaise; and desserts like rum cake with chocolate topping. House wines are good and the prices are right, also. There's been an Italian restaurant at 1512 Stockton since 1928, but it was only in 1970 — when Lorenzo Petroni joined with chef Bruno Orsi (brother of the downtown Orsi) — that it became not only above average but stratospheric. Alka-Seltzer is not a bad idea for an apéritif before settling down to this stomach-boggling dinner (I take one before every big dinner), and you'll need a place to rest afterwards.
Moderate to expensive. Open seven days. Lunch from 11:30 A.M. to 4 P.M. Dinner from 4 to 11:30 P.M. Reservations advised. All major credit cards. Full bar. Valet parking. Casual.

To obtain the best results from this Guide, be sure to consult the map on the various Northern California areas on page 28.

★
NORTH CHINA/Chinese/Mandarin
2315 Van Ness Avenue/San Francisco/Area 2/(415) 673-8201

The Lee family is responsible for opening the very first northern Chinese restaurant in Chinatown, and David Lee carries on the tradition in his North China restaurant on Van Ness. The tea duck, simmered for twelve hours in a broth of ginger, onion, and anise, is extraordinary for the delicate flavor. Other specialties here are the *kung pao* shrimp, the *mu shu* dishes, and the dry-braised beef. I would suggest you try one of the California gewurtztraminers as the best accompaniment of spicier fare.
Moderate. Open Monday through Saturday from 4 to 10 P.M. Reservations advised on weekends. Visa, MC. Wine and beer only. Street parking. Casual.

★ ★
NUT TREE/American/California
Nut Tree/Area 3/(707) 448-1818

An utter delight from the Bower family: authentic California cuisine (yes, there is such a thing—a reminder of our Spanish, Italian, Russian, Aztec and Mexican heritage) in a sparkling setting that includes a miniature railroad that shuttles to and from the airport (it's a popular "fly in"), a colorful and capricious toy shop, a gift shop, an art gallery and imaginative dining areas. Now, in its seventh decade, the cuisine has been improved by geniuses like Luther Burbank who blessed the vegetables and the fine chefs who adapted the dishes to western palates. It would take a volume simply to adequately describe the menu, but I'm certain that there's something for everyone, from the almond chicken to the Nut Tree tamale to the barbecued spareribs to the Swiss steak stew in a bread basket. There are salads, sandwiches and friendly people. Try the chess pie for desert—walnuts and raisins in a butterscotch filling—it's been a favorite for decades. And it's all garden fresh, wholesome and good, albeit not inexpensive. A must-see for visitors to the area.
Moderate to expensive. Open seven days. Breakfast from 7 to 11 A.M. Lunch from 11 A.M. to 5 P.M. Dinner from 5 to 9 P.M., summer months 10 P.M. Reservations accepted. Visa, MC, AX. Wine and beer only. Patio. View. Child's menu. Lot parking. Casual.

In order to obtain the best results from this Guide, please consult "A Few Inside Tips" on page 18.

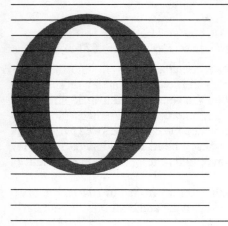

★ ★
OAKMONT INN/Continental/American
7025 Oakmont Drive/Oakmont/Area 3/(707) 539-3111

Although the Oakmont Inn does offer an impressive wine list, guests may be forgiven if they find the view alone intoxicating. Broad windows overlook the lush Oakmont golf course, beyond which rise the rugged mountains marking the boundary between Napa and Sonoma counties. However, hosts Bob Schreck, Jurgen Weise and Dieter Meier have gone to considerable lengths to ensure that the Inn's cuisine rivals the breathtaking landscape.

Diners can choose from a variety of tempting à la carte entrées that include filet mignon *Massena*, and roast duck *aux pruneaux* (flamed at your table with Armagnac). Among the dinner entrées are filet of salmon zinfandel, veal sauté Dijonnaise, breast of capon *Marengo*, and sweetbreads princess. Wine lovers can order the fixed-price "wine country dinner," which features premium wines (priced separately) by the glass, if desired, and a special menu that changes every two weeks.

As noted before, the wine list, carrying both leading California and imported labels, is impressive.

Moderate. Open seven days a week. Lunch Monday through Saturday from 11 A.M. to 3 P.M. Dinner Monday through Saturday from 5 to 9:30 P.M., Sunday from 3 to 8:30 P.M. Sunday brunch from 9 A.M. to 3 P.M. Reservations advised. All major cards. Full bar. Parking in adjacent lot. Casual to semi-dressy.

In order to obtain the best results from this Guide, be sure to read the French, German, Italian and Oriental menu translators on pages 399 to 404 of this Guide.

OCEAN/Chinese
726 Clement Street/San Francisco/Area 2/(415) 221-3351

Not long ago, while visiting New York, a friend told me that he had a great new Chinese restaurant to go to. He said this was currently *the place* in Chinatown, and that I should expect a wait. Was it a Hunanese restaurant, I asked, or perhaps a new Foo Chow style place, or one that serves incredible Shanghai style meals? Nope, said my friend, it's Cantonese. Amazingly, Cantonese cuisine was making a comeback in the Big Apple. And the food I ate that night at the Phoenix Garden was some of the best Chinese cuisine I've ever eaten, Cantonese or otherwise. It wasn't the old style of heavily cornstarched, steamed-to-death dishes of my youth, but rather a new, cleaner form of Cantonese cooking, that depended heavily on fresh ingredients and quick cooking. In essence, it was the equivalent of *nouvelle* cuisine Chinoise-style.

One of the centers in San Francisco for the rebirth of the long-maligned Cantonese style of cooking is the extremely popular Ocean restaurant, out in the New Chinatown section along Clement Street. So popular is Ocean that a wait is inevitable at any hour, in the restaurant's tiny vestibule, or out in the fog of the Avenues. You can tell those waiting by the number they clutch in their hands like a rosary.

Once seated, the experience at Ocean is one of speed and efficiency. Dishes emerge with disconcerting speed from the kitchen, in no particular order. Perhaps because of that speed, the dishes tend to be erratic, though they lean toward erratically good, rather than bad. Braised straw mushrooms with baby corn were a wonderful creation, tender and musky. Fried squab with special sauce tasted great, though several members of my party were disconcerted by the presence of the squabs decapitated head upon the platter. Dried squid with shrimp sauce was a bit of a disappointment, with the squid more rubbery than usual, and the shrimp sauce notable only for its nondescript nature.

Though there's strong leaning toward seafood at Ocean (for true sybaritic pleasure, try an order of prawns with pepper and salt, which come complete with heads), there are unexpected pleasures in some of the more prosaic sounding dishes. Try the beef with tender greens, or any of the egg foo yungs, and see what those old standbys should really taste like. Enjoy the house spareribs and the superb cold chicken salad. But don't expect fortune cookies. For whatever reason, Ocean does not end the meal with that most venerable of Cantonese traditions. **Moderate.** Open seven days. Lunch from 11:30 A.M. to 3 P.M. Dinner from 4:30 to 9:30 P.M. Wine and beer. Visa, MC. Street parking. Casual.

★

OLD EUROPE RESTAURANT/Continental
663 Lighthouse Avenue/Pacific Grove/Area 2/(408) 375-1743

Even the menu-sophisticated and cuisine-weary find here a new zest in dining out when they experience an evening meal cooked by owner/chef Gernot Leitzinger—a Swiss perfectionist of the old school, although still a comparatively young man. Gernot and his wife, Rosemarie, have one of the most appealing places on the Monterey Peninsula. The astute combination of wood and brick with many brass, copper and crystal artifacts results in a feeling that one is indeed in a European village.

For about eleven years, Gernot has been creating such inspired dishes as wild boar medallions, as well as veal *piccata,* veal *cordon bleu* and *champignon frites,* a supreme appetizer. Some come here just for his escargots. Specialties include venison, boar, and other game. The wine list matches the cuisine and you are fortunate that you're dining here today and not just a few years ago, when Pacific Grove forbade alcoholic beverages. This is a nostalgically appealing town of grand old homes and lovely little cottages dating back one hundred years and more. **Moderate to expensive.** Open Tuesday through Saturday (Sunday in summer) from 5:30 to 9 P.M. Reservations advised. Visa, MC, AX. Wine and beer only. Street parking. Semi-dressy.

★ ★

OLD POODLE DOG/French
161 Sutter Street/San Francisco/Area 2/(415) 392-0353

We're talking history here. There's been a Poodle Dog in San Francisco since 1890. Known initially by the first name "Ritz"— and said to be a corruption of "Poulet d'or"—this ancient establishment has known its ups and downs. It has probably never been better than today, now that the grandson of the original owner has taken charge, even though the location and some of the cooking concepts have been changed to accomodate the 1980s.

It is a spacious, luxurious restaurant, not entirely unmindful of its roots. Chicken "a la Ritz" is still served, though now a lighter and brighter dish in a sherry-cream sauce. Young Gary Jenanyan is at home on the ranges, transforming old familiars like rack of lamb into interesting and even exciting dishes. Jenanyan is a product of the Robert Mondavi Great Chefs of France cooking school where he picked up a few tricks from the likes of Paul Bocuse, Jean Troisgros, Michel Guerard and others of exalted station.

Dishes to recommend include appetizer tartlettes filled differently each week like a kind of Escoffier *dim sum*. The original crab or seafood "Louie" is said to have been developed here and it is still prepared with extra virgin French olive oil, champagne vinegar and Dijon mustard. Rex sole turned up in the 1950s and is a bit over rich, with clarified butter used in the reduction. Whatever you order is bound to be among the best dishes in the city and is appropriately expensive.

Moderate to expensive. Lunch weekdays from 11:30 A.M. to 2:30 P.M. Dinner Tuesday through Saturday from 6 to 9:30 P.M. Reservations advised. All major credit cards. Full bar. Valet parking for dinner. Dressy.

★
OLD SOUTH BBQ/Barbecue
27941 Manon Avenue/Hayward/Area 2/(415) 782-1163

Owner Harold Cox is proud of his homemade beef links, and with good cause. Spare ribs, chicken, sliced beef, and homemade sweet potato pie are served up by the Cox family in a spotlessly clean, comfortable forty-seat eat-in or take-out establishment that is a favorite of some of the '49ers, who could afford to eat anywhere. The hot sauce is really hot—the way I like it—but if you don't have callouses on your palate, you might start with the mild.

Inexpensive to moderate. Open Tuesday through Saturday from 11 A.M. to 10 P.M., Sunday noon to 8 P.M. No reservations. All major credit cards. Wine and beer only. Lot parking. Casual.

★ ★
OLD SWISS HOUSE/French/Swiss
Pier 39/San Francisco/Area 2/(415) 434-0432

Chef/owner Roger Braun and his lovely wife Marianne, both Swiss-born, describe their favorite of locals and visitors as a "French restaurant with Swiss touches." On the mark, for Roger's fame is now worldwide, considering the international mélange of travelers that has visited since its late 1978 opening, when this charming dining place was one of the original Pier 39 tenants.

Roger and Marianne won a most vocal claque of discerning diners when they owned and operated central Marin County's pet—The Swiss Cellar. Having to turn away as many as a hundred would-be diners nightly from their intimate premises offended both their sense of responsibility to patrons and their basic financial instincts, so their Pier 39 restaurant was the ideal solution.

On the upper level, wide windows open to spreading vistas of the Golden Gate Bridge, the Bay, Fisherman's Wharf, nearby piers, the City's Pacific Heights residential hills, even Marin County and Bay traffic. This is a captivating retreat, with lace curtain, white napery, colorful designs, costumed waitresses, and chef Roger's talents.

The menu opens with escargot Bourguigonne, *pâté maison* and smoked salmon. Soup du jour, possibly chowder. Entrées can be such as: wienerschnitzel, milk-fed veal, steak *morelle,* poached salmon (fresh, seasonally), lobster tail or prawns sautéed in white wine, fresh tomatoes and onions, with rice— *"Portugaise."* Roger's sensitive approach to cooking utilized the light touch years before its vogue. The Brauns make their own ice cream. A full bar for you tipplers. Choice wines, of course.

Moderate. Open seven days for lunch from 11:30 A.M. to 4 P.M. Dinner from 5 to 10 P.M. Reservations accepted. All major credit cards. Full bar. View. Validated garage parking. Semi-dressy.

★ ★
THE OLEMA INN/California/Continental
10000 Sir Francis Drake Boulevard/Olema/Area 3/(415) 663-8441

Few restaurants in the entire West can match this magnificently restored old hotel, at the entrance to the Pt. Reyes National Seashore. The Inn opened in 1876 as a hostelry where John Steinbeck, Jack London, Edwin Booth (actor-brother of John Wilkes Booth), Governor Hiram Johnson and the likes penned their names in the register.

Re-opened in July 1980, after four painstaking years of renovation, the Olema Inn (Olema is the Miwok Indian name for coyote) now has several cozy dining rooms and a spacious terrace. A wine and espresso bar lounge is a usually quiet retreat with chamber music (of course). The Inn is also quite a serious art gallery, with exhibits and showings of local artists. They still have three rooms upstairs, bed and breakfast.

Fresh, seasonal foods highlight the continental cuisine. All possible local products are utilized. Oysters come from Johnson's nearby; the fresh fish from Bodega Bay and veal is local Provimi. The kitchen has a sensitive touch and everything is reasonably priced, particularly the lunch. Tomales Bay's sea air will enliven your appetite.

Moderate. Open Thursday through Tuesday. Lunch weekdays from 11:30 A.M. to 3 P.M. Dinner from 5 to 9 P.M. Saturday 6 to 10 P.M. Sunday brunch from 10 A.M. to 3 P.M. Reservations advised. Visa, MC, AX. Entertainment. Full bar. Patio. Parking lot. Casual.

For best results, consult "How to Use This Guide" on page 25.

★★
OLIVER'S/Continental
1700 Second Street (entrance at 950 Washington)/Napa/Area 3/(707) 252-4555

Oliver's offers "one-of-a-kind cuisine" that early on made it the *Critic's Choice* and a member of International World Famous Restaurants. Now owned and operated by Julie Merdith, Oliver's has taken some exciting twists and turns along the way, and still ends up a winner. The menu tempts with such specialties as: rack of lamb, baby lobster tails, and beef medallions. Table side desserts and salads are especially good. This is a relaxing and enjoyable way to end a day of tasting and traveling through Napa Valley. None of this really sounds so unique as to be called "one-of-a-kind," but tasting may change your mind.
Moderate to expensive. Open seven days. Lunch served from 11:30 A.M. to 2:30 P.M. Dinner from 5:30 to 10 P.M. Reservations advised. All major credit cards. Entertainment. Full bar. Parking lot. Semi-dressy.

★
THE OMELETTE HOUSE/American
514 Peninsula Avenue/San Mateo/Area 2/(415) 348-9883

Some great philosopher once described the egg as the most nearly perfect object in an imperfect world. I would tend to agree, although I don't know where that leaves Raquel Welch. The Omelette House has taken the nearly perfect egg and perfected it. The three egg omelettes are fluffy, light and innovative. Selections range from shrimp curry (with raisins, chutney and coconut) to the Veronique (seasoned chicken, mushrooms, artichoke hearts and grapes sautéed in a white wine sauce), the Meridan (salami, green chiles and cheddar cheese) and Brazilian flambé (bananas, brown sugar, cinnamon, butter and flaming rum). Of course, there are more traditional standbys of avocado, ham, tomato, mushrooms, and onion which may be combined with the more creative selections of eggplant, bean sprouts, pineapple, and cinnamon. The "U-Do-It" invites you to make up your own combinations.

In addition to the extensive selection, the main claim to fame here is their record in the Guiness Book of World records. Owner Eleanor Woodman managed to serve one hundred people with *one* ostrich egg.
Inexpensive to moderate. Open weekdays from 8 A.M. to 2 P.M. Saturday and Sunday from 8 to 3 P.M. Reservations accepted. Visa, MC. Full bar. Patio. Child's menu. Street parking. Casual.

★

ONDINE/French/Continental
558 Bridgeway/Sausalito/Area 3/(415) 982-1740

Ondine has one of my favorite night views of the Bay—silvery and smudged beneath the city's glittering skyline. The cuisine is not quite up to the ambiance or the view, but it's still a worth-while experience. The *poulet sauté Patricia,* tournedos Rossini and the *quenelles* are fine. Best of all are the Grand Marnier soufflé (place your order at the beginning of the dinner, please) and the extensive wine list. If you can afford it, have a dessert sauterne, imported, with the soufflé or the dessert of your choosing.

Expensive. Open seven nights from 5:30 to 10:30 P.M. Sunday 5 to 10 P.M. Reservations advised. All major credit cards. Full bar. View. Valet parking. Semi-dressy to dressy.

★

ONE-UP RESTAURANT AND LOUNGE/Continental
Hyatt on Union Square/San Francisco/Area 2/(415) 398-1234

Elegantly placed atop the Hyatt on Union Square, occupying the thirty-sixth floor; this restaurant provides its patrons not only with choice cosmopolitan dining selections but with lofty views through glass expanses.

Hyatt hotels, from their Burlingame origin in 1960 (their first construction at the Los Angeles airport location was purchased intact) have always projected their restaurants for their businessmen patrons who possess civilized instincts and sophisticated tastes. This belief has encouraged this hotel chain to present better-than-expected food in compatible settings. One-Up, although not designated as a Hyatt Regency, demonstrates this concept.

The Sunday brunch, in the same high-ceilinged rooms, is rated as one of San Francisco's finest. Hyatt brunches rate high everywhere. What better way to launch a week—magnificent morsels and views.

Expensive. ($40 minimum). Open seven days. Lunch served weekdays from 11:30 P.M. to 2 P.M. Dinner served from 6 to 10 P.M. Sunday brunch from 10:30 A.M. to 2 P.M. Reservations advised. All major credit cards. Full bar. View. Garage parking. Semi-dressy to dressy.

To obtain the best results from this Guide, be sure to consult the map on the various Northern California areas on page 28.

★★
ON LOCK SAM/Chinese/Cantonese
333 South Sutter/Stockton/Area 6/(209) 466-4561

When On Lock Sam first opened in 1898, it was to serve the Chinese railroad workers, little more than slaves, who longed for the foods of Canton. As the area grew, the menu, written in Chinese characters, was enlarged to include English subtitles — a necessary metamorphosis to accommodate the Gold Rush prospectors and their ladies. That practice still continues, and the fried asparagus, stuffed chicken wings, prawns barbecued in the shell, garlic chicken and Chinese chicken salad are offered in both languages. This is Cantonese-creative, a far better representation of Chinese foods than you'll find in most "Chinese" restaurants.

Inexpensive. Open seven days. Sunday through Thursday from 11:30 A.M. to 10 P.M., Friday and Saturday till 11 P.M. Reservations accepted. Visa, MC. Full bar. Patio. Child's menu. Lot parking. Casual.

★★
OPERA HOUSE CAFE/American/California
145 Kentucky Street/Petaluma/Area 3/(707) 765-4402

Host/co-owner Charles Robbins describes the cafe's cuisine as "country style" in honor of the country American, country French and country Italian recipes that inspire chefs Lea Bergen and Kay Baumhefner. And they are inspired. Both the seasonally adjusted basic menu and the daily specials (fish and shellfish only when available fresh) reflect their creative approach to what is clearly a labor of love.

Noted for the freshness of its produce, the cafe also offers a different soup, made from that morning's chicken stock, each day. Desserts, concocted daily on the premises, vary endlessly, always in keeping with the season. Wine authority Don Baumhefner has crafted an interesting list of California wines, and some uncommon beers are offered as well. A small bar accomodates tasters. Though the cafe's atmosphere is informal, the staff is courteous and efficient.

Moderate. Open Monday through Saturday. Lunch Monday through Saturday from 11:30 A.M. to 2:30 P.M. Dinner Thursday through Saturday from 6:00 to 9:30 P.M. Reservations accepted. Visa, MC, AX. Wine and beer only. Street parking. Casual.

Please be sure to consult "Tipping Made Easy" on page 22 of this Guide.

★
ORI-DELI/Indonesian/Deli
5479 Snell Avenue/San Jose/Area 2/(408) 578-6262

Robert Tan has found an idea whose time has come – an Oriental deli. Part of the menu is Chinese, but Tan feels that the Indonesian selections are his specialties. The *nasi rames* with *sate* is an unusual combination of steamed rice, spiced beef, spiced potato chips, shrimp chips, *serundeg, sambel goreng* (spiced coconut), and *sambel* (chiles). The exotic-sounding *fu young hai* translates simply as an omelette with crab meat. The Chinese side of the menu offers very little creativity: almond chicken, cashew chicken, beef chow mein, spring rolls . . . all the usuals.

One part of the Ori-Deli is sectioned off to be a store that purveys Thai, Filipino and Dutch food in addition to the Chinese and Indonesian products. At the very least, it can be an interesting experience wandering through aisles of completely unrecognizable foodstuffs – and realizing many of these odd-looking things were used in your meal. **Inexpensive.** Open Tuesday through Friday from 10 A.M. to 8 P.M. Saturday from noon to 9 P.M. Sunday from 4 to 9 P.M. Reservations advised. Visa, MC. No alcohol. Adequate parking. Casual.

★ ★
ORIENT EXPRESS/Continental
1 Market Plaza/San Francisco/Area 2/(415) 957-1776

Named for the legendary, deluxe train that spanned the Continent from London to Istanbul, this beautifully designed dining place is architecturally so impressive that your trip to The City really must include at least a stroll through the outer lobby on One Market Plaza, with a pause for refreshment in the appealing cocktail lounge and bar adjoining the main dining room. Glass panels are etched with the name and insignia of the *Cie Internationale de Wagon-Lits,* which operated the Orient Express. Within, the exotic, enticing aromas of the southern European cuisine will arouse even the most laggard taste-buds. Luncheon, only, is serve to those who daily reserve one of the coveted tables. Many office workers come not only from nearby high-rise towers, but from all over the city (even the City Hall politicos), for the superior food and soul-soothing ambience.

There are nine, room-wide Byzantine arches, set at twelve-foot intervals, upon columns reminiscent of eras of the Pharoahs. Colors range from off-white to desert sand and complement the napery and chair cushions, even to the dusty rose carpeting, abundance of fresh flowers and the custom-made, heavy, blonde wood chairs. Owner/operator Khajag Sarkissian, a modest gentleman of incredible talent, comments: "A husky man likes a solid feel to his chair. He relaxes more while at his meal and returns."

The eclectic menu will divert your attention from the compelling design which is akin to that of an award-winning motion picture set. Selections range from calamari vinaigrette, smoked duck, Greek salad, cold cucumber and yogurt soup (my favorite) to unusual sandwiches and hot entrées such as baby salmon, rack of lamb marinated in pomegranate juice, veal *piccata*, fettuccine, and even that worldwide standard—New York steak. The food is an itinerary of special dishes that follows the path of the Orient Express—from London to Istanbul.

Moderate to expensive. Open weekdays for breakfast from 6:30 to 10 A.M. Lunch from 11 A.M. to 2:30 P.M. Reservations strongly advised. Visa, MC, CB, AX. Entertainment. Full bar. Public garage. Semi-dressy.

★
ORIGINAL JOE'S/Italian
144 Taylor Street/San Francisco/Area 2/(415) 775-4877

They're not original—even the location isn't where the late "New Joe's" (from which this descends) used to be, but it's been family operated since 1937 and you don't serve Italian food for that long in San Francisco unless you're filling a need as well as a stomach. The neighborhood is pornville and care should be used walking in the area at night, but Original Joe's somehow remains above it all and serves a respectable non-sleazy clientele who seriously study the massive à la carte menu. Minestrone is for real and the scalloppine with mushrooms is generous enough for a platoon and good enough for a gourmet. All portions are big here (even the French bread is served in quarter-pound loaves) and the cooking is exhibition style, in full view of the customers. The daily lunch specials have attracted a large and loyal following, and the *osso bucco*, braised veal, is admirable.

Moderate. Open seven days from 10:30 A.M. to 1:30 A.M. No reservations. No credit cards. Full bar. Street and lot parking. Casual.

In order to obtain the best results from this Guide, be sure to read the French, German, Italian and Oriental menu translators on pages 399 to 404 of this Guide.

★
ORIGINAL JOE'S/Italian
301 South First Street/San Jose/Area 2/(408) 292-7030

Louis J. Rocca Jr., son of the former proprietor of Original Joe's in San Francisco, operates this satisfying, middle-of-the-road Italian restaurant with an essentially à la carte menu, good soups, great grilles, huge portions and reasonable prices. In many respects, this is a good copy of the San Francisco Original, itself a descendant of the long-gone "New Joe's" that was a landmark. The bread is terrific and, along with minestrone and the good house Chianti, makes for a lunch in itself. The hamburgers are outrageous.
Inexpensive to moderate. Open seven days from 11 A.M. to 1:30 A.M. No reservations. No credit cards. Full bar. Child's menu. Street parking. Casual.

★
OSCAR'S BISTRO/French
21181 Foothill Boulevard/Hayward/Area 2/(415) 538-3522

Oscar" is neither the owner nor the chef. "Oscar" is the stuffed pheasant perched by the door in this ramshackle old cottage. Owner/partner/chef Don Buhrz does a spectacular veal Florentine, and the *grenouilles cannoise Provençale* frog's legs served French country style, are simply marvelous. Lobster thermidor and tournedos are another couple of his specialties. The rest of the menu we found not unordinary yet nothing is disappointing, and the wines are reasonable.
Moderate to expensive. Dinner Tuesday through Thursday from 6 to 9:30 P.M., Friday and Saturday from 6 to 10:30 P.M. Reservations accepted. Visa, MC, DC, CB. Wine and beer only. Child's menu. Street and lot parking. Semi-dressy.

★
OSPITAL'S VILLA BASQUE/Basque
448 South Hunter Street/Stockton/Area 6/(209) 462-4377

Pete and John Ospital have created a warm, friendly restaurant with hearty slap-on-the-back Basque cheer enough and to spare. They start their day's serving with a mid-day regale that can leave you ready for little other than an afternoon nap. Soup and salad (served with olive oil) are served in help-yourself, all-you-can-eat bowls. The French bread is tempting, the entrées worth demolishing and dessert and coffee are included in the feast. If this is indicative of Basque cooking, it is no wonder their province is heard of so infrequently—no one can move after such glutinous bachannals.

The Ospital's also create a hearty dinner that leaves the pocketbook intact. But quantity is not the only bonus – the food is innovative and always of high quality.
Moderate. Open for lunch Monday through Saturday from 11 A.M. to 3 P.M. Dinner served Tuesday through Saturday from 5 to 8 P.M. Reservations accepted. Visa, MC, AX. Full bar. Ample parking. Casual.

★
OTAFUKU TEI/Japanese
1737 Buchanan Mall/San Francisco/Area 2/(415) 931-1578

Teahouse of the happy facemask," as it was interpreted for me, is the best example of an uncomplicated, ungarish teahouse in San Francisco. The prices are snack-shop but the quality is quite high. A specialty of the house is *gyoza*, a Japanese version of the Chinese "pot sticker": seasoned gound pork wrapped in this pastry and steam fried. The *donburi* dishes (bowl of rice topped with assorted ingredients) are generally great eating and begin at pre-inflationary prices on complete dinners which include a savory soybean soup, pickled vegetables and green tea. The choice of toppings ranges from fishcakes with bamboo shoots and mushrooms in an omelette to beef sukiyaki with slightly cooked egg. There is a wide selection of wheat or buckwheat noodles, cooked *al dente*. Newer to Western palates is *ochazuke*, presented here in four variations of toppings over hot green tea and rice (try the salted salmon). Hitoshi and Shigeko Marumoto operate an exciting restaurant with unusual and exotic dishes, and their fifty-seat tearoom is often crowded in appreciation of that fact.
Inexpensive. Open Monday through Saturday. Lunch from 11 A.M. to 2 P.M. Dinner from 5 to 10 P.M. No reservations. No credit cards. Wine and beer only. Street parking. Casual.

★
OWL TAVERN/American
134 Mill Street/Grass Valley/Area 5/(916) 273-0526

Two years after the opening of Empire Mine in 1850, the first brick building was constructed and it was, naturally enough, a restaurant/saloon to accommodate the prospector's newly acquired affluence. The back bar is solid cherry wood and was assembled on the premises after being shipped from Austria. The bar/lounge with the antique cash register and ancient carvings is as comfortable today as it must have seemed back then, when meals were paid for in gold dust or coin. The dining room is a stark and pleasant contrast: natural rock slab walls, skylight fixtures supported by heavy beams, old brick, captain's chairs and natural woods. There are light sandwich lunches with soups and salad, but at dinner there's fine prime rib (as long as it lasts) and London broil steak and fresh Idaho trout. Note: You can tour the old mine by obtaining a pass at the administration building, and you can rent snowmobiles in the wintertime.

Moderate to expensive. Open seven days. Lunch Monday through Friday from 11 A.M. to 2:30 P.M., Saturday from noon to 3 P.M. Dinner Monday through Thursday from 5 to 10 P.M., Friday and Saturday from 5 to 11 P.M. Sunday from 4 to 9 P.M. Reservations accepted. Visa, MC, AX. Full bar. Lot parking. Casual.

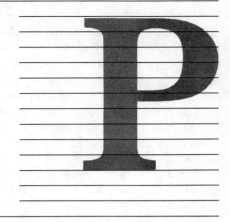

★
PACIFIC CAFE/Seafood
7000 Geary Boulevard/San Francisco/Area 2/(415) 387-7091
900 North Point/Ghirardelli Square/San Francisco/Area 2/(415) 775-1173
2151 Salvio/Concord/Area 2/(415) 687-3888
3560 Callan Boulevard/South San Francisco/Area 2/(415) 952-0666
850 College Avenue/Kentfield/Area 3/(415) 456-3898

That James Thomason and Thomas Hawker dared to open a sea-food house in the city of Tadiches and Sams is startling. That they were immediately successful when they opened little more than nine years ago is improbable. The reason is that, while their menu is minis-cule compared to the other venerable seafood emporiums, the food is excellent—mostly broiled sole, halibut, fresh salmon, abalone and lob-ster, along with oysters that have been deftly pan fried and firm shrimp (in shell, with a towel thoughtfully provided) with a simple garlic and wine sauce. The small wine card represents careful thought and there's even a fairly good house champagne.
Moderate. Open seven days. Dinner served Monday through Thurs-day from 5 to 10:30 P.M., Friday and Saturday from 5 to 11 P.M., Sun-day from 5 to 10 P.M. No reservations. No credit cards. Wine and beer only. Street parking. Casual.

To obtain the best results from this Guide, be sure to consult the map on the various Northern California areas on page 28.

DA ★★
THE PACIFIC EDGE/California/Continental
Highlands Inn/Highway One/Carmel/Area 1/(408) 624-3801

Literally millions of tourists and travelers have come to this great old inn, some only to stroll the grounds and have a libation, others for their honeymoon in one of the quaint cottages. Founded in 1916, the Highlands Inn continues with a new life (completely rebuilt and restored), a beautiful, contemporary world-class destination. The Pacific Edge exemplifies these high standards. In the beautiful two-level dining room, unsurpassed views of Carmel Bay, the Pacific and the forest of trees surrounding, all meals served are superb in concept and execution. To mention just a few of the chef's devisings: Monterey Bay salmon, Carmel River trout, fried calamari, Belon oysters, even clam fettuccine. My blackened swordfish was exceptional, as were my companions' grilled duck and roast pheasant. We ate a number of other items and found no fault. The bar lounge looked inviting. Perhaps another time. By then the sixty-odd townhouses should be complete. **Moderate to expensive.** Open seven days. Lunch from 11:30 A.M. to 2 P.M. Dinner 6 to 10:30 P.M. Reservations necessary. All major credit cards. Entertainment. Full bar. Valet parking. Semi-dressy to dressy.

★★
PACIFIC FRESH/Seafood
2203 Mariner Square Loop/Alameda/Area 2/(415) 521-6577
1130 North Mathilda Avenue/Sunnyvale/Area 2/(408) 745-1710
550 Ellinwood Way/Pleasant Hill/Area 2/(415) 827-3474

You who have eaten in some of those large, East Coast seafood restaurants will feel at home right off. Pacific Fresh takes full advantage of its nearly ten thousand square feet to accommodate over three hundred guests at once. The neat, clean lines of these additions to the ranks of the East Bay's leading dining places, suggest a nononsense approach to the business of feeding their patrons reasonably and very well indeed. Deft employment of brown, green and yellow in the airy, spacious rooms imparts a certain graciousness that is not as apparent in the New England establishments. The well-regarded Eve Tanovitz, graphic artist, created a series of seafood-related etchings in brass frames, mounted around the walls. Guests are seated comfortably in spindle-back chairs at well-spaced tables. No crowding at Pacific Fresh. While there are windows, there is no water view. Some folks have the interesting theory that the food is better if not served by or over the water.

These are basically dinner houses and meals here are planned, not spontaneously decided at the last minute. Therefore, as true seafood places, that is what they serve, except their New York steak and chicken breast, a concession to those who don't or won't eat fish and shellfish and to some of their banquet patrons. Managing partner Dan Laguna (with a name like that he'd have to go into the seafood business) has fishermen, some at Bodega Bay, who sell all their catch to him, often including less common varieties, like angel shark, butterfish, possibly a rare sock-eye salmon. Note of these is given on the lighted boards, announcing the day's specials. You'd do well with the mixed plate of calamari, fish, oyster and shrimp. Everything is good and fairly priced; just name your favorite. From 5 to 7 P.M. the "early catch" dinner is a bargain.

Moderate. Open seven days. Hours may vary. Lunch served weekdays from 11:30 A.M. to 2:30 P.M. Dinner from 5 to 10 P.M. Friday to 10:30 P.M. Saturday from noon to 10:30 P.M. Sunday from 10:30 A.M. to 9:30 P.M. Reservations accepted. Visa, MC, AX. Full bar. Child's menu. Parking lot. Casual.

PAM PAM EAST/American/Coffee Shop
The Raphael Hotel/398 Geary Street/San Francisco/Area 2/(415) 433-0113

The food need not be as good as it is here. The location just off Union Square is ideal for a twenty-four-hour-a-day restaurant, and one would expect it to be a greasy spoon. Actually, the French toast is nearly as good as at Sears, and the giant Belgian waffles, hangover omelette and the chef's chili are surprisingly good.

Inexpensive. Open seven days for twenty-four hours. No reservations. No credit cards. Full bar. Street parking and parking garage within one block. Casual.

★
PANOS'/American/Greek
4000 24th Street/San Francisco/Area 2/(415) 824-8000

Panos' food is immeasurably better than the concoctions that most Greek restaurants serve up. Here, it is as it should be, served by the John Panos Gianaras family. There are half a dozen fresh seafood entrées and another half dozen red meat main courses from which to choose. I particularly like the appetizers: *tsitsiki* (garlic and yogurt), feta cheese and Greek olives, *tarama* (creamed white caviar) and *riganita* (french fried zucchini). Open for Saturday and Sunday brunch featuring three egg omelettes, raisin spice pancakes, and more. They opened in 1978 to packed houses and they're still packing them in . . . for obvious reasons.

Moderate. Open seven days. Lunch weekdays from 11:30 A.M. to 2:30 P.M. Open nightly from 5 P.M. Saturday and Sunday brunch from 9 A.M. to 2:30 P.M. Reservations accepted. Visa, MC. Wine and beer only. Street parking. Casual to semi-dressy.

★ ★ ★
PAOLO'S/Continental/Italian
520 East Santa Clara Street/San Jose/Area 2/(408) 294-2558

Paolo's is the most-undiscovered, successful restaurant in all of Northern Callifornia. Owner Jack Allen says this with tongue-in-cheek despair for one always must reserve early to be certain of a table in this one-of-a-kind dining place. Opened in its current guise in 1959, it is now operated properly and efficiently by Jack's daughters, Carolyn and her sister, Jenny, with father occasionally present if only to answer a question or whip up a favorite dish. He likes what the girls are doing, even the redecorating. Very mellow.

Everything is made to order. Jack maintains that the essence of preparing food properly is *timing*, assuming that you have purchased the finest available ingredients (and he does – he does), and know your cooking thoroughly. Every dish here is served at that precise moment it reaches its peak of perfection. From childhood, Jack was fascinated with gourmet cookery– first as an avocation and, finally as his profession. He was heavily involved with food his entire life until he was strongly persuaded by friends to open the type of dining place where he could follow his percepts – Paolo's.

Italy's finest pastas are imported to make the delicate noodles from *capellini* to fettuccine, cooked al dente, using the true *parmigiano*, flown in at times. *Tortellini* and ravioli here clear your memory of all others. Jack has a dedication which the steak-and-potatoes diner – or better said, eater – could never appreciate. He is convinced that no other restaurant in this country – nay, in the world – is able to serve at one time as many fresh fruits as does Paolo's. Not only what is in season here – and that means everything the length of California and the western states, but prickly pears, figs, papaya, mangoes, raspberries – you name it, from the world over, appear on Paolo's tables.

Even the cheesecake here is one-of-a-kind, made from the original, now-vanished Lindy's recipe, bought from the pastry chef in the once-world-famous favorite of New York's cafe society and "in" people. While in the dessert mood, let me tell you about some of Paolo's special ones. The separate menu lists forty, count 'em, forty temptations, from raspberries in clotted cream, Comice pears with *teleme, hvarti* or Brie cheese, to fried cream with brandy; *zabaglioni;* Amaretto soufflé and about ten Gelato concoctions and, even, *granita di raspberry.* As you know, *granita* is pure fruit juice and water. Paolo's own equipment produces the *gelati* and *granita.* Where store ice cream checks out about twelve to fourteen percent butterfat, Paolo's is a whopping thirty-six percent. It's like being spoon-fed flavored whipped cream!

I skipped over much of the main courses. Space precludes my doing justice to the twenty appetizers, the eight special fish appetizers, the sixteen pastas, thirteen salads—don't miss "Jack's Empress Original"—an entire meal. Didn't I just mention sixteen pastas? Well, there are twenty-two more imported and homemade pastas! Sixteen fish, eleven poultry, fourteen veal and lamb specialties and bringing up the rear—twelve beef entrées. Even I can't believe this. Some favorites of mine—Icelandic *scampi livornese,* roasted quail and *spedini alla palermitana.*

Moderate to expensive. Open Monday through Saturday. Lunch served from 11 A.M. to 3 P.M. Dinner from 4:30 to 10 P.M. Reservations advised. All major credit cards. Parking lot. Dressy.

★ ★
PAPRIKAS FONO/Hungarian
Ghirardelli Square/900 North Point Street/San Francisco/Area 2/(415) 441-1223

Laszlo Fono is the man—for batter or for worse—who started the Magic Pan. The Quaker Oats Corporation became intrigued with his crêpe making machine and used it with some other ideas of the former Olympic skier as the basis for their growing Magic Pan empire. Mr. Fono found the corporate climate not to his liking, and returned to San Francisco with this restaurant jewel that serves authentic Hungarian foods (you know they're authentic when paprika is not used for cosmetic purposes but adds character to the construction of a dish). The dining room—called the Gulyas (goulash) room—is charming with a massive soup pot simmering at the center. The white walls are accented with colorful artifacts, and the outdoor terrace with fresh flowers everywhere provides a heart-stopping view of the Bay and the plaza below. *Palacsinta* (Hungarian for crêpe) is offered with luscious fillings like ham and asparagus or chicken strudel (chopped and rolled in paper-thin strudel dough). The menu is a lesson in Hungarian cuisine; try the "Farmer's Wife": layers of thinly sliced potato with bacon, sausage and eggs baked in a rich sour cream sauce and served with a red beet salad. Service is by colorfully costumed waitresses and our Hungarian wine was served by a waiter (sommelier? I don't think so) in an embroidered jacket.

Moderate. Open seven days. Lunch from 11 A.M. to 4:30 P.M. Dinner from 4:30 to 11 P.M. Reservations advised. Visa, MC, AX. Full bar. View of San Francisco Bay. Patio. Garage parking. Casual to semi-dressy.

PASAND/South Indian
1875 Union Street/San Francisco/Area 2/(415) 922-4498

A hard to find restaurant, but the rare and interesting cuisine of southern India is well worth the effort. Madras, the chief city in the state of Andra Pradesh, produces a somewhat different array of dishes than we have come to expect of an Indian restaurant. Appetizers include potato *pakora*, a delicious and somewhat spicy beginning to the dinner. Entrées include *ravva dosa* (crêpe with nuts and vegetables) and a splendid chicken *koorma* curry cooked in yogurt sauce. Lamb *biriani* with curry sauce was my favorite single dish. A family operation: the women do the cooking and just about any family member does the serving in this strange restaurant that claims to be the home of Luigi's Pizza as well.

Inexpensive to moderate. Open seven days from 11:30 A.M. to 10 P.M. Reservations advised. Visa, MC, AX, DC. Full bar. Entertainment. Patio. Street parking. Casual.

★
PASHA/Middle Eastern
1516 Broadway/San Francisco/Area 2/(415) 885-4477

B elly dancers performing naval manuevers are not generally associated with good food, in my experience, but an exception must be made for this mid-Eastern restaurant that is one of the outstanding late dining establishments in San Francisco. Located a little west of the Broadway tunnel, its business has grown in the more than a decade owner/manager Michael Deeb has been at the helm. These kind of restaurants usually offer a *prix fixe* menu with *b'stilla*, the Morrocan chicken/egg/almond and cinnamon pie, the most cherished course. Pasha is unique in that it is à la carte and you can compose your own feast with *harira* (spicy soup), fresh vegetables as a salad, and *cous cous* that is light grains of semolina steamed in a good stock. The rack of lamb is a long time favorite.

If you haven't tried it, eating with your fingers is a lot of fun and creates a friendly communal atmosphere. Dress casually, with loose clothing, and prepare for an evening of ritual, like the hand washing in warm rosewater to begin the evening. You can arrive as late as midnight and expect to be served.

Moderate. Open Tuesday through Sunday from 6 P.M. to 1 A.M. Reservations advised. All major credit cards. Entertainment nightly. Full bar. Valet parking. Semi-dressy.

★ ★
PATISSERIE BOISSIERE/French/Continental/Bakery
Mission Street between Ocean and 7th/Carmel/Area 1/(408) 624-5008

Why travel to France when you can have breakfast, lunch or dinner in this perfectly charming dining room of an upper-class French country domicile? After your meal, coffee or tea in what began as a *salon de tè*, is accompanied by exquisite pastries, compellingly displayed in the entry-way showcase. You'll want to have Madame Eliane Boissiere pack some for you to take along. In the windowed, intimate dining room, an inviting fireplace blazes on crisp days and evenings. While Pierre, Eliane's spouse, works his wizardry in the patisserie section behind the scenes, the separate kitchen turns out soups, salads, sandwiches, quiche, escargots, even *coquilles St. Jacques,* along with *bouchee à la reine,* scampi with a delectable sauce, beef Wellington, other beef specialties and fresh seafood.

Moderate. Open seven days from 9 A.M. to 10 P.M. Reservations necessary. No credit cards. Beer and wine only. Street parking. Casual.

★ ★
PAULI'S CAFE/Continental
2500 Washington/San Francisco/Area 2/(415) 921-5159

Every time I've gone to see a foreign film at the Clay Theatre I've noticed a charming little cafe called Pauli's. They feature a limited selection of those dishes they can do well—in welcome contrast to the restaurants that provide a menu about the size of *War and Peace.* There's a different chicken dish every day and fresh red snapper sautéed and served with lemon, butter and caper sauce. New York strip steak is served with blue cheese butter or sauced with cream, brandy, mustard and green peppercorns. Sausages include a *weisswurst* served with a special mustard. *"Petite"* entrées include a fine blue cheese house salad, a Mediterranean salad with fresh spinach, tomatoes, feta cheese, olives and a lemon-oil dressing; and a different pasta every night. Prawns are butterflied and sautéed in a white wine sauce and are also served alongside a New York strip steak. There are nightly soups and pâtés and a special of the chef. That's virtually the entire menu with each dish prepared with care. Desserts are all house baked and may include a walnut tart or a fudge pie. The wine list is intelligently selected. This place has a warm and friendly feeling.

Moderate. Open Tuesday through Sunday. Lunch served Tuesday through Friday from 11 A.M. to 2:30 P.M. Dinner Tuesday through Saturday from 6 to 10 P.M. Saturday and Sunday brunch from 10 A.M. to 2:30 P.M. Visa, MC. Wine and beer only. Street parking. Casual.

★
THE PAVILLION ROOM/American
The Claremont Resort and Tennis Club/Ashby and Domingo Avenues
Oakland/Area 2/(415) 843-3000

Just walking through the Claremont Hotel is a nostalgic step back into the not-so-distant past. If you have picked up a few years, memories of listening to the big band melodies of orchestra leaders like Russ Morgan and Jack Fina coming to you over nationwide radio broadcasts will return—"From high atop the Oakland/Berkeley hills we bring you the dancing music of," etc. Built over seventy years ago, this huge, rambling hostelry reminds one of an old-style Eastern place by the sea. Set in a twenty-two acre garden, there is a tennis club adjoining. The chef, Kurt, is a perfectionist and his creations demonstrate this vividly. All is fresh. Stop by the bar lounge, if only for the great views.

Moderate to expensive. Open seven days. Breakfast Monday through Saturday from 6:30 A.M. to 11 A.M. Lunch from 11:30 A.M. to 2 P.M. Dinner nightly from 6 to 10 P.M. Sunday brunch 10 A.M. to 2 P.M. Reservations necessary. All major credit cards. Full bar. Validated parking with hotel. Semi-dressy.

In order to obtain the best results from this Guide, be sure to read the French, German, Italian and Oriental menu translators on pages 399 to 404 of this Guide.

DA ★★
THE PEACOCK/Indian
2800 Van Ness Avenue/San Francisco/Area 2/(415) 928-7001

I **doubt** that the original owners of this gracious, stately Victorian home could ever have imagined that nearly eight decades later it would become a strikingly beautiful Indian dining place that is gradually taking its station among San Francisco's most highly respected restaurants. Constructed in 1903 and emerging unscathed from the 1906 fire-quake, this marvelous old mansion, until recently, served as an annex for television station KPIX. Now, one enters slightly up Lombard Street from Van Ness Avenue, through the bar lounge. Loiter here, if you would, before dinner or later—for a post-prandial libation. You will be conducted upstairs to the main dining room and a symphony of muted colors— mauve and white walls, salmon-color tablecloths, rich, thick red carpeting, commodious chairs, original globe chandeliers of brass, soft lighting and, that California touch—fresh flowers. A perfect setting for a civilized, romantic, dining experience, with touches reminiscent of the old India.

Every individual involved in The Peacock has had a multi-year background in Indian restaurants, and they have attracted their own following. It is essential that waiters are knowledgeable about Indian foods in all their complexity. The meats and chicken are cooked in the circular *tandoori,* well-like ovens lined with clay, where intense heat from the charcoal coals instantly seals in the juices and evenly cooks the product. Of breads, a variety of seven, some are also cooked in a *tandoor.* You can select as you wish, and I guarantee you'll want to try most of them.

For a first meal here, you order a combination special dinner for a sampling from *pakoras* and *samosas, chapatis* and *papadums,* to *tandoori* chicken, *murgh masala* or *kashmiri* lamb. Other breads accompany your meal—*masala kulcha* (mmmmm) and *pooris,* the latter deep-fried rather than *tandoori*-treated. If you are familiar with Indian cuisine, you will appreciate the kitchen's skill with the spices that can lift each dish to epicurean heights. If you are a novice, let your waiter advise. Beer or wine are a must.

Expensive. Open Sunday through Friday for lunch from 11:30 A.M. to 2:30 P.M. Dinner daily from 5:30 to 10:30 P.M. Reservations essential. All major credit cards. Full bar. Valet parking. Semi-dressy to dressy.

For best results, consult "How to Use This Guide" on page 25.

★ ★
THE PENINSULA RESTAURANT/California
Hyatt Regency Monterey/One Old Golf Course Road/Monterey/Area 1
(408) 372-7171

After the former Hyatt Del Monte hotel was redesigned as one of the Hyatt chain's top-drawer Regency operations (mid-1984), this beautiful dining room opened to both local and national attention. Karl Buchta, executive assistant to general manager Phil Lombardi, assumed the post of Director of Food and Beverage and has employed his expertise in creating this excellent restaurant. Guests dine in comfortable booths or at tables, with views of the golf course on one side, and the open exhibition kitchen on the other, where white-attired chefs work their magic. At dinner the mesquite grill turns out fresh fish, chops and steaks. The "All American Dinner," an appealing concept, includes bay shrimp cocktail, Monterey salad, prime rib, baked potato, corn on the cob and hot apple or hot cherry pie. À la carte orders of dinner entrées include a Monterey salad—fresh lettuce, bacon bits, chopped egg and a creamy French dressing. Luncheon features sandwiches, soups, salads and daily hot specialties. Guests often comment on the dining room's airy ambiance—soft pastel colors reflecting the designers' concept of California contemporary style, which is further softened in the evenings by astute lighting. We all appear younger. Perhaps Hyatt should bottle this boon. The hotel's cellar is a revelation. Incidentally, the adjoining Cafe Monterey has a delicious continental buffet breakfast from 6:30 to 9:30 A.M. and tea, finger sandwiches and various sweet cakes in the late afternoon, with several types of tea and coffee. In the adjacent bar area there is a happy hour with intriguing hot and cold hors d'oeuvres and a "bar snack" menu from 11 to 11. You'll never have to go hungry, or dry, in this handsome hotel. If you've never spent a night here, you could follow my example and ask to see some rooms. I've often done this, all over the world, and discovered some hotels and inns for a later stay that I might otherwise have overlooked.
Moderate to expensive. Open seven days. Breakfast 6:30 A.M. to 11:30 A.M. Lunch noon to 3 P.M. Dinner 5 to 11 P.M. Sunday brunch 10:30 A.M. to 3 P.M. Reservations necessary. MC, Visa, AX, DC. Entertainment. Full bar. Lot parking. Semi-dressy.

In order to obtain the best results from this Guide, please consult "A Few Inside Tips" on page 18.

DA★
PERRY'S/American
1944 Union Street/San Francisco/Area 2/(415) 922-9022
625 Redwood Highway/Mill Valley/Area 3/(415) 383-9300

Long the action spot and great for bird watching; the voguish, vagueish models that work in the boutiques and antique shops along Union Street like to pop in to give the lads a look and have spinach-stuffed crêpes. As one of my advisors puts it: "Busy, hectic, packed, popular, fashionable and with it." Perry Butler serves a good London broil, a fine fettuccine and a good interpretation of quiche Lorraine. The hamburgers are huge and juicy, served with homemade cottage fries. Fresh grilled fish are featured daily and the weekend brunch features a wide variety of Perry's specialties—eggs Benedict and eggs Blackstone. It's plain old-fashioned pub food— and it's good. There's a crush around noon and it's favorite for business lunches, if you don't let business interfere with your lunch. There are also population explosions at the cocktail hour, dinner hour and all through the night. Want to avoid the crowds? Try Perry's for breakfast.
Inexpensive to moderate. Open seven days. Breakfast from 9 to 11:30 A.M. Lunch from 11:30 A.M. to 6 P.M. Dinner from 6 P.M. to midnight. Saturday and Sunday brunch from 9 A.M. to 3 P.M. Reservations advised. Visa, MC, AX. Full bar. View in Mill Valley location. Patio. Child's menu. Garage parking. Lot parking in Mill Valley. Casual.

★
PETROUCHKA/Russian/Vegetarian
2930 College Avenue/Berkeley/Area 2/(415) 848-7860

Nazdroroval" (to your health) is the Russian toast my companion and I drank a few too many times in this pleasant oasis. Of course, as the cuisine is partially French, as well as Russian, we drank a few to "a 'votre santé" as well. The Russian openers can be black bread with sweet butter, salad, or any one of the *zakuski* (hors d'oeuvres). The nine varieties of salads range from the Byzantine salad of spinach and feta cheese to the *Caucasus* salad of cracked wheat, tomatoes, parsley and onion. Manchurian chicken *shashlyk* is a difficult dish which the chef handles very well. The red borscht comes with complete dinners, but it also serves as an excellent late night snack by itself.

I had recently become a hazelnut addict after trying Frangelico liqueur, so the Alexander torte (raspberry filling over a hazelnut crust) sounded too good to pass up. The house specialty dessert, Charlotte *malakoff*, is a rich end to the dinner.

Moderate. Open seven days from 11 A.M. to 10 P.M. Reservations accepted. Visa, MC. Entertainment on Friday and Saturday nights. Wine and beer only. Public lot. Casual.

DA★

THE PFEIFER HOUSE/European/Continental

760 River Road/Tahoe City/Area 6/(916) 583-3102

In 1954, under the sheltering branches of huge pines, this blend of the *gemütlich* and gastronomic opened to immediate acceptance of residents and visitors alike. In 1960, the premises became the unofficial gathering place for athletes from the world over who participated in the Winter Olympics at Squaw Valley, only five minutes north, and dinner in the two dining rooms and convivial drinks at the long mahogany bar became a tradition. Hermann Schaefer and his wife Lois founded the restaurant, selling out a decade back to Franz Fassbender and partner Henry Obermuller, both talented chefs, who still operate this mountain chalet, which could have been transported from Bavaria. The exterior is white stucco, stone walls and colorful roof flower boxes. Inside resembles a *gasthaus*—knotty pine and redwood walls, a huge tile stove, hand-hewn beams, old lanterns and polished hardwood floors. The two dining rooms carry out the theme—print curtains at dormer windows, mellow maple chairs and tables, pewter plates and tankards in wall niches.

Franz, Henry and congenial staff see to their patrons' comfort and pleasure, offering such European specialties as duckling *bigarde*, rack of lamb, fresh red snapper, sauerbraten and potato pancakes, pepper steak, Hungarian goulash, two double French lamb chops and choice New Yorks. The German potato salad is spicy and hot and vegetables are always fresh.

Moderate to expensive. Open Wednesday through Monday. Dinner served from 6 to 10 P.M. Reservations essential. All major credit cards. Full bar. Parking lot. Semi-dressy.

★ ★

PHIL LEHR'S STEAKERY/Steakhouse/Continental

Hilton Hotel Tower/330 Taylor Street/San Francisco/Area 2/(415) 673-6800

Owner/host Phil Lehr is something of a legend in his profession, nationally known and acclaimed for his innovations and professionalism. He is always concerned with providing his guests the ultimate in a dining experience. This praiseworthy concept has placed Phil Lehr's Steakery on a "reservations required" basis. Fortunately for those of us who can't resist that sudden urge to enjoy an unsurpassed steak (you select your own from the meat display cases, indicate type, thickness and weight desired and cooking degree, as you enter), you can often be seated after only a brief wait. The cosmopolitan ambiance with antiques, brass and polished metals, and commodious booths lends a feeling of well-being. Phil was the patented originator of his "Pay By the Ounce" theme, back in 1950, now copied here and there. Linda Lehr, Phil's daughter, is president of his operation and always on hand. Cart cooking by unique, magnetic energy is a tableside marvel. Sensational desserts.

Moderate. Open seven days. Dinner from 5 P.M. to midnight. Reservations advised. AX, Visa, MC. Full bar. Valet parking. Semi-dressy.

★
PIER 15/Seafood/Steaks
15 Harbor Street/San Rafael/Area 3/(415) 459-9978

An ebullient, clubby atmosphere that appeals to a youthful clientele who enjoy the glassed-in deck area, the fine seafood and really good broiled steaks. Boat docking is available, and the bar has been jumping with weekend sailors since 1956. Prices are as appealing as the view. A casual, friendly, happy place that's worth a visit anytime. **Moderate.** Open seven days. Breakfast 8 A.M. to noon. Lunch from noon to 5 P.M. Dinner from 5 to 10 P.M., 11 P.M. on weekends. Sunday brunch from 8 A.M. to 5 P.M. Reservations accepted. Visa, MC. Full bar. Patio. View of San Rafael Canal. Child's menu. Street and lot parking and boat docks. Casual to semi-dressy.

★ ★
PIERRE/French
Meridien Hotel/50 Third Street/San Francisco/Area 2/(415) 974-6400

The Meridien hotels have earned an enviable reputation for their restaurants, and this one will do nothing to contradict the good words. With a menu set by famed chef Alain Chapel—one of the jet-setting chefs who serve as consultants to U. S. restaurants—the food is good, if rich, and the service and surroundings are elegantly sophisticated. Chef in residence, Bruno Tison, works his magic in the kitchen on dishes like fish roe raviolis, trout with champagne sauce and stuffed baby vegetable, and grilled langoustines with coriander stems in a light mustard sauce. Among the favorites are an artfully arranged presentation of salad with duck liver, and rabbit meat seasoned with cloves and served with hot toast. The dessert cart displays a choice of sorbets as well as the rich pastries and tarts. I have it on good authority that this is one of the top three restaurants in the area. It is not, as my respected source pointed out, for everyone. But if you appreciate the fine art of French cuisine, Pierre affords a superb experience. **Expensive.** Open for lunch weekdays from 11:30 A.M. to 2 P.M. Dinner Monday through Saturday from 6 to 10 P.M. Reservations advised. All major credit cards. Full bar. Valet parking. Dressy.

★ ★
PILOU/Country French/California
464 First Street East/Sonoma/Area 3/(707) 996-2757

Highly regarded by local residents and tourists alike, Pilou is tucked away in a shop-lined alley across from the Sonoma Plaza. Its decor suggests a cozy French cafe, but the dinner menu reflects higher ambitions. Consider broiled sturgeon with sesame oil, oyster mushrooms and sweet red peppers, or Norwegian salmon poached in champagne and cream, garnished with kiwi fruit. Not light cafe fare by any means. Four or five specials at both lunch and dinner add variety to the selection.

Executive chef Francoise Guerra and chef de cuisine Grant Karle take particular pride in the freshness of the products entering Pilou's kitchen. All seafood is fresh, produce is from nearby farms, and the bread arrives daily from the Sonoma French bakery a few yards away. Soup stock and sauces are prepared from scratch each morning.

Though not extensive, the wine list features a carefully balanced array of California vintages. The staff is knowledgeable and attentive. **Moderate.** Open Tuesday through Saturday. Lunch Tuesday through Friday from 11 A.M. to 2:30 P.M., Saturday and Sunday 9 A.M. to 2:30 P.M. Dinner Wednesday through Sunday from 6 to 9:30 P.M. Sunday brunch from 9 A.M. to 2:30 P.M. Reservations advised. Visa, MC. Wine and beer only. Parking in rear lot and on street. Casual.

PINEHURST INN/Continental
1520 The Alameda/San Jose/Area 2/(408) 998-1415

A "P. T." (palate teaser) that looks good, but with food that is somewhat less exciting than an all day seminar on the mating habits of the tse tse fly. The room is pleasant enough with windows overlooking the garden and walkways below, and potted ferns hanging in abundance. It's when the food starts arriving that the trouble begins. The bread was so old it deserved to be retired. We should have taken this as an omen but we stayed anyway. The captain's seafood plate offered scallops, sole, shrimp and oysters. Unfortunately the fish had gone through the freeze-thaw cycle more often that your first lover—and had attained the same mushiness. The meat selections are a bit of an improvement. The prime rib was tender and rare, and the filet mignon topped with an adequate béarnaise sauce. To make up for any blandness in the other dishes, the pepper steak is a New York steak buried in coarse black pepper and mushrooms.

The Sunday brunch is adequate. The free-flowing champagne is in its favor—the salads are not. The buffet of "cold plates" is all promise with little delivery. The potato salad, bean salad and tuna salad are all the standard brunch offerings of an uninspired chef. The hot plates offer an abundancy of sausages, ham (quite good), scrambled eggs, pancakes with spiced apples, roast beef and ribs (also quite good). The surprising thing about this place is that it is always crowded—a few years back I would have said that was a comment on the lack of decent restaurants in the area. But San Jose has grown immensely, and there are other places around that offer more creative and inspired fare.

Moderate. Open seven days. Lunch weekdays from 11 A.M. to 3 P.M. Dinner from 5 to 10 P.M. Sunday brunch from 10 A.M. to 2 P.M. Reservations accepted. All major credit cards. Piano bar. Child's menu. Parking lot. Casual.

★
PISCES SEAFOOD RESTAURANT/Seafood
2127 Polk Street/San Francisco/Area 2/(415) 771-0850

This delightful place has been a hit from the day it opened in 1978—and for good reason. The service is excellent: as soon as you're seated, a basket of sourdough bread and a glass of white wine appear before you. The seafood is all fresh, and properly prepared to emphasize the freshness rather than the sauces. There are daily specials of such delicacies as salmon topped with crab, shrimp, mushrooms and a lemon butter sauce. Some of the daily specials are steamed clams, oysters Rockefeller, Blue Points and sand dabs. The cioppino comes in a kettle of delicious, rich broth packed full of clams, scallops, crabs, prawns, and other fish. All entrées come with salad or thick chowder, rice or French fries and a selection of fresh fruit. The best point of all this—if you can get any better—is the extraordinarily low prices for the quality and quantity. The early bird dinners are an extra value—$6.25 to $6.75 for a complete dinner.

Moderate. Open seven days. Lunch served Monday through Saturday from 11:30 A.M. to 3 P.M. Dinner from 5 to 10:45 P.M. Sunday from 4 to 10:45 P.M. Reservations accepted. All major credit cards. Wine and beer only. Child's menu at dinner. Public parking. Casual to semi-dressy.

★ ★
THE PLUMED HORSE/French/Continental
14555 Big Basin Way/Saratoga/Area 2/(408) 867-4711

When Klaus Pache assumed ownership of The Plumed Horse, he retained the decor which is a splendid renovated livery stable and former home of a village doctor. Two distinct dining atmospheres – one early American, the other mid-Victorian – provide a nostalgic background for such classic fare as rack of lamb, steak Diane, and Australian lobster tail. The wine list represents many of the California vineyards. **Moderate to expensive.** Open Tuesday through Saturday 6 to 11 P.M. Reservations accepted. Visa, MC, AX. Entertainment. Dancing. Full bar. Semi-dressy.

★
POMPEI'S GROTTO/Seafood
Fisherman's Wharf/340 Jefferson Street/San Francisco/Area 2/(415) 776-9265

Visitors should take a clue from the natives who scorn the plastic tourist haunts of Fisherman's Wharf in favor of this old-time wharf restaurant. The seafood is super-fresh and succulent – from sand dabs, steamed clams, and petrale sole to the remarkable, pale pink, moist salmon, poached in dill, lemon and butter. One bite and you're hooked. **Moderate to expensive.** Open seven days from 11:15 A.M. to 10:45 P.M. Reservations accepted. All major credit cards. Full bar. Casual.

★ ★
PREGO/Northern Italian
2000 Union Street/San Francisco/Area 2/(415) 563-3305

For the longest time, the spot where Prego now sits was a subspecies of Victoria Station called Thomas Lord's. It was a good place for drinking Irish coffee in front of the fireplace or for watching the wildlife on Union Street, but not for eating. Then, a couple of years ago, with a little help from Patrick Terrail of Los Angeles' Ma Maison, Thomas Lord's became Les Bistroit des Halles, which I am told was a simply wonderful establishment, serving good bistro fare at a fair price. For whatever reasons, the place never really caught on, it changed faces yet again, and turned into Prego.

According to the exquisitely designed menu at Prego, the name means something along the lines of "Please . . . not at all . . . that's all right . . . don't mention it . . . you're welcome." Something along those lines. To my surprise and delight, Prego is more than just a name at this very modern, very fine Italian restaurant. The rooms are light and airy, with big windows opening out onto Union Street, and the well-boutiqued throngs. Inside, walls are either brick or pastel, and factory lights hang low over the tables, giving a feeling of intimacy within all that space. In the back of the main room is a wood-burning pizza oven, manned by a chef who speaks no English, but will gladly open the oven for you if you make the right gestures.

Half the menu is a wine list on which the musky elegance of a 1977 Jordan cabernet sauvignon meets the ruby gaity of a Bersano Barolo. The dishes range from the *nouvelle* exotic to the downright motherly. There's a wonderful *carpaccio Giuseppe Cipriani*, a variation on the thinly-sliced raw beef appetizer, topped with roughly-shaved Parmesan cheese, olive oil, lemon and capers. The soup of *pasta e fagioli* is a thick stew that would do mama proud—heavily laden with red kidney beans and broken elbow macaroni, interspersed with the occasional sliver of rich *pancetta* bacon. The *insalata mista* gave me much pause, largely because of the oddness of the *radicchio* lettuce, which is red and curly, and the fresh fennel, which is quite strong.

The *trittico di gnocchi* puts most versions of these lovely little potato dumplings to shame—in this case, there are three sauces, one red tomato, one green *pesto*, and the third, a white *gorgonzola* which is not easily forgotten. The pizza from the wood-burning oven is good, though not great. My favorite was the one with four cheeses—mozzarella, provolone, fontina and gruyère. There's also a *pizza con tartufo blanco*—topped with white truffles—which I consider an excess. One simply must draw the line somewhere.

Moderate. Open seven days from 11:30 A.M. to midnight. Reservations for six or more only. Visa, MC, AX. Full bar. Street parking. Casual.

PRINCETON INN/Seafood/Continental
Capistrano Road/Princeton By the Sea/Area 2/(415) 728-7311

If **you** are driving up or down Highway One, you might spot this restored historical monument a few hundred feet off the road, only about a half block from the ocean. Built in 1906, the attractions have varied, at one period being quite lively. Now, with its handsome renovation (in Mission style), the Princeton Inn draws many customers from San Francisco as well as the local trade from Half Moon Bay, four miles south.

Seafood is the big thing here, where the catch of the day could be snapper or halibut. A number of continental items are always on the menu. Owner Marilu Sells and manager Felicia Bitter keep everything running (and tasting) as it should.

A bar lounge adjoins the simple, pleasant dining room, where waitresses serve patrons at tables in the many-windowed room which is attired with various greens. It has a rather old-fashioned feeling.

Sunday champagne brunch is a delight. Besides the bubbly, you are served orange juice, coffee or tea, chowder, and a main dish, such as steak and eggs, eggs Blackstone, seafood frittata, a couple of quiches, etc., buttermilk biscuits, jam and home fries.

Moderate. Open Tuesday through Sunday from 11:30 A.M. to 3 P.M. Dinner from 5 to 9 P.M. Friday and Saturday to 10 P.M. Reservations advised. Visa, MC, AX. Entertainment. Dancing. Full bar. Lot parking. Casual.

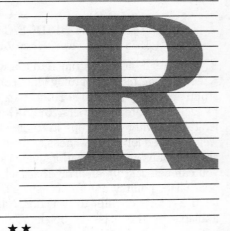

★ ★
RAFFAELLO/Northern Italian
Mission between Ocean and 7th/Carmel/Area 1/(415) 624-1541

A **northern Italian** restaurant where chef/owner Mrs. d'Agliano still sniffs, nibbles, pinches, prods and fondles the raw foodstuffs to make certain the Tuscan dishes are served at their peak. Host/manager/co-owner/son Remo d'Agliano runs the front of the house with efficiency and graciousness. The fettuccine *alla Romano* is sinfully good, a holdout in the lower calorie trend of *haute cuisine* and *alta cucina*. The *medaglioni à la piemontese* is a blend of tender veal, fontina cheese, white truffles and *pâté de foie gras* sauce. The modest canopied front looks like three individual shops (which it probably was) joined into a dramatically formal dinner house with gracious chandeliers and walls tastefully hung with a few—not cluttered—paintings. This is another restaurant that has the courage to go against the casual dress codes of Carmel and insist upon jackets and ties. But they're collaring enough new patrons each season until now it has become difficult to make reservations.

Moderate to expensive. Open Wednesday through Monday from 6 to 10 P.M. Reservations essential. Visa, MC. Wine and beer only. Street parking. Dressy.

Please be sure to consult "Tipping Made Easy" on page 22 of this Guide.

★ ★
RAINBOW BRIDGE/Creative American
1335 Pueblo Avenue/Napa/Area 3/(707) 255-2311

Stop here, at the entrance to the wine country, around mid-day for one of the most rewarding luncheons in the area. Ask for John Johnston (call him J. J.) or Dan Hunt, part owners, who are always around to accommodate the diners. Brain Guier, one-time original chef here, is still an owner and drops in to check the action. Rainbow Bridge is well regarded for the freshness of their ingredients, offering sandwiches, salads, soups and hot creations, such as eggplant parmesan. At dinner, you can select from an array that includes fresh pasta, prime rib, filet béarnaise, poultry and fresh fish. There is usually a wicked dessert for the calorie counter to consider. Napa Valley and Sonoma wines are available by the glass or bottle. They have all the best ones. Live entertainment nightly. Gene Nelson, morning man on KSFO radio really likes this—and he's fussy.

Moderate. Lunch 11:30 A.M. to 2 P.M., Monday through Friday. Dinner Monday through Thursday 5:30 to 10 P.M., Friday and Saturday 5:30 to 10:30 P.M. and Sunday 5 to 9 P.M. Reservations recommended. All major credit cards. Dancing Monday, Wednesday through Saturday. Full bar. Lot parking. Casual.

★
RAMIS/Continental/Middle Eastern
1361 Church Street/San Francisco/Area 2/(415) 641-0678

There is a Rami, he is a former dancer and actor who does virtually everything here, except the cooking. There is a revolving art gallery and an air of relaxed enjoyment one is not likely to find outside of a sidewalk cafe in Europe. Israeli specialties co-exist with chicken pasta, and it's hard to spend more than $10. The sit-down brunch is currently $5. There is a limited wine selection.

Moderate. Open Wednesday through Monday 5:30 to 10 P.M., Friday and Saturday till 10:30 P.M. Sunday brunch from 10 A.M. to 3 P.M. Reservations accepted. No credit cards. Wine and beer only. Street parking. Casual.

In order to obtain the best results from this Guide, be sure to read the French, German, Italian and Oriental menu translators on pages 399 to 404 of this Guide.

★
RAMONA'S/Mexican
1025 "C" Street/San Rafael/Area 3/(415) 454-0761

Perhaps a word of explanation is due. The reader may have noticed that I am underwhelmed by Mexican restaurants in Northern California, generally inferior to those in Southern California. The reason is that I have been to the source, and I have tasted the real foods of Mexico where tomatoes are ripe and red and bursting with the nearly forgotten flavor of . . . tomatoes. (We have been slowly and diabolically conditioned to regard those puny, yellow, hormone-injected things as "tomatoes" in the States). Avocado in Mexico, is soft and velvety, and sings with dimensions of flavor unlike the green putty of Stateside guacamole. *Molé* sauce, constructed of forty-eight spices and flavorings, including chocolate, is allowed to simmer for twenty-four hours, and when ladled onto chicken, is a sauce with a series of aftertastes that continue like a mild fireworks display. (It's fun to watch someone taste *molé* for the first time; they taste—and taste—and taste, their expression changing all the while.) So my condemnation of Mexican cooking in the United States may be too subjective, unfair and uncomfortable to those who have favorite "Mexican" restaurants.

Ramona's is a good example. This is a tasteful, subtle, colorful, interesting, sophisticated restaurant that comes as close as they can—fifty percent of the way—to authentic Mexican gourmet foods. The tortillas are made by hand, only the best lard is used, and the wide variety of dishes makes for an interesting, if not entirely exciting, occasion. Specialties of the house include chicken *molé (poblano), paella,* and *chile verde.*

Inexpensive to moderate. Open Tuesday through Sunday. Lunch served weekdays from noon to 2:30 P.M. Dinner from 5 to 10 P.M. Reservations accepted. Visa, MC. Entertainment. Wine and beer only. Parking lot. Casual.

★
RED'S/Chinese/Szechwan
1475 Polk Street/San Francisco/Area 2/(415) 441-7337

Not my favorite Chinese restaurant, it is, perhaps an indictment of the low level of mainland China's food preparation. Chef Lau is from China and he opened at this restaurant in 1983 which may be for those who are comfortable in a westernized version of the ambiance, with a piano tinkling in the background. They're open until 1 A.M. and specialties include lemon chicken, *kung pao* shrimp, and seafood, especially lobster.

Inexpensive to moderate. Open daily 11:30 A.M. to 10 P.M. Reservations accepted. Visa, MC, AX, DC. Entertainment. Full bar. Valet parking. Casual.

★ ★ ★
RENE VERDON'S LE TRIANON/French
242 O'Farrell Street/San Francisco/Area 2/(415) 982-9353

I first met Rene Verdon briefly when he was a consultant to a food chain and was lending his advice to the Chez Cary in Southern California. Monsieur Verdon had recently departed the White House, deploring the barbecue sauce of the Lyndon Johnson administration that replaced the béarnaise of the Kennedys and their friends. That he should end up in San Francisco was almost predestined—a talent like his needs to be appreciated. He took over an unimpressive operation and blessed it with his classic French cuisine. The *quenelles nantua* are as close to perfection as I've tasted, and the Old World luxuries like oysters in champagne or the *escalope de saumon* in sorrel or the *poulet au vinaigre* (chicken in a sauce of curacao, mixed with tomato and a soupçon of vinegar blended with cream and wine), are lovingly concocted. A cool, crisp salad of lettuce, apples and walnuts is served after the entrée, in the European manner, to clear the palate for the limited dessert list. The wine list is impressive—heavily into the imported superstars.
Expensive. Open Tuesday through Saturday from 6 to 10 P.M. Reservations advised. All major credit cards. Full bar. Street parking. Dressy.

★ ★
RENZO'S CONTINENTAL CUISINE/Continental
1700 West Campbell Avenue/Campbell/Area 2/(408) 379-9200

Renzo's opened in 1967 to local acclaim that has since burgeoned to international proportions, a source of pride to owners/hosts Tony Monsef and John Vossoughi. In bestowing its coveted recommendation, Travel/Holiday Magazine states, in part: "Handsome interior of rich woods, attractively dressed boothes and tables with fresh flowers and one of the finest menus in the area. The owners have quietly made legions of friends through a constancy of superb food and attentive service . . ."

The French-Italian-continental gourmet cuisine presents such standouts as tournedos *rossini,* veal *piccata,* chicken sauté, rex sole, sole Marguery, salmon steak and sweet basil, even abalone! Many of the well-dressed couples in the mirrored main room, where spotlighted paintings adorn walls, are anticipating their post-dinner dancing to a live band (9:30 P.M. to 1 A.M. Tuesday-Saturday) in the bar lounge. The music does not reach the dining room, so relax. Renzo's well-vintaged cellar stocks many of California's boutique wines. **Moderate to expensive**. Open weekdays for lunch from 11:30 A.M. to 2:30 P.M. Dinner served Monday through Saturday from 5:30 to 10:30 P.M. Reservations advised. All major credit cards. Entertainment. Full bar. Lot parking. Semi-dressy to dressy.

★
THE RICE TABLE/Indonesian
1617 Fourth Street/San Rafael/Area 3/(415) 456-1808

The Indonesian rice table is a potpourri of cuisines which have been adapted from those that have remained behind when visitors departed. The Dutch, Portuguese and English have all left their indelible culinary influence, but the *rijstaffel* has become a cuisine with an exotic personality all its own. Despite some of the unusual spices used to prepare the dishes here, the tastes and textures can be enjoyed by everyone. *Semur* (sautéed squares of beef in soy sauce, butter and cloves), the *bihun goreng* (chow mein with shrimp and noodles) and the banana fritters are a few of the more satisfying components. Decor features grass-matted walls and soft lighting. The *rijstaffel* may include as many as seven different dishes—some are very spicy. **Inexpensive**. Lunch Tuesday through Friday 11:30 A.M. to 2:30 P.M. Dinner Thursday through Saturday from 5:30 to 10 P.M., 5 to 9 P.M. on Sunday. Reservations advised. Visa, MC, AX, DC. Wine and beer only. Street parking. Casual to semi-dressy.

DA ★
RICK'S SWISS CHALET/Swiss/German
4085 El Camino Way/Palo Alto/Area 2/(415) 493-7575

The late John Herman Rickey, one of the Bay Area's most widely known and respected restaurateurs, founded this devotedly patronized restaurant in 1962. Before entering, one glance at the always full parking lot tells the story.

It isn't necessarily the Swiss-German-Austrian cuisine here that draws what seems to be an ever-increasing gaggle. The menu lists about twenty-five entrées, ranging from Australian lobster tail to prime rib (not my favorite here) to such Germanic dishes as sauerbraten, *wiener zweibel rostbraten,* smoked bratwurst and wienerschnitzel Holstein (a nice, small steak). Other nationalities are represented with: veal *cordon bleu,* brochette of beef, veal cutlet parmigiano and two quite enjoyable fondues. Good old Southern fried chicken and New York steak for us Mason-Dixon line straddlers. With your entrée comes a bottomless tureen of thick, homemade soup and salad with tangy dressings. Desserts include apple strudel — warm apples, raisins and flaky pastry.

The name exemplifies the ambiance — Swiss-Austrian, wood beams and paneling, many related artifacts, mugs, steins and Alpine scenes. A *gemütlich* bar, what else.

Moderate. Open seven days. Lunch served weekdays from 11:30 A.M. to 2:30 P.M. Dinner served Sunday through Thursday from 5 to 10 P.M., Friday and Saturday to 11 P.M. Reservations advised. All major credit cards. Entertainment and dancing on weekends. Child's menu. Parking lot. Casual.

★
RIERA'S RESTAURANT/Italian
1539 Solano Avenue/Berkeley/Area 2/(415) 527-1467

In this cheerful, popular little dining place, Russ Riera — youthful restaurant critic Sunday noon on KGO radio in San Francisco — practices what he preaches when he discusses what he considers good and poor restaurants. Russ puts out, with the help of his dedicated kitchen staff, very tasteful homemade pasta, homemade bread and unusual specialties, making use of fresh ingredients whenever possible. Desserts also made on the premises and, as Russ has a sweet tooth, you know they'll be O. K. Diners are refreshed by the garden view, where up to sixty varieties of flowers are in bloom. Credit Russ's dad for his all-around expertise, including the garden. The wine list is moderately priced and reflects the owner's taste and knowledge.

Moderate. Open Monday through Saturday for dinner from 5:30 to 10 P.M. Reservations recommended. MC, Visa. Wine and beer only. Street parking. Casual.

★ ★
RISTORANTE BUCA GIOVANNI/Northern Italian
800 Greenwich Street/San Francisco/Area 2/(415) 776-7766

Owner/chef Giovanni Leoni had been an important part of San Francisco culinary history for the better part of three decades. As chef and part owner of Vanessi's, he has seen northern Italian fare come into its own. As chef/proprietor of Buca Giovanni, he has developed his specialties — venison tortelli, medallions of veal with porcini mushrooms and shrimp ravioli — for his new customers. "Buca" means hole, and the restaurant is below ground level with brick walls and sand-blasted supports. The decor is simple and rustic, and there is a small additional room at the rear that could be used for a private party. The warm chicken salad with pine nuts and balsamic vinegar was a grand beginning, as was the *bruschetta* (a kind of garlic bread served with a tiny carafe of virgin olive oil on the side). Pastas are fresh, and the innovations—veal stuffed pasta with a walnut sauce—are as good as the classics. Tender veal in a delicate red pepper sauce was as good as I had hoped. Other favorites include chicken simmered with Italian black olives and garlic, and *fagioli alla Toscano*, a kind of Italian cassoulet made with red beans and garlic. The gelato was frozen hard, but the Italian cheesecake and expresso mousse were memorable. The waiters, the hostess, the customers . . . everyone is happy. It's the perfect place for a casual evening of hearty Italian fare.

Moderate to expensive. Dinner Monday through Thursday from 5:30 to 10:30 P.M., Friday and Saturday until 11 P.M. Reservations advised. Visa, MC. Wine and beer only. Garage one block away and street parking. Casual.

★ ★
RISTORANTE GRIFONE/Italian
1609 Powell Street/San Francisco/Area 2/(415) 397-8458

The old-time North Beach Italian ambiance pervades without the nice-but-dull cuisine so many once-popular places purvey. Here, pastas are treated respectfully and sauces are meticulously made. This one-time caffè has become an appealing dining place with ornate glass chandeliers, framed mirrors on dusty pink walls, wood banquettes and snowy-topped tables with bentwood chairs. Portofino murals are nice touches, very atmospheric. A second dining room, above, is a bit less lively. Herb Caen is credited with the column assist that sparked the transformation, and he knows his *cannelloni* better than most of us. Lovers of Caesar salad will revel in this garlicky version, replete with anchovies. You'll like the fresh garlic bread that starts you out. *Crème caramel* is the perfect dessert here.

Moderate to expensive. Open seven days. Dinner from 5 to 11 P.M. weekdays; Friday and Saturday till midnight. Reservations advised. MC, Visa, AX. Wine and beer only. Valet parking. Casual.

To obtain the best results from this Guide, be sure to consult the map on the various Northern California areas on page 28.

★ ★
RISTORANTE ORSI/Northern Italian/Grand
375 Bush Street/San Francisco/Area 2/(415) 981-6535

Chef Oreste Orsi was one of the most renowned and accomplished masters of the difficult Tuscan cuisine in America. His older son was brought up in his father's kitchen and has taken over since his father's death, while the younger son operates Orsi with Oreste's original partner, Joe Orsini. And their father taught them well . . . the *alta cucina* of northern Italy was, as admitted by *L'Escoffier*, the "inspiration" for much of the French *haute cuisine*. Pasta dishes like *fettuccine à la Romana* (or in champagne sauce) and *tortellini à la Bolognese* are served in formal surroundings more appropriate to their noble stature than the traditional Italian restaurant decor. Patrons are willing to dress up for baked shrimp à la "Orsi," Caesar salad, rich and succulent lobster thermidor and lamb served with prosciutto, cheese and sauce of Marsala wine *(lamb di Medici)*. The fried cream and baked Alaska are superbly prepared and presented. It is said that chef Orsi introduced *cannelloni* to San Francisco in 1957, but it is not my favorite dish here. I do enjoy the original chicken Etruscan which is cooked in a clay pot with herbs. The wine list is formidable. Prices are not expensive but this is one of the area's superstars – and they never come cheap.

Moderate. Open Monday through Friday from 11:30 A.M. to 11:30 P.M. Dinner only Saturday from 5:30 to 11:30 P.M. Reservations advised. All major cedit cards. Full bar. Valet and street parking. Dressy.

★
RIVE GAUCHE/French
33 West Portal Avenue/San Francisco/Area 2/(415) 566-0700

In this cheery French restaurant, hand-picked ingredients are used by the talented young chef to create some outstanding dishes, the ordinary becomes unordinary and even extraordinary as compared to the average Gallic-influenced establishment. The tournedos *au poure vert* is exquisite, and the *veau piccata* is a standout. The dessert choice of *crème caramel* is good, although the selection is pedestrian. The only gauche thing about the place is the service, which can be brisk, brusque and boorish.

Moderate. Open Tuesday through Sunday from 5:30 to 10 P.M. Reservations advised. All major credit cards. Wine and beer only. Lot and street parking. Casual.

★ ★
RIVER'S END/Continental
Highway 1/Jenner/Area 3/(707) 865-2484

Perched on a cliff above the mouth of the Russian River, this restaurant affords diners and overnight guests a striking view of not only the river's end, but also the land's end. Below them, the tireless Pacific lashes offshore rocks and smoothes the dark sand while sea birds wheel, calling in the breeze.

But the view is not the chief reason for occupying a table, or a cabin, here. The menu, which changes two or three times a year, offers an intriguing variety of dishes expertly prepared by owner/master chef Wolfgang Gramatzki. They include hearty German fare, Indonesian curries (with homemade chutney), coconut-fried shrimp, and even rackettes of venison. The fairly extensive wine list primarily honors Sonoma County labels, but a few French and German bottlings are also available. Local premium wines may be sampled by the glass.

Moderate. May through September: Dinner Monday through Saturday from 5 to 9:30 P.M., Sunday from 4 to 9:30 P.M. Brunch Saturday from 11 A.M. to 4 P.M., Sunday from 10 A.M. to 3 P.M. January-April, October-November: Dinner Friday through Sunday from 5 to 9:30 P.M. Brunch hours unchanged. Reservations advised. Visa, MC. Full bar. Parking off road in front. Casual.

★ ★
THE ROGUE/Seafood/Continental/Italian
Wharf #2—Waterside/Monterey/Area 1/(408) 372-4586

Perhaps, like me, you're what those jaunty yachtsmen call a landlubber (a "land-lover?"). Well, pay attention, for when you mount the stairway to the second level of this nautically conceived Monterey Marina landmark, to be greeted pleasantly by the smartly attired staff, you become a yachtsman. You're right off your sloop, dropping by the club for a libation and some seafod like calamari or a continental Italian specialty to savor as you leisurely survey one of Monterey's most panoramic views, from the Presidio to seaside, from the yacht harbor, just below, to Santa Cruz, across the bay.

The Rogue has an entire, now-retired, commercial fishing boat poised smack in the center of the main dining room. Mannequins attired in authentic working garb seem to be guiding their vessel right past your table; children even wave. The two dining rooms, another surrounding the bar lounge, are justly popular, especially at lunch. The Rogue serves only eastern corn-fed, aged beef. I like the large seafood salads and sandwiches, as well as both red and white chowders.

Moderate. Open seven days. Lunch served 11:30 A.M. to 2:30 P.M. Dinner from 5 to 10 P.M. Reservations advised. All major credit cards. Full bar. View. Public parking lot. Casual-chic to semi-dressy.

★
ROONEY'S GARDEN CAFE/Jewish Deli/Deluxe
38 Main Street/Tiburon/Area 3/(415) 435-1911

Kipling once called San Francisco a "mad city," and where else could a man named John N. Rooney open a delicatessen with the greatest home-baked Jewish rye in town? Now in the capable hands of owner/chef David Hinman (one of the original partners), it's still wrapped around the most succulent assortment of sandwiches since New York's Lindy's in the old days. He's also added some specials like hot chicken and spinach salad with pinenuts and steamed clams. Dinner here is a special find, as the neighborhood people are quickly discovering. The menu changes as David used the ingredients fresh that day, and entrées may include prawns *à la parilla* with spicy Créole sauce; grilled breast of chicken with apricot, walnut and wine sauce; cioppino; and steamed Pacific clams with onions, garlic, wine and butter. Whatever you try is going to be fresh and big and good. There's a popular patio that seats seventy-five during the spring and summer months.

Inexpensive to moderate. Open seven days. Monday through Thursday from 11:30 A.M. to 3:30 P.M., Friday through Sunday from 11:30 A.M. to 10 P.M. Reservations accepted. No credit cards. Wine and beer only. Patio. Lot parking. Validated parking at lunch. Casual.

★
ROSEBUD'S/Continental
370 Geary Street/San Francisco/Area 2/(415) 433-0183

The decor is scintillating, the tone authentic, the ambiance warm and appealing. If the food were up to the setting, Rosebud's would be one of the dozen best restaurants in San Francisco.

It has been called a tourist trap; and, tourists do find its sparkling appearance and central location hard to resist. Sophisticated San Franciscans will object to the "surf and turf"—crab and steak. But, many places feature this odd duo.

However, above and beyond these carping and, sometimes, unfounded criticisms, Rosebud's has one great virtue—its prices are very sensible! The food is really a good quality, adequately prepared—often with epicurean flourishes. A complete dinner can cost as little as $9; the wine prices are so low that you wonder if there has been some mistake. And, the list is most decently selected.

The house specialty is roasted prime rib and beef, served with a sunken Yorkshire pudding. A generous serving of above-average beef, bargain-priced. Breast of chicken Tiffany is an example of one of their more fanciful offerings. It contains a strange miscellany of ingredients: almonds, Canadian bacon, bananas and orange marmalade. Each adds its flavorsome bit to the mélange, and — surprise — it comes off far better than you'd expect.

Moderate to expensive. Open seven days. Lunch Monday through Thursday 11 A.M. to 3 P.M. Friday and Saturday till 5 P.M. Dinner Monday through Saturday from 5 P.M. to midnight. Open Sunday from 3 P.M. Reservations advised. Visa, MC, AX. Full bar. Street parking, garages nearby. Casual.

ROSE ET LeFAVOUR/French
1420 Main Street/St. Helena/Area 3/(707) 963-1681

Another successful storefront conversion in the wine country, this basically French restaurant is a bit more upscale than most, and serves the residue of the *nouvelle* cuisine hysteria in high style and at high prices. Perhaps $50 for a *prix fixe* dinner is really not high, considering the quality, and the dinner does take three hours — a bit longer that I like. Carolyn Rose and Bruce LeFavour may have been inspired by those wonderful dining adventures in Barbizon — an hours ride south of Paris — and their huge wine list — five hundred labels — is about half French, not a commonality in wine country restaurants. High ceilings, candles, framed paintings and lithos provide a lovely country setting for various interpretations of fresh salmon, grilled squab, good local lamb and fair desserts.

Expensive. One seating Wednesday through Sunday at 6:30 P.M. Reservations necessary. No credit cards. Wine only. Street parking. Semi-dressy to dressy.

★
ROSIE'S CAFE/American Regional
571 North Lake Boulevard/Tahoe City/Area 6/(916) 583-8504

Once this was the location of the funky Hearthstone, but all else is changed since this has been Rosie's Cafe for five years and the menu is now American regional. Never heard of such? Why, it's very simple — just ponder all the world's cuisines, realize that they have been transplanted into our culture and you have it.

That the cafe is popular is evident in the owners' request that you reserve for any night of the year (open 365 days) and take note that weekend reservations are a must. Call or write a week ahead, at least. The very able, professional chef and crew are turning out an astonishing variety of specialties which you can savor while viewing the beauty of Lake Tahoe through wide windows. Cheerful, happy and contemporary are perfect adjectives to describe Rosie's, a name that somehow portrays simplicity, honesty and a certain freshness.

Inexpensive to moderate. Open seven days. Breakfast and lunch from 7 A.M. to 2:30 P.M. Dinner served from 5:30 P.M. to 10:00 P.M. Reservations essential on weekends. Visa, MC. Full bar. View. Easy parking. Casual to semi-dressy.

DA ★ ★
RUSSIAN RENAISSANCE/Russian
5241 Geary Boulevard/San Francisco/ Map 2/(415) 752-8558

One would not expect the food to be particularly noteworthy in a restaurant garishly gilded in thirteenth-century Byzantine baroque. But one would be wrong.

Despite the atmosphere, which I find a bit grotesque and off-putting, the food is — as the menu proclaims — very Russian and owner/founder/chef Boris Vertloogin is the reason for the very good fare. The straight vodkas, served ice-cold by the shot, are sensational, particularly the *zubrovka,* or spicy buffalo grass (the grass is still in the bottle). My companion loved the *pertzovka* (vodka flavored with very hot chile peppers) and we managed to drink our way through the list on three visits . . . strictly for the purpose of research, of course.

Dinners can begin with any number of exotic appetizers, but if you can afford it, I'd recommend one of the caviar plates. Soups are excellent, and the borscht is served with *pirojok* (small meat pies). The long list of entrées is similar to that of the original restaurant in Shanghai (this one is an offshoot) with dishes representing all regions of Mother Russia. There's ground lamb American style, skewered and served with marinated fruits; *shashlik karsky,* rack of lamb marinated, carved into chunks and charcoal broiled on the skewer; and *golubtzy,* Ukranian stuffed cabbage garnished with sour cream and served with really fresh vegetables. Desserts are rich and good, particularly the Turkish baklava, thin-wafered pastry made with honey and chopped walnuts. The wine list is limited.

Expensive. Open seven days from 5 to 11 P.M. Reservations advised. Visa, MC, AX, DC. Piano bar. Full bar. Child's menu. Street parking. Semi-dressy.

★ ★
RUSSIAN RIVER VINEYARDS/Continental/Greek
5700 Gravenstein Highway North/Forestville/Area 3/(707) 887-1562

Continental with a Greek flair" is the description offered by chef Bob Engel and co-owner Michael Topolos, who, along with brother Jerry Topolos and his wife Christine, are responsible for this very pleasant dining spot. The Greek flair is seen in such dishes as *souvlaki* (marinated lamb en brochette) and *spanikopita* (a tasty mixture of spinach, eggs, cheese, and flaky filo); other, equally interesting, flairs account for duck with black currants and Madeira, and the catch of the day. Fish, always fresh, is a major menu category, varying seasonally.

The wine list is naturally devoted to Topolos wines, produced at Russian River Vineyards. The vineyards have provided a lovely background for weddings and receptions in the wisteria-bedecked courtyard, where a fountain plays.

Moderate. Open Wednesday through Sunday. Lunch Wednesday through Saturday from 11:30 A.M. to 2:30 P.M. Dinner Wednesday through Sunday from 5:30 to 9:30 P.M. Sunday brunch from 10:30 A.M. to 2:30 P.M. Closed all January. Reservations advised. Visa, MC, AX. Music Saturday and Sunday nights and for Sunday brunch. Parking in lot. Casual.

★
RUTHERFORD SQUARE/American
Rutherford Crossroads/Rutherford/Area 3/(707) 963-2317

There are three restaurants and an unusual bar in this unique cultural complex under the guiding hand of Mary Tilden Morton, the sculptor, rancher and owner of the Square. The Beaulieu Vineyards wine tasting center, which Morton designed, is a handsome, hexagonal tasting room on Highway 29, at Highway 128, and forms one corner of this Square. Another corner is occupied by The Cottage, a two-story country-comfortable, Victorian building from 1896, where homemade specialties are served in the original dining room and parlor. Food is continental, innovative and reservations are requested. The Garden Restaurant, outdoors and open only during the summer months, serves luncheon including homemade soups and salads. Both places offer Napa Valley wines, naturally including Beaulieu bottlings. Then, there is the Gourmet Deli, providing sandwiches, choice ice cream, soft drinks, wines and beers for guests desiring to picnic on the lush lawns, beneath shade trees. Visit The Corner Bar and Cellar Lounge, across from The Cottage. **Moderate.** Open seven days. Hours vary according to season. Reservations advised. Visa, MC. Dancing. Patio. Vineyard view. Adequate parking. Casual.

★
R. V.'S SUPER IT'S RESTAURANT/Filipino
6287 Mission/Daly City/Area 2/(415) 755-1330

When chef/owner Ray Villafranca opened this strangely named Filipino restaurant in the early 1980s, he must have been surprised at its success. His timing was perfect—San Francisco has become home to the fastest growing Filipino population in America and the soul food of this cuisine—lumpia, pork in sauces, catfish—is served generously and at bargain prices. Not much on atmosphere, but R. V.'s has some interesting entertainment on weekends.

Inexpensive to moderate. Open Monday through Thursday from 5 to 11 P.M., Friday and Saturday till 11 P.M. No reservations. No credit cards. Entertainment. Wine and beer only. Street parking. Casual.

DA ★★
THE SAILING SHIP RESTAURANT/Continental
Pier 42/San Francisco/Area 2/(415) 777-5771

Dolph Rempp's colorful, romantic restaurant, christened the Dolphin P. Rempp, overlooks San Francisco Bay. Here one dines on noteworthy cuisine created by the multi-talented French chef, Doug Achterberg. Your dining room is the salon of this private, three-masted schooner. Built in 1908, it first roamed the seven seas and then served in both World War I and II. Later, this vessel starred in three motion picures — *Hawaii, Mutiny on the Bounty,* and *Here Come the Brides.* Altogether, a veritable star ship. Some of the extraordinary dishes here are flamed baby pheasant breast with morels, wild hickory nuts and walnut sauce; Iowa milk-fed veal sautéed with Schramsberg champagne and black forest mushrooms. I enjoyed my fresh quail with pears and truffle sauce, and a guest savored the grilled filet cut of Black Angus beef with black peppercorns and sour mash whiskey. There are daily seafood specials of local and exotic fish. Over seventy-five different champagnes as well as California and imported wines.
Moderate. Open Tuesday through Saturday. Weeknights from 6 to 10 P.M. Weekends till 11 P.M.. Reservations advised. Entertainment. All major credit cards. Full bar. Lot parking. Semi-dressy.

In order to obtain the best results from this Guide, please consult "A Few Inside Tips" on page 18.

★ ★
ST. GEORGE/Mediterranean/Italian
1050 Charter Oak Street/St. Helena/Area 3/(707) 963-7938

I drove with my friend the winemaker to the Napa Valley Olive Oil Company on the outskirts of St. Helena to pick up some of the company's elegant, silky green olive oil, fresh pressed from California olives, and easily the equal of Italy's best. We also bought some wonderful *pesto* (packed in a mason jar) and a lusty hunk of romano cheese. As we rounded a corner on our way back into St. Helena, my friend pulled into a parking lot, and said, "Here's another one of those restaurants I like to eat at." My eyes boggles; my mouth dropped open. Since my last visit to St. Helena somebody had decided to build a castle on the outskirts of town, and use it as a restaurant.

I was intimidated. I was wearing workboots and jeans. I had the mud of the winery on my clothes. "Don't worry about it," said my friend the winemaker. And in we went. Inside the castle, I found a large room, decorated with a vast panorama of Yosemite Valley on one wall, and a few broken Rubenesque nudes scattered here and there. Unlike the formidable exterior of St. George, the interior was calm, non-effete, even fun. Young, silvery-tongued waitresses described the wonders of the menu—the pleasures of the *pasta al pesto,* the singular joys of the *pagello con pomodoro e capperi* (red snapper with tomato and caper sauce) and the *salsicce* (grilled Italian sausauge with *rositto*), and the unique virtues of the *lambughini* (ahem—a ground lamb burger on a hunk of sourdough bread). This being lunchtime, I also glanced at the dinner menu. It was filled with the most simple and beloved of Italian dishes—a homey minestrone, a humble plate of fried calamari and a friendly portion of broiled salmon steak. The simplicity of St. George taught me a valuable lesson, something along the lines of "Don't judge a restaurant by its battlements," or maybe, "People who dine in brick castles, won't necessarily get stoned."

Moderate to expensive. Open Wednesday through Monday. Lunch from 11:30 A.M. to 2:30 P.M. Dinner from 5:30 to 10 P.M. Sunday brunch from 11:30 A.M. to 2:30 P.M. Reservations advised. Visa, MC, AX. Full bar. Patio in summer. Street parking. Casual to semi-dressy.

Please be sure to consult "Tipping Made Easy" on page 22 of this Guide.

★
ST. MICHAEL'S ALLEY/Continental
800 Emerson Street/Palo Alto/Area 2/(415) 329-1727

I like the food at this university favorite, but their handling of customers can be a bit awkward at times. A friend of mine (who was never very good in the math department) once accidentally miscalculated what fifteen percent of the bill was, and inadvertently left a rather scant tip. Upon reaching the sidewalk, the hostess tapped my friend on the back and asked if there had been anything wrong with the lunch. She added that when people left less than fifteen percent it generally meant they had been displeased. While this may be an indication of proprietary concern, it is not considered the best form, and can create an embarassing situation. Even assuming that this is the exception rather than the rule, the service can still be a bit disorganized.

Dinners are handled with a bit more finesse than lunch in both the kitchen and dining room. The menu changes daily on a blackboard menu, and offers everything from chicken curry to veal scalloppine (considered the prize of the kitchen). The Greek lamb chops have a whispery marinade of light vinegar and garlic. The pasta *aglio* could leave you and anyone you're with in a slight state of garlic shock. It's heavily seasoned with garlic, onions and red pepper. The prawns Créole is good, as are most of the Créoles the chef prepares. The fish is always fresh. According to owner Vern Gates, if it's not fresh—it's not served.

The prices are a bit high and the service is a bit slow, but St. Michael's is still packing 'em in. Just remember to leave a good tip or they'll know the reason why.

Moderate to expensive. Open seven days. Lunch served Monday through Saturday from 11:30 A.M. to 5 P.M. Dinner from 5:30 to 10 P.M. Reservations accepted. Visa, MC. Entertainment. Wine and beer only. Child's menu. Street parking. Casual.

★
ST. ORRES/French
Highway 1/Gualala/Area 3/(707) 884-3303

This is the kind of place that produces a twilight-zone feeling of age. An architect's orgy of modern architecture is combined with the feel of a Russian countryside and located on the California coast. Whatever has been said about "too many cooks in the kitchen" cannot be applied to architects: the five architects and carpenters who purchased this site have worked together to create a fantasy atmosphere of lush greenery and airiness.

This coastal castle has pretensions toward *haute cuisine* . . . and it's good. The creativity exhibited in the architicture has been extended to the imaginative kitchen. Entrées come with soup, salad, and home-baked wheat loaves with an unusual orange butter. Both my companion and I had the rack of lamb Dijonnaise which was roasted to succulent perfection. A continental breakfast is served to overnight guests: a buffet of fresh fruit, fresh orange juice and homemade coffee cake. **Moderate to expensive.** Open for dinner from 5:15 to 9:45 P.M. Sunday brunch from 11:30 A.M. to 2:30 P.M. Reservations essential. No credit cards. Wine and beer only. Parking lot. Casual.

★ ★
SALUTO'S/Italian/American
1600 Old Bayshore/Burlingame/Area 2/(415) 697-6565

Consistency is the hallmark of this Mediterranean-style restaurant which is perched picturesquely — like an Italian palazzo — on the water's edge, with commanding vistas of the Bay and airport. Owned by Larry Geraldi, scion of the pioneer San Francisco Fisherman's Wharf restaurant family, it had garnered a three-star "excellent" award from *Mobil Guide* for nine consecutive years. It is a direct descendent of the celebrated Domino Club, Geraldi's first success story. Everything here is cooked fresh, with no prepared or frozen dishes. The Italian and fresh seafood menu offers sole Florentine, *cannelloni Roma,* veal parmigiana Sophia, and roast prime rib, all geared to a family budget. Complimentary cheese fondue precedes each dinner, salads are made tableside, and house wines are dispensed from a quaint Sicilian donkey cart. Echos of the Domino Club include complimentary buffets in the lounge. Don't miss some of the famed Domino Club art collection exhibited in the bar and banquet room. Non-stop live entertainment and dancing every night.
Moderate. Open seven days. Lunch served weekdays from 11:30 A.M. to 2:30 P.M. Dinner from 5:30 to 11 P.M. Reservations advised. Visa, MC, AX. Entertainment and dancing nightly. Full bar. Bay and airport view. Child's menu. Parking lot. Casual.

To obtain the best results from this Guide, be sure to consult the map on the various Northern California areas on page 28.

★ ★
SALVATORE'S/Italian
1000 El Camino Real/San Carlos/Area 2/(415) 593-1000

Although Sal Campagna's restaurant specializes in continental and Italian foods, if you're not a veal or pasta fancier, filet mignon is served with artichoke bottom and mushroom cap; and New York steak and prime steer beef are broiled to taste. Veal suggestions include veal *stecchine*, tender scallops of veal stuffed with mushrooms and ham; veal *melanzane*, sautéed eggplant between veal scallops served with a lemon butter sauce; and veal scalloppine Marsala, milk-fed veal sautéed in olive oil, shallots and Marsala wine. One of the most extensive wine lists on the peninsula.
Moderate to expensive. Open for lunch Monday through Friday 11:30 A.M. to 3 P.M. Dinner Sunday and Monday 5 to 10 P.M., till 11 P.M. Tuesday through Saturday. Reservations necessary on weekends. MC, Visa, AX. Full bar. Parking in rear. Casual.

DA ★
SAMOA COOKHOUSE/American/Family Style
445 W. Washington Street/Eureka/Area 4/(707) 442-1659

This is the place to indulge your fantasy of the unzipped dinner or eating like a lumberjack. The last surviving lumber-camp cookhouse on the Pacific Coast lives on, still serving man-sized meals family style across its oilcloth-covered tables. For more than thirty years after 1898, the large dining room was filled three times a day with the hubbub of hungry, and sometimes raucous, lumbermen. Today it is a glimpse into the past, its walls covered with old cooking implements and its small historical museum filled with tools from the early years of the logging industry. The Cookhouse opens at 6 A.M. seven days a week to serve the heartiest breakfast you're likely to see anywhere. Dinners are comprised of soup, salad, two meat courses, several vegetables and side dishes always including beans, homemade bread and fresh pie for dessert.
Inexpensive to moderate. Open seven days. Breakfast from 6 to 11 A.M. Lunch from 11 A.M. to 3 P.M. Dinner from 5 to 10 P.M. No reservations. All major credit cards. Child's menu. Lot parking. Casual.

For best results, consult "How to Use This Guide" on page 25.

★
SAM'S ANCHOR CAFE/Seafood/Continental
27 Main Street/Tiburon/Area 3/(415) 435-4527

Open-air dining on the famous deck where masses of tanned bodies watch the harbor action, the San Francisco skyline and sip a Ramos gin fizz or share an "Eggs Benedict and Champagne for Two" is just fine. Fine? This is good outdoor dining in the Bay Area, although there's a lot of drinking going on here, too. The huge, old (1920) facility has family dinners with family prices in the Blue Room, and the informal waterside dining (where I saw my first string bikini) is in view of their own docking facilities. My recommendations: boned rex sole, veal *champagne bleu* and shrimp *tetrazzini* are the best of the average fare. There are also boat docking facilities available for patrons.
Moderate. Open seven days. Monday through Friday from 11 A.M. to 10 P.M., Saturday 10 A.M. to 10:30 P.M., Sunday 9:30 A.M. to 10 P.M. Saturday and Sunday brunch. No reservations. Visa, MC. Full bar. Patio. View of San Francisco Bay. Child's menu. Lot parking. Casual.

★ ★ ★
SAM'S GRILL/Seafood
374 Bush Street/San Francisco/Area 2/(415) 421-0594

One of the best seafood restaurants in San Francisco is over a century old. This unpretentious, Yugoslavian-influenced establishment still prints new menus every day with twenty specials and almost one hundred à la carte dishes. Gary and Walter Seput, the proprietors, are not at all above taking a shift behind the old bar or helping clear the tables. Dishes like turtle soup, oyster cocktail, shellfish salad, boned rex sole and charcoal-broiled filet of petrale sole are worth lining up for. The financial community virtually monopolizes the restaurant at lunch; dinner lures a more varied clientele, although the restaurant closes at 8:30 P.M., early by San Francisco standards. The menu also provides a non-seafood variety of grills and poultry and omelettes and pasta — but going to Sam's and not ordering seafood would be like going to Tiffany's for a zircon. Vegetables are garden fresh and perfectly turned-out. (Asparagus is crunchy, served with a mustard mayonnaise.) The limited wine list is really not a fault here—there's an adequate selection of Wente (you might like to try their dry Semillon) and Krug whites, a few reds and a corkage charge if you want to bring your own wine (many do).
Inexpensive to moderate. Open Monday through Friday from 11 A.M. to 8:30 P.M. Reservations accepted for six or more. Visa, MC. Full bar. Street parking. Casual.

★ ★
SANPPO/Japanese
1702 Post Street/San Francisco/Area 2/(415) 346-3486

Most of the usual Japanese dishes are served in this simply deco-rated restaurant. The tempura, with its feather-light coating, and *gyoza* (thin pasta shells with a tasty filling) are notable. Add a hot sake and you'll find yourself deep in transdigestional meditation.
Moderate. Open Tuesday through Sunday. Lunch from 11:45 A.M. to 5 P.M. Dinner from 5 to 10 P.M., Sunday 3 to 10 P.M. No reservations. No credit cards. Wine and beer only. Lot parking. Casual.

SAN REMO/Italian/American
2237 Mason Street/San Francisco/Area 2/(415) 673-9090

A good thing about children and restaurant booths . . . both are washable – and they need to be at this family-style restaurant. Din-ners with entrées like veal scalloppine, veal parmigiana and fairly good sweetbreads are not exciting but they are good – hot and filling. You get soup, simple salad, a pasta, dessert and coffee with your choice of about a half dozen main courses. The decor is plain but honest.
Moderate. Open seven days from 5 to 11 P.M. Reservations accepted. All major credit cards. Full bar. Street parking. Casual.

★
SAN SIMEON RESTAURANT/Seafood/Italian/American
Highway 1/San Simeon/Area 1/(805) 927-4604

Just a short three miles south of Hearst Castle, on the east side of the highway, awaits this oasis of choice food and wine, plus a full bar. The interior is highlighted by various momentoes of the nearby Castle, giving the diner both a preview and a review, depending on which route you're pursuing. I would not deem it museum-like since the res-taurant has a lighter ambiance, but the artifacts bear study. While there are other dining places and just plain eateries nearby, the cuisine here is dependable and consistent. The steaks and prime rib are alone worth the trip, and the seafood is properly fresh.
Moderate. Open seven days. Breakfast from 7 to 11 A.M. Lunch 11 A.M. to 2 P.M. Dinner from 5 to 9 P.M.. Reservations advised. All major credit cards. Organ piano Tuesday through Saturday from 8 P.M. to midnight. Full bar. Ample parking. Casual.

★ ★
SANTA FE BAR AND GRILL/California/Nouvelle
1310 University Avenue/Berkeley/Area 2/(415) 841-4740

A **huge** and clattering old train depot, it is yet more evidence (as if that were needed) of the culinary magic that Jeremiah Tower has managed to impart to every restaurant with which he has been associated. There is a rumor, currently going the rounds, that Tower's restaurants (actually he has partners as well) are up for sale so that Jeremiah can move to New York. If the rumor is true – and most are not – it will be extremely difficult to find investors who can harness the kind of talent to keep this establishment in the gastronomic orbit it has attained. Much of the menu has been designed around a mesquite grill including several varieties of fresh fish, squab in raspberry vinegar and lamb. Salads at luncheon are the more exciting fare on the menu and the Sunday brunch in sumptious.

Moderate to expensive. Open seven days. Lunch 11:30 A.M. to 2:30 P.M. Dinner 5:30 to 10 P.M., Friday and Saturday until 11 P.M. Reservations accepted. Visa, MC, AX. Entertainment. Full bar. Lot parking. Casual.

★ ★ ★
SARDINE FACTORY/Continental/Seafood
701 Wave Street/Monterey/Area 1/(408) 373-3775

O**wners** Ted Balestreri and Bert Cutino continue to polish every facet of this crown jewel of the Monterey Peninsula, constantly seeking even more ways to add to their guests' fine dining experience. In 1984 they opened a unique Cellar Room, which is a "must-see" for wine buffs and those interested in planning parties and banquets. It was handcrafted within the building by one of the Factory's three sommeliers, even to a massive, long table and tall chairs. There are even alcoves with wine lockers for the regulars' own treasures. The restaurant has three entirely different dining rooms: the Conservatory, a veritable garden of blooming greenery enclosed in a lofty glass bubble, with center statuary fountain (very Italian); the Captains' Room, rich with ceiling to floor velvet drapes, marble fireplace, gold chairs and exquisite chandeliers; and the Cannery Row, front room, with casual decor, a fireplace, and daytime views out over The Row and bay. Many recognize the elevated long bar as that favored by Clint Eastwood in the movie *Play Misty for Me*. Clint still drops by, as do an impressive collection

of celebrities from pictures, TV, politics and the social scene, winery executives and the business world. The cuisine, created by executive chef Bert, is never static but always interesting, and has brought their restaurant the envied Travel/Holiday Magazine Award for Fine Dining for many consecutive years. Food and Wine Editor of Travel/Holiday, Robert Balzar, goes out of his way to visit here, a rare tribute. It is superfluous to cite individual dishes. The meats are all choice, seafood is fresh, local when possible, except for imported gourmet-type items. Be sure to have the abalone chowder. Photographs galore of this historied area adorn the bar area Wall of Fame. The very building in which you dine was one of Cannery Row's originals. The Row, itself, is but a block away, just a stroll from the Monterey Aquarium.
Expensive. Lunch Monday through Saturday from 11:30 A.M. to 2:30 P.M. Dinner Friday and Saturday from 5 to 11 P.M., Sunday 2 to 11 P.M. Reservations necessary. All major credit cards. Full bar. Lot parking. Dressy.

★
SARI'S/Indonesian
2459 Lombard Street/San Francisco/Area 2/(415) 567-8715

Julda and André Harsono are the delightful owners of this batik-covered restaurant. Indonesian artifacts abound and can make for interesting conversation pieces. The *rijstaffel*, Indonesia's most celebrated and varied dinner, is the specialty. Fried *krepuk* shrimp chips, *lumpia* (a kind of egg roll), *gado gado* (Indonesian salad), *ayam goreng* (lemon marinated chicken), *pergedel* (meatballs), *redang goreng* (shrimp with onions), rice and *sate daging* (beef marinated in Japanese spices and served with peanut sauce) make up this food heathen's heaven. In spite of some of the bland sounding translations, this cuisine is far from bland — it can, in fact, be more spicy than you bargained for. Boring it isn't.
Inexpensive to moderate. Open Tuesday through Sunday from 6 to 10 P.M. Reservations advised. Visa, MC, DC, CB. Wine and beer only. Street parking. Casual.

In order to obtain the best results from this Guide, be sure to read the French, German, Italian and Oriental menu translators on pages 399 to 404 of this Guide.

★

S. ASIMAKOPOULOS CAFE/Greek
288 Connecticut Street/San Francisco/Area 2/(415) 552-8789

The name means "silversmith of Akopoulos." And husband and wife team Spero and Barbara Asimos (a shortened version of the original) keep everything as shiny and bright as a new *drachma*. The butcher block tables, sparkling white walls and on-view kitchen set the scene for this haven from the Aegean. There's even a long counter for individual dining in this neighborhood favorite. A nice touch . . . they stay open during those "in limbo" hours between lunch and dinner. The menu is long on flavor and value. *Souvlaki,* a house specialty, is a hearty skewer of marinated, grilled lamb, pork and chicken, topping a pita bread pocket and a bed of vegetable tidbits. Try sliding the meat from the skewer into the pita in one deft move. Easier said than done. On Friday and Saturday nights, another "must try" is *goulbasi.* Tender lamb on the shank is braised, then wrapped around garlic slices, butter and Kaserai cheese—the whole thing is then wrapped in parchment and baked. Other entrées include a *kotokapama*, chicken sautéed in wine and tomatoes spiced with cinnamon, and *arni me anginares,* roasted lamb with artichoke hearts and topped with egg-lemon sauce. It's a thoroughly professional operation, mixing the right proportions of love and food and fun. **Inexpensive**. Open Monday through Friday from 11:30 A.M. to 10 P.M., Saturday from 5 to 10 P.M. No reservations. Visa, MC. Wine and beer only. Street parking. Casual.

★ ★

THE SAVOY/Continental
3131 North Main Street (adjacent to The Pleasant Hill Inn)/Pleasant Hill
Area 2/(415) 938-2911

This sophisticated, cosmopolitan dining place is regarded as one of the three leading restaurants in Contra Costa County, only about twenty minutes drive from Berkeley. Owner/host Sam Vassiliou was Doros' gracious *maître d'* nearly a decade ago, and he frequently greets patrons who have followed him from San Francisco. In this spacious, quietly elegant oasis, tuxedoed waiters present dishes such as a rack of lamb and veal *scalloppine à la Savoy,* both so simple in concept that only a talented chef can make their flavors sing. Try the kitchen again; order scampi with lemon garlic butter and white wine. Sam's wine cellar holds select vintages, California and imports. The bar lounge is one of the Walnut Creek area's favorites for all the right times.

Moderate. Open 11:30 A.M. to 10 P.M. Lunch Monday through Friday, dinner Monday through Saturday. Reservations recommended. AX, Visa, MC, DC. Entertainment. Full bar. Valet parking weekends. Casual.

★
SCANDINAVIAN DELI/Scandinavian
2251 Market Street/San Francisco/Area 2/(415) 861-9913

I can't see how Ernst Meyer can make money in this authentic Danish family restaurant. His prices are among the lowest in town for good, not great, dinners of herring and roast pork and beef soup and Swedish sausage. The *fläkesteg* is a pork roast with a good crust and is a favorite of the merchants in the area. Open-faced sandwiches in the style of Denmark are very reasonable.

Inexpensive. Open Monday through Friday from 9 A.M. to 8 P.M. No reservations. No credit cards. Wine and beer only. Street parking. Casual.

DA ★ ★
SCHROEDER'S GERMAN RESTAURANT/German/American
240 Front Street/San Francisco/Area 2/(415) 421-4778

There's *gemütlich* galore at this Teutonic legend, a financial district landmark which owner T. Max Kniesche, Jr. took over from his father. T. J. Maxim Kniesche III is the manager.

In 1893, the doors opened for the businessmen, sea captains, merchants and others who enjoyed the comraderie of the "men only" lunches. In 1935, the forerunners of today's lib movement prevailed upon the owners to accept the patronage of ladies after 1:30 P.M. That continued until 1970, when the last restriction was withdrawn, although the heavy food and massive, male-oriented interior still attracts a predominantly mens group.

For reasons that elude me, German food has never been popular in the United States—you can count the number of good German restaurants on one hand and still have a thumb left over. Here the sauerbraten is a revelation to those who thought they had tried sauerbraten before—it's well marinated, tender and served with potato pancakes that are made fresh in the kitchen. The wienerschnitzel with good German beer is as full-filling a dinner as I've had.

In the vast hall, heavy with dark wood and mahogany pillars, a half-mile of shelving displays a huge collection of beer steins. Above are the antlered stag trophies, but it is the seven-foot oil murals (*brauhaus* scenes), earthy and heavy-handedly humorous that are the decor highlights of the room. The all-German kitchen, staffed by four chefs and three assistants in the manner of the ancient grand hotels, turns out a wide range of victuals to an ample clientele that look like they are living beyond their seams.

Liver dumplings or pig's knuckles with sauerkraut, *schweizer* bratwurst with red cabbage, goulash and noodles, roulade of beef and roast duck with apple sauce give you a glimpse of the entrées. Strudel, multilayered tarts and fresh huckleberries with real whipped cream are a brief introduction to the desserts.

The food is amazingly inexpensive for the amount of effort and authenticity represented by this charismatic old restaurant which has a chalet front and copper-adorned main doors.

Inexpensive to moderate. Open Monday through Friday. Lunch from 11 A.M. to 4:30 P.M. Dinner from 4:30 to 9 P.M. Reservations advised. AX. Full bar. Child's menu. Validated parking in nearby lot. Casual to semi-dressy.

★ ★
SCOTT'S SEAFOOD GRILL & BAR/Seafood
2400 Lombard Street/San Francisco/Area 2/(415) 563-8988
#3 Embarcadero Center/San Francisco/Area 2/(415) 981-0622
2300 East Bayshore Road/Palo Alto/Area 2/(415) 856-1046
Jack London Square/Oakland/Area 2/(415) 444-3456

As long as there is a San Francisco, there'll be some excellent seafood restaurants. The City has its famous old favorites—Sam's Grill & Seafood Restaurant, Maye's Oyster House, Tadich Grill, and the East Bay has its Spenger's Fish Grotto, in Berkeley, but Scott's is a new "must" place for fish and shellfish. It is so handsomely and successfully operated that the owners have opened several sister restaurants on the Podium level of Embarcadero Number Three, in Palo Alto, and in Oakland.

This is a no-nonsense place; a two-story Victorian on the northwest corner of Scott and Lombard, with a front bar, open kitchen and display cases from which assorted shellfish and finny folk view you icily. Two dining rooms, neat and crisp with wood trim and some photos and pictures reflecting an older San Francisco, are always beset with Scott fanciers and I do not refer to Sir Walter. Incidentally, a subtle underliner of the name—ample wain*scot*ting throughout.

Opened in 1976 by Malcolm Stroud and Martin Newman, of The Coachman fame, and still operated judiciously and enthusiastically by same. The menu states "All seafood subject to season, weather & catch." Very honest—and that's what Scott's is about. Fine fish that receives superb treatment in all fashions, Eastern oysters are flown in whenever available. The chefs make knowing use of the best local seafood—even thresher shark, and there is a cheerful, professional staff. **Moderate.** Open daily from 11 A.M. to 11 P.M. Reservations advised. All major credit cards. Full bar. Street parking. Garage parking at Embarcadero. Casual.

★
SCOTTY CAMPBELL'S/Continental
2907 El Camino/Redwood City/Area 2/(415) 369-3773

James B. Sniadecki, a former '49er linebacker of fine repute, now owns and operates this Peninsula old-time favorite. A happy institution long-favored for its pleasant, cheerful, Scottish-influenced ambiance, long mahogany bar and good steaks.

The foyer could be that of a men's club; tailored and tartan-clad, with a glass-encased suit of armor. Dining rooms are also sheathed in red and black tartan plaid and embellished with prints while a formidable shield and escutcheon centers one wall. There are working, hooded fireplaces in the dining rooms and fringed, Tiffany lamps add their touch. Kilted and Scots-capped waitresses professionally go about their tasks with grace and charm. Many have been on staff here for donkey's years and recognize patrons by name. On our last visit, our server was the same woman who had so nicely taken care of us five years ago. Her speech-burr had not softened a vowel and recalled memories of my last trip to Edinburgh.

Dinner includes a basket of warm garlic bread, followed by choice of soup or salad. First, though, consider the barbecued spare ribs as an appetizer. Steaks appear in nine entrée listings, from the special prime club steak to the New York pepper steak. All are juicy and done exactly as you order. Steak and lobster, double-cut French lamb chops, half spring chicken, chicken à la Kiev, lobster tails, sole, trout, mahi-mahi and scampi are some of the other selections. I observed practically all of the above passing en route to various tables, but people primarily come to Scotty Campbell's for steaks.

Moderate to expensive. Open Monday through Thursday from 4:30 to 10:30 P.M., Friday and Saturday to 11 P.M. Sunday from 4 to 10:30 P.M. Reservations necessary. All major credit cards. Entertainment. Dancing. Parking lot. Casual to semi-dressy.

★ ★
THE SEA GULL/Continental
10481 Lansing (at Ukiah)/Mendocino/Area 3/(707) 937-5204

It's like dining in some eccentric's cleaned-up attic: antiques and Oriental carpets and stuffed animals and musical instruments and antlers and ship's wheels provide the whimsical setting for some really good food. The moderate prices include a relish dish of raw vegetables, fresh fruit, peppers, homemade soup, fresh green salad, crusty French bread and butter, and dessert. Entrées include red snapper or ling cod (when the boats come in), rainbow trout, shrimp sautéed with mushrooms and herbs, sweetbreads and the finest chicken Kiev outside of a Russian restaurant. The Sea Gull special salad with meat and cheese is a stomach-expanding meal in itself. For lunch, I like the mussels on the half shell in broth served for two people, or any of the gourmand sandwiches. Breakfast pastry is fresh from the kitchen. (Try to be seated in the cellar portion for the best "feel" . . . metal tables, classical music and low couches.) There is lodging here in the small bed and breakfast inn, with ocean views and very reasonable rates.
Moderate to expensive. Open seven days. Breakfast from 7:30 to 11:30 A.M. Lunch from 11:30 A.M. to 5 P.M. Dinner from 5 to 9 P.M. No reservations. No credit cards. Entertainment. Full bar. Child's menu. Lot and street parking. Casual.

★ ★
SEARS FINE FOODS/American
439 Powell Street/San Francisco/Area 2/(415) 986-1600

The late Dwight Eisenhower, Clint Murchison and J. Edgar Hoover were among the faithful who made this little bungalow, sandwiched between two brick and stone buildings on the Powell Street cable car line, the breakfast capital of the Western Hemisphere. It was founded more than seventy years ago by Ben Sears, a Ringling Brothers clown who built his second and more lucrative career with recipes for pancakes, inherited from his wife's Swedish family. He sold the business some thirty years ago, but the hungry hordes still wait until the 7 A.M. openings to have the eighteen feather-light Swedish pancakes arranged in small stacks and served with whipped butter and hickory smoked ham or country sausage. Syrups are homemade loganberry, wild blackberry, boysenberry and maple – and after breakfast, the lunches feature fresh vegetables (a specialty), roast beef, turkey or ground steak. There are sandwiches and salads, too. Sears *was* celebrated for the novelty of its Cadillac waiting room; the owners used to park two pink Cadillacs in front with the heaters and radios on to shelter the waiting

crowds. (I stood in line at the curb so long one morning that I expected to have my leg chalked by a meter maid.) Incidentally, this true value eating place still charges only fifteen cents for a cup of coffee that is ordered with food and it's a bottomless cup, at that. Also, the fresh fruit, cream-topped pies (in season) are so delicious and popular that many patrons order their selection as soon as they are seated, to avoid disappointment in the event that Sears "runs out." Owner Al Boyajian, a sturdy teddy-bear of a nice gentleman now has son Lee, a handsome former footballer, at his side. This is one of my favorite places in all of San Francisco.
Inexpensive. Open Wednesday through Sunday from 7 A.M. to 2:30 P.M. Reservations accepted. No credit cards. Street parking. Casual.

SEBASTIAN'S/Continental
1901 South Bascom Avenue/Campbell/Area 2/(408) 377-8600

If you know the way to San Jose, you might pass this restaurant, located just southwest of that city in Campbell. Perhaps its only redeeming quality is its location at the top of Pruneyard Towers and offers a splendid view of orchards and vineyards. Sebastian's specializes in lamb and veal, with dinners starting at $10. But don't go here to "get down" in your funky faded blue jeans—you won't get in the door. I get the impression Sebastian's is trying to upgrade the poor restaurant reputation San Jose has been cursed with . . . but they've got a long way to go.

Tour note: If you are in the area, don't miss the Winchester Mystery House just off U.S. 101. It's a giant, insane monstrosity built by an eccentric lady to baffle the "evil spirits" that haunted her. There are doors that open into brick walls, staircases that go nowhere, and a spy system the CIA would admire. You need a guided tour, because even the owner Sarah Winchester and her servants needed maps to find their way around. It cost $5 million of the Winchester Arms fortune—a sizeable amount in those pre-inflationary times.
Moderate to expensive. Open seven days. Lunch served from 11:30 A.M. to 3 P.M. Dinner from 6 to 11 P.M. Reservations essential. Visa, MC, AX. Entertainment. Full bar. Parking lot. Semi-dressy to dressy.

For best results, consult "How to Use This Guide" on page 25.

★
SEOUL GARDEN/ Korean
22 Peace Plaza, East Building/Japan Cultural Center/San Francisco
Area 2/(415) 563-7664

Some of the best Seoul food in town is served in this new restaurant adjacent to the Japan Center. Smoking or non-smoking rooms here could apply to the cook-it-yourself room where tables have a built-in grill from which the perfume of cooking beef emanates, or the other room where the food is brought to your table. Bowls of rice topped with grated vegetable—green and red cabbage, zucchini—with tidbits of fish or beef, are among my favorite dishes here, although I am addicted to *kimchee*, the wonderful pickled cabbage so hot it leaves an imprint on your palate for hours to come. Koreans use a lot of garlic in their cooking, and so it is with Seoul Garden. Virtually all meats are marinated before cooking, and the cuisine resembles that of Manchuria. Manager Steve Chu will help first-timers explore Korean food, which is closer to western cooking than any other Asian cuisine. Waitresses in spectacular costumes create much of the atmosphere.
Moderate. Open daily from 11:30 A.M. to 10:30 P.M. Reservations accepted. Visa, MC, AX. Full Bar. Parking in Japan Center garage. Semi-dressy.

★ ★
SEVEN SEAS/Seafood
682 Bridgeway/Sausalito/Area 3/(415) 332-1304

The informal, unusually competent seafood house that's located near the Ferry has been serving their everyone-knows-everyone clientele since 1959. The sign "keep clam" sets the tone of a restaurant that doesn't take itself too seriously yet manages an excellent bouillabaisse, serves eastern oysters and tells you what's fresh (most everything) and what isn't (still good). I once ate two dozen cherrystone clams here with good icy beer, a refreshing experience I recall fondly. The three-egg omelette is a favorite for hangovers with the "I take an occasional drink" set, particularly the hangtown fry. There may be fancier places, certainly most seafood houses are far more expensive, but owner Paul DeMoss need defer to no one in his efficient and popular establishment.
Moderate. Open seven days from 8 A.M. to 11:30 P.M., Saturday and Sunday brunch from noon to 3 P.M. Reservations accepted. All major credit cards. Full bar. Patio. Street and validated lot parking. Casual.

DA★★
SHADOWBROOK/American/Continental
Wharf Road at Capitola/Capitola/Area 1/(408) 475-1511

One of California's unforgettable restaurants clings to a steep slope, descending to the bank of Soquel Creek, four miles south of Santa Cruz. Its most persuasive attractions unfold in a fascinating sequence, level by level, reminiscent of a Swiss chalet. An eight-passenger cable car leisurely transports guests returning up the thirty-one-degree grade — primarily for those who have dined too well but also for sheer fun. If you prefer, there are two paths (one past a waterfall) down the foliaged hillside, past writhing oaks and shrubs, at every turn revealing pastoral vistas. I usually lead my guests down a path, later ascending by the European-style car.

Edmund F. Philippet bought this private property in 1946, a veritable "haunted house," for his own use. However, he saw the potential and renovated it as a dining place. New owners have not only maintained Shadowbrook but have continued to add some charming features.

The top level, the Rock Room, has a happy bar backed by the waterfall flowing down the exposed hillside rock, with fireplaces and tables. Next, descend to the main dining room with the mammoth fireplace and tilted view windows. Hanging pots of flowers, abundant rusticity, and ropes of ivy and wisteria cascade from eaves and beams. Somewhat below, the windowed Garden Room seats more diners and the Wine Cellar below is enclosed. Finally, the Greenhouse, a glass-ceilinged room on the river bank — an enchanting place for your memory book.

The menu is uncomplicated but certainly more than adequate. Prime rib, scampi, salmon with hollandaise, *mahi mahi* with macademian butter, and *coquilles St. Jacques* are some of the offerings. There is a daily fresh catch and steaks, and all are accompanied by breads from their own bakery, soup or salad, veggies and rice pilaf. Brunch is a special occasion with blueberry blintzes and almond French toast, among others. **Moderate to expensive**. Open seven days. Dinner is served Monday through Thursday from 5 to 9:30 P.M., Friday from 5 to 10:30 P.M., Saturday from 4 to 10:30 P.M., Sunday from 4 to 9 P.M. Brunch is served Saturday from 10:30 A.M. to 2 P.M., Sunday from 9:30 A.M. to 2 P.M. Reservations advised. Visa, MC. Entertainment. Full bar. View. Patio. Lot parking. Casual to semi-dressy.

Please be sure to consult "Tipping Made Easy" on page 22 of this Guide.

SHANGHAI STATION/Chinese
3565 Standish Avenue/Santa Rosa/Area 3/(707) 584-4881

Perhaps the most popular Chinese restaurant in the Santa Rosa area, owner/hostess Sally Lee's Shanghai Station owes its fame not only to its cuisine but to its charming decor – a blending of old railroad cars with a convincing reproduction of a vintage station. Surrounded by original mahogany paneling and stained-glass windows, guests can easily imagine that they're dining on a cross-country train of bygone days.

The menu, though not as extensive as those in larger Chinese restaurants, offers a good sampling of Cantonese, Hunanese, Szechwanese and Mandarin dishes. Diners can stay with old favorites or try such treats as beef with spicy tea sauce or chunky crispy chicken in ginger and garlic sauce (delicious). Bargain hunters can enjoy lunch specials. The wine list is limited but varied.

In the summer, meals are served under umbrellas on the rear deck by the garden, along with live music.
Moderate. Open seven days. Lunch Monday through Friday from 11:30 A.M. to 2:30 P.M. Dinner Monday through Saturday from 5 to 10 P.M., Sunday from 4:30 to 9:30 P.M. Sunday brunch from 10:30 A.M. to 2:30 P.M. Reservations advised on weekends. Visa, MC, AX. Jazz Friday and Saturday nights. Full bar. Parking in adjacent lot. Casual.

★ ★
SHARL'S/French
136 West Napa Street/Sonoma/Area 3/(707) 996-5155

Guests at Sharl's cannot help but feel pampered. Perfectionism impels Bob Subaie and Karl Rashash, hosts and operating partners, to personally shop for the freshest produce available, plan menus, keep an eye on preparation of cuisine, greet patrons, and even help to serve them in order to monitor presentation, which is a treat to behold. Thoughtful extra touches make diners feel very well cared for.

The tantalizing dinner menu offers a choice between the sumptuous many-course *prix fixe* dinner and such à la carte items as Sharl's filet of sole, whose sauce changes daily (all seafood is fresh), milk-fed loin of veal in apple brandy sauce (meat is also fresh), and duck with pink and green peppercorns and lemon leeks. Hors d'oeuvres include hot and cold specials of the day, oysters and escargots and two soups are offered. The half-dozen desserts range from the exquisite to the sinful. Though devoted largely to California bottlings, the extensive wine list also carries leading French and Italian labels.

The decor — white walls, ample greenery, indirect lighting, high ceiling, and nicely spaced tables — adds to guests' sense of well-being. A roofed terrace is pleasant in warm weather.

Expensive. Open Wednesday through Monday. Lunch Monday, and Wednesday through Saturday from 11 A.M. to 3 P.M. Dinner Monday, Wednesday and Thursday from 5:30 to 9 P.M., Friday and Saturday from 5:30 to 9:30 P.M., Sunday from 4:30 to 9:00 P.M. Sunday brunch from 11 A.M. to 2:30 P.M. Reservations advised. Visa, MC, AX, DC. Piano music Friday and Saturday nights. Full bar. Parking in adjacent lot. Casual to semi-dressy.

★ ★
THE SHERATON ROUND BARN INN/American/California
3555 Round Barn Boulevard/Santa Rosa/Area 3/(707) 523-7080

Called simply "the Restaurant," the Round Barn Inn's dining room offers a degree of sophistication rarely seen in laid-back Sonoma County. Dinner guests in particular are treated to high-level, formal service which includes tableside cooking. The care given to presentation is especially impressive. In other words, diners are acutely aware they are having an experience rather than a mere meal.

A few of the favorites include king salmon, medallions of veal Nagasawa (honoring an early resident of the historic Round Barn property), and double breast of pheasant Créole. Each day's hors d'oeuvres have a theme, representing different national cuisines. All seafood is fresh, the poultry and meat are California grown, and produce is local. The fairly extensive wine list carries mostly Sonoma and Napa County bottlings along with some leading French labels.

The restaurant is dramatically decorated in pinks and reds; and its hillside location affords a view of the Santa Rosa plain and the coastal hills beyond.

Moderate to expensive. Open seven days a week. Breakfast Monday through Sunday from 6:30 to 11 A.M. Lunch Monday through Sunday from noon to 2:30 P.M. Dinner Monday through Sunday from 5:30 to 10:30 P.M. Reservations advised. All major credit cards. Live music six nights a week. Full bar. Parking in adjacent lot. Tasteful casual to semi-dressy.

In order to obtain the best results from this Guide, please consult "A Few Inside Tips" on page 18.

★
SHOGUN/Japanese
4390 El Camino Real/Los Altos/Area 2/(415) 948-3327

Let's face it, the cooking at Shogun is not traditional Japanese cooking, but it's a cultural experience just the same. Diners are seated with perfect strangers, or imperfect as the case may be, around the teppan grill which covers the entire middle of the table. The chefs have trained as apprentices for years before they are allowed to cook before the customers — and you can see why: with all the tossing of salt shakers, twirling of gleaming knives and slashing of vegetables, one slight misstep could result in supreme embarassment if not outright pain. All the adroitness exhibited by the chef really dictates that you at least attempt the dexterity necessary to handle the chopsticks provided.

The chef, who is also your waiter, carefully explains the ingredients and sauces in any dish. As our chef distributed the sauces to all ten people at our table, he repeated for each person while pointing to the appropriate sauce, "hot sauce . . . not-hot sauce." My companion and I were giggling about the repetition involved in this serving process, figuring it had been indelibly etched into our minds. A few rounds of sake later, however, my friend and I were holding a muted conference to decide which one we had been told was hot.

The cuisine is described as "Japanese steak and seafood" which illustrates the Americanization in the kitchen. Scallops, shrimp, lobster, chicken or steak are all prepared with artistry right in front of you. The grilled vegetables, which seem to consist mainly of bean sprouts, are well seasoned and serve as a complement to any dinner. The teppan version of Japanese cooking will not leave you hungry as some of the sushi bars about town might, but neither will it have you walking away with that "I can't believe I ate the whole thing" feeling of many American steak 'n seafood restaurants.

Moderate to expensive. Open seven days. Lunch Monday through Friday from 11:30 A.M. to 2 P.M. Dinner from 5 to 10 P.M. Reservations advised. Visa, MC, AX. Full bar. Child's menu. Parking lot. Casual.

In order to obtain the best results from this Guide, be sure to read the French, German, Italian and Oriental menu translators on pages 399 to 404 of this Guide.

★
THE SHORE BIRD/Seafood/American
390 Capistrano Road/Princeton-by-the-Sea/Area 2/(415) 728-5541

Cape Cod on our California Coast? Believe it. The almost-too-popular Shore Bird is nested within a typical New England cottage, near Highway One but hidden from view, about fifty feet from the Pacific. You'll like your overall experience here so much that you won't mind waiting for a table. No reservations are accepted but if you'll phone, they'll put your name on a "waiting list" Mondays through Thursdays. Turn off the road at the stoplight.

In any weather, this is worth the drive. Guests on standby may order drinks in the garden patio. The three comfortable dining rooms are almost always full. Beamed ceilings, skylights, plants, local photographs, some paintings and a cheery fireplace in the bar lounge set the scene.

As you would expect, the kitchen's immediate concern is with fresh seafood. The Shore Bird purchases everything possible from Princeton-by-the-Sea commercial boats. Ship to Shore Bird—live! Most fish are broiled. Other items of note—chicken stuffed with crab, top sirloin and two daily specialties—dubbed "The Creative Urges." You are served a huge bowl of salad on your table, along with dressings and a rack of condiments, rather like a salad bar brought to you. Even bacon bits, sour cream and croutons. Everything comes in generous proportions. The famous Boudin French bread is so-o-o good. In the fall, there is pumpkin pie from the widely publicized pumpkin fields of Half Moon Bay. As a matter of fact, there are serendipitous benefits of driving to this place — whale watching cruises originate nearby from December to April; fishing party boats, Christmas tree farms where you cut your own; an award-winning winery (Obester Wines) and even a candle factory.

Moderate. Open seven days. Lunch served Monday through Saturday from 11:30 A.M. to 3 P.M. Sunday brunch from 10:30 A.M. to 3 P.M. Dinner is served Monday through Thursday from 5:30 to 10:00 P.M. (9:00 P.M. in winter), Friday from 5 to 10:30 P.M. (10 P.M. in winter), Saturday and Sunday from 4:00 to 10 P.M. (9:00 P.M. in winter). Preferred seating Monday through Friday for dinner. All major credit cards. Full bar. Lot parking. Casual.

To obtain the best results from this Guide, be sure to consult the map on the various Northern California areas on page 28.

★ ★
SIAM/Thai
5140 Stevens Creek Boulevard/San Jose/Area 2/(408) 243-5549

An amazingly inexpensive Thai restaurant in a bowling alley was a real find. It is difficult to properly describe the simple sounding dishes, but this restaurant produces dishes with all the subtle charm of bigger, fancier and more trendy establishments. *Sa-tay* is skewered strips of pork accompanied by a smooth peanut butter sauce or a chilled sweet and sour marinade with tiny pieces of hot green pepper.

Hot red and green pepper, lemon grass, garlic, peanuts, ginger and coconut are commonly used in Thai cuisine. *Pla jaramet* is a whole butterfish crisply fried in a special marinade. Thai beer is one of the best brews in the world and both "iced coffee" and "iced tea" are thick, sweet drinks despite their names. Owners are likely to do the serving here in this labor of love, and while you may not feel at harmony with the decor, you will enjoy the good food.

Inexpensive to moderate. Open seven days, Sunday through Thursday from 10:30 A.M. to 10 P.M., Friday and Saturday to 10:30 P.M. Reservations accepted. Visa, MC. Wine and beer only. Parking lot. Casual.

★
SILVER/Chinese
737 Washington/San Francisco/Area 2/(415) 433-8888

This upscale-looking, eclectic Chinese restaurant is noteworthy because it stays open until 3 A.M. and the food is at least on a par with the other inexpensive restaurants of the area. The name is a reflection of the chrome and silver decor with poster style scenes of Hong Kong. There are two menus, an ordinary Cantonese style dinner menu and the more interesting list of noodle and rice dishes. Chef Kwan Ng does a good Peking duck (call in advance), and while there are some wines available, you would do well to pay the $2.50 corkage charge and bring your own. (My favorite, with Chinese food is St. Jeans Gewurtztraminer). Chinese beer is also available and a perfect accompaniment to the cuisine. **Inexpensive.** Open daily from 7 A.M. to 3 A.M. Reservations accepted. Visa, MC. Wine and beer only. Street parking. Casual.

★ ★

SILVERADO COUNTRY CLUB & RESORT/California/Continental
1600 Atlas Peak Road/Napa/Area 3/(707) 267-0200

Always regarded as one of the finest out-of-town addresses, this marvelously restored and improved resort now boasts two good restaurants – The Vintners Court and the Royal Oak, the latter being the principal dining room until the opening of the Vintners Court in 1984. Let us attend to The Court (as the insiders call it) – a sterling room for fine dining. One of the significant new features in interior design is the prominent inclusion of some 123 oak wine lockers, each identified by the name of a Napa Valley vintner, such as Robert Mondavi, Beaulieu, etc. Of course, each holds representative wines. The Silverado's own cellar now carries 185 wines on the restaurant list and another 100 vintages on the "cellar list." The room is charming with its large, brass antique chandelier, creamy tablecloths and dusty rose napkins. A pianist entertains nightly from 5:30 to 10 P.M. The cuisine is Californian and contemporary, with detailed care for the freshness of each product. You can dine well on Sonoma lamb and Petaluma duck. Prime beef and the daily seafood specialties have their adherents here, after eighteen holes and a nineteenth hole tall-story recital. The pastas, made here, are special. I was taken with the warm duck salad, as well. The desserts, in addition to such tempters as the walnut torte, feature homemade ice cream. Or you could opt for the frozen orange soufflé. The Royal Oak dining room was the original restaurant here. It is still quite well patronized by those who value the atmosphere and dinners in this mellow place. Prime steaks, charcoal-broiled and the triple-cut lamb chops and fresh Main lobster are featured. On Fridays, there is a seafood buffet. The interior design blends open beams, brick-work, gleaming copper, high-back chairs and hand-carved tables. The garden views are lovely on summer evenings. The cellar offers the same bottlings, that add to the Vintners Court experience. We have Richard Fivis, Director of Food and Beverage, to thank for much of the above.

Expensive. Open for dinner from 6 to 10 P.M. six nights (days open vary during winter). Sunday brunch 10 A.M. to 2:30 P.M. Reservations necessary. Visa, MC, DC, AX. Entertainment. Full bar. Valet parking. Semi-dressy.

For best results, consult "How to Use This Guide" on page 25.

★
SILVER DRAGON RESTAURANT/Chinese
835 Webster/Oakland/Area 2/(415) 893-3748

Within the handsome interior of this inviting, three-level old favorite, Chef Wah Quon Chee and his sons, Lester and Wesley, operate that rare find, a restaurant that specializes in serving their distinctive cuisine to families. Within the last five years, the city of Oakland has made impressive strides in improving street lighting, and a number of new buildings have miraculously appeared in this general area of downtown. The city views from the Silver Dragon's upper levels are much more pleasant now. A BART station is but two blocks walk, and a large parking lot is opposite the restaurant.

Chef Chee's delectable cuisine presents two of my personal choices here, and you have to order them twenty-four hours ahead — Peking duck and stuffed crab claws. The daily *wo choy* has the attention not only of the Chinese-Americans, but of an appreciative claque of the Caucasian persuasion.

Moderate. Open seven days from 11:30 A.M. to 9:30 P.M. Reservations weekdays only. Visa, MC, AX. Full bar. Validated parking lot. Casual.

DA★
SINBAD'S PIER TWO/Seafood/California
Pier 2, Embarcadero/San Francisco/Area 2/(415) 781-2555

The ambiance and spectacular views of the Bay Bridge, Yerba Buena Island and the East Bay, combine with good food to make this a popular spot with younger business types and their attractive dates. Romance is here for the sharing. Ocean liners, freighters and all manner of water traffic cruise by while you enjoy sandwiches, salads and hot specialties from the uncomplicated menu. Fresh seafood can include even the elusive abalone. For meat lovers there is filet mignon and prime rib. Almost in the southern shadow of the landmark Ferry Building, hardier patrons favor the outdoor dining deck. Inside, the floor-to-ceiling windows set off the pleasing, contemporary design. My spies inform me that many of the city fathers (and a mother or three) like this unusual place, and it is no secret that even Mayor Feinstein is a fairly regular guest.

Moderate to expensive. Open Monday through Friday 11:15 A.M. to 4 P.M. for lunch. Dinner Monday through Friday 5:15 to 10:30 P.M., Saturday and Sunday from 4:30 to 10:30 P.M. Brunch/lunch Saturday and Sunday from 10:30 A.M. to 4 P.M. Reservations necessary weekends. All major credit cards. Entertainment. Full bar. View. Pier parking. Casual to semi-dressy.

★

SIXTEEN MILE HOUSE/American
448 Broadway/Millbrae/Area 2/(415) 692-4087

In the late 1800s, a stagecoach stop, exactly sixteen miles from San Francisco was established. It was later converted into a respectable restaurant and then moved to a new location in Millbrae. Newel posts, nickelodeons and knick knacks have all been carried along in the relocations and the place retains the atmosphere of a wayside tavern.

Dinners include gargantuan Idaho potatoes, sautéed vegetables, house salad and the soup du jour—possibly potato-leek. The chicken is marinated for hours in cognac and sauterne, then broiled with Italian herbs and flambéed with a quick shot of cognac. Veal *cordon bleu* with champagne sauce is another admirable selection and the rack of lamb is their specialty.

Moderate to expensive. Open Tuesday through Thursday from 5:30 to 9:30 P.M. Friday and Saturday to 10:30 P.M., Sunday from 5 to 9:30 P.M. No reservations. Visa, MC. Full bar. Child's menu. Ample parking. Casual.

★ ★

610 RESTAURANT/French
610 Petaluma Boulevard North/Petaluma/Area 3/(707) 762-6625

Many local residents still think of this pleasant establishment by its former name, 610 Main. In any case, the charming white Victorian house has not budged an inch, and the cuisine is still decidedly French. Jacques Constant and Michel Lalanne, tripling as owners/chefs/hosts, put together a new menu every four months, but an appealing variety is never lost.

The fish of the day, always fresh, may be what you want, or perhaps the scallops with cream and dill sauce, or the pork, the veal, the rack of lamb, or the New York steak. Naturally (this *is* Sonoma County), all produce is fresh. Lunch choices, equally varied, are as reasonably priced as those for dinner. The wine list, though not extensive, carries a good balance of California selections.

The simple decor and generally relaxed manner of the operation contribute to an atmosphere of informality.

Moderate. Open Monday through Saturday. Lunch Monday through Friday from 11:30 A.M. to 2 P.M. Dinner Monday through Saturday from 5:30 to 9:30 P.M. Reservations advised on weekends. Visa, MC. Wine and beer only. Parking in adjacent lot. Casual.

DA★
SKYWOOD CHATEAU/California/Continental
Skyline Boulevard at Woodside Road/Woodside/Area 2/(415) 851-7444

If you are one of this mountain-lodge-like dinner house's long-time patrons and have not been in since March 1982, you're due for some pleasant surprises. Ralph Oswald, a restaurant authority who has influenced many restaurateurs and restaurants, has completely renovated the mellow premises. Together with partner/host, Mike Sarno, the restaurant has successfully turned to California cuisine, winning staunch adherents from the entire Peninsula. This old favorite of some decades is even more appealing now, and the work has spread. Shirley Sarno, wife of Mike, is hostess.

Retaining the cheerful fireplaces and panoramic windows with tree-filtered vistas of the bay and beyond, they resurfaced the redwood walls, laid light carpeting, shifted the bar area and eased ready access to the outer decks. Everything is lighter, as the now emphasis of California cuisine dictates, except the libations. Now guests dine upon dishes prepared with the very freshest products, whether it be the seafood of the day, the crisp vegetables or the house-made fresh pasta, such as fettuccine, *tortellini* or *pasta con pesto*. Everything is à la carte and you can compose your meal. I like the romaine salad, with walnuts and Gorgonzola. The desserts will please and the cellar and full bar are tops.
Moderate. Open Tuesday through Saturday. Weekdays from 6 to 10 P.M.; Friday and Saturday till 11 P.M. Reservations essential on weekends. All major credit cards. Entertainment. Full bar. Patio. View. Parking lot. Casual to semi-dressy.

★
SONOMA CHEESE FACTORY/Deli
2 Spain Street (on the Historic Plaza)/Sonoma/Area 3/(707) 996-1931

Traveling through the luscious green wine country, flagging spirits can be resurrected by an extensive selection of cheese and spirits at this combination shop and cafe. The house specialty is Sonoma jack cheese, which you can watch being made from the recipe that has been in the family for over fifty years. There are also one hundred other kinds of cheese, fifty kinds of Italian cold cuts, Sonoma French bread, and a wine tasting bar. A charmingly country aspect of this place is that, as you browse through the shop, when you find a vintage wine you like you simply open it and pour.
Moderate. Open seven days from 9 A.M. to 6 P.M. (5 P.M. in the winter). No reservations. Visa, MC, AX. Wine and beer only. Patio. Parking lot. Casual.

★★
SONOMA HOTEL/California Country
110 West Spain Street/Sonoma/Area 3/(707) 996-2996

Owners/hosts Lisa and Scott Olmsted use the term "California country cuisine" to indicate their freedom from tired tradition, and their determination to use the best local raw materials. The Olmsteds find nearly all their produce within minutes of their kitchen and, in fact, grow herbs outside their door. The fish, though naturally grown a little farther away, is always fresh.

Changed weekly, the dinner menu is also modified according to the season. The fixed-price dinner offers a choice among four regular and two "evening's-special" entrées; one of the specials is always a seafood. Poultry, pork, beef, and lamb are all well represented. The wine list is interesting, and premium wines can be had by the glass.

Sharing the Sonoma Plaza with other early buildings, the newly restored Sonoma Hotel, furnished with antiques, is a charming setting for the restaurant. In May, the garden patio is opened for service. **Moderate.** Open Friday through Tuesday. Lunch from 11:30 A.M. to 3 P.M. Dinner from 5:45 to 9:30 P.M. Sunday brunch from 10:30 A.M. to 3 P.M. Reservations advised. Visa, MC, AX. Occasional live music. Full bar. Street parking. Casual.

★
SORABOL/Korean
372 Grand Avenue/Oakland/Area 2/(415) 839-2288

Sorabol is a decorator's example of understated elegance. Thick carpet, wide upholstered chairs, dry flowers in Korean vases and antique chests subtly transport you thousands of miles away. Korean food is influenced by both Japan and China but bases its own spicy flavor (when done properly) on garlic, chili, ginger, scallions and sesame oil. *Kimchee*, spiced Chinese cabbage, is served with all the house specials. The exotic sounding (and indeed exotic tasting) *ge-jige, nak-ji jungol* and *bibimnaengmyn* translate to crab casserole with hot bean paste, octopus casserole, and cold noodles with house special hot sauce. The pan-fried dishes include honeycomb tripe, squid with hot sauce, vegetable beef vermicelli and Mongolian beef.

Please be sure to consult "Tipping Made Easy" on page 22 of this Guide.

Ginsing root is an interesting spice (with many alleged restorative powers) that was once responsible for one of the worst concoctions I have ever had. Years ago, an acquaintance of mine proudly poured some rather healthy shots of ginsing vodka his father had made for a couple of friends and me. We all took rather hesitant sips and valiantly tried to smile our approval. Our host then momentarily disappeared to the kitchen, whereupon one friend promptly poured the rest of his glass into mine and the other sureptitiously emptied hers in a nearby plant. I must admit I expected the plant to keel over immediately (I suppose I've seen too many animated cartoons). The plant survived, however, after finishing my double dose, I was left a little the worse for wear and a little more leery of ginsing. I was with some surprise that I discovered Sorabol uses it in a few of their dishes and it is really quite good.

The luncheon menu is lighter, but equally intriguing. *Jogesalguyi* translates simply as marinated scallops but the taste is much more, and much spicier, than the name implies. *Bul-goki,* the marinated rib eye steak with special house sauce, is better than I have had at many other restaurants. The menu is fairly extensive so there's always something new to enjoy.

Inexpensive to moderate. Open seven days from 11 A.M. to 9:30 P.M. Reservations accepted. Visa, MC, AX. Full bar. Easy street parking. Semi-dressy.

★
SOUTH PACIFIC/Seafood
2500 Noriega Street/San Francisco/Area 2/(415) 564-3363

The decor could have you feeling like you are dining on the set of *South Pacific,* and some of the guests could make you feel like you're in the middle of that cast party (some people feel obliged to wear Hawaiian print shirts and dresses to theme restaurants of this ilk). There are tiki masks on the walls, bamboo everywhere, an outrigger canoe suspended from the ceiling and miniature Japanese umbrellas stuck in everything, from the daiquiris to the seafood curries.

Fortunately, and unusually I might add, the creative efforts have not been exhausted on the cosmetics; the kitchen does turn out some above-average talent. Seafood, naturally, is the specialty, with special attention paid to the jumbo prawns and Polynesian seafood curry on a scooped out papaya. Our dessert was coconut ice cream and a banana fritter—with an umbrella.

Moderate. Open Tuesday through Sunday. Tuesday through Thursday from 5 to 10 P.M., Friday and Saturday to 11 P.M., Sunday from 4 to 9 P.M. Lunch served Tuesday through Saturday from 11:00 A.M. to 2:30 P.M., Sunday brunch from 11 A.M. to 2:30 P.M. Visa, MC. Full bar. Child's menu. Street parking. Semi-dressy.

★ ★
SOUVERAIN RESTAURANT/Continental
Independence Lane/Geyserville/Area 3/(707) 433-3141

If you have ever motored through France's wine country, you will experience a sense of *déjà vu* when you approach this unique monument to fine dining. The hop-kiln design suggests an old chateau – a theme that is enhanced by the courtyard fountain, soaring interior, stone floors, high, glassed doors and the spreading terrace overlooking acres of Sonoma Valley Vineyards and beyond, Mt. St. Helena looming benignly in the distance.

You can dine outdoors, weather permitting, as well as within the impressive interior, attended with such true concern as to maintain the chateau image. The continental fare is exceptionally well prepared, from fresh calamari marinated in herbs with capers, hearts of butter lettuce with bay shrimp. Veal *cordon bleu,* duck *à l'orange,* breast of chicken with green peppercorn sauce and even hazelnut soufflé.

Reasonably enough, *only* Souverain wines are offered. Sunday brunch may well be, as the menu proclaims, "the most elegant brunch on the north coast."

Moderate to expensive. Open seven days for lunch 11 A.M. to 3 P.M. Winter dinner hours: Friday seafood buffet 5:30 to 9 P.M., Saturday 5:30 to 9 P.M. Dinner served Wednesday through Sunday from 5 to 9 P.M. Sunday brunch from 10:30 A.M. to 2:30 P.M. Reservations advised. Visa, MC, AX. Wine only. Patio. Vineyard view. Parking lot. Casual.

★ ★
SPENGER'S FISH GROTTO/Seafood
1919 Fourth Street/Berkeley/Area 2/(415) 845-7771

Breathes there a soul with a palate so dead that he hath not written to me and said – in effect –"Hey, where can I find a really good seafood restaurant?" There aren't many. Outside of San Francisco, they're about as plentiful as Kosher delis in Saudi Arabia. But here's a good one.

Everything is fresh–fresh–fresh, served faultlessly by longtime waiters who can deftly help you through the sixty-four entrées without making you feel they are pushing yesterday's leftovers.

This pioneering restaurant was originally the family home, grocery store and bait shop. If you stand in the parking lot and look at the rambling restaurant façade where you'll easily discern the outline of the first building, now vastly expanded to enclose five dining rooms and two spacious long bar rooms plus several banquet rooms. Since 1890, Spenger's growth has paralleled that of the Bay Area, becoming a many-chambered nautilus of excellent seafood. The fresh fish market within the main building draws literally thousands of Bay Areans weekly. Quality is supreme, quantity amazes and the prices seem lower than anywhere. Frank Spenger III (Spanky to all), son of Bud Spenger (Frank Jr.) and grandson of the late Frank Spenger, Sr., runs this complex operation, largest of its kind in the world. Bud still heads the family operation and is an avid fisherman (wall-mounted trophies attest) and hunter. The labyrinth of dining rooms resembles sailing ship salons, and the hundreds of marine artifacts, even to teak planks from old battleships and ocean liners, are of museum worth.

Inexpensive to moderate. Open seven days from 8 A.M. to midnight. Reservations for six or more only. All major credit cards. Full bar. Child's menu. Lot parking. Casual.

★
THE SPINNAKER/Seafood/Continental
100 Spinnaker Drive/Sausalito/Area 3/(415) 332-1500

Dramatically placed at the water's edge, with the eastern end of the long dining room actually over the bay, this nautical dining place was named for the billowing, huge sails that blossom from the sleek yachts racing across the panoramic view. The interior is maritime in theme and subtle in execution. Dark woods blend richly with deep red carpeting. As you relax in oversized chairs in the spacious cocktail lounge, you can observe the San Francisco skyline, water traffic, islands and the Bay Bridge. Nightfall brings guests the sensation of dining aboard an ocean liner. Gulls and pelicans fish in the reflected glow of the lights.

Spinnaker's menu is not highly priced yet yields considerable variety for any palate: oysters, a fruit cocktail of California's freshest, soups and large, crisp salads—even a Caesar. Since its 1960 opening, this properly tended restaurant has won as patrons thousands of locals. Tim McDonnell, general manager, is the son of Bill McDonnell, who also owns famous Tarantino's in San Francisco, on Fisherman's Wharf. Tim says that, oddly enough, their T-bone steaks and choice meats have as many adherents as the fresh seafood and fowl. Host/captain Mark Martini will be glad to consult with you about your meal, and he is most knowledgeable about wines.

Moderate. Open seven days. Lunch from 11 A.M. to 3 P.M. Dinner from 5 to 11 P.M. Reservations necessary during the summer months. Visa, MC, AX. Full bar. View. Valet parking. Casual.

★ ★
SQUARE ONE/California/Continental
190 Pacific Avenue/San Francisco/Area 2/(415) 788-1110

Like most graduates of Chez Panisse, owner/chef Joyce Goldstein believes that food is all, and the atmosphere in which it is served (bleak) or the view (of Golden Gate Park) is relatively unimportant. And the concentration has been on the food here, to the extent that since the restaurant opened in mid-1984 it has been serving hundreds of dinners each day. From the beginning, Square One began emitting those high frequency signals heard only by the food lemmings who flocked here, along with camera crew and restaurant writers.

The menu changes each day, one presumes to keep Goldstein interested, because the new breed of chefs are a restless lot. What doesn't change is the wonderful aromatic home-baked crusty Italian bread on which most of us could make a complete dinner. The "Daily Special" on one of my visits included fettuccine with chicken, white truffles and cream; grilled little chicken with oregano and garlic; grilled sausage with truffles and pistachios served with truffled potato gratin and wilted greens (the latter a sensational bargain); and pork scalloppine with Dijon mustard and cream, served with zucchini julienne. That particular day, the menu featured dishes inspired by the Burgundy region of France and wine was served by the glass to complement those specials.

Under soups was listed "white bean with escarole, pancetta, pasta and Parmesan." Desserts may include pears that have been poached in cassis and burgundy wine, then served with crème Anglaise and cookies; or *pain d'epices*, a Burgundian honey-spice cake with almonds, anise and candied fruit, served with a lemon mousseline. Ask your waiter if they have any of the 1983 Quady Essensia (orange muscat wine) that they sometimes serve by the glass at $3.

This is a superb place to restore your faith in innovative and exciting cookery.

Expensive. Open for lunch weekdays from 11:30 A.M. to 2:30 P.M. Dinner Monday through Saturday from 5:30 to 10:30 P.M. Reservations advised. Visa, MC. Full bar. View. Valet parking. Semi-dressy to dressy.

★
SQUIRE ROOM/French/Continental
Fairmont Hotel/San Francisco/Area 2/(415) 772-5211

Lace tablecloths, silver showplates and lavish presentation make this, a unique restaurant for a hotel location. The liver mousse is served with cocktails, intermezzo, before the main course, and Friandaise and petit fours finish the meal. Specialties are the *saumon au champagne* and *La côté de veau aux morilles* is veal "pink as a baby's ass," so the chef told us (not quite the first time we have heard that line). The Fairmont has made their restaurant worth venturing into. **Expensive.** Open seven days. Lunch weekdays from 11:30 A.M. to 2:30 P.M. Dinner nightly from 6 to 10 P.M. Reservations essential. All major credit cards. Full bar. Parking in hotel lot. Dressy.

★ ★ ★
STARS/California/Continental
150 Redwood/San Francisco/Area 2/(415) 861-7827

Jeremiah Tower may be the only superstar chef with a degree in architecture from Harvard, and his restaurant is undoubtedly the only restaurant named after (not before) the design in the carpeting. It takes a great deal of confidence, perhaps bordering on arrogance, to call a restaurant "Stars," but Tower is accustomed to making strong statements. When is was suggested that he was a protégé of Chez Panisse owner Alice Waters, he was quoted "to set the record straight" as saying he got the job as head chef "because they didn't have one." In those days Chez Panisse was a country French restaurant, but after Tower took over much of the buying and cooking, his subtle combinations of tastes became known as "California" cuisine. He left Panisse – after becoming a limited partner – and revived the failing Santa Fe Bar and Grill in Berkeley and then the Balboa Cafe, and he remains a principal in both. Stars, however, is *his* statement, and Tower – hatless in a white apron with pant cuffs scraping the floor – is here, there and everywhere – consulting, cajoling, explaining, inspecting and, obviously, having fun.

Perhaps the best way to understand Tower's cuisine is to regard him as a food historian. He pours over old *Escoffier* cookbooks and recipes from early California and imagines how they might be prepared today. He designed Stars with an exhibition kitchen, retaining the high ceilings of the Italian restaurant dungeon it had been, adding a forty-foot mohogany bar, transparent mosaic chandeliers, and tables covered with white linen throughout the massive multi-level interior.

Exciting tastes begin at the bar. A "Dorchester" cocktail is made with fresh strawberry juice and cherry liqueur in champagne, with a dash of lemon. Pepper vodka, one of my favorite drinks of the world, is made with vodka in which hot red chiles have marinated. The wine list includes twenty-five champagnes, boutique Californians and more, quite reasonably priced.

As an appetizer, the giant Shiitake mushroom with bone marrow and black forest ham was a smooth and textured combination with what Paul Prudhomme calls "second tastes," and even thirds. Perfect oysters are served with spicy lamb sausage, the oysters in a half-circle iced plate on the dinner plate, the sausage laid artfully in the center. For a main course, the braised lamb shank was a sensational dish served with a mint-aioli sauce, redolent of garlic. The lamb on a huge bone was surrounded by white beans and shredded red bell peppers. Another main course I tried was the somewhat less successful, yet interesting, presentation of walleye pike, poached and served with baby bok choy, garlic, ginger and black beans. It would be pointless to list more dishes on the menu which would probably not be available on any given night, but I do know that the appetizers of snails with ham, shallots, tarragon and chardonnay sauce, and the brioche with lobster, marrow, poached garlic and chervil are particular favorites among the cognoscenti.

Desserts included a magnificent orange-walnut soufflé (there is a toasted pecan soufflé on certain nights) and a marjolaine described as "four layers of nut meringue with chocolate, praline and vanilla buttercreams."

Moderate. Open seven days. Lunch from 11:30 A.M. to 2:30 P.M..; dinner from 5:30 to 11:30 P.M., Sunday from 5 to 10 P.M. Sunday brunch from 11:30 A.M. to 2:30 P.M. Reservations recommended. Visa, MC, AX. Full bar. Street parking. Chic casual to dressy.

★
STATION HOUSE CAFE/American/Seafood
3rd and Main Streets/Point Reyes Station/Area 3/(415) 663-1515

No, the name does not refer to "Barney Miller" or to "Kojak," or even to "Hill Street Blues." This unassuming, medium-size dining place is not far from the one-time station of the two railroads that junctioned here. Local residents, farmers, dairymen and visitors to the Point Reyes National Seashore come here for: the breakfasts (fresh-squeezed orange juice), lunch (cornbread, country fries and thick soups), and dinners. Your evening meal can include smoked salmon quiche, steamed clams or baby oysters. Complete dinners include soup, salad, a basket of popovers and cornbread, fresh vegetables, assorted pastas, and entrées such as fresh bay scallops, tempura, boned chicken breast, seafood, even New York steaks. Homemade desserts could be fruit pies, mousses, crèmes, perhaps coffee cake.

This is a casual, friendly, eater's paradise where owner and guiding light Pat Healy has a smile and an incredible variety of fine, fresh food. **Inexpensive to moderate.** Open Wednesday through Monday. Breakfast from 8 to 11:30 A.M. Lunch from 11:30 A.M. to 5 P.M. Dinner from 5 to 9 P.M. Reservations for six or more only. Visa, MC. Entertainment weekends. Wine and beer only. Street parking. Casual.

★
STEAMER GOLD LANDING/Seafood/Steak
1 Water Street/Petaluma/Area 3/(707) 763-6876

An aura of history surrounds Steamer Gold Landing. Located in the refurbished Great Petaluma Mill, the restaurant honors the Steamer Gold, which plied the waters of the Petaluma River (actually a slough) many years ago. Guests feel welcomed by the art-bedecked brick walls, two large stone fireplaces, richly figured blue/green carpet, polished wood and exposed beams and girders. On a cool winter's day, a table by a fireplace is particularly cheering. In April, the patio overlooking the river is opened for service.

Devoted to seafood (always fresh) and beef, the menu does carry a couple of good chicken favorites. Ocean catches include *mahi mahi*, beer-battered prawns, and stuffed English sole, while steak lovers can order top sirloin and Angus filet mignon, among others. Bargain seekers' "Sundowner Dinners" are served from 5:30 to 7:00 P.M. every day.

The wine list is limited but varied. There is live music nightly in the bar upstairs.

Moderate. Open seven days a week. Lunch Monday through Saturday from 11:30 A.M. to 2:30 P.M. Dinner Monday through Thursday from 5:30 to 9:30 P.M., Friday and Saturday from 5:30 to 10:30 P.M. Sunday brunch from 10:30 A.M. to 2:30 P.M. Reservations encouraged. Visa, MC, AX, DC. Jazz/country/rock nightly. Full bar. Street and lot parking. Casual.

In order to obtain the best results from this Guide, be sure to read the French, German, Italian and Oriental menu translators on pages 399 to 404 of this Guide.

★ ★
SUWA'S/Japanese
2262 Clayton Road/Concord/Area 2/(415) 825-3201

No tempura tantrums here. This authentic Japanese restaurant makes that delicate dish about as well as anyone can. Shrimp tempura is my favorite, served with sweet potato (I don't think there's anything better than the contrast of textures in this vegetable when it is tempuraed), string beans, asparagus and carrots. The sukiyaki is another traditional Japanese dish that is well prepared here. Sukiyaki, by the way, comes from two idiographs — *suki* means "plow" and *yaki*, "roasted." In early times, meat for sukiyaki was cooked on plow shares by farmers in their fields. Beef is the prime ingredient, although you may use chicken or even seafood.

There are some hearty combinations that won't leave you with that feeling some Americans complain about Asian food, "I can't believe I ate the whole thing . . . and I'm still hungry." The Suwa Special combination starts off with *sunomono* (bay shrimp and tomatoes with cucumbers, in a light dressing). Sashimi and that wonderful shrimp tempura are next, followed by chopped chicken in teriyaki, and finally sukiyaki.

Sushi is also a specialty of Mr. Suwa, and his knife is lightning fast — the mark of a good sushi chef. The menu for sushi and for complete dinners is extensive, but Suwa miraculously manages to keep the quality consistently high in all aspects of the selection.

Inexpensive to moderate. Open Tuesday through Saturday. Lunch served Tuesday through Friday from 11:30 A.M. to 2 P.M. Dinner Tuesday through Thursday from 5 to 9 P.M., Friday and Saturday to 10 P.M. Reservations accepted. Visa, MC. Wine and beer only. Parking lot. Casual.

★ ★
SWAN OYSTER DEPOT/Seafood
1517 Polk Street/San Francisco/Area 2/(415) 673-1101

This is really a fish market with the front and back connected by a white tile and marble counter, strewn with bowls of oyster crackers and lemon wedges. An energetic corps of young fishmongers man the counter, opening cherrystone clams — my theory: many is not enough — and Blue Point oysters, and shredding lettuce for the generous shrimp and/or prawn salads served with Louie dressing or oil and vinegar. A Boston-style clam chowder is the only hot dish offered, and it's full of fresh chopped clams. Only the largest eastern oysters are used — they're right out in plain view — so the oyster cocktail is a terrific bargain here. Another bargain is the open-faced sandwich of locally smoked salmon on French or rye with a healthy serving of shrimp Louie. The salmon is lightly

smoked, moist and carved from a great slab right before your eyes. A very fruity French Colombard wine is to be had and there's an assortment of beers. A stunning bit of the improbable is the "Swan sundae" of caviar from (believe it or not) the Sacramento River, served with a split of champagne. The fish market stocks really first-rate seafood for the housewives of nearby Russian and Nob Hills. Both the large deep-sea scallops and tiny bay scallops are there, as well as the enormous, milky-white abalone. More economical is the finnan haddie, lightly smoked haddock from Scotland.
Inexpensive. Open Monday through Saturday from 8 A.M. to 5:30 P.M. No reservations. No credit cards. Wine and beer only. Casual.

SWEDEN HOUSE BAKERY/Swedish/Konditori
35 Main Street/Tiburon/Area 3/(415) 435-9767

One of my favorite lunch places in Tiburon, this very Swedish, light-menu restaurant has a thriving take-out business, but it also has tables on a small patio overlooking the water. Open-faced sandwiches in a variety of combinations are authentic and good. The hot sandwiches include a fine homemade meatloaf with creamed mushrooms and crab and mushroom in wine sauce, all served on their freshly baked bread. Soup is home style, too—and filling. Dessert pastries are the best in the area—so fresh they're often still warm from the oven.
Inexpensive. Open seven days. Breakfast from 8:30 A.M. Lunch from 11:30 A.M. to 3 P.M. Sunday brunch all day. No reservations. No credit cards. Patio. View of San Francisco Bay. Lot parking. Casual.

★
SWISS ALPS/Swiss/Fondue
605 Post Street/San Francisco/Area 2/(415) 885-0947

On the site of the Old Zurich restaurant, Heinz Oetiker greets his mostly local following in the small, *gemütlich* ambiance of a Swiss (Swiss-German) country restaurant. The *geschnetzeltes* (veal) is lovingly handled, whether ordered *cordon bleu* or *"kalbfleisch"*—minced. The sauerbraten was prepared with a cheaper-than-choice cut beef, but it is only the Americans who demand tenderness in their meat, often at the expense of flavor. This beef held its marinade well and came served with *spatzle,* the delicate sautéed noodles. The fondues taste a bit strongly of wine, but they are acceptable (some of the worst fondue I've ever experienced have been in Lucerne). I wish they had a good dessert fondue, perhaps morsels of fresh fruit (pineapple and fresh cherries particularly) to dip into a gently simmering chocolate sauce; but the desserts

are otherwise good here. The wine list, featuring some imports, is reasonable. Swiss Alps is near the theatre district for a before-the-show snack (they close at 10 P.M.) for dinner.
Moderate. Open Tuesday through Saturday from 5 to 10 P.M. No reservations. Visa, MC. Wine and beer only. Street parking. Casual.

★★
SWISS LAKEWOOD LODGE/Swiss/Continental
5055 West Lake Boulevard/North Lake Tahoe (Homewood)/Area 6
(916) 525-5211

Since **1965** the knowledgeable have been aware of the consistently good dining experience in this authentic Alpine inn. Swiss chef Albert Marty and his attractive wife Helga serve noteworthy Swiss and continental creations in their delightful, knotty-pine-walled haven. Helga, the hostess, suggests from chef Albert's impressive menu — *emince de veau Zurichoise.* Outstanding quiche Lorraine and onion soup. Be sure to ask Helga about their daily special.
Moderate to expensive. Open seven days for dinner from 5:30 to 10 P.M. Closed Monday during winter. Reservations necessary. AX, Visa, MC. Full bar. Lot parking. Casual to semi-dressy.

★★
SZECHWAN VILLAGE/Chinese
427 Gellert Boulevard/Daly City/Area 2/(415) 992-2444
548 Contra Costa Boulevard/Pleasant Hill/Area 2/(415) 671-0655

The **hot spicy** dishes from Szechwan, the westernmost province of China, first surfaced in New York's Chinatown in the early 1970s. Now, this fiery fare has even become popular in such surprising locations as Pleasant Hill and Daly City.

After a long day, this place can be a little slice of nirvana. It's like an escape from the frantic commuter's world as you cross over the bridge by a peaceful rock garden and into a tranquil setting. (Unusual in a Chinese restaurant where bickering in the kitchen can usually be heard throughout the building). Beautiful wood partitions and long bamboo designs etched on smokey glass divide the dining areas. Oriental prints and vases on display are set amidst a tastefully done decor.

In order to obtain the best results from this Guide, please consult "A Few Inside Tips" on page 18.

If you like *kung pao* chicken, and I'm an addict, you'll find it done to perfection (which by my definition means fiery enough to keep the fire department standing by). *Mu shi* pork is another good dish (vegetables and pork wrapped in a Chinese pancake with plum sauce) that seems seems to have become an American favorite.

Inexpensive to moderate. Open seven days from 11 A.M. to 10 P.M. Reservations accepted. Visa, MC. Full bar at Contra Costa location. Wine and beer only at Gellert Boulevard. Parking lot. Casual.

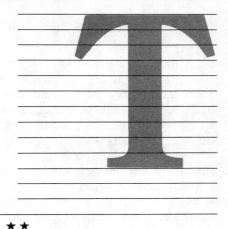

★ ★
TADICH GRILL/Seafood
240 California Street/San Francisco/Area 2/(415) 391-2373

This is one of the oldest restaurants in San Francisco, founded in 1849, and it has survived because of a stubborn dedication to preserve or bring forth the natural, unsauced and untampered-with flavors of seafood.

You can sit at the long counter, or, if you're lucky, in one of the wooden, uniquely San Francisco-style booths, and you can watch the cooks bustling to prepare your fresh fish to order. There's not a beat lost between the time the plate is "up" until it's delivered to your table piping hot. The à la carte menu lists more than sixty entrées, mostly seafood, but there are a few steaks to be ordered, I suppose, by those people who have to move their lips when they read freeway signs. There's charcoal-broiled brook trout, spring salmon steak, rex sole with pure butter, baked filet of turbot and crabmeat à la Newburg. Tadich's is always crowded, so you'll have to leave your name with the man at the door (no reservations are taken) and elbow your way to the cocktail lounge for what may be a lengthy wait. But it's worth it – even at lunchtime, when the line begins forming an hour before the noon opening. **Inexpensive to moderate.** Open Monday through Friday from 11 A.M. to 9 P.M. No reservations. No credit cards. Full bar. Street parking. Casual.

In order to obtain the best results from this Guide, be sure to read the French, German, Italian and Oriental menu translators on pages 399 to 404 of this Guide.

★
TAIWAN RESTAURANT/Taiwanese
2071 University Avenue/Berkeley/Area 2/(415) 845-1456

Although entitled "Taiwan," this restaurant offers the distinctive cuisines of the regions of Manchuria, Szechwan, Shanghai, Canton, Hunan and Peking, emblazoning their menu with the suggestion that the selections of Taiwanese specialties are "for the adventurous." Some of the specials are: sweet rice *en crock*, boneless duck web (pork, squid and celery in soup stock), and white turnip cakes.

You can combine adventuresome with unadventuresome, and fiery with subtly flavored dishes. Unlike many establishments, the serving staff here makes suggestions and tries to discourage diners from ordering beyond their spirit of adventure, while still providing new experiences. The half smoked tea duck was a dish I truly enjoyed. I'm told that it is marinated for several days in tea leaves and barbecued in a specially designed smoke oven. You also might want to try dessert—a recommendation I do not frequently make in Asian restaurants— specifically the glaced apples or bananas. There is also a weekend brunch that bears little resemblence to the *dim sum* brunches we have by now become accustomed to.

Inexpensive to moderate. Open seven days. Monday through Friday from 11:30 A.M. to 9:30 P.M. Saturday and Sunday from 10:30 A.M. to 9:30 P.M. Reservations accepted for five or more. Visa, MC, AX. Wine and beer only. Parking lot in back. Casual.

DA★ ★
TAJ OF INDIA/North Indian
825 Pacific Avenue/San Francisco/Area 2/(415) 392-0089

Indian restaurants in America had a timid, almost apologetic beginning. Until Taj opened in 1956 to accommodate palates grown sophisticated by the United Nations diplomats and workers who cooked *tandoori* in their homes and apartments, the Indian restaurant was usually an off-campus converted storefront with more optimism than talent. Decor was generally confined to a few Air India posters with Ravi Shankar kinds of records in the background and harassed students serving compromised curry in their perma-press saris.

At the Taj, many selections are from the Punjab, or northern, colder sections of India. Dinners prepared there are cooked only in *"ghee,"* purified butter, not oil. Curry is but half the secret in curry dishes. The other half is in the method of cooking, during which the curry is combined with the meats to allow the flavors to permeate. Curries are as individual as the restaurant in which they are served—differing widely from mild to hot—and in the spices which are used according to the composition of the particular chef.

Several informal rules should be observed, among them: one never mixes more than one curry at dinner, and bread is not eaten immediately before or after rice. A complete dinner here would include *rassam* (soup), *pulao* (savory rice sautéed in butter with onions and spices), *chappati* (Indian bread) or *paratha* (a wheel of buttered bread in thin layers), then the entrée (perhaps beef curry Punjab, prepared with black mushrooms) and dessert (sweetmeats or any of the exotic selections.)

Waiters and waitresses wear colorful, authentic costumes and are exceedingly patient and gracious when discussing the dinner selections or explaining the fine points of Indian dining. The foyer, cocktail lounge and dining rooms are Eastern with dramatic shadows, filigreed lanterns casting a lambent glow on coral walls and brass artifacts. Rooms are partitioned with intricately carved screens of Kashmir *shisham* wood, and the sounds of a soft sitar (still sounding much like a syncopated dial tone) provide background music. The Taj is owned by Raj Sanwal, and he has brought a Trader Vic kind of professionalism to the bar. How about a "cobra's kiss" made with light rum and fresh pomegranate with a slice of lime? Or a "white tiger": drambuie, light cream and nutmeg blended with crushed ice? There's all the Pimms cups from number one (gin) through number six (vodka). Pimms, in the event you didn't know, came from Pimms Tavern in London and is made with various whiskeys (hence the numbers—to denote which), served in a glass-bottomed tankard with a stick of fresh cucumber and a slice of fresh lemon topped off with a spritz of tonic water or soda.

Moderate to expensive. Open seven days from 5:30 to 11:30 P.M. Reservations accepted. All major credit cards. Entertainment. Full bar. Street and lot parking. Casual.

To obtain the best results from this Guide, be sure to consult the map on the various Northern California areas on page 28.

★
TAJ MAHAL/Indian
120 Hazelwood Drive/San Francisco/Area 2/(415) 952-8487

Recently moved from its original location on Columbus, Taj Mahal now has a *tandoor* oven in the kitchen and enough room to accommodate its following. As the menu wisely warns, the hot lamb curry, *lamb vindaloo*, is for pros only and is . . . "racy and could drive you crazy."

The complete dinners are the best buys — entrées like the assorted curries or chicken *tandoori* (marinated in spices and broiled) are served with soup, rice, condiments, bread, tea or coffee and dessert. Among the coyly named wine drinks there is a good one, Taj "delight," that's made with pomegranate juice, lemon and vermouth with crushed ice. As an added plus there is live music and belly dancing — the only Indian restaurant in town to offer entertainment.

Moderate. Open seven days from 5:30 to 10:30 P.M. Lunch from 11 A.M. to 2:30 P.M. Reservations accepted. All major credit cards. Wine only. Child's menu. Parking lot. Semi-dressy.

DA★★
TANDOORI/North and West Indian
420 Beach Street/San Francisco/Area 2/(415) 775-6366

We specialize in an ancient method of cooking done in a traditional clay oven — the *tandoor* — from India. Our special mild blend of Indian spices accentuates the taste of the food. Bread fresh-baked in the *tandoor* is unique." So speaks Ram Gulati, one of four brothers and two sisters with restaurants in Delhi, Bombay, London, and — hold it — Rockford, Illinois.

Serendipity led to the restaurant in San Francisco. Brother Dev married a girl from Iowa and came here to visit friends they had met in Rockford. As might be predicted, Dev and his bride fell in love with San Francisco and three days after arrival they took an option on this place.

It isn't often that a restaurateur describes his cuisine so precisely and with such modesty. The superlatives come from those who dine here; they say things like "undoubtedly the most distinctively delicious food I have ever encountered."

Although non-*tandoori* cooking is also served, the *tandoor* is the heart of its reputation. A clay oven shaped like a huge Grecian urn originally devised by the mogul rulers of northern India, it is entirely encased in firebrick overlaid with tile. The bottom is covered with several inches of real hardwood charcoal and fired to a white hot 650 degrees. The various breads are thrown on the inside walls and baked in just a few minutes — light, bubbly, a sensation!

Chickens are stripped of fat and skin, rubbed with exotic herbs and spices, put on skewers and set in the middle of the *tandoor*. The flesh is seared instantly, retaining all the succulent juices; in five minutes the cooking is finished to perfection.

Lamb, fish, prawns, chicken, liver—all achieve culinary heights with this ancient method of cooking. (The expected curries are here, too; while they are uncommonly delicious, they are not as distinctive as the *tandoori* dishes.)

Nothing is ordinary. Cauliflower, chick peas, lentils, okra, mushrooms—all are prepared with creativity. Recommended—*alu gobbi masala*—made with fresh cauliflower. It was delicious, unlike anything I have ever eaten (and I don't even *like* cauliflower).

While the food is exotic, the surroundings are neither mysterious nor Indian. Located within a Van Ness Avenue motel, it's an unpretentiously comfortable place where you don't mind accepting Ram Gulati's encouraging admonition: "Feel like a Maharaja . . . eat with your fingers, as they did."

Lighting is restrained and cozy; a few Indian artifacts on display, a splendid tapestry, and a fascinating series of eleven hammered aluminum scenes from the Royal Gardens.

There's a limited wine list at very modest prices. However, you might prefer the excellent Taj Mahal beer from Calcutta, which comes in oversized bottles. It will put out any fire lighted by the spices. So will a drink called *lassi*—yogurt and ice churned with fragrant orange flower water and sugar.

You'll want to return, for the menu is indeed extensive. Chances are, when you do, a member of this charming Indian family will greet you with one of the oldest welcomes in the world: "*Namaste* . . . to you I bow."

Moderate. Open seven days. Lunch served from noon to 3 P.M. Dinner from 5 to 10:30 P.M. Sunday buffet from 11:30 A.M. to 3:30 P.M. Reservations accepted. Visa, MC. Full bar. Parking lot. Casual.

To obtain the best results from this Guide, be sure to consult the map on the various Northern California areas on page 28.

★
TAO TAO/Northern Chinese
675 Jackson Street/San Francisco/Area 2/(415) 982-6125

Vintage photographs of Chinatown set the scene for the cultivated cuisine at Tao Tao. The menu offers a well-prepared, extensive variety of northern Chinese dishes with specialties including barbecued young quail and Manchurian beef. Chinese chicken salad with cashew nuts and crisped noodles; beef won ton, a soup-cum-entrée. Beef strips, stuffed dumplings and scallions in meat stock and Peking duck are part of the high-quality fare that traces its ancestors back several hundred years.
Moderate. Open seven days from 11 A.M. to 10 P.M., weekends till 11 P.M. Reservations accepted. Visa, MC, AX. Full bar. Street parking. Casual.

★
TAO TAO CAFE/Chinese
175 South Murphy Avenue/Sunnyvale/Area 2/(408) 736-3731

When this excellent Cantonese favorite opened in 1951, it was difficult to find a *really* good Chinese restaurant outside of San Francisco. Tao Tao is truly one of the Bay Area's best. Owner/host Frank Wong takes pride in his modern Chinese design, airy dining rooms, bar lounge and family dinners. Superb à la carte specialties include tossed shredded chicken salad, Tao Tao beef, and Peking duck (twenty-four hours notice).
Moderate. Open seven days for dinner only from 4 to 9:45 P.M. Reservations advised. AX, Visa, MC. Full bar. Parking in rear. Casual.

★ ★
TARANTINO'S/American/Seafood
206 Jefferson Street/San Francisco/Area 2/(415) 775-5600

Two Irishmen, Gene McAteer and Dan Sweeney, founded this American/seafood restaurant in 1945 — a daring move in the heart of Fisherman's Wharf, which was then a completely Italian preserve. This upper-level restaurant has continued to delight not only the visitors from the world over but a host of Californians as well who claim Tarantino's as a refuge from the hustle of the more touristy aspects of The Wharf.

Owned and operated by Bill McDonnell for over twenty years, Taratino's is regarded by many locals as "the" place to savor excellent meals and superb views of the inner Wharf, the Golden Gate Bridge, the Bay and the hills of the City and Marin County.

Moderate. Open seven days from 11:30 A.M. to 11 P.M. Reservations advised. Visa, MC, AX. Full bar. View. Parking lot across the street. Casual to semi-dressy.

★ ★
TAVERNA YAISOU/Greek
48 North San Pedro Road/San Rafael/Area 3/(415) 479-2991

Greek food in Greece can be so drenched in olive oil (remember all the olive orchards in the Greek Islands) as to be almost inedible for American palates. This candlelit cafe, while remaining faithful to the cuisine of Greece, cannot be said to be the cuisine of grease. *Moussaka,* the national dish of Greece, is the specialty: layers of lamb and eggplant topped with rich tomato sauce and cheese. The baklava is housemade—an unusual and delightful touch. This could be the best restaurant of its type in Northern California.
Moderate. Lunch served Monday through Friday from 11:30 A.M. to 1:30 P.M. Dinner Thursday through Saturday from 6 to 9:30 P.M. Visa, MC. Wine and beer only. Parking lot. Casual to semi-dressy.

★
THUNDERBIRD BOOKSTORE AND RESTAURANT
California/Continental
The Barnyard/Carmel/Area 1/(408) 624-1803

You may dine surrounded by fifty thousand books, magazines, art, classical music and a great stone fireplace. Sounds just right for Carmel? Well, that's the basic story about this unique book shop and dining place where they advertise, "Food for the body and soul." Surprisingly enough to a can-be-caustic critic like myself, the food is very good indeed.

Situated in The Barnyard, a picturesque collection of variously named "Barns" just off Highway 1 between Rio Road and Carmel Valley Road, about a mile and a half from central Carmel, this "largest bookstore on the Monterey Peninsula" serves lunch and dinner, during which you are invited to select a shelved book and browse (or read) while lunching on hearty beef soup, sandwiches and creamy cheesecake. At dinner, with that great old fireplace and all those warm woods, you'll be ready for early bird dinners (served from 5:30 P.M.): soup and salad, entrée, popovers and butter. Modest price but no reservations. On the regular menu are: roast prime rib of beef *au jus* with the above extras plus two fresh vegetables. Fresh fish is served in season. Recently, the patio was covered with a solarium-greenhouse retractable roof for "outside" dining year round.

Inexpensive to moderate. Open seven days. Lunch daily from 11 A.M. to 3 P.M. Dinner Tuesday through Saturday from 5:30 to 8:30 P.M. Sunday and Monday only soup and salad bar are available from 5 to 8 P.M. Reservations accepted. Visa, MC. Beer and wine only. Patio. Lot parking. Casual.

★

TIEN FU/Chinese
1395 Noriega/San Francisco/Area 2/(415) 655-1064

This little Chinese restaurant has had more ups and downs than a ferris wheel at carnival time. Currently, it's on an up-swing. On a menu as extensive as this one, it's agony trying to decide on just a few dishes and reject all those delicious creations on all the neighboring tables. I still haven't tried the green onion pancakes or hot sauce beef with spinach, although both have been recommended to me. The eggplant in Szechwan sauce had the distinct flavor of sesame and spice and happily had not absorbed the oil that frequently makes eggplant soggy and, in my opinion, inedible. The Hunan fish is a good choice, as is the hot-and-sour soup, made with pork, bamboo shoots, eggs and cloud ears. Cloud ears, by the way, is an enchanting name for the otherwise unappealing sounding tree fungus or tree ears. These cloud ears are rather alarming to cook with because when they are soaked before cooking (as they must be) they expand to about twenty times their original size. In spite of their origins, they're really very good when used in dishes like the hot-and-sour soup or *mu shu* pork.

Inexpensive. Open Wednesday through Monday from 11 A.M. to 10:00 P.M. Reservations necessary. Visa, MC. Wine and beer only. Street parking. Casual.

★

TOKYO CHICKEN/Japanese
3406 Mount Diablo Boulevard/Lafayette/Area 2/(415) 283-3890

Fortunately this place has improved with time and a new chef. I say fortunately because the chef they had on my first visit didn't know the difference between sushi and a soufflé. The only reason I returned was that a friend had enjoyed a dinner there recently and suggested I give the place another chance.

In order to obtain the best results from this Guide, please consult "A Few Inside Tips " on page 18.

The *miso* soup was thicker than most I have tasted which was a pleasant variation. The tempura was heavily battered vegetables and shrimp—the heavy batter a not-so-pleasant variation. The heaviness, in fact, seemed to extend to a number of items we tasted. The *karaage* chicken was an exception; it was lightly coated and deep fried so that it was non-greasy. Things have improved since my last disasterous visit, and in spite of some of the heavier dishes, I'm glad I returned. **Inexpensive to moderate.** Open Tuesday through Friday for lunch from 11 A.M. to 2 P.M. Dinner Tuesday through Friday from 5 to 9:30 P.M., Saturday and Sunday from 4 to 9 P.M. Reservations accepted. Visa, MC. Wine and beer only. Parking lot. Casual.

★ ★
TOMMASO'S/Italian/Pizza
1042 Kearny Street/San Francisco/Area 2/(415) 398-9696

Yes, Virginia, Francis Coppola really does show up at Tommaso's on occasion to cook pizza. I was there myself one night several years ago when in popped the great man, fresh from his triumphant *Godfather* movies, anxious to feed his guests with pizza made by his own hand. It was a fine piece of work, and I am happy to report that should Francis ever find himself flat broke, he could get a job just about anywhere making pizza.

Tommaso's is to San Francisco what Gino's Pizzeria is to Chicago—it's *the* cult pizzeria, and devotees happily wait in line for hours to sample just a little of the holy bread. The pizza served at Tommaso's really is superb, and the reason for this is a wood-burning oven in which the crust is cooked to absolute perfection—crispy, filled with woodsy flavor, and covered with one the the best tomato sauces in the West. The rest of the toppings, which are poured on generously and which never seem to make the crust soggy, are exceedingly traditional—cheese, ham, mushrooms, sausage, anchovies, pepperoni and a singular oddity—chicken.

There are some who find the *calzone* at Tommaso's even better than the pizza, and indeed *calzone* is a close blood relation. It's pretty much a pizza folded in half, and filled with gobs of ricotta and mozzarella cheese, mushrooms, sausage and tomato sauce. The rest of the dishes are not bad, but rarely come up to the pizza. There are several veal *scalloppines,* served *marsala, fiorentina, piccante, parmigiana, rolletini* and with peppers and mushrooms. The best appetizer is the toasted peppers with olive oil and lemon, though I would not turn down the chilled broccoli unless forced to under duress.

Moderate to expensive. Open Tuesday through Saturday from 5 to 10:45 P.M., Sunday 4 to 9:45 P.M. No reservations. Visa, MC. Wine and beer only. Street parking. Casual.

DA★
TOMMY'S JOYNT/Continental/Chuckwagon
1101 Geary (at Van Ness Avenue)/San Francisco/Area 2/(415) 775-4216

One of the tragedies of San Francisco was instigated by some idiotic city bureau that forced Tommy Harris to cover up his multi-colored façade with more modern and less meaningful supergraphics. Under Albert Pollack's new direction, it still is an outpost of independence, a short-order chuckwagon serving buffalo stew and dozens of other homemade dishes in an atmosphere that looks like utter pot and pandemonium. There are peculiar artifacts hanging from virtually every square foot of the ceiling and from the walls. The saloon portion is the friendliest place in town where visiting baseball players (many of them stay in the ugly, huge Jack Tar Hotel across the street) get in a shot or two before retiring. There's community sing-alongs, often vying in volume with the television set which seems to have no "off" button. Prices are very low for the giant sandwiches (try the dips) and the oxtail sauté, but even if they were substantially higher, the place would still be packed. This is San Francisco eccentric, unlike any other area, but perhaps combining, a bit of the Irish with the Barbary Coast to the absolute delight of the mixed clientele from whiskey-voiced old American Legion types to chinchilla clad lovelies with their escorts. A not-to-be-missed part of the scene, and one of my favorite places. **Inexpensive.** Open seven days from 10 A.M. to 2 A.M. No reservations. No credit cards. Full bar. Street parking. Casual.

★
TON KIANG/Chinese
683 Broadway/San Francisco/Area 2/(415) 421-2015
5827 Geary Boulevard/San Francisco/(415) 387-8273
3148 Geary Boulevard/San Francisco/(415) 752-4440

The Hakka are a non-native people who live near Canton but have retained their own dialect, customs and cuisine. The cuisine is a far cry from the frequent blandness of Cantonese and offers many unique and subtly spiced dishes of the Hakka. The menu, however, is quite large and if you're not feeling adventurous enough to make a complete dinner out of the more unusual sounding specialties, there are plenty of Cantonese and Mandarin dishes with a fair sprinkling of Szechwan entrées.

I have been amazed a number of times in Chinese restaurants by the attitude of the waiters. Some are unwilling to translate Chinese characters, assuming, I'm sure, that American palates would not be appreciative. At one restaurant, I asked our waiter for more plum sauce. His response, delivered as he ambled back to the kitchen, "If I have time." He never did. Ton Kiang is the happy exception to this, and waiters are more than willing to translate, describe and explain. Although sometimes, I confess, I found it nicer not to know.

Moderate. Open seven days. Lunch from 11 A.M. to 5 P.M. Dinner from 5 to 10 P.M., weekends 11 A.M. to 11 P.M. Hours may vary. Reservations essential. Visa, MC. Wine and beer only. Street parking. Casual.

★ ★
TOPAZ ROOM/Seafood/Continental
96 Old Courthouse Square/Santa Rosa/Area 3/(707) 542-7753

A Santa Rosa institution, the Topaz Room is particularly favored by lunching businessmen, though it offers a well thought-out dinner menu that features seafood. Fish and shellfish offerings include halibut sauté, stuffed trout, crêpes stuffed with seafood, abalone, and lobster tail. Other popular items are sweetbreads, frog legs, chicken Kiev, and filet mignon. Less expensive early bird dinners are available Monday, Tuesday, and Wednesday until 7 P.M., and a reduced-price special is offered on weekends. The wine list is devoted to California vintages.

Owner/host Neil Blumenthal has gone to considerable trouble and expense to provide diners with an elegant setting. The Topaz Room's flocked wallpaper, crystal chandeliers, large wall mirrors, and white tablecloths carry guests back to an earlier, less harried, time. Service is knowledgeable and efficient.

Moderate to expensive. Open Monday through Saturday. Lunch Monday through Saturday from 11 A.M. to 4:30 P.M. Dinner Monday through Saturday from 4:30 to 10 P.M. Reservations advised. AX, Visa, MC, DC. Full bar. Street and garage parking. Casual to semi-dressy.

Please be sure to consult "Tipping Made Easy" on page 22 of this Guide.

★
TORA-YA/Japanese
1734 Post Street/San Francisco/Area 2/(415) 931-5200
1914 Fillmore Street/San Francisco/Area 2/(415) 931-9455
1695 Solano Avenue/Berkeley/Area 2/(415) 524-7000

Tora-ya, which means Place of the Tiger, has dishes ranging from the above average, if ordinary, noodle dishes to the exotic, which can be . . . interesting. The *yakinori* (toasted seaweed) comes in a beautiful lacquered box, but looks something like burned paper. The pork *miso nabe* is strips of pork, green onion, mushrooms, bean and fish cakes in a surprisingly good bean paste soup. Yoshinori Takao has managed to keep all three of his restaurants operating smoothly at a very moderate cost. My own favorite is the cozy Fillmore Street location which also has a sushi bar, but is closed for lunch.
Inexpensive to moderate. Days and hours may vary. Open Tuesday through Sunday from 11:30 A.M. to 10 P.M. Post Street location open seven days. Reservations advised for six or more. Visa, MC. Wine and beer only. Casual.

★ ★ ★
TRADER VIC'S/Polynesian/International
9 Anchor Drive/Emeryville/Area 2/(415) 653-3400

When I started in the restaurant business, I did everything to get customers—I sang, I even let them stick an icepick in my wooden leg," said Trader Vic Bergeron, entrepreneur, artist, adventurer and head of a Polynesian empire that stretches from America to Japan to Europe and above, in a real sense, for Trader Vic's is the food and menu consultant to United Airlines. Here is where it all started, an unlikely area to spawn such a sophisticated and successful operation.

The Trader began his career with a hamburger stand in Oakland. As business grew, he traveled throughout the world discovering exotic foods, observing methods of preparation and collecting recipes. His rum drinks require the use of scores of different shaped glasses to accommodate the perfect blend—the result of the Trader's research. That the blend in the drinks and all the sauces remain perfect is a tribute to what must be one of the world's great quality control systems.

The term "commissary operation" usually denotes a coffeehouse chain where food is pre-cooked and delivered to the locations. Here, the commissary is an exacting laboratory that blends myriad spices and herbs and other substances into the precise formulas the Trader developed. Dishes like poached salmon with red caviar co-exist with Indonesian lamb roast in peanut sauce and other fine dishes from the Pacific.

These are extraordinary restaurants that rise above the levels of mediocrity that have become a national malaise. Every detail is checked and double-checked in each of the far-flung operations. Trader Vic Bergeron died in late 1984, but all his staffs are loyal almost beyond belief and reflect their meticulous training. Promotions come from within the ranks, rewarding sincere effort. This location is a derivative of the original founded in Oakland in 1934, and first famous as Hinky Dink's. Genial manager, Fred Fung, who has overseen this large location for decades, says of their December 1972 move here from Oakland, "It was both sad and happy. But now we have wide water and hill views, and can accommodate many more guests." Ask for Fred. His menu is the same as in all the other Vic's but he feels, naturally, that his place is a bit better. **Expensive.** Open Monday through Friday from 11:30 A.M. to 3 P.M. Dinner from 5 to 10:30 P.M. Reservations advised. All major credit cards. Full bar. Ample parking. Dressy.

DA ★ ★ ★
TRADER VIC'S/Polynesian/Continental
20 Cosmo Place/San Francisco/Area 1/(415) 776-2232

A brief history of the colorful Trader and his Polynesian empire is found under "Trader Vic's" in Emeryville (previous entry). Suffice it to say that of all the Trader Vics, from New York to Japan, this one is perhaps the smartest and most loyally attended. The quality of the varied cuisine is constant, the drinks are superb, and you will be lucky to get a table here even on a Tuesday evening.

The decor is colorful—fish nets and ships' masts and the like—the service is impeccable and the dishes are marvelously different. You'll find French sweetbreads on the same menu with snow peas and my favorite, the Indonesian lamb roast with peanut sauce.

Definitely not for the thin of wallet or the timid. This version caters to the uptrodden of the world and is frequented by San Francisco high society. Coats and ties required for gentlemen—a rarity in customarily casual Polynesian restaurants. Lynn Bergeron, son of the late and widely missed Trader Vic, directs the entire galaxy of his worldwide operations from his main office here and watches personally over this remarkable institution.

Expensive. Open weekdays for lunch from 11:30 A.M. to 2:30 P.M. Dinner Monday through Sunday, 5 P.M. to 12:30 A.M. Reservations advised. All major credit cards. Full bar. Valet parking. Dressy.

DA ★★
THE TRELLIS CAFE/California
7115 Greenback Lane/Citrus Heights/Area 3/(916) 969-1580

If you have not been fortunate enough to visit Sacramento for several years, you will be astonished at the development of the contingent areas. All the best restaurants are no longer downtown, although The Trellis Cafe is easily reached by freeway. The Trellis Cafe is situated within the Fountain Square Nursery and the air is refreshing, cleansed and perfumed by the thousands of plants, many blooming, that surround you here. You lunch and dine on such innovative creations as chicken and ham *pithivier* — breast of chicken marinated in mustard sauce and filled with ham and cheese, in a puff pastry. At dinner, try the veal medallions, stuffed with prosciutto, garlic and parsley, coated with walnut bread crumbs, then sautéed with light cheese sauce. Creative owners/hosts Diane and Tom Struhm will greet you, describe their dishes and discuss your dining experience. **Moderate to expensive.** Open Monday through Saturday 11:30 A.M. to 2:30 P.M. Tuesday through Saturday 5:30 to 9:30 P.M. Sunday brunch 10:30 A.M. to 2:30 P.M. Reservations necessary weekends. All major credit cards. Beer and wine only. Ample free parking. Casual.

★★
TRICOLOR RESTAURANT FRANCAIS/French Country
4233 Geary Boulevard/San Francisco/Area 2/(415) 752-9974

When asked to suggest his specialty de maison, Monsieur le proprietor Jacques Janot replied: "Every meal." While I don't fully agree, the attitude is commendable. Each dinner includes soup du jour, salad, fresh vegetables, potato, dessert and coffee — all especially prepared for your enjoyment — and if you don't finish your dinner, you'll be asked to explain. I don't know if the chef will ever forgive me for merely tasting his *lapin au vin rouge* or tripe *à la mode de Caen,* but perhaps when he reads that his was the seventh restaurant I visited in one day — simply to taste — he will forgive. The decor is charmingly French-country with flowered wallpaper, old-fashioned lamps and a brick fireplace at one end. Tables are simply appointed with white linen, red napkins and sturdy, no-nonsense chairs. Prices on the wine list seem to have changed little since 1941. **Moderate.** Open Wednesday through Saturday from 5 to 10 P.M. Sunday from 4 to 9:45 P.M. Reservations accepted. Visa, MC. Wine and beer only. Child's menu. Street parking. Casual to semi-dressy.

★ ★
TUBA GARDEN/Continental
3634 Sacramento Street/San Francisco/Area 2/(415) 921-8822

Luncheon only is served here, and is frequently so popular reservations should be made days in advance. Anthony LaCavera, host/partner and chef/co-owner Gerd (call him Ben) Wenske have drawn a discerning clientele with their appealing old Victorian home, with its romantic, nostalgic ambiance and Ben's excellent cuisine. The gourmet dishes are served traditionally, impeccably. The imaginative menu changes weekly and some regulars come in that often. Be sure to have their Tuba Flower Pot dessert.
Moderate. Open seven days. Monday through Friday 11 A.M. to 2:30 P.M. Saturday and Sunday brunch 11:30 A.M. to 2:30 P.M. Reservations accepted. All major credit cards. Beer and wine only. Lot parking across the street. Casual.

★ ★
TUNG FONG/Chinese/Dim Sum
808 Pacific Avenue/San Francisco/Area 2/(415) 362-7115

Almost all the *dim sum* parlors in Los Angeles, and most of the tea houses in San Francisco, are of the vast-hall-and-rolling-cart type, seating hundreds of diners at once amidst a maniacal cacophony of clinking cups of tea, rattling plates and waitresses explaining the nature of the pastries on their carts in an endless singsong. Tung Fong is different. Sandwiched as it is between the massive Hong Kong Tea House, and the awesome Asia Garden, Tung Fong is a tiny place by comparison, with only room for some twenty or so formica-topped tables.

Waitresses at Tung Fong don't roll carts around loaded down with only one type of *dim sum* at a time. Instead, they carry large trays (in the style of New York's legendary Nom Wah Tea Parlor) stacked high with a dozen or so different items, each tempting you into grabbing far more dishes than you could ever finish. But there's a lot more going on at Tung Fong than diminuitive size and multitudinous trays. Tung Fong is easily San Francisco's best *dim sum* house for a variety of good reasons.

First of all, there's the matter of the tea. At most tea houses, the teapot just appears, and you get whatever the waiter has opted to serve you. At Tung Fong, as soon as you are seated, the first thing you're asked is which of the seven house teas you'd like to have—jasmine, chrysanthemum or a fascinating green tea called dragonwell are a few.

Then, as I've said, there's the matter of the large trays, each covered with an assortment of a dozen or more different *dim sum*. And what *dim sum* these are! The *har gow* are lovely, translucent crescents, shimmering with an inner glow that emanates from the filling of chopped shrimp, vegetables and spices. The *cha sui bow*, which looks a little like a tennis ball, only white and puffy, is light and flavorful, overflowing with hunks of barbecued pork. There's an imcomparable paper-wrapped chicken, and lovely, succulent spareribs. And there are two of the great triumphs of Tung Fong—the pickled mustard greens and the hot black bean sauce, both of which are also available bottled, to go.

At Tung Fong, the pastry always seems a little crisper, the food a little less oily, and the service a little friendlier. All *dim sum* tea houses are good; Tung Fong is just that much better.

Inexpensive. Open Thursday through Tuesday from 9 A.M. to 3 P.M. No reservations. No credit cards. Beer only. Street parking. Casual.

★
UNCLE RUGBY'S GALLEY/Continental
905 Los Osos Valley Road/Los Osos/Area 1/(805) 528-4449

Conveniently sited halfway between Morro Bay and San Luis Obispo, only twelve minutes to either town, Uncle Rugby's Galley shares ownership with the noted Galley in Morro Bay. Bud's talented and personable offspring—Jeff and Rodger Anderson and sister Mollie (worth the trip just to receive one of her smiles)—run this charming dining place much of the time, and help out as hosts at their dad's sea-food Galley. The interior displays casual elegance throughout its two dining rooms, one with antique oak fireplace and sofas, the other with booths and a tableside fern garden. The menu includes steaks, chicken, lamb and seafood. The various appetizers tempt—won tons, escargot, steamed clams, Blue Points and hearts of palm. The soups are made fresh daily: chicken almond and clam chowder may be choices. Gracing the menu are scampi, petrale sole almondine, breast of chicken casserole and the house special treat—steak Bercy.

Moderate. Open nightly for dinner from 5 to 9 P.M. Reservations necessary on weekends. MC, Visa. Wine and beer only. Child's menu. Lot parking. Casual.

In order to obtain the best results from this Guide, be sure to read the French, German, Italian and Oriental menu translators on pages 399 to 404 of this Guide.

DA★
UNION HOTEL/Italian
3703 Main Street/Occidental/Area 3/(707) 874-3555

Sixty miles north — across the Golden Gate Bridge — is an old-time lumber town that has been a gastronomic mecca for the fishing towns nearby. The aroma of garlic and pungent sauces wafts in the air, like a beautiful song, from the huge Italian and Basque restaurants that vie for favor among locals and visitors alike. The best of these, Union Hotel, offers a multitude of seven-course dinners from which to choose, but be sure to save room for the zucchini fritters during dinner and the banana fritters as dessert. The ravioli here is a house specialty — and so is the pan-fried chicken with mashed potatoes and country gravy. The restaurant is past its hundredth year and the gracious old building, with a canopy and sign projecting out into the street, radiates the hospitality that has become a tradition for many generations of fishing families. **Moderate.** Open seven days from 11:30 A.M. to 9 P.M., Sunday till 8 P.M. Reservations accepted. Visa, MC, AX. Entertainment Friday. Full bar. Child's menu. Street and lot parking. Casual.

★
THE UPPER CRUST/Pizza/Pasta
2415 Mission Street/Santa Cruz/Area 1/(408) 423-9010

The pasta is not the most exciting, but then with a name like Upper Crust you would expect an emphasis on good pizza if not pasta. They have Neopolitan Rounds, regular pizza, which is just that — pretty regular. The Sicilian-style, however, is an extra thick square pizza that is worth the extra money.
Inexpensive to moderate. Open seven days from 11 P.M. to 11 P.M., Friday till 1 A.M. Saturday till midnight. Visa, MC. Wine and beer only. Parking lot. Casual.

★
UPSTAIRS AT THE CLIFF HOUSE/Omelettes
1090 Point Lobos Avenue/San Francisco/Area 2/(415) 386-3330

This island of order is perched bravely between the ruins of the Sutro Baths and the urbanely renewed Playland at the Beach. The preferred technique for surviving expeditions to Seal Rocks is to view them from the warmth and comfort of the great indoors. Downstairs at the Upstairs, is a spacious bar decorated in traditional San Francisco attic treasures — the walls hung heavy with historic photos of the former Cliff House's glory, some shipwrecks and other memorable occurrences. The decor winds its way upstairs to the Upstairs, where omelettes are served from a menu listing forty-five varieties. They could probably play "stump the chef" and give a prize to anyone who could come up with yet another combination. The specials are "Aloha"—ham and pineapple; German—ham and potato; Italian—sausage and artichoke; Greek—shrimp and feta cheese; and Spanish. There are salads, chili, chowder and sandwiches, and a nicely sized wine list. The staff may exhibit that dull blankness that comes from staring into a fog too long, but that's preferable to the ruin and tackiness and tour buses outside.

Moderate. Open seven days from 9 A.M. to 10:30 P.M. No reservations. Visa, MC, AX. Full bar. View. Public parking. Casual.

★
U. S. RESTAURANT/Italian
431 Columbus/San Francisco/Area 2/(415) 362-6251

Here's an interesting one: an Italian restaurant, called the U. S. Restaurant, and managed at one time by a Chinese couple. Luigi Borzoni is the current owner/manager of this anomaly that has been a family tradition for well over fifty years. Your taste buds may have forgotten the taste of thick tomato sauce, homemade and simmered for hours. The spaghetti and rigatoni are covered in Mrs. Borzoni's tomato-y culinary coup. The veal parmigiana and ravioli *al pesto* are similar feats. The daily specials are the real bargains and they're likely to run out of these early in the evening—particularly when the special is baked lasagna. The cheeseburger is not just an Italian's concession to American palates, but an enormous burger of ground beef on French bread that has even made me pass up the lasagna—but only once.

Inexpensive Open Tuesday through Saturday. Breakfast from 6 A.M. to 3 P.M. Lunch and dinner from 11 A.M. to 9 P.M. Reservations accepted. No credit cards. Beer and wine only. Street parking. Casual.

★ ★
VANESSI'S/Italian/Continental/Landmark
498 Broadway/San Francisco/Area 2/(415) 421-0890

There are restaurants that are older, better and more interesting, but there is no restaurant that so captures the essence of San Francisco as Vanessi's. Once it was "the" restaurant—I recall an uncle who, when he felt I was ready for my introduction to the good life, took me here, where I was properly intimidated by waiters who seemed as old as Solomon (most of them are still here). The veal dishes and *cannelloni* are still as good as they ever were, and the wine list is second to none. My favorite lunch is the calamari at Vanessi's on Friday. It's the best late evening spot I know of, open until 1:30 A.M. when most everything that's legal has closed, anyway. For the authentic San Francisco experience, you should work Vanessi's in. But be prepared for the crowd.

Moderate to expensive. Open Monday through Saturday from 11:30 A.M. to 1 A.M., Sunday from 4:30 P.M. to midnight. Reservations accepted. All major credit cards. Full bar. Lot parking. Casual.

VANNELLI'S SEAFOOD/Seafood
Pier 39/San Francisco/Area 2/(415) 421-7261

Chef Claus Iversen's recipe for crab cioppino and crab Mornay won the 1980 Crab Olympics, and though the cioppino is not as good as the stuff you'll find at some of San Francisco's smaller Italian restaurants, the view is better. The menu is one of the simplest of the seafood restaurants on the pier, which means the kitchen is able to work harder at perfecting fewer dishes. The cold seafood platter is an intriguing combination of Pacific smoked salmon, calamari vinaigrette, lobster pâté, prawns, a clam and an oyster, mushrooms and artichokes. The oysters Rockefeller is made better, not only in New Orleans, but also in San Francisco. But the baked bass Farallon is an honest dish, topped as it is with green peppercorns and sour cream. And the baked salmon Wellington is an interesting idea — salmon stuffed with scallops and spinach and served *en croute,* with a bit of basil sauce on the side. The side of potato skins is usually good.

Moderate to expensive. Open weekdays for lunch from 11 A.M. to 4 P.M. Dinner weekdays from 4 to 10 P.M. Weekends to 11 P.M. Saturday and Sunday brunch from 10:30 A.M. to 3 P.M. Reservations advised on weekends. All major credit cards. Full bar. View. Validated parking at Pier 39. Casual.

★
VEGI FOOD/Chinese Vegetarian
1820 Clement Street/San Francisco/Area 2/(415) 387-8111
2083 Vine Street/Berkeley/Area 2/(415) 548-5244

As Chinese cooking is probably the healthiest cuisine in the world, I'm not exactly sure what the point is in removing the use of meat — which is limited normally anyway. Be that as it may, apparently someone felt that California's craze for Chinese food could be coupled with the craze for vegetarian food — and someone (owner David Chan) was right.

The non-usage of meat does not spark any real vegetarian creativity, as most of the dishes are the same as their meaty counterparts only without the meat. *Mu shu* pork becomes *mu shu* vegetables; sweet 'n' sour pork becomes fried walnuts with sweet 'n' sour sauce. One exception to this is the gluten puffs. I guess I'm just too much a traditionalist when it comes to my Chinese food, but I think this is going a bit too far.

Inexpensive. Open Tuesday through Friday for lunch from 11:30 A.M. to 3 P.M. Dinner from 5 to 9 P.M. No reservations. No credit cards. Street parking. Casual.

To obtain the best results from this Guide, be sure to consult the map on the various Northern California areas on page 28.

DA ★★
VENTANA INN/California
Highway One/Big Sur/Area 1/(408) 667-2332

This lovely restaurant and inn offers cushioned bentwood chairs, subtle lighting, and fresh flowers for your pleasure. At dinner, classical music mellows the air and the presentation of the superb food is further assurance that your meal will be a treasured memory. Naturally, everything that can and should be fresh *is* just that, from the bounty of the ocean and rivers to the crisp greens and fruits. Meats have been properly aged. Boar from the Santa Lucia range is a rare treat. A magnificent stone fireplace in the bar area can be a comfort in less clement weather, although there are terraces for outdoor dining. A connoisseur's cellar.
Moderate. Open for lunch Monday through Friday from noon to 3 P.M., Saturday and Sunday 11 A.M. to 3:30 P.M. Dinner nightly from 6 to 9 P.M. Reservations necessary. All major credit cards. Full bar. Lot parking. Casual.

★
VIA VENETO/Italian/Seafood
Ghirardelli Square/San Francisco/Area 2/(415) 673-4088

A long, swinging balcony-bar overlooking the plaza at Ghirardelli Square with a light menu – salads, lasagna, drinks – but a heavy view of everything. It's a pleasant way to spend an afternoon, and the Hontalas (owner John, manager Larry and Verna) have seen to it that there's more than the dreaded veal cutlet of other outdoor trattorìas.
Inexpensive. Open seven days noon to 10 P.M. No reservations. AX only. Full bar. Patio. View of San Francisco Bay. Garage parking. Casual.

★★★
VICOLO/Italian/Pizza
201 Ivy Street/San Francisco/Area 2/(415) 863-5355

Nothing seems to arouse passion for debate more than trying to determine who has "the best of" anything. Pizza is particularly crucial; each gourmand has his favorite, and terms like Chicago style, "deep dish," thin crust, most eclectic toppings, etc. roll off the palate as each extolls the virtues of his or her favorites. Vicolo has done more than that. They published a flyer purporting to show the difference with a slice of "theirs"– commercially prepared tomato sauce, rubbery cheese (often frozen), a few chunks of sausage with preservatives and soy extender, and too much crust made of bleached white flour and cottonseed oil – as compared to "ours" (Vicolo's) with a sauce of marinated whole tomatoes with fresh herbs, grated aged, Reggiano parmigiano, roasted marinated green peppers, crisp crust of unbleached cornmeal, imported olive oil and French yeast and a thick layer of creamy whole milk mozzarella.

Vicolo is certainly the classiest pizzeria in town. The exterior is of corrugated iron, but the interior, with rose walls inset with windows at fey angles, art pieces and sculpture, is a setting for people on the move, rushing into or out-of nearby Davies Symphony Hall. What's more it's brought to you by the same four partners who own Fourth Street Grill. Somehow they've managed to get hold of real Coca-Cola in the original little green bottles to serve along with the Heineken on draft and Italian ice cream. It's all in what they describe as a "glamorous shed" in Ivy alley. There's seating for forty and Vicolo's enjoys a big take-out business.

Moderate. Open Monday through Friday from 11:30 A.M. to 11:30 P.M., Saturday and Sunday from 3 to 11:30 P.M. No reservations. No credit cards. Wine and beer only. Street and nearby lot parking. Casual.

★ ★
VICTORIAN HOUSE ANTIQUES GARDEN RESTAURANT
Continental/Italian
476 South First Street/San Jose/Area 2/(408) 286-1770

My first word of this colorful dining place came from one of the deans of San Jose's finest restaurants, Emile Mooser, proprietor of the highly regarded Emile's. Owner Patrick Mormon proudly gave me the royal tour. First, we cruised through the two initial dining areas, passing beneath thirty or forty Tiffany-inspired hanging lamps, spaced by profusely growing plants. There is a player-piano that Patrick started for me. Every note was clear and crisp—a joy that bore me back to childhood. Along our route, which took us out the rear door, I was impressed by the scores of antiques (all of which are for sale), occupying every inch of free space as well as wall areas. Glass-front cabinets displayed treasures of the past.

Once in the splendid, bricked-in, tree-shaded garden, I had to exclaim at the spaciousness. My host confided that he found everything in concrete when he acquired the property and had to dig it out so as to plant and lay brick. Lunch and brunch are served here in fine weather.

It seems that Patrick opened here in mid-1975 as a tea garden restaurant but soon learned that his guests demanded more. In a few months the Victorian began serving complete meals, with immediate success, so much so that reservations are now strongly suggested.

Among dishes that my guests and I have tried and enjoyed are scampi and large prawns, both in garlic sauce, as appetizers; delicious soups, such as cream of broccoli; salads of merit (the blue cheese dressing is a prize); *scalone amandine,* veal scalloppine, calamari marinara, broiled lobster tail and a sensational boneless chicken parmigiana. There are several veal specialties, as well as other chicken creations, roast prime ribs of beef and a New York steak. Ten à la carte appetizers and extra dishes will tempt you, and the rich desserts include a fantastic Grand Marnier frozen mousse covered with raspberry purée.

Moderate to expensive. Open seven days. Lunch served weekdays from 11 A.M. to 4 P.M. Dinner served Sunday through Thursday from 4 to 10 P.M. Friday and Saturday to 11 P.M. Sunday brunch from 10:30 A.M. to 2:30 P.M. Reservations advised. All major credit cards. Full bar. Patio. Child's menu. Parking at motel next door. Semi-dressy to dressy.

★ ★
VICTOR'S/California/Continental
Westin St. Francis Tower/San Francisco/Area 2/(415) 956-7777

Honoring Victor Hertzler, the internationally famous executive chef of the Hotel St. Francis from 1906 to 1926, this splendid restaurant was designed to enhance his memory while affording a memorable dining experience.

From its site on the 32nd floor of the Westin St. Francis Tower, Victor's commands a panorama of The City through solar bronze glass. Warm earth hues and chandeliers impart an air of muted elegance. Cocktails in the club-like, library lounge are a natural preface to the unusual dining experience awaiting you here.

The menu, under the direction of chef Joel Rambaud, has taken a delicious turn toward California cuisine, while continuing to uphold the tradition of the meal as a total culinary experience. On a recent visit, the appetizer of poached filet of trout with chives and golden caviar simply melted on my tongue, an ambrosial medley of tastes and textures. Grilled squab sausages with Perigourdine sauce and black bean purée were as savory (Joe Elmiger, Director of Food and Beverage for the hotel, has to share credit for this one) as they were innovative. Maine lobster ragoût with fresh morrels and angel hair pasta was a generous portion of lobster chunks bedded on delicate al dente pasta. The grilled East Coast scallops were tender and served on fresh spinach with a light red pimento sauce. The underlying complexity of these seemingly simple dishes is morning-fresh ingredients (and Rambaud's ingenuity) choreographed into a mélange of at once contrasting and complementary flavors. For a double treat, rabbit filet and veal liver are served with a honey and caraway sauce. Desserts are on par with the rest of the meal and include baked to order fruit pies, chocolate ganash with Grand Marnier and Sabayon sauce and a pastry wagon that will keep you calorie-counting for weeks. Enjoy your choice with a rich coffee, prepared to order at your table-side.

Any concern that they may not stock your favorite vintage is unfounded. There are over thirty thousand bottles. David O'Connor, one of only three sommeliers in San Francisco, is extremely knowledgeable and will be happy to guide you to a satisfying choice.

Expensive. Open for dinner Monday through Sunday from 5:30 to 10:30 P.M. Sunday brunch from 10 A.M. to 2:30 P.M. Reservations advised. All major credit cards. Full bar. View. Hotel valet parking. Dressy.

★
VIET-NAM RESTAURANT/Vietnamese
1010 Doyle Street/Menlo Park/Area 2/(415) 326-2501

Vietnamese restaurants are rare finds in California, and what ones there are, are generally heavily influenced by the French and Indian cultures. Not so at Viet-Nam. Decor is really the absence of decor— it's just plain missing. There's a narrow room with only eight tables, connected to a small Vietnamese grocery store—your first clue that the food is authentic. Clue number two: English is the foreign language. In fact, to avoid confusion, it is wise to order by the number given to each dish.

Many of the dishes sound like Chinese food, but if that's what you're expecting, you're a few thousand miles off base. Rice noodles with barbecue shrimp comes with cucumber, scallions and peanuts. Barbecue beef rolled in green leaves is a large dish of chicken, pork, onions, and spicy beef wrapped in green grape leaves with lemon grass. In a city that is beginning to see so many Vietnamese, Korean, Thai, etc. restaurants, this one is an authentic anomaly that can provide a real dining adventure.

Inexpensive to moderate. Open for lunch weekdays 11:30 A.M. to 2 P.M. Dinner Monday through Friday from 5 to 9 P.M. Saturday and Sunday from 10 A.M. to 9 P.M. Reservations advised. Visa, MC. Wine and beer only. Street and lot parking. Casual.

Please be sure to consult "Tipping Made Easy" on page 22 of this Guide.

★
THE VILLA/Italian/Seafood
3901 Montgomery Drive/Santa Rosa/Area 3/(707) 528-7755

Perched on a hilltop overlooking Santa Rosa, The Villa provides a particularly romantic dinner setting. The attractive room's mellow illumination allows diners to enjoy the lights of the city below, a reliable catalyst for the chemistry of romance. Tall windows afford luncheon guests a pleasant view of the hills surrounding Santa Rosa.

Owners/hosts Gaspare Bernardo and John Vicini, offering fresh fish and produce every day, have developed a menu that overflows with possibilities. Dinner seafood selections (to barely scratch the surface) include crab cioppino, steamed clams Bordelaise, sea bass, filet of sole *all'agro,* and abalone in season. Steak and veal are available, both alone and in combination with seafood. Pasta dishes include linguine and ever-tasty *cannelloni.* "Petite" dinners are offered for small appetites, as is a daily early-bird special.

Though it features California labels, the wine list also carries a few leading French and Italian vintages. The staff is professional and attentive. **Moderate.** Open seven days. Lunch Monday through Friday from 11:30 A.M. to 3 P.M. Dinner Monday through Thursday 5 to 10:30 P.M., Friday and Saturday from 4 to 11 P.M., Sunday from 4 to 10 P.M. Reservations advised. Visa, MC, AX. Live music Tuesday through Saturday from 9 P.M. to 1:30 A.M. Full bar. Parking in adjacent lot. Casual.

★
THE VILLAGE PUB/Continental
2967 Woodside Road/Woodside/Area 2/(415) 851-1294

Unique — in the heart of the "deep Peninsula," this resembles a true European country inn, with paneled walls, equestrian prints and a comfortable ambiance. Jack Shutz, congenial owner, shares host duties at lunch and occasional evenings. Manager Antoine de Vos knows everyone, their tastes in wines and food. He cooks tableside, creating such worthies as beef Antoine (also beef *Fantastique,* honored by the California beef council) and fresh salmon Antoine. Chef Frank Perez is a master — the rex sole *meunière* (my favorite) and roast Long Island Duckling are unsurpassed. Proper, professional service, of course. Woodside is "horse country" and The Pub is a solid favorite, very "in," since its 1958 founding. You'll like it anyway.

Moderate to expensive. Open Tuesday through Saturday from 11:30 A.M. to 10 P.M., Sunday from 5 to 10 P.M. Reservations essential on weekends. All major credit cards. Full bar. Parking lot. Semi-dressy.

★ ★
VIVANDE PORTA VIA/European Deli/Caterer
2125 Fillmore Street/San Francisco/Area 2/(415) 346-4430

Carlo Middione and his wife, Lisa, are still glowing from the exceptional compliments of Horace Stone, a gentleman internationally
respected for his knowledge in the world of food, cooking and dining.
"I rank your Vivande Porta Via as one of only seven such ultimate European delis in the entire world," was his statement. A visit here will
enable you to observe this remarkable couple orchestrating the complete preparation, presentation and delivery of perfectly fresh, good
food from their open kitchen. Their principal business is catering, along
with take-home (Porta Via) meals and snacks. The few diners' tables
face the working kitchen, sans glass dividers, a veritable ballet of pots,
pans and an occasional flame. Carlo Middione is absolutely dedicated
to his unusual profession and, when you wander through his long establishment, past cases of cheese and items from the world over, all
that a true food-lover will treasure, you understand. Before your eyes,
white-attired kitchen workers make pasta, roast and bake, carefully,
surely, deftly. Only luncheon is served (but long hours) daily, with Sunday
brunch. No reservations, but what a marvelous waiting room!
Moderate. Open Monday through Friday, 10 A.M. to 7 P.M., lunch
11:30 A.M. to 4 P.M. Saturday 10 A.M. to 6 P.M., lunch 10 A.M. to 4 P.M.
Sunday 10 A.M. to 5 P.M., lunch/brunch 10 A.M. to 4 P.M. No reservations. MC, Visa, AX and DC. Wine and beer. Street parking. Casual.

★
VLASTA'S/Czech/German/European
2420 Lombard Street/San Francisco/Area 2/(415) 931-7533

If the light of your life is the one in the refrigerator, then I suggest
you check into this European family restaurant that serves generous
portions at budget prices. While the Vlastas describe their small restaurant as "Czech," the menu speaks more of central Europe; the
wienerschnitzel and *kassler rippchen* and *rouladen* are more closely associated with the foods of Germany. The *szekeley* goulash is from Prague,
however, and attracts homesick sailors and students to this motel-row
site. The German beer and Hungarian wines are interesting to explore,
and well suited for these multi-course dinners.
Moderate. Open Tuesday through Sunday 5:30 to 11 P.M. Reservations accepted. All major credit cards. Full bar. Child's menu. Lot parking.
Casual.

★
WALKER'S PIE SHOP/American Pie/Coffee Shop
1491 Solano Avenue/Albany/Area 2/(415) 525-4647

One of the best coffee shop kind of restaurants in the area, Walker's is whimsical (paintings on display—sophomoric newsletters) but good, with prime rib as fine as you'll find in the uptown restaurants. Doug Walker and his cheerful family turn out great pie, too. You can bring your own wine from one of the nearby tasting rooms.
Moderate. Open Tuesday through Saturday. Breakfast from 8 to 11 A.M. Lunch from 11 A.M. to 3 P.M. Dinner from 5 to 8 P.M. Friday and Saturday until 9 P.M. Sunday 1 to 9 P.M. No reservations. No credit cards. Wine and beer only. Child's menu. Street parking. Casual.

★
WAREHOUSE CAFE/American
5 Canyon Lake Drive/Port Costa/Area 2/(415) 787-1827

The namesake of this restaurant (formerly called Juanita's Warehouse) is a real character who also happens to be somewhat of a restaurant gypsy—starting one restaurant and moving on as soon as it gets a foothold. Juanita has opened restaurants in such unlikely locations as on a dry-docked Sausalito ferryboat, and an El Verano chicken farm and, sadly for Port Costa, she has now left the Warehouse to open a successful business in (of all places) a bowling alley. Juanita's tremendous sense of humor has been retained and the menu proclaims that the "food is guaranteed, but the disposition of the cook is not."

For best results, consult "How to Use This Guide" on page 25.

Prime rib is the specialty. A hefty one-pound cut. Or choose a whole Maine lobster, breaded prawns or Australian lobster tail for your entrée. The dinner buffet also includes an appetizer, a salad bar, soup or chili and dessert. Monday night is all-you-can-eat-spaghetti-night for $5. **Moderate to expensive.** Open seven days. Lunch from 11 A.M. to 4 P.M. Dinner from 6:30 to 10 P.M. Visa, MC. Full bar. View of water. Child's menu. Parking lot. Casual.

DA★
WARSZAWA/Polish
1730 Shattuck Avenue/Berkeley/Area 2/(415) 841-5539

This northside Berkeley house has been transformed into an elegant restaurant where a waterfall and indoor garden help to create the atmosphere of a charming Polish country inn. Most Polish menus look like eye charts, but this one's annotated. Herring and apples in sour cream or coarse country-style chopped liver is served for openers, followed by a manly bowl of cold borscht. Salad is served with a traditional sour cream dressing. The house specialty is *pierogi,* pasta shells stuffed with meat, cheese and mushrooms, lightly fried in butter and served with sour cream. The same mixture stuffed in crêpes is called *nalesniki,* while beef stroganoff appears in Polish as *wolowina.* The most hearty of the dishes if *bigos,* a hunter's stew of beef, pork, sausages and bacon in sauerkraut. Desserts include a strawberry crêpe, homemade cheesecake and a marvelous rum walnut torte. The wine list has also been selected with obvious care, with the unusual choice of a dry Olorosa sherry as an apértif. Louis Martini zinfandel or Wente grey riesling, are excellent choices to complement this sturdy fare. **Moderate.** Open seven days 5:30 to 10 P.M., to 11 P.M. on weekends. Reservations advised. Visa, MC. Wine and beer only. Street parking. Casual to semi-dressy.

To obtain the best results from this Guide, be sure to consult the map on the various Northern California areas on page 28.

★
WASHINGTON SQUARE BAR & GRILL/Saloon/Italian
1707 Powell/San Francisco/Area 2/(415) 982-8123

If you want to see "somebody," this is the place to do it. If not, the city view is exceptional, with a window-wall overlooking Washington Square Park and the North Beach side of Telegraph Hill.

The food is down home Italian—hearty and plentiful, if not particularly exciting. Veal, pasta and fish dishes cover most of the entrées, although there are daily specials, which tend to be a bit more innovative. Or maybe you'll try that old North Beach favorite called "Joe's Special" with scrambled eggs, spinach and ground beef. They're open late and WSB & G may be just the place to cap an evening.

Moderate. Open seven days. Lunch Monday through Saturday from 11:30 A.M. to 3 P.M. Dinner Sunday through Thursday 6 to 11 P.M., 6 to midnight on Friday and Saturday. Sunday brunch 10 A.M. to 3 P.M. Reservations essential. All major credit cards. Entertainment nightly. Full bar. View of Washington Square Park. Garage parking. Casual.

★
WATERFRONT RESTAURANT/Seafood/Continental
Pier 7/San Francisco/Area 2/(415) 391-2696

When you're looking out the window, you're not eating . . . the real problem with the food in "view" restaurants. Too many restaurateurs think a tidy window-washer is better than a good chef.

Al Falchi knows better, but then he has been in this business for a long time. His view restaurant lets you see the sparkling bay through great, tall windows; the tables are arranged on different levels, rather like box seats at a fancy theater, giving you a sweeping panorama. It's most exciting at night; at lunch time it's almost too popular and the crush distracting.

Historically, the location of this restaurant is most appropriate. More than a century ago this was the Broadway Pier—the site of the city's first Fisherman's Wharf. Each morning, captains and their crews would come to the pier to peddle their finny wares, after which they'd hoist a tankard or two in celebration (or for any other reason).

Today it's called Pier 7, and the modern setting is considerably more elegant, and the kitchen far more sophisticated than in earlier days. Best of all, the fish is as fresh as it was then.

There's soup, pasta, steaks, and seafood—plus an outstanding wine list. Entirely from California, it was obviously planned by a knowledgeable, persuasive, and very determined cellarmaster. Here you'll find rarities like Acacia chardonnay and Cakebread sauvignon blanc—at very agreeable prices since supplies of these "boutique" offerings are long sold out. Our only complaint; vintages are not shown on the wine list, though Chuck, our waiter, seemed to have them memorized.

An auspicious way to start dinner is by ordering the ceviche supreme as an appetizer (it's also served as a salad). Fresh sea bass and salmon are marinated in lemon juice with onions, tomatoes, and wild coriander. What makes this distinctive is a piquant dash of chile—just enough.

Pasta is an equally good way to begin, dividing an order. Recommended is the *linguine alle vongole Waterfront,* the thick, fresh cream sauce teeming with baby clams, seasoned with garlic and parsley. Also superb—fettuccine Alfredo, a version with smoked salmon that puts the famous Italian original to shame.

Fish is handled properly. Orders from the broiler arrive golden brown on the exterior, moist and flaky, within. The Waterfront scampi—baby lobster tails sautéed in lemon butter and wine—is most subtly seasoned, equally recommendable.

If you love good coffee, the blend of pure Colombian here or the excellent espresso offers a proper way to end your meal. And, if you *don't* like coffee, there's a snifter of cognac. But, if you like *both* coffee *and* congnac . . . well.

Moderate to expensive. Open seven days from 11:30 A.M. to 10:30 P.M. Saturday and Sunday brunch from 10 A.M. to 3 P.M. Reservations advised. All major credit cards. Full bar. View. Valet parking. Semi-dressy.

★★
WHALING STATION INN/Seafood/Italian
763 Wave Street/Monterey/Area 1/(408) 373-3778

A special dining experience awaits you in John Pisto's reincarnation of what was loved at the turn of this century. Once a Chinese grocery store that catered to the workers of Cannery Row, a block away, the building has been rebuilt and converted to a low-key, woody and verdant dinner house. This is a rare find, an honest, regional restaurant where owner-perfectionist Pisto prepares and serves some of the finest food around. Sicilian-descended and Monterey-born, the owner/executive chef, assembles artichokes fresh from nearby Castroville fields, lettuce from Salinas, the freshest of Monterey and Carmel Bays' seafood, choicest of meats and fowl, and baked-here breads and desserts. John's pasta machine turns out pasta daily, offering artichoke ravioli and several seafood pastas. His artistic bent and appreciation of the past led to the various stained-glass panels that enliven the cozy bar area. Hanging plants and petal lamps enhance the beguiling ambiance. The menu prices are remarkable for all this bounty. The restaurant looks expensive but is really quite inexpensive for both the quality and the generous quantity of what you receive. John's kitchen pioneered the mesquite broiler and currently offers delicious variations of fish not commonly found on restaurant menus. Try the barbecued lamb with herbs, the stuffed veal medallions, fresh calamari and abalone, or rock cod stuffed with fennel. Finish with a piece of his home-baked cheesecake, New York style. There is fresh fruit, even Comice pears in season. As you might expect, John Pisto's California wines include a wealth of lesser known but often interesting labels. Dress here as you wish; to many the Whaling Station Inn calls for "dressing up," others come Carmel-casual; everyone is at home here in this mellow oasis where the staff gives warm welcome.

Moderate to expensive. Open seven days 5 to 10 P.M. Reservations accepted. Visa, MC, AX, DC. Full bar. Valet parking on weekends. Casual.

★
THE WHITE ELEPHANT/English/Continental
480 Sutter Street/San Francisco/Area 2/(415) 398-8900

S ome of the best food to be found in England is in pubs. If that sounds a bit dogmatic so be it, but English cuisine is often lamentable except in those pubs where you can order such delicacies as Scotch eggs and cold mutton. The White Elephant does not limit itself entirely to "English cuisine" and that, perhaps, is to its credit. The decor is decidedly British with hunting prints, wainscoting, white linen tablecloths with single rosebuds set in high-fluted vases on each table, tulip lamps, and high-backed cushioned chairs.

A seasonal menu uses the freshest products available and the Sunday brunch buffet (particularly in summer—the fresh fruit season) is, as they say, smashing. All the fresh fruit you can imagine; watermelon, crenshaw melon, honeydews, cantaloupe, strawberries and . . . well, you get the idea. Croissants, muffins, pastries and bagels, chicken liver pâté and a number of cheese selections. On the brunch menu are many more continental favorites like: *coquilles St. Jacques,* eggs Neptune, and of course, "London" mixed grill and eggs Benedict.

Moderate to expensive. Open seven days. Breakfast served Monday through Saturday from 7 to 10:30 A.M. Lunch served Monday through Saturday from 11:30 A.M. to 2:30 P.M. Dinner from 6 to 10 P.M. Sunday brunch from 10:30 A.M. to 2:30 P.M. Reservations accepted. All major credit cards. Full bar. Hotel parking lot. Semi-dressy.

★
WHITE HORSE TAVERNE/Continental/Seafood
637 Sutter Street/San Francisco/Area 2/(415) 771-1708

People are beginning to rediscover this old restaurant that handles seafoods well, has one of the best salad bars in town and features dishes like the artichoke omelette. Located in the Beresford Hotel and open for lunch and breakfast only, it's a favorite with the white-collar workers in the area.

Inexpensive. Open weekdays for breakfast from 7 to 10:45 A.M., Saturday 8 A.M. to 2 P.M. Lunch served 11:30 A.M. to 2:15 P.M. No reservations. All major credit cards. Full bar. Street parking. Casual.

★★
WILL'S FARGO/American
Carmel Valley Village/Carmel Valley/Area 1/(408) 659-2774

Stepping through the tall, carved doors leads you into the nostalgic gas-light era of a gentler America to be greeted by Barbara Fay, hostess/partner. Pause for a bit at Will Fay's old-fashioned bar and exchange thoughts with him over a potent libation or a glass of Calistoga. I'm one of those who always secretly wanted to emulate Will, running a rendezvous where sophisticated folks with a nod to subtle humor might exchange news and views regularly. Oh, well . . .

Every table views, through floor-to-ceiling windows, the tree-shaded garden patio, rich with blooms, an oasis for weary eyes. The comfortable dining room is woodsy, with antique sideboards, prints, photos, signs and compatible appointments.

The dressings with the house salad are offered for your decision; personally, I like the avocado mixture on one side and the blue cheese dressing on the other. Steaks here are always so remarkable that I can't bear to have another elsewhere for a few weeks. Over the years I have enjoyed other entrées, of course, and chef/partner Clifford H. Washington's talents are such that you'll be planning your next meal here after just a few bites. His lamb chops (super-thick) with mint sauce, broiled chicken basted with butter, tarragon and wine, swordfish, filet of sole, even abalone are the yardstick by which you can measure true quality. On Friday and Saturday only, many diners come just for the prime eye of the rib. Exemplary desserts – all chocolate torte, fresh Carmel Valley walnut pie and '49er cheesecake with apricot glaze.

Expensive. Open Tuesday through Sunday. Dinner Tuesday through Thursday from 6 to 10 P.M., Friday and Saturday from 6 to 10:30 P.M., Sunday from 5 to 10 P.M. Reservations advised. All major credit cards. Full bar. Patio. Child's menu. Street parking. Semi-dressy.

★
THE WINDFALL/French/Continental
228 Main Street/Salinas/Area 1/(408) 758-6452

At one time, Salinas did not exactly have as many fine restaurants as did San Francisco, but since 12 September 1978 there has been at least one event that has brightened the dining-out lives of businessmen, ranchers, businesswomen, and those individuals who, from dining experiences away from the nation's lettuce bowl, have acquired epicurean tastes. On that fateful date, The Windfall opened its doors, under the ownership of Bob Farahmand, who oversaw every detail of the construction and watched his architect's concepts flower.

This lovely place, with five separate dining areas plus the bar lounge, expresses casual elegance in the truest sense of the abused term. There is inspired employment of redwood, copper, stained glass, and color photograph murals. The large booths are comfortable, uncrowded, almost designed to deter too early a departure. Ample greenery lends its cool touch which is welcome in the summer, even with the perfect air-conditioning.

Bob tells me that their French-American-continental cuisine has no specials. He smiles, "With us, there are no specials but we think that everything we do is special." Despite this, let me say that not only do I know that The Windfall would be successful in any city, just as it is, but that I have been told and have observed that this is "the" place, with some patrons even driving over twenty five miles from Monterey. One recommendation – order the "Chocolatey Chocolate" – chocolate and coffee ice cream mixed with brandy and covered with dark hot chocolate. They have an ideal wine list with many of my favorites.

Moderate to expensive. Open for lunch weekdays from 11:30 A.M. to 2:30 P.M. Dinner daily from 4:30 to 9:30 P.M. Sunday brunch from 10:30 A.M. to 2 P.M. Reservations advised. Visa, MC, AX. Full bar. Child's menu. Parking lot. Semi-dressy.

In order to obtain the best results from this Guide, please consult "A Few Inside Tips" on page 18.

★ ★
WULFF'S/French
2333 Fair Oaks Boulevard/Sacramento/Area 3/(916) 922-8575

Some years ago, writing about Sacramento, I mentioned that the area was virtually a gustatory wasteland, except for a few expensive places frequented by lobbyists entertaining and educating our legislators. I did praise Wulff's in moderate degree and an now amplifying my comments. Jury is still out about the wasteland.

Horace Wulff opened his French country inn-like dining place in January 1972, to immediate local acceptance. There was only one other restaurant at that time regarded as in a class with some of San Francisco's better places. Horace, a perfectionist, set about providing a worthwhile dining experience. He has never let down his standards of quality food, properly presented and served. Waiters and waitresses are from local colleges, prompt, pleasant.

Wulff's interior is appealing, from the beamed ceiling, the creamy walls, with reproductions of Gobelin tapestries, to the wooden sideboards, ladder-back chairs, mirrors, curtained windows, lampshaded chandeliers, pictures and authentic tile floor. The bar area is apart from the spacious, airy, main room.

Eleven entrées at dinner include a choice *suprême de volaille en croute, rôti de porc à la Robert, coquilles St. Jacques à la Parisienne, lapin sauté au vin blanc, canard à la crème* and other inspired dishes. You are blessed with both soup and *salade* with your dinner main course. Six desserts are highlighted with *profiteroles* —the menuese being cream puff sundae. Espresso, cappuccino and Horace's fine vintages.

Moderate to expensive. Lunch Tuesday through Friday 11:30 A.M. to 2 P.M. Dinner Tuesday through Thursday 6 to 9:30 P.M. Friday and Saturday to 10:30 P.M. Reservations advised. Visa, MC, AX. Full bar. Parking lot. Semi-dressy.

DA★★
XENIOS/Greek/Mediterranean
2237 Polk Street/San Francisco/Area 2/(415) 775-2800

This is The City's first truly elegant, authentic Greek dining place. Owner/host Peter Stavros, in his family tradition, offers classic Greek cuisine from Greece and all the Mediterranean islands—even eight appetizers, the best of which is the eggplant Mama Stella. There are thirteen main courses with nightly specials such as *moussaka, kalamair* (prepared lovingly from Monterey Bay squid with its tender flesh either fried or sautéed in red wine sauce), and *souvlakia,* (broiled *kebab* of marinated spring lamb) that are to marvel over. All are served with an array of fresh vegetables. Another Xenios special, *vlahiko,* consists of marinated lamb cubes with cheese and vegetables, wrapped in *filo* then baked in an earthenware casserole. Alexander must have loved this dish—a world beater. As is the *avgolemono.*

The brick walls, inset with arches, and the placement of mirrors in the intimate dining rooms tend to reflect sound, but the Mediterranean ambiance, complete with tile floor and richly ornate chandelier, flowers, pink linen and slender tapers, bestows a romantic aura. There is a new bar adjoining the restaurant, which incidentally, has doubled the capacity. The sidewalk cafe is nice on a sunny day.

Moderate. Open seven days from 5 P.M. to 1 A.M. Lunch weekdays from 11 A.M. to 3 P.M. Saturday and Sunday brunch 11 A.M. to 3 P.M. Reservations advised. All major credit cards. Full bar. Valet parking. Casual to semi-dressy.

Please be sure to consult "Tipping Made Easy" on page 22 of this Guide.

★ ★ ★
YAMATO/Japanese
717 California Street/San Francisco/Area 2/(415) 397-3456

Japanese fare is light, delicate, cultured cuisine, artfully arranged and ceremoniously served to entice the senses with color, smell, texture – even sound. At Yamato, random words from the menu ripple as musically as water in a pebbly brook – *suimono, miso shiru, sunomono, sashimi;* how much more caressing to the ear than the English translation – broth, bean soup, salad, filet of raw fish.

The menu is constructed around four basic dishes – shrimp tempura, sukiyaki, salmon, and chicken teriyaki – accompanied by a variety of beef, chicken, and lobster dishes. The Imperial Dinner begins with *suimono* (clear broth), crisp *sunomono* (fresh vegetable salad with sweet vinegar), followed by shrimp tempura and seasonal vegetables, dipped in batter and deep-fried. Skewered chicken teriyaki is next; then sukiyaki made with sliced tender beef, *tofu* (soy bean curd), young bamboo shoots, spinach, fresh mushrooms, celery, green and sweet onion, and *shirataki* (yam noodle), prepared at the table by the kimonoed waitress. American potables are available, though sake and Japanese beer make the experience more tranquil. Several years ago, a sushi bar was added to the already extensive menu. Owner Joe Ishizaki cautions against strong drinks before sushi as "you want your taste buds sensitive to the nuances of flavors."

To obtain the best results from this Guide, be sure to consult the map on the various Northern California areas on page 28.

Yamato's distinctions are architectural as well as gastronomical. The interior of forty native woods and fifteen varieties of bamboo was fabricated in Japan and assembled in San Francisco. Shoji-screened private rooms, tatami-matted floors, peeled and polished posts and — spanning the pond — the *nari bashi* or "sound" bridge (with a built-in squeak that announces a patron's passage) create a timeless environment exquisitely appropriate to the cuisine and service.

Moderate to expensive. Open Tuesday through Sunday. Lunch Tuesday through Friday from 11:45 A.M. to 2 P.M. Dinner from 5 to 10 P.M. Reservations advised. All major credit cards. Full bar. Child's menu. Street and garage parking. Casual to semi-dressy.

★ ★
YANK SING/Chinese/Dim Sum
427 Battery Street/San Francisco/Area 2/(415) 362-1640

First, there was the Yank Sing at 671 Broadway, a good (if ordinary) *dim sum* parlor just down the street from the Broadway tunnel. Then, a few years ago, Yank Sing opened a second branch at 53 Stevenson which was, well, different. It had bare brick walls, and a skylight, and colorful banners. It was light and airy and didn't look at all like your basic *dim sum* parlor.

Then, early in 1981, the people behind Yank Sing experienced a profound cultural breakthrough. They opened their third branch, in the midst of San Francisco's financial district, and in the process changed the way that *dim sum* is eaten in San Francisco. By tradition, *dim sum* is served as a late breakfast/lunch. At Yank Sum it is served all day long, a radical departure from the way it used to be done, and a significant blending of the styles of East and West.

For the love of me, the new Yank Sing looks like a good *nouvelle* cuisine restaurant. The rooms are big, the colors subdued, the service (even though it's via rolling carts) is understated, and the help is quite glad to tell you what's what. I asked one waitress to tell me what a particular dish was, and she informed me that it was akin to a Russian *piroshki*. Usually if you ask what a dish is, you get the dish handed to you, so you can find out yourself.

Even though the *dim sum* at Yank Sing is served with certain concessions to western styles, taste remains uncompromised. This is easily some of the best *dim sum* I've ever had. There are three types of spareribs, which are more meaty than they are fatty. The *char siu bao* looks like a Hostess Snoball, but tastes like a dream. There are fine *har gow* and, should dumplings not be right at the moment, excellent orders of chow mein and chow fun (yes, Virginia, chow mein can be a terrific dish if prepared properly). Dishes are a bit more expensive, but a *dim sum* meal at Yank Sing is still cheaper than lunch most anywhere else. And I'm told that the place's to-go annex is changing the eating habits of the entire financial district.

Inexpensive to moderate. Open seven days from 11 P.M. to 3 P.M. Saturday and Sunday from 10 A.M. to 4 P.M. Reservations necessary. All major credit cards. Full bar. Casual to semi-dressy.

★ ★

YENCHING/Chinese/Mandarin

2017 Shattuck Avenue/Berkeley/Area 2/(415) 848-2200

★

939 Kearny Street/San Francisco/Area 2/(415) 397-3543

An offspring of the Yenching on Kearny Street in San Francisco, the Berkeley version is both similar—the northern Chinese menu with Peking duck, princess prawns—and different, in that it is a contemporary, attractive restaurant unlike the stark and sometimes forbidding ancestor. The menu is so vast and unfamiliar to Westerners that it is essential to ask for guidance. All of the employees are gracious and accustomed to such requests, and you will assure yourself of a balanced dinner—the correct proportion of spicy to non-spicy dishes—rather than a come-and-guess-it feast (although the latter can be fun). Cantonese restaurants generally add dishes to the dinner for every person over two ("with three there's egg roll"). Mandarin restaurants, more wisely I think, reduce the price of the individual dinner instead. Lichee fruit is a specialty at Yenching and makes a splendid and refreshing dessert.

Moderate. Open Wednesday through Monday. Lunch from 11:30 A.M. to 3 P.M. Dinner from 5 to 9:30 P.M. San Francisco location open Thursday through Tuesday. Reservations accepted. Visa, MC, AX. Full bar. Wine and beer only at Berkeley location. Street parking. Casual.

In order to obtain the best results from this Guide, please consult "A Few Inside Tips" on page 18.

DA ★ ★
YE OLDE HOOSIER INN/American
1537 North Wilson Way/Stockton/Area 6/(209) 463-0271

I **was** first alerted to this fantastically popular institution when motoring (yes, that's what they used to call it, especially on Sundays) through the Delta town of Stockton one summer day about twenty years back. I spied what appeared to be a menacing crowd attacking a single-story building bearing an ancient buggy on its flat roof. Closer looks revealed that they were quite nicely dressed and, now I could see, were lined up expectantly before an open doorway. Then I spied the lantern-topped tall sign—Ye Olde Hoosier Inn.

Occasional visits over the years have made me a convert, even though absolutely no liquor of any kind is served or welcome. Once, back in 1933, it was a "truck stop" and continued that humbly until 1946 when Charles and Charlotte Dyer came to Stockton from Indiana. Understand that "Hoosier" now? They made an almost instant hit, improving the design over the years.

You will be impressed with The Red Parlor and its antiques, which are not confined to the one room. There are marble-topped tables, tapestried chairs, be-frilled couches, you-name-it. The five dining rooms are rich in red wallpaper with beamed ceilings sporting thought-provoking verse. Over the front door is a flattering proclamation: "Through this portal pass the world's finest people."

On the dinner menu, you will have soup and salad, entrée, dessert and all of the marvelous rolls you can eat. That's real old-time, hot, homemade yeast bread (at breakfast, it's hot muffins, fresh from the oven). Every day of the week there is a special entrée on the dinner— ground beef with garlic butter on Monday, pounded steak with garlic butter on Tuesday, and so on. Sunday's special entrées: baked ham with spiced crab apples, old-fashioned chicken and dumplings, roast turkey with cranberries, or Swiss steak. Always on the menu are: Southern fried chicken, fried prawns, grilled chicken livers, choice steaks with garlic butter, and extra special spareribs with their own barbecue sauce. **Inexpensive to moderate.** Open daily from 7 A.M. to 10 P.M. No reservations. No credit cards. No alcohol. Child's menu. Ample lot parking. Casual.

For best results, consult "How to Use This Guide" on page 25.

★ ★

YET WAH/Northern Chinese

(Locations in San Francisco—three on Clement Street; Larkspur Shopping Center; Concord; Sausalito and Foster City. See phone book for listings.)

The most popular Chinese restaurant among the locals may just be one of the best. A massive menu with literally hundred of dishes is all the more remarkable because every dish is created carefully, no matter how busy all the locations may get or how long the lines. Add the fact that the prices are moderate, the service competent and swift, and you have a restaurant that needs some talking about.

Bill Chan's first location on Clement Street was so well received—some called it a fluke—that when he opened his second one, his loyal patrons began to stir uneasily. By some epicurean miracle, however, since expanding, Yet Wah has attained even greater heights and continued to attract an ever-widening following, though not yet among the tourist or convention groups.

It's difficult to recommend specific dishes because they're all good, but I'll give you a sampling. The lemon chicken (cubed chicken in lemon slices), *kubla* lamb, fish balls with vegetables, frog legs in ginger sauce, barbecued crispy duck with scallions and *hoison* sauce, *musee* pork and pork with fruit sauce are all masterpieces.

And you will find, if you try to get in at the dinner hour, Yet Wah is no longer a discovery, but has been mutually acclaimed by restaurant writers and the general public alike.

Moderate. Hours vary at different locations. Reservations for six or more only. All major credit cards. Full bar. Valet or lot parking. Casual to semi-dressy.

★

YOSHIDA-YA/Japanese

2909 Webster Street/San Francisco/Area 2/(415) 346-3431

Entering the brick tile foyer of Yoshida-Ya Restaurant is like stepping onto the streets of Kyoto, Japan. The restaurant's vivid color and nooks and niches, as well as the arresting sight and scent of food preparation, are an invitation to explore and enjoy Japanese food in a gracious, traditional setting.

Kushiyaki—a traditional favorite that is served in open air stalls on Japan's city streets—is Yoshida-Ya's specialty. This style of cuisine is distinguished by the *"kushi"* or bamboo skewer on which chunks of fresh seafood, meat and vegetables are impaled. Popular variations of the *"kushi"* theme are *yakitori* (chicken, beef, seafood and vegetables dipped in a special *yakitori* sauce and broiled over a charcoal fire) and *kushi-katsu* (breaded beef, chicken, pork, seafood or vegetable cutlet deep-fried on a skewer and served with a special sauce).

Given two days notice, the chef will plan and prepare a personalized *omakase* (or "leave it up to the chef") dinner including special appetizers. *Omakase* dinners with six or more courses begin at $35 per person. **Moderate to expensive.** Open Sunday through Thursday for dinner from 5:30 to 10:30 P.M. Friday and Saturday to 11 P.M. Reservations required. All major credit cards. Full bar. Street parking. Semi-dressy.

★
YUET LEE/Chinese
1300 Stockton Street/San Francisco/Area 2/(415) 982-6020

A h, the painful frustrations of those elusive items that are written in Chinese on walls and on mirrors. I'm in agreement with food maven Calvin Trillin that those mysteries written in cursive Mandarin script are what most Chinese restaurants really make well. Consider then Yuet Lee, where the writing on the walls is in Chinese, but the waiters show an uncommon willingness to do a bit of translating. Mysteries revealed! The secrets unfurled! With a bit of patience, you can discover that the writing on the walls refers not only to the generalized dishes of the day, but also to the specific seafoods that are available. Thus, a type of seabass stir-fried with mushrooms and (in season) asparagus is touted, along with those tiny black shelled clams that you can purchase by the bucket load at any good Chinese market. Here, they're sauced with a purée of brown beans and lubricated with enough garlic and ginger to notably raise your body temperature.

Stick to the printed menu and you'll eat well, if less adventurously. *Jook* is popular here, as it is in much of China, as an inexpensive early meal. This ubiquitous rice gruel comes garnished with anything imaginable—from preserved duck eggs (an acquired taste) to more easily accepted slivers of chicken, beef and fish. Noodles (chow mein and chow fun) are available in copious varieties, in soup and not. My favorite dish, though, is *lo han chai*, a vegetarian plate which I first tasted in a version cooked by the Taoist Society of Hong Kong. Yuet Lee's rendition offers only a fraction of the vegetables served by the Taoist's, but its flavors are elegantly melded. This is vegetarian cooking at its very best. **Inexpensive.** Open Wednesday through Monday from 11 A.M. to 3 A.M. No credit cards. No alcohol. Street parking. Casual.

Please be sure to consult "Tipping Made Easy" on page 22 of this Guide.

★

ZACK'S BY THE BAY/American/Burgers
Bridgeway and Turney Street/Sausalito/Area 3/(415) 332-9779

Where the action is. Where the girls are. Where the boys are. This huge multi-level swingery has bands from Wednesday through Sunday, turtle racing every Wednesday night and live music and dancing every night, and filling, youth-oriented food like broiled burgers and tuna salad. The shish kebab steak and salads are above average. Sam Zakessian has catered to swarms of tourists and several generations of locals since 1958.

Inexpensive to moderate. Open seven days. Monday through Thursday from 7 A.M. to 7 P.M. Friday through Sunday from 7 A.M. to 10 P.M. No reservations. No credit cards. Entertainment. Full bar. Patio. View of Richardson Bay. Lot parking. Casual.

★ ★

ZOLA'S/French
1722 Sacramento Street/San Francisco/Area 2/(415) 775-3311

After the enthusiastic recommendation of a number of foodies, that breed of hardy diners who relentlessly seek out the best food wherever it may be, I couldn't wait to go to Zola's. And they were right. In this simple, whitewashed atmosphere, chef/co-owner Catherine Pantsios serves some marvelous dishes that are creating as much excitement as the Jeremiah Tower era at Chez Panisse. Pantsios likes to research recipes and is somewhat of a food historian. Many of the dishes and combinations on the small menu that seem new, are not. They are old dishes brought up to date in a flawless manner. Sautéed calf's liver with mustard butter, roast pork with homemade sauerkraut, and an array of stews, make a personal statement about the careful preparation and presentation that sets this small restaurant (opened in 1983) apart. Slow cooked braises of lamb shanks, cassoulets of lamb with homemade pork sausages, sweetbreads braised with black mushrooms, and an extraordinary veal tongue served with French lentils are among the favorites here.

Desserts may include whole pears poached in wine with peppercorns and orange peel, or the "fresh fruit fool," a heavy cream whipped with rhubarb and served in a wine glass, or espresso custard. Wines are fairly priced, intelligently selected accompaniments to the menu. **Expensive.** Open for dinner Tuesday through Sunday from 6 to 11 P.M. Reservations advised. Visa, MC, DC. Wine and beer only. Lot parking. Semi-dressy.

★
ZUNI CAFE/California/Continental
1658 Market Street/San Francisco/Area 2/(415) 552-2522

The immediate impression here is southwest, with whitewashed walls, a high ceiling and Indian-print woven upholstery. There is an American-California feeling to the fresh simple foods. The cold seafood bar offers an endless choice of oysters (Cape Cod, Portugese, Kumamoto . . .), clams and even Dungeness crab. The menu changes daily and offers innovative appetizers; a variety of salads (always a mixed garden lettuce combination with a savory cheese); light entrées (a good idea in body health-conscious California) like grilled scallops with ginger *buerre blanc* and shoestring potatoes and varying presentations of risotto. Main courses may include grilled rib-eye steak with bourbon-mustard butter and rabbit braised with chanterelles, Smithfield ham and tarragon. Desserts are surprisingly good, with unexpected choices like walnut torte with maple crème Anglaise and Indian corn pudding. The wine list is sizeable and apt for this small, multi-level establishment. Fresh juices, hot Ovaltine, espresso and cappucino are extra touches as well as a list of bottled waters. Brunch is a special pleasure at the Zuni. **Moderate.** Open Tuesday through Sunday. Lunch weekdays from 11:30 A.M. to 3 P.M. Dinner Tuesday through Sunday from 6 to 11 P.M. Brunch Sunday from 11 A.M. to 3 P.M. Reservations advised. Visa, MC, AX. Full bar. Street parking. Casual.

In order to obtain the best results from this Guide, be sure to read the French, German, Italian and Oriental menu translators on pages 399 to 404 of this Guide.

MENU TRANSLATOR

Guide to German Menus

German	English
Abendessen	Dinner
Apfel	Apple
Apfelmus	Applesauce
Auflauf	Soufflé
Austern	Oysters
Backhuhn	Breaded, fried chicken
Backwerk	Cakes
Belegte Brote	Open sandwiches
Bier	Beer
Birnen	Pears
Blumenkohl	Cauliflower
Bockwurst	A rather heavy type of frankfurter
Brathuhn	Roast chicken
Bratwurst	A pork sausage
Brot	Bread
Brüehe	Consommé
Eiskaffee	Iced coffee
Ente	Duck
Erbsen	Peas
Erdbeeren	Strawberries
Fisch	Fish
Forelle	Trout
Fruchtsalat	Fruit salad
Frühstück	Breakfast
Garneien	Shrimp
Gebratene Lammkeule	Roast leg of lamb
Gekochte Eier	Boiled eggs
Gemischter Salat	Mixed salad
Gemüse	Vegetables
Grüne Bohnen	Green beans
Grüner Salat	Lettuce
Gurke	Cucumber
Gurken	Cucumbers
Gut durchgebraten	Well-done
Halb roh	Rare
Huhn	Chicken
Hummer	Lobster
Kaffee	Coffee
Kaffeekuchen	Coffee cake
Kalbfleisch	Veal
Kalbskotellett	Veal cutlet
Karotten	Carrots
Kartoffeln	Potatoes
Käse	Cheese
Käseplatte	Cheese platter
Knoblauch	Garlic
Lammscrippchen	Lamb chop
Milch	Milk
Mittagessen	Lunch
Muschein	Mussels
Nachspeisen	Desserts
Obst	Fruit
Omelette	Omelette
Pfannkuchen	Pancakes
Pfirsich	Peach
Pfaumen	Plums
Quark	Cottage cheese
Rindsbraten	Roast beef
Roggenbrot	Rye bread
Rosenkohl	Brussel sprouts
Rosinen	Raisins
Rühreier	Scrambled eggs
Salz	Salt
Schweinsrippchen	Pork chop
Schweizerkäse	Swiss cheese
Senf	Mustard
Speck	Bacon
Spiegeleier	Fried eggs
Tee	Tea
Tomaten	Tomatoes
Weissbrot	White bread
Würstchen	Sausages
Zitrone	Lemon
Zucker	Sugar
Zwieback	A type of dry-toast

Guide to French Menus

Abricôt	Apricot	**Châteaubriand**	Filet of steak
Agneau	Lamb	**Chaud**	Hot
Ail	Garlic	**Choix**	Choice
Airelles	Berries	**Chou**	Cabbage
Alose	Shad	**Choucroute**	Sauerkraut
Aloyau	Sirloin of beef	**Chou-fleur**	Cauliflower
Ananas	Pineapple	**Citron**	Lemon
Apértif	Any appetizer drink taken before a meal	**Coq au vin**	Chicken cooked in a wine sauce containing on-ions, ham, mushrooms, etc.
Artichaut	Artichoke		
Asperges	Asparagus		
Assiette	Platter; a plate	**Coquilles St. Jacques**	Scallops in sauce
Babeurre	Buttermilk		
Béchamel	A thick white sauce	**Côte de boeuf**	Ribs of beef
Beurre	Butter	**Crème**	Cream
Bifteck	Beefsteak	**Crevettes**	Shrimp
Bisque	A soup made from shellfish	**Croissant**	A typical breakfast or teatime pas-try made in the shape of a cres-cent (roll)
Blanquette d'agneau	A stew of lamb made with mushrooms and onions		
Blinis	Thin, unsweetened pancakes	**Cuiller**	Spoon
		Déjeuner	Lunch: also used occasionally to mean breakfast (*petit déjeuner*)
Bombe	Dessert of ices, whipped cream and various fruits		
Bordeaux	Claret (wine)	**Digestif**	Any after-dinner liqueur
Bouillabaisse	A fish stew made with saffron, wine and herbs	**Dindon**	Turkey
		Douce	Sweet
Bouillon	Broth	**Eau**	Water
Bourgogne	Burgundy (wine)	**Entrecôte**	Rib steak
Brocoli	Broccoli	**Entrecôte chateau**	Large, thick steak
Brouillé	Scrambled		
Brut	Dry (as applied to wines); unsweetened	**Epinards**	Spinach
		Escalopes de veau	Thin slices of veal; veal scallops
Cacao	Cocoa		
Café au lait	Coffee with hot milk	**Escargots**	Snails
Canard	Duck	**Faisan**	Pheasant
Caneton	Duckling	**Filet de boeuf**	Filet of beef
Carotte	Carrot	**Foie**	Liver
Carré de porc	Filet of pork	**Fourchette**	Fork
Cerises	Cherries	**Froid**	Cold
Cervelles	Brains	**Fromage**	Cheese
Champignons	Small mushrooms	**Gâteau**	Cake
Chantilly	Served with whipped cream	**Gigot d'agneau**	Leg of lamb
		Glace	Ice; ice cream
Chapon	Capon	**Hareng mariné**	Pickled or mari-nated herring

Haricots verts	Green beans	**Pomme de**	Potato
Homard	Lobster	**terre**	
Huîtres	Oysters	**Porc**	Pork
Jambon	Ham	**Potage**	Soup
Jus de fruit	Fruit juice	**Poulet**	Chicken
Lait	Milk	**Prix fixe**	At a fixed price
Laitue	Lettuce	**Ragoût**	Stew
Langouste	European lobster; crawfish	**Riz**	Rice
		Rosbif	Roast beef
Lapin	Rabbit	**Rôti de veau**	Roast veal
Légumes	Vegetables	**Salade**	Salad
Lyonnaise	Served with onions	**Sauce**	A cream sauce
Mignons de	Very small cuts of	**Allemande**	made with egg
boeuf	beef		yolks and
Moules	Mussels		lemon juice
Moutarde	Mustard	**Sauce Barcey**	Sauce made from
Noisettes	Boneless lamb		fish concen-
d'agneau	chops		trate, white
Oeufs	Eggs		wine, and
Oeufs pochés	Poached eggs		shallots
Oeufs sur la	Fried eggs	**Sauce**	A sauce made with
plat		**béarnaise**	eggs, butter,
Oignon	Onion		shallots etc., a
Omelette	Omelette		classic sauce
Pain	Bread		with steak
Pain grillé	Toast	**Sauce**	Orange sauce for
Pâté de foie	Fine goose liver	**Bigarade**	duck
gras	paste with	**Saucisson**	Sausage
	truffles	**Sec**	Dry
Pâtisserie	Pastry	**Sel**	Salt
Pêche	Peach	**Service**	Service (charge)
Petit marmite	A classic French	**compris**	included
	beef soup con-	**Service non**	Service (charge)
	taining vegeta-	**compris**	not included
	bles, toasted	**Sucre**	Sugar
	bread, etc.	**Tasse**	Cup
Petits pois	Small green peas	**Thé**	Tea
Poire	Pear	**Truite**	Trout
Poisson	Fish	**Veau**	Veal
Poitrine de	Breast of veal	**Verre**	Glass
veau			
Pomme	Apple		

Guide to Italian Menus

Acqua	Water	**Formaggio**	Cheese
Aglio	Garlic	**Fragole**	Strawberries
Agnellino	Baby lamb	**Frittata**	Omelette
Agnello	Roast lamb	**Frutta**	Fruit
arrosto		**Funghi**	Mushrooms
Al burro	With butter	**Gamberi**	Shrimp
Al forno	Baked	**Gelati di frutta**	Fruit ices
Alla	Broiled	**Gelato**	Ice cream
griglia		**Gelato di**	Ice cream
Anitra	Duck	crema	
Arancia	Orange	**Granatina**	Hamburger patty
Arista	Roast loin of pork	**Granchio**	Crab
Birra	Beer	**Insalata**	Salad
Biscotti	Cookies	**Insalata mista**	Mixed salad
Bistecca	Steak	**Istingolo**	Stew; *ragoût*
Brodo	Broth	**Lardo**	Bacon; lard
Bue	Beef	**Lasagne**	Broad noodles
Burro	Butter	imbottite	baked in layers
Caffé	Coffee		with sauce and
Caldo	Hot; warm		cheese
Cannelloni	Rolled noodles,	**Latte**	Milk
	stuffed with	**Lattuga**	Lettuce
	meat, baked in	**Legumi**	Vegetables
	sauce	**Limone**	Lemon
Cappone	Capon	**Linguini**	Narrow noodles
Carciofi	Artichokes	**Lumache**	Snails
Carne	Meat	**Maiale**	Pork
Carne tritata	Chopped meat	**Manzo**	Beef
Castrato	Mutton	**Mela**	Apple
Cioccolata	Chocolate	**Merenda**	Snack, small in-
Cipolle	Onions		between meal
Colazione	Lunch	**Meringa di**	Chocolate
Coltello	Knife	cioccolata	meringue
Costolame di	Ribs of beef	**Minestra**	Entrée; either
bue			pasta or soup
Costolette di	Lamb chops	**Montone**	Mutton
agnello		**Mostarda**	Mustard
Costolette di	Pork chops	**Muscoli**	Mussels
maiale		**Noci**	Nuts
Cozze	Mussels	**Olio**	Oil
Crostacei	Shellfish	**Ostriche**	Oysters
Dolci	Sweets, desserts	**Pane**	Bread
Fagiano	Pheasant	**Pane tostato**	Toast
Fegatini di	Chicken livers	**Panna**	Cream
pollo		**Pasta**	Noodles, macaroni,
Filetto alla	Filet of beef		spaghetti
mignon		**Patate**	Potatoes
Filetto di	Creamed breast of	**Pepe**	Pepper
tacchino alla	turkey	**Pera**	Pear
crema		**Pesca**	Peach
Forchetta	Fork		

Pesce	Fish	**S.Q.**	An abbreviation indicating that the item is charged according to size
Pesto	Green garlic sauce		
Piatti del giorno	The daily specials		
Piselli	Peas		
Pollame	Poultry	**Stracciatella**	Bouillon containing beaten eggs and cheese
Pollo	Chicken		
Polpette	Meatballs		
Pomidoro	Tomato	**Stufatino**	Veal stew
Pranzo	Dinner	**Succo di arancia**	Orange juice
Prima colazione	Breakfast		
		Succo di frutta	Fruit juice
Prosciutto	Smoked ham, served paper thin	**Tacchino**	Turkey
Riccio	Sea urchins; a Mediterranean shellfish	**Tavola fredda**	Cold buffet (literally cold table)
		Tè	Tea
Riso	Rice	**Tordi allo spiedo**	Small birds roasted on a spit
Risotto	Rice dish	**Torta**	Cake; pie, tart
Rosbif	Roast beef	**Trota**	Trout
Sale	Salt	**Turnedo**	Filet of beef
Salsa	Sauce	**Umido**	A stew
Salsicci	Sausage	**Uova**	Eggs
Saltimbocca alla romana	Veal and ham cooked in wine	**Uva**	Grapes
Scallopine di vitello alla bolognese	Veal slices, with ham and cheese	**Valdostana di vitello**	Veal with ham and cheese
		Vermicelli	Very fine variety of spaghetti
Scungilli	Conch, a shellfish	**Vitello**	Veal
Sogliola alla belia mugnaia	Filet of sole with sauce	**Vongole**	Clams
		Zabaglione	A foamy egg dessert, made with wine
Sorbetto	Sherbet		
Spezzatino di vitello	Veal stew	**Zucca**	Squash
		Zucchero	Sugar
Spinaci	Spinach	**Zuppa**	Soup
Spumoni	A rich ice cream usually filled with fruit and nuts		

Guide to Oriental Menus

Bulkogi	Korean barbecued beef, usually cooked at table on a *hwaro*	**Huo Kuo**	Chinese hot pot, in which various ingredients (fish, vegetables, meat) are cooked at table
Cha su	Barbecued pork		
Gyoza	Pan fried pork dumplings		

Hwaro Korean gas brazier used for cooking *bulkogi*

Kim chee (Hot! hot!) Any number of Korean pickles, all of which are very hot

Koo jul pan A Korean appetizer plate, in which sundry cold ingredients are served on a Lazy Susan for wrapping in pancakes

Mee krob The classic Thai dish of crisp rice noodles, egg, pork and shrimp

Miso Fermented soy bean paste

Miso cha su Fermented soy bean paste and barbecued pork, in this case used as a flavoring for noodles

Onigiri Japanese rice balls, wrapped in seafood, usually containing pickled plum bits or salted salmon

Oshinko Pickled vegetables

Oshi-style A variety of sushi in which the rice is formed within a box press rather than being wrapped in seaweed

Pud Thai Thin Thai noodles flavored with peanuts, chile, bean sprouts and shrimp

Ramen Chinese noodles served in pork broth in Japanese restaurants

Sake Japanese rice wine, usually served warm, and consumed from porcelain thimbles

Sashimi Slivers of raw fish or other seafood, served as a rule in a simple yet elegant fashion

Shinsulla A Korean hot pot, in which various ingredients are stewed at table

Sushi Japanese canapés of vinegared rice topped with seafood (but not always) and eaten by hand

Tanmen A noodle dish containing Chinese cabbage, mushrooms, bamboo shoots, carrots, and spinach in a pork broth

Tempura A school of Japanese cooking involving deep-frying just about anything in batter

Teriyaki Beef, chicken or fish grilled with a sweet sauce

Udon Thick, wheat flour noodles

Wonton Meat and shrimp filled dumplings in thin egg noodle wrappers

Yakatabune Combination dish of two types of cold noodles served with a side of tempura in a small wooden boat-like container

Yaki soba Chinese noodles cooked on a grill with a variety of vegetables and meats and served in Japanese restaurants

WHAT YOU NEED TO KNOW
ABOUT SEAFOOD

Species	Other Names	Where Caught	Ways Most Often Served
Catfish	Bullhead, Blue Channel	Great Lakes, other United States lakes, inland rivers, ponds, creeks	Southern Catfish Stew, Deep-fried Catfish with Hush Puppies
Ocean Catfish	Wolf Fish	Iceland, Germany, England, Denmark, Norway	
Cod	Codfish, Scrod (Baby)	New England, Middle Atlantic, Pacific Coast, Iceland, England, Norway, Germany, Denmark, Canada	Baked Cod with Cream, Stick or Portions, Served with Zesty Mustard Sauce, Sandwich Portions, Fish and Chips
Croaker	Hardhead	New Jersey, Atlantic Coast to Texas Gulf	Chowder, Fish Chowder, Pan-fried, Deep-fried
Flounder	Sole, Fluke, Blackback Yellowtail	Northwest Coast, Gulf Coast, New England, Middle Atlantic, Canada, Denmark, England, Iceland	Grilled Steaks, Baked Fillets in Orange Sauce, Pan-fried, Deep-fried
Grouper	Red, Black, Yellowfin, Speckled Hind, Gag, Scamp	South Atlantic, Gulf	Fillet Rollup with Spanish Sauce
Haddock	Scrod (Baby)	New England, Canada, Iceland, Norway, England	Fillets in Wine and Tarragon Sauce, Finnan Haddie, Baked au Gratin, Hearty Fish Sticks, Portions in Sandwiches
Hake	White, Red, Squirrel, Ling, "Deep-sea Fillet"	Gulf of St. Lawrence south to North Carolina	Baked, Chowder
Halibut		Pacific Coast, Alaska, New England	Halibut Steaks in Herb Sauce, Baked, Stuffed, Broiled
Lake Perch	Yellow Perch	Great Lakes, other United States lakes, inland rivers	Deep-fried, Pan-fried
Lake Trout	Togue	lakes of North America	Trout Amandine, Baked Whole with Herb Stuffing

Species	Other Names	Where Caught	Ways Most Often Served
Mackerel Spanish	Blue, American	New England, Norway, South Atlantic, Gulf	Broiled or Baked, Seafood Casserole
King	Cero, Kingfish	South Atlantic, Gulf	
Mullet	Striped, White, Jumping, Silver	Atlantic (Florida to North Carolina), Gulf (Florida to Texas)	Baked atop Herb-Seasoned Stuffing
Ocean Perch	Rosefish, Redfish	New England, Northwest Coast, Iceland, Germany, England, Norway, Canada	Pan-fried, Baked in White Wine Sauce, Perch Amandine
Pollock	"Deep-Sea Fillet," Boston Bluefish	Cape Cod to Cape Breton	Baked, Broiled with Herb Sauce
Rainbow Trout		Northwestern United States (commercial fish farms), Denmark, Japan	Trout Amandine, Charcoal Broiled or Baked with Lemon Butter, Sauté Meunière
Red Snapper		Gulf, Middle Atlantic, Formosa	Poached Snapper, Snapper Fillet Amandine, Planked, Charcoal Broiled
Salmon Sockeye Chinook Silver Pink Chum	Red Spring, King Silversides, Coho Humpback Fall	Pacific Coast, Alaska, North Atlantic, Great Lakes	Poached or Baked, Salmon Steaks Florentine, Planked, Charcoal Broiled
Scup	Porgy, Paugy	Southern New England to North Carolina	Baked, Broiled with Lime and Butter, Pan-fried
Sea Bass Black and White		Pacific Coast	Sautéed Bass with Tartar Sauce, Baked Stuffed Bass, Pan-fried
Common	Blackfish, Black Sea Bass	New England, Middle and South Atlantic	
Sea Herring	Atlantic Herring, Pacific Herring	New England, Middle Atlantic, Iceland, Denmark, Norway, Germany, England, Scotland, Holland, Sweden (virtually worldwide)	Herring in Sour Cream or Wine Sauce

Species	Other Names	Where Caught	Ways Most Often Served
Sea Trout Gray Spotted White	Weakfish, Squeteagues Speckled Trout White Trout, Sand Trout	Middle and South Atlantic Middle and South Atlantic, Gulf Gulf	Canapés, Fish Cakes, Trout Amandine, Pan-fried Trout, Sauté with Lemon Butter
Shad	Buck, Roe or White Shad	coastal rivers Maine to Florida, Washington to California	Broiled with Bacon, Baked with Toasted Sesame Topping, Pan-fried
Smelts	Whitebait, Surf Smelt, Grunion, Eulachon River Smelt, Columbia River Smelt, Silverside, Jack Smelt, Bay Smelt	North Atlantic, Pacific Coast, Columbia River, and bays from Mexico to Canada, Great Lakes	Pan-fried, Broiled
Sole	Rex, Petrale, Sand, Grey, Lemon Sole Dover, English	Pacific Coast, Alaska, Canada, Atlantic Coast, England, Holland, Belgium, Denmark, England	Sole Amandine, Baked Fillet of Sole with Seafood Stuffing, Charcoal Broiled with Lemon Butter
Striped Bass	Rock, Rock Bass, Rock Fish	Atlantic Coast, Pacific Coast	Baked with Herb Stuffing, Pan-fried with Mushrooms
Tuna Albacore Yellowfin Skipjack Blue Fin Little		Pacific Coast Pacific Coast Southern waters Atlantic and Pacific Coast Atlantic (all tuna worldwide)	Tuna Salad Scalloped Tuna Casserole Marinated and Grilled
Whitefish		Great Lakes, Minnesota, Canada	Baked, Broiled, Poached with Hollandaise
Whiting	Frostfish, Silver Hake	New England, England	Breaded and Deep-fried

Species	Other Names	Where Caught	Ways Most Often Served
Clams			
Butter		Pacific Coast, Alaska	Scalloped Clams, New England Quahog Cakes, Clam Chowder, Fried, Paella, Clam Cocktail
Hard	Quahog, Hard Shell,	New England, Middle and South Atlantic	
Littleneck	Cherrystone	Pacific Coast, Alaska	
Razor		Pacific Coast, Alaska	Steamed Clams
Soft	Soft Shell	New England, Middle Atlantic	
Surf	Skimmer	Middle Atlantic	
Crabs			
Blue		Middle and South Atlantic, Gulf	Deviled Crab Cakes, Crab Mornay, Crab Bisque, Crab Louis, Avocado Stuffed with Crab Salad, Sautéed in Butter
Dungeness		Pacific Coast, Alaska	
King		Alaska	
Stone		Florida, Texas	
Lobsters			
Northern	Maine	New England, Canada	Lobster Thermidor, Lobster Newburg, Lobster Stew, Broiled Lobster, Broiled Stuffed Lobster
Rock	Rock Lobster Tail	South Africa, South Atlantic, Gulf, Pacific Coast, Australia, New Zealand, Brazil, Equador,	
Spiny		British Honduras, Haiti	
Oysters			
Eastern		New England, Middle and South Atlantic, Gulf	Oyster Stew, Oysters Rockefeller, Oysters on the Half Shell, Fried Oysters
Pacific	Japanese	Pacific Coast, Japan	
Olympia	Western	Pacific Coast	
Scallops			
Bay		Middle and South Atlantic, New England, Gulf, Canada, New England, Middle Atlantic, Australia, Alaska	Scallops au Gratin, Fried, Scallop Stew, Broiled Scallops
Calico			
Sea			
Shrimp	Prawn	South Atlantic, Gulf	Shrimp Creole, Paella, Shrimp de Jonghe, Shrimp Egg Foo Young, Shrimp Curry, Pickled Shrimp, Shrimp Cocktail, Shrimp Newburg, Breaded, Deep-fried, Tempura, Jambalaya
White			
Brown and		Alaska,	
Pink		Maine, Mexico,	
Alaska		French Guinea, Dutch	
Pink		Guinea (imports virtually	
California		worldwide)	
Gay			

REGIONAL STYLES OF CHINESE COOKING
by Hugh Carpenter

Chinese cooking can be divided into four regional styles located around the major areas of Canton, Szechwan, Peking and Shanghai. As for the term "Mandarin," rather than denoting a style, this term is used by Chinese restaurants to indicate that they offer some of the best known dishes from all the various regions of China.

Cantonese food: Cantonese cooking emphasizes color and textural contrasts, strives to accent the natural flavor of ingredients, and excels in quick stir-fry dishes. This region is famous for steamed dumplings (*dim sum*), shark's fin soup, frogs' legs, pigeon recipes, and snake. Among their favorite seasonings, they prefer light soy sauce over heavy soy, and cook with ginger, garlic, salted, fermented black beans, oyster sauce, sweet and sour concoctions, and curry.

Szechwanese food: The Szechwanese use more seasonings and in greater variety than other provinces. Authentically prepared, their food tastes fiery hot and spicy. Besides relying heavily on fresh and dried chiles, their cooks use hot chili oil, chili paste, hot bean sauce, ginger, lots of garlic, heavy soy rather than light soy, the highly aromatic Szechwanese pepper, sesame oil, sesame seed paste, star anise, and cinnamon.

Peking food: A wheat (not rice) growing area, the northern Chinese eat a geat deal of noodles, steamed breads and stuffed dumplings, and season their food with lots of garlic, scallions, leeks, as well as using brown bean sauce, heavy soy sauce, wines and vinegars. The province of Shantung is known for its fruits, apples and pears, as well as for its great chefs. Many refer to Peking as the culinary center of north China, but it has no native cooking style, borrowing instead on styles of the surrounding provinces and from chefs who journey to the capital from all over China.

Shanghai food: Shanghai and the cooks of eastern China excel in cooking fresh and salt water fish and shellfish to bring forth the natural flavor. But many dishes have more sauce and are more robust tasting than the foods found elsewhere in China. Meats cook longer, often seasoned with generous amounts of soy sauce and rock sugar, or her cooks braise meat in a "master sauce" kept "alive" by reserving a small amount of the sauce to add to the next braised dish. Even when stir-frying, the cooking process is lengthened by reducing the heat and simmering the food until tender.

SOME WINE TALK

by Paul Wallach

If it is true, as the professional wine experts enjoy telling us, that in vino veritas ("In wine there is truth"), it should also be known that in wine there is pompous pettifoggery as well.

I vividly recall attending a Bacchus Society dinner presided over by a renowned guru of wines and attended by the practitioners of the new wine snobbism. Eyes closed, Mr. Guru solemnly cupped his hands tightly over his glass, then fluttered his hands toward his head as though washing his face with the scent. Immediately the fifty-odd diners began their fluttering and laving, a spectacle that unnerved the professional serving staff, who struggled—as I did—to retain composure. To give you an idea of the pretense in the room, I was the only one to identify the mystery wine (a Muscadet) and my palate is a mere notch or two above Archie Bunker's.

I don't mean to imply that everything about the study of wine is similarly silly. On the contrary, it is a deeply enriching form of art appreciation for those who are seriously inclined. It's negative value, however, is the mystique imposed by many would-be experts that makes simple enjoyment of wine a complex and confusing ritual.

While most restaurants seem to perpetuate ritual for ritual's sake, there is actually sound, practical reasoning behind most of wine's pomp and circumstance. If you understand the reasons behind this seeming fal-da-ra, you'll be one step ahead of your waiter, because very often he doesn't have the slightest idea why he's doing what he's doing.

Hopefully, after reading this brief chapter you will feel more secure about ordering wine in restaurants, and in dealing with sometimes pompous waiters.

First of all you are the *boss!* Order the wine *you* want to drink, with the dish *you* want to order. If you enjoy a dry white chardonnay with prime rib or a steak, it is your palate and your right to do so. If you wish to drink Chateau d'Yquem (the world's greatest white dessert wine) with enchiladas, or a rich red pinot noir with trout, that is your business.

If the waiter looks at you a little funny or tries to talk you out of a personal favorite, ignore him. Always remember two things: he is there to serve you, and you are the one that is paying the check. On the other hand, if you really don't know what to order, you're almost forced to trust his judgement.

Basically, there are two ways to order wine in a restaurant: house wine (by the litre, half-litre or glass) and corked wine (usually by the bottle or half-bottle). Let's deal with house wine first.

Almost without exception, house wines are the same wines you can buy at your local retail store in gallon or half-gallon jugs. While there are many sound, pleasant "jug" wines (in fact, with the present surplus of quality grapes, they're better than ever), unfortunately, most restaurants select their house wine on the basis of price alone. Therefore, where the house wine at one restaurant may be a crisp, dry wine produced in the North Coast, another may offer some too-sweet wines from the Central Valley. You'll usually pay as much for the bad as the good.

Keep in mind also that terms such as chablis and burgundy have no real meaning when it comes to house wines. These terms indicate nothing more than blended white and red wines, respectively.

As to price, a good house wine in most restaurants sells for $5 to $7 the liter—$1.00 to $2.00 the glass. If the wine list is reasonably priced, you can usually find more dollar value by purchasing a cork-finished bottle for only a dollar or two more.

Discussing bottle wines is a whole different ball game. Here is where most of the ritual comes in, and here, also, you have to do more than choose a color (red, white or pink). On a good wine list there may be eight or ten wines of the same type from different producers and different vintages. In such a case you should order something you're familiar with, be prepared to pay the price of being adventurous, or, if he or she seems knowledgeable, trust your waiter to make a recommendation.

Assuming that you have the wine list in hand, and making the further assumption that you are bravely selecting your own wine, I highly recommend that you order the wine by the number that proceeds each wine on almost every wine list you're likely to come in contact with.

The reason for this is two-fold. First off, it saves you the embarrassment of trying to pronounce some exotic French or German name; and secondly, even if you did say it properly, the waiter probably wouldn't understand you, because chances are he doesn't know how to pronounce it. Besides, if it is an extensive wine list, the wines are stored by number, not name, and the waiter will have to either ask you for the number or take some time to look it up himself.

Now the service ritual begins in earnest. First, the bottle is presented. All that is really required of you is a nod of approval or some comment to the effect that this is the wine you ordered. You'd be surprised how often a different brand, or vintage, or even kind of wine is brought to the table. It is definitely worth your while to look up for a moment and make sure you're getting what you're paying for.

Next comes the cutting of the foil and the opening of the bottle. More ritual — the cork is removed and placed, usually , at your left hand. This presentation of the cork has its purpose, too.

For a cork to properly seal a bottle of wine, the bottle should be stored on its side, keeping the wine in contact with the cork. This keeps the cork wet and swollen, providing the seal that was intended. If a bottle is stored upright for any length of time, the cork will dry out permitting the entrance of minute quantities of air which start the wine on its way to becoming vinegar.

When the cork is presented, pinch it up between thumb and forefinger, squeeze gently at the end which has been (or should have been) in contact with the wine. The cork should be slightly pliable. If you want to really get into cork inspection, wave the wet end, gently, just under your nose, about an inch away; it should smell of wine, not cork. If you feel uncomfortable about this particular part of the ritual, simply ignore the cork and the waiter will go ahead with serving.

Now the pour. The waiter will pour a small portion, perhaps a half-ounce into the glass of the host (or the person who ordered the wine). This is your opportunity for final approval. It is extremely rare to receive a bad (unsound) bottle of wine, but it does happen.

Swirl the wine in the glass a bit to release its fragrance. Don't be bashful about smelling it because much can be discovered from the aroma; take a small sip, work it around your mouth; swallow. Nine hundred and ninety-nine times out of thousand the wine will be fine, and with another nod of approval the waiter will proceed to pour for the rest of your party, filling your glass last.

So, you see, the "ritual" has its purpose, and it is all very simple when you understand it. But if it still makes you uncomfortable, simply instruct the waiter to go ahead and pour as soon as he opens the bottle.

A couple of added notes that should add to your enjoyment:

Do not overchill your white wines. The colder a wine is, the less of it you can taste or smell. In fact, this has long been a trick of wine merchants and restaurateurs. When they have a mediocre white or rose wine with many faults, they will chill it almost to the point of freezing. The customer can smell nothing and can taste little more than alcohol.

If you are going to drink red wine with your meal, ask that it be brought to the table and opened immediately. Without going into great detail and explanation, red wines, almost without exception, taste better if the bottle is opened awhile before you are going to drink them. Even if the entrée with which you will drink your red wine is an hour away insist that your red wine be opened to "breathe." You needn't sample it until the companion course appears, just let the open bottle sit on the table.

As mentioned before, if you have a favorite wine-food combination, no matter how unorthodox, please your own personal tastes. If you are still learning and experimenting, though, you will be better off staying with the traditional combinations that have proved themselves to suit most people's tastes. Red wine with red meat, white wine with fish and fowl is a good general guideline. But common sense must always be employed. If your seafood is prepared in a sauce of red wine, for example, then a red wine will more likely be a suitable accompaniment. Barbecued anything, including chicken, goes better with red wine than white.

The old saying that, "Rosé goes with anything," is a copout. I personally feel that rosé goes well with no dish, or at least that there is a white or red that would be more appropriate. Rosés can be fun, though as an apéritif, a substitute for a cocktail or as "summer sippers." (That's an editorial opinion.) Once again personal taste is the key, and if you really like such overpriced pink wines as Lancers and Mateus then drink them by all means.

Which wines are best, imported or domestic? You can't imagine how tired I am of hearing that question. There is no answer to such a general question. Give me two glasses of wine, one imported and the other a California wine of the same type, and I'll tell you which of *those* two I like the best. When it comes to wine, each bottling has its own unique qualities. Generalities do not apply.

I enjoy some wines from most of the world's wine-producing countries, and as you expand your own wine-drinking experience you too will find may different wines that appeal to your personal taste. Explore.

Since we're discussing wine in restaurants, I would suggest that California wines will provide the best drinking at the best price. As part of a latent, European wine-snobbism, many restaurants take a higher markup on imports than they do on domestics.

As with the house wines, I'll make a few suggestions out of the thousands of wines available to the restaurant trade. I'd like to preface these recommendations with a few comments. First, there are certain grand European wines for which there is simply no California counterpart. For instance, the exquisite wines of the Sauternes' district of France will probably never be equaled by a California wine labeled sauterne. The same applies to port, with the possible exception of Ficklin's California Port which compares well to all but the finest vintage ports of Portugal.

Unfortunately, these grand European wines cost an arm and a leg, especially in a restaurant, so I'll limit my recommendations to the wines of California.

The prices you will pay for wine in a restaurant will, generally speaking, be somewhat higher than the retail price you would pay at your local wine shop. Thankfully, the trend is toward more reasonable wine prices in restaurants, mainly due to more public awareness of what prices should be. There are even a few establishments doing a booming business by charging strictly retail prices.

There is some justification for restaurants to charge more than a retail store; they do not have the same volume and they do provide service and stemware. An elegant house that serves your wine in expensive imported crystal, must, therefore, charge more for their wine than a steak house that employs good old American jelly-glass.

There are still price gougers who charge way too much, mark up the most popular wines even more and the public be damned. These people should never receive a second visit; you should drink iced tea instead of wine while you're there, and make sure they are aware of your displeasure when you leave.

Most restaurants use a standard percentage markup for their wine list. The only problem with this is that while an inexpensive wine may sell for only a dollar or two above retail, more expensive wines can end up costing many dollars above retail. This, I think, is self-defeating for the restaurant.

My suggestion to restaurateurs: try using a uniform service charge: Take the basic retail price, add $2-$3 service charge, uniformly, to each bottle, and watch your wine sales multiply. Your customers will be happy, the additional volume will more than pay the bill, and you will probably discover many customers.

WINE RECOMMENDATIONS

ALL WINES ARE RETAIL-PRICED*

Here is a list of wines which I think offer good value. A few are from France or Germany, but the majority are made in California. Many appear on the restaurant wine lists throughout California and other sections of the United States. California retail prices and vintages are shown for each wine where possible. A good index price formula for restaurant wines is *three times wholesale or retail plus about three dollars*. Sparkling wines are likely to be higher.

*Prices provided by John Vincenti of Red Carpet Liquors in Glendale, California.

OUTSTANDING EUROPEAN WINE VALUES

Beaumes de Venise – Red Côtes du Rhone $5.00
    Canteval – Red and White Burgundy $3.25
    Chantefleur – Red and White Burgundy $3.99
    Entre-Duex-Mers, Barton White Bordeaux $3.99
    Green Label Moselle, Deinhard $5.25
    St. Macaire, Barton, White Bordeaux $4.29
    Vouvray, Henri Leger, White Loire Chenin Blanc $3.99

CALIFORNIA

Barbera
Papagni $3.95; Louis Martini $4.50; Heitz $4.75; Sebastiani $4.95
Black Muscat
Novitiate $5.50
Burgundy
Gallo Hearty Burgundy $2.25; Inglenook Navalle $3.25; Taylor California Cellars $3.25; San Martin 1.5L $4.99; Heitz $4.25; Franciscan (Cask 318) $3.75; Souverain $3.75; Beaulieu '76 $3.90
White Burgundy
Foppiano $5.95; Mirassou $6.50
Cabernet Sauvignon
Colony $2.25; Stone Creek $4.99; Sebastiani Mountain $3.49; Los Hermanos 1.5L $6.29; Louis Martini '80 $5.99; Caymus Liberty School '79 $5.00; Fetzer Mendocino '80 $7.00; Beaulieu Beautour '80 $7.00; Spring Mountain $13.00; Dehlinger '78 $8.75; Diamond Creek '80 $20.00; Jordon '76 $35.00 or '77 $20.00; Caymus '79 $12.50
Chablis
Gallo (Chablis Blanc) $1.89; Stone Creek $3.50; Los Hermanos 1.5L $6.29; Almaden Mountain $3.25; Taylor California Cellars $3.25; CK Mondavi $2.75; Geyser Peak (Summit) $3.59; Paul Masson $2.95; Beaulieu $4.99
Charbono
Inglenook $7.95; Souverain $7.59
Chardonnay (Pinot Chardonnay)
Stone Creek $5.49; Sebastiani $10.00; Louis Martini $7.00; San Martin $6.89; Wente $7.25; Sonoma $8.49; Parducci '81 $7.75; Mirassou $8.25; Beringer $9.50; Dehlinger $9.00; Fetzer $8.50; Estrella River $10.00; Burgess Cellars $12.00; Lambert Bridge $14.00; Château St. Jean (Robert Young) $12.00; Château Montelena $16.00; Grgich Hill $17.50; David Bruce $19.50

Chenin Blanc
Stone Creek $3.49; Inglenook Navalle $5.00; Los Hermanos 1.5L $5.19; San Martin $4.99; Charles Krug $5.50; Mirassou $6.00; Dry Creek (dry) $6.00; Callaway Sweet Nancy (sweet) $35.00

Chianti
Gallo $2.25

French Colombard
Gallo $2.50; Foppiano $3.95; Sonoma $5.89; Parducci $4.50

Fumé Blanc
Christian Bros. Napa Fumé $5.50; Beringer $7.35; Dry Creek $8.50; Robert Mondavi '78 $9.75

Gamay
Christian Bros. Gamay Noir NV $6.50; Charles F. Shaw (Napa) $5.00

Gamay Beaujolais
Louis Martini $4.49; Inglenook $4.95; Stag's Leap $5.50

Gewurztraminer
Almaden $5.75; Louis Martini (dry) $5.50; Geyser Peak $6.25; Firestone $6.50

Green Hungarian
Weibel $4.75

Grignolino
Heitz $4.75

Johannisberg Riesling
Monterey Vineyard $5.95; Paul Masson (Pinnacles) $5.95; Saint Michelle '78 $6.50; Jekel $6.50; Llords & Elwood $7.25; Château Montelena $7.75; Château St. Jean $7.50; Joseph Phelps $20.00

Merlot
Louis Martini $5.00; Firestone (Aroyo) $5.35

Malvasia
Beringer Malvasia Bianca $5.00

Moscato Amabile
Sutter Home $4.75; Angelo Papagni $5.50

Muscat Blanc (Canelli or Frontignan)
Christian Bros. Château La Salle (sweet) $4.00; Concannon '79 (semi-dry) $6.59

Petite Sirah
Cresta Blanca $4.49; Almaden $5.25; Wente $5.00; Mirassou $5.49; Concannon $6.29; Fetzer $5.50; Callaway $9.00

Pinot Blanc
Paul Masson $6.29; Wente $5.29; J. Lohr '78 $6.95; Fetzer $8.50

Pinot Noir
Pedroncelli $4.50; Louis Martini $5.00; Foppiano $6.95; Mill Creek $7.50; Souverain $6.89; Beaulieu (Beaumont) $7.00; Stonegate $6.50; Robert Mondavi $8.50; Firestone $8.25; Gundlach-Bundschu $13.75; Beaulieu (Carneros) '76 $9.25

Pinot Noir Blanc
Sebastiani $4.99; Caymus $4.75; Gemello $6.75

Port
Novitiate $3.49; Almaden Ruby $3.25; Ficklin $7.25; Llords & Elwood Proveab Port $5.50

Rosé
Christian Bros. La Salle $6.50; Mirassou Petite Rosé $3.50; Llords & Elwood Rosé of Cabernet $4.75; Heitz Grignolino Rosé $4.75

Ruby Cabernet
Colony $2.25

Sauvignon Blanc
Wente $6.25; Monterey Vineyard (Botrytis, sweet) $10.25; Santa Ynez Valley (dry) $7.50; J. Lohr (dry) $7.49

Sherries
Llords & Elwood Dry Wit Sherry $5.50; Gallo Livingston Cream Sherry $2.39; Cresta Blanca Triple Cream Sherry $5.39

Sparkling Wines
Le Domaine Champagne $4.65; Hanns Kornell Champagne $10.75; Angelo Papagni Spumante d'Angelo $6.75; Almaden Blanc de Blancs $9.39; Domaine Chandon Napa Valley Brut $13.25; Mirassou Au Natural Champagne $14.00; Korbel Natural $10.95

Spanish Sparkling Wines
Codornieu Brut $8.00; Freixenet Carta Nevada $7.39

Zinfandel
River Oaks P.R. Zinfandel $8.50; Almaden NV $3.75; Stone Creek $4.39; Sutter Home $6.25; Souverain $4.79; Dehlinger $7.50

White Zinfandel
Sutter Home $4.75

Restaurants By City and Area Number

Alameda—Area 2
Acapulco
Pacific Fresh
Alamo—Area 2
The Elegant Bib
Albany—Area 2
Chin Szchawn
Walker's Pie Shop
Auburn—Area 5
Auburn Hotel
Cafe Delicias
Belmont—Area 2
Horky's
Iron Gate
Berkeley—Area 2
Augusta's
Bette's Oceanview
  Diner
Blue Nile
Cafe at Chez Panisse
Cafe Fanny
Cafe Pastoral
Caffe Giovanni
Casa de Eva
Chez Panisse
China Station
Fourth Street Grill
Good Earth
India Kashmir
La Val's Gardens
LoCoco's
McCallum's
Norman's
Petrouchka
Riera's
Santa Fe Bar & Grill
Spenger's Fish Grotto

Taiwan Restaurant
Tora-ya
Vegi Food
Warszawa
Yenching
Big Sir—Area 1
Deetjen's
Nepenthe
Ventana Inn
Bodega—Area 3
Bodega Gallery
Booneville—Area 4
New Booneville Hotel
Burlingame—Area 2
Benihana of Tokyo
Kee Joon's
La Piñata
Saluto's
Calistoga—Area 3
Calistoga Inn
Mount View Hotel
Cambria—Area 1
Brambles Dinner House
Cambria Pines
Grey Fox Inn
Campbell—Area 2
Fung Lum
Renzo's
Sebastian's
Capitola—Area 1
Shadowbrook
Carmel—Area 1
Anton & Michel
The Carmel Butcher Shop
Clam Box
The Covey
French Poodle
L' Escargot

Marquis
Pacific Edge
Patisserie Boissiere
Raffaello
Thunderbird
  Bookstore
Will's Fargo
Chico — Area 5
Italian Cottage
Citrus Heights — Area 3
Trellis Cafe
Columbia — Area 6
City Hotel
Concord — Area 2
The Good Earth
La Tour
The Melting Pot
Pacific Cafe
Suwa's
Yet Wah
Crescent City — Area 4
Harbor View Grotto
Cupertino — Area 2
Anthony's Pier 9
Benihana of Toyko
Chili's
Daly City — Area 2
R.V.'s Super It's
Szechwan Village
Emeryville — Area 2
Trader Vic's
Eureka — Area 4
Lazio's Sea Food
Samoa Cookhouse
Fairfax — Area 3
Deer Park Villa
Fair Oaks — Area 3
Bon Appétit
Folsom — Area 3
Koya's

Forestville — Area 3
Russian River Vineyards
Foster City — Area 2
The Customs House
Yet Wah
Fremont — Area 2
Mission Deli
Garberville — Area 4
Benbow Inn
Geyserville — Area 3
Souverain Restaurant
Gilroy — Area 2
Digger Dans
Grass Valley — Area 5
Owl Tavern
Gualala — Area 3
St. Orres
Hanford — Area 6
Imperial Dynasty
Hayward — Area 2
Bancheros
Old South B.B.Q
Oscar's Bistro
Healdsburg — Area 3
Giorgio's
Madrona Manor
Incline Village, Nev. — Area 6
Hugo's Rotisserie
Inverness — Area 3
Manka's
Jenner — Area 3
River's End
Kentfield — Area 3
Pacific Cafe
King's Beach — Area 6
Cantina Los Tres Hombres
Lafayette — Area 2
Cape Cod House
La Rue
Tokyo Chicken
Lake Forest — Area 6
Bacchi's Inn

Larkspur—Area 2
Firehouse Bar-B-Que
Good Earth
Lark Creek Inn
Yet Wah
Little River—Area 4
Heritage House
Ledford House
Los Altos—Area 2
Columbus Street
Mac's Tea Room
Shogun
Los Molinos—Area 5
N-B Cafe
Los Osos—Area 1
Uncle Rugby's Galley
Marin—Area 3
Yet Wah
Mendocino—Area 3
Cafe Beaujolais
The Sea Gull
Menlo Park—Area 2
British Bankers Club
Dal Baffo
Golden Acorn
Late For The Train
Le Pot Au Feu
Viet-Nam Restaurant
Millbrae—Area 2
Sixteen Mile House
Mill Valley—Area 3
California Cafe
El Paseo
Le Camembert
Perry's
Modesto—Area 6
Carmen's
Monte Sereno—Area 1
La Hacienda Inn
Monterey—Area 1
Clock Garden
Consuelo's

Domenico's on the Wharf
Fresh Cream
Mark Thomas' Outrigger
Neil de Vaughn's
Peninsula Restaurant
The Rogue
Sardine Factory
Whaling Station Inn
Moraga—Area 2
Mondello's
Morro Bay—Area 1
The Fondue Pot
Galley Restaurant
Mountain View—Area 2
El Calderon
Mekong
Napa—Area 3
The Carriage House
Grape Vine Inn
Jonesy's Famous Steak
   House
La Boucane
Oliver's
Rainbow Bridge
Silverado
North Lake Tahoe—Area 6
Swiss Lakewood Lodge
Novato—Area 3
Charlie Bolton's
Hilltop Cafe
Nut Tree—Area 3
Coffee Tree
Nut Tree
Oakland—Area 2
Bay Wolf Cafe
Broadway Terrace Cafe
Chris' Hot Dogs
Dutch East Indies
Equinox
Flints
Gingerbread House
The Grotto

Jade Villa
La Mexicana
LoCoco's
Mirabeau
New Sunshine Pizza
Pavillion Room
Scott's Seafood
Silver Dragon
Sorabol
Oakmont — Area 3
Oakmont Inn
Occidental — Area 3
Negri's
Union Hotel
Olema — Area 3
The Olema Inn
Orinda — Area 2
Aux Delices
Marcello's
Pacifica — Area 2
Moonraker
Pacific Grove — Area 2
Old Europe
Pebble Beach — Area 1
Club XIX
Palo Alto — Area 2
Chantilly
Chez Louie
China First
Dinah's Shack
Ecco
Gaylord
Good Earth
Kirk's
Liaison
MacArthur Park
Maddalena's
Mama's
Ming's
Rick's Swiss Chalet
St. Michael's Alley
Scott's Seafood

Penryn — Area 6
The Ground Cow
Pescadero — Area 2
Duarte's Tavern
Petaluma — Area 3
Farrell House
Opera House Cafe
610 Restaurant
Steamer Gold Landing
Pleasant Hill — Area 2
Pacific Fresh
Savoy
Szechwan Village
Pleasanton — Area 2
Good Earth
Point Reyes — Area 3
Station House
Point Richmond — Area 3
Hotel Mac
Port Costa — Area 2
Bull Valley Inn
Warehouse Cafe
Princeton-By-The-Sea – Area 2
Princeton Inn
The Shore Bird
Redding — Area 5
Italian Cottage
Jack's Grill
Redwood City — Area 2
Gypsy Cellar
La Guinguette
L'Auberge
Scotty Campbell's
Reno — Area 5
Cafe Gigi
Roseville — Area 5
Cafe Delicias
Ross — Area 3
Coquelicot
Rutherford — Area 3
Auberge de Soleil
Rutherford Square

St. Helena—Area 3
  Abbey
  California Cafe
  La Belle Helene
  Miramonte
  Rose et LeFavour
  St. George
Sacramento—Area 3
  Aldo's
  Cafe La Salle
  The Firehouse
  Fuji Sukiyaki
  Good Earth
  Hong Kong Cafe
  Hungry Tiger
  Maleville's Coral Reef
  Movable Feast
  Wulff's
Salinas—Area 1
  The Windfall
San Carlos—Area 2
  Salvatore's
San Francisco—Area 2
  Adolph's
  Akasaka
  Alejandro's Sociedad
    Gastronomica
  Alexis
  Alfred's
  Alta Plaza
  Amelio's
  Archil's
  Asia Garden
  Atlantis Seafood
  Bagatelle
  Balboa Cafe
  The Bank Exchange
  Bardelli's
  Basque Hotel
  Basta Pasta
  Beethoven's
  Benihana of Tokyo

Bentley's
Beppino's
Bertolucci's
The Big Four
Billboard Cafe
Bill's Place
Blanche's
Blue Boar Inn
Blue Fox
Blue Light Cafe
Brentwood Lodge
Buena Vista Cafe
By The Square
Caesar's
Cafe Americain
Cafe du Nord
Cafe Gitanes
Cafe Jacqueline
Cafe Riggio
Cafe Royale
Cafe Sn. Marcos
Caffe Sport
Caffe Trieste
California Culinary
  Academy
Campton Place
Caravansary
Carnelian Room
Cars
Casablanca
Castle Grand Brasserie
Celadon
Cheers
The Cherry Flower
Chez Marguerite
Chez Michel
Cho Cho
Ciao
Coatepeque
Coffee Cantata
Columbus
Cordon Bleu

The Courtyard
Cuba
Dante's
David's
The Deli
De Paula's
Des Alpes
Diamond Street
Di Grande
Doidge's Kitchen
Donatello
Doros
Double Rainbow
Drake's Tavern
E' Angelo
The Elite Cafe
El Sombrero
El Tazumal
El Zarape
Empress of China
The English Grill
Enrico's
Ernie's Neptune Fish
   Grotto
Ernie's
Far East Cafe
Fior D'Italia
Firehouse Bar-B-Que
Fishermen's Grotto
Fleur de Lys
Fournou's Oven
Four Seas
The French Room
Fuki-Ya
Gaylord
Gelco's
George's Specialties
German Cook
Gino's
Golden Turtle
Gold Mirror
Gold Spike

Good Earth
Good Karma Cafe
Graziano's
Great Eastern
Greens
Hahn's Hibachi
Hamburger Mary's
Hana
Hang Ah Tea Room
Hans Speckmann's
Harbin
Harris'
Hayes Street Grill
The Hippo
Hog Heaven
House of Prime Rib
Hunan
Hunan Village
Hungry Tiger
Il Giglio
Imperial Palace
India House
Ino Sushi
The Iron Horse
Jack's
JoAnn's
John's Grill
Julius Castle
Kabuto
Kan's
Khan Toke
Kichihei
Kinokawa
Kirin
Korea House
Kum Moon
Kundan
La Bodega
La Bourgogne
La Fuente
La Mirabelle
La Pantera

La Pergola
La Piñata
La Quiche
La Rocca's
La Rondalla
La Scala
Las Mañanitas
Le Candide
Le Castel
Le Central
Le Club
Le Cyrano
Lehr's Greenhouse
L'Entrecôte de Paris
L'Etoile
Lichee Garden
Lipizzaner
Little Joe's
Liverpool Lil's
L'Olivier
Lung Fung
Luzern
MacArthur Park
Mai's Vietnamese
Mama's
Mamounia
The Mandarin
Mandarin Delight
Marrakech
Masa's
Maxwell's Plum
Maye's Oyster House
Meat Market
  Coffeehouse
Mekong
Mifune
Mike's Chinese
  Cuisine
Mitoya
Modesto Lazone's
Modesto Lanzone's
  Opera Plaza

Monroe's
Nam Yuen
Napoli
Nautilus
The Neon Chicken
Neptune's Palace
New Pisa
New San Remo
Nicaragua
Nob Hill Cafe
North Beach
North China
Ocean
Old Poodle Dog
Old Swiss House
One-Up Restaurant
Orient Express
Original Joe's
Otafuku Tei
Pacific Cafe
Pam Pam East
Panos'
Paprikas Fono
Pasand
Pasha
Pauli's
The Peacock
Perry's
Phil Lehr's Steakery
Pierre
Pisces
Pompei's Grotto
Prego
Ramis
Red's
Rene Verdon's Le Trianon
Ristorante Buca Giovanni
Ristorante Grifone
Ristorante Orsi
Rive Gauche
Rosebud's
Russian Renaissance

Sailing Ship
Sam's Grill
Sanppo
San Remo
Sari's
S. Asimakopoulos
  Cafe
Scandinavian Deli
Schroeder's
Scott's Seafood Grill
Sears Fine Foods
Seoul Garden
Silver
Sinbad's Pier 2
South Pacific Seafood
  Grotto
Square One
Squire Room
Stars
Swan Oyster Depot
Swiss Alps
Tadich Grill
Taj of India
Taj Mahal
Tandoori
Tao Tao
Tarantino's
Tien Fu
Tommaso's
Tommy's Joynt
Ton Kiang
Tora-ya
Trader Vic's
Tricolor
Tuba Garden
Tung Fong
Upstairs At The Cliff
  House
U. S. Restaurant
Vanessi's
Vannelli's
Vegi Food

Via Veneto
Vicolo
Victor's
Vivande Porta Via
Vlasta's
Washington Square Bar &
  Grill
Waterfront Restaurant
The White Elephant
White Horse Taverne
Xenios
Yamato
Yank Sing
Yenching
Yet Wah
Yoshida-Ya
Yuet Lee
Zola's
Zuni Cafe

San Jose — Area 2
Bini's Bar & Grill
Don The Beachcomber
Emile's Swiss Affair
Gervais
The Good Earth
Harry's Hofbrau
La Foret
Mama's
Menara
Ori-Deli
Original Joe's
Paolo's
Pinehurst Inn
Siam
Victorian House
San Juan Bautista — Area 1
Cademartori's Casa Maria
San Luis Obispo — Area 1
Madonna Inn
San Mateo — Area 2
La Bonne Auberge
La Cigogne

Lanai
Mama's
The Omelette House
San Rafael — Area 3
Andalou
Dominic's Harbor
Guido's
La Petite Auberge
Le Chalet Basque
Mamounia
Maurice et Charles
  Bistrot
Pier 15
Ramona's
The Rice Table
Taverna Yaisou
San Ramon — Area 2
California Cafe
San Simeon — Area 1
Cavalier Inn
San Simeon
  Restaurant
Santa Clara — Area 2
Buy-Th-Bucket
The Good Earth
J. R. Chops
Santa Cruz — Area 1
The Crow's Nest
The Upper Crust
Santa Rosa — Area 3
Cricklewood
The Good Earth
J. M. Rosen's
John Ash & Co.
La Gare
La Province
Los Robles Lodge
Shanghai Station
Sheraton Round Barn
  Inn
Topaz Room
The Villa

Saratoga — Area 2
Le Mouton Noir
The Plumed Horse
Sausalito — Area 3
Alta Mira Hotel
Caffe Trieste
Casa Madrona
François' Coffee House
Guernica
Ondine
Seven Seas
The Spinnaker
Yet Wah
Zack's By The Bay
Sebastopol — Area 3
Le Pommier
Sonoma — Area 3
Au Relais
La Casa
Pilou
Sharl's
Sonoma Cheese Factory
Sonoma Hotel
South Lake Tahoe — Area 6
Chez Villaret
Christiania Inn
The Cook Book
Harrah's Tahoe
Harvey's Resort
Stockton — Area 6
On Lock Sam
Ospital's Villa Basque
Ye Olde Hoosier Inn
Sunnyvale — Area 2
Michael's
Pacific Fresh
Tao Tao Cafe
Tahoe City — Area 6
Fire Sign Cafe
Jake's On The Lake
The Pfeifer House
Rosie's Cafe

Tahoe Vista — Area 6
   Le Petit Pier
Terra Linda — Area 2
   LoCoco's
Tiburon — Area 3
   The Caprice
   The Dock
   Rooney's Garden
     Cafe
   Sam's Anchor Cafe
   Sweden House
     Bakery
Vacaville — Area 3
   Murillo's
Walnut Creek — Area 2
   Affagottso's

California Cafe
Grison's
Le Virage
The Melting Pot
Woodside — Area 2
   Skywood Chateau
   The Village Pub
Yosemite — Area 6
   The Ahwahnee
Yountville — Area 3
   The Chutney Kitchen
   Domaine Chandon
   The French Laundry
   Le Chardonnay
Yuba City — Area 5
   Lee's Canton

Types of Cuisine

American
   The Ahwahnee
   Alfred's
   Balboa Cafe
   Bette's Oceanview Diner
   Bill's Place
   Bini's Bar & Grill
   Blue Light Cafe
   Brambles Dinner House
   Buena Vista Cafe
   Buy-Th-Bucket
   Cademartori's Casa Maria
   Cafe Beaujolais
   California Cafe
   Cambria Pines
   Cape Cod House
   The Carmel Butcher Shop
   The Carriage House
   Chili's
   Chris' Hot Dogs
   Chutney Kitchen
   Coffee Tree

The Cook Book
Cricklewood
The Crow's Nest
Deetjen's
Digger Dans
Dinah's Shack
The Dock
Duarte's Tavern
Ecco
The Elegant Bib
Fire Sign Cafe
The Fondue Pot
Gingerbread House
Grape Vine Inn
Grison's
The Grotto
Ground Cow
Hamburger Mary's
Harris'
Harry's Hofbrau
Heritage House
The Hippo

House of Prime Rib
Hungry Tiger
Jack's Grill
Jake's On The Lake
J. M. Rosen's
JoAnn's
John's Grill
Jonesy's Famous
  Steak House
Kirk's
La Casa Rosa
Late For The Train
Ledford House
Lee's Canton
Lehr's Greenhouse
MacAuthur Park
Mac's Tea Room
Maleville's Coral Reef
Mama's
Masons
N-B Cafe
The Neon Chicken
Nepenthe
The New Booneville
  Hotel
Nut Tree
Oakmont Inn
The Omelette House
Opera House Cafe
Owl Tavern
Pam Pam East
Panos'
Pavillion Room
Perry's
Phil Lehr's Steakery
Pier 15
Rainbow Bridge
Rosie's Cafe
Rutherford Square
Saluto's
Samoa Cookhouse
San Remo

San Simeon Restaurant
Schroeder's
Sears Fine Foods
Shadowbrook
Sheraton Round Barn Inn
The Shore Bird
Sixteen Mile House
Station House Cafe
Steamer Gold Landing
Tarantino's
Tommy's Joynt
Upstairs At The Cliff
  House
Walker's Pie Shop
Warehouse Cafe
Will's Fargo
Ye Olde Hoosier Inn
Zack's By The Bay

Alsatian
La Cigogne
Le Castel

Armenian
Caravansary

Barbecue
Firehouse Bar-B-Que
Flint's
Hog Heaven
Old South BBQ

Basque
Auburn Hotel
Basque Hotel
Cafe Du Nord
Des Alpes
Guernica
Le Chalet Basque
Ospital's Villa Basque

Belgian
Chez Marguerite

Brazilian
De Paula's

California/Continental
Abbey
Alta Plaza
Amelio's
Andalou
Billboard Cafe
Blue Boar Inn
Bodega Galley
Broadway Terrace
   Cafe
Cafe Fanny
Cafe Pastoral
Cafe Royale
California Cafe
Campton Place
Cars
Casa Madrona
Cheers
The Courtyard
Farrell House
The French Laundry
Hayes Street Grill
John Ash & Co.
Madrona Manor
Movable Feast
New Booneville Hotel
Norman's
Nut Tree
Olema Inn
Opera House Cafe
Pacific Edge
Peninsula Restaurant
Pilou
Santa Fe Bar & Grill
The Sheraton Round
   Barn Inn
Silverado
Sinbad's Pier 2
Skywood Chateau
Sonoma Hotel
Square One
Stars

Thunderbird Bookstore
Trellis Cafe
Ventana Inn
Victor's
Zuni Cafe

Chinese
Asia Garden
Cafe Pastoral
Celadon
China First
China Station
Chin Szchawn
Empress Of China
Far East Cafe
Four Seas
Fung Lum
Great Eastern
Hang Ah Tea Room
Harbin
Hong Kong Cafe
Hunan
Hunan Village
Imperial Dynasty
Imperial Palace
Jade Villa
Kan's
Kee Joon's
Kirin
Kum Moon
Lanai
Lee's
Lichee Garden
Lung Fung
Maleville's Coral Reef
The Mandarin
Mandarin Delight
Mike's
Ming's
Nam Yuen
North China
Ocean
On Lock Sam
Red's

Shanghai Station
Silver
Silver Dragon
Szechwan
Tao Tao
Tao Tao Cafe
Tien Fu
Ton Kiang
Tung Fong
Vegi Food
Yank Sing
Yenching
Yet Wah
Yuet Lee

Coffeehouse
Cafe Trieste
Enrico's
François Coffee
  House
Meat Market
  Coffeehouse
Pam Pam East

Continental
Abbey
The Ahwahnee
Aldo's
Alexis
Alta Mira Hotel
Amelio's
Anthony's Pier 9
Anton & Michel
Bagatelle
The Bank Exchange
Bardelli's
Beethoven's
Benbow Inn
Beppino's Ristorante
The Big Four
Blanche's
Blue Boar Inn
Blue Fox
Bon Appétit

Brentwood Lodge
British Bankers Club
Bull Valley Inn
By The Square
Cafe Americain
Cafe Beaujolais
Cafe at Chez Panisse
Cafe La Salle
Cafe Sn. Marcos
California Culinary
  Academy
Calistoga Inn
Cambria Pines
The Caprice
The Carmel Butcher Shop
The Carriage House
Casablanca
Charlie Bolton's
Christiania Inn
Chutney Kitchen
Clock Garden
Coffee Cantata
The Covey
The Customs House
Dal Baffo
Deetjen's
The Deli
The Dock
Doidge's Kitchen
Doros
The Elegant Bib
El Paseo
Emile's Swiss Affair
The English Grill
Enrico's
Equinox
The Firehouse
Fournou's Oven
Fourth Street Grill
François Coffee House
The French Room
Fresh Cream

Gelco's
Golden Acorn
Graziano's
Grey Fox Inn
Grison's
Harrah's Tahoe
Harvey's Resort
Hilltop Cafe
Hotel Mac
Hugo's Rotisserie
Imperial Dynasty
Iron Gate
The Iron Horse
Jake's On The Lake
J. R. Chops
Julius Castle
Koya's
La Foret
La Hacienda Inn
La Mirabelle
La Petite Auberge
La Province
Lark Creek Inn
La Rue
Ledford House
Liverpool Lil's
Los Robles Lodge
Maddalena's
Madonna Inn
Manka's
Maxwell's Plum
Michael's
Mirabeau
Monroe's
Moonraker
Mount View Hotel
Neil de Vaughn's
Nob Hill Cafe
Norman's
North Beach
  Restaurant
Oakmont Inn

Old Europe
Oliver's
Ondine
One-Up Restaurant
Orient Express
Paolo's
Patisserie Boissiere
Pauli's Cafe
The Pfeifer House
Phil Lehr's Steakery
Pinehurst Inn
The Plumed Horse
Princeton Inn
Ramis
Renzo's Continental
  Cuisine
River's End
The Rogue
Rosebud's
Russian River Vineyards
Sailing Ship
St. Michael's Alley
Sam's Anchor Cafe
The Sardine Factory
Savoy
Scotty Campbell's
Sea Gull
Sebastian's
Shadowbrook
Souverain Restaurant
The Spinnaker
The Squire Room
Swiss Lakewood Lodge
Tommy's Joynt
Topaz Room
Trader Vic's
Tuba Garden
Uncle Rugby's Galley
Vanessi's
Victorian House
The Village Pub
Vivande Porta Via

Vlasta's
Waterfront Restaurant
The White Elephant
White Horse Taverne
The Windfall

Créole
The Elite Cafe
The Gingerbread
    House

Cuban
Cuba

Czechoslavakian
Gypsy Cellar
Manka's
Vlasta's

Deli
Balboa Cafe
David's
The Deli
Mission Deli
Ori-Deli
Rooney's Garden
    Cafe
Scandinavian Deli
Sonoma Cheese
    Factory
Vivande Porta Via

Dessert
Double Rainbow
McCallum's

English
Blue Boar Inn
Drake's Tavern
The White Elephant

Ethiopian
Blue Nile

Fast Food/Take-Out
Bill's Place
Buy-Th-Bucket
Chris' Hot Dogs

Filippino
R. V.'s Super It's

Fondue
Fondue Pot
The Melting Pot
Swiss Alps

French
Alexis
Auberge de Soleil
Au Relais
Basque Hotel
Blue Boar Inn
Bon Appétit
Cafe Du Nord
Cafe Gigi
Cafe Jacqueline
The Caprice
Carnelian Room
Casablanca
Casa Madrona
Castle Grand Brasserie
Chantilly
Chez Louis
Chez Marguerite
Chez Michel
Chez Panisse
Chez Villaret
City Hotel
Club XIX
Coquelicot
Domaine Chandon
El Paseo
Ernie's
Fleur de Lys
French Poodle
Gervais
Guernica
Jacks
John Ash & Co.
La Belle Helene
La Bonne Auberge
La Boucane
La Bourgogne
La Gare

La Guinguette
La Mirabelle
La Petite Auberge
La Quiche
La Rue
La Tour
L'Auberge
Le Camembert
Le Candide
Le Central
Le Chalet Basque
Le Chardonnay
Le Club
Le Cyrano
Le Mouton Noir
L'Entrecôte de Paris
Le Petit Pier
Le Pommier
Le Pot Au Feu
L'Escargot
L'Etoile
Le Virage
Liaison
Lipizzaner
L'Olivier
Luzern
Marquis
Masa's
Maurice et Charles
    Bistrot
Mirabeau
Miramonte
Mount View Hotel
Old Poodle Dog
Old Swiss House
Ondine
Oscar's Bistro
Patisserie Boissiere
Pierre
Pilou
The Plumed Horse
Rene Verdon's Le
    Trianon

Rive Gauche
Rose et LeFavour
Sharl's
St. Orres
610 Restaurant
The Squire Room
Tricolor
The Windfall
Wulff's
Zola's

German
Beethoven's
German Cook
Hans Speckmann's
Rick's Swiss Chalet
Schroeder's
Vlasta's

Greek
Panos'
Russian River Vineyards
S. Asimakopoulos
Taverna Yaisou
Xenios

Hungarian
Gypsy Cellar
Paprikas Fono

Indian
Diamond Street
Gaylord
India House
India Kashmir
Kundan
Pasand
The Peacock
Taj of India
Taj Mahal
Tandoori

Indonesian
Dutch East Indies
Ori-Deli
The Rice Table
Sari's

Italian

Adolph's
Affagottso's
Alfred's
Augusta's
Bacchi's Inn
Bancheros
Basta Pasta
Beppino's
Bertolucci's
Blue Fox
By the Square
Cademartori's Casa
 Maria
Caesar's
Cafe Riggio
Cafe Giovanni
Caffe Sport
Caffe Trieste
Ciao
Columbus
Columbus Street
Dante's
Deer Park Villa
Di Grande
Domenico's On The
 Wharf
Dominic's Harbor
Donatello
E'Angelo
Ecco
Fior d'Italia
Gino's
Giorgio's
Gold Mirror
Gold Spike
Grape Vine Inn
Graziano's
Guido's
Il Giglio
Iron Gate
Iron Horse
Italian Cottage
La Hacienda Inn
La Pantera
La Pergola
La Scala
La Val's Gardens
Liaison
Little Joe's
LoCoco's
Marcello's
Modesto Lanzone's
Modesto Lanzone's Opera
 Plaza
Mondello's
Napoli
Negri's
New Pisa
The New San Remo
New Sunshine Pizza
North Beach Restaurant
Original Joe's
Paolo's
Prego
Raffaello
Riera's
Ristorante Buca Giovanni
Ristorante Grifone
Ristorante Orsi
The Rogue
St. George
Saluto's
Salvatore's
San Simeon Restaurant
San Remo
Tommaso's
Union Hotel
The Upper Crust
U. S. Restaurant
Vanessi's
Via Veneto
Vicolo

Victorian House
The Villa
Washington Square
  Bar & Grill
Whaling Station

Japanese
Akasaka
Benihana of Tokyo
Cho Cho
Fuji Sukiyaki
Fuki-Ya
Hana
Ino Sushi
Kabuto
Kichihei
Kinokawa
Mifune
Mitoya
Otafuku Tei
Sanppo
Shogun
Suwa's
Tokyo Chicken
Tora-ya
Yamato
Yoshida-Ya

Korean
Hahn's Hibachi
Korea House
Seoul Garden
Sorabol

Mediterranean
Bay Wolf Cafe
Caravansary
St. George
Xenios

Mexican
Acapulco
Cafe Delicias
Cantina Los Tres
  Hombres

Carmen's
Casa de Eva
Consuelo's
El Calderon
El Sombrero
El Tazumal
El Zarape
Horky's
La Casa
La Fuente
La Mexicana
La Piñata
La Rondalla
Las Mañanitas
Murillo's
Ramona's

Mid-Eastern
Marrakech
Pasha
Ramis

Moroccan
Mamounia
Menara

Nicaraguan
Nicaraga

Polynesian
Don The Beachcomber
Lanai
Mark Thomas' Outrigger
Trader Vic's

Polish
Warszawa

Russian
Archil's
George's Specialties
Petrouchka
Russian Renaissance

Salvadorean
Coatepeque
El Calderon
El Tazumal

Scandinavian
Scandinavian Deli
Sweden House
Bakery
Seafood
Anthony's Pier 9
Atlantis Seafood
Augusta's
Basta Pasta
Bentley's
Calistoga Inn
Cape Cod House
Cavalier Inn
Clam Box
The Crow's Nest
Di Grande
Domenico's on The
Wharf
Dominic's Harbor
The Elite Cafe
Ernie's Neptune Fish
Grotto
Fishermen's Grotto
Fourth Street Grill
Galley Restaurant
The Grotto
Harbor View Grotto
Hayes Street Grill
Hugo's Rotisserie
Hungry Tiger
La Guinguette
La Rocca's
La Scala
Lazio's
Madonna Inn
Masons
Maye's Oyster House
Michael's
Moonraker
Nautilus
Neptune's Palace
Pacific Cafe

Pacific Fresh
Pier 15
Pisces
Pompei's Grotto
Princeton Inn
Rogue
Sam's Anchor Cafe
Sam's Grill
San Simeon Restaurant
The Sardine Factory
Scott's Seafood
Seven Seas
The Shore Bird
Sinbad's Pier 2
South Pacific Seafood
Grotto
Spenger's Fish Grotto
Spinnaker
Station House Cafe
Steamer Gold Landing
Swan Oyster Depot
Tadich Grill
Tarantino's
Topaz Room
Vannelli's
Via Veneto
The Villa
Waterfront
Whaling Station Inn
White Horse Taverne
South American
Alejandro's Sociedad
Gastronomica
Spanish
Cuba
La Bodega
La Fuente
Swiss
Emile's Swiss Affair
La Gare
Luzern
Old Swiss House

Rick's Swiss Chalet
Swiss Alps
Swiss Lakewood
   Lodge
Taiwanese
   Taiwan Restaurant
Thai
   Khan Toke
   Siam
Tunisian
   Cafe Gitanes
Vegetarian/Organic
   Diamond Street
   The Good Earth
   Good Karma Cafe
   Greens
   Late For The Train
   Petrouchka
   Vegi Food

Viennese
   Lipizzaner
Vietnamese
   Aux Delices
   The Cherry Flower
   Cordon Bleu
   Golden Turtle
   Mai's Vietnamese
   Mekong (Mountain View)
   Mekong (San Francisco)
   Viet-Nam Restaurant
Yugoslavian
   Gelco's

BRUNCH

The Ahwahnee
Alta Mira Hotel
Anthony's Pier 9
Anton and Michel
Augusta's
Au Relais
Bay Wolf Cafe
Benbow Inn
The Big Four
Blue Light Cafe
Bodega Gallery
Bon Appétit
Broadway Terrace Cafe
Bull Valley Inn
By The Square
Cafe Sn. Marcos
California Cafe
The Caprice
Caravanasary

Carnelian Room
City Hotel
Clock Garden
Club XIX
Coffee Cantata
Consuelo's Mexican Restaurant
Customs House
Digger Dans
The Dock
Domenico's on The Wharf
Dominic's Harbor
Don The Beachcomber
Dutch East Indies
Ecco
The Elite Cafe
Farrell House
The French Room
Fung Lum
Gaylord

The Good Earth
Greens
Grey Fox Inn
Heritage House
The Hilltop Cafe
Hotel Mac
Italian Cottage
John Ash & Co.
Koya's
La Belle Helene
La Casa
La Foret
Lark Creek Inn
Le Camembert
Le Chalet Basque
The Ledford House
Lehr's Greenhouse
L'Entrecôte de Paris
Liverpool Lil's
MacArthur Park
Madrona Manor
Mama's
Manka's
Mark Thomas' Outrigger
Mount View Hotel
One-Up Restaurant
Oakmont Inn
Olema Inn
Panos'
Pauli's Cafe
Pavillion Room
Peninsula Restaurant
Perry's
Pier 15

Pilou
Pinehurst Inn
Ramis
River's End
Russian River Vineyards
St. George
St. Orres
Sam's Anchor Cafe
Seven Seas
Shadowbrook
Shanghai Station
Sharl's
The Shore Bird
Silverado
Sinbad's Pier 2
Sonoma Hotel
South Pacific
Souverain
Stars
Steamer Gold Landing
Sweden House Bakery
Tandoori
Trellis Cafe
Tuba Garden
Vanelli's
Victorian House
Victor's
Vivande Porte Via
Washington Square Bar & Grill
Waterfront Restaurant
The White Elephant
The Windfall
Xenios
Zuni Cafe

CHILD'S MENU

Abbey
The Ahwahnee
Anthony's Pier 9
Bacchi's Inn
Bagatelle
Banchero's
Basque Hotel
Bertolucci's
Bill's Place
Caesar's
Cafe Du Nord
Cambria Pines
Carmel Butcher Shop
Cavalier Inn
Chutney Kitchen
Clam Box
Coffee Tree
Coquelicot
Crow's Nest
Cuba
David's
Deer Park Villa
Digger Dans
Dinah's Shack
Dominic's Harbor
Ecco
The Elegant Bib
El Tazumal
The English Grill
Fishermen's Grotto
The Fondue Pot
Galley Restaurant
Giorgio's
Gold Mirror
Gold Spike
Grape Vine Inn
Grison's
The Grotto
The Ground Cow
Gypsy Cellar
Harbor View Grotto

The Hippo
Horky's
House of Prime Rib
Hungry Tiger
Iron Gate
Italian Cottage
La Foret
La Piñata
Lazio's
Le Chalet Basque
LoCoco's
Mama's
Mark Thomas' Outrigger
Michael's
Murillo's
Nam Yuen
Negri's
Neil de Vaughn's
New Pisa
The Nut Tree
The Omelette House
On Lock Sam
Original Joe's (San Jose)
Oscar's Bistro
Pacific Fresh
Perry's
Pier 15
Pinehurst Inn
Pisces
Rick's Swiss Chalet
Russian Renaissance
St. Michael's Alley
Saluto's
Samoa Cookhouse
Sam's Anchor Cafe
Sardine Factory
Schroeder's
Sea Gull
Shogun
Sixteen Mile House
South Pacific Seafood Grotto
Spenger's Fish Grotto

Taj Majal
Tricolor
Uncle Rugby's Galley
Union Hotel
Victorian House
Vlasta's

Walker's Pie Shop
Warehouse Cafe
Will's Fargo
The Windfall
Yamato
Ye Olde Hoosier Inn

DANCING

The Bank Exchange
The Dock
Gaylord
Hamburger Mary's
La Fuente
Los Robles Lodge
Maddalena's
Madonna Inn
Mark Thomas' Outrigger

Mount View Hotel
The Plumed Horse
Princeton Inn
Rainbow Bridge
Rick's Swiss Chalet
Rutherford Square
Saluto's
Scotty Campbell's

DINING ADVENTURES (DA)

The Ahwahnee
Alta Mira Hotel
Basque Hotel
Basta Pasta
Buena Vista Cafe
Cafe Trieste
California Culinary
    Academy
Carnelian Room
Carriage House
Chutney Kitchen
Coatepeque
Deetjen's
De Paula's
Empress of China
Enrico's
Ernie's
The Firehouse
Fournou's Ovens
François' Coffee House

Gaylord
Greens
Hang Ah Tea Room
Hilltop Cafe
Hunan
Imperial Dynasty
Imperial Palace
John's Grill
Julius Castle
La Hacienda Inn
La Rondalla
The Ledford House
Lehr's Greenhouse
MacArthur Park
Mamounia
The Mandarin
Manka's
Marrakech
Maxwell's Plum

Negri's
Neil de Vaughn's
Nepenthe
New Bonneville Hotel
Pacific Edge
The Peacock
Perry's
The Pfeifer House
Rick's Swiss Chalet
Russian Renaissance
Sailing Ship
Samoa Cookhouse
Schroeder's

Shadowbrook
Sinbad's Pier 2
Skywood Chateau
Taj of India
Tandoori
Tommy's Joynt
Trader Vic's — San Francisco
Trellis Cafe
Union Hotel
Ventana Inn
Warszawa
Xenios
Ye Olde Hoosier Inn

ENTERTAINMENT

The Ahwahnee
Aldo's
Alejandro's Sociedad
    Gastronomica
Alexis
Auberge de Soleil
Auburn Hotel
Bentley's
Beppino's Ristorante
Bon Appétit
Bodega Gallery
Bull Valley Inn
Cafe La Salle
Cafe Royale
Caffe Trieste
Cambria Pines
Cape Cod House
Castle Grand Brasserie
Charlie Bolton's
Chez Louis
Chutney Kitchen
Coffee Cantata
The Crow's Nest
The Customs House
De Paula's

Digger Dans
Dinah's Shack
The Dock
Dominic's Harbor
Ecco
El Calderon
The Elegant Bib
El Zarape Room
Equinox
Farrell House
Fournou's Ovens
Four Seas
The French Room
Gaylord
Gingerbread House
Good Karma Cafe
Grape Vine Inn
Great Eastern
Grison's
Guernica
Gypsy Cellar
Harrah's Tahoe
Harvey's Resort
Hugo's Rotisserie
Iron Gate

J. M. Rosen's
John Ash & Co.
Khan Toke
Kinokawa
Koya's
La Bodega
La Foret
La Fuente
La Petite Auberge
La Piñata
La Rondalla
La Scala
Las Mañanitas
L'Etoile
Le Virage
Little Joe's
MacArthur Park
Maddalena's
Madonna Inn
Mandarin Delight
Mark Thomas' Outrigger
Marrakech
Meat Market Coffeehouse
The Melting Pot
Menara
Michael's
Mirabeau
Mitoya
Mount View Hotel
New Bonneville Hotel
New San Remo
Old Poodle Dog
The Olema Inn
Oliver's
Orient Express
Pacific Edge
Pasand

Pasha
Peninsula Restaurant
Petrouchka
Pinehurst Inn
The Plumed Horse
Princeton Inn
Ramona's
Red's
Renzo's
Rick's Swiss Chalet
Russian Renaissance
Russian River Vineyards
R.V.'s Super It's
Sailing Ship
Saluto's
San Simeon Restaurant
Santa Fe Bar & Grill
Savoy
Scotty Campbell's
Sea Gull
Sebastian's
Shadowbrook
Shanghai Station
Sharl's
Sheraton Round Barn Inn
Silverado
Sinbad's Pier 2
Skywood Chateau
Sonoma Hotel
Station House Cafe
St. Michael's Alley
Steamer Gold Landing
Taj of India
Union Hotel
The Villa
Washington Square Bar & Grill
Zack's By The Bay

INEXPENSIVE

Balboa Cafe
Bancheros
Bette's Oceanview Diner
Bill's Place
Bini's Bar & Grill
Blanche's
Blue Nile
Buena Vista Cafe
Cafe Delicias
Cafe Fanny
Caffe Trieste
Cantina Los Tres Hombres
Carmen's
Casa de Eva
The Cherry Flower
Chili's
Chris' Hot Dogs
Chutney Kitchen
Clam Box
Coatepeque
Coffee Cantata
Coffee Tree
Consuelo's
Cordon Bleu
Double Rainbow
El Calderon
El Tazumal
Firehouse Bar-B-Que
Fire Sign Cafe
Flint's
Good Karma Cafe
Hahn's Hibachi
Hamburger Mary's
Hang Ah Tea Room
Harry's Hofbrau
The Hippo
Hong Kong Cafe
Italian Cottage

JoAnn's
Kirk's
La Piñata
La Rondalla
Late For The Train
La Val's Gardens
Lee's Canton
Little Joe's
Liverpool Lil's
McCallum's
Meat Market Coffeehouse
MeKong (San Francisco)
The Melting Pot
Mission Deli
Murillo's
N-B Cafe
Nicaragua
On Lock Sam
Ori-Deli
Otafuku Tei
Pam Pam East
The Rice Table
Rooney's Garden Cafe
S. Asimakopoulos Cafe
Scandinavian Deli
Sears Fine Foods
Silver
Swan Oyster Depot
Sweden House Bakery
Tien Fu
Tommy's Joynt
Tung Fong
U. S. Restaurant
Vegi Food
Via Veneto
White Horse Taverne
Yuet Lee

444

LATE DINING

Adolph's
Akasaka
Alejandro's Sociedad
  Gastronomica
Basta Pasta
Blue Light Cafe
Buy-Th-Bucket
Cafe at Chez Panisse
Cafe Sn. Marcos
Caffe Giovanni
Caffe Trieste
Cars
Castle Grand Brasserie
Chantilly
Cheers
Chez Michel
Chez Panisse
Chili's
China Station
Chris' Hot Dogs
Ciao
Coffee Tree
Cuba
Dante's
David's
The Deli
De Paula's
Double Rainbow
Enrico's
Fishermen's Grotto
Flint's
Fuki-Ya
The Good Earth
Great Eastern
Hamburger Mary's
Harrah's Tahoe
Harris'
Harry's Hofbrau

Harvey's Resort
The Hippo
Imperial Palace
Italian Cottage
Kinokawa
Korea House
La Bourgogne
Lanai
La Rondalla
La Scala
Las Mañanitas
La Val's Gardens
Liverpool Lil's
Maxwell's Plum
Mitoya
Modesto Lanzone's
Nicaragua
Original Joe's
Pam Pam East
Pasha
Perry's
Phil Lehr's Steakery
Prego
Ristorante Grifone
Rosebud's
Seven Seas
Silver
Spenger's Fish Grotto
Stars
Taj of India
Tommy's Joynt
Trader Vic's - San Francisco
The Upper Crust
Vanessi's
Vicolo
Washington Square Bar & Grill
Xenios
Yuet Lee

PATIO DINING

Abbey
Alta Mira Hotel
Andalou
Anton & Michel
Auberge de Soleil
Augusta's
Au Relais
Bay Wolf Cafe
Benbow Inn
Bill's Place
Bull Valley Inn
Cademartori's Casa Maria
Cafe La Salle
Cambria Pines
The Carriage House
Cars
Casa Madrona
Chantilly
Chutney Kitchen
Clam Box
Clock Garden
Club XIX
Coffee Cantata
Consuelo's
The Cook Book
Conquelicot
The Crow's Nest
The Customs House
Deer Park Villa
The Deli
The Dock
Domaine Chandon
Dominic's Harbor
Dutch East Indies
Enrico's
The Firehouse
Gingerbread House
Grey Fox Inn
The Ground Cow
Harbin
Heritage House

Kirk's
La Casa Rosa
La Fuente
Lark Creek Inn
La Scala
Las Mañanitas
Le Camembert
Le Chalet Basque
L'Entrecôte de Paris
MacArthur Park
Madrona Manor
Maxwell's Plum
McCallum's
Meat Market Coffeehouse
The Melting Pot
Mount View Hotel
Nepenthe
New Bonneville Hotel
New Sunshine Pizza
Nut Tree
The Olema Inn
The Omelette House
On Lock Sam
Paprikas Fono
Pasand
Perry's
Pier 15
Rooney's Garden Cafe
Rutherford Square
St. George
Sam's Anchor Cafe
Seven Seas
Shadowbrook
Skywood Chateau
Sonoma Cheese Factory
Souverain
Sweden House Bakery
Thunderbird Bookstore
Via Veneto
Victorian House
Will's Fargo
Zack's By The Bay

446

THREE STARS

~~Amelio's~~
~~The Big Four~~
Bill's Place
Broadway Terrace Cafe
Campton Place
Chantilly
Chez Panisse
The Covey
Doros
Ernie's
Fournou's Ovens
The French Laundry
Gaylord
George's Specialties
Greens
Hang Ah Tea Room
Harris'
Imperial Dynasty
Imperial Palace
Kee Joon's
Khan Toke
Kichihei
La Bourgogne
Le Castel
Le Club
Le Mouton Noir
The Mandarin
Maurice et Charles Bistrot
Miramonte
New Booneville Hotel
Paolo's
Rene Verdon's Le Trianon
Sam's Grill
Sardine Factory
Stars
Trader Vic's
Vicolo
Yamato

VIEW

Abbey
The Ahwahnee
Alta Mira
Auberge de Soleil
Bodega Gallery
Broadway Terrace Cafe
Buena Vista Cafe
The Caprice
Carnelian Room
Casa Madrona
Cavalier Inn
Club XIX
The Covey at Quail Lodge
Crow's Nest
Deer Park Villa
The Dock
Dominic's Harbor
Empress of China
Fournou's Ovens
Galley
The Grotto
The Ground Cow
Harbor View Grotto
Heritage House
Hugo's Rotisserie
Jonesy's Famous Steak House
Julius Castle
Kee Joon's
Kichihei
La Casa
Lazio's
Le Chalet Basque
Ledford House
Le Petit Pier

Madrona Manor
Manka's Czech Restaurant
Mark Thomas' Outrigger
Masons
Maxwell's Plum
Nepenthe
Neptune's Palace
New Booneville Hotel
Nut Tree
Old Swiss House
Ondine
One-Up Restaurant
Paprikas Fono
Perry's
Pier 15
The Rogue
Rosie's Cafe
Rutherford Square
Saluto's

Sam's Anchor Cafe
Shadowbrook
Sinbad's Pier 2
Skywood Chateau
Souverain
Spinnaker
Square One
Sweden House Bakery
Tarantino's
Trader Vic's
Upstairs At The Cliff House
Vanelli's
Via Veneto
Victor's
Warehouse Cafe
Washington Square Bar & Grill
Waterfront Restaurant
Zack's By The Bay